AN EXPLORER'S GUIDE TO RUSSIA

Robert Greenall

ZEPHYR PRESS • BOSTON
CANONGATE PRESS • EDINBURGH

Editor & Project Director
Ed Hogan

Copy Editing
Maia Anderson, Ed Hogan, Peter McIsaac, Lisa Sapinkopf

Proofreading
Michael Kimmage, Peter McIsaac, Lisa Sapinkopf

Design
Ed Hogan

Production
Ed Hogan, Peter McIsaac, Alison Rakoske, Leora Zeitlin

Russian Keyboarding & Proofing
Natasha Derevianko, Yelena Lisovich

Maps created by
Viktor Yakovlev

This edition first published in 1994 by
Zephyr Press, 13 Robinson Street, Somerville, MA 02145, U.S.A. Write for a catalog of titles in Eastern European travel and books about Russia.
Published in the United Kingdom and Western Europe by
Canongate Press Ltd., 14 Frederick Street, Edinburgh EH2 2HB, Scotland.

ISBN 0-939010-41-0 (Zephyr Press)
Library of Congress Catalog Card No. 94-60751
ISBN 0 86241 474 1 (Canongate Press)
British Cataloging-in-Publication Data: A catalogue record for this book is available on request from the British Library.

Printed in the United States of America by
Cushing-Malloy, Inc., Ann Arbor, Michigan

To Ch, without whom none of this would have been possible

ROBERT GREENALL would like specially to thank Natasha Perova, Tom Birchenough, Natasha Lapayeva, Pavel Larin, Katya Volodina, Villi Pshenichny, and Patriarchi Dom Tours. Also Yelena Kuzmina, Galina Nosova, Arina Kuznetsova, Guy Pugh, and Giles Butler in St. Petersburg; Dima Glumov and Olga Shimanskaya in Nizhny Novgorod; Lidia Biryukova in Pskov, Tanya Kulikova in Yaroslavl; and Tatyana Bestuzheva on the Solovki cruise. Also to the tour guides, museum staff and other knowledgeable people all over Russia who made my task so much easier and more interesting.

THE PUBLISHERS gratefully acknowledge the assistance of Helen Kates, Alla Kashtanova, and Katya Cherkasova for making possible our supporting services for travelers; Yelena Kuzmina for corrections and elaborations of the St. Petersburg chapter; J. Kates for translations of Russian poetry; and the Widener Library of Harvard University and Renata Dmowska for assistance with photo research. We would also like to thank Grigory Benevich, Natasha Derevianko, and June Gross.

Although he took Russian at Claremont Preparatory School in Hastings, England and deepened those studies at the University of Durham, Robert Greenall writes that "nothing could prepare me for this great country, where a combination of perestroika, kitchen philosophizing, vodka, Russian girls, and the beauty of the land set my head spinning."

"Abject boredom with England took its toll too," he adds. "At the first opportunity, I was back in Moscow correcting the appalling English of Mikhail Gorbachev's speech translators, in a poky corner of a Moscow publishing house.

"But it wasn't just Russia I fell hopelessly in love with. Oksana, now my wife, played a big part in fuelling my mania. Apart from following the daily lives of Moscow's street sellers, my main theme is travel – sneaking around Russia with the goal of exposing unknown destinations to the outside world."

PHOTO AND ILLUSTRATION CREDITS

Maia Anderson (25, 26, 28[2], 59, 87)

Borodino, Planeta Publishers (Moscow, 1991), photo by **Vyacheslav Tsoffka** (166)

"Detskaya Kniga" postcard (1990), photo by **H. Samsonenko** (175)

Robert Greenall (19, 97R, 99, 109, 110, 111, 112, 113, 114, 119, 121[2], 122L, 124R, 125T, 130, 131, 151, 159, 161, 162[2], 168, 176, 186, 198R, 206, 210, 212, 217, 241, 242, 243[2], 247T, 251, 258, 261, 262, 264, 274, 279, 282, 286[2], 287, 288, 290, 292, 293, 297, 299, 300, 304, 306, 312, 313, 315, 316[2], 317, 322[2], 323, 324, 328, 331, 336, 337, 338, 342[2], 343, 344, 351, 353, 356, 358, 359, 361, 364, 365, 367[2], 368, 374, 375, 376, 378, 379, 382, 387, 388, 391, 394, 395, 396, 397, 398, 400, 401, 404, 410, 411, 412, 414)

Ed Hogan (33, 56, 63, 67, 86, 94, 95, 97L, 101, 116, 117[2], 120, 122R, 124T, 124L, 127, 128, 129, 137, 158, 163, 171[2], 172, 173, 184, 188, 189, 190, 191, 194, 195, 196, 199, 204, 207[2], 208, 209, 213[2], 234, 235, 245[2], 247B, 285)

House-Museum of P. I. Tchaikovsky in Klin (Moscow: Moskovsky Rabochiy, 1990), photo by **V. Dorozhinsky** (169)

Moscow Guardian [15 Jan. 1993](40)

New York Public Library (278)

Pamyatniki Otechestvo (No. 2/1991), photo by **Sergey Barsegyan** (260)

Planeta Publishers postcards (Moscow, 1983), photos by **V. Babailova** (165[2])

Russland **by Hans von Eckardt** [Leipzig, 1930] (16, 18, 27)

The Story of Moscow **by Wirt Gerrare** [London, 1900] (108, 126, 152)

Uglich, Planeta Publishers (Moscow, 1991), photo by **Sergey Bulavsky** (272)

Photos on pages 39 and 377[2] are from private collections.

Illustrations on pages 13, 14, 17, 23, 32, 34, 36, 37[2], 69, 91, 92, 102, 125B, 149, 181, 183, 187, 198L, 200, 201, 202, 205, 211, 214, 215[2], 224, 229, 233, 236, 240, 248, 254, 265, 266[2], 267, 270, 271, 307, 308, 329, 339, 383, 402, 403 are from pre-1973 Soviet sources.

Russian book titles are given above in translation.

POINTS OF DEPARTURE

PREPARATIONS

SURVIVAL GUIDE

MOSCOW

ST. PETERSBURG

VOLGA VALLEY

OKA VALLEY

WESTERN DEFENSES

CITY STATES

THE RUSSIAN NORTH

LIST OF MAPS

Maps & Russian Glossaries

Outside of Moscow and St. Petersburg, each chapter surveys a separate Russian region, or *oblast*. Most chapters include a map of that region's principal city. Each map is accompanied by two directories comprised of transliterated and Cyrillic entries: streets, followed by a Map Key with numbered points of interest. (Note that the maps do not include every street.) Each chapter concludes with a bilingual Russian Glossary of regional geographical features and points of interest not shown on the city map.

The transliterations were prepared, for the most part, on a letter-by-letter basis from Russian to English, using an informal blend of the various recognized transliteration systems. A notable exception is the ending *ogo* (in Russian, ого). In the maps themselves, this common suffix is spelled *ogo* (e.g., Ulitsa Mayakovskogo) However, in the accompanying directories and the Russian Glossaries, we adopt the spelling *ovo*, which accords more closely with the way this suffix is actually pronounced (e.g., Ulitsa Mayakovskovo).

QUICK REFERENCE

LIST OF ADVERTISERS

Basic Weights & Measures

Length
.39 inches = 1 centimeter (cm) / сантиметр (см)
3.28 feet = 1 meter (m) / метр (м)
.62 miles = 1 kilometer (km) / километр (км)
1.61 km = 1 mile (U.S./British) / миля
1.07 km = 1 verst (archaic Russian) / верста

Weight
.0353 oz. = 1 gram (g) / грамм (г)
1 ounce = 28.35 grams
2.2 lbs. = 1 kilogram (kg) / килограмм (кг)
1 pound = .454 kilograms (kilos)

Temperature Conversions
°C to °F:
Multiply by 1.8 and add 32
°F to °C:
Subtract 32 and multiply by .55, rounding the result to the nearest whole number

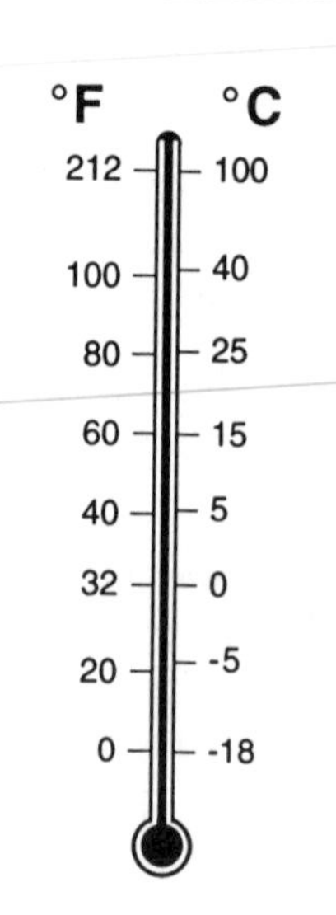

opening somewhere nearby. You will be intrigued by what you find – disused churches and country estates forgotten by time and the Revolution are common features of the Russian countryside.

Of course, contact with people is the best way to begin your explorations, and in Russia this is perhaps truer than in most countries – in a social environment that is often coarse on the surface, personal relationships and mutual support are a vital means of compensation.

In order to provide such opportunities, we have arranged our own recommended contacts for **bed & breakfast**, **guide/interpreters**, and **cars with drivers** for Moscow and St. Petersburg. You can arrange bed & breakfast stays prior to your departure from the U.S. or Europe, for $20 to $35 per night, the lowest published rate we are aware of. Some of our interpreters are available to accompany *Explorer's Guide* users on trips into provincial Russia – which can otherwise be challenging for unaccompanied people who don't speak Russian. In Moscow, we recommend **Moscow Bed & Breakfast**, and in St. Petersburg, **Shakti – the Center for Advanced Studies of History & Culture**. For further details on their services, as well as a sampling of hosts and guides, see the "Practical Matters" sections of the Moscow and St. Petersburg chapters.

We also suggest that you take a look at Jim Haynes' unusual directory – *Russia: People to People* (published by Canongate Press and Zephyr Press in summer 1994) – which provides names and brief information about Russian citizens interested in meeting foreigners.

The principle of Haynes' unusual guidebook, part of a series which also covers Eastern Europe and the Baltic republics, is that you write to people who seem interesting, several weeks before your departure. (Try to write at least two months in advance, as the mails can be very slow.) With luck, a number of Russians will respond with invitations to meet. Some might also offer accommodation, but given the current hard times, you should offer a payment, or reciprocate in some other tangible way – their costs for hosting you are likely to be substantial, relative to their budget. Some might even accept an offer to take a few days off as your guest and guide on explorations of the provinces.

This first edition of *An Explorer's Guide to Russia* covers, in addition to Moscow and St. Petersburg, seventeen other regions, or *oblasts*. This territory encompasses the lion's share of early Russian heritage (I say "Russian" rather than "Russia's," because the Russian Federation comprises many nations and heritages), and is also reasonably accessible from Moscow and St. Petersburg. If you plan trips further afield, to the south, the Urals and Siberia, don't feel abandoned. Our second edition should give you many interesting ideas for places to visit in these areas, too.

You may wonder why I rarely use the term "Golden Ring," one usually closely associated with travel in European Russia. This expression was invented purely as a convenient way of introducing tourists to the sights of Vladimir, Suzdal, Yaroslavl, and other ancient monastery towns northeast of Moscow. Indeed, the so-called "Golden Ring" area has decent roads, signposts in English, and a number of high standard hotels and restaurants, all of which are rare in most of the country. However, by giving up the option to go where he or she pleases, the explorer is no longer an explorer. Therefore I have left the itinerary for you to decide, and have organized this guide by regions – with each adminis-

POINTS OF DEPARTURE

What dreams and what storms, Russia,
Await you in the coming times?
–Alexander Blok *

So you've decided to go to Russia. Let me congratulate you on your choice. A vast wilderness of a country, its enigmatic people and undisclosed treasures are an explorer's dream! So many books have been written about Russia and yet it remains a mystery to all but an initiated few.

During the last few years the lifting of travel restrictions has given foreigners an unprecedented freedom to move around as they please. In theory it is now possible to visit places that no non-Russian has seen before. And yet, well-meaning officials still try to direct those they see as pampered Westerners away from poor living conditions, or may be reluctant to expose them to features of Russian life they regard as inadequate or embarrassing. Ideas about the country are likewise clouded by the ignorance of Westerners who persist in believing, because of outdated guidebooks or simple lack of information, that they are restricted. The real Russia remains largely undiscovered.

In most of the country today, the tourist industry is practically non-existent. Intourist (no longer the monolithic organization it was) and its new competitors continue to ply the best known routes with group tours. But elsewhere, what was once a fairly efficient structure for serving Soviet tourists is collapsing because of declining demand under present conditions. Provincial areas are slow to awaken to the possibility of receiving travelers from abroad. These destinations remain the natural territory of the explorer, to whom this guide is specially offered.

I have tried to point out in these pages the best places to visit, and to suggest how to survive in what can be a difficult and infuriating country. But within the territory of European Russia covered here, there is yet much more. Seek help from local people, and chances are you will make additional discoveries and learn the stories behind them. Even the smallest village has its *znatok*, or know-all. Also take some time to explore on your own, and don't be put off by closed gates or fences – chances are there will be an

---

* from the long poem, "Retribution" (1911), trans. Jon Stallworthy and Peter France in *20th Century Russian Poetry: Silver and Steel,* ed. Albert C. Todd and Max Hayward (New York: Doubleday, 1993), p. 67.

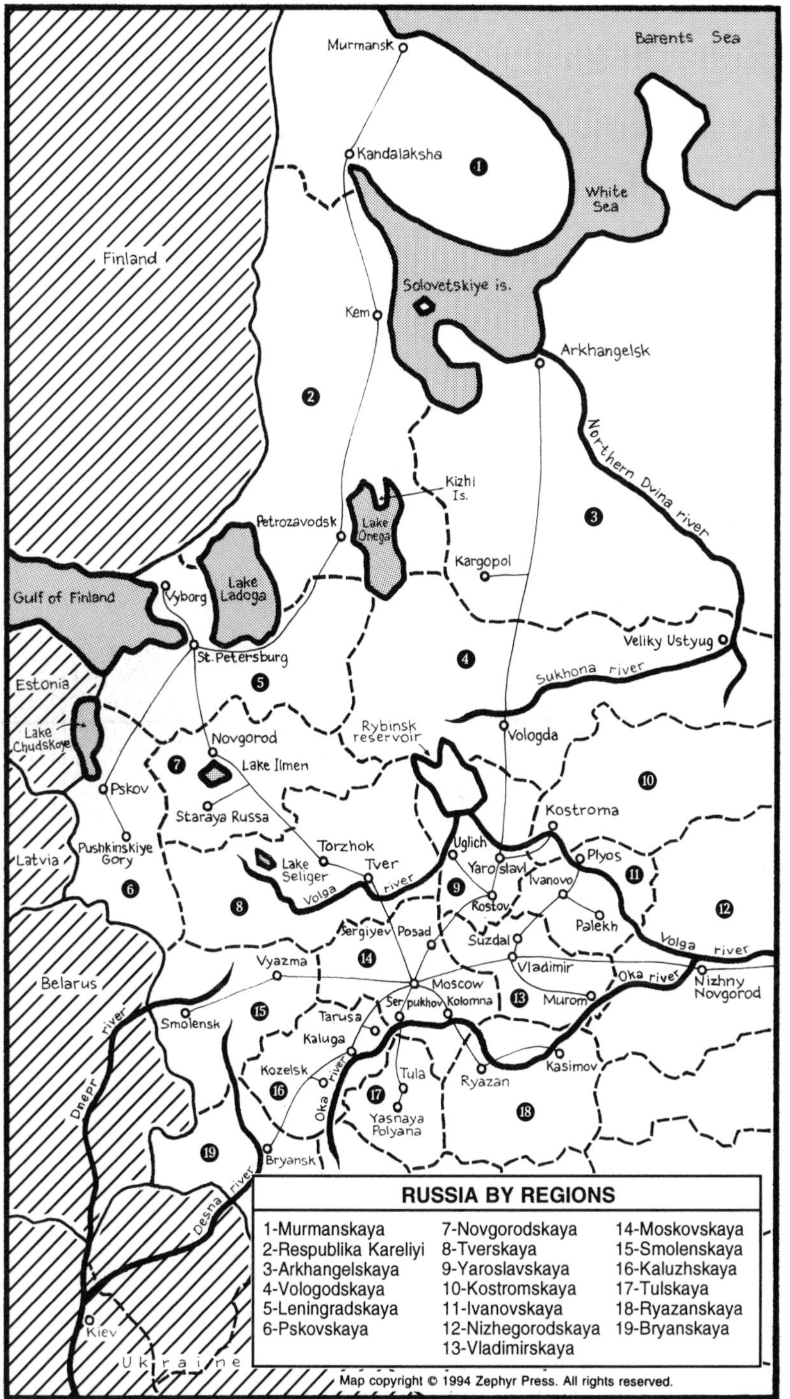

Barents Sea
Murmansk
Kandalaksha
White Sea
Finland
Solovetskiye is.
Kem
Arkhangelsk
Northern Dvina river
Kizhi Is.
Petrozavodsk
Lake Onega
Kargopol
Gulf of Finland
Vyborg
Lake Ladoga
Veliky Ustyug
St. Petersburg
Sukhona river
Estonia
Rybinsk reservoir
Vologda
Lake Chudskoye
Novgorod
Lake Ilmen
Pskov
Staraya Russa
Kostroma
Latvia
Pushkinskiye Gory
Torzhok
Uglich
Plyos
Lake Seliger
Tver
Yaroslavl
Ivanovo
Volga river
Rostov
Palekh
Sergiyev Posad
Suzdal
Volga river
Vyazma
Vladimir
Belarus
Moscow
Oka river
Nizhny Novgorod
Serpukhov
Kolomna
Murom
Smolensk
Tarusa
Dnepr river
Kaluga
Kasimov
Kozelsk
Tula
Ryazan
Oka river
Yasnaya Polyana
Bryansk
Desna river
Kiev
Ukraine
RUSSIA BY REGIONS
1-Murmanskaya
2-Respublika Kareliyi
3-Arkhangelskaya
4-Vologodskaya
5-Leningradskaya
6-Pskovskaya
7-Novgorodskaya
8-Tverskaya
9-Yaroslavskaya
10-Kostromskaya
11-Ivanovskaya
12-Nizhegorodskaya
13-Vladimirskaya
14-Moskovskaya
15-Smolenskaya
16-Kaluzhskaya
17-Tulskaya
18-Ryazanskaya
19-Bryanskaya

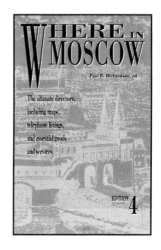

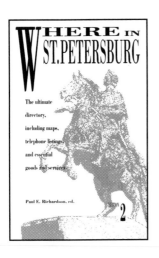

trative center (generally the largest city) acting as a base from which to see that region. To introduce some order into this system, I have organized it to reflect Russia's oldest communications network – its rivers. If, however, you're traveling by car to the Golden Ring cities, the chapters on Vladimir, Ivanovo, Kostroma and Yaroslavl have everything you need. Bear in mind, though, that many places are better seen from a Volga river cruise.

Here again, we have a recommendation: the cruises operated by the Center for Creative International Programs, Russia's first Glasnost-era charitable organization. CCIP's tours to old Russian towns, each including several days in Moscow and/or St. Petersburg, are a remarkable value. Cruise proceeds support CCIP's charitable programs. For more information, see their "Best of Russia" advertisement.

I shall refrain from welcoming you to Russia; it is not my place to do so, and I know that your Russian friends-to-be will do this infinitely better. Instead, let me wish you a happy and eye-opening trip, and extend the hope that Russia will reward you with as rich an adventure in life as it has given me.

– R.G.

Russian History in a Nutshell

Few countries in the world have as long and turbulent a history as Russia. Occupying a vast expanse of land virtually undefended by mountains or seas, the Russian state has always been prone to invasion from outside, finding strength only in its distant borders and the unusual resilience of its people, who have endured centuries of oppressive rule punctuated by intervals of rapid change.

Russia had its historical beginnings during the 9th to 11th centuries A.D., as city states of varied origin combined, seceded, were subjugated, and finally found in Moscow a strong and worthy center. The first Russian state began in Kiev in the 9th century, formed by a Slavic tribe called the Polyane. Shortly afterwards, Novgorod became an important center in the north, and it was the latter's Norse leaders who united the two in 882.

Following the Christianization of Russia in 988, and the coming to power of Yaroslav the Wise in 1019, Rus', as it was then known, developed for the first time into a major European and international power.

But the hodge-podge of principalities which made up Kievan Rus' was soon weakened by disputes, and in 1237–38, a Tatar invasion ended the independence of all but two, Novgorod and Pskov. These two cities

The Battle on the Ice (1242) Miniature from 16th century chronicles

kept a nominal Russian sovereignty alive for the next 150 years, and the great warrior Alexander Nevsky kept at bay both the Swedes (1240) and the German Teutonic Knights (1242) in resounding victories.

The principal burden of the "Tatar Yoke" was tribute, which impoverished the towns and led to cessation of stone church building for two centuries. The resistance of enslaved Rus' came to be centered more and more around the remote city of Moscow. It was a Muscovite prince, Dmitry Donskoy, who dealt an almost fatal blow to the Tatars at Kulikovo Field, near present-day Voronezh, in 1380.

The next hundred years saw the consolidation of Moscow's position as Russia's new center. Still powerful, Novgorod resisted this influence for some time, but was finally absorbed during the reign of Prince Ivan III (1462–88). Meanwhile, the "Golden Horde" of the Tatars failed to maintain its domination of Rus', and 250 years of foreign rule ended.

In the 16th century, the Tatar power bases of Kazan and Astrakhan were destroyed, and Russia began the first of many eras of strong and tyrannical rule. With the coming of Ivan IV (the Terrible) in 1533, the Russian state became a single unit, and just before Ivan's death in 1584, the conquest of Siberia began. Ivan also unleashed a terror against the *boyars*, a group of influential noblemen, and established the principle of personal rule.

Ivan IV. Portrait on wood by an unknown artist, late 16th–early 17th centuries

The vacuum left by Ivan's death led to a bloody interregnum, in which the great Tsar's heirs perished and power was usurped by Boris Godunov, brother-in-law of Ivan's eldest son Fyodor. Two pretenders, both claiming to be Ivan's second son Dmitry (who had been murdered by Godunov), appeared in quick succession, each supported by invading Polish armies. But in 1612, Russians rallied to the defense of their new nation, drove out the Poles, and the following year elected a new tsar, Mikhail, the first of the Romanov dynasty, whose 300-year rule extended until the First World War and the revolutions of 1917.

The 18th century saw new attempts to bring Russia into parity with Europe. Tsar Peter I (the Great) promoted Western customs, culture, and science for the first time. It is questionable to what extent Peter succeeded in Westernizing Russia, but, as with other more physical invasions, complete conquest was always impossible. Russia's dilemma over whether to look eastward or westward became more acute, and evolved into a battle of ideas between *Slavophiles* and *Westernizers*, one which rages with renewed vigor today.

Peter's achievements in other spheres were, however, substantial: he built Russia's first navy, defeated the Swedes again at the Battle of Poltava (1709), and raised a new capital city, St. Petersburg, from the northern marshes on the Gulf of Finland.

Russia's Leaders

Kievan Princes

882–912	Oleg
912–945	Igor
964–972	Svyatoslav I
978–1015	Vladimir Svyatoslavovich (I)
1019–54	Yaroslav the Wise
1073–76	Svyatoslav Yaroslavich (II)
1078–93	Vsevolod Yaroslavich (I)
1113–25	Vladimir Monomakh (II)
1139–46	Vsevolod Olgovich (II)
1155–57	Yuri Dolgoruky

Princes of Muscovy

1276–1303	Daniel
1303–25	Yuri Danilovich
1325–41	Ivan Kalita
1340–53	Simeon the Proud
1353–59	Ivan II (Krasny)
1359–89	Dmitry Donskoy
1389–1425	Vassily I
1425–62	Vassily II (the Dark)
1462–1505	Ivan III (the Great)
1505–33	Vassily III
1533–47	Ivan IV (the Terrible)

Tsars

1547–84	Ivan IV (the Terrible)
1584–98	Fyodor Ivanovich
1598–1605	Boris Godunov
1605–13	(Time of Troubles)
1613–45	Mikhail Romanov
1645–76	Aleksey Romanov
1676–82	Fyodor Alekseyevich (III)
1682–89	Ivan V and Peter I (with Sofia as Regent)
1689–1725	Peter I (the Great)
1725–27	Catherine I (his wife)
1727–30	Peter II
1730–40	Anna Ioannovna
1740–41	Ivan VI (with Anna Leopoldovna as Regent)
1741–61	Elizabeth

Tsar Nicholas II and Alexandra in old Moscow coronation dress. Petersburg, 1897

1761–62	Peter III
1762–96	Catherine II (his wife; the Great)
1796–1801	Paul
1801–25	Alexander I
1825–55	Nicholas I
1855–81	Alexander II
1881–94	Alexander III
1894–1917	Nicholas II

March–Nov. 1917	Provisional Government

Soviet Communist Party General Secretaries (or equivalent)

1917–24	Vladimir Lenin
1924–53	Joseph Stalin
1953–64	Nikita Khrushchev
1964–82	Leonid Brezhnev
1982–84	Yuri Andropov
1984–85	Konstantin Chernenko
1985–Sept. 1991	Mikhail Gorbachev

Soviet President

March 1990–Dec. 1991	Mikhail Gorbachev

Russian President

March 1991–	Boris Yeltsin

Peter the Great

But while Russia was creating the foundations of one of the world's great cultures, it remained a backward, feudal, absolute monarchy throughout the Age of Enlightenment. More Westernizing monarchs – the German Catherine the Great and her grandson Alexander – completed Russia's evolution into a great power, but life grew more oppressive still for the Russian peasant with the strengthening of serfdom under Empress Anna in 1736.

In 1812, Napoleon Bonaparte's invading army reached the gates of Moscow, but his triumph was entirely hollow. He had lost a large part of his army at nearby Borodino Field and entered an abandoned city, which he soon quit. He never recovered from his Russian fiasco.

A possible legacy of Napoleon was the appearance of liberalism as a tendency in Russia during the early 19th century. In 1825, a group of young officers instigated the Decembrists' revolt in an attempt to introduce a constitutional monarchy. Though the Decembrists failed and their leaders were exiled to Siberia, their ideas remained and the advent of another enlightened tsar, Alexander II, led to a major reform, the emancipation of the serfs in 1861. As was often the case with reformers, however, this tsar met a violent end at the hands of anarchists, and the emancipation actually brought little improvement to the lives of the peasants.

Liberal opinion went underground to reappear during the dramatic year of 1905. In January of that year, Russia suffered a disastrous naval defeat by Japan at Tsushima. Meanwhile, Russian Socialists first demonstrated political strength, with the urban Social Democrats and rural Social Revolutionaries both gaining broad mass appeal. The Revolution of 1905 ensued, as workers' *soviets*, or councils, were established in major cities, and the Tsar acceded to the establishment of a *duma*, a weak representative assembly. An attempt at agricultural reform was made by Prime Minister Pyotr Stolypin, but his assassination in 1911 by anarchists put an end to this.

The ravages of the disastrous 1914 war delivered Russia into economic collapse and revolution. In February 1917, the last tsar, Nicholas II, abdicated and a provisional government was set up by members of the *duma*. At the same time, workers and peasants again set up *soviets*, which became stronger as their demands became more radical. The Provisional Government, led by Social Democrat Alexander Kerensky, proved incapable either of conducting the war effectively or dealing with the economy. It was finally overthrown in November 1917 by what historians describe variously as a proletarian revolution or a *coup d'état* led by the Bolsheviks, who had formerly been the radical wing of the Social Democrats.

Civil war broke out. Although it ini-

Early 1920's **agit-prop** ***against vodka drinking***

tially controlled only a small territory around Moscow and St. Petersburg, the Bolshevik Red Army gradually cleared their foreign-backed but disorganized White Army (conservative and monarchist) opponents from the country. The last White army left the Crimea in 1921.

Iron discipline and one-party rule under Lenin saw Russia through the Civil War, and was subsequently modified by Lenin's New Economic Policy (NEP), an experiment with limited capitalism which brought a measure of prosperity during the early and middle 1920's.

These policies were reversed following Lenin's death in 1924, by the man who emerged on top following a complex power struggle among Communist Party factions. By 1928–30, Russia was moving toward totalitarian rule and the personality cult of Josef Stalin, a pedestrian but wily Georgian. Massive industrialization, forced collectivization of agriculture, secret police terror and the creation of a huge army of political prisoners in the *Gulags* delivered Russians into a new and terrible kind of serfdom.

On the eve of World War II, the Soviet Union was an industrial nation, but Stalinist purges of the Red Army's officer corps rendered it ineffective against Hitler's blitzkrieg of 1941. After immense effort and loss of life, including the Nazi slaughter of millions of civilians, the Russian people finally turned back the invader and the Soviet Union emerged as the principal victor of the war. By 1948, nearly all of Eastern Europe was in the Soviet sphere of influence.

Stalin's rule continued for another five years, until his death in 1953. Three years later, a "thaw" began, initially with the delivery of a special report on the Stalin era to the 20th Communist Party Congress by Nikita Khrushchev, the new General Secretary and effective ruler of the country. In a significant break with Stalinism, millions of political prisoners were pardoned and released, and political and cultural life was allowed a measure of breathing space. However, Khrushchev's half-hearted reforms and often eccentric policies alienated his more conservative colleagues, and he was overthrown in 1964. However, unlike the "Old Bolsheviks" who had been convicted during show trials and shot during the Great Terror of the late 1930's, Khrushchev was permitted to retire and live out his life.

Emerging from a collective leadership to assume absolute power in the 1970's, the dull and aging Leonid Brezhnev plunged Russia into a period of deathly stability, known nowadays as the "great period of stagnation." The costs of an aggressive policy abroad (notably the invasion of Afghanistan) and the squandering of natural resources left a legacy of economic ruin which the next generation of leaders has not yet been able to deal with effectively. Nevertheless, the Brezhnev era left a complex legacy. Most Russians, whatever their political beliefs, remember those years as ones of relative prosperity, with many elements of a decent life, including abundant and inexpensive food, more or less assured. However, by the time Brezhnev and his fellows left the scene in the early 1980's, the Communist Party was suffering an irreversible diminution of power, at first psychological and then political.

The watchwords of the new General Secretary, Mikhail Gorbachev – *perestroika* and *glasnost* – brought immediate enthusiasm and relief from an uncertain interregnum, but this was followed by disillusionment, as political reform was not matched in the economic sphere. The country teetered toward crisis. The coup of August 1991, a botched attempt to return to old-style Communism, finally destroyed the power of the Party, and

Russian White House, Moscow, after the October 1993 rebellion

the country itself. The Soviet Union, founded in 1922, broke up into constituent republics. Russia once again became a sovereign state, as President Boris Yeltsin and his reformers attempted to create a functioning market economy, simultaneously contesting this new direction with a parliament still dominated by former Communists.

Confrontational politics continued. Economic hardship and steep inflation caused, depending on your opinion, by the policies of the reformers themselves or by the obstructive tactics of their opponents, fueled growing opposition to the new Russian government. Communists and nationalists, now in opposition, found new champions in disillusioned reformers like parliamentary leader Ruslan Khasbulatov and Yeltsin's own vice president, Alexander Rutskoy. Deadlock deepened between the executive and legislative branches of power, culminating in an absurd and tragic confrontation in September and October 1993. On September 21st Yeltsin dissolved parliament. His opponents responded by impeaching him and declaring Rutskoy president. Although Yeltsin's surprise tactics had gained him the advantage, he was unable to dislodge the parliamentarians from their headquarters in the White House – the very site where Yeltsin and his erstwhile allies had stared down the tanks of '91. Finally on October 3rd violence erupted, supposedly provoked by parliament supporters, and the White House was stormed, amid bloodshed. With the support of the armed forces, and probably of a majority of ordinary Russians, Yeltsin prevailed. New parliamentary elections, set by Yeltsin for the end of 1993, yielded disappointing results for the liberal, market-oriented parties, who were outpolled by nationalists and reorganized Communists, leaving the future path of political and economic reform very much in question. Amid continuing turmoil and shocking contradictions, the Russian experiment remains arguably the greatest historical drama of our day.

Geography and Resources

The collapse of the Soviet Union still leaves Russia by far the world's largest country, covering 17.8 million square kilometers (11 million square miles) of eastern Europe and northern Asia. The population is close to 150 million, of which 80 percent is Russian and the remaining 20 percent consists of over 100 other nationalities. As well as 49 regions (*oblasty*, plural of *oblast*) and six territories (*kraya*, plural of *kray*), the Russian Federation comprises 33 autonomous groupings, including 20 ethnic republics (such as Karelia and Tatarstan), with varying degrees of independence from the central government.

Russia's topography is almost uniformly flat or gently rolling, though much of the far east is covered by mountains. The highest, however, are further west, in the Altai Region bordering on Mongolia. The Caucasus are European Russia's only substantial mountain range. The famous Urals, dividing Europe and Asia, are very old and worn down, and in this way comparable to the North American Appalachians.

In most of Russia, the climate is continental, changing to marine in the northwest and monsoon in the far east. Much of the country is covered by taiga (pine forest), mixed forest and steppe, which give way to Arctic tundra in the far north and desert in the south. Temperatures range from -50°C (-58°F) in Siberia in winter to 25°C (77°F) along the Black Sea in July.

Much of Russian industry is still geared toward military production, into which some inroads have been made by "conversion" (to civilian output), a concept introduced by Mikhail Gorbachev as part of his initiatives to ease Cold War tension. Lighter industries, such as food processing and textiles, remain underdeveloped.

Russia's disadvantages in this respect have always been compensated by an abundance of raw materials for export. The oil industry, despite current setbacks, is still significant on the world market, with large oil and gas reserves in the Caucasus, Komi, Tatarstan, and Tyumen in Siberia. Substantial coal fields exist in the Kuzbass in Siberia, Pechora in northern Komi, and Irkutsk, while the Republic of Yakutia is now able to market its own diamonds without interference from Moscow, thus giving it the lion's share of an industry second only to South Africa's.

Despite its huge areas of agricultural land, Russia is unable fully to feed itself as a result of centuries of backward and inefficient farming methods. This seems unlikely to change in the near future as the economy flounders and wrangles over land ownership continue. The Chernozemye (Black Earth Region), reaching from the north Caucasus, and the Volga and Don Valleys into the Urals and southwest Siberia, is a reliable provider, but the rich farming lands of the Ukraine, once a vital part of the Soviet economy, are all but lost to Russia.

Nature and Environment

Russia is a country of enormous natural beauty, a land of forests, lakes, marshes and pasturelands rich in wildlife. The endless tracts of taiga forest and the rolling pastures of the steppe also encompass hidden beauties – rare flora and fauna and geological wonders, such as Kamchatka's volcanoes or the cave formations near Arkhangelsk and Perm. There is mountainous beauty too, from the Himalayas in Altai (southern Siberia) and the rocky, romantic Caucasus, to the gentler rolling hills of the Urals and the Kola Peninsula.

But years of breakneck industrialization and total disregard for pollution have taken an incalculable toll on people and nature alike. Radiation from the Chernobyl accident is the most obvious example, but even in the nuclear field it is not the only one. Nuclear testing on the northern island of Novaya Zemlya has virtually poisoned the Barents Sea, while plutonium dumping in southern Siberia has left the large city of Chelyabinsk a radioactive hell. Other problems include chemical pollution, which is destroying huge tracts of forest, and direct interference in ecosystems, such as the creation of the huge Rybinsk reservoir in north-central Russia which flooded the natural habitat of thousands of birds and animals.

The early perestroika period saw a rise in the power and influence of environmental movements, and some efforts at least were made to check the enormous and incompetently used power of central officialdom. Many grandiose building programs were stopped in their tracks and a (relatively) more responsible attitude was taken towards the environment. But other problems soon came to the fore and in recent years environmentalism has declined again. Western groups like Greenpeace, now firmly established in Moscow, are thinly spread. Dangerous and outdated atomic power stations continue to operate; industrial enterprises on the verge of bankruptcy cannot afford to "go green"; and, most dangerous of all, independent Ukraine is sitting on an aging nuclear stockpile which is rapidly approaching lethal obsolescence.

But though large areas have been hit by ecological disasters of various kinds, other vast territories are clear and untouched wilderness. Despite its deadly danger zones, it is often overlooked that Russia has areas which are safer and less polluted than anywhere in Europe. These may be difficult to find, and a long way from civilization. However, a series of maps (available in map shops on Ulitsa Kuznetsky Most, Moscow) has now been produced in Moscow showing levels of pollution, a good idea for those in quest of countryside and clean air.

An Economy in Crisis

If the news reports and shifts in public opinion between 1985 and the present are anything to go by, it's easy to get an impression of a country grinding itself slowly into an abyss of lower production levels and cutbacks in services, while the more enterprising members of society are increasingly forced to make money buying and selling imported goods, hard currency and government bonds.

This is just how things are. And yet Russia's decline began long before perestroika. In the 1970's, the Soviet Union was relatively prosperous, living off an oil boom, but once that was over, the weaknesses of the economic system began to show through. The Communists had given the country a centrally planned economy, in which production was effectively in the hands of government ministries and no account was taken of the consumer. The important thing was quantity. If a tractor plant produced tractors according to plan, this was enough, even if 80% of them might not work – the farmers would just have to go without equipment. How were they, then, to fulfil their own plan? Simply by falsifying records.

The Soviet economy was top-heavy with factories producing goods for the weapons industry – so that the country could be defended to the teeth and its Cold War proxies abroad could fight their local wars. Consumer products, meanwhile, were basic and of poor quality, sometimes virtually inedible or unusable, and many goods were rationed, or altogether unavailable outside the main cities.

Gorbachev's advent in 1985 brought changes to the economy, but only in such a way as to destroy the mechanism that was already there. Tentative moves toward creating a market, rumblings of political discontent, the breaking of links with Eastern Europe and the eventual break-up of the Soviet Union all added to the chaos, while no real economic program was adopted.

Only the last of these factors, allowing power to pass into the hands of Russia's radical reformers, facilitated genuine economic change in the new Russian state, with President Yeltsin bringing in a team of young whiz-kid economists to run the government under Prime Minister Yegor Gaidar. As 1992 was rung in, Russia underwent a transformation, with state-regulated prices being freed and goods, previously scarcer and scarcer, appearing in the shops. People suddenly found themselves unable to afford many ba-

Pride of Soviet times: Leningrad's Kirov works

sic things, and were forced to go out on the streets to sell their belongings – these spontaneous "markets" are still common today. Not only that, but their wages were suddenly in a race against inflation which they couldn't hope to win.

Meanwhile the government's privatization plan went into action, with the young and energetic Anatoly Chubais heading the State Property Commission. Government bonds, known as "vouchers" or "checks" were issued to the whole population, which they were expected to invest in major enterprises which were being sold off.

The fate of the voucher program is typical of reform in Russia as a whole. Dogged by lack of confidence, opposition claims of the unsuitability of shock methods to Russia and "dollarization" of the economy, the voucher, and reform, has often floundered and sometimes seemed in danger of collapse. The mafia operates virtually unchecked and often strangles weak new enterprises. Moscow becomes increasingly expensive and vulgar while small towns and villages die away in abject poverty. The outcome is still very much in question.

The state of the economy is all too visible to the visitor. The throes of transition are marked by strange juxtapositions – decrepit buses and slick Mercedes, filthy student hostels and luxury foreign hotels, tasteless cafeteria food and stylish restaurants. But the greatest contrast is in people – elderly pensioners begging on the streets, while young entrepreneurs make money their parents wouldn't have dreamed of.

People

Thought to be originally from Scandinavia, the Russian people are descended from those northeastern Slavic tribes which increasingly centered around Moscow in the Middle Ages. Originally fair and with high cheekbones, they mingled with Tatars and other invaders of their soil, though these features are often still seen today.

The characteristics of their land, vast, wild, low-lying and peaceful, seem to have rubbed off on the nation. Having lived a backward rural lifestyle for hundreds, even thousands of years, Russians are periodically dragged into the present kicking and screaming. But the modern world never seems to fully penetrate Russia; there are some areas that progress never quite reaches. Peasant life seems simple, even primitive, to outsiders.

And yet Russia is constantly changing, moving from what at the end of the last century was a rural nation to an advanced industrial and urban one. Rural communities are losing their vitality, and folk traditions are dying. Attracted by the big city lights, young people desert the towns and villages to live in overcrowded high-rises of flats, and often find themselves dogged by poverty and unemployment.

Russians' tolerance is high. Centuries of suffering, either at the hands of foreign invaders or of their own incompetent rulers and officials, has given them a high pain threshold and an amazing capacity to persevere. They will stand in line for hours, even days, for something they need, or take on the colossal task of organizing a trip abroad to sell the family silver for good money.

In their personal relations, Russians are very warm, emotional and honest, once they have overcome their initial natural suspicions of each other. If they like or don't like a person they will show it, and their relationships can veer between open hostility and undying love in a matter of minutes. To Westerners, their behavior can sometimes seem overpowering, both physically and mentally. Physical contact is common, no less between men than women, and a hand round the shoulders or on the knee has no homosexual overtones. People stand surprisingly close together, in a way that for Americans at least is clearly an invasion of personal space. They are generous; many will be prepared to give you the shirts off their backs, but will expect the same in return.

Russians share a surprising sense of community, a concept for which they have a special word, *sobornost*. A gathering of complete strangers will appear to know and understand each other in a matter of minutes. This can make foreigners feel uncomfortable, and not part of things. The position of honored guest can be a hard one to relinquish.

Russians at Work and Play

While in America it is common to put work before personal lives, in Russia the opposite is almost always the case. The pressures of work are miniscule compared with the difficulties of feeding yourself, bringing up children and living in overcrowded accommodation. Thus it is that women, still very much regarded as the housekeepers, have the toughest lot in life, but are also better prepared to cope than the men, whose inability to fulfill themselves leads often to alcoholic oblivion.

Work, meanwhile, is not taken seriously, with absenteeism rife and usually unpunished. Many blame Communism for making Russians "forget how to work," but there is something deeper than this. Things always get done here, but only at the last minute, after hours of idling and getting nowhere. Only the adverse intervention of some outside force seems to galvanize Russians into action.

If Russians don't know how to work, though, they certainly know how to play. Their ability to cast aside formality and simply be human should be a lesson to the rest of us. They celebrate in Asiatic fashion, long and hard, with large quantities of food and alcohol, and wild dancing and singing, often all

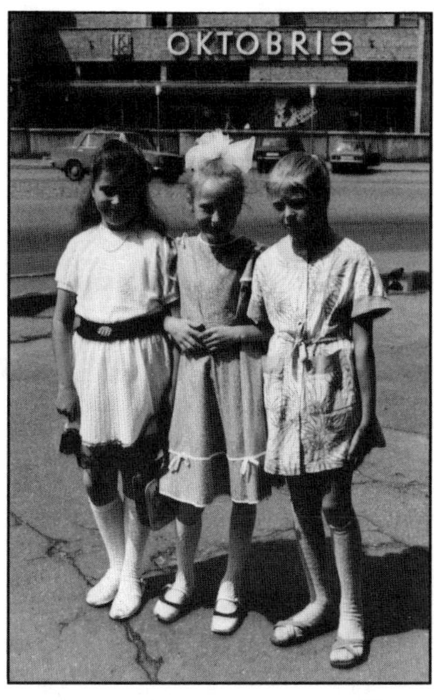

night. Alternatively, small groups gather, in the kitchen or on a park bench, to drink tea or vodka and solve the world's problems, or pour out their own – the nearest thing in Russia to a session with a psychoanalyst.

Russians Today

Whatever their attitudes to work and home life, the realities of today are harsh even by Russian standards. Wages are unable to keep up with runaway inflation, and most jobs that provided a means of existence are no longer capable of doing so. Those still holding white-collar jobs in education, medicine, and other professions, receive hopelessly low salaries. Many families where both husband and wife work are unable to make ends meet on their official income alone. The circumstances of pensioners are especially precarious, as they rely on the state not to neglect them, something which it can come very close to doing.

No one, however, at least so far, is starving. People always manage to find ways of making extra money, and the possibilities are now almost unlimited. Russia today is a capitalist jungle, with commercial structures and individuals ranging from the legal to the openly criminal living their cutthroat lives.

But some, obviously, live a lot better than others. While pensioners struggle on packed trolleybuses and haunt shops and markets looking for an ever decreasing number of bargains, the young nouveau riche cruise the Western supermarkets and expensive restaurants and drive imported cars, often living just as well their Western counterparts.

The fairly well-off city family lives in conditions closer to the first group than to the second – average incomes are much lower than in the West. They will probably earn the equivalent of about $50–100 a month, depending on where they live, but may add to this by what is known as *pereprodazha*, buying and reselling things for profit. This could be clothes, food, or even hard currency or privatization vouchers.

Inflation renders savings worthless, and people are unlikely to be able to save much money anyway. Food takes up a large part of their earnings though families will manage to afford things like meat and milk products, shopping mostly in state stores. For vegetables they will rely more on their *dachas* (country cottages or simply garden plots) where they usually spend their weekends. Kiosks and private food stores mainly sell imported products, beyond their everyday means, but for special occasions or treats they may shop there.

Such a family will probably be a little more extravagant with clothes, the wife at least allowing herself reasonable quality imported goods, perhaps from Turkey or the Middle East.

Dacha

Children will also be given the best possible toys, clothes and education, if extra lessons can be afforded. The principal factor that allows this moderately well-off urban family to maintain these elements of a decent life is low housing costs. While prices of most goods have soared, Russians generally pay under 10 percent of their income for shelter and utilities; if it comes to more than this, they get a government benefit to help them pay.

Attitudes Toward Westerners

Russia's relationship with the West has always been highly contradictory. While some are deeply suspicious, to the extent of wanting to cut off all relations, others seem almost excessively receptive to Western ideas and materials. Throughout history these two groups have been struggling for power and influence, and at various stages each has had its way.

Recently, the second group has been very much dominant. This is because years of enforced ignorance about and negative reporting on the West by the Communists has made people hungry to know the truth. However, they are so convinced that the Communists lied about everything that many are now prone to believe that the West is a paradise, full of golden people living golden lives. Don't be surprised by such naiveté.

There is another aspect to this. Some unscrupulous people regard Westerners as a source of unlimited wealth, and may try to overcharge you for things, or even ask you to buy them expensive things. More commonly, people will ask you to embark on business ventures with them. This could indeed be lucrative, but try not to be too trusting – Russians have a great ability to talk, but tend to be less capable when it comes to follow-through.

Whatever their financial aspirations, Russians' earthy generosity and hospitality will inevitably make you feel at home and secure. Try to respond in kind, and don't be afraid to show emotions – all too often Westerners are seen to be cold and unfriendly. If you do, chances are you will find loyal friends and lasting friendships.

Return of the Faiths

When people think of Russia, especially when shorn of that "empire" known as the Soviet Union, their visions are likely to include the Russian Orthodox Church, historically a rigid, monolithic, and conservative branch of imperial power, and at the same time a courageous and magnificent thorn in the side of the country's leadership in the days of Communism.

Tsar Aleksey, the tsarina, Patriarch Nikon, Byzantine Emperor Constantine and Empress Helen gathered around the Russian Cross

Orthodoxy, the religion of Byzantium, was officially adopted in 988, and was spread throughout the country over the centuries using varying degrees of force, which sometimes, as was the case with the Kazan Tatars, amounted to conversion at the point of a sword. Byzantine liturgical traditions were borrowed from the outset and remain virtually unchanged to this day.

The only major attempt at church reform was made in the 16th century by the Patriarch Nikon. One innovation was to change the number of fingers used when crossing oneself from two to three. This seemingly minor detail helped cause a schism in the Church. Many different sects of Old Believers, as they called themselves, broke away. Some have survived to this day, despite centuries of persecution by tsarist authorities. They continue to worship at two Moscow sites, at a monastery in Borovsk outside the city, and in remote northern areas.

The other major split came four centuries later, and was political rather than procedural. Under the tsars, the Orthodox Church had been a branch of the state; as such, it became a target of the Bolsheviks when they came to power. But while many priests left the country with the Whites, and most of those who remained were killed or sent to labor camps, some sought a way to collaborate with their upstart masters. They set up their own tame and limited church, from which emigrés carefully distanced themselves. The two branches have never fully been reconciled.

The moral and spiritual vacuum caused by the demise of socialism in Russia has given the church, now rapidly recovering from its near extinction under the Soviets, a tremendous impetus. In the late '80's it even became "trendy" to get baptized. Reconsecration of churches goes ahead all over Russia at breakneck speed, restoration rather more slowly. Such absurdities as services being held in side-chapels of churches used as timber warehouses, or to the sound of OMON (tactical police) cadets taking shooting practice are not uncommon. Meanwhile, in settlements built after the Revolution, people are now demanding places to worship.

However conservative the Russian Orthodox Church may be, its atmosphere of antiquity, where the smell of incense combines with the booming voice of the priest, the flickering of hundreds of tapers, and the golden glitter of iconostases, rarely fails to deeply affect the firstcomer.

Services are long, and the worshippers stand throughout. Certain courtesies should be observed. You should refrain from photography (although

Preparations for a christening

you can try asking for permission), and women should wear a scarf, while men should remove any headgear. However, walking around and even talking is tolerated within reason, which sometimes conveys the feeling of being in a market. Candles and pocket icons are sold in stalls at the back of the church, and beggars will often be found supplicating outside.

Other branches of Christianity are variously represented in Russia. Some western cities still have Catholic, mainly Polish, communities. Baptist groups exist, most concentrated in the Urals and western Siberia.

But while these communities are relatively established in Russia and are fighting to restore their identity, American evangelical Christians are also making thousands of converts. Their often unscrupulous methods have found easy prey among people whose lifelong faith in Communism has been undermined. While mainstream preachers like Billy Graham have been at pains to emphasize the overriding importance of faith in God, others have deeply angered the Orthodox Church by their sectarian approach.

Despite centuries of Orthodoxy as the state-sponsored religion and decades in which religion itself was anathema, Russia's diverse ethnic fabric has led to the appearance on its territory of many of the world's other faiths. Like Orthodoxy, these are in the process of revival and a genuine pluralism of faiths is at last developing.

Islam is Russia's second largest religion. Its 18 million believers are found mainly in the now semi-independent republics of Tatarstan and Bashkortostan (mainly Sunnis, and ethnically Tatar), and in the smaller mountain nations of the north Caucasus (mainly Shiite), though cities such as Moscow, St. Petersburg, and Yekaterinburg also have large communities. Islam's revival has the advantage of healthy financial backing. Both Saudi Arabia and Iran have contributed generously to the construction and renovation of mosques, *madrassas*

ARCHITECTURAL ELEMENTS: 14TH CENTURY, NOVGOROD
Church of St. Theodore Stratilites on the Brook, 1361

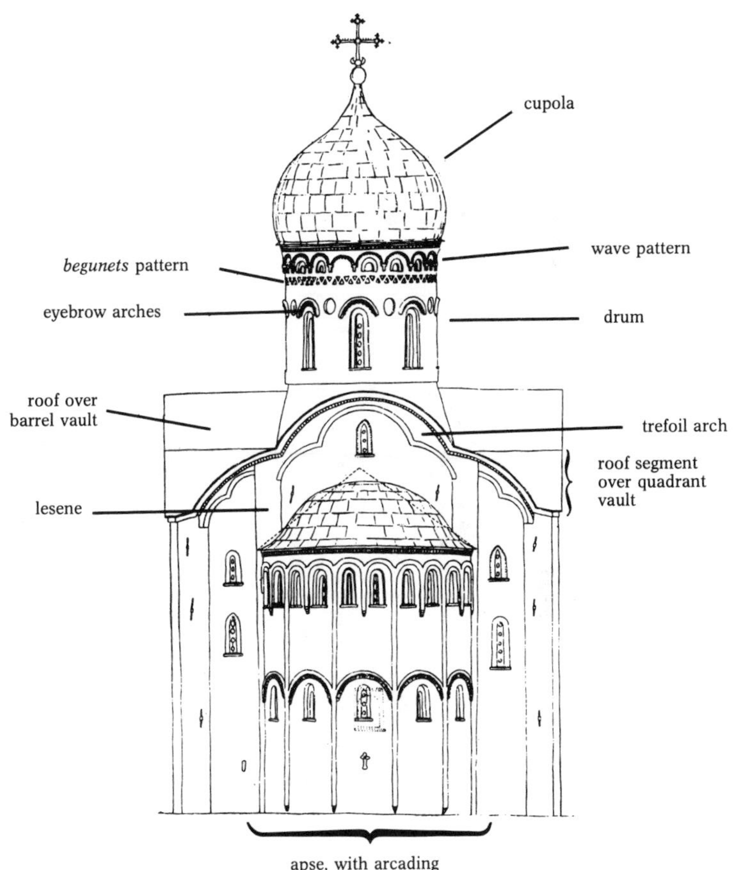

Adapted from *A History of Russian Architecture*
by William C. Brumfield (Cambridge University Press, 1993)
by permission of the author

ARCHITECTURAL ELEMENTS: 15TH CENTURY, MOSCOW
Cathedral of the Dormition, the Kremlin, 1475–79

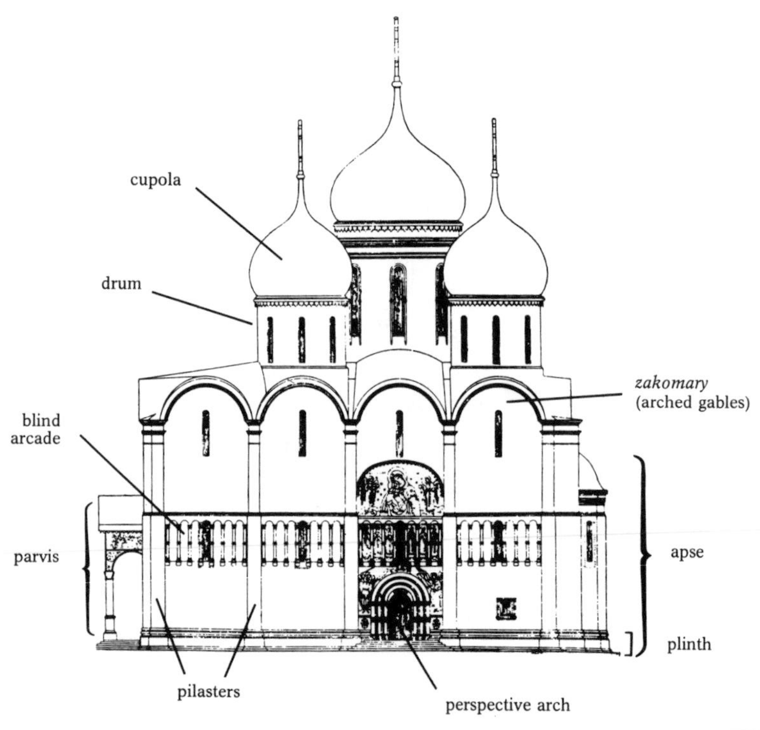

Adapted from *A History of Russian Architecture*
by William C. Brumfield (Cambridge University Press, 1993)
by permission of the author

(schools), and cultural centers.

The revival of Judaism in Russia has been far more muted. The growth of anti-semitism and the general frustration with life in Russia has led to mass emigration in the last few decades. Indeed, the more devout members of the community see moving to the Promised Land, rather than building the faith in Russia, as the ultimate goal.

In three autonomous republics, Buryatia and Tuva in Siberia, and Kalmykia in the southern steppe, Buddhism flourishes. All Russian Buddhists belong to the Gelugpa Tibetan sect, which takes its leadership from the Dalai Lama.

One Caucasian tribe, the Adygs, and several northern peoples including the Yakuts and Evenki invoke the worship of spirits in objects of the natural world, contacted through shamans, or witch doctors.

Cultural Development

Architecture

As with every other aspect of Russian life, the tendency to mingle Eastern and Western influences is strikingly apparent in its architecture, which draws admiration from the world over.

Early Russian building design is best represented today by churches, which for centuries were the only stone structures. Their design borrowed from the Byzantine "cross in square" plan (the shape of a cross filling a square base), they were topped by an onion dome or cupola, giving them an Eastern feel.

The first wave of stone construction began in the 11th century during the reign of Yaroslav the Wise, who presided over the Golden Age of Kievan Rus'. Huge, elaborate cathedrals were constructed, like St. Sophia's in Kiev, which, despite much alteration in the 17th century, is still a reminder of the might of that princedom.

After Kievan Rus' began to break up in the 12th century, Russian architecture became more regional, with individual schools appearing in such cities as Novgorod and Vladimir. There was a tendency toward smaller and more modest churches, with high domes and smaller bodies, like the Church of the Intercession near Vladimir, startlingly white beside the river Nerl, or the Church of the Arkhangel Michael at Smolensk, elegantly gracing a hillside above the Dnieper river.

In the 13th and 14th centuries, during the Tatar occupation, times were hard and resources few, so virtually no stone building was carried out. New styles were tried on wooden constructions. Though unfortunately none from this period have survived, the designs of those from the 15th and 16th centuries were little changed. Greater emphasis was put on interiors, the aim being to focus the attention of the worshipper fully on the iconostasis.

In the 15th century, the center of Russian architecture shifted firmly to Moscow. Intensive building during that period led to its being christened "the city of 40 times 40 churches." The Cathedral of the Intercession (St. Basil's) on Red Square, with its covered stairways and blind arcades, is the epitome of the tent-roofed church, a style that remained popular for centuries.

Meanwhile, the Kremlin's Assumption Cathedral, built by the Italian Aristotele Fioravanti in 1475–79, combines Renaissance style with architectural features of pre-Mongolian

Yaroslavl Station, Moscow

Russia. Italian architects were frequently engaged for important Russian building projects of this period.

The Westernizing influence of Peter the Great was strongly felt in architecture. At the end of the 18th century, the Baroque made its appearance in Russia, with the building of huge, ornate palaces, especially in and around the new capital of St. Petersburg. But by the end of the 18th century, tastes had changed, and austere classical (sometimes called neo-classical) forms became prevalent. Many rooms in baroque palaces were later redesigned in classical style.

Classicism was in decline by the middle of the 19th century, and its pre-eminent place was taken by Historicism, or Eclecticism. Among the great diversity of styles employed in varying combinations, the most significant was the attempt to revive elements of early Russian architecture, both monumental and folk. By the last quarter of the century, architects and artists were working in concert to rediscover and celebrate the Russian past in buildings whose character made a dramatic impact. This was particularly true in Moscow, where several notable examples – the State Historical Museum, the GUM department store, and the former Lenin Museum (built in 1890–92 as the City Duma) – stand on or near Red Square.

Toward the turn of the 20th century, Eclecticism yielded partly, and rather gracefully, to Art Nouveau or *Style Moderne*, whose flowing and naturalistic lines combined modern techniques and stylistic influences from Europe with a revival of traditional Russian forms. Although the buildings in this style are relatively few in number, Art Nouveau has made a significant impact on some cities, including St. Petersburg, whose Kamennoostrovsky prospekt merits special attention in this respect. Two of the best-known art nouveau buildings are Moscow's Yaroslavl Station (Fyodor Shekhtel, 1902–04) and Petersburg's Dom Knigi, originally built as the Singer Building (Pavel

Syuzor, 1902–04).

War, revolution, and civil war brought most building to a halt for ten years. But in 1925, at the International Exhibition of Decorative Arts in Paris, young Russian architects led by Konstantin Melnikov (1890–1973) placed a revolutionary style before the world. Constructivism fused the starkly modern visions of the Russian Futurists with the late-19th century Chicago School principle that form in architecture should follow function. The poor economic conditions of the 1920's meant that vastly greater numbers of constructivist buildings were designed than erected, but the offices of *Izvestiya* (1927) and the private house of Melnikov (1928), to cite two examples from Moscow, still seem fresh and inspired today.

Although Constructivism made a long-lasting impact on Europe and North America through its progeny, Bauhaus and the International Style, it was dead in the Soviet Union by 1935, victim of a culturally conservative leadership. Historicism was brought back into favor, but this time it was monumental and bland, often with classical overtones. After the war the great avenues of the capital were lined with block after block of flats and offices in what was dubbed "Stalin Baroque." The most dominant examples of the style are Moscow's seven nearly identical "wedding cake" skyscrapers, which include the Foreign Ministry and Moscow State University.

In the 1960's and '70's, Russian architecture awoke from its 25-year sleep, but the results brought little comfort to ordinary Soviet citizens, as modern blocks of flats became progressively uglier, taller, and less habitable. They now epitomize the suburban hell of cities worldwide, with their skylines of 15-story abominations. Nowadays, lack of funds has made the huge building projects of the Communist era impossible. Most new construction – typically offices, country cottages for the nouveau riche, or expensive hotels – is financed privately or by foreign capital. There is also a tendency toward restoration or even rebuilding of ancient monuments, a striking example being Moscow's Kazan Cathedral. At least some of Russia's 20th century uglification is being reversed.

Art

Prior to Christianization in 988, the only art which existed in Russia was sculpture – the depiction of heathen gods in wood or stone. The Byzantine church, however, brought with it the art of icon-painting, which spread throughout Russia and became established in a number of major cities. For the first few centuries, Byzantine canons were rigidly observed. Icons were considered to be the work of God,

Pre-Christian totem, recovered from the Dniepr River, Kiev

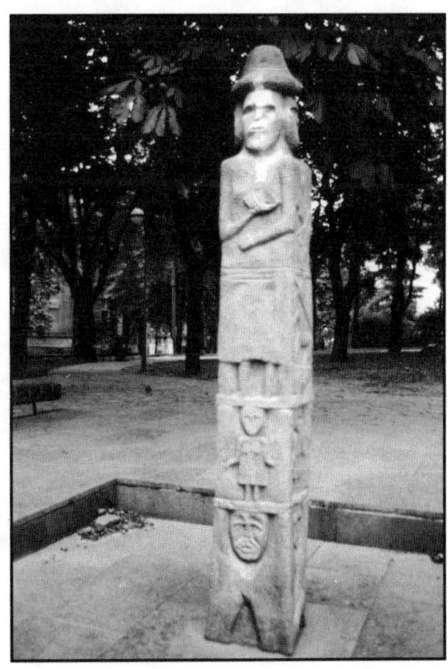

and any change in form was deemed unholy. The artists were merely anonymous servants of God's will.

As the individual princedoms became more independent, they began to develop their own schools of art. Particularly influential was the Vladimir and Suzdal school, best illustrated by the stone carvings of Vladimir's St. Demetrius Cathedral, a feast of pre-Christian motifs, flora and fauna.

In the 11th to 13th centuries, Novgorod and Pskov also emerged as important artistic centers. The *Ostromir Codex* (1056–57), a richly colored and decorated collection of readings from the gospels, establishes Novgorod as an early literary and educational center. Townspeople, including even the most lowly merchants, are known to have sent each other letters on birch bark, centuries before any but the most privileged Russians elsewhere had learned to write.

It wasn't until the 14th century that the first moves were made toward greater subjectivity in icon-painting. Theophanes the Greek, working initially in Novgorod then moving to Moscow, painted expressively, expressing open and acute emotion in the faces of his subjects.

It was only with Andrey Rublyov (c.1360–c.1430) that the first truly Russian school was created. The work of Rublyov and his pupils, unlike the Byzantine art which preceded it, was highly poetic and contemplative, capturing Russia's suffering at the hands of the Tatars while at the same time observing Hellenic traditions of harmony, color, and beauty. Rublyov's major work included the Annunciation Cathedral in the Moscow Kremlin, the Assumption Cathedral in Vladimir, and the Trinity Cathedral in Sergiyev Posad (formerly Zagorsk).

Andrey Rublyov, "The Holy Trinity," early 15th century. State Tretyakov Gallery, Moscow

After the fall of Byzantium to the Turks in 1453, Moscow became increasingly the center not just of Russia but of the Orthodox world as a whole. During this period, Russian icon-painting continued to evolve on an independent basis. Dionysius (c.1440–c.1508), the best known artist of this period, is noted for his moderation of expression and sparseness of detail in subtly colored portrayals of heavenly bliss.

In the 16th century,

icon art became once again rigidified, this time to serve the purposes of the Russian state. Depth of expression and inner meaning now were sacrificed for the sake of outward beauty.

The split in the church precipitated by Nikon's 17th century reforms was reflected to some extent in art. The pro-Nikon faction, known as the Kremlin Armory artists, brought some Western influences to icon-painting, for instance by introducing buildings and landscapes into the backgrounds of their compositions. A classic example is the Assumption of the Virgin Mary in the Kremlin's Assumption Cathedral, painted in 1658 by Fyodor Kondratyev and Luka Afanasyev.

By the end of the 17th century, icon-painting began to lose its significance as an art form, as European influence led to the rise of portraiture. By the middle of the following century, such secular painters as Fyodor Rokotov and Dmitry Levitsky were known throughout the continent. Meanwhile, artists such as Vladimir Borovikovsky began to make the transition through sentimentalism to the heroism and romanticism of the early 19th century.

The mid–19th century onset of realism included attempts to mix the earthly and the ideal. Perhaps Karl Bryullov's *The Last Day of Pompeii* (1830–33), now in St. Petersburg's Russian Museum, best expresses this aspiration.

In 1870, the founding of the Association of Itinerant Art Exhibitions firmly established realism in Russian painting. The painters Isaac Levitan, Vassily Surikov, and Ilya Repin are well known to the discerning Western public today.

As the turn of the century approached, Russia was developing economically and evolving socially at a breathtaking pace. This unprecedented era was reflected among artists in a conscious search for new expression, commonly known as the "Great Experiment" in Russian art. This took many directions, from the formalism of Boris Kustodiev and Aristarkh Lentulov to the abstraction of Kazimir Malevich and the primitivism of Natalya Goncharova and Marc Chagall.

Kazimir Malevich,* The Woodcutter *(1911). Stedelijk Museum, Amsterdam

This artistic ferment continued after the Revolution, though many artists became carried away by political fervor. In any case, the freedom for experiment was closed off by the early 1930's, when the realistic traditions of the 19th century were rigidified into the totalitarian art of the Stalin era, Socialist Realism. Artists were told they had to portray things as they should be, not as they really were. Socialist it may have been, realist it certainly was not.

The last few decades have seen the appearance of an underground movement to challenge official culture. Initial attempts to bring it to the surface in the 1950's failed, when an abstractionist exhibition visited by Khrushchev was damned as "dogshit." Until 1986, dissident artists were threatened, exiled, and their works even bulldozed, as was the case with one unapproved open-air show in the 1970's. Many artists held exhibitions in their private flats to avoid interference by the authorities.

Glasnost engendered a flood of enthusiasm for Russian art both inside and outside the country. While catching up with 50 years of works lost, forgotten, or hidden away in the store rooms of museums, the public was confronted by the often highly rebellious and political style of present-day artists. After a while, though, interest waned and while pluralism of form remained, financial considerations came to take priority for many. Now the situation is stabilizing, as private art galleries have sprung up in Moscow and St. Petersburg. A small but knowledgeable public appreciates contemporary Russian art.

Literature

Literature has long held a special place in the lives of Russians, and not only for its artistic merits. Because of political repression, dissent could often be expressed only "between the lines" of poetry.

The earliest work of Russian literature is considered to be the anonymous 12th century epic, *The Lay of Igor's Host,* which lauded a campaign against the Turkic Polovtsy tribe. This patriotic poem called for unity of the Russian princes against the Mongol threat.

A rich literature, mainly of religious inspiration, developed during subsequent centuries, composed in Old Slavonic, the high language of the church, by anonymous authors. Two medieval authors whose names come down to us are Kievan Grand Prince Vladimir Monomakh (ruled 1113–25), whose *Instruction* is a blend of autobiography and good advice to his sons, and Ivan the Terrible (1533–84) who used secular Old Russian to compose literary parodies and letters.

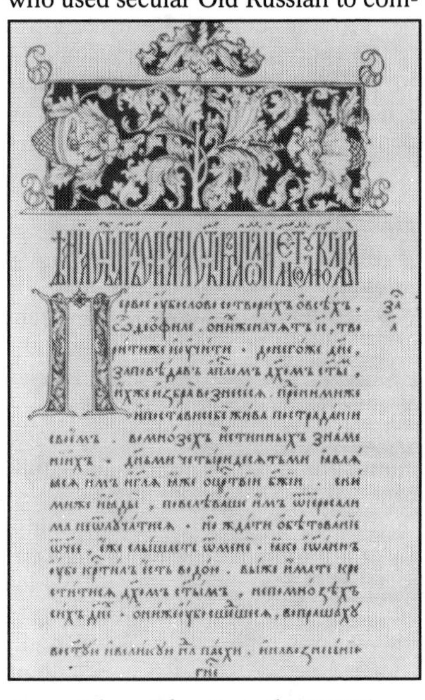

A page from* The Apostle *(1564), the first Russian printed book

Only in the 18th century did the language assume essentially its modern shape, when scientist, poet, and humanist Mikhail Lomonosov (1711–65) did much to regularize it. Modern Russian literature came into flower with the arrival of Alexander Pushkin (1799–1837).

"Leaving aside ... the luminosity of his achievements in a dazzling array of genres or the ability of his texts to capture and define the crucial conflicts of Russian culture (Russia/the West, folk/gentry, religious/secular, state/individual), Pushkin's [preeminence] rests primarily on the seminal nature of his writing," writes scholar William M. Todd (*Handbook*

Alexander Pushkin, 1827

of Russian Literature, ed. Victor Terras; Yale University Press, 1985).

In the "Golden Age" of Russian poetry, Pushkin was succeeded by the romantic Mikhail Lermontov and the tragic and psychologically profound Evgeny Baratynsky.

The second half of the century saw the appearance of the novel in Russian literature, which originated with Lermontov's *A Hero of Our Time*, a closely woven collection of tales about Pechorin, his bored, superfluous antihero. Similar characters were cast by such writers as Ivan Goncharov and Ivan Turgenev. The novel matured in Russia with Lev Tolstoy and Fyodor Dostoyevsky. Tolstoy's *War and Peace* (1863–69) was a chronicle of the Napoleonic Wars through the eyes of several aristocratic families, while *Anna Karenina* told the story of a "misfit" who is brought to grief by the strict moral codes of the late 19th century. Dostoyevsky, meanwhile, investigated the psychological worlds of tortured heroes, such as Raskolnikov in *Crime and Punishment* and the three *Brothers Karamazov*.

In drama, the new realism of Anton Chekhov at the turn of the century, combined with the acting "Method" of director Konstantin Stanislavsky, did much to sweep away the pompous operatic pretensions of the old theater throughout the world.

In the early 20th century, the Symbolists, who included the eclectic and erudite poets Dmitry Merezhkovsky and Alexander Blok, and novelist Andrey Bely, turned away from the realistic and often naturalistic prose of the previous decades. Symbolism reimagined earthly existence as a reflection of a higher, perhaps divine, reality. It also largely broke with the social and political engagement of its predecessors, in search of philosophical understandings.

It was from the Acmeist school, the natural successor to Symbolism, that two of the finest poets of the Soviet period, Anna Akhmatova and Osip Mandelstam, emerged. Intending to reform rather than destroy Symbolism, its advocates nonetheless devel-

Lev Bakst, frontispiece to* **The Snow Mask**, *a book of poems by Alexander Blok (1907)

oped a more down-to-earth style, using concrete imagery and emphasizing "the precise embodiment of emotional experience," in the words of its leader, Nikolay Gumilyov. Gumilyov's poetry also introduced an element of macho romanticism.

Soon after, Acmeism found its diametrical opposite in Futurism, exemplified by the anarchic verse of Velimir Khlebnikov and the booming revolutionary voice of Vladimir Mayakovsky. These poets, like their revolutionary soulmates, sought to destroy established forms and build from scratch.

But as the fervor of revolution subsided at the end of the 1920's and Socialist Realism became the norm in literature as well as in art, some writers continued to produce classic works underground. Mikhail Bulgakov's fantastic satire, *The Master and Margarita*, was written at the height of the Great Terror of the 1930's.

Persecution of writers became unusually severe during and after this decade under a pervasive system of Stalinist rewards and punishments that sought to transform writers, for the purposes of "socialist construction," into "mouthpieces and transmission belts of party policy," as scholar Jane Taubman once expressed it. Some who refused to conform, such as Mandelstam, perished in the Gulag; after the war the expulsion of Akhmatova and satirist Mikhail Zoshchenko from the Union of Soviet Writers rendered the latter totally loyal to Stalin. Even the "thaw" of the Krushchev era failed to halt this persecution completely. The hounding of Boris Pasternak after his novel *Dr. Zhivago* was awarded the Nobel Prize in 1959, is believed to have hastened his death.

In Brezhnev's time, writers' fates became less dire, although the means of censure, such as banishment or confinement to psychiatric hospitals, could still be severe. Alexander Solzhenitsyn, Russia's greatest living writer and author of the most renowned indictment of Communism, *The Gulag Archipelago*, suffered the former. His return to Moscow from a reclusive life in Vermont is expected in 1994.

During the 1970's, underground literature (not only works by repressed Soviet-era writers, but even those of the "decadent" Silver Age poets) became more and more widespread in the form of *samizdat*, self-produced books typed or photocopied at the risk of KGB persecution for writer, disseminator, and reader.

Glasnost brought literary revelations to a broader Russian public, and for a few years people were avidly reading anything that had been banned during the previous decades. Now the novels of Bulgakov and Solzhenitsyn have yielded much ground to detective stories and pulp fiction, as people seek to escape life's present uncertainties. Many traditional writers, such as Valentin Rasputin, a member of the important and interesting "Village Prose" movement which appeared in the mid-1950's, remain deeply bogged down in politics, often in opposition to the current reforms, while the avant garde has removed itself to the realms of postmodernism.

But Russia is still to an unparalleled degree a nation of readers. Much current poetry and fiction is shadowed by the past, still in reaction to the Soviet period. In periodicals such as *Novy mir* (New World) and *Literaturnaya gazeta*, critics are debating the contours of the truly post-Soviet literature to come. The present literary ferment can be glimpsed in English translation in the unique, Moscow-based journal, *Glas: New Russian Writing*. (*Glas* is available in bookstores in North America and Britain, or by contacting Zephyr Press, 13 Robinson Street, Somerville, MA 02145, U.S.A.)

Music

Evolving from the twin sources of Orthodox chant and folk melodies, Russian musical composition first rose to prominence in the early 19th century with the works of Mikhail Glinka. He initiated two main genres, popular musical dramas with *Life for the Tsar,* and folk operas with *Ruslan and Ludmila.*

Glinka provided the inspiration for the *Moguchaya Kuchka* (roughly, "The Mighty Handful"), a group of five composers without formal musical training who continued to develop Slavic traditions in music. Of these the best known are Modest Mussorgsky, famous for *Pictures at an Exhibition,* his work for piano (subsequently orchestrated by Ravel and others), and the opera *Boris Godunov,* and Alexander Borodin, for the opera *Prince Igor.*

Toward the end of the century, it was Pyotr Tchaikovsky who placed Russian music firmly on the world stage. He is perhaps most renowned for his ballets *Swan Lake* and *The Nutcracker,* which with the help of the prestigious ballet schools of Moscow and St. Petersburg made Russia the world leader in classical ballet, a position it still claims today.

The present century saw the appearance of such experimentalist composers as Alexander Scriabin and Igor Stravinsky, as well as the more traditionally grounded Sergey Rachmaninov. But like many other intellectuals, Stravinsky and Rachmaninov left after the Revolution, and much of Russia's musical heritage was lost to emigration. Of those composers who remained in, or returned to, Russia, Dmitry Shostakovich and Sergey Prokofiev in particular demonstrated that it was possible to write great music, and sometimes even to find critical success for it, under the new

Igor Stravinsky

conditions. Examples may be found in works as contrasting as Prokofiev's *Peter and the Wolf* (1936) and Shostakovich's splendid *Preludes and Fugues* for piano (1951). Nevertheless, each was forced at times to compromise with the commissars.

Recently, Russian classical music has developed a form of academic avant garde, led by such figures as Edison Denisov, Sofia Gubaidullina, and Alfred Schnittke.

American trends in jazz in the 1930's found some reflection in the Soviet Union. Though jazz was often officially disapproved of, there were some wonderful exceptions, including the widely popular Leonid Utosov, who was really the founder of Russian jazz. Louis Armstrong once spoke of Soviet jazz musicians as some of the best in the world.

More recently, Soviet rock music has made its mark. Beginning as a pale imitation of Western music (in the '60's, some 95% of Russian groups were unashamed Beatles wannabes), it was held back because performance and radio broadcast were not permitted. Until the 1980's, rock lived an almost underground life in Russia. Then it burst to the surface and developed rapidly, with groups such as Aquarium, Strange Games, and DDD

***Russian supergroup Akvarium, led by singer/songwriter Boris Grebenshchikov* (lower left, with acoustic guitar)**

expressing the discontents of a new generation. The effect of rock music at that time was very similar to that of 1960's and '70's rock in the West. Rock & roll's popularity was preceded during the 1970's by anti-establishment bards, including Vladimir Vysotsky, Alexander Galich, and Bulat Okudjava, whose simple melodies and memorable lyrics became known to everyone.

In Russia today, all three genres are struggling. Classical music lacks funding, jazz players have no decent permanent venues, and rock is in the throes of a severe identity crisis. Now musicians of all kinds are out on the streets of Moscow and St. Petersburg, busking their way through popular tunes to scrape together a few extra rubles.

But all is not lost. International musicians of all kinds visit Russia, from the emigré Russian conductor and cellist Mstislav Rostropovich, always ready to give democracy a boost with his presence, to androgynous superstar Michael Jackson, adored in Russia but unable to break even on his Moscow concerts. And homegrown talent is still there, and developing along Western lines, playing in rock venues and dance clubs, touring and releasing compact discs and promo videos in the West.

Film

Russian film has always enjoyed prestige among world cinema lovers, though in reality this standard has been set by a very few films, while the rest have fallen far short.

The tradition matured in the 1920's with Sergey Eisenstein, whose films *Battleship Potemkin* and *Ivan the Terrible* rocked audiences with their grandiose scenes and emotional poignancy.

But the young art inevitably fell prey to the state propaganda machine. As in Nazi Germany, film seemed a perfect tool for manipulating the masses. At the same time, comedy films offered distraction from the black realities of oppression.

But as cinematography became more sophisticated, its makers became less tame. Since the 1960's, the unusual nature of Soviet cinema has meant almost unlimited funding for the making of films, while tight censorship has meant that the best films were shown only to selected audiences or banned altogether. This fate befell Alexander Askoldov's *The Commissar*, shown for the first time more than 20 years after it was made, as well as the works of the great Andrey Tarkovsky.

In recent times, the story is a familiar one. The initial enthusiasm for shelved films has dissipated as people turn to American war, horror, and porno movies. All over Russia, cinema screens have become deluged with third-rate U.S. fare. The industry's financial paralysis has brought a drastic reduction in purely Russian films. A handful of directors struggle on, including Alexander Sokurov (*Spasi Sokhrani*, approximately translated as *Save, Preserve*) and Sergey Solovyov (*House under a Starry Sky*). The appearance of an annual Russian film festival, the Kinotavr at Sochi, provides some hope for the future. Co-productions have also had some success, as with the films of Nikita Mikhalkov (*Urga, Territory of Love*) and Pavel Lungin (*Taxi Blues*).

PREPARATIONS

Visas

There are three types of visa for the Russian Federation:

Ordinary. This requires an invitation from a Russian citizen from the first city you wish to visit, which must be processed by the local branch of the OVIR (*Otdel Viz i Registratsiy*, Visa and Registration Department).

Business. Similar to the above, except that private individuals are replaced by the company you wish to visit or are going to represent. If you have a contact at an enterprise or other legitimate organization, you may be able to solicit from them a "business visit" invitation letter. Their letter can be very brief and vague as to your purposes, and will still likely be accepted by the Russian consulate or embassy to which you are applying.

Tourist. This is the kind of visa you will get if you join a group tour, although individuals can also travel this way by purchasing a special Intourist voucher with their visa. For individual travel, this is the least flexible visa, as it all but requires an advance-booked hotel and/or organized tour itinerary for every day of the trip. If you book your hotel accommodations through Intourist, you should be aware that these are nonrefundable, which makes it quite costly if you decide you'd like to change your itinerary after arrival. All in all, these restrictions ought to persuade most individual travelers to attempt to obtain one of the other two types of visa.

Fortunately, various organizations will assist you in applying for an ordinary or business visa. They include travel agents who specialize in Russia and other CIS destinations. Others who do this are: the three youth hostels mentioned in the "Practical Matters" sections of the Moscow and St. Petersburg chapters; the Center for International Education in Alexandria, VA (tel. [800] 343-7114, fax: [703] 931-4085); and Russian Travel Service in Fitzwilliam, NH (tel. & fax: [603] 585-6534), who are also the agents for our recommended Moscow and St. Petersburg bed & breakfast services.

Whether you request the application from the Russian embassy or consulate and submit it on your own, or do it through a visa support agent, all applications require you to supply two passport-size photos and your passport (or a photocopy of the main pages will do), plus the processing fee. For the U.S., the following fees and schedules were in effect at the time of writing: $30 for 5 working days, $60 for 48-hour service, and $100 for same-day service. Apply in person if possible, for the standard ("5-day") service in particular, as it often takes longer if you apply by mail.

Travel Restrictions

All three types of visa will state which city or cities you are traveling to. However, apart from the tourist visa's itinerary requirements, any restrictions to the cities named on your visa are nominal, and no one will stop you from going anywhere else. The lifting of travel restrictions in 1991 has meant that foreigners can go anywhere they please, excepting a few closed areas. To find out where these are, contact the Security Ministry in Moscow (tel. [095] 924-4150). However, if you are found driving through one of these areas, the penalty is unlikely to be high. None of the places mentioned in this guide is off limits.

On arrival in each city, you are supposed to register with OVIR or the local militia, although in hotels they will generally do this for you. In some remote areas you may still be reproached by hotel receptionists or militia (police) if you don't have that place written on your visa. All this means is that they see few foreigners and are unfamiliar with the new law. Even so, it's probably not worth trying to persuade them, so be humble, apologize and say you didn't know.

What to Take with You

Food and drugs. Nowadays, most Western food items and basic medications are easy to obtain in Moscow and St. Petersburg, though very often the prices are higher than at home. Still, it's a good idea to take things like vitamins and dietary food. Some form of insect repellant is vital in summer – the mosquitoes, especially in northern areas, are vicious, and shop supplies get snapped up quickly during the season. If you're traveling outside Moscow and St. Petersburg, be sure to take whatever items of personal comfort you hold dear – chances are you won't find them where you're going.

Clothing. If you're traveling between April and October, some form of waterproof clothing is essential, plus Wellingtons or gumboots if you like country walks – the ground in many places is swampy. The weather can be very warm and dry, but there will be plenty of chilly spells, especially in the north. In winter, take layers of warm clothing, and a hat; temperatures are generally below freezing. There will almost certainly be snow and ice, so wear shoes that have a good grip; pavements can be treacherous.

Presents. You should be prepared to give plenty of small gifts to Russian friends, but this doesn't necessarily mean lugging them all the way from home with you. Most major brands of alcohol, cigarettes, sweets, and the like are available in Moscow, so while still at home think along the lines of things special to where you come from. Books or magazines in a foreign language spoken by the recipient are always appreciated, as are records and cassettes, though bear in mind that the average Russian family doesn't have a CD player! You might make copies of a cassette of some of your favorite music.

Vaccinations

Recent outbreaks of contagious diseases in Moscow and other areas mean that some vaccinations are now necessary. Diptheria jabs are essential for Moscow, where dozens of people have died of the disease. If you are going to southern Russia you should also get vaccinated against typhoid. Should you fail to do so before departure, the American and European Medical Centers in Moscow and St. Petersburg provide this service.

Travel into Russia

Almost all major airlines have flights to Moscow and St. Petersburg,

Embassies & Consulates

U.S.A.

Russian Embassy: 1115–1125 16th Street, N.W., Washington, D.C. 20036; tel. (202) 628-7551, 7554

Russian Consulate General: 9 East 91st Street, New York, NY 10020; tel. (212) 348-0926; fax: (212) 831-9162

Russian Consulates: 2790 Green Street, San Francisco, CA 94123, tel. (415) 202-9800, fax: (415) 929-0306; 2323 Westin Building, 2001 6th Avenue, Seattle, WA 98121, tel. (206) 728-1910, fax: (206) 728-1871

Ukrainian Embassy: Consular Section, 3350 "M" Street, N.W., Washington, D.C. 20007; tel. (202) 333-0606, fax: 333-0817

Canada

Russian Embassy: 52 Range Road, Ottawa, Ont. K1N 8G5; tel. (613) 236-7220, fax: (613) 238-6158

Russian Consulate: 3655 Avenue du Musée, Montreal, P.Q. H36 2E1; tel. (514) 843-5901, fax: (514) 842-2012

Ukrainian Embassy: 331 Metcalfe Street, Ottawa, Ont. K2P 1S3; tel. (613) 230-8015 (visa section); 230-2961, fax: (613) 230-2655

United Kingdom

Russian Embassy: 18 Kensington Palace Gardens, London W8 4QP; tel. (071) 229 6412, 727 6888

Russian Consulate: 5 Kensington Palace Gardens, London W8 4QP; tel. (071) 229 3215, 3216

Ukrainian Embassy: 78 Kensington Park Road, London W11 2PL; tel. (071) 243 8923 (visa section); (071) 727 6312, fax: (071) 792 1708

Western Embassies & Consulates in Russia

Moscow

Australia: 13 Kropotkinsky pereulok, metro Park Kultury; tel. (095) 956-6070

Austria: 1 Starokonyushenny pereulok, metro Kropotkinskaya; tel. (095) 201-7307

Belgium: 7 Ulitsa Malaya Molchanovka, metro Arbatskaya; tel. (095) 291-6027

Canada: 23 Starokonyushenny pereulok, metro Kropotkinskaya; tel. (095) 241-5070, 5882

Denmark: 9 Ostrovskovo pereulok, metro Kropotkinskaya; tel. (095) 201-7860

Finland: 15/17 Kropotkinsky pereulok, metro Park Kultury; tel. (095) 230-2143

France: 45 Ulitsa Bolshaya Yakimanka, metro Oktyabrskaya; tel. (095) 236-0003

Germany: 56 Mosfilmovskaya ulitsa, metro Kievskaya then trolleybus #34 or #17; tel. (095) 956-1080

German Consulate: 95A Leninsky prospekt, metro Leninsky Prospekt then trolleybus #33 or #62; tel. (095) 936-2401

Ireland: 5 Grokholsky pereulok, metro Prospekt Mira; tel. (095) 288-4101

Italy: 5 Ulitsa Vesnina, metro Smolenskaya; tel. (095) 241-1533, 1536

Netherlands: 6 Kalashny pereulok, metro Arbatskaya; tel. (095) 291-2999

New Zealand: 44 Ulitsa Vorovskovo, metro Barrikadnaya; tel. (095) 956-3581

Norway: 7 Ulitsa Vorovskovo, metro Barrikadnaya; tel. (095) 290-3872

Spain: 50/8 Ulitsa Gertsena, metro Barrikadnaya; tel. (095) 202-2180, 2161

Sweden: 60 Mosfilmovskaya, metro Kievskaya, then trolleybus #34 or #17; tel. (095) 147-9009

United Kingdom: 14 Naberezhnaya Morisa Toreza, metro Biblioteka imeni Lenina, Borovitskaya; tel. (095) 230-6333

U.S.A.: 19/23 Ulitsa Chaikovskovo, metro Barrikadnaya; tel. (095) 252-2451, 2459

St. Petersburg Consulates

Finland: Ulitsa Chaikovskovo 71, metro Chernyshevskaya; tel. (812) 272-4256

France: Naberezhnaya reki Moiki 15, metro Nevsky Prospekt; tel. (812) 314-1443

Germany: Ulitsa Furshtatskaya 39, metro Chernyshevskaya; tel. (812) 273-5598

Italy: Teatralnaya ploshchad 10, metro Sennaya Ploshchad; tel. (812) 312-3217

Sweden: 10-ya Liniya 11, metro Vassilyeostrovskaya; tel. (812) 218-3526

United Kingdom: Ploshchad Proletarskoy Diktatury 5; metro Chernyshevskaya, tel. (812) 119-6036

U.S.A.: Furshtatskaya 15, metro Chernyshevskaya; tel. (812) 274-8235, 8568, 8689

Embassies of Former Soviet Republics

In the United States

Armenia: 122 "C" Street, N.W., Suite 360, Washington, D.C. 20001; tel. (202) 628-5766, fax: (202) 628-5769

Azerbaijan: 927 15th Street, N.W., Suite 700, Washington, D.C. 20005; tel. (202) 842-0001

Belarus: 1619 New Hampshire Avenue, N.W., Washington, D.C. 20009; tel. (202) 986-1606, fax: (202) 986-1805

Estonia: 1030 15th Street, N.W., Suite 1000, Washington, D.C. 20005; tel. (202) 789-0320, fax: (202) 789-0471. No visa required for U.S. citizens.

Georgia: 1511 "K" Street, N.W., Suite 424, Washington, D.C. 20005; tel. & fax: (202) 393-6060

Kazakhstan: 3421 Massachusetts Avenue, N.W., Washington, D.C. 20007; tel. (202) 333-4504, fax: (202) 333-4509

Kyrgyzstan: 1511 "K" Street, N.W., Suite 705, Washington, D.C. 20005; tel. (202) 347-3732, 3733, fax: (202) 347-3718

Latvia: 4325 17th Street, N.W., Washington, D.C. 20011; tel. (202) 726-8213, fax: (202) 726-6785

Lithuania: 2622 16th Street, N.W., Washington, D.C. 20009; tel. (202) 234-5860, fax: (202) 328-0466

Moldova: Moldova Mission to the United Nations, 573-577 Third Avenue, New York, NY 10016; tel. (212) 682-3523, fax: (212) 682-6274

Tajikistan: c/o International Commodities Traders, Inc., 1825 "I" Street, N.W., Suite 400, Washington, D.C. 20006; tel. (202) 429-2026

Turkmenistan: Turkmenistan Mission to the United Nations (c/o Russian Mission to the United Nations), 136 East 67th Street, New York, NY 10021; tel. (212) 472-5921, fax: (212) 628-0252

Ukraine: 3350 "M" Street, N.W., Washington, D.C. 20036; tel. (202) 333-7507, fax: (202) 333-7510

Uzbekistan: 1511 "K" Street, Suites 619 & 623, Washington, D.C. 20005; tel. (202) 638-4266

In Moscow

Armenia: 2 Armyansky pereulok, metro Kitai-gorod; tel. (095) 924-1269

Azerbaijan: 16 Ulitsa Stanislavskovo, metro Pushkinskaya, Tverskaya; tel. (095) 229-1649

Belarus: 17 Ulitsa Maroseika, metro Kitai-gorod; tel. (095) 924-7031

Estonia: 5 Sobinovsky pereulok, metro Arbatskaya; tel. (095) 290-5013

Georgia: 6 Ulitsa Paliashvili, metro Arbatskaya; tel. (095) 290-6902

Kazakhstan: 3A Chistoprudny bulvar, metro Chistiye Prudy; tel. (095) 208-9852

Kyrgyzstan: 64 Ulitsa Bolshaya Ordynka, metro Novokuznetskaya; tel. (095) 237-4882

Latvia: 3 Ulitsa Chaplygina, metro Chistiye Prudy; tel. (095) 925-2707

Lithuania: 10 Ulitsa Pisemskovo, metro Arbatskaya; tel. (095) 291-1698

Moldova: 18 Kuznetsky Most, metro Kuznetsky Most; tel. (095) 928-5405

Tajikistan: 19 Skaterny pereulok, metro Arbatskaya; tel. (095) 290-6102

Turkmenistan: 22 Aksakova pereulok, metro Arbatskaya; tel. (095) 291-6636

Ukraine: 18 Ulitsa Stanislavskovo, metro Pushkinskaya, Tverskaya; tel. (095) 229-2804

Uzbekistan: 12 Pogorelsky pereulok, metro Polyanka; tel. (095) 230-0076

In Kiev

Russia: Vul Kutuzova 8, metro Klovska; tel. (044) 296-4504, 294-6631, 6389 and there are an increasing number of new routes to provincial cities. Try to avoid having to buy your ticket back at the Russian end – it'll work out to be a lot more expensive. Flying Aeroflot – the Russian state airline – is not recommended for everyone; on-board comforts do not meet the norms for international flights, although they are improving steadily. Two important considerations, however, are flexibility and price. Aeroflot tickets are generally unrestricted; they are good for up to 12 months, and the return can be open. You also might save several hundred dollars over the cost of a ticket on Delta, British Airways, or even Finnair. The price of an off-season economy roundtrip ticket between New York and Moscow in early 1994 was as low as $550, with not much difference between low and high season prices. Two travel agents specializing in Russia and Aeroflot are **Intermeet** in New York, NY (tel. [800] 888-4895; fax: [212] 856-9743) and **The Travel Team** in Des Plaines, IL ([708] 297-8484).

Arrival by train, via Europe or China, can be fun for meeting people, although journeys are very lengthy. If you want good scenery, avoid the northern routes, via Poland and Helsinki, and go either from Czechoslovakia or Romania through the Carpathians. The Trans-Siberian runs between Moscow and Peking, and you have a choice of whether to go through Mongolia. The China–Russia only route's trains are more comfortable. A new route has just opened up through Kyrgyzstan which promises to be spectacular. Remember to get transit visas for the CIS republics you're travelling through. (See boxed listing of CIS embassies.)

Train tickets straight through to Moscow or St. Petersburg are probably not any cheaper than flying, after all the various transit visa costs are figured in. But based on your individual trip itinerary, there may be opportunities for a little added adventure and saving some money. If you are already in Europe, going by rail – when planned with care – will probably be cheaper than flying. One possible budget option would be to go to Budapest, book a train ticket to Chop (the Ukrainian border town, which is reached in the wee hours of the morning on the Budapest–Moscow *Tisza Express*), purchase a ticket in Ukrainian coupons on a later train from Chop to Kiev, and in Kiev, buy another ticket for the final leg to Moscow. A good part of the savings comes from the fact that a dollar stretches a very long way in Ukraine right now. This route is probably best not attempted unless you have some knowledge of Russian or Ukrainian. Another, less complicated option on this same route is Budapest–Kiev–Moscow. In mid-1993, the second-class sleeper fare was about $120 from Budapest to Kiev, when purchased in Budapest, and under $15 for Kiev–Moscow, when purchased in Kiev. Overall journey time was a little under 48 hours. See the Survival section for more information on rail travel, including descriptions of the different classes of accommodation.

There are also a number of bus routes from Germany and Finland. Check locally for details.

Customs Regulations

On entering the country, you are expected to fill in a customs declaration form stating the amount of currency you have in cash, travelers' cheques, etc. You should keep this form throughout your stay – when you leave it will be compared with the exit form you fill in. There is no limit to how much you can bring in, but the

amount you take out should not exceed it by more than $50. (By the way, it's a good idea to make photocopies of credit cards, the main pages of your passport, and your visa, and to keep them in the same safe place as your customs declaration.)

It is forbidden to bring in (or take out) Russian currency and other purchasing documents, narcotics, and weapons, with the exception of those required for hunting, which need a special permit from the Interior Ministry.

There are also restrictions on what you can take out of Russia. Carpets, furs, and jewelry are forbidden to those with tourist or private visas (but not to those with business visas), as is red and black caviar if the quantity exceeds two small tins. Objects of artistic, historical, or other cultural value, such as icons, may be taken out, but require authorization by the Ministry of Culture and payment of a special duty.

SURVIVAL GUIDE

Accommodation

In a country still lacking an effective system of private accommodation, the independent traveler is likely to have a hard time, unless she or he plans carefully or has friends or acquaintances to stay with. The hospitality of Russian people makes this option an extremely attractive one, although it may not always give the truly independent spirit the desired freedom.

An option that you may find combines the benefits of independence and contact with ordinary Russians is **bed & breakfast**. A few b&b booking services are appearing, including several based in the U.S., but the per-night cost of the latter tends to be out of the budget category, beginning at about $50 per night. In response to this, we have made arrangements with reliable agents in Moscow and St. Petersburg who can provide b&b host, guide/interpreter, and other contacts for independent travelers at a more reasonable cost. For further information, see advertisement for **Russian Travel Service** in this section and "Practical Matters" in the Moscow and St. Petersburg chapters. The following U.S.-based bed & breakfast services can book accommodation in other cities, as well as Moscow and St. Petersburg: **American-International Homestays, Inc.** ([800] 876-2048; Irkutsk/Lake Baikal, Russia, and Kiev, Ukraine); **Home & Host International** ([612] 871-0956, fax: [612] 871-8853; they claim they can make arrangements for b&b homestays "coast to coast" – St. Petersburg to Vladivostok); **International Bed & Breakfast** ([215] 663-1438, fax: [215] 663-8580; Irkutsk, Kiev, Tashkent, Samarkand and other places in the CIS).

For those who prefer to go their own way, there are a number of possibilities. Western-built hotels are beginning to appear in major cities, although as yet only Moscow, St. Petersburg, and Novgorod have them. These are generally very expensive ($100–$350 a night for a single); so far, very little has been done in this category to cater for the middle and lower end of the market.

Intourist hotels. These were once top quality but now tend to occupy the middle range. They are usually found in the most established tourist centers, and single room rates range from $40 in the provinces to $150 in the major cities. In summer, most are crowded with tour groups.

Municipal and "tourist" hotels come in several classes but standards are generally mediocre. Many are afflicted with bad plumbing, cockroaches, faulty electrical equipment, etc. You will need to ask if rooms have adjoining bathrooms (*s udobstvami*, с удобствами). Although foreigners generally have to pay three to five times the usual tariff, it often works out very cheaply indeed ($5–$30). You may be refused a room on the grounds that you're a foreigner, whether because of municipal law or simply due to the inferiority complex of the administrator (who has decided her hotel isn't good enough for you). In either case, stand your ground – it usually pays off. If you're told there is no room, again, don't be discouraged. Alternatively, at the sight of your foreign passport the administrator may "suddenly remember" that a room is available. Persistence is the key; do keep in mind, however, that the hotel may genuinely be full, though nowadays this is rare.

Communal hotels are a kind of Russian version of Youth Hostels, with four- and eight-room dormitories and strict rules. Facilities consist of washbasins and toilets on each floor (sometimes without running water), and a jar of water on the table in each room. They may not know how to cope with foreigners, but if they let you stay, you'll probably be able to buy up a whole dormitory without feeling a serious drain on your pocket. (If they charge the equivalent of $3 a night, it's expensive.)

Private hotels. Still very thin on the ground, but generally a godsend if you find one. Class and price vary.

Private apartments. If you have contacts, you should be able to find a place to live on your own reasonably cheaply (under $10 a night). In some major tourist centers and resort towns, there are special bureaus dealing with private flats, and privateers circling nearby.

Doma otdykha (Дома отдыха) and **tourist bases** (Turbazi, Турбазы). These holiday homes, often situated in beautiful countryside, used to be full of groups from the various organizations that owned them, such as trade unions or ministries. People would buy tickets in advance known as *putyovki* (путёвки), and worries about food and accommodation would be removed for the rest of the holiday. Nowadays most are in financial difficulty and have opened their doors to all comers. Turning up at the gate and "negotiating" with (i.e., bribing) the director is as good a way as any to get a room. The most exclusive of these places, former party and government sanatoria, can be booked in Moscow through an organization called Dipservis. Contact Mr. Pavel Larin (tel. [095] 143-3967).

A note on water. Every Russian dwelling connected to the mains hot water system has periods when there is no hot water. For a full month in the summer, the tanks of the central plant are emptied and overhauled, causing grief and discomfort for millions of local residents. There may be other, shorter periods (even in winter) when this is the case. In some places, hot water may only be provided morning and evening. Some major hotels and enterprising private landlords have installed their own heaters, but this is still quite rare. Cold showers may not be a good idea – the water is icy. For comments on drinking water, see "Food and Drink" later in this chapter.

Camping. If you are well-prepared and can stand the vicious mosquitoes (July and August are the worst), camping in Russia could be an appealing summer holiday. You can camp almost anywhere in her vast tracts of forest without fear of being chased away. If you are in a rural area, you can feel quite safe, although the same precautions in the vicinity of wild animals apply in Russia as anywhere else. You're more likely to come across bears and wolves in northern areas such as Kostroma, Vologda, and Arkhangelsk, but they're unlikely to be interested in you. As for crime, no self-respecting criminal gang would waste their time combing the taiga for unsuspecting tourists. With the possible exception of the Caucasus, these types keep to the cities.

If you prefer more organized facilities, there are official campsites, which range from clearings with hole-in-the-ground toilets to sites adjacent to Intourist motels with all modern conveniences. These are operated by various entities, but with the exception of the Intourist-operated ones, it's usually only possible to find out about them by inquiring locally. It should be possible to learn about some of the Intourist campsites from Intourist offices in the U.K. (292 Regent Street, London W1; tel. [071] 580 1221 or 631 1252) and U.S. (630 Fifth Avenue, Suite 868, New York, NY 10011; [212] 757-3884). After arrival in Russia, query at Intourist desks, usually located in the main tourist hotels.

Currency

Rubles or dollars?

After years during which the dollar functioned as an alternative currency on Russian territory, a new law which took effect on 1 January 1994 made rubles the only legal tender. Now all shops and other enterprises take rubles only, although some street- or market-sellers may still accept cash dollars. Be discrete when purchasing with dollars on the street. Don't be fooled by prices in former hard currency outlets written in dollars or deutschmarks: payment is by rubles at the current exchange rate, or by credit card. Credit cards and travelers' cheques, however, are at present accepted in a very limited number of places, and rarely outside Moscow and St. Petersburg. Bring with you a good supply of $1, $5, $10, and $20 bills for purchases, and $100 bills for changing into rubles.

Exchange

Changing money is never a problem, in Moscow and St. Petersburg at least. Exchange offices are now everywhere, with banks, shops, kiosks, and even holes in the wall offering to buy your dollars. A recent tightening of the law means that all of these options are now fairly safe. Another innovation is heavily guarded minibuses and vans – don't feel intimidated about climbing inside. Be wary, however, of changing with people on the street, especially if they appear from nowhere – chances are they'll disappear again with your money. Sometimes people standing in line with you will offer to sell you rubles – they'll give you a better rate but make sure they produce their rubles before you show them your dollars.

Travelers' cheques can be changed in some hotels and banks, but don't rely on finding one of these places. Make sure you always have some cash with you just in case. If you want to draw cash in dollars, this is even more difficult. The best place to go is Moscow's Dialogbank at the Slavyanskaya Radisson Hotel, Berezhkovskaya nab. 2, right beside the Kievsky Vokzal. Otherwise go to the old and inefficient Foreign Trade Bank at Serpukhovsky Val 8, metro Tulskaya. American Express cardholders can draw out dollars either on their cards or with traveler's cheques at the following AmEx branches: Sadovaya-Kudrinskaya 21a in Moscow, or in St. Petersburg inside the Grand Hotel Europe at Mikhailovskaya, 1/7.

Bills

At present, ruble bills range from 100 to 50,000 rubles. Old Soviet bills, dated 1961–91, are no longer legal tender. They have been replaced by coins in denominations of 1, 5, 10, 20, 50, and 100 rubles. Make sure when you change money that you receive valid notes – your 10,000's should be green, your 5,000's red, and your 1,000's should *not* have Lenin's portrait. Pre-1993 notes of 5,000 and 10,000 rubles are also invalid.

Postal Services

The Russian post office is notoriously inefficient, with ordinary airmail taking up to a month to get to Western Europe and up to two when going in the other direction, although letters to the U.S. sometimes arrive in 10 to 14 days. The

stamps and special airmail envelopes (*myezhdoonarodniye kan-vyerty*) you need are not always available in post offices. Registered (*zakazniye*) and express mail are only moderately faster and more reliable, although they are at least much less expensive than Western postal charges. If you want to be really sure, though, there are only three realistic options:

(1) Do as Russians do and send your mail via someone flying out to the West.

(2) Find a Western company sending regular packets.

(3) Use one of the international mailing services (Federal Express, TNT Mailfast, etc.) based in Moscow and St. Petersburg. These can generally be found in major hotels, while the more reasonably priced **EMS Garantpost** is based in several major Moscow post offices (including the Glavpochtampt, Myasnitskaya 26, metro Chistiye Prudy, and at 22 Novy Arbat, metro Arbatskaya), as well as at St. Petersburg's main post office, Glavpochtampt, Pochtamskaya ul., 9, just off ploshchad Dekabristov. Figure four days to a week if using Garantpost.

The same applies to parcels. If sending them by post, the usual practice is to take them to the post office unwrapped, where you will be given string and brown paper for them after they have been inspected.

For sending mail within the CIS, you need to write the six-figure index in the bottom left corner of the envelope (for international mail this is just three – 500). The address should start with the town and finish with the recipient's name. Unless you know how to write in Russian, capital letters are usually best. Domestic mail is considerably less reliable than international. Another accepted way of sending things is by train. You can pay a carriage attendant a small sum to take letters or packages, but make sure there is someone to collect them at the other end.

Telephoning

International Calls

Recently it has become infinitely easier to make calls out of the CIS. There is now a 24-hour direct dial service to Europe and the U.S. from Moscow and St. Petersburg, with cheaper rates for calls made between 8 p.m. and 8 a.m. Dial "8" then wait for the tone and dial "10" and the country code. From other cities, you'll still have to book a call through the operator; check locally for the number to call to make bookings. For information in Moscow on international calling, dial "08," wait for tone, then 196;

all the staff speak English. In St. Petersburg, dial 315-00-12 and ask for an English-speaking operator: *Puzaveetye, pahzhal'sta, anglaguvaryaschooyoo tiliphaneestkoo.*

Ordinary telephone company tariffs are lowest from homes and state-financed organizations. Ordered calls and offices are charged about twice the home rate, so dial direct from a home if you can. In Moscow, you can find out rates for calls by dialing "07"; in St. Petersburg, the number is 315-00-12.

Internal Calls

Unfortunately the situation is not so good here. The nightmarish difficulties of getting a line are matched only by the gargantuan complexity of the system itself. Here is a guide to its major features:

Dialing from an apartment. First bear in mind that local calls are free, so nobody minds you calling, or for how long, although it's polite to ask all the same. For calls to other major cities or places within the region, you can call direct. Dial "8," wait for the tone, then dial the city code and number. It sounds simple, but there are a number of complications:

(1) If you're calling *outside* the region, the sum total of digits you dial (without the initial "8") should always be 10. If not, you need to add one or two "2's" after the city code. For instance, to call a six-digit number in Yaroslavl you need to dial "8," then the city code "085," then "2," then the number; or to call a five digit number in Kaluga, dial "8," then the city code "084," then "22," then the number.

(2) In some cities, and in a number of Moscow areas, you may be required to dial your own number after the number you are calling.

To call villages or small towns outside your region, you will need to book a call by dialing "07" (though in Moscow this number is only an information service – they will tell you the number to ring, which is different for each area of the country). Expect to be called back within the hour (or half-hour if you booked it "urgent," *srochny*, for three times the price).

Note: What might seem to you like a cheap phone call could be expensive for your host, so be sure to agree beforehand about reimbursement.

Dialing from a hotel. If you have a direct dial phone in your room, which outside Moscow and St. Petersburg is quite rare, the same applies as above. The bills will arrive downstairs. If your phone is only a local one, or if you have to use the floor lady's phone, you will probably need to pay in advance at the reception desk for a stated period. You will be given a slip of paper (*talon*), whose number you need to quote to the operator when you make the booking.

Moscow's Central Telephone & Telegraph office, #7 Ul. Tverskaya, metro Okhotny Ryad

Dial "07" as above. International calls are made in the same fashion when you are phoning from a hotel room.

Dialing from the Post Office. You can book a call to just about anywhere (though you may not be able to make it right away, or even on the same day if you are in some really remote location), just by writing the town, phone number and duration of call on a piece of paper and paying the cashier. You can also state whom you want to speak with, to avoid being charged for the call if that person is not in. You will be directed to one of the numbered phone booths to take your call.

Pay phones. The ordinary ones – таксофоны (*taksofony*) – that you see on the street are for local calls only, and you cannot ask people to call you back on them. In theory, each coin should give you three minutes, but in fact most seem to carry on indefinitely without your putting more money in. Inflation-induced chaos has created some confusion about payment – in some cities calls are now free, in others there is a token (*jeton*) system. Moscow is now switching to the telephone token system, while St. Petersburg uses metro tokens.

If you see a sign saying, междугородныи телефон (inter-city pay phone) don't rejoice too soon. Chances are it requires special tokens or coins which are impossible to find, or else is simply broken. However, there are such pay phones that work on the street and also in post offices, or sometimes in special halls marked переговорный пункт (calling station). If they take tokens, they'll probably swallow them quite avidly. Other places have worked out an ingenious system whereby the caller pays a cashier in advance for a specified period of time, and then can dial freely from the alloted booth. This arrangement applies only to calls within the region or to major cities outside. Sometimes you don't need to dial 8, and sometimes you need to press a button to be heard by the person receiving the call.

Telegrams. This is an effective and cheap way to reach people, both inside and outside the former Soviet Union. Telegrams can be sent from any post office, or over the phone by dialing 927-2002 (in Moscow). If you want to dictate a telegram by phone, you'll need to speak Russian. However, post offices should be able to handle telegrams given to them on paper in English.

Useful Numbers (Nationwide)

	City Codes		
Fire – 01 Militia (police) – 02 Ambulance – 03 Local information – 09 **Time:** Moscow – 100 St. Petersburg – 08	Arkhangelsk – 818 Bryansk – 083 Ivanovo – 093 Kaluga – 084 *Moscow* – 095 Murmansk – 815 Nizhny Novogorod – 831 Novgorod – 816 Petrozavodsk – 814 Pskov – 811 Ryazan – 091 *St. Petersburg* – 812 Smolensk – 081	Suzdal – 09231 Tula – 087 Tver – 082 Vladimir – 092 Vologda – 817 Yaroslavl – 085 Kiev, Ukraine – 044 **Country Codes** USA and Canada – 1 Great Britain – 44 France – 33 Germany – 49

Travel within Russia

Air

Until recently there was only one airline, **Aeroflot**, for the whole Soviet Union, whose internal flights were always regarded with great trepidation by Westerners. Tales of boozing pilots, rattling fuselages, and rocky landings were commonplace. This is still more or less true, but there have been some changes. While the CIS republican airlines breaking away from Aeroflot are just as bad and often worse, one new Russian carrier, **Transaero**, is proving a leaner, fitter competitor. Co-founded by Aeroflot itself, Transaero now flies most major domestic routes. While charging identical prices as Aeroflot, Transaero provides a higher standard of service, including in-flight meals and a business class option.

Air travel for foreigners is without exception much more expensive than it is for Russians, and there's no way of getting round that, as passports always have to be shown. Tickets should be bought at the places indicated in the Moscow and St. Petersburg city sections, or in smaller cities at Intourist desks, which are usually found in one or more of the main tourist hotels.

Upon arrival for your flight, you go to a special check-in desk and waiting room for foreigners, which is generally less crowded and seedy than the regular one. If you are traveling with Russians, you can ask for them to accompany you. On a long flight, don't expect to be fed well; take along snacks.

Rail

There are three types of trains in Russia:

Prigorodniye poyezda (пригородные поезда) – known colloquially as *elektrichki*, these are short distance local trains serving city and country areas. They are currently Russia's cheapest form of out-of-town transport, and it shows. In summer they are stifling, in winter freezing cold, and often dirty, smelly, slow, and packed tight. Tickets are bought at the *prigorodnaya kassa* (пригородная касса).

Skoriye poyezda (скорые поезда) – the fastest trains, but that's not saying a lot. There are four classes, all requiring a reservation.

(1) *Spalniy* or *Lyuks* are first class, two-berth sleeper compartments; usually, but not always, the cleanest.

(2) *Koopeyniy* are second class, four-berth couchette-type.

(3) *Platskartniy* are open compartments with extra window-side berths across the corridor. There's no privacy, and you risk being kept awake by screaming children or drunken soldiers.

(4) *Obshchy* are the same as above, except that a bunk to sleep on is not guaranteed, and you don't get bed linen.

Classes 1–3 have a carriage attendant *(provodnik)* to distribute linen. He or she should also in theory provide tea, though this rarely happens. Still, there is always a water heater (*titan*) at the end of the carriage, so you can make your own. There are toilets at both ends, which should be approached with care – some require a sustained holding of breath. Bring your own paper and soap, as these are frequently not available.

For longer than overnight trips, there is usually a restaurant or buffet car, but it's a good idea to bring your own food. Almost everyone else does so, and it's good to have something to share with your fellow travelers. Anyway, train food is usually especially poor, with very little choice.

Each train has a guard (*nachalnik poyezda*). Any queries or problems with fellow passengers or *provodniks*

should be addressed to him.

The third type of train, *Passazhirskiye poyezda* (пассажирские поезда), is almost identical to *skoriye*, except that they stop at every station, and tend to be seedier.

The best trains are the *skoriye* between Moscow and St. Petersburg, most of which run overnight. The famous *Red Arrow* (*Krasnaya strela*), as well as the Intourist trains operated mainly for foreigners, come very close to Western standards.

When traveling by intercity train in Russia, consider the advantages and disadvantages of traveling by first-class (two berths) or second-class (four berths). Second-class, while seedier, will almost certainly throw you together with Russians, which can be a lot of fun, as you and your fellow travelers produce various provisions for the window table, and much reference is made to dictionaries. On the Moscow–Petersburg route in particular, a first-class booking will likely put you in the company of another foreigner.

If you are worried about personal security, some suggest bringing a two-foot length of nylon cord to tie shut the door to the corridor, which is not very secure, even when locked. On overnight trips, it's best to store your most valuable luggage in the compartment underneath the lower berths.

Buying Tickets

Foreigners are required to buy tickets separately from Russians, paying three times more for the privilege and often having to stand in line longer at special ticket offices. It may be easier to book through Intourist, though they charge a few dollars more. However you get them, tickets are cheaper than in most Western countries, although the gap seems to be closing steadily. At time of writing (spring 1994), fares for foreigners on the Moscow–St. Petersburg overnight trains were the equivalent of $36 for first class and $20 for second class. There was also a special student fare of about $20 for first class.

In the provinces, it is often unclear how foreigners are supposed to obtain tickets. If you're having difficulties, it's usually worth applying to the duty officer (*dezhurny po vokzalu*) or the station master (*nachalnik vokzala*). This approach could also prove useful in the case of trains that are supposedly fully reserved.

There are usually hawkers around mainline stations selling tickets at what for Russians are inflated prices, but for foreigners often work out to be cheaper. Also, if your Russian is good, or if you are traveling with Russian friends, you can try getting a ticket at the ticket office for Russian prices. Only bear in mind that they have to include the name of the holder, so think up a Russian name for yourself. *Provodniks* are required to check passports, but this rarely happens even on major routes – it's more than their jobs are worth. Just try not to stand out too much or speak English in their presence. As a last resort, if you're too late to buy tickets (the ticket office stops selling five minutes before the train leaves) or know that they are sold out, try offering a *provodnik* a few dollars and you'll probably get on the train.

Buses

These are often the most efficient and comfortable means of traveling shorter distances, that is, within or between regions. For foreigners there is no extra charge, so they are also much cheaper than long-distance trains, though the ticketing system is archaic. Tickets, together with a seating list, are generally written out by hand. If

you're traveling on Friday, Saturday morning, or Sunday evening, you should get tickets at the advance booking office (*predvaritelnaya kassa*). On short local routes, ticket selling doesn't stop when there are no seats left, only when the bus is packed full. On longer journeys, approaching the driver directly can usually get you a standing place.

Buses are normally quite comfortable, but without air-conditioning, and can get stiflingly hot owing to Russians' dislike of draughts (which they fear carry germs), even in high summer.

River Boats

Russia's extensive waterway system is covered by a surprisingly good network of long- and short-distance river transport. Unfortunately, it has been severely hit by the recession and decimated by service cutbacks in recent years. But even now, if you're traveling between May and September, boats are a more pleasant and sometimes more convenient option than buses or trains.

Shorter routes are serviced by fast *raketa* hydrofoils or slower "Moskva"-class river buses, especially useful in such areas as the Gulf of Finland, Lake Onega or on the River Volga.

For longer journeys and leisure cruises, there are now a host of travel firms offering package deals, mostly on the upper Volga and the northern lakes. (One of these, which we can book for you, is the "Best of Russia" cruises operated by the **Center for Creative International Programs** [CCIP]. For further information, see the Introduction or their advertisement.) For the budget traveler or anyone wanting to travel on obscure routes such as the Oka River, the state-run river fleet (Rechflot) sells tickets for its own dilapidated diesel boats (*teplokhody*). These do not include food and excursions, but are identically priced for Russians and foreigners alike. There are several classes of cabin.

Municipal Transport

All major Russian cities have buses and trolleybuses, and some also have trams (streetcars) and a metro system. All except the metro, which uses tokens, now use the universal *talony* system, whereby strips of tickets are purchased from the driver or from kiosks near stops. For each journey, you punch your ticket in one of the gadgets along the walls of the bus. Some cities, just to be confusing, use different tickets for different means of transport, but you won't encounter this very often. You can get monthly passes, too (*prayezdneeye*, проездные), which are cheap enough to be worth buying for the convenience even if you're only staying a few days. Combined passes for surface and metro travel are called *yedeeniye* (единые).

Many small-town and country services still use an older system, whereby you put money in a box and roll out tickets yourself by hand. More commonly, though, you pay the driver, who may or may not give you a ticket, depending on availability or mood.

Inspectors are rare, and never appear during rush hour or late at night, and fines are even cheaper than monthly passes. Watch out for them particularly at weekends – they will show identification and expect you to produce a monthly pass or punched ticket. If you don't you will have to leave the bus with them at the next stop and pay the fine. Sometimes tickets are checked as people leave the bus at the end of the route.

City transport in Russia is often

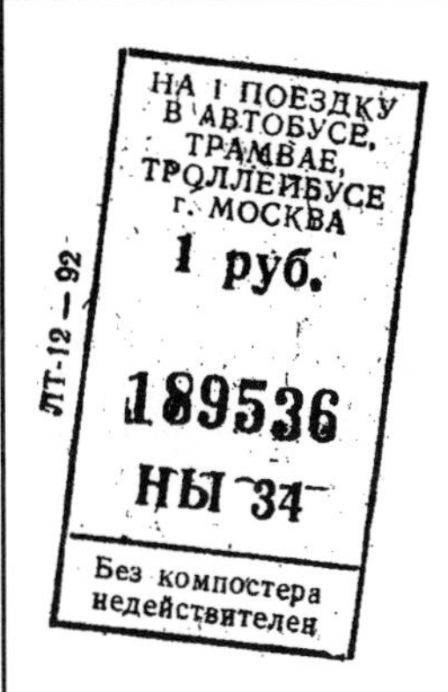

Moscow bus, tram and trolleybus ticket; St. Petersburg trams

overburdened and sometimes there can be terrifying crushes. At such times pushing and shoving, within reasonable limits, is acceptable. If you are stuck a long way from an exit and need to get out, ask the question *vy vykhoditye*? (are you getting out?) and if they are not, the person will try to make way for you. You can also ask people to punch your ticket for you – just say, *prabivayitye pahzhal'sta*?

Public transport works, in theory, from 5:30 a.m. or 6 a.m. to 12:30 a.m. or 1 a.m., depending on the city and form of transport. This should be confirmed locally, though, because recent cutbacks have led to some services stopping earlier. If you are trying to go somewhere at, say, midnight, don't rely on public transport to take you there.

On the metro, on local trains, and sometimes also on buses and other surface transport, stations or stops will be announced over a loudspeaker. Usually, the name of the station will be given first, followed by connections from that station. Just before the doors close you will hear the warning *astarozhna, dveeri zakrivayootsa* ("attention, the doors are closing"), followed by the name of the next station. (Note that in St. Petersburg the name of the next station is announced before the doors are closed.) On overland transport you will normally have to ask where you should get off, as there is no other way of knowing. If you don't speak Russian, try writing down your destination on a scrap of paper, referring to the Cyrillic glossaries provided in each chapter of this book.

In the metro, if you wish to change to another line, look for the sign with the man walking down steps and the word переход. Exits from stations are marked simply by the word выход. Many stations have two exits, and there are signs on the platform indicating which exit leads to which bus, trolleybus, and tram routes, and also directions to nearby streets and landmarks.

In St. Petersburg, a metro map, and also a transport map called Skema Passazhirskovo Transporta (Скема пассажирского транспорта), can be purchased at Rospechat kiosks and others, and at some bookstores. They are in Russian with some English and the route numbers are clear.

Marshrutniye taksi, or *marshrutki* (маршрутные такси, route taxis) can be more convenient. Unlike with buses, you can stop them anywhere along their given route. These are usually minibuses, and are slightly more expensive.

Taxis

Taxis are not always easy to find, but in big cities you won't have much trouble getting a lift. Just hold out your arm at the roadside (with your palm spread, not with thumb extended as in the West). You can flag down almost anyone, from trucks to Mercedes, and at night even buses. If you're going a short distance, ambulance drivers usually offer the best rates and almost always stop. Don't worry about interfering with their work; they won't pick you up unless they're off duty!

When the car stops for you, you need to state your destination and agree on a price with the driver, even if the car appears to have a meter. Many will try to overcharge foreigners, so try to get an idea of approximate rates beforehand. Airport and train station taxis are expensive, and occasionally unsafe, so try to get someone to meet you.

You can book radio taxis by phone. These are reliable, and can work out cheaper despite the booking fee. For telephone numbers, consult the books *Where in Moscow*, *Where in St. Petersburg*, or *The Traveller's Yellow Pages* for each of the cities. (See Booklist.)

If you're in a rural area and you want to hitchhike, bear in mind that in theory the same procedures apply as in town. In practice, many people will give you lifts for free, but it's polite to offer them some money anyway.

Travel by Car

Car journeys through the wide open spaces of Russia can be a rewarding experience, but require some serious preparation. To begin with, your choice of car is very important. American and Japanese makes are not recommended for trips outside Moscow and St. Petersburg – you'll rarely find spare parts or decent roads, and Russian petrol will cripple your engine. Simpler European cars are likely to perform well here. Volvos, Peugeots and Volkswagen Posads are the best choices. Perhaps best of all is a Russian car, such as a Lada – nothing else is better equipped to deal with the legions of ruts and potholes you'll come across.

Make sure no parts are about to drop off your car, and check that the suspension is healthy – it's going to be a bumpy ride! Take a couple of full extra gas cans, too; you might need them, if only in searching for gas stations. Avoid speculators – you might find yourself with a tank full of a gas/diesel mix and an astronomical repair bill.

If you're bringing a car in from Europe, check on insurance and customs regulations beforehand, as these are constantly changing.

Car hire. Most foreign firms restrict clients to very limited areas around Moscow and St. Petersburg. However, some offer the whole country, including three of the major companies: Europcar, Hertz, and Avis. If you're planning to visit other republics of the former Soviet Union, check whether the rental company's insurance covers that area. The Moscow phone numbers of these firms are:

Avis: (095) 930-1323, Peugeots and Toyotas

Europcar, Sheremetyevo-2 Airport: (095) 578-8236; Novotel Hotel: (095) 578-9407; Mezhdunarodnaya Hotel: (095) 253-2477; Olympic Penta Hotel: (095) 971-6101; Pullman Iris Hotel: (095) 488-8000; Peugeots, Volvos, and Mercedes

MTDS-Hertz: (095) 448-6728, Ladas and Volvos

Try to return the car with a full tank, otherwise you'll get charged a

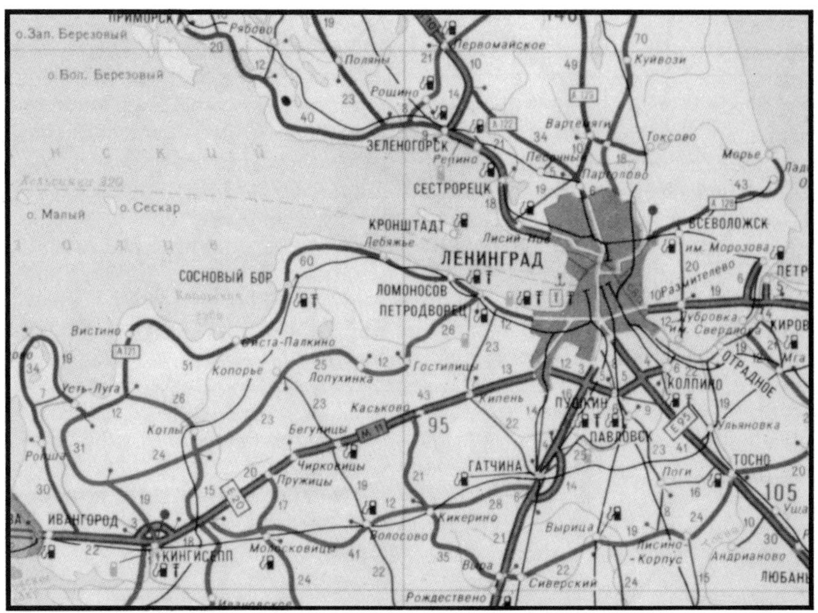

The vicinity of St. Petersburg, from the **Automobile Atlas of the USSR**

much higher price for the gas than you would have paid for it at a station.

A road atlas is essential. Try to get a copy of the *Atlas Avtomobilnykh Dorog SSSR* (*Атлас Автомобильных дорог СССР*). Different editions are different colors, the most readily available being the brown 1991 edition (hardback, 25 cm x 17 cm). It includes relatively simple maps of the former Soviet Union, plus major cities and an explanation of road signs in Russian, and can usually be obtained from sidewalk booksellers on Ploshchad Revolyutsiyi in Moscow and on Nevsky prospekt near the Kazan Cathedral in St. Petersburg.

Note that on all but the principal tourist routes, such as Moscow–St. Petersburg and the Golden Ring, signs are in Russian only, so be sure to learn the Cyrillic alphabet.

Roads are classified according to the following system:

"E" roads: European road numberings, for routes of continental significance. Be aware that this doesn't mean they are of European *standard.*

"M" roads: Magisterial roads ("motorways," if you like) of national significance, but bear in mind that in terms of quality they are a far cry from their British or American equivalents. Few even have two lanes in each direction. Some "M" roads also have accompanying "E" numbers (e.g., the M10 Moscow–St. Petersburg highway is also the E95).

"A" roads: Other major roads of national significance.

"R" roads ["P" in Russian]: Other routes of national significance, which are sometimes unpaved. They are not numbered in standard Soviet road atlases, only on regional maps.

City driving. Traffic rules in Russia are often quite bizarre, with elaborate one-way systems, U-turns and lack of legal left-turns, which often require a U-turn followed by a right turn, or vice versa. You will probably find that you are pulled over by the *militia*

Name Changes

There is currently a lot of confusion in major cities about old (Communist era) and new (often prerevolutionary) street names. Sometimes the names have been changed on the streets themselves, but not on maps, and sometimes there has simply been a decision made to change them which has not been implemented. In this guide, new names have been given for the most progressive cities (Moscow and St. Petersburg in particular) and old ones in the provinces. These may not always be correct, as things are changing all the time. Local people will know the old names, so always ask if things seem to be different. A list of "Old & New Street Names" will be found in both the Moscow and St. Petersburg chapters.

(GAI, ГАИ) quite regularly; they usually stand by the roadside and usher you aside with hand signals. On such occasions, indicating that you don't understand, and failing that the proffering of a few dollars, should satisfy them. Be warned also that Russians drive aggressively, and often fail to heed the rules.

A note on distances: The distances in kilometers for car journeys given in this book are approximate.

Shopping

However glitzy shopping streets in Moscow and St. Petersburg may now seem to Russians, they're unlikely to impress the Western eye. Despite liberation of prices in 1992, which released goods of every kind onto the market, the absence of an effective distribution system and a lack of retail space means that many basic products are still in short supply while luxury goods are abundant relative to demand. In these confusing times, there are basically four types of retail outlet:

State or former state stores, still often poorly stocked and inefficiently staffed. In some shops you'll see piles of useless and unwanted goods sitting on the shelves gathering dust while others are snapped up within minutes of being set out. This situation is a leftover of the old "command economy" system in which production levels were all important, and no one cared about quality.

The frustrations of standing in lines are often compounded by the *kassa* system, which requires that you queue up in one place to pay and receive a chit, and then in another to pick up what you have purchased. In some food shops, you may also have to wait to get the item weighed and priced in the first place before you can stand in the cashier's line!

Markets. Once places where peasants simply came to sell their excess produce, these have grown into huge, unruly bazaars, including imported or speculated local goods, which are often sold by people simply standing on the street displaying a single item. Many new markets have recently sprung up spontaneously. Sometimes it may be worth haggling over prices there.

Kiosks. One answer to the retail space problem has been to build kiosks in heavily frequented public areas (especially in the plazas surrounding metro entrances), or to take over old newspaper or *kvas* kiosks and fill them with profitable, nonper-

St. Petersburg covered market near Moskovsky Vokzal

ishable items such as confectionery, savory snacks, alcohol, soft drinks, coffee, and tea. These places are operated by the new entrepreneurs of Russia, who are not always paragons of honesty. Therefore, if you buy there, check that products are what they say they are, and are not past their sell-by dates. When buying wines and spirits, make sure the tops are fixed firmly on the bottles – if they seem inexpensive they may be adulterated or even poisonous. The advantages of kiosks are quick service and flexible hours – they are quite often open round the clock. Thanks to kiosks, there is no longer a danger of going hungry or thirsty on the streets of Moscow and Petersburg at night.

Western-type shops. These have been sprouting almost as fast as kiosks and can range from simple basement stores selling a few items of clothing to full-fledged supermarkets. They provide similar types of products as the kiosks but on a larger scale.

Other shopping notes. Always take along your own bags when you go shopping as stores rarely sell them. A new pricing practice has emerged recently. Because of inflation, some prices may be stated in dollars, but payable only in rubles at the current exchange rate. Be sure to have small bills and coins with you, whether paying in rubles or dollars.

Keep in mind that small shops and pleasant cafés and restaurants may be located in unexpected places – such as in the courtyards of apartment buildings or up a flight of dark stairs – and also may be poorly marked. Your Russian contacts may be able to help you find such places.

Eating and Drinking

People don't go to Russia for its cuisine, which has neither the rich variety of southern European cooking nor the spicy intrigue of Asian dishes. But it has enough tasty and filling choices to keep you satisfied and interested for some time at least, especially if you don't rely too much on restaurants, and accept offers of Russian hospitality.

The basic Russian diet is a simple one. Traditional peasant cooking usually involves one or more of the following staple vegetables: potatoes (*kartoshka*), turnips (*repa*), onions (*luk*), cucumbers (*ogurtsy*), beets (*svyokla*), and cabbage (*kapusta*), of which the perishable ones are pickled for the winter. Salted cabbage or cucumbers are commonly used as garnishes.

Other fruits and vegetables appear in season, so look in July for strawberries (*klubnika*) and raspberries (*malina*), and August and September for melon (*dynya*) and watermelon (*arbooz*). Sour cranberries (*klyukva*) help to liven up the monotonous winter diet, while apples (*yabloka*), and to some extent tangerines (*mandariny*) and persimmons (*khurma*), are the only source of winter vitamins for most Russians. Vegetables are generally served in salads as *zakuski*, or appetizers, while fruit is served as a dessert.

Mushrooms (*griby*) are widely enjoyed, and one of the most popular Russian pastimes is an outing to the forest for mushroom-picking. They can be fried (*zharenniye*), pickled (*marinovanniye*), or baked in a delicious sour cream sauce to produce *zhulyen* (julienne). They can be served as a main dish or as a first course, instead of soup.

Soup (*sup*) is a vital part of lunch (*obyed*) in Russia. In fact, it is commonly held that eating lunch without it will upset your stomach. The most famous variety is *borscht*, its deep red color emanating from its main ingredient, beets. Others include the hearty *solyanka*, with tomato, fish, and meat as the main ingredients, which in more sophisticated company may be topped with olives and lemon. *Shchi* is cabbage soup, and *okroshka* is a cold soup made with *kvas* (see Drinking).

Milk products, like *smetana* (sour cream) and yogurts of various flavors and thicknesses, originated in the south. Today, many of these are unobtainable in northern Russia, though you are bound to come across kefir, a kind of plain, drinkable, sometimes salty-tasting yogurt. Others are *prostakvasha*, similar to petits suisses, and *ryazhenka*, a delicious creamy yogurt. *Tvorog* is similar to cottage cheese, and normally eaten with *smetana*. It's also a nutritious source of vitamins and protein if you're having diet problems. Milk can be scarce, especially in summer, and the flavor is not very pleasant to the Western palate – Russian pasteurizing techniques leave something to be desired. Sterilized milk is probably the safest, but is available only in Moscow. On the other hand, nothing beats the creamy unpasteurized stuff you'll find in country markets.

Bread is normally eaten with every meal, traditionally black rye bread (*rzhanoy khleb*), heavy and slightly sour tasting. Wheat bread has appeared more recently and is regarded as something of a delicacy in rural areas, where it is scarce. Russians love to bake all kinds of pastry (*pirogi*) with fillings ranging from fish to cabbage to cranberries. Pancakes (*bliny*) are virtually a national dish, and date from pagan times. Pancakes with caviar (*bliny s ikroy*), originating from the Volga valley, are a particular favorite.

Cereals are a staple, especially in villages, where there is little else to eat. They are usually prepared as a *kasha*, that is, boiled in water with salt and butter. Most common are *grechka* (buckwheat), *mannaya* (semolina) and *ovsyanka* (oats).

Meat (*myasa*) was rarely eaten in old Russia, as people gave it up during Lent and other fasts, which totalled about 240 days a year. Peasants ate lots of fish, however, with plentiful river species proving a favorite for feast days. Herring (*selyodka*) became a fitting accompaniment to vodka, while the traditional dried fish called *vobla* was eaten with beer. Fish were the source of old Russia's only delicacies: red salmon caviar (*krasnaya ikra*) or black sturgeon caviar (*chornaya ikra*) and sturgeon itself (*osetrina*). Today, raw or smoked fish is often served as an appetizer.

Although meat became widespread in Russia only during this century, it is now firmly established as the main source of protein, at least in urban areas. *Kolbasa* (German or Polish sausage) is also very popular, particularly as an appetizer or as a snack with bread (*buterbrod*). Much of today's Russian cuisine is centered around meat. Vegetarianism is virtually nonexistent despite the previously cited strong Orthodox Christian traditions. Typical meat dishes include *pelmeni* – a kind of ravioli or dumplings, and *zharkoye* – a hotpot which, if prepared properly, ends up covered in dough, sealing the top so that the flavor is cooked in. *Kotlety* (cutlets) are the Russian equivalent of hamburgers, while *shashlyki* are shish kebabs, a very popular import from the Caucasus, especially for picnics.

"Night Blinis" – 19th century poster

At the end of a meal, tea (*chay*) is normally drunk, though coffee (*kofye*) is now popular too. Russians take both without milk but with lots of sugar. Indian tea is the most popular, and is sometimes supplemented with herbs. Tea is often served with *varenye*, a very sweet, liquid jam, almost always homemade and delicious. Alternatives are cake (*tort*) and sweets (*konfyety*), or in poorer families *pryaniki* – heavy, hard little cakes originating from the special patterned cakes prepared for festivals.

Drink

As everyone knows, the Russian national drink is vodka, consumed copiously by the working male (and sometimes female) population. The most common brands, "Russkaya" and "Pshenichnaya," vary greatly in taste depending on the factory where they were produced – Kristall in Moscow is said to be the best, while the Azerbaijani version is pure paint-stripper. Nowadays imports are flooding the market and the better Russian vodkas are increasingly rare, but the options are enticing if you can find them. Other than brands familiar in the West, vodkas like "Posolskaya," "Zolotoye Koltso" and "Sibirskaya" are a must for the connoisseur. If you like flavored vodkas, the fruity "Kubanskaya," herbal "Zubrovka" (bison vodka!) and the butterscotchy "Starka" should not be missed.

The other popular hard liquor in Russia is *konyak* (cognac), mainly a Caucasian drink, but widespread in Russia, too. Quality ranges from Azerbaijani (again, paint-stripper), through Dagestani and Georgian, to Armenian "Ararat" brands and the excellent Moldavian "Bely Aist" (White Stork).

Wine (*vino*) has never been popular in northern Russia, with the exception of some cheap Azerbaijani and

Dagestani sweet wines, known deceptively as *portvein* and favored by drunks who can't afford vodka. Dry wines are enjoyed only in the most enlightened circles, and availability of the local Georgian and Moldavian types is very poor. If you can find them, try semi-drys like "Tsinandali" (white) or "Kindzmarauli" and "Odzhareshi" (red). Drier wines like "Ereti" and "Mukuzani" are slightly sour, but this does not detract from their appeal. The top Moldavian wines are those which mix together the best grape varieties, although the Moldovian Cabernets, Sauvignons, Aligotes and Rkatsitelis are good on their own, too. The best sweet wines – a glorious range of sherries, ports and madeiras – are from the Crimea's "Massandra" factory. Have fun trying to find them in Russia.

Sparkling wine (*shampanskoye*) on the other hand, is cheap, popular and abundant, a must for any celebration and a staple for many women who drink. It is usually quite drinkable, but though the labels are uniform, quality varies. Nowadays, though, you can tell the Azerbaijani brands because the labels are written in Turkish. The best is the "Novy Svyet" label from the Crimea.

Beer (*pivo*) for Russians is scarcely considered an alcoholic drink, though their own is generally double the strength of Western varieties. More commonly it is treated as a soft drink by men, sometimes to chase down vodka or as "hair of the dog." Contrary to expectations, and to the convictions of many Russians, their beer is often better than many of the weak European imports now so common in Russia. But while Russian beer is considerably cheaper, it is rarely pasteurized, so be sure to check production dates. If it's cloudy, or has plankton swimming in it, don't touch it. The most common brands – "Zhigulyovskoye," "Yachmenny Kolos" and "Moskovskoye" – are nothing to write home about. The best is "Tverskoye" from Tver, whose brewery produces both lager (*svetloye*) and ale (*tyomnoye*). The latter in particular has a strong, sweet, heady flavor (try the "Prazdnichnoye" brand if you can find it). There are a growing number of beers brewed in Moscow for export, such as "Mamovniki" and "Troika"; these are also recommended.

Russia's western neighbors, Belarus and Ukraine, produce even better beer, but the best of all comes from the Baltics. Try the Lithuanian "Porteris" (porter) or Latvia's "Rigas Alus," not to be confused with Russian "Rizhskoye."

Then there is *kvas*, also treated as a soft drink although it is slightly alcoholic. Made from fermented black bread, it is sold widely on tap in summer. Among traditional drinks, there is a stronger alternative, *myod* or *myedovukha*, a kind of mead, found only in old Russian cities. It may seem at first to be nonalcoholic, but just try standing up after a few glasses!

A note about drinking water. Always boil tap water. In St. Petersburg, unboiled water may cause severe stomach problems, and while Moscow's water is generally considered safe, there were several cases of cholera in the city recently. Elsewhere the water is probably okay, but better to boil it all the same. Western mineral water can generally be found as an alternative. The Russian variety is usually fizzy and often tastes strongly of minerals. The best are "Narzan" (almost tasteless) and "Yessentuki" (with a thick, salty taste), both from the northern Caucasus spas.

Dining Out

While Moscow and St. Petersburg now boast an impressive array of foreign, private, and cooperative restau-

Sample Russian Dishes

Закуски	**Zu*koo*skee**	**Appetizers**
Черная икра	***Chor*naya eek*ra***	Black (sturgeon) caviar
Красная икра	***Kras*naya eek*ra***	Red (salmon) caviar
Шпроты	**Sh*proty***	Sprats
Лосось, Семга	**La*sos'*, *syom*ga**	Salmon
Колбаса	**Kulbas*sa***	Sausage
Ветчина	**Vitchi*na***	Ham
Язык	**Ya*zeek***	Tongue
Рулет (из говядины)	**Rool*yet* (eez gov*ya*diny)**	Collared beef (meat loaf)
Студень, холодец, заливная рыба, заливное мясо	***Stoo*din', hulad*yets*, zuleev*naya* *rey*ba, zuleev*noye* my*a*so**	Various types of jellied cold meat or fish

Мясо	**My*a*so**	**Meat**
Бифштекс	**Bifsh*teks***	Steak
Шашлык	**Shash*leek***	Shish kebab
Шницель	***Shnee*tsel'**	Shnitzel
Пельмени	**Pelm*ye*nee**	Dumplings, similar to ravioli
Говядина	**Guv*ya*dina**	Beef
Жаркое	**Zhar*koye***	Meat roast with onions in stock and red wine
Котлеты	**Kotl*ye*ty**	Cutlets
Котлеты по-киевски	**Kotl*ye*ty pa *Kee*yevski**	Chicken Kiev
Цыплята табака	**Tseepl*ya*ta Taba*ka***	Young chicken, fried in sour cream and oil, with garlic sauce

Рыба	***Rey*ba**	**Fish**
Осетрина фри, жаренная	**Ase*tree*na free, *Zha*rennaya**	Fried sturgeon
Судак варёный	**Soo*dak* var*yon*ny**	Boiled pike, perch
Треска запечённая	***Tris*ka zapi*chon*naya**	Cod baked with potatoes, onions, tomatoes
Форель	**Fo*rel'***	Trout

Блюда без мяса	**Bl*yoo*da byez my*a*sa**	**Non-Meat Dishes**
Блины, оладьи	**Bli*nee*, a*la*di**	Pancakes, with jam or sour cream added
Каша	***Ka*sha**	Boiled cereal with butter
Пироги с рисом, луком, грибами, картошкой, яблоками	**Pira*gee* s *ree*sum *loo*kum, gri*ba*mee, kar*tosh*kuy, *ya*blakumi**	Pies with rice, onion, mushroom, potato, apple filling
Сырники	***Syr*niki**	Curd, cottage cheese pancakes
Вареники	**Var*yen*iki**	Dumplings with mushroom or potato filling
Омлет	**Aml*yet***	Omelette
Яичница	**Ya*eesh*nitsa**	Fried eggs

Первые блюда	**P*yer*vye bl*yoo*da**	**Soups/First Course**
Борщ	**Borsch**	Beet and cabbage soup
Щи	**Schee**	Cabbage soup
Солянка	**Sal*yan*ka**	Thick meat/fish soup
Окрошка	**Ak*rosh*ka**	Cold soup with kvas, sausage and vegetables
Рассольник	**Ras*sol*nik**	Hot soup with pickled vegetables
Бульон с яйцом	**Bool*yon* s yait*som***	Egg broth
Бульон куриный	**Bool*yon* s koo*ree*ny**	Chicken broth
Уха рыбная	**Oo*ha* *ryb*naya**	Fish soup
Жульен с грибами	**Zhool*yen* s gree*ba*mee**	Mushrooms baked in sour cream sauce

Салаты	**Sa*la*ty**	**Salads**
Столичный салат	**Sto*leech*ny sa*lat***	Potato, meat, pickled vegetable and mayonnaise salad
Салат из помидоров	**Sa*lat* eez pumi*do*rov**	Tomatoes in sour cream, mayonnaise or oil
Салат из огурцов	**Sa*lat* eez agoort*sov***	Cucumber as above

Салат витаминный	**Salat vita*meen*ny**	Cabbage, carrots, apples and spring onions in oil, sugar, wine and lemon juice
Салат из капусты	**Salat eez ka*poo*sty**	Fresh or pickled cabbage
Винегрет	**Vinegr*yet***	Potatoes, beets, carrots and cucumbers in oil, vinegar, salt, pepper and mustard
Сладкие	***Slad*kiye**	**Desserts**
Мороженое	**Ma*ro*zhenaye**	Ice cream
Пирожные	**Pi*rozh*niyeh**	Cakes, pastries
Торт	**Tort**	Cake (in slices)
Конфеты	**Kanf*ye*ty**	Sweets, chocolates
Яблоки	***Ya*bloky**	Apples
Арбуз	**Ar*booz***	Watermelon
Шоколад	**Shoka*lad***	Chocolate bar
Напитки	**Na*peet*ki**	**Drinks**
Напиток, морс	**Na*pee*tok, morss**	Fruit squash
Газированный напиток	**Gazi*ro*vanny na*pee*tok**	Fizzy drink, soda
Минеральная вода	**Mine*ral*naya va*da***	Mineral water
Сок	**Sok**	Fruit juice
Пиво	**Pee*vo***	Beer
Вино	**Vi*no***	Wine
Шампанское	**Sham*pan*skoyeh**	Sparkling wine
Водка	***Vod*ka**	Vodka
Коньяк	**Kan*yak***	Cognac
Кофе	***Kof*yeh**	Coffee
Чай	**Chay**	Tea

rants, the same cannot be said for the provinces, though things are beginning to improve. For now, it's still not an exaggeration to say that most Russian restaurants are dirty, smoky, noisy, greasy, virtually devoid of menu choice, and have poor service. I call attention in the following pages to the happy exceptions as often as possible.

When you enter a restaurant, making it obvious you are a foreigner should be enough to ensure you an immediate place, excepting higher-class establishments in Moscow and St. Petersburg. Even so, it is considered courteous to wait in the entrance to be seated, at least in the evenings.

If you are hoping for a quiet evening meal, chances are you will be disappointed. Traditional Russian restaurants have music – the latest home-grown pop played loudly and often badly by local bands. (Even the more sophisticated private restaurants usually have live music of some kind and many now charge an admission fee.) The clientele, meanwhile, comes to party, get drunk, and pick up members of the opposite sex – in small towns the local restaurant is the only place where this is possible.

The alternatives are probably worse – street vendors selling cold, greasy meat pies, or seedy *shashlyk* bars. This does not apply to ice cream (*morozhenoye*), which is always worth trying. Though not native to Russia, it is generally creamy and tasty, and is frequently sold on street corners or from special kiosks. Cafés rarely serve food other than stale open sandwiches, and food in *stolovayas*, cheap cafeterias, is often inedible (though now and then you may find one where they really care about what they serve). Expect to find the local menfolk swigging vodka by the beakerful and the fiercest and most unpleasant local *babushkas* working behind the counter.

Customs and Habits

Russians have always been known for their public sullenness and reserve. While recent events seem to have made them more open and able to express themselves to strangers, they are still very modest in public and shun unnecessarily overt displays of emotion. Foreigners, on the other hand, particularly some Americans, often stand out like sore thumbs for doing just this. Attitudes toward foreigners here vary, and while you are unlikely to meet open hostility, some may resent loud behavior. Try to be restrained, without going to the other extreme and becoming excessively timid.

The Rigors of Life

In some respects, assertiveness is necessary in Russian daily life. In public transport, in shops, and in lines generally, some extra effort may be needed to get what you want, as staff are often infuriatingly passive and unhelpful. If you find shop assistants chatting to each other or to one of the customers, don't be afraid to interrupt or surprised if they seem annoyed at the interruption – that's what everyone does.

Lines in Russia have their own special rules, which are essential to know. The first thing you should do before joining one is to establish who is last. Ask *kto paslyedny* and expect the reply *ya* (I am). Failing to do this, particularly if the line is an ambiguous one, with people standing or sitting around in no obvious order, will result in people not remembering when you arrived and refusing to let you go ahead of them.

Don't be too abashed by the foregoing comments. If you get lost or are in need of other information, don't be afraid to ask. People are almost always helpful and in major cities often have some understanding of English.

Visiting Friends

The Russian home is very different from the fast, savage world of the street. You will be given a lavish welcome and considered an honored guest, so try to rise to the occasion. Bring flowers for the hostess (make sure there's an odd number of them; even-numbered bouquets are for funerals) and chocolates, alcohol, biscuits, books, cassette tapes from your own country, or anything you think is suitable. Children will like any Western sweets, chewing gum, coins, badges, or other trinkets.

You will be fed sumptuously. Don't be afraid to help yourself or ask for more – it can only please your hostess. If you're drinking, try to master the Russian down-in-one vodka technique, but know your limits. Do as everyone else does and take a long drink of juice or eat a pickled cucumber to take the taste away. And remember the common sense of eating food with your drink if possible. It may make a big difference in how you handle your vodka. After everyone's had a few drinks it's easier to keep your glass full and avoid inviting further refills.

It is worth knowing a few basic codes of etiquette. Men always shake hands in greeting, while hugs and kisses are reserved for more emotional occasions. Women kiss, but not always. Never greet someone across the threshold, as it is considered bad luck. Use the more formal greeting when first being introduced to someone, especially when they are of an older generation. (See "Basic Expressions" in the Language section.)

If you're drinking, remember that bottles should be finished, and then removed from the table.

In Church

If you visit a Russian Orthodox church or monastery, note that men are required to remove their hats, and women to wear some form of headgear. Shorts and miniskirts are also frowned on, and taking photos inside a church is generally not allowed, although you may certainly request permission.

"Avdotya was a typical grocery-store granny, a type unrecognized by socialist statistical science..."

It was never calm in the big shop. When you plunged in there, the waves grabbed you and bore you away... From the grocery section to the delicatessen, from the delicatessen to the meat section... And always elbows on every side, elbows and shoulders, more elbows... The good thing was they couldn't nudge you here – there was nowhere to fall. But an elbow to the face, the "mug" – nothing could be simpler.

Now they've wheeled out a trolley piled high with fat tins of herring. This kind of situation is mannah from heaven to Avdotya... No queue or order of any kind, straightforward pillage. Free-for-all grabbing. It's not the cunning of the fox Avdotya requires here, but the cunning of the mouse. Just like a circus act: hup, one, two – and the trolley's empty. People look around to see who's holding what. The men have grabbed one or two... Some folk have grabbed nothing but empty air, they're furious. The leaders of the pack are the strong, skilled housewives, with three or four tins. A few little old women are up there with them. Avdotya has three tins in her little bag.

Now you've got your fatty herrings, you get out of there, Avdotya, while you're still in one piece. Get out, Avdotya...

– excerpted from "Bag in Hand" by Friedrich Gorenstein, trans. Andrew Bromfield, from Issue #4 of *Glas: New Russian Writing*

The Banya

The *banya* (baths) occupies a traditional place in Russian life. After a hard day's work or strenuous exercise, men in particular often retire to the bathhouse. Technically speaking, it differs little from a sauna, with a hot room and shower or pool. However, the activities of its users lend it a very special flavor. Every session inevitably involves drinking large quantities, as you might expect, but the most distinctive custom is the use of *veniki*, bunches of twigs for beating the sweat out of each others' bodies.

Crime and Safety

Although you may have heard about the rising crime rate in Russia, don't expect the streets of Moscow to be any worse than those of New York; in fact, they are considerably safer. The flood of Western-style clothing into Moscow and St. Petersburg during the past few years means that you are much less likely to stand out as a foreigner than in the past, as long as you avoid dressing in a way likely to attract special attention.

However, precautions should be taken, and you should keep in mind that crime-fighting in Russia is of a very poor standard. Take all the precautions you would in any large city, and don't expect the *militia* (police) to be of much help if you become a victim.

One common phenomenon in major cities is gypsies, who may approach you and offer, for instance, to read your palm for a fee. In this case the best thing to do is get away from them as fast as possible. They can be very persistent, and it may be necessary to show more aggression than you are used to, or would like, to keep them away.

As in many European cities, gangs of children can be the most visible and aggressive thieves. Beware of unkempt, poor-looking children (often under age 14, because they cannot be arrested) and resist being sympathetic to their condition. You could actually be in danger of being robbed as they surround you. Giving them money to get rid of them often, unfortunately, has the opposite effect.

On the other hand, it is undeniably true that many of the people begging on the street or at the doors of churches are in real need. Once you are feeling reasonably acclimated, and especially when not alone, you might consider on occasion that a 100 ruble note or two (worth a small fraction of a dollar) might help quite a lot.

Be especially careful at night. Foreigners are always assumed to be loaded with money, and can therefore attract crime. Avoid hanging around metro stations, train stations or airports at night, and don't carry excessive amounts of money if you can avoid it. Don't get into private cars or taxis if there are two or more people inside already. You might consider carrying a pocket flashlight, as many entrance halls and stairways have no lights.

When staying in hotels, it is particularly important to keep a low profile. In big city hotels, you will often find among the guests members of the local Caucasian mafia. Caucasians, or "southerners," are similar in appearance to Arabs or Iranians. They often hang around in large groups at hotel entrances, and if there are any women with them they will almost certainly be Russian. Don't take unnecessary risks with these people, but also remember they may be genuinely friendly. If in doubt, ask the hotel staff.

When traveling outside Moscow and St. Petersburg, try not to take too many valuables as hotel door locks are rarely a reliable protection against crime. Don't leave valuables in your room and avoid hotel bars in the evening where local criminals often congregate. Unless you're a seasoned traveler and/or fluent enough in Russian to pass as a native, it's probably best not to travel on your own.

If you're renting an apartment, never give your home address to a stranger. Often, Russians don't even let taxi drivers know exactly where they live.

A note to women. Many Western women have had harassment problems from Russian men, so be warned. You might get accosted on the street. Try not to be too friendly; even if a man seems nice, chances are it's not friendship he's after. Even looking him in the eye could be interpreted as a direct come-on. You'll notice that Russian women are much more restrained and surly with men, until they know and trust them. Try not to walk alone at night; if it's really necessary, walk briskly and don't turn your head if someone calls out to you.

Language

While in some parts of the former Soviet Union speaking Russian may be met with disapproval or even incomprehension, this is not the case in the Russian Federation, despite all its minority nations, except possibly in the Caucasian republic of Chechenia, which no longer considers itself part of Russia anyway.

Other tongues, however, are now enjoying a revival. They include Tatar, spoken in the upper Volga valley; languages from the Finno-Ugric group such as Karelian, Komi, Mordovian, and Udmurt; north Caucasian languages related to Georgian; and Ossetian, which is similar to Persian.

Russian

Russian is a language in the eastern Slavonic group, using the Cyrillic alphabet, devised in the 9th century and based on the Greek alphabet. Its closest relatives are Ukrainian and Belorussian, but a knowledge of Polish, Bulgarian, Czech or Serbo-Croatian also makes learning easier.

The Alphabet

А а	*a*, as in "car"
Б б	*b*, hardening to "p" at the end of a word or before another consonant
В в	*v*, hardening to "f" at the end of a word or before another consonant
Г г	g, hardening to "k" at the end of a word or before another consonant. -его or -ого at the end of a word or in сегодня is always pronounced *yevo* or *ovo*
Д д	*d*, hardening to "t" at the end of a word or before another consonant
Е е	*ye*, as in "yesterday"

Ё ё	*yo,* as in "yob," always stressed
Ж ж	*zh, j, g* as in the second "g" in "garage"
З з	*z*
И и	*ee*
Й й	*y* (at beginning or end of word – at the end to lengthen a vowel; does not have its own sound)
К к	*k*
Л л	*l*
М м	*m*
Н н	*n*
О о	*o,* as in "short"; when unstressed becomes like the "a" in ran
П п	*p*
Р р	*r,* rolled as in Scottish
С с	s
Т т	*t*
У у	*oo*
Ф ф	*f*
Х х	*kh,* like the German or Celtic "ch"
Ц ц	*ts,* as in "floats"
Ч ч	*ch,* as in "check"
Ш ш	slightly hard *sh,* as in "shop"
Щ щ	*shch,* as in "Khru*sh-ch*ev"
Ъ ъ	the hard sign: a prerevolutionary letter, now used in only a few words to denote a break between letters, as in въезд (driveway) – vuy-yezd
Ы ы	a soft *i* with a hint of the "ir" sound in "bird"; like the French sound *oeu* in *boeuf*
Ь ь	the soft sign, used only to soften consonants
Э э	*e,* as in "egg"
Ю ю	*yu,* as in "yule"
Я я	*ya,* as in "yarn"

Stress. Every word of two or more syllables in Russian is stressed, but the place of stress is rarely predictable. To help with pronunciation, we have italicized each stressed syllable in this brief introduction to Russian.

Pronouns and proper forms of address. In Russian as in some other European languages, different pronouns are used depending upon the speaker's relationship to the listener. When addressing a stranger, an acquaintance or an elder, the *plural* pronoun вы (*vy*) is used. (You might think of it this way: that the speaker does not, in more formal situations, differentiate the listener very much from the mass of "others." For good friends, relatives and children, on the other hand, the singular form ты (*ty*) is acceptable. In the examples which follow, the singular form is always given first.

In the following transliterations, the English letters used do not necessarily correspond to those given above, but are intended to aid in the most accurate pronunciation. They differ in turn from transliterations of place-names elsewhere in this guide, which are the generally accepted English spellings and not always a reliable guide to exactly how they should be pronounced.

Note that the single-letter word **"s"** (in Russian, "C") is pronounced by combining it with the next word; for example, **"piragee s reesum"** (p. 72).

Basic Expressions

Yes

Da Да

No

Nyet Нет

Good day, afternoon

***Do*bry den** Добрый день

Good morning

Doe*broy*ah *oo*tra Доброе утро

Good evening

***Doe*bry *vyech*er** Добрый вечер

Goodnight

Spa*koi*ny *noch*i Спокойной ночи

Hello (formal)

***Zdrast*vooy / *zdrast*vooytye** Здравствуй / Здравствуйте

Hi!

Priv*yet!* Привет!

Goodbye

Da svi*dan*ya Досвидания

'Bye

Pa*ka* Пока

All the best

Vsi*vo* kha*ro*sheva / Vsi*vo do*brava

Всего хорошего / Всего доброго

How are you?

Kak dye*la?* / Kak *zheez*n'? Как дела? / Как жизнь?

Nice to meet you.

***Otch*in pry*at*no.** Очень приятно.

It's good to see you.

Rud tib*ya* / Vas *vi*dit. Рад тебя / Вас видеть.

Basic Expressions

Do you speak English?

Ty guvar*eesh* / Vy guvar*eet*ye pa-ang*lee*sky?

Ты говоришь / Вы говорите по-английски?

Thank you very much

Bal*shoye* spah*see*ba Большое спасибо

I don't understand Russian.

Ya nye puni*ma*yu pa-*roo*ski. Я не понима ю по-русски.

Please; you're welcome

Pah*zhalu*sta Пожалуйста

Sorry; excuse me

eezvee*nee* / eezvee*neet*ye Извини / извините

That's okay; it's nothing

neeche*vo* ничего

Good; fine

khura*sho* хорошо

I'm okay; it's okay

Nar*mal*na Нормально

bad

***plo*kha** плохо

My name is...

Min*ya* zu*voot*... Меня зовут...

What is your name?

Kak tib*ya* / Kak vus zuv*oot*?

Как Тебя / Как Вас зовут?

I'm American, English (male, female)

Ya ameri*kan*yets. / Ya ameri*kan*ka.

Я американец. / Я американка.

Ya anglee*cha*nin. / Ya anglee*chan*ka.

Я англичанин. / Я англичанка.

I (don't) want...

Ya (nye) khu*choo*... Я не хочу...

How old are you?

***Skol*ka tib*ye* / *Skol*ka vam lyet?**

Сколько тебе / Сколько Вам лет?

Congratulations

Puzdravl*ya*yu Поздравляю

Basic Expressions

Help me.

Puma*geet*ye mnye. Помогите.

I'm hungry.

Ya khu*choo* yest'. Я хочу есть.

I'm thirsty.

Ya khu*choo* peet'. Я хочу пить.

I'm tired.

Ya oo*stahl*. Я устал.

I'm lost.

Ya zabloo*deel*siya. Я заблудился.

It's very important.

***Eta otch*in *vahzh*na.** Это очень важно.

It's urgent.

***Eta sroch*na.** Это срочно.

Questions

Where?

gdye? где?

When?

kag*da*? когда?

What?

shto? что?

How?

kak? как?

How much?

***skol*ka?** сколько?

Who?

kto? кто?

Why?

pache*moo*? почему?

Orientation

How can I get to (by foot)… / How can I get to (by car)…?

Kak mnye prai*ti*… / Kak mnye pra*ye*khat da…?

Как мне пройти… / Как мне проехать до…?

Where is…?

gdye zdyes…? где здесь…?

How long does it take to get to (by foot)… /…(by car)…?

***Skol*ka eet*ee*… / *Skol*ka *ye*khat' da…?**

Сколько идти… / Сколько ехать до…?

To the left

nahl*ye*vo налево

To the right

nah*pra*va направо

Straight ahead

pr*ya*ma прямо

Far away

dahlie*ko* далеко

Nearby

***bleez*ka** близко

Transport

The metro

mi*tro* метро

Where's the nearest metro station?

Gdye blee*zhai*shaya *stant*seeya mi*tro*?

Где ближайшая станция метро?

token, jeton

zhi*ton* жетон

monthly pass

prayezd*noy* проездной

exit

***vy*khud v *go*rud** выход в город

walkway (to another station)

pierie*khod* переход

metro station

***stant*siya** станция

Transport

train station

vak*zahl* вокзал

train

***po*yezd** поезд

railway

zhel*yez*naya du*ro*ga железная дорога

airport

aera*port* аэропорт

airplane

sumal*yot* самолёт

enquiries

sprah*vachnuye byoo*ro справочное б юро

Are there any tickets for…?

Yest beel*ye*ty da…?

Есть билеты до…?

Can I have a ticket for…?

***Dai*tye mnye beel*yet* da…?**

Дайте мне билет до…?

sleeper (sleeping car)

es veh СВ

couchette

koo*peh* купе

check-in

rigi*strat*seeya регистрация

boarding

pu*sad*ka посадка

flight number

***nom*er *rei*sa** номер рейса

taxi

tuk*see* такси

bus

av*to*boos автобус

trolleybus

trull*yey*boos троллейбус

tram

trum*vai* трамвай

Transport

route taxi

marsh*root*ka / marsh*root*noye tuk*see*

маршрутка / маршрутное такси

Hotels

hotel

gus*tee*nitsa гостиница

receptionist

udmeenee*stra*tur администратор

passport

***pass*part** паспорт

visa

***vee*za** виза

luggage

bu*gash* багаж

floor lady

di*zhoor*naya дежурная

maid

***gor*nichnaya** горничная

room

***no*mer** номер

key

klyooch ключ

Does the room have a bathroom?

***No*mer s oo*dob*stvumee**?

Номер с удобствами?

Does the room have a phone?

***No*mer s tielie*pho*num**?

Номер с телефоном?

How can I phone long distance?

Kak zva*neet'* pa myezhg*o*rudoo?

Как звонить по межгороду?

How can I make an international call?

Kak zva*neet* zuh gru*neet*soo?

Как звонить заграницу?

Eating Out

restaurant
ristа*ran* ресторан

café
ku*feh* кафе

cafeteria
stu*lo*vaya столовая

I'd like to book a table for two / three / four.
Ya khu*choo* zuka*zat sto*lik na d*voye* / *tro*ye / *chet*vera.
Я хочу заказать столик на двое / трое / четверо.

hors d'oeuvres
zah*koo*skee закуски

first course
p*yer*vuye bl*yoo*da первые блюда

main course
ftu*ri*ye bl*yoo*da вторые блюда

meat
myas*ni*ye bl*yoo*da мясные блюда

fish
***ryeb*nuye bl*yoo*da** рыбные блюда

poultry
p*teet*sa птица

salad
su*lat* салат

vegetables
***o*vashee** овощи

cheese
seer сыр

fruit
***frook*ty** фрукты

dessert
des*sert* десерт

ice cream
mu*rozh*ennuye мороженое

wines, spirits
speert*ni*ye na*peet*ki спиртные напитки

Eating Out

boiled
vur*yon*ny варёный
fried
***zhah*renny** жареный
baked
zupi*chon*ny запечёный
Can I have the bill, please?
Pushi*tait*ye, pah*zhahl*sta? Посчитайте, рожалуйста?

Numbers

one **ah*deen*** один
two **dva** два
three **tree** три
four **chi*teer*ye** четыре
five **p*yat'*** пять
six **shest'** шесть
seven **syem'** семь
eight ***vo*syem'** восемь

d*yev*iat' matr*yo*shek
девять матрёшек

nine **d*yev*iat'** девять
ten **d*yes*iat'** десять
eleven **ud*yeen*natsat'** одиннадцать
twelve **dvye*nat*sat'** двенадцать

Numbers

twenty **d*vat*sat'** двадцать
thirty ***trid*sat'** тридцать
forty ***so*rak** сорок
fifty **pidis*yat*** пятьдесят
sixty **shestdes*yat*** шестьдесят
seventy ***syem*desyat** семьдесят
eighty ***vo*syemdesyat** восемьдесят
ninety **divya*no*sta** девяносто
one hundred **sto** сто
two hundred **dv*yes*ti** двести
five hundred **pit*sot*** пятьсот
one thousand ***ty*siacha** / [informal] ***tee*shcha** тысяча / тыща
a thousand rubles [slang] ***shtoo*ka** штука
one million **meelee*yon*** миллион

Shopping

How much does it cost?
***Skol*ka *sto*yit?** Сколько стоит?
Could I have a look at...?
Puka*zheet*ye pah*zhal*usta...? Покажите пожалуйста...?
shop assistant
prudav*yets* / prudav*sheet*sa продавец

Puka*zheet*ye pah*zhal*usta...?

Shopping

Who's last in line?

Kto pusl*yed*ny? Кто последний?

cashier's desk

***kas*sa** касса

Do you have any...?

Oo vus yest...? У вас есть...?

Russian Words to Recognize

администратор

udmeenee*stra*tur hotel receptionist

касса

***kas*sa** cash desk, ticket office

театр

tee*atr* theater

кинотеатр

keenatee*atr* cinema

сувениры

sooveneery souvenirs

хлеб

khlyeb bread, baker's

овощи

***o*vashee** vegetables, vegetable shop

рынок

***ry*nak** market

продукты

pra*dook*ty grocer's

гастроном

gastra*nom* food shop

туалет

twal*yet* toilet

аптека

up*tye*ka drugstore

книги

kn*yee*gee [hard "g"] bookstore

Russian Words to Recognize

почта
  ***poch*ta** post office

банк
  bunk bank

обмен вал юты
  ubm*yen* vul*yoo*ty exchange office

молоко
  mula*ko* milk store

мясо-рыба
  m*ya*sa-*ry*ba meat and fish store

камера хранения
  ***ku*mera khrun*yen*iya** left luggage office

закрыт на ремонт
  zuk*rit* na ri*mont* closed for repairs

закрыт на учёт
  zuk*rit* na oo*chot* closed for inventory

перерыв
  piri*riv* lunch break

здесь не курят
  zdyes nye *koor*yat no smoking

вход
  fkhod entrance

выход
  ***vy*khad** exit

переход
  piri*khod* crossing, walkway between adjoining metro stations

посторонним вход воспрещён
  pusta*ron*nim fkhod vuspri*shyon* no admission

Geography

бульвар
  bul*var* boulevard

мост
  most bridge

Geography

набережная
_na_berezhnaya embankment
переулок
per_yu_lok lane
площадь
plosh_chad'_ square
проспект
pros_pekt_ avenue
река
re_ka_ river
улица
_u_litsa street
шоссе
show_seh_ highway
вокзал
vak_zal_ station

MOSCOW

MOSKVA

Moscow ... how vast is your house!
Every Russian is – homeless.
We shall all make our way toward you.

– after lines of Marina Tsvetaeva (1916)

No city reflects the confusions and contradictions of the Russian national spirit more fully than that unwieldy giant, Moscow. Beauty and gracelessness compete at every turn in a scramble of monstrously wide streets and quiet lanes; concrete blocks and charming mansions, austere "culture palaces" and ornate churches, hideous suburbs and attractive old quarters. Every turn of Russian history can be sensed in its houses, monuments and street names – from the Tatar invasion, to the unification of Russia, to the disastrous fire of 1812, to the building of socialism. East clashes with West, too – while the aspiring middle classes seek an enlightened, Western-oriented existence, the city's markets and railway stations resemble oriental bazaars.

A key to understanding the city's rather undisciplined growth lies in its shape, the typical Russian town formation, accreting from the center in concentric circles. In medieval times Russia's vast countryside was not organized by feudal law. Whereas in crowded western Europe expanding cities had to buy separate land and start new settlements, nothing prevented Russian builders from using the land immediately around the city.

Today, Moscow seems almost immeasurably huge, 878.7 sq. km of urbanity enclosed within the limits of the Outer Ring Road. Yet this is no sprawl. Although the city is already creeping systematically beyond this limit, its boundary generally remains intact, as housing estates end abruptly to be replaced by green fields and forests.

Nevertheless, there is no shortage of space inside the city. Russians still build up rather than out, and while people's living conditions are cramped and box-like, they have acres of space for recreation throughout the city. One huge park, Losiny Ostrov ("Deer Island") covers most of northeast Moscow, an area larger than the center itself. But space is not always so well used – much land seems wasted, a rubbish-strewn sludge churned out by failed building projects and industrial pollution.

History

Founded in 1147 by Yuri Dolgoruky, Moscow had a late and modest beginning compared to many Russian towns. Dolgoruky, a powerful warrior prince of Rostov-Suzdal, later won the throne of Kiev. From the beginning he obviously liked the place – its first mention in the chronicles refers to a banquet he held there for his southern ally, Prince Svyatoslav.

This little settlement in the forest on Borovitsky Hill (now the Kremlin) did not prove much of an obstacle for the Tatars in 1238. Perhaps that was why the enemy saw fit to make Muscovy the center of their vassal Russian state and collector of their taxes. In 1328, Muscovite prince Ivan Kalita, renowned for his greed (his name means "money-bags"), was made Grand Prince by the Khan, and the *metropolitan* (the name at that time for the head of the Russian Church) moved from Vladimir to Moscow.

Moscow, wooden Kremlin, 1340
Artist: A.M. Vasnetsov

But from then on Moscow started to take its fate into its own hands. In fact, it was Moscow's Prince Dmitry who first united Russia against the Khans. He defeated them on the Don River at Kulikovo Field, thus earning himself the title "Donskoy" (of the Don).

Moscow went from strength to strength, and with the fall of Byzantium in 1453, Ivan III hastened to proclaim it the center of the Orthodox world. It became known as the Third Rome, and received its first stone buildings as well as its earliest influence from western architecture – a magnificent Kremlin built in part by Italians.

A century later, the fall of Novgorod and demise of the Tatars put Moscow in control of a united, centralized Russian state – but not for long. The death of its architect, Ivan the Terrible, led to the "Time of Troubles," and to Polish invasion and occupation. Moscow was saved by a militia from the Volga, and by Mikhail Romanov, elected tsar by the boyars meeting in council. Tsar Mikhail, just 16 at his election, proved capable of uniting the squabbling nation.

Moscow suffered terribly at the hands of Peter the Great, who hated the city and built his own capital at St. Petersburg. After a brief return to favor under Peter's successor Peter II, Moscow went into a protracted decline, hovering dangerously on the brink of provincial obscurity.

Still, it continued to develop, in its own special way. A decree by Catherine the Great in 1762 freed the nobility from most of its obligations to the monarch. As a result, Moscow became a "Nobles' Republic," a freer city unrestrained by the oppressive officialdom of St. Petersburg. Now the city flourished, intellectually and culturally.

Then Napoleon's invasion in 1812 brought disaster. Moscow's inhabitants burnt the city to prevent looting by the French, and Napoleon, departing with his demoralized army, decided to blow up the Kremlin. Only the sturdiness of the fortress prevented its destruction.

A new city quickly rose from the ashes of the "Nobles' Republic." In just over 10 years it had a magnificent new appearance. Growth continued throughout the century, and accelerated in the later decades of industrialization.

Moscow played almost as large a role in Russia's various revolutions as did St. Petersburg, and in October 1917 was a Bolshevik stronghold. When White armies threatened the northern capital during the Civil War, it was moved hastily back to the southern city.

Even since then, Moscow has seen many changes. In the 1930's old buildings, including many churches, were pulled down, and replaced by grandiose granite structures generally described as "stalinist." Some streets were widened (as Tverskaya/Gorky Street); others were built from scratch (as Prospekt Mira or Leninsky prospekt).

World War II spared Moscow its ravages, but only just. The "Battle for Moscow" in winter 1941 stopped the first German advance within tens of kilometers of the capital.

A second wave of modernization came in 1954, this time causing what can only be described as monstrous mutilation of large areas of the city. Prospekt Kalinina (now Novy Arbat) was driven through an old quarter and lined with enormous shops, and building programs in the suburbs went into overdrive, creating *"khrushchoby,"* five-story apartment blocks whose nickname was word-play on the name of General Secretary Khrushchev and the word for "slum" (*trushchoba*). But the effects were not entirely lamentable – at last, people were able to move out of their overcrowded communal flats and into places of their own.

With the even more gargantuan projects of the '60's and '70's – the enormous housing estates which define (some would say defile) the suburban skyline – Moscow assumed its current appearance.

In the post-perestroika era, the city is again witness to major political upheaval. As in 1905, the focus is not the Kremlin, but the western *Presnya* area. In both 1991 and 1993, the House of Soviets, better known as the "White House," became a battleground, first between the Russian government and pro-Communist coup plotters, then between Russia's own estranged branches of state power.

People

Muscovites are likely to be the first Russians that foreigners meet when they arrive in Russia. This should do something to allay the potential culture shock of a visitor from the West. People here are for the most part friendly and helpful to foreigners, and many have at least a smattering of English and a good idea of what foreigners are likely to be interested in. However, the picture you will probably get of Russians from contact with Moscow friends is not going to be completely accurate.

Muscovites have all the basic traits of Russianness – strong emotions and moods, a love of celebrating, straightforwardness, and hospitality – but, almost inevitably, big city life has gotten

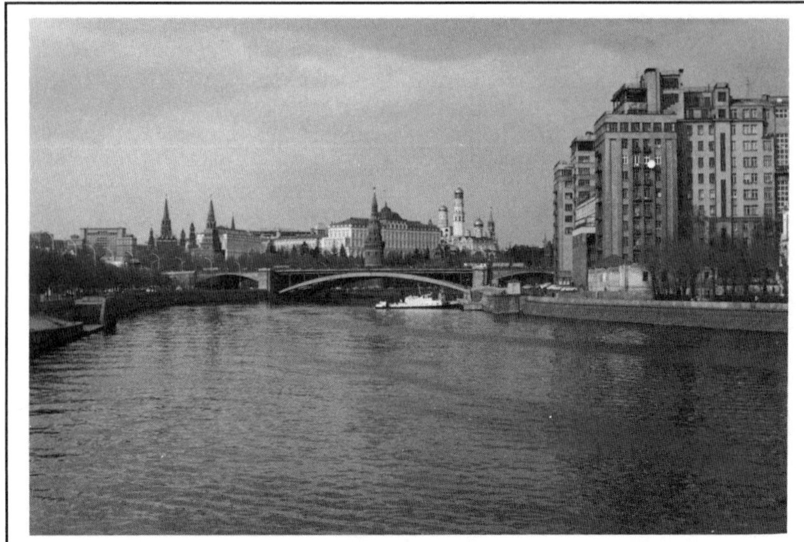

Moscow River and the Kremlin

to them. They are also worldly wise, cosmopolitan and thrusting. Provincials usually treat them with disdain, seeing them as spoiled, loudmouthed and unruly, an impression which they do sometimes give when outside their home environment.

Moscow Today

Today's Moscow offers something for everyone. In prices and facilities it is fast approaching the standards of any Western city. However, the process is far from an easy one, and it seems as if two different worlds are existing side by side: the old, crumbling Soviet one for the ordinary citizen, and a new, expensive and exclusive superculture of fast cars, night clubs and restaurants – the realm of the nouveau riche and foreigners – completely out of his reach. Every Russian city has this dichotomy, but not as blatantly as in Moscow, where the gap between the two worlds seems at its widest.

If you want to get to know Moscow properly, and avoid the superculture, which in the main is either completely tacky or so Westernized that there's nothing Russian left in it, you may have some hard days ahead of you. To take one example, getting into restaurants or cafés serving good Russian food at reasonable prices may require some ingenuity and a great deal of patience. Having (or making) local contacts is of course a great bonus. This is one of the strongest arguments for seeking out a hospitable bed & breakfast host, or writing well in advance of your trip to listees in *Russia: People to People*. (For both of these, see the Survival Guide.)

As for getting to know the city's history and monuments, the situation is very similar. Apart from a few obvious central areas, Moscow requires exploration, mostly on foot, as public transport will rarely take you through the most interesting streets. In this you can be as thorough as your length of stay allows, but don't expect to see much in less than a week.

The key is not to give up too easily. Moscow richly rewards the persistent.

WALK 1: THE KREMLIN

A walk through Moscow's central fortress, the seat of government from 1276 to 1712, and then again from March 1918 to the present day (Metro Bibliotyeka imeni Lenina/Arbatskaya/Alexandrovsky Sad).

Exit the metro toward the **Alexander Garden,** deposit any bags you have in the left luggage, buy your tickets in the kiosk and set forth. (Remember that the Kremlin is closed on Thursdays... and may occasionally be closed on other days as a result of political events!) As you enter, note the **Kutafya Tower**, a curious squat structure, which takes its name from an archaic Russian word meaning "clumsy old woman."

Cross the bridge over the Alexander Garden up to the Kremlin wall, beneath which used to flow a river, the Neglinka. At its confluence with the Moskva, by what is now the **Borovitsky Tower**, Yuri Dolgoruky founded the city. The Neglinka was diverted into underground pipes after the fire of 1812, and Osip Bove, the main architect of the city's reconstruction, replaced it with the present garden.

Trinity Tower

Entering the Kremlin by the **Trinity Tower**, pay attention to the walls, which are at their highest elevation here. They date from the 15th century, when Ivan III was building his "Third Rome." There were three previous walls, the most famous ones built in the 14th century. Made of white stone, they earned Moscow the nickname *Belokammennaya* (white stone), which stuck, even though the walls fell into ruin.

Immediately on the left side as you enter is the **Arsenal**, now the headquarters of the Kremlin Guard. Built by Peter the Great for weapon manufacturing and storage, in 1812 it became a museum commemorating the victory against Napoleon. Most of the cannons displayed outside were captured from the retreating French army.

To your right is the only recent building in the Kremlin, the **Palace of Congresses**. It was built in 1961, in the Khrushchev days of bravado and Communist rhetoric, to host the upcoming Communist Party Congress. For many years it has served as a venue both for gatherings of top Soviet Party officials and for cultural performances such as ballet. The latter has now become its only occupation. Interestingly, the builders sank the structure 15 meters into the ground, so that it wouldn't overshadow the other Kremlin buildings.

As you continue past the Palace of Congresses, you'll see on the left, across the drive, a bright yellow building in classical style behind a small garden. This is the **Senate**, one of the many Moscow masterpieces of architect Matvey Kazakov, favored by Catherine the Great for his restrained, functional style. Its most notable feature is the rotunda, a symbol of happiness, which Catherine hoped to establish through the rule of law. Inside the building, the offices used by Lenin after the Revolution have been preserved, but are no longer open to the public.

To the right of the Senate is a much later building painted in a similar color, perhaps to camouflage its architectural deficiencies. Built in 1935, it formerly housed the **Presidium** of the Supreme Soviet, a kind of inner standing parliament. (In pre-perestroika days the full parliament only needed to meet for a few days a year, since there was little genuine debate.) Now it is the official residence of the Russian President.

As you approach Cathedral Square, you will see the Kremlin's twin oddities: the largest cannon in the world, which has never been fired, and the largest bell in the world, which has never been rung.

The **Tsar Cannon**, weighing 40 tons and boasting a barrel five meters long, never really had any occasion to be used; Moscow's enemies would take one look at it and turn tail. It was commissioned by Ivan the Terrible's son Fyodor, and has a relief of him just behind the muzzle. On the carriage, meanwhile, the depiction of a

"A ghostly choir of white-stoned cathedrals"

As you walk over the crinkled pink flagstones of Cathedral Square, the air grows foggy with imagined incense, and with the shades of those terrible elder tsars. Ringed by their draughty forests at the antipodes of Christendom, their reigns black with superstition and chaos, these sixteenth and early seventeenth century tyrants come down to us in a light eerily magnified and intense. Ivan the Terrible, Fyodor I, Boris Godunov, the False Dimitry – they process across the inner eye in a queue of ruthless autocrats or vacuous simpletons: religious, half-savage, melancholy-mad. Around their great square the white-stoned cathedrals lift in a ghostly choir.... They inhabited these cathedrals with familiar ease. The two-hour morning liturgy broke over them like the waves of some benedictory ocean, while they deliberated with their councillors in the nave. This was their natural and exotic habitat. In its softly-domed interiors, among a liana jungle of hanging lamps and blazing copses of candles, their most secular and atrocious decisions took on the sanctity of gospel.

– Colin Thubron, from *Where Nights Are Longest: Travels by Car through Western Russia* (New York: Atlantic Monthly Press, 1987)

Left: ***Assumption Cathedral portal, decorated with mosaic panels***
Right: ***Assumption Cathedral, center; statue of Lenin in foreground***

lion savaging a snake symbolizes Russian power, always victorious over its enemies.

The **Tsar Bell**, weighing 200 tons, was an impossible proposition right from the start. Things kept going wrong as it was being made, until it finally cracked during a fire. Begun in the 1730's during Anna Ivanovna's reign, it was only lifted out of its pit, into which it had fallen during a casting misshap, 100 years later. An 11-ton piece broke off then, and has lain beside it ever since.

On entering Cathedral Square, your attention will be taken immediately by the largest of the churches, the magnificent **Assumption Cathedral** (also called Dormition Cathedral or, in Russian, *Uspensky sobor*) on your right.

During the process of unification of Russia under Moscow in the 15th century, Tsar Ivan III decided to create a cathedral that would become the focal point of Russian Orthodoxy. He needed a highly skilled architect, of a kind Russia was at that time unable to provide. Obliged to look abroad, he finally chose the Bolognese, Aristotle Fioravanti, to build Russia's greatest church. Fioravanti was dispatched to Vladimir, Pskov and Novgorod to acquaint himself with the varieties of Russian style. This he did, thoroughly, and Assumption Cathedral (1475–79) is the result.

Most of all, the Cathedral resembles the Assumption Cathedral in Vladimir, its massive bulk topped by *zakomary* and five domes. The belt of **arcades** intended to relieve the austerity of the walls (located just below mid-height), and the large window slits below the semicircular arches that crown the walls, are also features of the older cathedral.

Assumption Cathedral served as a burial place for patriarchs and for the coronation of tsars. Inside, the walls were painted mainly in the mid-17th century, their themes copied from original 15th century works by the great Russian master Dionysius. A few of his simple and delicate earlier paintings are preserved below the main iconostasis. Their main theme is the Assumption of the Virgin Mary into heaven, the backbone of the new dogma of Russian Orthodoxy. This replaced the Byzantine tradition of devoting the main cathedral to St. Sophia, or the Wisdom of God – the Assumption, in Orthodoxy, was the means by which that wisdom was brought to humankind.

The iconostasis also has a purpose – to demonstrate the unity of Russia. The lowest tier contains icons captured from Moscow's defeated rival cities, most notably Novgorod and Vladimir. On the rear wall to the right of the entrance is another of these, a 15th century copy of the Virgin of Vladimir, a Byzantine icon used by successive Russian capitals to proclaim their superiority. The original arrived in Moscow in 1395, but after the Revolution was transferred by Lenin to the Tretyakov Gallery.

Note also the solid silver chandelier. Napoleon, who used the cathedral as a stable while he was here, on departure looted all the gold and silver inside. This was later recaptured, and the silver remoulded into the chandelier.

The second of the existing Kremlin churches to be built was **Annunciation Cathedral** (in Russian, *Blagoveshchensky sobor*), on the back of the square to the left. As this was intended for the tsars' private worship, it was built by Pskov masters without foreign help. The original, also in the Vladimir style, was quite modest, but was enlarged in Ivan the Terrible's time. The result is a festive nine-domed church with gilded copper roofing. One necessary innovation was a porch, built when Ivan was forbidden to enter the church for services after he contravened Orthodox doctrine by marrying a fourth time. (Only three marriages were permitted.)

The most interesting features inside are the early 15th century icons, preserved from the previous cathedral on the site and miraculously rediscovered, under layers of later painting, in the 20th century. They demonstrate a rare collaboration between the two greatest artists of the day – Theophanes the Greek and Andrey Rublyov. Compare Theophanes' harsh, dramatic figures in the deisus tier (second from the bottom) with Rublyov's rounder, softer images (St. Peter and the Archangel Michael).

The **Cathedral of the Archangel Michael** (*Arkhangelsky sobor*), the third on the square, shows a much more obvious foreign influence. In fact, it is commonly referred to as a "Russian church in an Italian robe." Its builder was a Venetian called Alevisio, who was commissioned by the dying Ivan III in 1505. Alevisio's most noticeable contribution was the scallop-shell decoration inside the semi-circular *zakomary*, later copied by other Russian architects.

The interior of the cathedral is a burial place of grand princes and tsars, from Ivan Kalita in the 14th century to Fyodor II. Peter the Great then decreed that tsars should be buried in the SS. Peter and Paul Cathedral in St. Petersburg. Nonetheless his Moscow-loving son Peter preferred to stay here, and after dying of smallpox in 1730 was buried in the *Arkhangelsky sobor*.

The frescoes were painted by talented 17th century masters, including the great Simon Ushakov (see walk #2), mostly on historical and military themes. The cathedral's patron was Michael, captain of the heavenly host, and consequently a number of the paintings celebrate Russia's cam-

Ivan the Great Belltower

paigns. Many tsars are depicted, and there also are likenesses of all of the Russian princes whose principalities had joined Moscow.

On the right side of the entrance to the square is the bell-tower, known as **Ivan the Great** (1329; not to be confused with Ivan III, who shared this title) after the patron saint of its builder, Grand Prince Ivan Kalita. The upper portion, which brought the tower to a height of 270 meters, was added by Tsar Boris Godunov in 1600.

The last structure in the square, opposite Ivan the Great, is the **Palace of Facets**, designed for the great feasts of the tsars, particularly the one that followed the capture of Kazan. The building work going on currently at its side is the reconstruction of the Red Staircase, which the Tsar used to ascend to his coronation. The original was destroyed in 1933 to make way for a dining room for delegates to the 17th Party Congress. In 1993, Boris Yeltsin donated 240 million rubles from his personal fund toward the rebuilding.

Two other Kremlin churches are open as museums. The **Church of the Deposition of the Robe** stands just behind Assumption Cathedral. It was built in 1486, in celebration of what was thought to be a case of divine intervention. A Tatar army en route to another sacking of Moscow suddenly got cold feet and withdrew. This miracle happened on the eve of the feast of the Deposition. The church now houses a wooden sculpture exhibition.

The **Church of the Twelve Apostles**, behind and to the right of the Assumption Cathedral, was built later by Patriarch Nikon, and replaced the Deposition church as a private place of worship for the patriarchs. It combines the drums of Annunciation Cathedral, the *zakomary* of the Assumption, and the size of the Archangel Michael, and is now a museum of the applied religious arts of the Kremlin.

Cross the square again to the viewing platform by the wall on the river side. The tower ahead of you, **Tainitskaya** or Secret Tower, is the oldest in the Kremlin. It is thought to conceal a passage down to the river, which provided a source of water when the fortress was under siege. The tower is also one of the possible repositories of Ivan the Terrible's famous library, full of rare and fabulous manuscripts, a treasure which remains undiscovered.

Turn your back to the river once again. To your left is the **Great Kremlin Palace**, built by Konstantin Thon after the triumph of 1812 and used as a Moscow residence of the tsars. There is no public access to the spectacular interior, but it frequently appears on television as the official Presidential reception area for foreign delegations.

Gaze farther to your left, down the long avenue toward the Borovitskaya

Tower, the visitors' exit from the Kremlin, and you will see the **Armory** to the right, past the façade of the palace. Also built by Thon, the Armory is Russia's oldest and most treasured museum. Although established as an armory by Vassily III in 1511, its collection originated much earlier, from the weapons and battle regalia that each Muscovite prince received from his ancestors. However, as the Tsar's court grew rich under Ivan III, it became a workshop for craftsmen of many trades. Peter the Great packed it off to St. Petersburg. The collection was poorly looked after, and many items were lost, especially during the 1812 war, when it was evacuated to Nizhny Novgorod. Only in 1851 was it installed in its current location.

Its earliest exhibits, which include the chalice that belonged to Yuri Dolgoruky, date from the 12th century. Its exhibits are not organized chronologically; rather, each room is devoted to a particular kind of artifact – weapons, vestments, or carriages. Although the golden age of the Armory was in the 17th century under Tsar Alexey Mikhailovich, some of the finest treasures are gifts from abroad, such as two thrones, one made of diamonds and the other of gold leaf studded with precious stones, both sent by Persia, or the carriage given to Boris Godunov by Elizabeth I of England.

The other part of the museum contains a collection of diamonds, opened to public view only in 1967. Its treasures include a diamond and pearl tiara made for Catherine the Great by the 18th century craftsman Posier. There is also a collection of exquisitely worked Fabergé eggs and other jewelry produced by the firm opened in Petersburg in 1842 by Gustave Fabergé. The museum has numerous exhibits from this century, when the opening of new mines made the Soviet Union one of the world's largest diamond producers.

The two parts are open by excursion only, each requiring a separate admission.

WALK 2: THEATERS, RED SQUARE AND KITAI-GOROD

This tour of the center and the old trading quarter begins at metro Okhotny Ryad/Teatralnaya/Ploshchad Revolyutsii, and concludes at metro Lubyanka.

Emerge from the eastern exit of Okhotny Ryad or the northern exit of Teatralnaya onto **Teatralnaya ploshchad** (Theater Square). From its current appearance it's difficult to imagine that this area was once a stinking bog, used as a rubbish dump by the well-to-do inhabitants of the city center. Only after the 1812 fire was it filled in and a parade ground built, surrounded by a classical ensemble built on piles. The square's present layout dates from 1911.

The most well-known building is the **Bolshoy Theater** (to your left), built in 1824 by Osip Bove. Its ponderous eight-columned ionic portico does little to betray the luxurious and acoustically excellent auditorium within.

Ahead of you across the square is the **Maly Theater**, once a private theater owned by the Vargin merchant family. It was famous in the early part of the last century as a catalyst for the intellectual opposition, performing plays by such irreverent figures as Griboyedov, Gogol, and Ostrovsky; a statue of the latter now stands outside the entrance. It remains today a good

Metropol Hotel

venue for classical Russian theater.

Across the main thoroughfare, Okhotny Ryad, is the **Metropol Hotel**, probably Moscow's finest example of Art Nouveau. Built by W.F. Walcott at the turn of the century, it was recently restored by a British/Russian joint venture from Intourist drabness to its former five-star glory. Look up to see the two large mosaics executed by Mikhail Vrubel in rounded pediments at gable height directly above the main entrances. They were inspired by Edmond Rostand's play *La Princesse Lointaine*. Brunch in a splendid dining room with a concave painted glazed roof will set you back about $25, but might be worth it.

Further to the right are the remains of the walls of **Kitai-gorod**, the main trading area of the city, which we shall visit later on this walk. Tradition differs on the origin of this name. Some say that Kitai-gorod comes from *kita*, the word for the baskets filled with earth that were used to build the wall. Historians agree that it does not mean, literally, "China-town."

Follow Okhotny Ryad ("Hunter's Row") away from Theater Square as far as its junction with Tverskaya ulitsa (to your right), and cross the former via the underpass to reach the entrance to Red Square.

Red Square, despite its obvious Communist overtones, came by its name much earlier, and is not on the mayor's list of city names to be changed. In Russian it is **Krasnaya ploshchad**, the word *krasnaya* meaning "beautiful" in old Russian. Over the centuries the square has served various functions – as a market and as a place of execution and of ceremony, from the defeat of Kazan to the spectacles of military strength of the Soviet May-Day parades.

Straight ahead you will see the Cathedral of the Intercession, better known as **St. Basil's**. Built in honor of Ivan the Terrible's capture of Kazan (1552), the stronghold of Russia's traditional Tatar enemy, its more common name, paradoxically, is taken

Communist Icons and the Changing Center

Lenin's funeral, Red Square, January 1924

In the days of Communism, central Moscow was of a place of pilgrimage for Communists the world over. People could visit the Central Lenin Museum, its great halls filled with every imaginable Lenin saying, scrap of writing, photograph and genuine (or fake) historical document, as well as the ubiquitous statues and busts. They could queue up on the edge of Red Square and pass solemnly through the Lenin Mausoleum, to see the great leader's enshrined waxen body. Next, they could walk over to the Kremlin wall and visit the graves of idealistic international Communists, such as the American John Reed, rubbing shoulders with dictator Josef Stalin or *apparatchik*-in-chief Leonid Brezhnev. Finally they could seek out monuments to secret police chief "Iron Felix" Dzerzhinsky, outside the Lubyanka KGB headquarters, and to Soviet heads of state Yakov Sverdlov (by Ploshchad Revolyutsii metro station) and Mikhail Kalinin (on Prospekt Kalinina, now Ulitsa Vozdvizhenka).

Today, most of these icons are gone. The failed coup of August 1991 led to the removal of the three statues; Dzerzhinsky's was dragged off its pedestal to the boisterous cheers of a crowd. The Lenin Museum struggled on under pressure to close, trying to justify itself by seeking the truth about Lenin, while at the same time it became a gathering-place for Russia's pro-Communist opposition. In November 1993 it finally gave up the ghost, yielding to the new Moscow City Duma. The fate of Lenin himself, meanwhile, is in the balance. It seems likely that he will be removed to be buried. The mausoleum, Alexey Shchusev's masterpiece in red marble for Communism and black marble for mourning, remains in place, as does Karl Marx's statue in front of the Bolshoy Theater, in a well known gay pick-up area.

from a ragged holy man who predicted the evil deeds of the Tsar and condemned him to eternal damnation.

Despite its throng of brightly patterned domes and cupolas, the core church is quite simple, built with a tent-roof of the kind that would be banned in the 17th century by Patriarch Nikon. Most of its features are borrowed from Russian wooden architecture.

Inside St. Basil's is a branch of the State History Museum which stands opposite it on the square. The latter was built in 1883 in the ostentatious pseudo-Russian style of the day. Its size, though, is astounding – 47 rooms and four million exhibits, not just Rus-

ARCHITECTURAL ELEMENTS: 16TH CENTURY, MOSCOW
Cathedral of the Intercession (St. Basil's), 1555–60

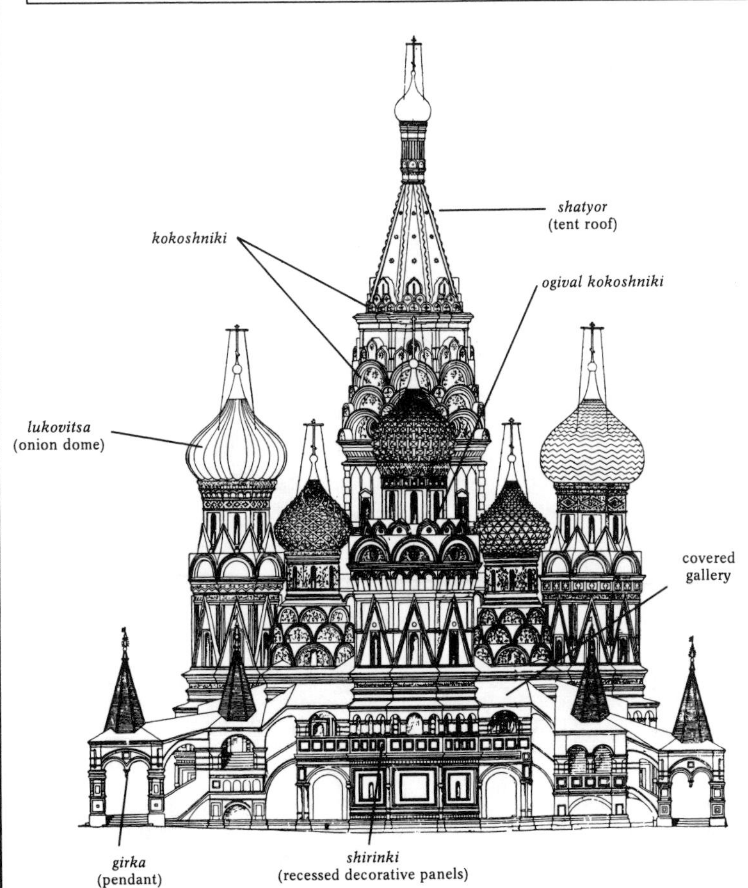

Adapted from *A History of Russian Architecture*
by William C. Brumfield (Cambridge University Press, 1993)
by permission of the author

sian – from the Stone Age to the present day.

The side of the square opposite the Kremlin Wall is occupied by **GUM** (meaning State Department Store, although it is now a joint-stock society). Formerly known as the Upper Trading Arcades, this splendid glass-roofed three-storied shopping center was built at the end of the last century to replace old merchant stalls. Once rather drab and frequented mainly by provincials, it has recently gone sharply upmarket, its valuable real estate leased by multinational retailers like Benetton and Karstadt.

Two monuments stand on Red Square, at the St. Basil's end. One is

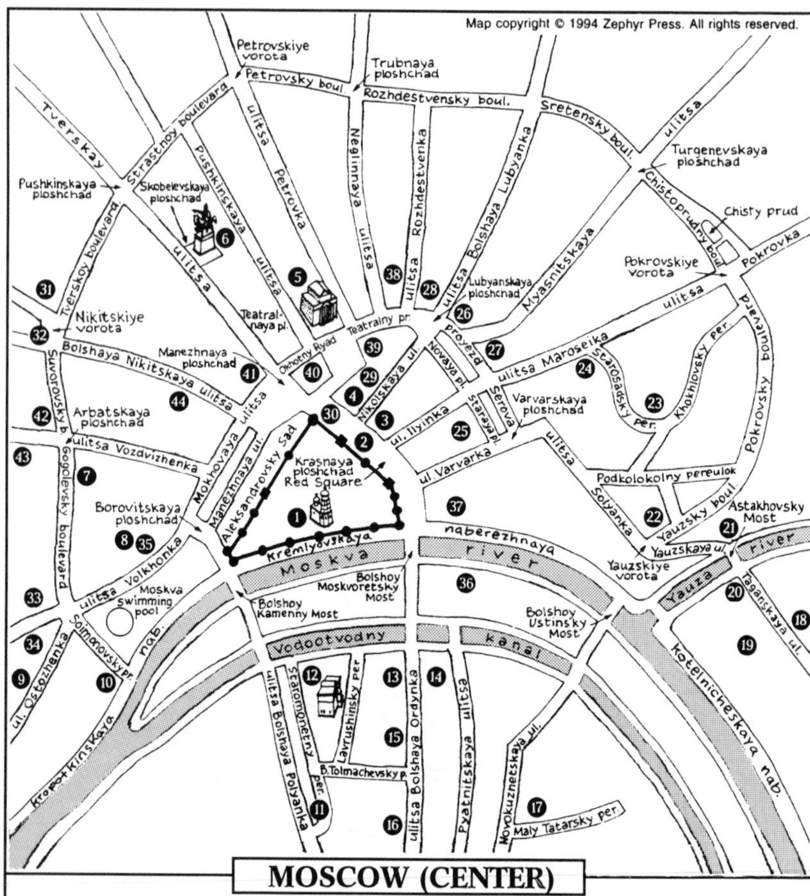

MOSCOW (CENTER)

Alexandrovsky Sad
Александровский сад
Arbatskaya ploshchad
Арбатская площадь
Astakhovsky most
Астаховский мост
Ulitsa Bolshaya Lubyanka
Улица Большая Лубянка
Ulitsa Bolshaya Nikitskaya
Улица Большая Никитская
Ulitsa Bolshaya Ordynka
Улица Большая Ордынка
Ulitsa Bolshaya Polyanka
Улица Большая Полянка
Bolshoy Kamenny Most
Большой Каменный мост
Bolshoy Moskvoretsky Most
Большой Москворецкий мост
Bolshoy Tolmachevsky pereulok
Большой Толмачевский переулок
Bolshoy Ustinsky Most
Большой Устинский мост
Borovitskaya ploshchad
Боровицкая площадь
Chistoprudny bulvar
Чистопрудный бульвар
Chisty prud
Чистый Пруд
Gogolyevsky bulvar
Гоголевский бульвар

Ulitsa Ilyinka
Улица Ильинка
Khokhlovsky pereulok
Хохловский переулок
Kotelnicheskaya naberezhnaya
Котельническая набережная
Kremlyovskaya naberezhnaya
Кремлёвская набережная
Kropotkinskaya naberezhnaya
Кропоткинская набережная
Lavrushinsky pereulok
Лаврушинский переулок
Lubyanskaya ploshchad
Лубянская площадь
Maly Tatarsky pereulok
Малый Татарский переулок
Manezhnaya ploshchad
Манежная площадь
Ulitsa Maroseika
Улица Маросейка
Ulitsa Mokhovaya
Улица Моховая
Moskva River (Reka Moskva)
Москва река
Ulitsa Myasnitskaya
Улица Мясницкая
Neglinnaya ulitsa
Неглинная улица
Nikitskiye Vorota
Никитские ворота
Nikolskaya ulitsa
Никольская улица
Novaya ploshchad
Новая площадь
Novokuznetskaya ulitsa
Новокузнецкая улица
Okhotny Ryad
Охотный ряд
Ostozhenka
Остоженка
Ulitsa Petrovka
Улица Петровка
Petrovskiye Vorota
Петровские ворота
Petrovsky bulvar
Петровский бульвар
Podkolokolny pereulok
Подколокольный переулок
Ulitsa Pokrovka
Улица Покровка
Pokrovskiye Vorota
Покровские ворота
Pokrovsky bulvar
Покровский бульвар
Prechistenskiye Vorota
Пречистенские ворота
Pushkinskaya ulitsa
Пушкинская улица
Pyatnitskaya ulitsa
Пятницкая улица
Ulitsa Rozhdestvenka
Улица Рождественка
Rozhdestvensky bulvar
Рождественский бульвар
Proyezd Serova
Проезд Серова
Skobelevskaya ploshchad
Скобелевская площадь
Soimonovsky proyezd
Соймоновский проезд
Ulitsa Solyanka
Улица Солянка
Sretensky bulvar
Сретенский бульвар
Staraya ploshchad
Старая площадь
Staromonetny pereulok
Старомонетный переулок
Starosadsky pereulok
Старосадский переулок
Strastnoy bulvar
Страстной бульвар
Suvorovsky bulvar
Суворовский бульвар
Taganskaya ulitsa
Таганская улица
Teatralnaya ploshchad
Театральная площадь
Teatralny proyezd
Театральный проезд
Trubnaya ploshchad
Трубная площадь
Turgenevskaya ploshchad
Тургеневская площадь
Tverskaya ulitsa
Тверская улица

Tverskoy bulvar
Тверской бульвар
Varvarskaya ploshchad
Варварская площадь
Ulitsa Varvarka
Улица Варварка
Vodootvodny Kanal
Водоотводный канал
Ulitsa Volkhonka
Улиц Волхонка
Vozdvizhenka
Воздвиженка
Yauza River
Река Яуза
Yauzsky bulvar
Яузский бульвар

MAP KEY

1. **The Kremlin**
Кремль
2. **Lenin Mausoleum**
Мавзолей Ленина
3. **GUM department store**
ГУМ
4. **Kazan Cathedral**
Казанский Собор
5. **Bolshoy Theater**
Большой Театр
6. **Yuri Dolgoruky statue**
Памятник Юрию Долгорукому
7. **Gogol monument ("The Soldier")**
Памятник Гоголю
8. **Vyazemsky/Dolgoruky Palace (former Marx-Engels Museum)**
Усадьба Вяземских
9. **Australian Embassy**
Австралийское посольство
10. **Pertsov House**
Дом Перцова
11. **Church of St. George Neokesariisky**
Церковь Георгия Неокесарийского
12. **Tretyakov Gallery**
Третьяковская галерея
13. **Resurrection Church in Kadashakh**
Церковь Воскресения в Кадашах
14. **Church of St. John the Baptist beneath the Forest**
Церковь Иоанна Предтечи под Бором
15. **Transfiguration Church**
Преображенская Церковь
16. **The Sisterhood of SS. Martha and Mary**
Марфо-Мариинская обитель
17. **Former Mosque**
Бывшая мечеть
18. **Golitsyn Hospital**
Голицынская больница
19. **St. Nikita Church beyond the Yauza**
Никитская церковь за Яузой
20. **Illuzion Cinema**
Кинотеатр «Иллюзион»
21. **Trinity Church in Serebryaniki**
Троицкая церковь в Серебряниках
22. **SS. Peter and Paul Church**
Петропавловская церковь
23. **St. Vladimir's Church in the Old Gardens**
Владимирская церковь в Старых Садах
24. **SS. Kosmas and Damian Church**
Космодемьянская церковь
25. **Trinity Church in Nikitniki**
Троицкая церковь в Никитниках
26. **Security Ministry**
Министерство Безопасности
27. **Mayakovsky Museum**
Музей Маяковского

the **Lobnoye Myesto**, a podium used to read edicts and decrees. The second is an 1818 statue by Ivan Martos of **Kosma Minin and Prince Dmitry Pozharsky**, who liberated Moscow from the Poles in 1612. Now dwarfed by the cathedral, this statue once stood in a more prominent position, in front of the little pink church on the corner of Nikolskaya ulitsa, at the other end of the square.

The **Cathedral of Our Lady of Kazan**, as this is called, is a reconstruction, built at lightning speed just last year on the site of the one that was pulled down in the 1930's. Fortunately, as it was being demolished, leading Soviet restorer Pyotr Baranovsky took photos and measurements in the hope that it might one day rise again. It, too, commemorates the events of 1612, and takes its name from the icon of the Kazan Virgin, which accompanied Pozharsky on his campaigns. Church processions, attended by the Tsar himself, would come here from the Kremlin's Assumption Cathedral.

Proceed to Nikolskaya, one of the three main streets of Kitai-gorod, which begins to the left of GUM's long Red Square frontage. Though originally a quarter inhabited by merchants, most were kicked out by Ivan III and replaced by nobles and clergy who had previously resided in the Kremlin. But the trading stalls remained until the Revolution, and the bazaar-like atmosphere still survives today. Nikolskaya in particular is now flush with expensive shops and banks.

Enter the first courtyard on the left, which is graced by a fascinating Moscow baroque church with balconies. This is all that remains of the **Monastery of the Savior behind-the-Icon-Stalls**. Once part of Moscow's first higher education establishment, where scientist and linguist Mikhail Lomonosov once studied, it is now in a semi-derelict condition, though the lower church is once again functioning.

Turn right down Bogoyavlensky pereulok past the derelict monastery of the same name (that is, "Epiphany"). Cross Ulitsa Ilyinka and follow Rybny pereulok. The right-hand

28. **Detsky Mir Children's Shop**
    Детский Мир
29. **Moscow City Duma**
    Московская Городская Дума
30. **History Museum**
    Исторический музей
31. **Gorky House Museum**
    Дом-музей Горького
32. **Great Ascension Church**
    Церковь Большого Вознесения
33. **Pushkin Museum**
    Музей Пушкина
34. **Tolstoy Museum**
    Музей Толстого
35. **Pushkin Fine Arts Museum**
    Музей Изящных Искусств имени Пушкина
36. **Baltschug Kempinski Hotel**
37. **Rossiya Hotel**
    Гостиница «Россия»
38. **Savoy Hotel**
39. **Metropol Hotel**
40. **Moskva Hotel**
    Гостиница «Москва»
41. **Intourist Hotel**
    Гостиница «Интурист»
42. **Gogol Museum and Monument**
    Музей и памятник Гоголя
43. **Irish House Supermarket**
44. **Conservatory**
    Консерватория

Ilyinka Gate, Kitai-gorod
19th century engraving

side of this back street is dominated by the **Old Merchant Arcade**, a classical pre-Napoleonic masterpiece by Giacomo Quarenghi. Now used as warehouses, it merits exploration nonetheless.

Coming out onto Ulitsa Varvarka, the third of Kitai-gorod's roughly parallel thoroughfares, you will find one of the most extraordinary sights of contemporary Moscow: a cluster of attractive merchant churches and 16th century secular stone buildings, all dwarfed by the hideous eyesore of the '60's-era **Hotel Rossiya**. And the post-Communist era has added another twist. Most of these ancient buildings are now occupied by souvenir shops catering to tourists staying at the hotel.

The so-called **Old English Embassy** dates from Ivan the Terrible's honeymoon with Elizabethan England. The Tsar was charmed by Sir Richard Chancellor, a sea-captain shipwrecked off what is now Arkhangelsk, to such an extent that he even asked Her Majesty to marry him. Though this was not to be, England got "most favored nation" status, and this well-located little house was made available for trade missions.

Nearby is a small **museum** devoted to the lives of the Boyar Romanovs, who once occupied this now reconstructed house. The head of the household was Nikita Romanov, grandfather of Tsar Mikhail. Ivan the Terrible's brother-in-law, Nikita had a softening influence, and probably curbed some of the regime's worst excesses while he was held in favor.

Walk down Varvarka to the end, the Kremlin at your back, then turn left onto Staraya ploshchad, one side of the huge Ilyinsky Square, which stretches up the hillside. Just on the left down a side street, you will see the fairytale **Church of the Trinity at Nikitniki**, considered to be the finest of Moscow's merchant churches. Its striking feature is the painting inside, done by Moscow master Simon Ushakov. In a color-livened tableau, he was able to convert the stories of the New Testament into a visible language for ordinary people, sometimes adding a humorous detail from contemporary life to spice it up. It is now a museum.

Return to Staraya ploshchad (Old Square). At the upper end of the square is the building that once made this name notorious. The headquarters of the Soviet Communist Party Central Committee was there; now it is occupied by the Russian Government.

If you want to see more of Kitai-gorod, turn left from here, down either Ilyinka or Nikolskaya, which will take you back to Red Square. Otherwise, continue straight to Lubyanskaya ploshchad, a feature of Russia's more immediate past.

The building ahead of you as you enter the square is **Dyetsky Mir** (Children's World), the biggest children's shop in the country. With its labyrinthine halls and corridors and impossible crowds, it gives a much better idea of Soviet-era shopping than the modernized GUM.

In a bizarre juxtaposition, Dyetsky Mir has three notorious neighbors farther around to your right. The **Lubyanka** was the headquarters of the variously named Soviet secret police, best known to us as the KGB but now regularly undergoing name changes. In the cellars of the middle building, Stalin's police chief Beria used to interrogate prisoners before they were shipped off to the Gulag – if they survived.

Speaking of which, the memorial stone in the center of the square is from the Solovyetsky Islands (see Arkhangelsk Region), one of the worst of the 1930's labor camps. It was brought there in 1990 by "Memorial," an organization devoted to discovering the truth about the Stalinist repressions.

A Feast of Futurism

If the culmination of this walk should seem too gloomy, you can strike a more lighthearted note by walking a few yards up Myasnitskaya ulitsa to a bust of a bald-looking man and what looks at first sight like a pile of junk. This is the entrance to the innovative **Vladimir Mayakovsky Museum**, opened in 1989.

Here is a shrine to Russia's greatest futurist poet, a man who devoted his life to the Revolution and then lost his way just as Stalin was beginning to flex his muscles. From top to bottom, it feels something like the backstage area of a modern theater, with mangled iron railings and furniture suspended at inconceivable angles. Mayakovsky's manuscripts hang frozen in glass while writing implements lie chaotically on sloping, sawn-off desks.

The museum traces his life, starting from childhood in Georgia and moving to his earliest involvement with the underground revolutionary movement. His attitude to power is summed up in one exhibit, a giant green armchair with a cracked portrait of Tsarist Prime Minister Stolypin on the seat. This reformist politician was a hateful figure for revolutionaries.

You now climb right to the top of the building, to the room where Mayakovsky shot himself, and work your way down. Other rooms demonstrate his talent for making revolutionary posters, and his impressions from trips abroad. But once Soviet power was firmly established, clouds appeared on the horizon – the death first of Lenin (1924), then of rival poet Sergey Yesenin (1925), occupy prominent positions. Then, in the penultimate room, a sinister picture of Stalin, in negative, appears on a heap of pipes, screws and machinery.

The year 1930 is upon us. In the final room, Mayakovsky's death mask lies on top of a huge white coffin, too large for a man who seemed larger than life.

WALK 3: FOREIGNERS' MOSCOW

During this long, meandering excursion through little-known parts of the city, you will find a calm almost inconceivable after the noise and crowds of the center. (Begins at metro Kitai-gorod, concludes at metro Taganskaya)

Exit Kitai-gorod metro at the Maroseika end and head for the beginning of this street. Looking back onto the square you will see a monument, a celebration of the taking of Pleven in 1877, Russia's contribution to the liberation of the Bulgarians, their fellow-Slavs, from the Turks.

Maroseika takes its name from its inhabitants, the *malorossy* or "little Russians," as Ukrainians were then called. They settled there after Ukraine was devastated by war with Russia and Poland, and dismembered by a treaty signed in 1683. The house at No. 11 became their first legation.

Pass between two buildings by Kazakov – on the left a mansion with fine sculptures now used as the **Belarussian Embassy**, on the right the austere green **Church of SS. Cosmas and Damian**, its cubes and cylinders hidden gracefully behind willows, then turn right down Starosadsky pereulok. The name, meaning "old garden," is most fitting for this quiet back street, once the site of orchards, where green-thumbed Tsar Vassily III grew and tended his rare plants.

Pleven Monument

After a sharp bend to the right, a huge 18th century gothic cathedral, surprisingly well obscured by trees, suddenly comes into view. Now a film studio, the Church of SS. Peter and Paul was once a Lutheran church used mainly by Germans who lived in the area.

You now emerge onto one of Moscow's most attractive hills, whose first landmark is the gleaming white **Church of St. Vladimir-in-the-old-Gardens**, the work of Alevisio, best known as the architect of the Kremlin's Archangel Cathedral.

This light, airy church is a contrast to the bleak, ruined towers and strange broad-domed church of the **St. John's Convent**, opposite. Not surprisingly for an institution founded in thanks for the birth of Ivan the Terrible, it had an unpleasant history, becoming a prison for noblewomen such as the ill-fated Elizabeth, illegitimate daughter of the Empress of the same name, and then much later for Stalin's NKVD.

Turn left down Khokhlovsky pereulok. This was once the heart of the Ukrainian community. Its name comes from *khokhly*, tufts of hair Cossacks wore on their shaven heads; the word has unfortunately been preserved to the present day as a derogatory term for Ukrainians used by some Russians.

Take the next right onto Podkopayevsky pereulok. About halfway down is a large red-brick manor house, lately guarded by savage dogs for reasons unclear. This is the former summer residence of "Time of Troubles" Tsar Vassily Shuisky. When his brief and bloody reign ended in 1610, his wife Maria became the first prisoner in nearby St. John's.

Turn left past the crumbling but still functioning St. Nicholas Church and take the next right, Petropavlovsky pereulok. The main landmark of this tiny street is the **SS. Peter and Paul Church**, a typical example of late Baroque with a number of famous icons. These include the **Bogolyubskaya Virgin**, one of the few Orthodox images of Mary without the Child.

Turn right onto the silent Yauzsky boulevard, the southern end of the Boulevard Ring (the inner ring road, which doesn't continue to the south side of the river), and left onto Yauzskaya ulitsa. The beautiful turquoise baroque bell-tower in front of you is part of the ensemble of the **Trinity Church in Serebryaniki (of the Silversmiths)**. This area was home to the guild which minted coins and made icon frames for the Tsar.

Now cross the Yauza, Moscow's second river. This waterway has had a very checkered history. Beginning as a trade route to the Volga in the 14th century, it declined during the next 400 years, gradually deteriorating into a rubbish dump. It was reclaimed for a time during the era of building grand estates and gardens, but then the arrival of the Industrial Revolution in Russia finally made of it the grimy wasteland of today.

On the right after the embankment is a huge 1950's-era building, one of Stalin's so-called "wedding cakes." These huge landmarks should on no account be used as reference points – just about every area of the city has one and they're all very similar. The one you see now is the "Illuzion" cinema, with residential flats behind it.

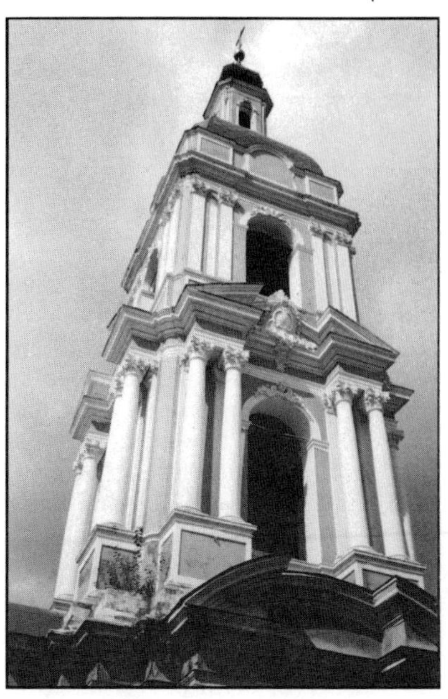

Bell-tower of Trinity Church in Serebryaniki

Take the smaller right fork up the hill (Bolshoy Vatin pereulok). This brings you to the **Church of St. Nikita Beyond the Yauza**, a little pillarless 17th century construction, with excellent views of the Moskva River and the south bank. Another site of feverish restoration work, this is a Serbian Orthodox monastery, linked to the one at Mount Athos in Greece.

Leaving the monastery, turn right down Ulitsa Volodarskovo and take the next left onto Ryumin pereulok. This will take you straight to the front gates of the "Golitsyn Hospital."

This palace (now Clinical Hospital No. 23) was built in 1798 to a design of Matvey Kazakov by the iron foundry owner Ivan Batashov. His homicidal maniac brother Andrey, the original manager of the foundries, bribed investigators copiously to keep them away from the piles of bones in his cellar. After his brother's death, Ivan took over the foundries, improved conditions and compensated the families of the deceased, for which he received the Order of St. Vladimir. Later bought by Prince Golitsyn, the palace is marvelous, both as a whole and in its details – such as the gates with their unusual sculpted lions. It is a highly imaginative classical ensemble, and rewards careful attention.

Turn left on Tagannaya ulitsa and descend toward Taganskaya ploshchad past the slender early 18th century Church of St. Nicholas in Bolvanovka. On your left is the modern red brick **Taganka Theater**. During the "stagnation years" of the 1970's and early 1980's, this experimental theater stood out as about the only center of cultural resistance to the Brezhnev regime. Most of the credit for this goes to Yuri Lyubimov, its brave and talented director, and to actor and gravelly-voiced bard Vladimir Vysotsky, whose social comments struck many chords in the hearts of his countryman.

But before entering the square, retrace your steps to the fork before the church and take a left down Uspensky pereulok. This will bring you to the festive **Assumption Church in Gonchary**, its ceramic tiles and gleaming cupolas now fully restored. Built in 1654, this five-domed pillarless church was decorated by ceramicists (*gonchary*) such as the renowned Stepan Polubes, who lived in the quarter. The church is now the headquarters of the Bulgarian Orthodox Church in Moscow.

Icon on Church of the Assumption of the Virgin in Gonchary

WALK 4: THE SOUTH BANK

(Begins and ends at metro Novokuznetskaya)

Exit the metro onto Pyatnitskaya ulitsa, a busy shopping street and one of the main arteries of the area known as *Zamoskvorechye* (the part beyond the Moskva River), Moscow's soft underbelly. This marshy lowland area, so exposed to attack from the south, did not seem a likely place for people to settle. Nonetheless it was on the southern trade route, so people came there. By the 17th century it was inhabited by traders, craftsmen and the crack regiment of *streltsy* (musketeers). Following the latter's rebellion against Peter the Great, the area became much less significant in the overall scheme of things. This situation only changed in the last century, when its status grew again with the replacement of rural estates by town houses and shops of the new educated bourgeoisie.

St. Clement's Church, by Novokuznetskaya metro

Now Zamoskvorechye is distinguished as the area least affected by the rigors of modern life – it even seems to have been passed over during the bouts of name-changing that periodically grip the city.

Walk toward the Moscow River, taking the first left turn off Pyatnitskaya, Chernigovsky pereulok. The small baroque church on the left is of **St. John the Baptist beneath the Forest**, built on the site of the oldest church in the Zamoskvorechye. The rather unlikely name is explained by the features across the river – in the days of the first church, the Kremlin was still a forested area.

Just opposite is the **Church of SS. Michael and Theodore of Chernigov**, built on the site of the grisly demise of these two martyrs in the year 1330. They were trampled to death underneath wooden planks by the soldiers of Tatar leader Batiy Khan for refusing to worship his gods.

You emerge onto Ulitsa Bolshaya Ordynka, a street still graced by wooden houses and beautiful churches that was once the main route taken by Moscow's attackers. Its name implies just this – the Russian word *orda* means Horde.

Now head for another side street just across and to the right. The lane you are now on is Vtoroy Kadashevsky pereulok, once the center of the Zamoskvorechye and the home of barrel-makers for the Tsar's household. Their Moscow baroque **Resurrection Church** is the most notable landmark of the area. The main body and nearby bell-tower are so slender that they seem stretched from above. The Resurrection Church also includes a number of motifs from both wooden Russian and classical architecture, repeated in many later Moscow churches.

Return to Bolshaya Ordynka by Trety Kadashevsky, circling the church, and turn right, away from the river. Walk a block or so to Tretyakovskaya metro station, then turn right again down Bolshoy Tolmachevsky pereulok.

If your appetite for Moscow-style churches is not yet sated, continue past the gallery and turn left into Staromonetny pereulok, site of the Mint in the 17th century. This will lead you onto Ulitsa Polyanka, Zamoskvorechye's third main street. The rather faded church dominating the skyline is **St. Gregory Neokesariisky**. Built by Tsar Alexey Mikhailovich in 1679, it was the first Moscow church worked on by the aforementioned Stepan Polubes. His "peacock's eye" tiling, in a band below the eaves, was first employed on the New Jerusalem Monastery, outside the city.

Otherwise, return to Bolshaya Ordynka and turn right. Two more churches appear, on your right the **Church of St. Nicholas in Pyzhakh**, another fine example of the Moscow ornamental style so effectively embodied in the Trinity Church at Nikitniki

The Tretyakov Gallery

On the corner of Bolshoy Tolmachevsky and Lavrushinsky pereulok is a modern red brick structure, the new annex of the **State Tretyakov Gallery**.

Wealthy 19th century merchant Pavel Tretyakov was not so much a patron of the arts as a man with a civic conscience, and a passionate collector. His interests went well beyond paintings – he kept an aviary, a pedigree milk herd and a valuable collection of violins, all of which he willed to interested societies at the early age of 28.

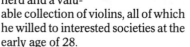

His gallery had its beginnings in 1856. He and his brother Sergey acquired a wide range of works of Russian art, in particular supporting painters of the "Itinerant" group such as Vasily **Polyenov**, Ilya **Repin**, and Vasily **Surikov**. Thirty-five years later, on Sergey's death and just six years before his own, Pavel presented his paintings as a gift to the city of Moscow (1892).

The Tretyakov Gallery was the first museum of painting entirely devoted to Russian works of art. The collection increased rapidly in size after the Revolution – notably at the expense of churches and private collectors. Its collection of icons is now indisputably the finest in the world.

Before entering the gallery, take a few steps to the right to see the original building, whose unusual art nouveau façade was designed in 1898 by the brilliant artist of many media, Viktor Vasnetsov. The original building soon became too small to hold the exhibits. Construction of the new building continues today, and currently only a fraction of the gallery's works are on display.

Begin with the icons. Every famous school and individual painter is included – bright and bold Novgorod icons from the 12th–15th centuries, the dramatic Byzantine masterpieces of **Theophanes the Greek**, and works by the first recognized Russian artist, **Andrey Rublyov**, represented by the most famous of all Russian icons – the Trinity from the Trinity and St. Sergius Lavra (monastery) in Sergiyev Posad.

The three remaining galleries are for each of the last three centuries. Quality far exceeds quantity, particularly in the 19th century room, with its fine portraits of Tolstoy and Tretyakov by Ivan Kramskoy, Isaac **Levitan**'s landscapes and **Repin**'s social studies. Though there are rarely more than two paintings by each artist, they are usually their best.

(see Walk #2). Its builders, the *streltsy* from Colonel Pyzhov's regiment, participated in the rebellion against Peter the Great and were executed in 1698.

Just opposite, barely visible through the trees, is the **Sisterhood of SS. Martha and Mary**. This remarkable little art nouveau church was commissioned by Princess Elizabeth, the last Tsar's sister-in-law, in 1908, after a terrorist bomb had killed her husband. The contrast between the fate of this woman, later beaten to death by the Bolsheviks, and that of the architect Shchusev, who went on to design the Lenin Mausoleum, is extraordinarily ironic. With its simple, squat white stone body, this church is most reminiscent of early Pskov architecture, although it is in fact conceptually closer to Moscow's Church of the Savior in the Forest, a charming, simple church built in the Kremlin in the 14th century, and destroyed by Stalin in the 1930's. Inside SS. Martha and Mary are some paintings and icons by Vasnetsov's contemporary, Mikhail Nesterov, but you'll need a special pass to get inside.

Return by Klimentovsky pereulok to Novokuznetskaya Metro station. On the right you won't have much trouble finding **St. Clements**, a palatial baroque church, built by local aristocrat Alexey Bestuzhev-Riumin to celebrate the successful *coup d'état* of his lover, Empress Elizabeth.

If you still have strength, continue behind the metro to the modern street with tram-lines, Novokuznetskaya ulitsa, and turn right. Walk for about five minutes until you arrive at a gap in a multi-story building on the left. Walk through here onto Malo-Tatarsky pereulok. While Tatar armies came via Ordynka to attack Moscow, their more peaceful brothers came to trade, and settled in the Zamoskvorechye. Though their community has long since been dispersed to the modern housing estates, some traces remain. Note the house at #8, with its Islamic-style portals – this used to be the community's mosque, and there are hopes for its revival. Meanwhile, further down on the right is the Islamic Cultural Center, whose aim is to restore a sense of religion and nationality to the Tatars (and other Muslims) of the Russian Federation.

WALK 5: LITERARY MOSCOW

This exploration of the haunts of Pushkin, Gogol, Bulgakov and others begins at metro Smolenskaya (dark blue line) and concludes at metro Mayakovskaya. In fact, almost every classic Russian writer has lived somewhere in this area.

Leaving the metro brings you out onto the *Sadovoye Koltso* (Garden Ring road). Turn left and keep left round the Smolensk food store. This brings you to the **Arbat**, the city's first pedestrian street; another of the "wedding cake" buildings – this one the Ministry of Foreign Affairs – looms over the intersection.

Originally a quiet old street, then a traffic trap, the Arbat was converted to a pedestrian precinct at the beginning of perestroika. It became an embodiment of the new Soviet Union, a celebration of artistic and religious freedom, thronged with buskers, street actors, artists, and even followers of Krishna.

Eight years on, the Arbat has become a noisy, crowded thoroughfare full of youths peddling clichéd souvenirs – Yeltsin matryoshka dolls, fake Palekh boxes, t-shirts, and lurid landscapes of the Moscow Kremlin. So if you shop here, do so with care, and be especially conscious of your belongings! Here, too, you can obtain almost any kind of hard drug available on the Russian market. Still, there is a positive side – though the Arbat has lost its monopoly on buskers, some still draw a crowd, and the cafés here are okay, so you can always rely on getting something decent to eat.

A short distance along on the right-hand side is the **Pushkin Flat-Museum**, the poet's Moscow residence after 1826. He lived here while courting his future wife, Natalya Goncharova. Here his "head spun" for two years before he finally won her hand in marriage in 1830. From then on, though, Moscow began to go sour on Pushkin, as he was worn down by the local gossip. "I'm not alone, nor are there two of us," he wrote, referring to that most pernicious element of the Russian family, the meddlesome mother-in-law. The couple departed soon after for St. Petersburg, never to return.

The ground floor of the museum has nothing to do with Pushkin's life in the flat, as indeed he lived on the first floor. Instead it is a unique and fascinating exhibition on Moscow at the time of Pushkin's childhood, that is, before the fire of 1812. Upstairs the arrangement is a little peculiar. Almost devoid of Pushkin's belongings, the museum is made up of a series of what seem like little shrines – tables or desks adorned with portraits of Alexander and Natalya. Of all Russia's literary heroes, so many of whom are lovingly remembered with house museums, Pushkin is the most worshipped. In the area covered by this guidebook, there are at least twelve museums solely devoted to him. (See Walk #6, and also St. Petersburg, and the Tver and Pskov Regions).

As coincidence has it, another part of the building is occupied by a tiny museum to **Andrey Bely**, the prominent symbolist writer from the beginning of this century best known for *Petersburg*, his satirical lyric novel on Russian statehood. Born there in 1880, Bely spent the first 26 years of his life in the flat, which became one of the spiritual and intellectual centers of the city and remained so after his

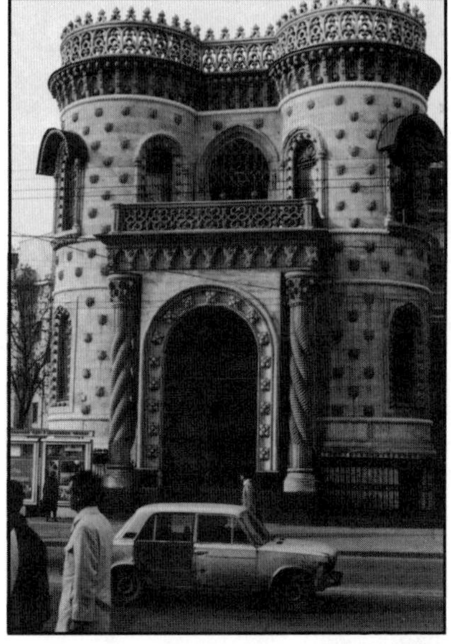

Former A.A. Morosov mansion, #16 Novy Arbat (1894–98)

departure. The most interesting exhibit is the "Line of Life," a complex diagram showing how moods, relationships and cultural influences affected his compositions.

If you wish to avoid the crowds of the Arbat, take the next right turn (Nikolsky pereulok) and join a quieter parallel street, Sivtsev Vrazhek, which is in any case more representative of how this area used to be. Its most notable landmark is the museum at #27 devoted to Alexander Herzen, the 19th century writer and proselytizer seen by revolutionaries as the link between the liberal Decembrist rebellion and the rise of socialism at the end of the century.

Eventually you emerge on Gogolyevsky bulvar, part of the Boulevard Ring and so called because of the statue at its beginning, where it intersects with the Arbat. Cross to the park area in the middle, turn left and walk up to the statue of **Nikolay Gogol**, Russia's greatest satirist. Known as "the soldier," this haughty and grandiose monument is one of the more unlikely attempts by Stalin to "reconstruct" Moscow. Riding down the boulevard one day in the 1950's, the great dictator decided that the original 19th century statue looked too forlorn and pathetic, and so promptly had it replaced by something more to his taste. Unfortunately, "the soldier" has nothing remotely in common with the sad and complex character that was Nikolay Gogol.

Now cross the square (Arbatskaya ploshchad) and Novy Arbat ulitsa, keeping on the left, outer side of the Boulevard Ring, to Suvorovsky Boulevard and enter a small courtyard. This is where the original statue, a slumped, suffering, contemplative figure, now sits above a frieze depicting tragi-comic animated characters from various of his works. Its new site is actually more appropriate – the building to the right, now a library, was where he instructed a servant to burn the manuscript of *Dead Souls*, the masterpiece that had become too great for him to finish and which seems to have killed him. He died there two days later.

Walk up the boulevard to the Nikitskiye Vorota (Nikita Gates), a square dominated by the huge ITA TASS building, home of the news agency once notorious as the mouthpiece of Soviet ideology. Turn instead toward the severe classical church on the left of the square. Although it was only finished in 1840, Pushkin chose the **Church of the Great Ascension** for his wedding in 1831. This was not an auspicious occasion, however – a dropped crucifix and candles blown out by a draught were taken as a bad omen, and six years later Pushkin was killed in a duel.

The other entrance to the church is on Ulitsa Malaya Nikitskaya, and across from it stands the **Gorky House-Museum**, otherwise known as the **Ryabushinsky Mansion** after the art-conscious banker for whom it was built in 1902-06. This is one of

Left: *Church of the Great Ascension.* Right: *Ryabushinsky Mansion (Gorky House-Museum)*

Moscow's best examples of Art Nouveau architecture, the work of Fyodor Shekhtel. It's interesting particularly for the amazing wavy staircase inside, as well as for an exterior which Catherine Cooke describes as follows: "There can be few more lyrical architectural sites than this house on a sunny spring day, with its strong square proportions and its strong curves, its gold touches amid floral mosaic behind the flowering fruit trees of its open garden; or rising from a sparkling, reflective layer of snow." (*Twilight of the Tsars*: *Russian Art at the Turn of the Century*; London, 1991). In 1931 it became the residence of Maxim Gorky, the writer considered to be the father of Socialist Realism, upon his return from several years abroad.)

The museum is at the corner of Ulitsas Malaya Nikitskaya and Alekseya Tolstovo. This quiet but proud street preserves much of the self-satisfied air of the turn of the century, when it was colonized by the progressive elements of the prosperous young merchant class of the day. At #17 is the **Morozov Mansion**, a baronial castle that is also the work of Shekhtel, though its style is a complete contrast to the other. It was built for Savva Morosov, member of a progressive family of Old Believers who arrived in Moscow in the early 1800's, entered textile manufacturing, and soon came to lead the cultural, social, and financial life of the city, right up to the Revolution. The building is now used by the Foreign Ministry for receiving guests from abroad.

Turn right onto Ulitsa Adama Mitskevicha and walk through to the tree-shaded park surrounding calm waters. This is **Patriarch's Ponds** (*Patriarshiye Prudy*), once a system of reservoirs created to provide fish for the Patriarch's table. Over the centuries the ponds fell into disuse, but after 1812 one was restored, and remains here today.

Patriarch's Ponds
Photo: Fiona Hill

Along the northern edge of the pond are a series of animals carved in relief on stands, characters from the stories of 19th century fabulist Ivan Krylov. This place is better known, however, for its part in the fantasy novel of **Mikhail Bulgakov**, *The Master and Margarita*. It is here, on the long-defunct tram lines beside the pond, that the novel opens. Berlioz, an editor at a Soviet-style literary organization, slips on some spilt sunflower oil and is decapitated by a passing tram, the first of many outrageous acts of sorcery that engulf the city.

Turn left onto Ulitsa Malaya Bronnaya, continue to the Sadovoye Koltso, and turn right. A few blocks up at #10, a plaque on the wall indicates the house where Bulgakov lived. Through the courtyard and up a stairway on the left is his flat, No. 50, portrayed in *The Master and Margarita* as the headquarters of the demons who

"As far as Anna could tell, this weird sleepwalker had flown out of the house like a bird, leaving not a trace. She crossed herself and thought, 'It's that No. 50! No wonder people say it's haunted.'"

– from *The Master and Margarita* by Mikhail Bulgakov, trans. Michael Glenny (New York: Harper & Row, 1967)

wreak havoc on the city's complacent officialdom. In the pre-perestroika days when Bulgakov was still officially disapproved of, this stairwell became a gathering place for Moscow's rebellious youth, with whom the novel struck a chord. Artists painted characters from the book, Christ figures and abstractions on the walls, interspersed with quotes and slogans. Meanwhile punks, hippies and other "outcasts" gathered on the landings and sang songs. Some of the paintings remain today, though the standard of recent contributions has fallen. The flat was briefly opened as a museum, but is currently under restoration, dogged by financial problems.

Leave the building and walk on to **Mayakovsky Square**, dominated by a huge statue of the great revolutionary poet. This is the boulevard's junction with Tverskaya ulitsa, still widely known among Muscovites as Gorky Street. Tverskaya is the city's showcase street, its mainly stalinist façades now transformed awkwardly into Western-style shops and restaurants.

WALK 6: NOBLES, PRECHISTENKA & MOSCOW CLASSICISM

You exit Kropotkinskaya metro onto the end of the Garden Ring boulevard at Kropotkinskaya ploshchad. When you pick out the monument (a statue of Friedrich Engels) on one side of the square, turn in the opposite direction and cross to the left-hand side of Ulitsa Volkhonka. On your left is the neo-classical facade of the **Pushkin Fine Arts Museum**, the second largest collection of Western European art in Russia (after St. Petersburg's Hermitage). It's useful to be more selective here than at the Tretyakov Gallery. You can probably skip the plaster copies of Greek and Roman sculptures in favor of a collection of genuine Ancient Egyptian art, and a

"What Are You, Jealous" (1892) by Paul Gauguin, collection of Pushkin Museum of Fine Arts

smattering of Botticellis and Rembrandts. Best of all are the Impressionist and Post-Impressionist galleries, featuring paintings from collections begun in Moscow before the artists were even recognized in France. Auguste Renoir's *Bathing in the Seine,* Monet's *Déjeuner sur l'herbe,* several works by Van Gogh, a gallery of Gauguins, and many Matisses are the pride of the museum. There is also an exhibition hall, generally occupied by those blockbuster shows of international art that reach Moscow. The Pushkin Fine Arts Museum (opened in 1912) was founded at the initiative of I.V. Tsvetaev, a professor of art history at Moscow University and father of the great poet **Marina Tsvetaeva**.

Walk round the swimming pool by the river side and turn back toward the metro. The extraordinary house on the corner of Kropotkinskaya naberezhnaya and Soymonovsky prospekt, with the triangular shapes and fairytale illustrations, is the Pertsov House. Built by the "Itinerant" (*peredvizhnik*) Talashkino artist

The Moskva Swimming Pool

This huge, circular, open-air heated swimming pool, surrounded by parkland and seats for spectators, is a truly Russian phenomenon: supremely glorious, awe-inspiring, and wasteful. Passing by here in winter, one used to see a cloud of steam blanketing the entire area, steadily eroding the foundations of old buildings nearby.

Those days are gone; the swimming pool has been closed while its fate is being deliberated. The pool also represents one of the greatest grievances that Muscovites had against Stalin – the destruction of the Cathedral of Christ the Savior to make room for it. Footage of the collapse of this enormous church has now been widely seen throughout the world, including in a 1991 film about poet Anna Akhmatova shown on American public television.

But despite the time it took to build (it was intended as a monument to the victory of 1812, but was begun only in 1837, and finished 46 years later), the cathedral was by no means a beauty. Rather it represented a kind of 19th century stalinism, the epitome of the pompous and falsely patriotic Byzantine style so loved by the conservative tsarist regime, and built on the site of the lovely Monastery of St. Alexey, also mercilessly torn down to make way for it.

The fate of the swimming pool seems uncertain. Many would like to see the church rebuilt, though finances are clearly a problem. Moscow's builders should stop and think before doing anything else there; perhaps they'll conclude that this time the Communists didn't do so badly after all.

View of Prechistenka, and detail of a mansion

Sergey Malyutin (see Smolensk Region), it is really just a block of flats from the turn of the century and serves as an excellent example of how the Itinerant movement applied its art to the architecture of Art Nouveau.

Return to the metro and take the second left, after the Engels statue, which is Ulitsa Prechistenka. This street is more representative than any other in Moscow of the post-1812 reconstruction, lined with **Osip Bove**'s Empire style houses (almost every one of which the architect worked on himself) for the enlightened nobility of the era. The sheer quantity of columned porticos seems to hem the street in, fronting directly onto it and probably suffering terribly from the effects of exhaust fumes and foundation-shaking juggernauts.

Two of the best examples of these houses can be spotted after a couple of blocks, almost opposite each other. Both are made of wood reinforced with stucco, and both contain museums to Russia's most revered writers, Leo Tolstoy and Alexander Pushkin, though neither ever actually lived there.

The first, the **Selesnyov House** at #12, is the more elegant, with its two columned façades and sculpted reliefs over the windows, and raised on a stone base in the tradition of Russian peasant architecture. A museum to Pushkin was opened in 1961, but rather too hastily, as it didn't yet contain a single exhibit. By now it appears to have gone to the opposite extreme, and is fairly bursting with Pushkiniana. Note the room devoted to the poet's childhood, a rare reconstruction of a pre–1812 Moscow interior.

The Lopukhin House at #11 is smaller and more conventional. It's interesting for its *War and Peace* section, but unless you're a real Tolstoy fanatic you'll do better to save your energy for his estate, the culmination of this walk.

For a view behind the façade of a Prechistenka mansion, go to #32, the house of the Okhotnikov family and now a music school. The outbuildings to the rear form a semicircular courtyard, now residential apartments, to judge by the laundry lines hanging between the gaps.

Turn left onto Kropotkinsky pereulok and walk down to Ulitsa Ostozhenka. This is a particularly attractive street to walk on. Novelist Ivan Turgenev lived at #37. On the way you will also pass the Australian Embassy, barely visible through the trees, an unusually austere and geometrical art nouveau masterpiece by Fyodor Shekhtel.

Turn right onto Ostozhenka and almost immediately you will pass a heavily guarded gateway, from which black government cars occasionally emerge. Walk on across the Sadovoye Koltso (Zubovsky bulvar) to the Park Kultury metro station forecourt to get a better view of this series of three huge former food storage warehouses. The Proviant Warehouses were also built during the 1812 reconstruction, but are currently a focus of controversy. They are used as a garage for the Ministry of Defense, and gasoline fumes are eating away at the buildings from within. Despite calls to move the cars out, however, the generals who are chauffeured in these cars are in no hurry to do so.

You have now reached the ending point of the walk, but it would surely be incomplete without visiting two more sites which lie a short distance ahead. Just down Komsomolsky prospekt on the right is the **Church of St. Nicholas in Khamovniki**, the most colorful in Moscow, thanks to an exterior based on the embroidery for which members of its patron community were known. Inside are several purportedly miracle-working icons.

Turn right at the corner of Ulitsa Lva Tolstovo and walk to the **Leo Tolstoy Museum Estate**, a wooden cottage

Lev Tolstoy Museum Estate

once surrounded by countryside – at the turn of the century this area was still outside the city limits. Tolstoy lived there with his family from 1895–1901, an increasingly isolated figure leading an unnecessarily austere existence, though his way of life is treated very positively in the museum. The great man's bicycle occupies a prominent position among his belongings.

Church of St. Nicholas in Khamovniki

BEST OF STALIN'S MOSCOW: THE METRO

Despite the indignation that mention of Stalin usually arouses when walking around Moscow, there are at least two 1930's features in today's city which can genuinely be appreciated.

Construction of the **Metro**, or *Metropolityen imeni Lenina*, as you'll see it written, commenced in 1931, and the first line opened four years later. Ever since, building has continued at a steady rate, and even economic crisis does not seem to have slowed it. Every year, you can be sure a new map will appear with more projected lines and stations.

Everything is designed to facilitate a hyper-efficient service, though in recent years it has lost a little of its edge. Trains run at intervals of between one and 10 minutes, stations are scrupulously scrubbed every night by armies of elderly women, and escalators are supervised by attendants in booths. Most impressive, though, are the extravagantly conceived and executed stations, which reflect seven decades of Soviet architecture. A suggestion: Try to bring a camera with fast film on the following tour of Metro highlights.

Begin with the red Sokolnicheskaya Liniya (Sokolniki Line), the oldest one, and in many ways unsurpassed. Note the rich, earthy colors of such older stations as the vast, simple, and columned **Kropotkinskaya (Кропоткинская)**, or **Komsomolskaya (Комсомольская)**, with its upper walk-through galleries, a feature never repeated.

Cross over to the circle line station at Komsomolskaya, the network's busiest. This glittering palace is one of two that won a prize at the New York International Exposition (1958). Its mosaics are by Pavel Korin, one of the leading Soviet artists of the day. The overall design was by the highly versatile (and by then quite elderly) architect Alexey Shchusev, who based it on the trapezium of a 17th century church in Rostov the Great.

Board a train in counter-clockwise direction, stopping briefly at **Novoslobodskaya** (look for **Новослободская** as the second station name displayed on the platform signs) to admire this station's stained-glass panelling, then continue one stop farther to **Belorusskaya (Белорусская)** and cross there to the Zamoskvoretskaya (green) line, chronologically the second to be opened. There are some interesting stations on the northern part of this line, notably **Sokol (Сокол)** with its unique double staircase, but the real masterpiece is one stop to the south, **Mayakovskaya (Маяковская)**, with its columns of stainless steel and red marble. The mosaics on the ceilings are copies of Alexander Deineka's socialist realist paintings.

At **Teatralnaya (Театральная)**, two stops past Mayakovskaya, cross to the Arbatska–Pokrovskaya (dark blue) line at **Ploshchad Revolyutsii (Площадь Революции)**. This station is one of the most striking, its every archway guarded by lifelike sculptures of Red Army soldiers and partisans, truly haunting at night. This line was built in 1944, and its three other stations within the circle line are also devoted to war themes.

For a look at '60's and '70's style, visit the purple Taganska-Krasnopresenskaya line, some of whose stations are truly hideous, especially at the southern end. For the latest constructions, try the grey Serpukhovskaya line, bland but rather more tasteful than the above.

Moscow Metro

Top & left: *Mayakovskaya station.* Right: *Ploshchad Revolyutsii*

VDNKh

Finally, take the orange Kaluzhsko–Rizhskaya line, the longest single stretch of underground railway in the world, to **VDNKh**, the former **Exhibition of Economic Achievement**. This was once a great showcase of socialism, proclaiming the Soviet Union's progress in all branches of science and technology. Several years ago, however, when it was decided that there were no more achievements, the name was changed to the All-Russian Exhibition Center, and the pavilions were filled with foreign products.

The central squares of the complex, a mingling of the former republics'

VDNKh, Space Pavilion

stock display circuit to the right. Pavilions devoted to hunting and fur displays (one of the few still being used for its original purpose) represent the zenith of the Stalin era classical style, so often seen in Soviet sanatoria and rest homes, with its idyllically posed lads and maidens.

various architectural styles, are a testament to the USSR's former glories. They are interspersed with golden fountains and monuments such as a copy of *Vostok*, Yuri Gagarin's first spaceship.

Take a look inside some of the pavilions – such as Animal Feed, now a furniture showroom, or Sheep Farming, with its rather bare shoe and boot shop. But the ultimate sell-out is the **Space Pavilion**. Built for the purpose of celebrating the Soviet Union's very real achievements in space flight, it is now a showroom for American cars, still under the gaze of a huge photo portrait of Yuri Gagarin.

There remain some exhibitions of genuine interest, though. Visit the Central Pavilion, with its City of Discovery and Creation, full of high-tech toys and holograms for children of all ages. The Cultural Pavilion, to the right, displays arts and crafts from various regions of the Russian Federation.

Many of the pavilions to the right and rear of the Space complex (to be found at the opposite end of the main entrance), seem almost forgotten but are no less magnificent, like the disused Meat Industry pavilion, its roof crowned with a statue of a man and bull, and those past the deserted live-

Before you leave, note the statue of the "Worker and Woman Collective Farmer" at the northern (main) entrance. Designed by Vera Mukhina in 1937, and familiar to many as the emblem of Mosfilm, it is considered to be one of the paragons of socialist realist art.

"Worker and Woman Collective Farmer" by Vera Mukhina

GREATER MOSCOW: THE MONASTERIES

The remaining places of interest to be described lie outside the center but are all easily reached by metro.

The monasteries – a chain of six fortresses along the city's southern flank – were a defense against the Tatars. **St. Daniel's (Danilovsky) Monastery** (metro Tulskaya; address: Danilovsky Val) is the oldest, founded in the 13th century by Prince Daniel, who was later canonized. It is now the headquarters of the Patriarchate of the Russian Orthodox Church, which returned there from Zagorsk (now Sergiyev Posad) in 1983. The most interesting building is the 17th century Church of the Seven Ecumenical Councils, built to celebrate the unity of Russia, Byelorussia and Ukraine, and including some features of the Ukrainian Baroque style. Many of the other buildings are brand new, and in the rather bland retrospective style used by today's church.

Danilovsky Monastery
19th century engraving

The **Monastery of the Savior and Andronicus** (metro Ploshchad Ilyicha; address: Ploshchad Pryamikova). Built at the time of Prince Dmitry Donskoy, this powerfully fortified but undefended monastery became something of a Christian sanctuary from the Tatars. As soon as you enter you see the **Cathedral of the Savior**, a beautiful single-domed church which, while preserving features of the pre-Mongolian school of architecture of Vladimir/Suzdal, included such innovations as *kokoshniki* or gables, later employed widely in Moscow churches. Built in 1427, the cathedral was painted by Andrey Rublyov; three years later, he was buried in the monastery. His remains have never been located, although a headstone was uncovered during restoration in the 1920's. Unfortunately, it was lost again the next day in the mud and rubble. Some traces of Rublyov's frescoes can be seen in the most remote window areas, and another monastery building now contains a museum of his work. These are mainly copies, as the originals are in the Tretyakov Gallery.

St. Simon's Monastery (metro Avtozavodskaya; Vostochnaya ulitsa, 4). Founded in 1370 and repeatedly sacked during Moscow's various troubled times, it also fell foul of Stalin, and was partially destroyed to make way for the Zil Culture Palace, a masterpiece of constructivism. In the process, the monastery graveyard was desecrated. St. Simon's produced a wealth of eminent church figures, the most notable being the monk Kirill of Beloozersk (see Vologda Region). It became immortalized in the 18th century, when a nearby stagnant pond was used by the sentimentalist writer Nikolay Karamzin as the place where

Novodevichy Convent

his abandoned heroine was drowned in his tale "Poor Liza." The monastery is currently under restoration.

The **New Monastery of the Savior** (metro Taganskaya; Krestyanskaya ploshchad, 10). Originally situated in the Kremlin, this monastery was removed by Ivan III during Kremlin rebuilding to be established as a superfortress down-river. The monastery was later chosen by the Romanovs as their burial place. In 1649, the Transfiguration Cathedral, an imitation of the Kremlin's Assumption Cathedral, was built over the family tombs, and painted with frescoes demonstrating the holiness, erudition, and majesty of the young Romanov dynasty.

Just south of the monastery is the **Krutitsky Mission**, residence of the Moscow metropolitans from the 13th to 16th centuries, before they moved into the Kremlin. Subsequently it became a country residence, and after 1693 was announced by a fabulous new entrance gate. The chamber walls above the entrance were covered with an unbroken layer of ceramic tiles decorated with patterns in relief.

Novodevichy Convent (metro Sportivnaya; Novodevichy proyezd, 1). Founded in 1524 by Grand Prince Vassily III to celebrate the capture of Smolensk from the Lithuanians, the Novodevichy (New Virgin) Convent, nestled in a bend of the Moscow River, soon occupied a prominent position among the southern fortifications. It also became a place of exile for high-ranking women in disfavor or mourning. Boris Godunov's sister lived there, and it was there that Boris was called upon to be become Tsar by the crowds. Peter the Great's reactionary sister Sofia, and the wife she forced on him, Yevdokia Lopukhina, both were banished there. From her cell, Sofia organized the 1698 coup against Peter, and as punishment her followers were strung up outside her window, driving her mad. The monastery's principal building is the **Cathedral of the Virgin of Smolensk**, built in 1525 as a more dynamic version of the Kremlin's Assumption Cathedral. Inside is a museum, telling the story of the monastery and displaying 16th century frescoes on the theme of the Muscovite princes being the heirs to the Kievan Rus' throne.

Outside the monastery walls to the right is **Novodevichy Cemetery**, Moscow's most celebrated place of burial. Among its distinguished interred, marked by monuments of exceptional and pleasing variety, are the writers Nikolay **Gogol** and Anton **Chekhov**, opera singer Fyodor **Chaliapin**, disgraced Soviet leader Nikita **Khrushchev** (not buried by the Kremlin wall like his more conservative predecessors and successors, though they may soon be joining him here) and Stalin's second wife **Svetlana Alliluyeva**.

Don Monastery (metro Shabolovskaya; Donskaya ploshchad, 1), was founded in 1591 by Tsar Fyodor as the last stopgap in the line of defenses. That year had been a trying one for Moscow, which had almost been captured by the Crimean Tatars. Dmitry Donskoy's miracle-working icon was brought into play as it was in 1380, and Khan Kaza Girei got cold feet and retreated. The new monastery was dedicated to the icon. In the same year, the tiny "Old" Cathedral was built, a beautifully proportioned church with a slender dome and stepped layers of *kokoshniki*. Beside it, in total contrast, is the "New" Cathedral, a massive baroque structure; both churches are now functioning. The cemetery contains some fine sculptures by Ivan Martos and famous graves, notably of artist Valentin **Serov** and architect Osip **Bove**. Along the back wall are some marble haut-reliefs saved during the destruction of the Church of Christ the Savior. (See Moscow Walk #6.)

Rogozhskoye Cemetery (metro Ploshchad Ilyicha; Ulitsa Voitovicha, 29) was established on land allotted to

Grave of Chekhov, Novodevichy Cemetery

the Old Believer sect in 1771 to bury their dead from the plague. Patriarch Nikon's 17th century reforms led to a split in the Orthodox Church, as many believers refused to accept them and were consequently persecuted. The Old Believers survived, however, to be granted freedom of worship during the reign of Catherine II, and they built a community around the new cemetery, including two fine churches. Their interiors are truly magnificent, with an old-world feel unmatched anywhere else in Russian Orthodoxy. The main reason is the icons, which all date from before the schism. The classical Intercession Cathedral houses a collection that almost matches the Tretyakov Gallery's, including a deisis row by the Rublyov school, with a Savior by the master himself. Take a stroll in the cemetery, too, which has tombs and mausoleums of merchant families such as the Ryabushinskys and the Morozovs.

THE ESTATES

Once the country residences of tsars or nobles, these mansions and parks now fall within the boundaries of the city.

Kolomenskoye (metro Kolomenskaya). This village, whose name may derive from refugees of Kolomna who fled there from the Mongols, became an out-of-town residence of the tsars as early as the 14th century. Ivan the Terrible built a magnificent wooden palace there, described at the time as "one of the wonders of the world"; foreign ambassadors were ferried across the Moscow River to be received there. Although Catherine the Great knocked it down, two churches and several smaller buildings remain, notably the **Ascension Church** (1530–32) by the river, built by Grand Prince Vassily III to celebrate the birth of his son, Ivan (the Terrible). This was once the tallest church in Russia, and its slender tent-roof, one of the first tent-rooves typical of northern Russia to be executed in stone, still makes it one of the prettiest. The wooden buildings on the site are not native to Kolomenskoye; in fact they could hardly be more diverse. They include a watchtower from Bratsk on Lake Baikal, and Peter the Great's cottage from Arkhangelsk in the far north.

Church of the Ascension, Kolomenskoye

The most arresting thing about Kolomenskoye is that one can find such a rural atmosphere just four metro stops from central Moscow. There is even a collective farm across the river, connected to the estate by Moscow's last remaining ferry service. The Kolomenskoye museum plans to restore the village as an open-air exhibition.

On the next hill is the site of the village of **Dyakovo**, which is known to have been settled as early as the 1st century B.C. The hilltop Church of St. John the Baptist (1540's or '50's) also represents the transition to the tent-roof form; it is regarded as the forerunner of St. Basil's on Red Square.

Izmailovo (metro Izmailovsky Park) is a royal residence dating from the 17th century. In 1683, Tsar Alexey Mikhailovich organized an experimental farm there, importing Western technology to cope with demand for silk, cotton, paints, medicinal herbs, and other products. Izmailovo is also one of the dozen or so places in Russia which claim to be the birthplace of the Russian fleet – Peter the Great found an old boat here and took it sailing on the nearby ponds, thereby cultivating an interest in ships. Much has been destroyed, but two interesting buildings remain: the beautifully tiled Interces-

Bridge Tower, Izmailovo Estate

sion Cathedral and the Bridge Tower, all that is left of a giant bridge crossing the estate's system of lakes.

Izmailovsky Park is also the venue of a huge souvenir market, Moscow's largest, held every weekend. (See p. 151.)

Kuskovo (metro Ryazansky Prospekt; address: Ulitsa Yunosti, 2; bus #133 or #288), the Sheremetyev family estate since the 16th century. This palace and park ensemble, built by serfs of its wealthy owners in the 18th century, was once described as the "Moscow Versailles." Unfortunately the main palace has not survived, but the classical wooden mansion that replaced it seems no less fine. The interior, open to the public, has what is probably Russia's best display of 18th century furnishings.

The park is imaginatively conceived, and amply endowed with follies in various European styles – a Dutch House, Swiss House, Italian House and Hermitage, the latter with a hint of the French. The orangery, meanwhile, houses a ceramics museum with 18th–20th century services and figurines from various Russian china factories. Sheremetyev's serfs could act, too – the park's open-air theater attracted the cream of Moscow society. Kuskovo Park is also a fine place to while away a summer afternoon. The opposite side of the central lake is a popular spot for sunbathing.

Ostankino (metro VDNKh; address: Pervaya Ostankinskaya, 5) is another Sheremetyev residence built by serfs, but here the palace is the focus of admiration. Rejecting Giacomo Quarenghi's proposed designs as inadequate for his purposes, Nikolay Sheremetyev instead commissioned Argunov, his serf architect, to build it. The palace features elaborate wood carving and a theater with a floor that can be raised to the level of the stage for balls.

The Trinity Church outside is unconnected with the palace. It was built at the end of the 16th century by Mikhail Cherkassy, the only man in Peter the Great's court exempt from the Tsar's edict to shave off his beard.

When you're in the area you won't fail to notice the Ostankino television tower, at 540m the second tallest free-standing structure in the world after the CN Tower in Toronto. Completed in 1967, its original plan resembled the Eiffel Tower, and as built still shows some features of that structure, in particular the spread legs at the base. The observation tower 337m up is open to the public, as are a restaurant and night club. Nearby are the offices of CIS television, also called Ostankino, and Russian Television and Radio, in the building stormed by pro-Communist supporters during the rebellion of October 4, 1993.

Tsaritsyno (metro Tsaritsyno), a huge palace commissioned by Catherine the Great, has throughout its existence remained a utopian dream. The Empress took a fancy to a piece of land south of Moscow called *Chornaya Gryaz'* (Black Mud), proclaimed it "heaven on earth," and promptly renamed it Tsaritsyno, the Empress's village. Vassily Bazhenov began work on the project, but the Moorish-gothic neo-Russian buildings he created were not to Catherine's lik-ing, and despite attempts by architect Matvey Kazakov to revive the project, funds ran out.

What remains, then, is a superb ruin of something that never quite existed: enormous palace walls with no floors, windows or roof, a paradise for children of all ages, stunt men, absailers, and the romantically inclined. Tsaritsyno has a reputation for supernatural happenings, too, including a bridge that moved several meters, and even sightings of "humanoid aliens."

Tsaritsyno Palace

Now there is a new burst of activity at Tsaritsyno. Many of the smaller buildings have been restored and there are plans to open a museum. Oddly, one was created in 1984, although there was no permanent place to display exhibitions. Fine collections of icons, glass, china and Fabergé eggs are stored in cellars under the ruins, occasionally surfacing for exhibitions abroad.

OLD & NEW STREET NAMES

Former ("Soviet") Name	New Name
Ulitsa Gertsena	Ulitsa Bolshaya Nikitskaya
Ulitsa Gorkovo	Tverskaya ulitsa
Ploshchad Dzerzhinskovo	Lubyanskaya ploshchad
Ulitsa 25-ovo Oktyabrya	Nikolskaya ulitsa
Internatsionalnaya/Verkhnyaya Radischevskaya ulitsa	Taganskaya ulitsa
Ulitsa Kachalova	Ulitsa Malaya Nikitskaya
Prospekt Kalinina	Ulitsa Vozdvizhenka/Novy Arbat
Ulitsa Bogdana Khmelnitskovo	Ulitsa Maroseika
Ulitsa Kirova	Myasnitskaya ulitsa
Kropotkinskaya ulitsa	Ulitsa Prechistenka
Ulitsa Kuibysheva	Ulitsa Ilyinka
Prospekt Marksa	Mokhovaya/Okhotny Ryad/ Teatralny proyezd
Ploshchad Nogina	Varvarskaya ploshchad
Ploshchad 50-letiya Oktyabrya	Manezhnaya ploshchad
Ulitsa Razina	Ulitsa Varvarka
Sovyetskaya ploshchad	Skobelevskaya ploshchad
Ploshchad Sverdlova	Teatralnaya ploshchad
Ulitsa Ulyanova	Nikolo-Yamskaya ulitsa
Ulitsa Chernyshevskovo	Ulitsa Pokrovka

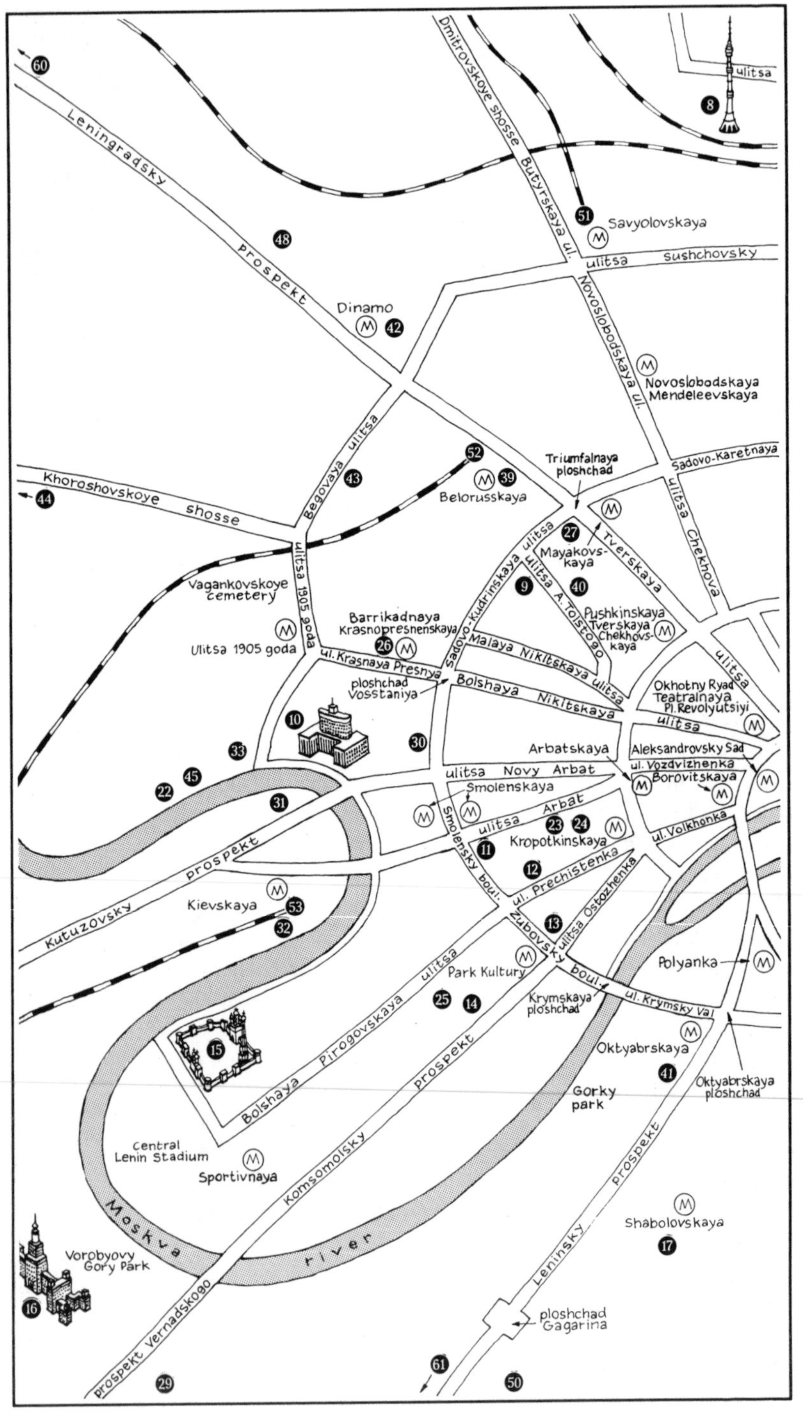

Dmitrovskoye shosse
Butyrskaya ul.
ulitsa
Leningradsky prospekt
Savyolovskaya
ulitsa Sushchovsky
Novoslobodskaya ul.
Dinamo
Novoslobodskaya
Mendeleevskaya
Begovaya ulitsa
Triumfalnaya ploshchad
Sadovo-Karetnaya
Khoroshovskoye shosse
Belorusskaya
ulitsa Chekhova
Tverskaya
Mayakovs-kaya
Sadovo-Kudrinskaya ulitsa
ulitsa A. Tolstogo
ulitsa 1905 goda
Vagankovskoye cemetery
Barrikadnaya
Krasnopresnenskaya
Pushkinskaya
Tverskaya
Chekhovs-kaya
Ulitsa 1905 goda
ul. Krasnaya Presnya
Malaya Nikitskaya ulitsa
ulitsa
ploshchad Vosstaniya
Bolshaya Nikitskaya
Okhotny Ryad
Teatralnaya
Pl. Revolyutsiyi
ulitsa
Arbatskaya
Aleksandrovsky Sad
ulitsa Novy Arbat
ul. Vozdvizhenka
Borovitskaya
Smolenskaya
ulitsa Arbat
Smolensky boul.
Kropotkinskaya
ul. Volkhonka
Kutuzovsky prospekt
ul. Prechistenka
Kievskaya
ulitsa Ostozhenka
Zubovsky boul.
Polyanka
Park Kultury
Krymskaya ploshchad
ul. Krymsky Val
Bolshaya Pirogovskaya ulitsa
Komsomolsky prospekt
Oktyabrskaya
Oktyabrskaya ploshchad
Gorky park
Central Lenin Stadium
Sportivnaya
Leninsky prospekt
Moskva river
Shabolovskaya
Vorobyovy Gory Park
ploshchad Gagarina
prospekt Vernadskogo
60 8 51 48 42 52 39 43 44 27 9 40 26 10 30 33 45 22 31 23 24 11 12 53 32 13 25 14 15 41 17 16 61 50 29

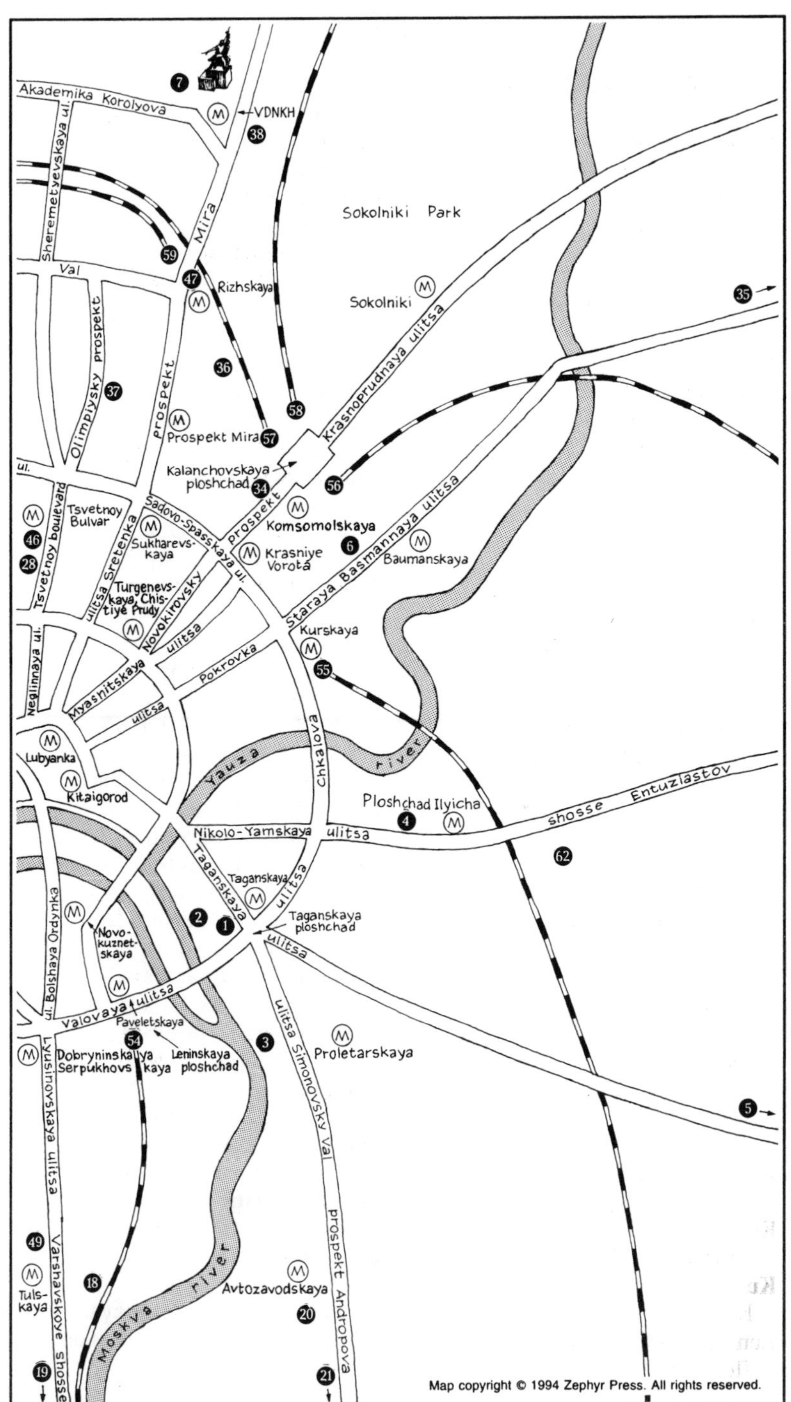

Akademika Korolyova
VDNKH
Sheremetyevskaya ul.
Sokolniki Park
Mira
Val
Rizhskaya
Sokolniki
Olimpiysky prospekt
prospekt
Krasnoprudnaya ulitsa
Prospekt Mira
Kalanchovskaya ploshchad
prospekt
Tsvetnoy Bulvar
Tsvetnoy boulevard
Sadovo-Spasskaya ul.
Sukharevskaya
Komsomolskaya
Krasniye Vorota
Staraya Basmannaya ulitsa
Baumanskaya
ulitsa Sretenka
Turgenevskaya, Chistiye Prudy
Novokirovsky
ulitsa
Kurskaya
Neglinnaya ul.
Myasnitskaya
Pokrovka
ulitsa
Lubyanka
Yauza
river
Chkalova
Kitaigorod
Ploshchad Ilyicha
shosse Entuziastov
Nikolo-Yamskaya ulitsa
Taganskaya
Taganskaya
ulitsa
Taganskaya ploshchad
ul. Bolshaya Ordynka
Novokuznetskaya
ulitsa
Valovaya ulitsa
Paveletskaya
ulitsa Simonovsky Val
Proletarskaya
Dobryninskaya Serpukhovskaya
Leninskaya ploshchad
Lyusinovskaya ulitsa
Varshavskoye shosse
Tulskaya
Moskva river
Avtozavodskaya
prospekt Andropova
7
38
59
47
35
36
37
58
57
34
56
46
6
28
55
4
62
2
1
54
3
5
49
18
20
19
21

MOSCOW

Ulitsa Akademika Korolyova
Улица Академика Королёва
Prospekt Andropova
Проспект Андропова
Ulitsa Arbat
Улица Арбат
Ulitsa Begovaya
Улица Беговая
Ulitsa Bolshaya Pirogovskaya
Улица Большая Пироговская
Butyrskaya ulitsa
Бутырская улица
Central Lenin Stadium
Центральный стадион
имени Ленина
Ulitsa Chekhova
Улица Чехова
Ulitsa Chkalova
Улица Чкалова
Dmitrovskoye shossé
Дмитровское шоссе
Dynamo Stadium
Стадион «Динамо»
Shossé Entuziastov
Шоссе Энтузиастов
Ploshchad Gagarina
Площадь Гагарина
Gorky Park
Парк Горького
Kalanchovskaya ploshchad
Каланчёвская площадь
Khoroshovskoye shossé
Хорошовское шоссе
Komsomolsky prospekt
Комсомольский проспект
Ulitsa Krasnaya Presnya
Улица Красная Пресня
Krasnoprudnaya ulitsa
Краснопрудная улица
Krymskaya ploshchad
Крымская площадь
Krymsky val
Крымский Вал
Kutuzovsky prospekt
Кутузовский проспект
Leningradsky prospekt
Ленинградский проспект
Leninskaya ploshchad
Ленинградская площадь
Leninsky prospekt
Ленинский проспект
Lyusinovskaya ulitsa
Люсиновская улица
Malaya Nikitskaya ulitsa
Малая Никитская улица
Prospekt Mira
Проспект Мира
Moskva River
Москва река
Nikolo-Yamskaya ulitsa
Николо-Ямская улица
Ulitsa 1905 Goda
Улица 1905 года
Novokirovsky prospekt
Новокировский проспект
Novoslobodskaya ulitsa
Новослободская улица
Ulitsa Novy Arbat
Улица Новый Арбат
Oktyabrskaya ploshchad
Октябрская площадь
Olimpiysky prospekt
Олимпийский проспект
Ulitsa Prechistenka
Улица Пречистенка
Ulitsa Sadovo-Karetnaya
Улица Садово-Каретная
Ulitsa Sadovo-Kudrinskaya
Улица Садово-Кудринская
Ulitsa Sadovo-Spasskaya
Улица Садово-Спасская
Sheremetyevskaya ulitsa
Шереметьевская улица
Simonovsky val
Симоновский вал
Smolensky bulvar
Смоленский бульвар
Sokolniki Park
Парк «Сокольники»
Ulitsa Sretenka
Улица Сретенка
Ulitsa Staraya Basmannaya
Улица Старая Басманная

МОСКВА

Sushchevsky Val
Сущевский Вал
Taganskaya ploshchad
Таганская площадь
Triumfalnaya ploshchad
Триумфальная площадь
Tsvetnoy bulvar
Цветной бульвар
Vagankovskoye Cemetery
Ваганьковское кладбище
Valovaya ulitsa
Валовая улица
Varshavskoye shossé
Варшавское шоссе
Prospekt Vernadskovo
Проспект Вернадского
Vorobyovy Gory
Воробьёвы горы
Ploshchad Vosstaniya
Площадь Восстания
Yauza River
Река Яуза
Zubovsky bulvar
Зубовский бульвар

MAP KEY

1. **Taganka Theater**
Театр на Таганке
2. **Assumption Church in Gonchary**
Успенская церковь в Гончарах
3. **New Monastery of the Savior**
Новоспасский монастырь
4. **Monastery of the Savior and St. Andronicus**
Спасо-Андрониковский монастырь
5. **Kuskovo Palace and Bykovo Airport**
Кусково/Аэропорт Быково
6. **Epiphany Cathedral**
Богоявленский собор
7. **All-Russian Exhibition Center (VDNKh)**
Всероссийский Выставочный Центр
8. **Ostankino Tower**
Останкинская башня
9. **Morozov Mansion**
Усадьба Морозова
10. **White House**
Белый Дом
11. **Foreign Ministry**
МИД
12. **Okhotnikov Mansion**
Усадьба Охотникова
13. **Proviant Warehouses**
Провиантские склады
14. **St. Nicholas Church in Khamovniki**
Никольская церковь в Хамовниках
15. **Novodevichy Convent**
Новодевичий монастырь
16. **Moscow State University**
Университет
17. **Don Monastery**
Донской монастырь
18. **St. Daniel's Monastery**
Даниловский монастырь
19. **Tsaritsyno Palace and Domodedovo Airport**
Царицыно/Аэропорт
20. **St. Simon's Monastery**
Симоновский монастырь
21. **Kolomenskoye**
Коломенское
22. **Expocenter**
Экспоцентр
23. **Pushkin Flat-Museum**
Музей-квартира Пушкина
24. **Herzen Flat-Museum**
Музей-квартира Герцена
25. **Tolstoy House-Museum**
Музей-усадьба Толстого
26. **Zoo**
Зоопарк

27. Tchaikovsky Concert Hall
Концертный зал имени Чайковского
28. Old Circus
Старый цирк
29. New Circus
Новый цирк
30. U.S. Embassy
Посольство США
31. Ukraina Hotel
Гостиница «Украина»
32. Slavyanskaya Radisson Hotel
33. Mezhdunarodnaya Hotel
Гостиница «Международная»
34. Leningradskaya Hotel
Гостиница «Ленинградская»
35. Izmailovo Hotel, Vernissazh (Market) and Estate
Гостиница «Измайлово», Вернисаж, Усадьба
36. Travellers' Guest House
37. Olympic Penta Hotel
38. Cosmos Hotel
Гостиница «Космос»
39. Palace Hotel
40. Presnya Hotel
Гостиница «Пресня»
41. President Hotel
42. Dynamo Stadium
Стадион «Динамо»
43. Hippodrome
Ипподром
44. Serbryany Bor beach
Серебряный Бор
45. Sadko Arcade
46. Tsentralny Market
Центральный рынок
47. Rizhsky Market
Рижский рынок
48. Leningradsky Market
Ленинградский рынок
49. Danilovsky Market
Даниловский рынок
50. Cheryomyshinsky Market
Черёмышинский рынок
51. Savyolovsky Vokzal
Савёловский вокзал
52. Belorussky Vokzal
Белорусский вокзал
53. Kievsky Vokzal
Киевский вокзал
54. Paveletsky Vokzal
Павелецкий вокзал
55. Kursky Vokzal
Курский вокзал
56. Kazansky Vokzal
Казанский вокзал
57. Leningradsky Vokzal
Ленинградский вокзал
58. Yaroslavsky Vokzal
Ярославский вокзал
59. Rizhsky Vokzal
Рижский вокзал
60. Sheremetyevo Airport
Аэропорт Шереметьево
61. Vnukovo Airport
Аэропорт Внуково

PRACTICAL MATTERS

Transport

Metro. Moscow has a vast metro system which is still being added to even now – it's amazing how many remote housing estates are yet cut off from the center. There is a circle line intersected by numerous radial lines. Payment is by green plastic *jeton* (token). However, the number you are allowed to buy at one time is often restricted, so it may be more sensible to try to get a monthly pass – which goes on sale toward the end of each previous month – even if you are only staying a few days. These are on sale for a week or two before the beginning of the month, from metro ticket offices, and from kiosks and street sellers. (See Metro map on the next page.)

Overland Transport. The trolleybus system is extensive, and can be useful for such routes as the Sadovoye Koltso (Garden Ring road), served by #10 and Б, or for shorter distances along major radial routes. Non-electric buses serve more obscure areas. Try to avoid trams in Moscow – they almost always take roundabout routes and are never convenient in the center. A word of warning: Moscow public transport has been seriously cut back in recent years and seems to get less frequent and more crowded as time goes on. *The Traveller's Yellow Pages* (see publications section) has a detailed map of all routes.

A Moscow tram on the Boulevard Ring, at Pokrovsky Gate Square

Suburban and Inter-city transport. Moscow's train, bus, and boat stations (*vokzaly*) and airports are as follows:

Leningradsky Vokzal (metro Komsomolskaya): trains to Tver, St. Petersburg, Novgorod, Pskov, Karelia, Estonia, and Finland (tel. 266-9111; 262-4281)

Yaroslavsky Vokzal (metro Komsomolskaya): trains to Sergiyev Posad, Yaroslavl, Vologda, Arkhangelsk and the Trans-Siberian route (tel. 266-0218)

Kazansky Vokzal (metro Komso–molskaya): trains to Ryazan, Tatarstan, Central Asia, western Siberia, Samara, and some southern destinations

Kursky Vokzal (metro Kurskaya): trains to Tula, Vladimir, Nizhny Novgorod, eastern Ukraine, Crimea, and the Caucasus (tel. 266-5846)

Paveletsky Vokzal (metro Paveletskaya): trains to central southern Russia – Voronezh, Volgograd, Astrakhan (tel. 233-0040)

Kievsky Vokzal (metro Kievskaya): trains to Kaluga, Bryansk, Chernigov, Kiev, western Ukraine, Odessa, and central and southern Europe (tel. 240-7345)

Byelorussky Vokzal (metro Belorusskaya): trains to Smolensk, Minsk, Poland, Germany and Lithuania (tel. 253-4464; 266-9213)

Savyolovsky Vokzal (metro Savyolovskaya): trains to Uglich and Rybinsk (tel. 285-9000; 266-9007)

Moscow Metro

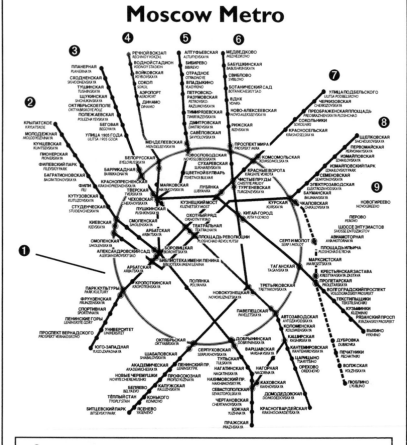

❶ **CIRCLE LINE**
❷ **FILEVSKAYA LINE**
(Krylatskoe–Aleksandrovsky Sad)
❸ **TAGANSKO–KRASNOPRESNENSKAYA LINE**
(Planernaya–Vykhino)
❹ **GORKOVSKO–ZAMOSKVORETSKAYA LINE**
(Rechnoy Vokzal–Krasnogvardeyskaya)
❺ **SERPUKHOVSKAYA LINE**
(Altufyevskaya–Prazhskaya)
❻ **KALUZHSKO–RIZHSKAYA LINE**
(Medvedkovo–Bitsevsky Park)
❼ **KIROVSKO–FRUNZENSKAYA LINE**
(Ulitsa Podbelskovo–Yugo-Zapadnaya)
❽ **ARBATSKO–POKROVSKAYA LINE**
(Sholkovskaya–Smolenskaya)
❾ **KALININSKAYA LINE**
(Novogireevo–Tretyakovskaya)

■ ■ ■ ■ ■ Lines under construction or planned

◉ Transfer stations

Rizhsky Vokzal (metro Rizhskaya): trains to Riga (tel. 266-1372; 266-9535)

(For 24-hour general inquiries about train services, call any number between 266-9000 and 266-9999.)

Tsentralny Avtovokzal (metro Sholkovskaya): all long-distance bus services (tel. 468-0400)

For suburban bus services, there are local stations at the following metros:

VDNKh – north (tel. 181-9755)

Vykhino – southeast (tel. 371-5254)

Izmailovsky Park – east

Tushinskaya – northwest (tel. 490-2424)

Yugozapadnaya – southwest

Severny Rechny Vokzal (metro Rechnoy Vokzal): hydrofoils to Moscow Canal and reservoirs, long-distance boats to Nizhny Novgorod and St. Petersburg (tel. 457-4050; 459-7465)

Yuzhny Rechnoy Vokzal (metro Kolomenskoye; address: Prospekt Andropova, 11): boats along southern Moskva river and Oka route to Nizhny Novgorod

Sheremetyevo 2 airport (bus #517 from metro Planernaya): virtually all international flights (tel. 578-5633; 578-5614; 578-5634)

Sheremetyevo 1 airport (bus #551 from metro Rechnoy Vokzal): Aeroflot flights to St. Petersburg and Russian north (tel. 578-5971), all Transaero internal flights, and some CIS and international destinations

Vnukovo airport (bus 511 or 511Э from metro Yugo-Zapadnaya): flights to most southern and Siberian destinations (tel. 234-8656; 234-8655)

Domodedovo airport (suburban train from Paveletsky Vokzal): flights to Central Asia and some Siberian destinations (same telephone numbers as Vnukovo)

Bykovo airport (suburban train from the Kazansky Vokzal): short flights to some central Russian destinations (tel. 155-0922)

Aerovokzal (metro Dynamo, Leningradsky prospekt, 37a): express buses to all internal flight airports, with connecting buses also running between each airport (tel. 155-0922)

Ticket Offices. ***Rail*** (international tickets): Intourtrans, Ul. Petrovka, 15/13, 1st floor (metro Teatralnaya/Okhotny Ryad); (domestic) Ul. Griboyedova 6/4, right-hand building (metro Chistiye Prudy), or Intourtrans, at Leningradsky Vokzal, 2nd floor. Advance booking for CIS citizens is at the building between Yaroslavsky and Leningradsky Vokzals, except for St. Petersburg tickets, which are at Leningradsky Vokzal, 2nd floor. ***Air:*** (domestic Aeroflot) Intourtrans, Ul. Petrovka, 15/13 (metro Teatralnaya/Okhotny Ryad), 3rd floor. The domestic booking office for Transaero is on the Tverskaya ulitsa side of the Moskva Hotel building on Manezhnaya ploshchad. ***River:*** Leningradsky prospekt, 1 (metro Belorusskaya). Tickets for river cruises to Nizhny Novgorod and St. Petersburg, food and excursions not included.

Car Hire. In addition to those firms mentioned in the introduction allowing unlimited travel in the Russian Federation, the following provide driverless cars for Moscow or the Moscow Region:

InNis, Ul. Petrovka, 15/13 (tel. 155-5021; 578-7532)

Rolf rent-a-car, Ul. Kulakova, 20 (tel. 241-7715): Mitsubishis and Fords, within Moscow only

Autosun (tel. 280-3600): Nissans and Sunnys in Moscow and the Moscow Region

Olga (tel. 927-6139; 927-6140): Sunnys and Opels, Moscow and the Moscow Region

Car Repair. Garages specializing in the servicing of Western cars in general: ABC Opel, Ul. Sergiya Eyzenshteyna, 2 (tel. 181-0407); Autodesignservice, Trubnikovsky pr., 1 (tel. 290-2327); Moscow X-Service, Ul. Mytnaya, 18/2 (tel. 238-6634); Nefto Agip, Bolshoy Cherkassky per., 7/D (tel. 930-7973); Sims & Klein, Ul. Tverskaya, 36 (tel. 251-8950); Service Station #7, 2nd Selskokhozyaisktvenny proyezd, 6 (tel. 181-1374; 181-2169); Sovinteravtoservice, Institutsky per., 2/1 (tel. 299-7773; 299-5900); Spetzavtotsentr, Kievskaya, 8 (tel. 240-2092; 240-4330).

Accommodation

While Moscow bends over backward to cater to the business community, the poor tourist still suffers from a lack of cheap, decent accommodation. Bureaucracy and skyrocketing real-estate prices have hampered any fledgling private sector developments, and while Western superhotels mushroom, ordinary mortals have to be content with a dwindling number of aging and overpriced Soviet-era monsters.

If you're handsomely rich or on an expense account, the choice of five-star properties is overwhelming – expect to pay $250–$350 for a single room. A few hotels deserve special mention. Two in the center should attract the discerning visitor: the **Metropol** (7 Okhotny Ryad, tel. 927-6000 to -6002), with its glamorous art nouveau decor and stylish cafés, and the **Baltschug Kempinski** (Ul. Baltchuga 1, tel. 230-6500 to -6507), overlooking the Kremlin and boasting a little-known top floor bar with a library of classic novels. Marco Polo's **Palace** is also conveniently located, at Tverskaya-Yamskaya, 19 (tel. 956-3152) and quite excellently run.

Somewhat cheaper ($100–$200 for a single) are the top Russian hotels, such as the **Intourist** (Tverskaya 3/5, tel. 203-4008; metro Okhotny Ryad), bang in the center, with decent restaurants and notorious for its prostitutes, or the **Cosmos** (150 Prospekt Mira, tel. 217-8680; metro VDNKh), great for the Exhibition Center but not so good for the Kremlin. Note also a small, exclusive-looking place called **Hotel Club Kachalova 27**, at the same address as its name, located in a quiet area just off the Garden Ring (metro Barrikadnaya).

Medium range ($40–$100) in Moscow generally means Soviet-type ordinariness, sleaziness, and mafia activity. However, there are several hotels of this type whose convenient location could make your stay worthwhile:

Budapest, Petrovskaya Liniya 2/18, tel. 921-1060, metro Teatralnaya/Okhotny Ryad, quiet and mafia-free; **Minsk**, Tverskaya 22, tel. 299-1300, metro Pushkinskaya/Tverskaya; **Rossiya**, Varvarka 6, tel. 298-5400, metro Kitai-gorod; **Ukraina**, Kutuzovsky pr. 2/1, tel. 243-3030, metro Kievskaya; **Leningradskaya**, Kalanchovskaya ul. 21/40, tel. 975-3008, metro Komsomolskaya; **Pekin**, Ul. Bolshaya Sadovaya 1/5, tel. 209-2442, metro Mayakovskaya; **Moskva**, Okhotny Ryad 7, tel. 292-1100, metro Okhotny Ryad. One other hotel with good facilities but outside the center (close to the flea market) is the **Izmailovo Tourist Complex** (Izmailovskoye shossé 71, tel. 166-0145; metro Izmailovsky Park).

As for cheap hotels, there is good news and bad news. The good news is that there is youth hostel-style accommodation at the **Travellers' Guest House** (Bolshaya Pereyaslavskaya 50, tel. 971-4059; metro Prospekt Mira). This oasis in the Moscow desert provides visa support, and cheap rail and air tickets, and also helps arrange travel on the rail routes to China. Sleeping two to four in a room, they

May We Recommend

MOSCOW BED & BREAKFAST

Get a taste of how Muscovites live, and let your host help acclimate you to the city! The bed-and-breakfast option is just arriving in Moscow, and so to open up opportunities for the independent traveler, the publishers of *An Explorer's Guide to Russia* have initiated a new service.

We are pleased, through Moscow Bed & Breakfast, to offer accommodation, guide/interpreter, and other contacts, bookable from the U.S. at a cost substantially below the rates of other such organizations.

Moscow B&B can meet you at the airport or train station, bring you to your bed & breakfast host, and pick you up at the end of your stay. They have also engaged 15 guide/interpreters who are available to take you on excursions in and around the city, for either individual sight visits, or for engagements lasting several days or more. Another service is ticket purchase, for the Bolshoy and other performances as well as for railroad, bus or boat travel. You pay the cost of the ticket plus a small service charge. Visa support is available as well.

For **bed & breakfast**, daily rates range between $20 and $35, depending upon whether your host speaks English and on the location of the apartment (the center or suburbs). **Guide/interpreters** are available at a daily rate of $25–$50, depending upon level of experience and other factors. (They can be engaged for half-days of four hours as well.) Guides with less formal training are suitable for most tourists. A **car and driver** may be hired for traveling within the city or outside. You can also book an interpreter (with or without a car) to accompany you on explorations of the Yaroslavl, Vladimir, and Tver Regions, as well as of more distant places. For further information, advice, visa support, and complete booking assistance, please contact Russian Travel Service, our U.S. agent. If you speak Russian, you may contact Moscow Bed & Breakfast directly, by fax:

Russian Travel Service
Attn: Helen Kates
P.O. Box 311
Fitzwilliam, NH 03447
tel. & fax:
(603) 585-6534

Moscow Bed & Breakfast
Alla Kashtanova, Director
Moscow, Russia
fax: (7)(095) 152-7493
tel: (7)(095) 193-2514;
457-3508

◆ SAMPLE LISTINGS ◆

These are some of the Moscow hosts and guide/interpeters who are available for booking through Moscow Bed & Breakfast.

BED & BREAKFAST

Metro KIEVSKAYA, just west of the center, across the Moscow river. **Evgeny** and **Galina** are actors, and live in a 2-room apartment with their 9-year old daughter, Daria. They speak English, and also have a car.

BED & BREAKFAST (Continued)

Metro KANTEMIROVSKAYA, south of the center near Kolomenskoye Museum Preserve. **Dina** lives alone in a 2-bedroom apartment. She speaks English.

Metro CHISTY PRUDY, in the center near the Garden Ring, a very beautiful part of old Moscow. **Galina** is 36, and lives in a 4-bedroom apartment with her 16- and 12-year-old sons, Ivan and Sergey. They can accommodate 4 guests in 2 rooms.

Near Metro FILI, a little NW of the center. **Pavel** has a one-room apartment. He speaks English, and can offer his apartment for any length of time.

Metro KRASNOPRESENSKAYA, on the Circle Line. **Boris** is an actor, and has a one-bedroom apartment. He speaks English, and offers his apartment for short lengths of time.

Near Metro DINAMO, north of the center. **Yelena** is a 35-year-old economist, and lives alone in her 2-room apartment, in a green and peaceful part of Moscow. She speaks English.

Near Metro OKTYABRSKOYE POLE, Khoroshovskoye shossé district, NW of the center. **Tatyana** is 45 years old, and lives in a 2-room apartment. She speaks English and French.

Metro TUSHINSKAYA, NW from the center. **Malika** is a vibrant middle-aged woman who has a two-room apartment. She teaches Russian language and literature, and speaks Spanish.

Metro KIEVSKAYA, on the Circle Line. Both **Lucia** and her husband **Sergey** are philologists. They have a small black poodle; Lucia speaks English.

Near Metro RECHNOY VOKZAL (River Station), north of the center. **Galina** is 50, and lives in a very comfortable 2-room apartment. She is an engineer, and has a dog named Collie.

Metro UNIVERSITET, near Moscow State University. **Alexender** is 60, and has a 3-room apartment. He offers two rooms for accommodation in this peaceful area.

Metro UNIVERSITET, near Moscow State University. **Olga** is an assistant director of the Moscow Art Theater. She lives with her mother and 8-year-old daughter in a 2-room apartment, and offers one room for accommodation of guests.

GUIDE / INTERPRETERS

Twenty-year-old **Vadim** lives in a Moscow suburb. He's studied in the U.S., where he practiced his English a lot, and can take part in some excursions outside of the city. He enjoys swimming, science fiction, theater, and music.

Olga is an actress who manages an art gallery. She's 35, and is fond of music, poetry, theater, and the piano. A very helpful and charming person.
Nadezhda is 40 years old, has worked as a dealer in an art gallery, and as an interpreter with Gosconcert, the state concert organization. She is an expert in Russian literature and art, and also enjoys traveling. She is willing and able to travel with visitors. She is an Orthodox Christian.
Natalya has been an interpreter with Aeroflot, and is now a supervisor with El Al Airlines in Moscow. She has worked as a tour guide, and also interpreted at meetings of all kinds. She is sometimes available to travel with tourists. She likes literature, theater, music, and art.
Lucia has graduated from the University of Sofia, Bulgaria. She teaches English and is also a professional interpreter, and likes to read history and French literature, and to attend theater, especially opera.
Raisa, 40, is a graduate in Technical Translation from the Institute of Foreign Languages, and worked abroad as an interpreter for several years. She is available to accompany visitors on trips outside of Moscow.
Forty-year-old **Marina** has three years experience as a guide/interpreter on Russian-American cruises. She can accompany visitors on tours of Moscow, and also of old Russian towns nearby.
Natalya likes literature, classical music, opera, and ballet. She is a teacher of English, and teaches Russian to foreigners. She is 39.
Lyuba has interpreted for American and Canadian tourists, and has served as an interpreter at international competitions. Her personal interests include music, theater, art, and politics; she also collects stamps. She can travel with tourists. Christian.

charge $10–$13 per person. They have only one floor of a multi-story building and 46 beds but have access to more rooms in summer.

The bad news is there's virtually nowhere else. Three hotels of the youth travel organization Sputnik are twice as expensive and poorly positioned. They are:

Molodyozhnaya, Dmitrovskoye shossé 27, tel. 210-4838, metro Timiryazevskaya; **Orlyonok**, Ul. Kosygina 15, tel. 939-8845, metro Leninsky Prospekt; **Sputnik**, Leninsky pr. 38, tel. 938-7096, metro Leninsky Prospekt. If location is important to you, the **Tsentralnaya** (Tverskaya 10, tel. 229-8539; metro Pushkinskaya/Tverskaya) certainly lives up to its name, but lacks conveniences in the rooms.

Apartment rental is another possibility, though while on the topic it's also worth mentioning the self-catering **Tsaritsyno Hotel** (Shipilovsky prospekt 47/1, metro Orekhovo). Close to the Tsaritsyno Palace, it provides fully furnished one- to five-room apartments, ranging from $80–$180 a night and with no restrictions on number of guests.

The best way of finding an apartment short term is probably through personal contacts, but if you have none the following firms offer rented accommodation:

Jupiter, Butyrsky val 7, tel. 250-2300; metro Byelorusskaya. Minimum of 3 days stay, $7–$15 a night, all over Moscow.

Unifuturer, tel. 473-4428. No details available at present.

Express, tel. 227-5827. Minimum one-month stay, $100–$500, all over Moscow.

Classified ads in newspapers such as the Moscow *Times* and *Tribune* are another useful source.

The most attractive option for budget travelers – or for anyone seeking a genuine experience of the city – may be **bed-and-breakfast**, which is just now becoming available in Moscow. To assist users of *An Explorer's Guide to Russia* in finding congenial accommodations and friendly local contacts, we have initiated **Moscow Bed & Breakfast**, a new service bookable through Helen Kates of Russian Travel Service, **phone & fax: (603) 585-6534**. (For more information, see previous pages.)

Eating Out

The rather unhappy state of affairs with accommodation is repeated also on Moscow's restaurant scene, with an abundance of expensive restaurants, mostly serving European cuisine, at one extreme, and a few sleazy cafeterias with mostly inedible food at the other.

If you tend toward the first, you would do well to obtain a thin volume called *Maitre D'* (published in Russia by the Bucephalus Agency and available in most major hotels and supermarkets). The guide describes the fifty best restaurants in Moscow as determined by a group of independent experts. It also includes a handful of somewhat less-pricey establishments.

What follows is a smaller selection of the most expensive restaurants ($30–$70+ for a three-course meal without drinks) serving "CIS" cuisine:

Anchor, Palace Hotel, tel. 956-3152. A fish restaurant which is shipshape. Excellent service, ingredients shipped in from the U.S., but some cooked in local style.

Sirena, Bolshaya Spasskaya 15, tel. 208-1412; metro Komsomolskaya. Another fish restaurant, this time fully Russian. Generally recognized as the best Russian private restaurant.

Boyarsky Zal, Metropol Hotel, tel. 927-6089. A restaurant that takes you back to the 16th century and the feasts of the powerful Boyar families. The prices are princely, too.

Kropotkinskaya 36, Prechistenka 36, tel. 201-7500; metro Kropotkinskaya. Moscow's first cooperative restaurant, it presents excellent cuisine, genuine Russian hospitality and gentle piano music.

Rus, 1-y Golutvinsky per. 2/10, tel. 238-7276; metro Oktyabrskaya. Excellent cuisine but not so hot on atmosphere and drinks are expensive. Full of nouveau riche Russians.

Golden Ostap, 3 Shmitovsky proyezd, tel. 259-4795; metro Ulitsa 1905 Goda. European/Georgian cuisine in an elegant, cozy restaurant with jazz improvisation and a small casino.

Savoy, Savoy Hotel, 3 Rozhdestvenka, tel. 929-8600. Prestigious like the Boyarsky, but in a more kingly way. The decor really is lavish. Cuisine is a Euro-Russian mixture.

Rather gentler on your pocket, the following should still provide you with a civilized meal:

Nemetskaya Sloboda, Ul. Baumanskaya 23, tel. 267-4476; metro Baumanskaya. Attractive, intimate restaurant reviving the traditions of the foreign community that lived in this district during the 18th century. Food, however, is Russian and very cheap.

Razgulyai, 11 Ul. Spartakovskaya, tel. 267-7613; metro Baumanskaya. Another early co-op restaurant, instead of basking in its success and be-

coming overpriced, it has stayed inexpensive. Food is decent and decor distinctly Russian.

Margarita, Malaya Bronnaya 28, tel. 299-6534; metro Pushkinskaya/Tverskaya. Formerly a trendy, slightly seedy café, it recently went upmarket and features a pianist in the evening. Food variable but always Russian, reliable for daytime snacks and popular with foreigners.

Guria, Komsomolsky pr. 7/3, tel. 246-0378; metro Park Kultury. Seedy, delicious, chaotic, and dirt cheap, everything a Georgian restaurant should be. Bring your own booze.

Danilovsky Monastery, hotel complex of the St. Daniel's Monastery, Bolshoy Starodanilovsky per., tel. 954-0566; metro Paveletskaya. As befitting the Patriarch's restaurant, the food is exquisite and prices moderate, though you must book in advance and be a representative of a reputable firm or organization.

Edem, Ul. Ostuzheva 22/2, tel. 200-0742; metro Pushkinskaya/Tverskaya. Clean, polite and efficient restaurant, little known and a good back-up if you can't get into Margarita.

Golden Horseshoe Club, Leningradsky pr. 32/2; metro Dynamo. Traditional gypsy food and entertainment; make a night of it.

Iberia, Ul. Rozhdestvenka 5, tel. 928-2672, 924-8694; metro Kuznetsky Most. Very reasonably priced and civilized Georgian restaurant with Spanish music in the evenings.

Bistro, Ul. Chekhova 6, tel. 299-3073; metro Chekhovskaya. A quite decent café, nothing special but good, cheap food. Very central, and not too crowded.

Orient, Nikoloshchepovsky per. 1/9, tel. 241-1078; metro Smolenskaya. A host of culinary delights and innovations; borders on the expensive.

U Babushki, Ul. Bolshaya Ordynka 42, tel. 239-1484; metro Tretyakovskaya. Despite the name, meaning "At Grannie's," this restaurant is run by actresses and the fare is more imaginative and even tastier than home cooking.

Arkadiya, 3 Teatralny proyezd, tel. 926-9008; metro Lubyanka. Cheap Russian fare and great jazz later on.

Artisticheskoye, Khudozhestvenny proyezd 6, tel. 292-0673; metro Okhotny Ryad. Tries to capture the old world atmosphere of the Moscow Art Theater opposite. Food is fair to good.

Snacks. Moscow is not the sort of place where you can just walk into a café wherever you happen to be and get a snack. You have to know where to find such places, as they are not very common. Here are a few:

Union Café, Bernikov per. 2/6, tel. 277-2805; metro Taganskaya. Slightly chaotic, cheap Western-style café.

Gelateria, Prospekt Mira 58, tel. 280-9679; metro Prospekt Mira. Lively Italian café, with pizza, ice cream, coffee, and alcoholic beverages at reasonable prices.

Holsten Bistro, Taganskaya ploshchad; metro Taganskaya. Small and plasticky, but the delicious Italian sandwiches are surprisingly cheap. Holsten beer on tap.

Kombi's, Prospekt Mira 46/48, tel. 280-6402, metro Prospekt Mira; and Tverskaya 32, metro Mayakovskaya. Great sandwiches. Popular hang-out for Russian yuppies. Eat in or take out.

Sverchok, Ul. Moskvina 10, metro Pushkinskaya, Tverskaya. Very informal café, with reasonable choice of starters and main courses. Not too busy at peak times. Folksy wooden decor.

Vareniki, Ul. Paliashvili, metro Arbatskaya. Typical Russian café specializing in a Ukrainian version of *pelmeni* called *vareniki*; go during the day to get a place.

Rosa, Arbat 31, metro Smolenskaya. The best of the Arbat's large and rather mediocre selection of cafés.

Fast food. Unlike cafés, fast food joints in Moscow are on the rise. Most common are *shashlyk* and pizza kiosks at metro stations, markets, or on busy shopping streets, but there is also an impressive array of Western-style restaurants – three **McDonald's**, at Pushkinskaya ploshchad (metro Pushkinskaya/Tverskaya), Ul. Ogaryova off Tverskaya (metro Okhotny Ryad), and Smolenskaya ploshchad (metro Smolenskaya); two **Pizza Huts**, at Tverskaya, 12 (metro Pushkinskaya/Tverskaya) and Kutuzovsky prospekt, 17 (metro Kievskaya); a PepsiCo.-run **taco bar** inside metro Park Kultury, a **Burger Queen** at Suvorovsky bulvar, off Nikitskiye Vorota (metro Arbatskaya), the Lebanese **Baku-Livan** kebab house at Tverskaya, 24 (metro Pushkinskaya/Tverskaya) and **Rostik's** spicy chicken in GUM.

Nightlife

Moscow is not exactly the most glamorous or stylish place to be for creatures of the night, but nowadays there's pretty much something for everyone.

Discos

Hermitage, Karetny Ryad 3, tel. 299-9774; metro Chekhovskaya. Set in a theater, reasonably cheap and popular with a trendy arts crowd. Techno disco and retro-type café.

011, Sadovaya Kudrinskaya 19, metro Mayakovskaya. A good mix of music but without techno-pop. Run by a Serb and frequented by Americans.

Mir, Mir Cinema, Tsvetnoy bulvar 11, metro Tsvetnoy bulvar. Though often labeled as a gay disco, this is a buzzing center of Moscow's dancing youth. Friends and lovers of all orientations gather here in this fun club's relaxing atmosphere.

Dom Kultury MELZ, Culture house setting for what is currently the gay community's most popular disco, Saturdays only.

Lis's, Olympiisky prospekt, tel. 288-4027; metro Prospekt Mira. Huge, mainstream disco in the Olympic Stadium complex, with casino, foodstalls, and bars. If you want to see a tasteless, tacky Russian nightclub, this is the place to go.

Pilot, Tryokhgorny val 6, tel. 255-1552; metro Ulitsa 1905 Goda. Bizarre new disco with a 1930's aviation theme; there's a cockpit on the dance floor you can climb in. Young, trendy crowd.

Manhattan Express, Rossiya Hotel, tel. 298-5355; metro Kitai-gorod. An interior copied from New York's Studio 54. Just like an expensive Western nightclub. Rich, mostly trendy crowd.

Rock, Jazz, and Blues

Arbat Blues Club, Aksakova per. 11, tel. 291-1546; metro Arbatskaya. Decent, homely little club using premises of Theater Studio. Unfortunately little known to Russians; mainly an expat hang-out.

Sexton FOZD, 1-y Baltiisky proyezd 2, metro Sokol. Gritty, rocker–frequented, somewhat mean and macho club, very characteristic of the local scene, with occasional good live music.

Bunker, Ul. Trifonovskaya 56, metro Rizhskaya, tel. 278-7043. Dark basement club with trendy local crowd and music, and tasteful decor. Justifiably known as Moscow's No. 1 rock club.

"A" Culture Center, Berezhkovskaya nab. 28, tel. 954-9193; metro Kievskaya then four stops by any bus or trolleybus from outside the *vokzal*. Very cheap and popular if you can get through the crowd of penniless teenagers scrambling at the door. Reminiscent of St. Petersburg's Indie Club. Fridays only.

Jerry Rubins, Profsoyuznaya 31, tel. 120-7006; metro Noviye Cheryomushki. Intimate and rather eccentric basement club, offering twice-weekly gigs and non-commercial art exhibitions.

Armadillo, Khrustalny per. 1, tel. 298-5258, 298-5091; metro Kitaigorod/Ploshchad Revolyutsii. Tex-Mex bar in the heart of Moscow's old Kitaigorod district, interesting for the local versions of live country and rockabilly music.

Jazz in Moscow is hard to come by. Try the Arcadia restaurant (see Eating Out) or the Arbat Blues Club; otherwise check the local press for occasional concerts or possible new venues.

Bars

Here you'll have difficulty in finding anything that's really Russian, as most are run by and for foreigners.

Shamrock, Irish House, Novy Arbat 19, tel. 291-7641; metro Arbatskaya. Now long-established as the main foreigners' night spot in Moscow. Live music some evenings.

Rosie O'Grady's, Znamenka 9/12, tel. 203-9087; metro Arbatskaya. Another expat bar but more traditionally Irish and down-to-earth. Too bad the beer's so expensive.

News Bar, Petrovka 18, tel. 921-1585; metro Kuznetsky Most. International newspapers to read during the day, live music at night. Popular and atmospheric.

TrenMos Bar, Ostozhenka 1/9, tel. 202-5722; metro Kropotkinskaya. Tastefully American and well-run, with friendly service, and an attached Bistro for food. If you're perishing for an American-style deli sandwich, there's also **TrenMos Restaurant**, Komsomolsky prospekt 21, tel. 245-1216; metro Frunzenskaya.

El Rincon Español, 2 Okhotny Ryad, tel. 292-2893; Hotel Moskva. Popular, traditional Spanish bar and restaurant.

Mayakovsky Theater Bar, in a back room of the theater, Ul. Bolshaya Nikitskaya (formerly Ul. Gertsena) 19. A café whose prices, clientele, and fortunes seem to change regularly. Can be chic, can be empty and overpriced.

English Pub, in Hotel Budapest. Little known bar with authentic decor. Quiet and frequented by middle-aged Western businessmen.

Gosser Bar, 46 Novy Arbat (at back of 1st floor supermarket), tel. 291-2025; metro Arbatskaya. Lively bar frequented by Russians. A kind of poor relation of the Irish House down the road.

Shopping

Department Stores

The great **GUM**, on Red Square, should look after most if not all of your shopping needs, and is beautiful to boot. The **Petrovsky Passazh** (Petrovka 10, metro Okhotny Ryad/Teatralnaya), similar in decor, was recently rebuilt by Turks and is now

more upmarket than GUM – favored by the Russian nouveau riche. **TsUM**, just down the road at Petrovka 2, on the other hand, still has some downmarket parts and is good for cheap souvenirs. Otherwise each district has an "Univermag," the central ones being the **Moskovsky** next to the Kazansky Vokzal, and the **Tsentralny Voyenny** (Central Army Store) on Ul. Vozdvizhenka (metro Biblioteka imeni Lenina).

Many Western-type stores sell a wide range of goods other than food. They are generally aimed at foreign residents and difficult to reach without a car. The Irish House (Novy Arbat 19, tel. 291-7461; metro Arbatskaya) has a good selection of household goods. If you're feeling homesick and have transport, take a walk in the huge and empty Swiss-run **Sadko Arcade**, with its endless shops, cafés, and restaurants (in the Expocenter, Krasnogvardeisky 1, metro Ulitsa 1905 Goda).

Food

The number of Western-style food stores in Moscow is now surprisingly large. With economic liberalization many Russian stores are closing the gap in terms of quality and choice, and are often much cheaper. In the first category are:

EML, Nab. Smolenskaya 2/10, tel. 241-9281; metro Smolenskaya. A 24-hour supermarket

Garden Ring, Ul. Bolshaya Sadovaya 1, tel. 209-1572; metro Mayakovskaya. Rather disorderly Irish supermarket, but well stocked

Tverskoy, Ul. Tverskaya 6, metro Okhotny Ryad. Belgian supermarket with cheap wines and liquors; one of city's best Russian stores, also called Tverskoy, is next door.

Galerie du Vin, Kutuzovsky pr. 1/7, tel. 243-0365; metro Kievskaya. Cheapest French wines and liquors in town

Supermarket Union, 2/6 Bernikov per., tel. 277-2805; metro Taganskaya. Good value if you're buying in bulk

Virginia, 24/7 Malaya Bronnaya, tel. 290-3531; metro Pushkinskaya/Tverskaya. Specializes in American junk food

Danone, Tverskaya 4, metro Okhotny Ryad. Good selection of milk, yogurt, and other dairy products

There is also a supermarket open late at Tverskaya 22, in the building of the Minsk Hotel.

Russian stores

Yeliseyevsky Gastronom, 14 Tverskaya, metro Pushkinskaya, Tverskaya. Come here for the lavish art nouveau interior rather than the food, which is cheap nonetheless.

Novoarbatsky Gastronom, Novy Arbat 19. The first privatized foodstore in Moscow, and it shows in the range of products, though lines are as long as ever, especially for European Community beef. Makes a good tandem with the Irish House above.

Gastronom #20, 14 Ul. Bolshaya Lubyanka. Proximity to the former KGB building guarantees a good choice of products.

Novy Arbat 46. Well-stocked 24-hour supermarket, with Russian and imported goods

The city's main covered markets are as follows:

Cheryomyshinsky, Lomonovsky pr. 1; metro Universitet. The biggest and most expensive

Danilovsky, Mytnaya 74; metro Tulskaya

Dorogomilovsky, Mozhaisky val 10; metro Kievskaya

Leningradsky, Ul. Chasovaya 11; metro Sokol/Aeroport. Well stocked and very clean

Rizhsky, Prospekt Mira 94/6; metro Rizhskaya

Tsentralny, Tsvetnoy bulvar 15; metro Tsvetnoy Boulevard. Especially good for rare products such as beans, pulses, spices, and other items

Souvenirs, Works of Art

The obvious place to go for such things is **Izmailovsky Park**, the huge market, or *Vernissazh,* in the east of the city, open on Saturdays and Sundays. Here you'll find everything from carpets to trinkets, from lacquer boxes to *matryoshka* dolls. Quality varies widely, so take your time.

Try to avoid shops marked "Suveniry," whether state or private. An exception is the one at **St. George's Church** (Varvarka, 12) in front of the Rossiya Hotel, which has beautiful toys and gifts by local craftspeople.

A better bet are the **Art Salons** (Khudozhestvenny Salony), at Ul. Petrovka, 12 and 16 (metro Ohkotny Ryad/Teatralnaya), Ukrainsky bulvar, 6 (metro Kievskaya), Ul. Dimitrova, 54 (metro Oktyabrskaya), and Ul. Pyatnitskaya, opposite metro Novokuznetskaya. For serious art collectors, here are some of Moscow's top galleries:

Art Moderne, Ul. Bolshaya Ordynka 39, tel. 242-0175; metro Tretyakovskaya. Exhibitions of mainly 1960's artists, including those well known in the West. Situated in a former church, with particularly beautiful third floor.

M'ARS, Malaya Filyovskaya ul. 32, tel. 146-2029; metro Pionerskaya. Moscow's first private gallery, organized by previously underground artists. Works with 3,000 artists.

Ridzhina, 36 Myasnitskaya, tel. 921-1613; metro Chistiye Prudy. Despite the clean and sober appearance of the premises, this is Moscow's most outrageous art gallery.

Moscow Gallery Exhibition Cen-

Doll seller, Izmailovsky Market

ter, 11 and 20 Kuznetsky Most, tel. 925-4264; metro Kuznetsky Most. State-run gallery, non-commercial. The second hall is generally better for local artists' exhibitions.

Contemporary Art Center, 6 Bolshaya Yakimanka, tel. 238-2454; metro Polyanka. Five progressive galleries in one. If you're serious about buying something, this is the place to start.

Central House of Artists, 10 Krymsky val, tel. 230-0091, 238-0457; metro Oktyabrskaya. A huge exhibition hall opposite the entrance to Gorky Park. A mixture of sellable and not-for-sale, with so many different halls there's something for just about everyone.

Books

Zwemmer's English bookshop at Kuznetsky Most, 18 features London selection and London prices. Good for novels, art books and the like, it's rather short on guidebooks. Two shops sell cheap secondhand paperbacks in English and other languages: **Inostranniye Knigi**, at Kachalova, 16 (metro Barrikadnaya), good for browsing away the hours, and **Akademkniga**, at Tverskaya, 19 (metro Pushkinskaya / Tverskaya), with a much smaller selection.

Spassky Tower of the Kremlin
19th century engraving

Guidebooks are probably best found in hotel shops, but street sellers around Ploshchad Revolyutsii metro station and **Dom Knigi** on Novy Arbat also have some. For older and used books, try the shops on the Arbat or the stalls at Nikitskiye Vorota, midway between Pushkinskaya and Arbatskaya metros.

A book market has recently appeared in the Olympic Stadium on Prospekt Mira (metro Prospekt Mira), open Saturdays and Sundays.

Theater, Concerts, Circus

Bolshoy Theater, Teatralnaya ploshchad, tel. 292-9986; metro Teatralnaya/ Okhotny Ryad. Still the #1 choice for an evening's entertainment, especially if it's ballet night. Tickets can always be purchased at the entrance before the performance if you don't have a hotel to book through. Don't bother trying the *kassa*, though sometimes the cheapest tickets can be bought at the city's "Teatralniye Kassy" kiosks.

Old Circus, Tsvetnoy bulvar 13, tel. 200-0668, metro Tsvetnoy bulvar and **New Circus**, pr. Vernadskovo 7, tel. 930-2815, metro Universitet. Both of a phenomenally high standard, though the New Circus narrowly edges out the other. Russian circuses make more use of animals than those in the West.

Tchaikovsky Hall, pl. Mayakovskovo 4/31, tel. 299-3681, metro Mayakovskaya, and **Conservatory**, Ul. Bolshaya Nikitskaya (formerly Ul. Gertsena) 13, tel. 299-0658, metro Arbatskaya. The city's top concert venues

Glinka Museum of Musical Culture, Ul. Fadeyeva 4, tel. 972-3237; metro Mayakovskaya. A broad selection of music, from the Middle Ages to the avant-garde.

Obraztsov Puppet Theater, Sadovaya-Samotyochnaya 3, tel. 299-3310; metro Tsvetnoy bulvar. Hilariously funny and for children of all ages; has evening performances too, often silent or mimed.

Lenkom Theater, Ul. Chekhova 6, tel. 299-0708; metro Chekhovskaya. Along with the Taganka Theater, the principal brave, experimental theater of the Brezhnev stagnation years. But while the Taganka troupe has splintered, the Lenkom continues to produce good drama.

Sovremennik Theater, Chistoprudny bulvar 19a, tel. 921-6473; metro Chistiye Prudy. Famous 1960's theater, still popular today.

Chekhov MKhAT, Kamergersky per. 3, tel. 229-8760; metro Okhotny Ryad. Better known as the Moscow Art Theater, this is where Chekhov and Stanislavsky revolutionized drama in the early part of the century.

Leisure

When talking about Moscow parks, what leaps to mind is **Gorky Park** (main entrance between Oktyabrskaya and Park Kultury metros). Rather gaudy and crowded in summer, it nonetheless has the best amusements in Moscow – the Big Wheel is certainly a hair-raising experience. For a quieter stroll, go to the southern end, formerly the Neskuchny Sad, once part of a noble's estate, and now badly neglected.

The view from the Big Wheel is probably better than that from the **Sparrow Hills** (*Vorobyovy Gory*) in the south, overlooking the Moskva River. Formerly the Lenin Hills, behind the main building of Moscow State University, this is a popular viewpoint nonetheless, especially for newlyweds. The park below is good for picnics.

The older parks at Tsaritsyno, Kuskovo, Izmailovsky, and Sokolniki are good places to wander, and large enough to get lost easily. If you need wide expanses for skiing, cycling, or other recreation, Losiny Ostrov, in the northeast, is a must. A beautiful 110 sq. km. of evergreen and deciduous forest, it is known as the "lungs of Moscow," and is populated by elks (the Russian word *los* means elk). It's reachable from Sholkovskaya metro, or from Yauza station on suburban trains from the Yaroslavsky Vokzal.

For swimming, Muscovites usually head out to Serebryany Bor (metro Polezhayevskaya, then any bus west), beaches on a lake formed at a bend in the Moskva river. It's very popular, and understandably so, but not very clean. To escape pollution, go farther west and out of the city to the untainted upper waters of the Moskva and Istra rivers. (See "Toward Tver" in Moscow Region chapter.)

Places of Worship

Russian Orthodox:

Epiphany (Yelokhovsky) Cathedral, Spartakovskaya 15; metro Baumanskaya

Trinity Cathedral, St. Daniel's Monastery, Danilovsky val 22; metro Tulskaya

Other Faiths:

Anglican Church, St. Andrew's Church, Ul. Stankevicha 9, tel. 143-3562; metro Pushkinskaya/Tverskaya

Baptist, Maly Vuzovsky per. 3, tel. 297-5167; metro Kitai-gorod

German Evangelical, German embassy, tel. 238-1324

Greek Orthodox, Telegrafny per. 15a, tel. 923-4605; metro Chistiye Prudy

Krishna Consciousness Society, Prospekt Mira 5/8, tel. 207-0738; metro Prospekt Mira

Mosque, Vypolzov per. 7, tel. 281-3866; metro Prospekt Mira

Roman Catholic (French), St. Louis, Ul. Malaya Lubyanka 12; metro Lubyanka

Roman Catholic (Polish), Church of the Immaculate Conception, Malaya Gruzinskaya; metro Byelorusskaya

Synagogue, Ul. Arkhipova 8, tel. 923-9697; metro Kitai-gorod

Medical Care

There is now quite a wide range of medical services for foreigners:

American Medical Center, Shmitovsky Proyezd 3, tel. 256-8212, 256-8378, 259-7181; metro Ulitsa 1905 Goda, behind the Mezhdunarodnaya Hotel. Has five Western doctors and 13 nurses. Provides emergency room, immunization, and evacuation home, and will see non-members during working hours Monday–Friday.

European Medical Center, Gruzinsky per. 3/2, tel. 253-0703; metro Byelorusskaya. A smaller operation (one doctor and two nurses) providing emergency care, routine examinations, and treatment.

British Embassy Clinic, Nab. Morisa Toreza 14, tel. 231-8511 (ask for clinic); metro Biblioteka imeni Lenina. Routine treatment during office hours.

SANA, Ul. Nizhnaya Pervomaiskaya 65, tel. 464-1254, 464-2563; metro Pervomaiskaya. Russian-French joint venture clinic with additional inpatient care in nearby Republican Hospital.

Athens Medical Center, Michurinsky pr. 16, tel. 143-2387, 143-2503; metro Prospekt Vernadskovo. Offers 24-hour emergency assistance and transportation, outpatient services, and hospitalization in a special ward.

For inpatient care, the AMC sends people to the former Communist Party **Clinical and Diagnostic (Kremlin) Hospital**. Tourists can apply directly to the **Botkin Hospital**, 2-y Botkinsky proyezd 5/5, tel. 255-0015, metro Dynamo, but should only do so as a last resort.

For a more complete list of recommended hospitals, see *The Traveller's Yellow Pages*.

As well as the municipal 03 Ambulance Service, there are two reliable fee-paying private services, **Ambulance Ltd.**, tel. 924-6472, and **VYEK Ltd.**, tel. 350-0131, 200-5851.

AMC, EMC, and SANA all have a decent selection of drugs. Other places to try are **Pharmacon**, Tverskaya 2, metro Okhotny Ryad; **Medicine Man** at Ul. Cheryakhovskovo 4, tel. 155-7080, 155-8788, metro Aeroport; or **Unipharm**,

Skatertny per. 13, tel. 202-5071, metro Arbatskaya. There is a 24-hour chemist next to Pharmacon.

Publications in English

Newspapers and Magazines

In Moscow, there's a dazzling array indeed. The following could be useful for the tourist.

Moscow Times: A respectable free daily and a permanent feature of everyday life, providing local, CIS-wide and international news, culture, business, and sport coverage written mainly by expats. Tends to regard itself as the mouthpiece of the foreign community and gets pompous at times. Also publishes an excellent quarterly color magazine called *Moscow Guide* aimed mainly at tourists for $5.

Moscow Tribune: A slightly weaker version of the above, but without pretensions and less opinionated.

Moscow Magazine: A thicker, glossier, bimonthly version of *Moscow Guide*, but same price and not really any more useful information.

What & Where in Moscow: Rather bland and colorless listings of hard currency shops, restaurants, etc. Published by Russians and free.

Time Out: This Russian-produced monthly color newspaper with information on the arts is not very well-edited, but it's readable enough and can be interesting. Rather naive in a Russian way.

Moscow Life: Russian-edited weekly with a rather odd style

Russia Now, Russia How: Large bimonthly color magazine good for practical information (i.e., laws) but short on entertainment value.

Two other publications, *Delovoy Mir/Business World* and *Moscow Business Telephone Guide*, provide information useful mainly to business-people. The second has a fairly thorough and regularly updated directory.

Guides and Directories

The Traveller's Yellow Pages: an idea originally started in St. Petersburg but recently brought out in Moscow, too. Includes a very good pull-out street map; essential for the first-time visitor. See Reading List for ordering information.

Where in Moscow: a more selective version of the above, plus a business telephone directory and a very handy bound-in sectional street map. Given Moscow's rapid changes, it tends to get out of date quickly. So be sure to get the most recent edition of this regularly-updated publication. See Reading List for ordering information.

Information Moscow: the very first Moscow telephone directory, dating back to the Brezhnev era. It is updated regularly and compares favorably to the many rivals it now has. Expensive but can be useful for tourists.

Tours

It seems especially appropriate to mention **Patriarchi Dom**, (tel. 255-4515), an organization run by an American and two Russians, which provides small group excursions to every imaginable place inside and outside the city. You can enquire with them about organized excursions, usually one every two or three days, or arrange your own. Occasionally they do a special "Moscow Orientation Tour," designed to familiarize bewildered newcomers with practicalities of city life. City tours cost $5 and generally last about 2–3 hours.

Other tour possibilities: See advertisement for **Galaxy** in this section, or contact Helen Kates at **Russian Travel Service** (see p. 53).

RUSSIAN GLOSSARY

"A" Culture Center
Культурный центр «А»
Aerovokzal
Аэровокзал
Akademkniga bookshop
Академкнига
Budapest Hotel
Гостиница «Будапешт»
Central House of Artists
Центральный Дом Художника
Chekhov MKhAT (Moscow Art Theater)
МХАТ имени Чехова
Dom Knigi
Дом Книги
Dom Kultury MELZ
Дом культуры «МЭЛЗ»
Edem Restaurant
Ресторан «Эдем»
Glinka Museum of Musical Culture
Музей музыкальной культуры имени Глинки
Guria Restaurant
Ресторан «Гурия»
Inostrannyie Knigi bookshop
Магазин «Иностранные книги»
Kremlin Palace of Congresses
Кремлёвский дворец съездов
Krutitsky Mission
Крутицкое подворье
Lenkom Theater
Театр Ленком
Lis's Disco
Дискотека «Лисс»
Losiny Ostrov
Лосиный остров
Maly Theater
Малый театр
Café Margarita
Кафе «Маргарита»
Mayakovsky Theater
Театр имени Маяковского
Minsk Hotel
Гостиница «Минск»
Mir Cinema
Кинотеатр «Мир»
Molodyozhnaya Hotel
Гостиница «Молодежная»
Moskovsky Univermag
Универмаг «Московский»
Nemetskaya Sloboda Restaurant
Ресторан «Немецкая слобода»
Novoarbatsky Gastronom
Новоарбатский гастроном
Obraztsov Puppet Theater
Театр кукол Образцова
Orlyonok Hotel
Гостиница «Орлёнок»
Patriarshiye Prudy
Патриаршие пруды
Hotel Peking
Гостиница «Пекин»
Petrovsky Passazh
Петровский пассаж
Pilot Disco
Дискотека «Пилот»
Razgulyai Restaurant
Ресторан «Разгуляй»
Rogozhskoye Cemetery
Рогожское кладбище
Café Rosa
Кафе «Роса»
Sadovoye Koltso
Садовое кольцо
Sovremennik Theater
Театр «Современник»
Hotel Sputnik
Гостиница «Спутник»
Café Sverchok
Кафе «Сверчок»
Tsentralnaya Hotel
Гостиница «Центральная»
Tsentralny Avtovokzal
Центральный Автовокзал
Tsentralny Voyennyi Univermag
Центральный Военный Универмаг
TsUM
ЦУМ
Tverskoy Gastronom
Тверской гастроном
U Babushki Restaurant
Ресторан «У бабушки»
Café Vareniki
Кафе вареники
Yeliseyevsky Gastronom
Елисеевский гастроном

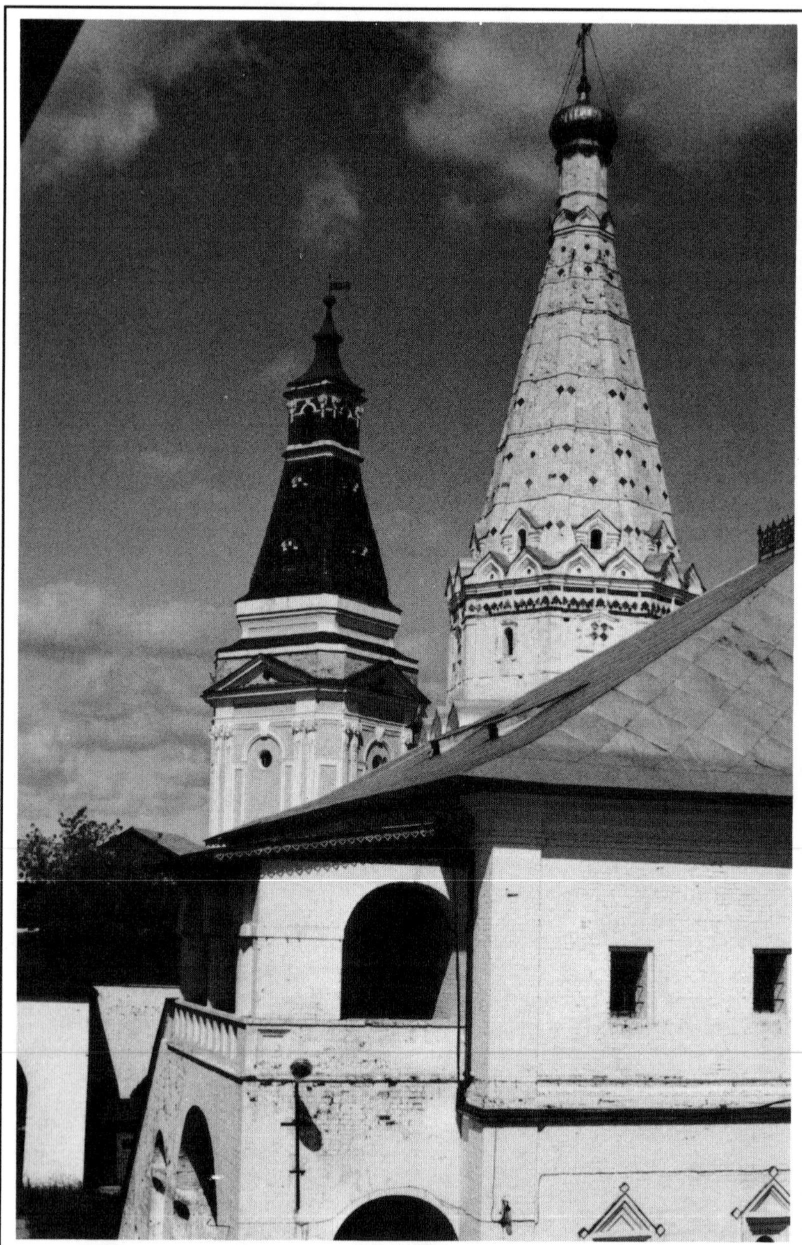

Trinity-St. Sergius Monastery, Sergiyev Posad. Hospital and the Church of SS. Zosima and Savvaty. To the rear: ***Kalichya Tower***

MOSCOW REGION

MOSKOVSKAYA OBLAST

This huge expanse of forest, marsh, and rolling hills has inevitably suffered from its closeness to the capital. All but the most remote areas are dotted with suburban development and Muscovites' holiday homes. Lines of communication run radially and are otherwise poor, which effectively renders the region into a series of linear peninsulas. Nevertheless, this is more than just the token countryside of the city-dweller. Dacha life exists side by side with that of the village, and wild animals roam remaining areas of virgin forest.

Most trips suggested here can be completed in a day, and if public transport is poor, taxis, when available, are cheaper than in Moscow.

TOWARD RYAZAN

The southeastern part of the Moscow Region is distinguishable by marshy and flat countryside; its dominant feature is the Moskva River. But occasional treasures can be found among the industrial wastelands of Lyubertsy, Voskresensk, and Golutvino. At the point where the Moskva joins the Oka is **Kolomna**, the area's most beautiful town, once a frontier post for both Muscovy and its rival princedom of Ryazan. This harmonious feast of churches, monasteries, ancient walls, wooden houses, and an attractive waterfront was one of the last places in the region to be opened up to foreigners, due to the presence of some defense-related industries.

The nearly complete absence of tourists and the dispersed nature of the town's attractions make Kolomna perfect for the explorer. Approaching the center from the railway station, you will discover old wooden houses and ruined churches which will whet the appetite without betraying too much of what is in store.

Approaching instead from the main road, visitors get a more immediate sense of history. The remains of the magnificent 90-foot-high walls of the Kremlin, built by Italians in the 16th century, are still imposing, in particular the section looming over the Moscow-Ryazan road. These battlements withstood numerous Tatar invasions. Walking down from them past the tiny Brusensky Monastery, now a museum, you will find the town's central square, dominated by the 17th century Assumption Cathedral, recently renovated, and its bell-tower. Behind them is the New Golutvin Convent, now being lovingly restored by its nuns. Leaving the Kremlin through the magnificent Pyatnitskiye Gates, you enter the central village street, which slopes gently toward the river. This area preserves Kolomna's peaceful atmosphere from the ravages of the nearby modern sprawl of Golutvino.

The best view of the town is from across the Moskva River, where a dirt track leads to Bobrenyovo Monastery, also picturesque although sadly derelict.

About 32 km to the south is **Zaraisk**, another ancient border town of the Ryazan princedom. A compact and well-kept regional center, its principal attraction is the smallest 16th century kremlin in Russia. The 17th century St. Nicholas Cathedral and 19th century Church of St. John the Baptist are undergoing restoration by local craftsmen, amid weed-ridden surroundings. The tiny town museum in the nearby square has, apart from historical exhibits, one notable painting, Lev Bakst's *A Portrait of Countess Keller*. Further up the main street is the birthplace of early 20th century sculptor Anna Golubkina, now a house-museum.

Ten kilometers away near the village of Darovoye is the estate of Cheremoshnya, where Fyodor Dostoyevsky (1821–81) spent his childhood and youth. It now houses a museum.

Various smaller places of interest lie aong the Moscow–Kolomna route. At the village of **Dzerzhinsky**, just outside the suburb of Lyubertsy, is the Nikolo-Ugreshsky Monastery. Although founded as early as the 14th century, most of its buildings date from the 19th century and are in pseudo-Russian style. The monastery's most distinctive feature is the Palestinian or Jerusalem Wall, a huge façade representing an ancient city in icon-like form.

Further south is the village of **Faustovo**, site of the Krasnokholmskaya Solovetskaya Pustyn, a tiny hilltop monastery with views of the Moskva River valley.

TOWARD TULA

Due south of Moscow is an area containing much of the forest land once characteristic of the Moscow Region, and a favorite place for holiday homes.

Not far from the station at Rastorguyevo is the village of **Sukhanovo,** site of one of Stalin's most horrific prisons. Located in a former monastery (now returned to the Orthodox Church), and bordering on a militia training school, "Sukhanovka" witnessed shootings and interrogations by torture. This was Beria's favorite prison – he often spent the night there. It also figures prominently in Alexander Solzhenitsyn's *Gulag Archipelago*.

Today, monks and church volunteers are trying to restore both the monastery buildings and the spiritual cleanliness of Sukhanovka. They do not seem overawed by this task, though some local people are still fearful of a return to the days of terror. Some also believe there is a curse on the place.

The cell blocks are falling down now, but some of the subterranean isolation and interrogation rooms remain. The former are too small to lie down in, and prisoners confined there were either shrouded in darkness or dazzled by bright electric light. In the latter, bits of iron tubing stick up out of the floor, remains of the table and two chairs which were the sole furniture of each room. The ground floor of the main church, site of executions, is currently a militia garage but the monastery is negotiating for its return.

Nearby is the Sukhanovo estate, built for Prince Volkonsky by some of the finest classical architects of the early 19th century. It now houses a sanatorium.

Away to the southeast is the estate of Gorki, better known as Leninskiye Gorki. This early 19th century mansion was taken over by the Moscow Committee of the Communist Party after the Revolution, supposedly for use as a rest home. Instead, it became Lenin's favorite place in his last years, and he died there in January 1924. Though not the great place of pilgrimage it once was, it is still of historic interest and a reasonable day trip.

The next main artery out of Moscow to the west, running due south in the general direction of the Crimea, is Varshavskoye shossé, paralleled by the railway line from the Kursk Station (*Kursky Vokzal*). For steam engine enthusiasts, the town of **Shcherbinka** hosts one of the country's few railway exhibits. On the grounds of a research institute, Russia's first-ever steam museum is being organized. Currently the center has just a few restored engines, which are occasionally operated "in steam."

A little further is **Podolsk**, a rather drab town whose only claim to fame is that Lenin lived there for ten days in 1900. Consequently, there is a museum dedicated to him. Just to the west, however, are three large and interesting estates. **Ivanovskoye** was originally the home of Count F.A. Tolstoy, and boasts a fine six-column portico, small theater, and landscape garden, as well as a recently opened museum of science education.

Five kilometers further is **Dubrovitsy**. Dating from the late 17th century, this estate changed hands many times, and was even owned by Catherine the Great. She didn't buy it for herself, however – it was a present for one of her favorites, Matvey Dmitriyev-Mamonov, a man who was nevertheless unfortunate enough to spend half of his life under house arrest. Twice, at its inception and during the period prior to the Revolution, it belonged to the powerful Golytsin family. While the mansion itself is ornately classical and mildly interesting, the jewel in Dubrovitsy's crown is the rather imposing Church of Our Lady of the Sign. This remarkable white tower, surmounted by a great gold tiara and cross, stands as a landmark over the beautiful Pakhra River to the unknown Italian artists who built it. The estate grounds are now used by a livestock research institute. Still further west is Polivanovo, an 18th century estate believed to have been built by the architect Vassily Bazhenov.

Our Lady of the Sign, Dubrovitsy

Despite its name, the town of Chekhov just to the south is not a major attraction. **Anton Chekhov**, playwright and master of the short story,

Chekhov Museum, Melikhovo

lived in nearby **Melikhovo**, and only came to the town (then known as Lopasnya) for his mail. The old post office is now a museum and archive of his letters. Chekhov's former estate, also a museum, is away to the east. In tiny, sleepy Melikhovo, he wrote the plays *The Seagull* and *Uncle Vanya*, and many short stories. A doctor and local philanthropist, he also fought a cholera epidemic and built three schools.

The ancient southern defenses of Muscovy in this part of the region were concentrated on the town of **Serpukhov**. Some spots are picturesque when seen from the twin heights of the Kremlin on Krasnaya Gora and the Vysotsky Monastery at the other end of town, especially in winter when the River Nara is in view. But one must also accept the disharmonious intermingling of the Krasny Tekstilshchik textile factory's tall red smokestack and the Kremlin towers. A forlorn broken bell-tower lying in between provides an enduring reminder of the ravages of the Second World War. Across the Nara is the fine 16th century Vladychny Convent.

Just to the west of Serpukhov is the **Prioksko-Terrasny Nature Reserve**, a haven of flora and fauna normally found only in the steppe of southern Russia, 650 km away. Its 40 sq. km of virgin forest shelters breeding grounds for large mammals, among them a nursery for European Bison, a species first reintroduced to the Soviet Union in 1948 in a last attempt to save it from extinction. The plan worked, and numbers worldwide have increased from a low of 47 to more than 3,000 today.

TOWARD KALUGA

The southeasterly route out of Moscow brings you into some of the clearest and freshest air around the city, acres of forest interspersed with sanatoria and dachas. Among them is **Peredelkino**, the famous Russian writers' village. Though now undergoing yuppification, it still has some literary residents, such as novelist Andrey Bitov and poet Andrey Voznesensky. Here Boris Pasternak spent half of his life and completed his Nobel Prize-winning novel, *Dr. Zhivago*. Just three years ago, a museum opened in his former house. The village graveyard, now rather neglected, includes

Pasternak's own grave, which stands in a quiet pine grove. This romantic spot was once a gathering place for the literary youth, and is still a place of pilgrimage for many.

Nearby is the tiny Transfiguration Church, frequently visited by high-ranking Orthodox priests and even by the Patriarch. It has survived well through the Communist era; its interior has several ancient icons. Now the daily peal of its bells can again be heard, at 6 p.m.

Pasternak House-Museum, Peredelkino

Down the road is one of Moscow's few hard currency country restaurants, the **Villa Peredelkino** (tel. 435-1478, 435-1211) on Chobotovskaya alleya, serving Italian food and offering skiing facilities in winter.

Just beyond Kaluzhskoye shossé to the south is the estate of Valuyevo, built by archaeologist and historian A.I. Musin-Pushkin, best known for his discovery of the epic poem of ancient Rus', *The Lay of Igor's Host.* Valuyevo's buildings in classical style dating from the 18th and 19th centuries are tasteful and harmonious; its landscaped gardens and summer houses reward leisurely exploration.

Further south, in the neighboring Kaluga Region but still within day-trip distance of Moscow, are several towns which have been involved in the defense of Moscow from the southwest throughout the centuries – from the days of Muscovy, though the Napoleonic Wars to Hitler's invasion. East of Balabanovo is **Borovsk**, where 19th century scientist Konstantin Tsiokolsky lived and taught mathematics. Except for a number of unspectacular churches and 18th century houses, though, the town itself has little to offer. Three kilometers outside, however, is the **Pafnutyev-Borovsky Monastery**, built in the fifteenth century and used as a frontier post by the Muscovites against independent princes. In the 17th century, Avvakum, leader of the Old Believers who had split from the Russian Orthodox Church, was imprisoned here for two years.

Once a defense against Caucasian tribes to the south, and Poles from the west, **Vereya** became an important trade center in the 17th century. Many of the houses and stone churches built at the time have been preserved, as have the market stalls in the town's central square. Behind the district college opposite is the Kremlin, surrounded on three sides by steep slopes and providing a magnificent view of the river Protva. There, too, stands the attractive 16th century Cathedral of the Nativity, unfortunately much obscured by later buildings.

Just to the south, **Maloyaroslavets** is best known as the place where Napoleon's march on Moscow was finally halted. Monuments to this war and the one against Hitler abound. On Moskovskaya ulitsa is a branch of the Borodino museum (see Toward Smolensk) and in a nearby chapel, a diorama of the Battle of Maloyaroslavets. On the battle site is the monastery of

St. Nicholas Chernoostrovsky, whose current buildings date from the early 19th century. The huge St. Nicholas Cathedral was built by A. Vitberg, one of the architects of the Cathedral of Christ the Savior in Moscow.

TOWARD SMOLENSK

Upstream (west) from Moscow, the Moskva River is a much more attractive proposition than the polluted waters to the southeast – nowhere more so than in and around 12th century **Zvenigorod**, one of the oldest settlements in the region. Swimming here in summer is excellent, and can be complemented by a visit to the town.

At the center of Zvenigorod is the Assumption Cathedral (c. 1400), the most ancient fully preserved architectural monument of old Muscovy. If you're lucky enough to visit when a service is taking place (6 p.m. Sundays and holidays), you'll be able to get in to see a fresco by master icon-painter Andrey Rublyov and his pupils.

Just west of the town is an area known as **Podmoskovnaya Shveitsariya** (Moscow Switzerland), whose beautiful landscapes of woodland and valleys have long been favored by party and government elites for short holidays. The most stunning scenery is along the valley of the Storozhka River, which was often visited by 19th century realist painter Isaac Levitan.

At the confluence of the Moskva and the Storozhka is the Savvino-Storozhevsky Monastery. Most of the current buildings are 17th century, but there is one outstanding exception. The Cathedral of the Nativity dates from the monastery's founding in 1398, and now stands in splendid isolation in the center. An exhibition inside contains some of Russia's finest 17th century icons. Other parts of the museum include a family chapel and the country's largest wickerwork collection. A century ago, Zvenigorod's monastery was one of the most important in Russia.

Restoration work plods on slowly in typical Russian fashion, but here there is a difference. Director Vladimir Kovtun, a man of great energy, has embarked on extraordinarily ambitious projects such as rebuilding the monks' living quarters from scratch.

The monastery is really quite magnificent, though this is frustratingly difficult to perceive visually, except from the high bell-tower or from across the river in winter.

Often described as a Versailles outside Moscow, **Arkhangelskoye** is a gem among the region's estates. Although it was originally built in the 1660s, most of today's buildings date from a hundred years later, when the Golitsyn family, prominent since the time of Peter the Great, poured large sums of money and attention into its reconstruction. When Prince Nikolay Yusupov bought the estate in 1810, he added new buildings and filled the main house with one of Europe's finest art collections, including works by Van Dyck and Tiepolo.

Unfortunately, the main house museum has been closed for a long time, but the park and outer buildings, entered through a gap in the fence near the bus stop, are still worth visiting. A combination of formal gardens near the house and a landscape park further away, the palace grounds are filled with classical statues and pavilions. The serf theater, just to the west, contains decorations by the Italian master Pietro Gonzaga dating from the late 18th century. The Bridge over the Ravine is perhaps the most unusual outbuilding, consisting of an archway above which is a wooden structure in pseudo-gothic style. Finally, the

Arkhangelskoye: Entrance arch and statue of Artemis with doe

Church of the Archangel Michael – the only survivor from the original estate – should be seen. Small and fairy tale-like, it now houses exhibitions.

Near Arkhangelskoye are two of the very few country restaurants outside Moscow offering more than primitive fare. The **Arkhangelskoye Restaurant** (tel. 562-0328) is just across the road from the museum. The pricey **Russkaya Izba** (tel. 561-4244) is near the Moskva River bridge in the village of Ilyinskoye.

Just beyond Ilyinskoye is the recently restored **Petrovskoye** estate, another of the many properties of the Golitsyn family. The main house is a specimen of 19th century Classicism, though two pseudo-gothic outbuildings remain from the 18th century. A landscape garden slopes down to the Moskva and Istra rivers.

To the south, toward the railway line to Mozhaisk, is the estate of **Zakharovo**, where Alexander Pushkin spent many childhood summers. Set high above the Vyazyoma river and surrounded by gardens, the house is now a museum. In 1949 (the 150th anniversary of Pushkin's birth), a black marble obelisk was erected on the grounds; on the first Sunday in June every year, people gather here for festive recitations of his poetry.

Twenty kilometers to the west of Zvenigorod is the ancient town of **Ruza**, situated on the hilly banks of the river of the same name, a deep and lush tributary of the Moskva. The old citadel there was once an outpost of Muscovy and even became a princedom in its own right, before being liquidated by Ivan the Terrible in the 16th century. Though its wooden walls have not survived, two churches have. The unusual Church of Dmitry has a bell-tower as its central feature. The Church of the Protection and Intercession of the Virgin houses the local history museum.

To the north of Ruza is a classic example of the excesses of Communist

Bas-relief from monument to General M.I. Kutuzov, commander of the Russian army at Borodino

planning. While not submerging whole villages and ancient churches as Rybinskoye Reservoir in north Russia did, the **Ozyorninskoye Reservoir** has nevertheless done significant damage to one of the Moscow Region's areas of natural beauty. Built amid the industrialization fervor and ecological irresponsibility of the 1960's, the reservoir is best seen from the **Volynshchino-Poluektovo** estate. This is one of the most magnificent mansions in the Region, but its park is now under water – the reservoir laps at the white stone terrace below the house, which is currently used as a sports center.

The town of **Mozhaisk** is best known as the main provider of the capital's sterilized milk. It is indeed the region's chief industrial center west of Moscow, but is also of historical interest. Komsomolskaya Square, in the west of the town, is the old center. Close by is the Kremlin, set on a massive rampart. Today's churches – the New St. Nicholas Cathedral and the Church of St. Peter and St. Paul – are both 19th century constructions but contain remnants of older buildings, notably the Church-over-the-Gate, dating from 1685.

Leaving the town to the north by the picturesque Ulitsa Krupskaya (named after Lenin's wife), visitors will first cross the Mozhaika River and then walk to the **Luzhetsky Monastery**, attractively situated on the banks of the Moskva River. Most of its buildings date from the 16th century, and were financed by Makary, a major religious and political figure during the reign of Ivan the Terrible.

Some six kilometers to the north, the Moskva River is dammed. Upstream is the so-called **Sea of Mozhaisk**, created in 1961. This "sea" is a favorite place for fishing, with an abundance of pike, perch, and tench. It's probably best to start trips from the base at **Staroye Selo**, to the northwest.

The furthest point of interest within day-trip distance on the road to Smolensk is the battlefield of **Borodino**. Although this huge museum preserve, covering an area of 130 sq. km, is impossible to see in its entirety, its main features can be taken in without great fuss. They are: a museum, less than 1 km south of Borodino village; a hilltop monument to Prince Bagration, a Georgian general who fell in battle nearby; the Russian headquarters in Gorki, marked by an obelisk; and Napoleon's camp, similarly indicated, at Shevardino. Almost 3 km from the latter were Bagration's positions, which bore the brunt of the French attack. In the 1830's, the Convent of the Savior of Borodino was built on the site and one of its churches dedicated to the fallen. The convent saw service as a hospital during World War II; it is now a museum dealing with Borodino during the 1939–45 war. Just opposite is a former hotel where Leo Tolstoy stayed in 1867 while researching his epic novel, *War and Peace*. This, too is now a museum. On the western end of the battlefield are the remains of the Kolotsky Monastery, with its Assumption Cathedral dating from the 17th century, another scene of fierce fighting.

TOWARD RZHEV

While many Russian monasteries seek to fill their visitors with awe, the subtle ingenuity and architectural excellence of **New Jerusalem** give it an appeal of a different kind. It was built in the 17th century by the colorful and controversial Patriarch Nikon, who sought to gain for Russia leadership of the Christian world. A part of his grand design was the rebuilding of sacred places on Russian soil.

Nikon chose this site on a bend in the river Istra because he felt it resembled the Holy Land's topography. The Istra became the Jordan, the hill beside it Mount Zion, and the monastery, Jerusalem itself. New Jerusalem's most extraordinary feature is the Cathedral of the Resurrection, completed in 1686 in the "image and likeness" of Jerusalem's Holy Sepulcher, though in contemporary Russian architectural style. Blown up by the retreating Nazis in 1941, it is undergoing painfully slow reconstruction. Yet this somehow seems to add to the attraction – the cathedral's interior appears to be discreetly crumbling before your eyes. In stark contrast is the white plastered underground church of Konstantin and Yelena. Entering by a doorway from the draughty cathedral, the cozy heated stairway gives one the feeling of descending into the bowels of the earth. This subterranean church is the only one of its kind in Russia; its base is six meters below ground level and its belfry just a couple of meters above the grass of the courtyard.

While it is accessible by guided tour only (on Sundays, May–September), at time of writing the rest of the museum was open every day except Sundays and included icons, tapestries, samovars, and 1970's dissident art, scattered through various monastery outbuildings. However, the monastery has recently been returned to the church, and the museum seems threatened with at least partial closure.

Outside the walls are the "Gardens of Gethsemane," known for their holy water spring. A wooden chapel, a folly, and a windmill complete a rich and pleasing scene.

Moscow's northwestern outskirts soon give way to acres of beautiful mixed woodland combined with such picturesque river valleys as the Sinichka, Banka, Nakhabinka, and the Malaya Istra, stretching from the Istra River in the south to the St. Petersburg rail and road routes in the north. This is fine walking country.

Not far from the village of Opalikha, the first rural settlement encountered by the Moscow-based traveler, is another mansion in the Golitsyn holdings, **Nikolskoye-Uryupino.** Resembling Arkhangelskoye in style and features, it has one outstanding treasure –the lavishly decorated and beautifully situated St. Nicholas Church, similar in period and style to Arkhangelskoye's.

Situated on the river route from Moscow to Novgorod, the town of **Volokolamsk** was always a bone of contention between these two rival princedoms. Now just a small provincial town, it lies beneath its tiny Kremlin, a cozy, fenced enclosure with two churches. One of these, the 17th century Resurrection Cathedral, houses the local museum. The town's center looks initially like a bustling shopping center until its drabness becomes apparent.

Some 24 kilometers northwest of Volokolamsk is the village of **Teryayevo** and nearby the Monastery of St. Joseph of Volokolamsk. The latter was founded in 1479 by Joseph Volotsky, a powerful political and religious figure of his time, known for his unbending spiritual discipline and dislike of heretics. His monastery became

Teryayevo Monastery, view from church-over-the-gate

a center both for education and for charitable activity. Legend has it that Volotsky's generosity to the poor upset local entrepreneurs by forcing up their prices. Most of the current buildings date from the late 17th century, when they were decorated with strikingly colored tile friezes, notably the Assumption Cathedral's "peacock's eye," created by Stepan Polubes, the famous Moscow ceramicist. Now returned to the church, the monastery has once again become an educational center, teaching the ancient art of manuscript-writing right down to such details as traditional methods of preparing ink, and collecting bibles from all over the world. A bible museum (the largest in Russia and the third largest in the world) displays the nucleus of the collection, including the first complete printed Slavonic bible.

Just to the west are two estates in the village of **Yaropolets,** owned by maverick Ukrainian hetman (general) Doroshenko in the 16th century. Having dared to take the side of the Turks in a war against Russia, Doroshenko was eventually captured by his fellow Slavs and died in prison. His two sons each inherited one of these estates.

The southern one is **Yaropolets Goncharovykh,** a fine classical mansion and outbuildings with elements of the pseudo-gothic. Most haunting and romantic are the walls at the southern edge of the grounds, reminiscent of Moscow's Tsaritsyno. The stately **Yaropolets Chernyshovykh** was built by Pyotr Nikitin, a contemporary of architect Vassily Bazhenov. It was reduced to a ruined shell during World War II and still awaits restoration. Its condition is in stark contrast to that of its brightly painted and well-maintained neighbor. Just opposite the main house is the Church of Our Lady of Kazan, a magnificent two-domed classical church with porticos and columns, now also a sad ruin.

TOWARD TVER

To the north and northeast of Moscow are two more in the ring of towns which were the outposts of ancient Muscovy. On the road to St. Petersburg is **Klin**, once a post station and stopping place for merchants. Now it is best known as the home of composer **Pyotr Tchaikovsky**. His mansion is set in woods below the town and is now a house-museum. It was here that he wrote his Sixth Symphony and the *Nutcracker* ballet. The birch table where he worked on the former has been preserved as an exhibit. In 1964 a concert hall seating 400 was added, where visitors can listen to tape recordings and watch films about Tchaikovsky.

Study and sitting room, Tchaikovsky House-Museum

The town itself has retained some of its charm, though it has suffered badly from heavy traffic and uglification. The Kremlin is now barely noticeable, its main church shorn of its cupola, painted a lurid green and used as a "Culture House." The nearby 19th century pseudo-Russian style market stalls have fared better, though, and exploration behind the façade reveals an 1886 shop sign, workplace of the trader Timofey Chelyshov. Two churches in the town are worth a look: the Assumption Church on Ulitsa Papivina, a forlorn but durable white building set back from a busy road, and the Church of the Prelate Tikhon on Sportivnaya, a gleaming, festive structure in a grim suburban wasteland, built and opened just last year by the Patriarch.

To the east of Klin, and due north of Moscow, is **Dmitrov,** founded by Yuri Dolgoruky in the 12th century. The town's history is turbulent: It was contested by the Muscovy and Vladimir-Suzdal princedoms, then sacked by the Lithuanians and Poles in the 17th century. The earthen ramparts of the Kremlin remain, shielding the churches within from the incursions of the modern world. The large Assumption Cathedral combines a working church and below it one of the area's best history museums. Behind the Kremlin stands the charming Monastery of SS. Boris and Gleb, a real find for lovers of crumbling ruins.

The village of **Rogachovo**, between

the two larger towns, is also worth a visit. Its huge Smolensky Cathedral is perhaps the closest extant approximation of the Cathedral of Christ the Savior in Moscow, the 19th century giant demolished by Stalin in the 1930's to make way for a swimming pool (see Moscow Walk #6). A few kilometers east of Rogachovo is the **Nikolo-Peshnoshsky Monastery,** another northern outpost of Muscovy built in the 14th century. The ensemble currently houses a sanatorium and is under restoration.

Closer to Moscow on the Dmitrov road is the estate of **Marfino**, with a magnificent 19th century gothic palace. Once frequented by literary figures in the last century, it was recently used as a location for the filming of the Satanic Ball in Bulgakov's satirical novel, *The Master and Margarita*. Though the building is now a sanatorium, visitors still come to admire the gardens, and particularly the front steps and stunningly romantic bridge over an ornamental pond.

Just a few kilometers away is the sleepy village of **Fedoskino**, nestled in the valley of the River Ucha. This is the original center of the production of Russia's famous lacquer boxes. Though begun in 1795, the industry faced new competition in the 1930's, when icon-painting centers such as Palekh and Mstyora began to adopt the craft (see Ivanovo Region). However, Fedoskino continues to produce boxes in its own 19th century classical, non-religious style. Though suffering from lack of a museum and relative obscurity, its reputation still brings regular visitors. Most of the artists now live in the modern residential blocks beyond the river opposite the factory, and they always welcome visits from potential buyers.

One of Stalin's more successful grandiose construction projects during the 1930's was a canal connecting Moscow to the River Volga at Dubna. The **Moscow Canal** was built with forced labor, and casualties ran into the thousands. It runs from the Moskva River in the city to the town of Kimry, via a number of artificial reservoirs – now Muscovites' favorite recreational areas for swimming, windsurfing, sailing, and fishing. The canal includes 11 immense locks and eight hydroelectric power stations.

Of the six reservoirs, perhaps the **Rlyazminskoye** is the most popular, and is one of the country's most important sailing centers. Here visitors can arrange Saturday and Sunday outings accompanied by an experienced crew from a wharf at the Vodniki end.

For swimming, try the adjacent **Pirogovskoye Reservoir**. Just 35 km from the city, it is nearly unspoiled and surrounded by forest. Fish swim in the shallows unperturbed by pollution, and the water sparkles.

Farther west, near the town of Solnechnogorsk, is another, much older artificial reservoir. **Senezhskoye Lake** is all that remains of a canal built in the early 18th century to carry stone to Moscow for the building of the Cathedral of Christ the Savior. Once frequented by such famous anglers as Lenin, poet Alexander Blok, and Soviet writer Maxim Gorky, it remains a prominent fishing center.

Completing the picture of Moscow's northern lakes is **Kiyovo** in the town of Lobnya. Though tiny and stagnant, it is an important nature reserve, and home to several thousand gulls.

TOWARD YAROSLAVL

Yaroslavskoye shossé, the road from Moscow to Sergiyev Posad and beyond, is one of the best-maintained in the region, the beginning of the

Abramtsevo Church and Folk Museum

Golden Ring tourist route and therefore frequented by coachloads of foreigners whom the Soviet government was always anxious to please. But even so, not all the area's treasures have been readily appreciated by visitors.

Take for instance **Klyazma,** a small village two kilometers off the main road with a handful of architectural gems to delight lovers of Art Nouveau. The **Church of Veronica's Veil** is its centerpiece – a stone structure with unique colored tiles over the belfry and entrance portraying Christ and the angels. It was built two years before the Revolution and services were never held there at the time. Just after reconsecration two years ago, the church was damaged by fire but remains largely intact. Restoration continues. Two doors away is the earlier wooden village church, also art nouveau, but nowadays locked up by the local gymnastics club. The Alexandrenko family, who sponsored these buildings, has a dacha nearby. Unfortunately a shady cooperative now owns it and the determined visitor will have to negotiate a high wall and vicious dog to see its modest architectural merits.

Just beyond the town of Ashukino is the pretty estate of **Muranovo.** Although virtually unknown to Golden Ring tourists, it has a museum dedicated to two of Russia's finest 19th century poets, Yevgeny Baratynsky and Fyodor Tyutchev. The former praised this "happy house" in a poem and declared that even in the throes of old age he would not grow cold there. The most endearing thing about Muranovo is its setting; the ideal season for visits is the autumn, when the mixed foliage around the estate is alive with color. A small church on the grounds houses the Tyutchev family burial vault.

The lush, green countryside in this part of the Moscow Region has inspired artists and writers for centuries,

The Jewel of Orthodoxy

It would be difficult to imagine Orthodox Christianity or indeed Russia itself without the city of **Sergiyev Posad** (formerly Zagorsk) or its centerpiece, the **Trinity-St. Sergius Lavra**. The origins of the monastery founded in the 1340's by St. Sergius of Radonezh are modest. Sergius was an ascetic monk who settled in the forest with his brother and gradually built up a community of like-minded people. With his followers he played a major role in the spiritual consolidation of a Russia demoralized by Tatar oppression.

Though destroyed during a Tatar raid in 1408, the monastery was soon being rebuilt, and 15 years later the **Trinity Cathedral**, the oldest and perhaps still the finest of the monastery's churches, was completed on the site of Sergius' grave. Though made of white stone and pre-Mongolian in style, it was the first church to include *kokoshniki*, a type of awning over the façades. It formerly housed Andrey Rublyov's *Old Testament Trinity*, the finest surviving work of ancient Russian art, which is now on display in the Tretyakov Gallery in Moscow. Rublyov's work is replaced here by a copy.

Nearby stands the shorter and slenderer **Church of the Descent of the Holy Spirit**, the second oldest in the ensemble, built in 1476 by Pskov masters. This is the oldest surviving church in Russia with a bell-tower contained under its roof.

In the 15th century, the monks decided to fortify the Lavra, and raised a huge brick fortress complete with moats and stakes. One result was to dwarf the Trinity Cathedral. In 1559 Ivan the Terrible commissioned a new cathedral, the blue and gold domed **Assumption**, which when finished 30 years later became the monastery's dominant structure, and remains so today.

Church of the Descent of the Holy Spirit

The monastery survived a bitter siege at the beginning of the 17th century. A hundred years later, after supporting Peter the Great in his struggle for power, it was rewarded with many of the exquisite buildings which grace its precincts today. Most notable of these is the **Refectory**, whose walls seem carpeted with lush decoration.

Building continued into the 18th century with a magnificent **bell-tower** which, although the tallest in Russia, nonetheless preserves the harmony of the ensemble; its successive layers are equal in height to that of other buildings in the monastery.

The **museums** of art and history

now on the site boast a rich collection of every conceivable form of ancient Russian art. One genre in which it excels above all other collections, however, is tapestry. It also includes a full-length portrait of St. Sergius, possibly made by Rublyov himself.

Although hundreds of visitors may mingle on its grounds with monks and theological students during a mid-summer day, the monastery's serenity seems never to be dispelled. To take stock of the Trinity-St. Sergius Lavra from a distance, walk to the village of **Blagoveshchenye** – the view from there is superb. Sadly, this village's fine 17th century wooden church can no longer be appreciated – it collapsed recently, leaving just the lower beams.

The Sergiyev Posad area has long been known for handmade wooden toys. The city has a very fine collection of historic toys, housed in a museum on Shkolnaya ulitsa, and you are likely to find on sale outside the monastery wonderful examples of the contemporary craft.

and made it an attractive setting for **Abramtsevo**. This small country estate was acquired by the devout Slavophile writer Sergey Aksakov in the mid-19th century because of its proximity to the Trinity-St. Sergius Lavra. For a time it became a kind of headquarters of the Slavophiles in their intellectual battle with the Westernizers. Later in the century, the estate was bought by the progressive industrialist and art patron Savva Mamontov, who invited such artists as Viktor and Apollinarius Vasnetsov and Ilya Repin to work on collective projects there. Even after the Revolution, artistic traditions continued, as painters Aristarch Lentulov and Robert Falk, among others, lived and worked there.

Abramtsevo is now a museum preserve, best appreciated by wandering around the grounds to see the outbuildings constructed by several of the resident artists. The neo-Russian **Church of Spas Not Made By Human Hand** (1880–82), designed by Apollinarius Vasnetsov with interior icons and other decoration by Viktor Vasnetsov and Vasily Polenov, is white, unimposing, and asymmetrically pleasing to the eye – a perfect site for peaceful contemplation. The Teremok baths, with their traditional but unorthodox folk carvings, and the ceramics on display in the studio should not be missed. The main part of the exhibition, though, is a rather colorless display of photographs and personal belongings of the estate's two famous owners.

The Abramtsevo museum is closed during the months of April and October, on Mondays and Tuesdays, and on the last Thursday of each month. On other days it is open 10 a.m. to 5 p.m.

Traveling to Abramtsevo by car you will pass the Convent of the Protection and Intercession of the Virgin at **Khotkovo**, originally built as a female complement to the nearby Trinity-St. Sergius Lavra. However, most of today's buildings date from much later. The ensemble is dominated by the St. Nicholas Cathedral, built at the beginning of this century in Russo-Byzantine style. The older Church of the Protection and Intercession of the Virgin was once frequented by Mamontov, and in recent years Abramtsevo people have worked tirelessly to restore it. It now gleams brilliantly among derelict surroundings. A small branch of the Abramtsevo museum devoted to local crafts can be found over the monastery gate.

Those with an interest in Scottish history or an abundance of Celtic blood should consider a deviation from Yaroslavskoye shossé to the village of Monino and the small estate at **Glinki.** It belonged to James William Bruce, a direct descendent of the Scottish King Robert and a commander of Peter the Great's artillery at the battle of Poltava. In addition to his military skills, he was known to practice the black arts, and on one occasion succeeded in hypnotizing the Tsar and his courtiers into believing they were about to be washed into the River Neva by a flood. The main house is now a sanatorium and the inside has been completely refurbished, but there is a small museum nearby devoted to Scottish-Russian relations of that era.

DIRECTIONS

Kolomna: take the M5 Ryazanskoye shossé to the southeast. The town is on your left after the Kolomna River bridge, approximately 93 km from the center of Moscow. By train, go from the Kazansky Vokzal to Kolomna, journey time 2½ hours.
Zaraisk: by M5 beyond Kolomna to the town of Lukovitsy, then right. By bus from Vykhino metro station, journey time 3 hours, or from Golutvino, the next rail station after Kolomna.
Dzerzhinsky: by M5 to Lyubertsy, then right, or turn off the Moscow Circular Road between the M5 and Domodedovo airport turn-offs. By train, to Lyubertsy 1 Vokzal, then by bus to the village.
Faustovo: by M5 to Bronnitsy, left as far as Yurovo (Bronnitsy rail station), then right for about 5 km. By train to Faustovo from the Kazansky Vokzal.

Sukhanovo: leave Moscow by Varshavskoye shossé and continue to the town of Butovo. Turn left there, then right 5 km later. By train to Rastorguyevo from the Paveletsky Vokzal, then by local bus.
Gorki: take Kashirskoye shossé, M4/6, 8 km out of Moscow and turn left to Gorki-Leninskiye. By train from the Paveletsky Vokzal to Leninskaya.
Shcherbinka: 3 km south of Butovo on Varshavskoye shossé, turn right and continue for another 1½ km. By train from the Kursky Vokzal.
Podolsk: continue another 6½ km past Butovo. For **Dubrovitsy**, leave the town by the A101 and turn right immediately. For **Polivanovo**, take a right turn further down the same road after **Oznobishino**. By train from the Kursky Vokzal.
Melikhovo: by M2 Simferopolskoye shossé, 48 km from central Moscow, then turn left, away from the town of Chekhov. By train from the Kursky Vokzal to Chekhov, then by local bus.
Serpukhov: by M2, another 32 km beyond Chekhov, and turn right. By

train $2^1/_4$ hours from the Kursky Vokzal.
Prioksko-Terrasny: turn left off the M2 where the right turn goes to Serpukhov. From Serpukhov by bus to Danki.

Peredelkino: by car leave Moscow by Minskoye shossé (M1) and at the 21 km post turn left. By train half an hour from the Kievsky Vokzal.
Valuyevo: take Kaluzhskoye shossé, M3, out of Moscow (called Leninsky prospekt as far as the ring road). After 5 km turn left to Moskovsky and continue through the village toward Verkhnyaya Valuyevo. By public transport, take the Vnukovo airport bus to the Peredeltsy stop, then on by local bus.
Borovsk: by the M3 to the town of Balabanovo, then turn right. By train from the Kievsky Vokzal to Balabanovo, then on by bus.
Vereya: by Minskoye shossé (M1) to Dorokhovo, then left. Continue 13 km to the hamlet of Kolodkina and turn right. By train from the Belorussky Vokzal to Dorokhovo, then by bus.
Maloyaroslavets: by M3 to Obninsk, then right, or direct by A101 (130 km). By train from the Kievsky Vokzal.

Arkhangelskoye: leave Moscow by Volokolamskoye shossé, then turn left onto Ilyinskoye shossé; or take Moscow bus #549 from Tushinskaya metro.
Petrovskoye: Some 6 km beyond Arkhangelskoye on Ilyinskoye shossé. By bus from Arkhangelskoye.
Zakharovo: take the M1 out of Moscow, then turn right on the A100 for Odintsovo. Continue 32 km past the town to Bolshiye Vyazyomy, then turn right. At the village of Shkolnaya, turn left. By train from the Belorussky Vokzal to Shkolnaya on the Zvenigorod branch line.
Zvenigorod: turn off the Moscow ring road onto Rublyovskoye shossé and continue for 40 km to the town. By train from Belorussky Vokzal.
Ruza: continue beyond Zvenigorod to a point just outside of Kolyubakino and turn right, then drive 27 km further. By train from the Belorussky Vokzal to either Tuchkovo or Dorokhovo, then on by bus.
Mozhaisk: direct by the A100 or 97 km on the M1 and turn right, for another 5 km. By train from the Belorussky Vokzal.
Borodino: continue through Mozhaisk on the A100, 13 km further to the village of Borodino. By train from the Belorussky Vokzal.

New Jerusalem: leave Moscow by the M9 Volokolamskoye shossé and

New Jerusalem: Yefrem's Tower (1694)

continue for 65 km. The monastery is just beyond the town, on a hill to the right. By train, go from the Rizhsky Vokzal to either Istra or Novoierusalimskaya, then take a local bus to the "Musei" stop.

Nikolskoye-Uryupino: by Rizhskoye shossé 10 km and turn right, or by train from the Rizhsky Vokzal to Opalikha, then 4 km on foot.

Volokolamsk: 130 km on the M9, or 2½ hours by train from the Rizhsky Vokzal, then on by local bus.

Teryayevo: by M9 approximately 105 km to the village of Chismena, then right though the village and another 24 km. By train to Volokolamsk and another 27 km by bus.

Yaropolets: by car to Volokolamsk, then right for another 13 km to the village of Kashino, then left. By bus 16 km from Volokolamsk.

Klin: by the M10 for 65 km, or by train to Klin from the Leningradsky Vokzal, then a short bus ride.

Dmitrov: 48 km by A104, or by train to Dmitrov from Savyolovsky Vokzal.

Rogachovo: by A104 for 16 km, then turn left toward Lobnya and continue for another 48 km. By bus from Dmitrov.

Marfino and **Fedoskino:** by A104 to the village of Sukharevo, then right, or by train to Katuar from the Savyolovsky Vokzal, then by bus.

Moscow Canal: In summer the canal and its main reservoirs are served by *Raketa* speedboats from Moscow's Northern River Vokzal *(Severny Rechny Vokzal).* Otherwise they are best reached by car along the A104 Dmitrovskoye shossé (**Klyazminskoye** and **Ikshinskoye**) or M8 Yaroslavskoye shossé (turn left at Mytishchi for **Pirogovskoye** or left at Pushkino for **Uchinskoye**). By train go to Vodniki for the **Klyazminskoye** or to Iksha for the **Ikshinskoye** from the Savyolovsky Vokzal, or to Pirogovsky for the **Pirogovskoye** or Pushkino for the **Uchinskoye** from the Yaroslavsky Vokzal.

Senezhskoye Lake: by M10 Leningradskoye shossé 40 km to the town of Solnechnogorsk. By train to the same from the Leningradsky Vokzal.

Kiyovo: by A104 Dmitrovskoye shossé for 16 km, then left to the

Teryayevo Monastery

town of Lobnya. By train to Lobnya from the Savyolovsky Vokzal.

Klyazma: by M8 about 24 km from Moscow, then turn left into the village. By train to Klyazma from the Yaroslavsky Vokzal.
Muranovo: by M8 for 40 km to the village of Rakhmanovo, then left and continue for 5 km. By train to Ashukinskaya, then 3 km on foot or by bus.
Abramtsevo: by M8 for 72 km to the village of Vozdvizhenskoye, then left to **Khotkovo.** Before reaching the entrance to the convent, turn left again for Abramtsevo. By train to Abramtsevo (just one stop further to Khotkovo).
Sergiyev Posad: take the M8 Yaroslavskoye shossé and continue for 80 km. By train from the Yaroslavsky Vokzal.
Glinki: by M7 Gorkovskoye shossé for 40 km, then left to Monino. By train from the Yaroslavsky Vokzal to Monino on the Fryazevo branch, then by bus to the "Sanatorium" stop.

RUSSIAN GLOSSARY

Abramtsevo
Абрамцево
Church of the Apparition of the Virgin
Знаменская церковь
Church of the Arkhangel Michael
Церковь Архангела Михаила
Arkhangelskoye
Архангельское
Ashukinskaya
Ашукинская
Assumption Cathedral
Успенский собор
Assumption Church
Успенская церковь
Balabanovo
Балабаново
Blagoveshchenye
Благовещенье
Bobrenyov Monastery
Бобренёв монастырь
Bolshiye Vyazyomy
Большие Вязёмы
Monastery of SS. Boris and Gleb
Борисоглебский монастырь
Borodino
Бородино
Borovsk
Боровск
Bronnitsy
Бронницы
Brusensky Monastery
Брусенский монастырь
Butovo
Бутово
Chekhov
Чехов
Cheremoshnya
Черемошня
Chismena
Чисмена
Chobotovskaya alleya
Чоботовская аллея
Danki
Данки
Darovoye
Даровое
Church of St. Demetrius
Дмитриевская церковь
Dmitrov
Дмитров
Dmitrovskoye shossé
Дмитровское шоссе
Dorokhovo
Дорохово
Dubrovitsy
Дубровицы
Dzerzhinsky
Дзержинский
Faustovo
Фаустово
Fedoskino
Федоскино

Glinki
Глинки
Golutvino
Голутвино
Golubkina House-Museum
Дом-музей Голубкина
Gorkovskoye shossé
Горьковское шоссе
Iksha Reservoir
Икшинское водохранилище
Ilyinskoye shossé
Ильинское шоссе
Church of the Intercession of the Virgin
Покровская церковь
Convent of the Intercession
Покровский монастырь
River Istra
Река Истра
Ivanovskoye
Ивановское
Church of St. John the Baptist
Церковь Иоанна Предтечи
Monastery of St. Joseph of Volokolamsk
Иосифо-Волоколамский монастырь
Kaluzhskoye shossé
Калужское шоссе
Kashino
Кашино
Kashirskoye shossé
Каширское шоссе
Khotkovo
Хотьково
Kiyovo
Киёво
Klin
Клин
Klyazma
Клязьма
Klyazma Reservoir
Клязьминское водохранилище
Kolomna
Коломна
Kolotsky Monastery
Колоцкий монастырь
Kolyubakino
Колюбакино
Komsomolskaya ploshchad
Комсомольская площадь
Krasnaya Gora
Красная Гора
Krasnokholmskaya Solovyetskaya Pustyn
Краснохолмская Соловецкая пустынь
Ulitsa Krupskaya
Улица Крупская
Leninskaya
Ленинская
Leninskiye Gorki
Ленинские Горки
Lobnya
Лобня
Lukovitsy
Луковицы
Luzhetsky Monastery
Лужецкий монастырь
Lyubertsy
Люберцы
Maloyaroslavets
Малоярославец
Marfino
Марфино
Melikhovo
Мелихово
Minskoye shossé
Минское шоссе
Monino
Монино
Moscow Canal
Московский канал
Moskovskaya ulitsa
Московская улица
Mozhaisk
Можайск
Mozhaisk Sea
Можайское море
Muranovo
Мураново
Mytishchi
Мытищи
River Nara
Река Нара

Nativity Cathedral
Собор Рождества Христова
New Golutvin Convent
Новоголутвинский монастырь
New Jerusalem
Новый Иерусалим
New St. Nicholas Cathdral
Новоникольский собор
St. Nicholas Cathedral
Никольский собор
Monastery of St. Nicholas Chernoostrovsky
Никольский Черноостровский монастырь
Monastery of St. Nicholas Peshnoshsky
Николо-Пешношский монастырь
Nikolo-Ugreshsky Monastery
Николо-Угрешский монастырь
Nikolskoye-Uryupino
Никольское-Урюпино
Novoierusalimskaya
Новоиерусалимская
Obninsk
Обнинск
Odintsovo
Одинцово
Opalikha
Опалиха
Church of Our Lady of Kazan
Казанская церковь
Oznobishino
Ознобишино
Ozyorninskoye Reservoir
Озёрнинское водохранилище
Pafnutyev-Borovsky Monastery
Пафнутьев-Боровский монастырь
Ulitsa Papivina
Улица Папивина
Church of St. Peter and St. Paul
Петропавловская церковь
Petrovskoye
Петровское
Pirogovo Reservoir
Пироговское водохранилище
Podmoskovnaya Shveitsariya
Подмосковная Швейцария
Podolsk
Подольск
Polivanovo
Поливаново
Church of the Prelate Tikhon
Церковь прелата Тихона
Prioksko-Terrasny Nature Reserve
Приокско-террасный заповедник
Protva River
Река Протва
Pushkino
Пушкино
Pyatnitskiye Gates
Пятницкие ворота
Rakhmanovo
Рахманово
Rastorguyevo
Расторгуево
Resurrection Cathedral
Воскресенский собор
Rogachovo
Рогачёво
Rublyovskoye shossé
Рублёвское шоссе
Ruza
Руза
Ryazanskoye shossé
Рязанское шоссе
Savvino-Storozhevsky Monastery
Саввино-Сторожевский монастырь
Senezhskoye Lake
Сенежское Озеро
Sergiyev Posad
Сергиев Посад
Serpukhov
Серпухов
Shcherbinka
Щербинка
Shevardino
Шевардино

Shkolnaya
Школьная
Shkolnaya ulitsa
Школьная улица
Simferopolskoye shossé
Симферопольское шоссе
Smolensk Cathedral
Смоленский собор
Solnechnogorsk
Солнечногорск
Church of Spas-Not-Made-by-Human Hand
Церковь Спаса Нерукотворного
Staroye Selo
Старое Село
Storozhka River
Река Сторожка
Sukhanovo
Суханово
Sukharevo
Сухарево
Tchaikovsky House-Museum
Дом-музей Чайковского
Teryayevo
Теряево
Transfiguration Church
Преображенская церковь
Trinity-St. Sergius Lavra
Троице-Сергиева Лавра
Tuchkovo
Тучково
Uchinskoye Reservoir
Учинское водохранилище
Varshavskoye shossé
Варшавское шоссе
Vereya
Верея
Verkhnyeye Valuyevo
Верхнее Валуево
Vladychny Convent
Владычный монастырь
Volokolamsk
Волоколамск
Volokolamskoye shossé
Волоколамское шоссе
Volynshchino Poluektovo
Волынщино Полуэ́ктово
Vozdvizhenskoye
Воздвиженское
Vysotsky Monastery
Высоцкий монастырь
Yaropolets
Ярополец
Yaroslavskoye shossé
Ярославское шоссе
Yurovo
Юрово
Zakharovo
За́харово
Zaraisk
Зарайск
Zvenigorod
Звенигород

Title page photo: *Bell-post, village of Melikhovo*

ST. PETERSBURG

SANKT-PETERBURG

And he thought:
From here we'll frighten off the Swede.
Here a city will be raised
To spite our overbearing neighbor.
Here for us, designed by nature,
Opens a window to the West
And on this shore we shall stand fast.

– from *The Bronze Horseman*
by Alexander Pushkin
(trans. J. Kates)

It is difficult to imagine a more extraordinary place than St. Petersburg, a city built by Europe's finest 18th and 19th century architects on the marshes of the broad Neva delta, for a huge, backward nation living obstinately between orient and occident. It sometimes seems miraculous that Petersburg has survived at all, and not sunk, Atlantis-style, without a trace or dwindled to obscurity like other once-great Russian towns. There are many occasions when this could have happened, beginning with the uncertain period following its founder's death, up to its near-annihilation by Nazi Germany. Petersburg remains today Russia's second largest city. Its survival demonstrates something typically Russian – the way in which society forces itself to adapt to conditions imposed from outside, or by its own leaders.

In many ways the city is leading a troubled life, amid crumbling façades and economic hardships. For the creative mind, though, this moodily romantic city is still fertile ground. Amid its grand squares, palaces, golden domes and spires, canals, embankments, and carefully planned prospects, poets, artists, and lovers all feel their lives infused with drama. When one thinks about Petersburg, its poets must surely come to mind, and none more so than Anna Akhmatova.

Not for anything would we exchange
this splendid
Granite city of fame and calamity,
The wide rivers of glistening ice,
The sunless, gloomy gardens,
And, barely audible, the Muse's
*voice.**

St. Petersburg will grandly woo you, as well.

People

Petersburgers have a decidedly more Western air. Unlike the traditionally warm and earthy Russian soul of Muscovites, Petersburgers are often seen as both more reserved and more refined. These traits can be traced back in part to the old aristocracy, whose imprint was never completely obliterated by the Soviet era. There is a strong rivalry with Moscow, which is somewhat looked down on, for example in pronunciation. Petersburgers claim to speak the purest Russian.

Still, the city is not without a streak of bohemianism, originating in the early years of this century. This, fused with the universal Russian tendency to drink, befriend, talk and dance all night, creates an amiable and lively climate that is once again attracting kindred spirits from all over Europe.

History

The Neva River delta which is now St. Petersburg was always an outpost of Slavic territory, the northernmost part of the great trade route from Scandinavia to Greece that the Slavs controlled. In the 10th century, Kievan Rus' extended this far; two hundred years later the site was in Novgorod's sphere, falling under Moscow's control at the end of the 15th century. The customary enemy was Sweden, whose interest in the Baltic coast led her to attack regularly. After three centuries of attempts, the Swedes finally cut Russia off from the Baltic in 1617. They built a fortress called Nienschantz at the mouth of the River Okhta. Who could have guessed that in a hundred years' time Russia's capital city would be standing just across the Neva?

In 1703, in the course of his northern campaigns, Peter the Great recaptured the Baltic coastal area that had been lost. To ward off further Swedish invasion, the small Hare Island (*Zayachy ostrov*) in the Neva delta became the site of the Peter and Paul Fortress. But right from the beginning Peter had more grandiose plans for these marshy islands. As the fortress was founded, he proclaimed that a city would be built, and as early as 1712 St. Petersburg became the capital of Russia.

The rapid development of the city over the next dozen years was due almost entirely to Peter himself. While the newly erected Admiralty Wharf, Foundry (*Liteiny Dvor*) and Tar Yard (*Smolny Dvor*) provided for the city militarily, the Tsar relocated the best noble families and artisans there virtually by force.

The rude new settlement was not a popular place to live, and when Peter's immediate successors, Catherine I and Peter II, took steps to return to Moscow, St. Petersburg was threatened with extinction not long after its birth. Tsarina Anna Ioannovna, however, shared the enthusiasm of her half-brother, and her accession in 1730 heralded the beginning of a prolonged Golden Age of building, one that reached its zenith during the reign of Catherine the Great (1762–96), with the creation of entire classical architectural landscapes.

---

* Translated by Judith Hemschemeyer, from *The Complete Poems of Anna Akhmatova* (Zephyr Press, 1992), p. 191.

In the 19th century, St. Petersburg assumed a new role, as the center not only of tsarist power but also of opposition to it. Early revolts – those of the Decembrists and to a certain extent of the bomb-throwing populists of the 1870's and '80's – were intellectual. By the turn of the present century, however, the rise of a powerful working class engendered the potent mixture of theorists and proletariat which ultimately brought about the collapse of the tsarist regime. The Bolshevik revolution was made and carried out here.

In 1918, the loss of Petrograd's* status as capital neither halted its growth nor diminished its significance. In 1941–43 it became the foremost symbol of Russia's heroism during the Second World War: attack by Nazi Germany led to an almost 900-day siege, the obliteration of 650,000 lives and 10,000 buildings, but not of the spirit of its people. Leningrad* held out, and further amazed the world after the war with great feats of reconstruction, as one by one the city's architectural treasures were restored to their original appearance.

St. Petersburg Today

In 1991, following a referendum, Leningrad went through another change of name, reverting to St. Petersburg. You will, however, find foreigners much more likely than Russians to call the city by its new/old name. "Leningrad" is still widespread, as is the ancient nickname, "Peter," which survived the Communist era.

The city has seen rapid change in recent years. While the transition to capitalism has been extremely painful, it seems to have had a more positive effect here than in Moscow. Prices are generally lower than in the capital, and state and nouveau riche privilege less ostentatious. Its culture – from architecture to public life – is more European and democratic. At the same time, much of the city's fabric is crumbling away, and there are only enough resources to selectively arrest this process.

Unlike Moscow, the splendor of this city is laid out for all to see. Though its heart is along Nevsky prospekt and the environs, it has another focus, the "square" bounded by the mainland and the Vassilyevsky and Petrogradsky Islands, and filled by the wide expanse of the Neva. At a glance you can see the stages of development of the city, moving from the Peter and Paul Fortress, to the new center envisioned on the Strelka, and finally settling on the magnificent squares and palaces of the left bank.

Above all, St. Petersburg invites and rewards exploration, whether of the canals and courtyards, the quiet back streets of the Petrograd Side, the dachas of Kamenny Island, or the parks of the out-of-town estates. Stray from the beaten track; you won't regret it.

* The city was renamed by Nicholas II during the First World War because the original name sounded too Germanic; in 1924, it became Leningrad.

General Staff Building Arch, Palace Square

WALK 1: PETER'S CITY

This tour of some of the oldest historical sites in St. Petersburg begins outside Gorkovskaya metro station on the Petrograd Side, on the islands where Peter originally intended his new capital.

As you follow Kamennoostrovsky prospekt from the metro down toward the river, it may seem tempting to head for the Peter and Paul fortress, whose slender spire dominates the skyline to your right, but this is not the oldest area of the city. Turn left along the embankment and walk to **Peter the Great's cottage**, the Tsar's first abode as he oversaw the fulfillment of his dream: the raising of a new northern capital on bare marshland.

This simple wooden hut, built in three days in the summer of 1703, seems an odd beginning for the "Northern Palmyra" he intended. It looks like the dwelling of a hermit, an industrious and self-denying monk. But Peter was not at all typical of Russia's extravagant rulers. He had an ascetic side, and also became a multi-skilled craftsman, often working incognito among his laborers.

Today Peter's cottage has all the trappings of a shrine. The approach from the river is flanked by two Manchurian Lions, used in China to guard palaces and burial vaults; they were brought from Manchuria in 1907. The Tsar's bust and garden were set here in the middle of the last century. The cottage was enclosed in a brick building much later. It is a place where you can get a glimpse into Peter's astonishingly modest and rational style of life.

Looking directly across the Neva you will see Peter the Great's **Summer Palace**, designed by Domenico Trezzini in 1710–14. It is one of the ironies of St. Petersburg that this once out-of-town residence, whose magnificent garden is dotted with marble statues, has long since become just one of the city's central landmarks. (See also Walk #4.) The wrought iron railing that screens it, added later in the 1770's, is itself a marvelous artifact. It is said that this fence gave such esthetic satisfaction to an eccentric English lord visiting the city during the last century, that he returned home without so much as a glance at the rest of the city! This story is not quite so far-fetched as it may seem, for the decorative wrought iron railings along Petersburg's bridges and embankments are one of the city's special delights.

Return to Revolution Square and cross the bridge past the souvenir peddlers to Zayachy Island and the **Peter and Paul Fortress.** In 1703 Peter declared that a city would be built on this strategically important island which guarded the approaches from three branches of the Neva delta against Swedish attack. According to legend, at this moment an eagle soared into the sky, an obvious borrowing from Rome's story, when Romulus' words prompted the flight of twelve kites. The fortress's shape is that of a six-pointed star. Its original walls were earthen. Later, after it was no longer used for defensive purposes, the walls were rebuilt in stone, purely for effect.

Leave the fortress by the Nikolsky Gate behind the **Botny Dom**, the pavilion which once housed Peter the Great's boat, and look across the Kronverksky Strait at the horseshoe-shaped building opposite. This was formerly the city's northern defense, **the Kronverk**, whose rampart and moat date from Peter's time. The original buildings were replaced in 1850 by

Peter and Paul Fortress

Peter's fortress was a deliberate attempt to upstage Moscow's Kremlin. The 122m spire of its belfry is still the highest point of the city. It was the first signal of the sustained goal of enriching the flat, monotonous landscape with architecture. The cathedral was designed by Domenico Trezzini as the royal place of worship. Russia's tsars, grand princes, and members of the Romanov family lie encased in rows inside the cathedral; a small white pavilion on the fortress's central square formerly housed the "granddad of the Russian fleet," the boat Peter used to "play sailor" in his childhood as he dreamed of Russia's own navy.

Indeed the fortress became the embodiment of Russian autocracy, combining within its walls the empire's lighter and darker sides. As well as the soaring splendor of the cathedral, it contains a notorious political prison whose inmates included Alexander Radishchev, a son of the Enlightenment, and radical thinker Nikolay Chernyshevsky, author of the visionary socialist novel, *What Is to Be Done*? The members of the Provisional Government were among the last imprisoned there, in 1917.

The entire fortress, including all of the structures within, forms the city historical museum. One of the newest and most peculiar monuments to be found on the grounds is a statue of Peter the Great created by the "unofficial" artist Mikhail Shemanka, who was expelled from the Soviet Union in the 1970's. The sculptor used as his models the death mask of Peter, as well as a unique wood and wax effigy of the Tsar, created just after his death and now in the Hermitage, whose moving limbs gave it the disquieting capability of standing up.

Peter and Paul Cathedral

Some of the treasures acquired by the museum in the last 10–15 years can be seen in three rooms, from a miniature version of Rastrelli's statue of Peter the Great (see Walk #3), to turn-of-the-century typewriters and sewing machines. There's also a room full of unusual musical instruments, demonstrated on Mondays and Thursdays between 3 and 4 p.m.

City life is illustrated by a rich collection of sketches and photos, amplified by reminiscences of Pushkin, Gogol and others. The reconstructed clerk's room seems to have jumped straight out of Gogol's black fantasy, "The Overcoat."

the **Arsenal**, now one of the world's largest military museums.

Leave Zayachy Island by the small bridge on the west side and follow Kronverkskaya naberezhnaya to the left, toward Birzhevoy most (formerly Most Stroiteley). This bridge leads to **Vassilyevsky Island**, the largest in the Neva delta, facing the Gulf of Finland.

The spit of Vassilyevsky, called the **Strelka** ("arrow"), now ahead and to your left, is a fine maritime ensemble from the early decades of the 19th century which stands as a brilliant example of the fusing of art and function. The strictly symmetrical plan was as follows. Wharves flared from the tip of the spit. Two Rostral Columns stood just behind them. These were another attempt to Romanize the city, and are decorated with the bows (*rostres*) of ships which were intended to equate Russia's naval victories with those of Rome over Carthage. At their bases are allegorical representations of the Dnieper, Neva, Volga, and Volkhov Rivers. They also served to warn pilots navigating the often foggy Neva passage. Goods were transferred to two modest, yellow classical warehouses flanking the sides of the Stock Exchange, the imposing building in the form of a Greek temple designed by Thomas de Thomon in 1805. Its portico is decorated with a sculptural group whose focus is Neptune. It became a naval museum after the port facilities were transferred downstream in 1855.

But to discover Petrine Vassilyevsky, you must look behind the traffic and bustle of Pushkin Square. Walking between the warehouses and the Stock Exchange, you will find a

An Urban Vision

When St. Petersburg became Russia's capital in 1712, Vassilyevsky Island became the focal point of the city and intensive building was carried out there. This was Russia's first planned city, its streets running in grid-like fashion with large east-west avenues crossing smaller north-south "lines," which were initially intended to be canals, in accordance with Peter's desire to make the city a northern Venice. The plan had to be abandoned when it was found that the water had become stagnant and unsanitary.

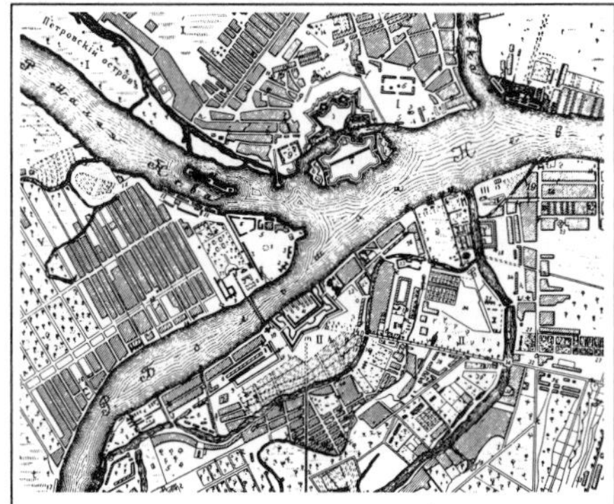

Plan of St. Petersburg, 1738

Peter's will was carried out, at least in the form which the city took. However, the absence of bridges to the mainland, as well as continual danger of flooding, soon left Vassilyevsky out of the mainstream of the city's development. Nevertheless, the impulse to elaborate the city according to a rational plan, first applied on Vassilyevsky Island, was later implemented in a new setting across the Neva. Vassilyevsky, however, kept its maritime role.

The Strelka at dusk

quiet square. In addition to enjoying the same buildings from an unusual angle, you will see ahead a long terraced row, the **Twelve Colleges**. These buildings, completed by the busy Domenico Trezzini in 1718, were instrumental in Peter's civil service reforms, an attempt to coordinate and organize the functions of state institutions. Like the reforms themselves, they survived a difficult 100 years. Then, in 1819, the ministries that replaced them moved to the mainland and St. Petersburg University took over the premises. The island subsequently became the scientific and academic center of the city.

Turning left to Universitetskaya naberezhnaya, again along the side of the warehouse building, brings you to the **Kunstkammer**, notable for its fine octagonal tower, a building in Petrine baroque style. Exotic items and curiosities attracted the Tsar's interest; the Kunstkammer was begun in the later years of his reign to house the country's first natural history museum, bringing human embryos, a two-headed foal, and other pale bodies in glass jars, as well as minerals and plant specimens, to the attention of the as yet ignorant Russian public, free of charge. Though the exhibition was greatly expanded over the following 200 years, the nucleus remained, and remains, Peter's collection. The Kunstkammer also houses a museum of anthropology and the museum of Mikhail Lomonosov, a great scientist, linguist, and poet who worked here for 25 years (1741–65).

Several blocks down from the Kunstkammer is the **Menshikov Palace**, the finest building of the city's early period. Ironically, the modest Tsar was upstaged by his extravagant lieutenant, Alexander Menshikov, the first governor of Petersburg, a childhood friend of Peter's who rose to the position from that of a street peddler. In 1707 Peter gave Menshikov the whole of Vassilyevsky Island and this palace, a luxurious residence unique in the city for its obvious Dutch influences, was one of the results. Some rooms of the equally extravagant interior are now open as a museum, visits by excursion only.

Walking down Universitetskaya naberezhnaya, which extends to the

Lieutenant Schmidt Bridge (1843–50), the first to span the Neva, you can sense the will of the great Tsar in later buildings and other features. Grand façades like the **Academy of Arts** (1767–88) are accompanied by ornate steps leading down to the river, a place for pontoons and ferry landings in pre-bridge days. In front of the Academy are two ancient Egyptian **Sphinxes**, brought here in 1834 as another imperial symbol.

Peter's second great dream, Russia's attainment of naval power, is closely linked with St. Petersburg, and its fulfilment is also evident here. Further down the embankment is the statue of Admiral **Ivan Kruzenstern**, the first Russian to sail round the world (in 1803–06). Not only was Russia able to bring the best products of other civilizations to its heart, now it could spread its own civilization round the world. On the pedestal is a bas-relief depicting a Negro and a Malayan with the navigator's coat-of-arms. It was built in 1873 in the heyday of colonialism, the natural extension of Peter's dreams.

Take any one of the lines (*linii*) inland, and follow Sredny prospekt to Vassileostrovskaya metro station.

WALK 2: GRAND CENTRAL SQUARES TO MOIKA EMBANKMENT

This visit to the city of governments, sailors, and Decembrists begins at **Palace Square** *(Dvortsovaya ploshchad)*, reached by the #2 trolleybus which picks up at the Nevsky Prospekt metro. Palace Square, often compared with Moscow's Red Square because it is similarly a focal point of the city, may be the best known landmark of St. Petersburg. The buildings which form it were built over a span of 80 years, and three of the city's

Palace Square

most notable architects took part in their construction.

In 1762 Bartolomeo Rastrelli completed the **Winter Palace** for Catherine II. With a single exception – that of Paul – it remained the principal residence of the tsars until the Revolution. The *risalits* and recesses of this glittering giant of Russian Baroque stretch for 200 meters along the square and almost as far back to the Neva embankment. There is something uneasy about its statues and carvings – a fear of floods, perhaps. For almost 125 years it was the largest, tallest edifice in the city; construction of anything taller was banned until the latter part of the 19th century. Its most famous historical role was as seat of the Provisional Government in 1917. The Bolsheviks stormed it and arrested their opponents, thus carrying out their coup.

The **General Staff Building** rose later, after the government removed townspeople and their houses from the south side of the square. Carlo Rossi was commissioned for the project in 1819, and designed a complex system of buildings and courtyards in classical style, a contrast to the palace opposite. The massive triumphal arch at its center was the first monument to Russia's 1812 victory over Napoleon, during the reign of Alexander I. Fifteen years later,

Pushkin's Last Address

While you're in the Palace Square you may want to look in on one of the city's literary museums, the **Pushkin Apartment** at Moika, 12. Of the country's numerous sites dedicated to Russia's greatest poet, this one is concerned mainly with the last five months of his life.

Pushkin had long struggled against the tsar's desire to make him a court poet, and society's to bend even his private life to its strict rules. He was one of the first Russian intellectuals to seek to establish an autonomous life of independent thought and action. In a way, the duel was the tragic climax of this struggle. Advances made to his wife, Natalya Goncharova, by his brother-in-law, forced him to challenge George Dantes to a duel on January 27, 1837. He died of his wounds in this flat two days later.

Everything here, from the tone of the excursion to the arrangement of the furniture, betokens Pushkin's agony, his death, and the ensuing sorrow of his nearest and dearest. His bed, the chair where his wife sat beside him, the room where well-wishers paid their respects, and his last portrait all capture those terrible two days and render them a monument to human suffering.

Moika embankment looking toward Pushkin apartment

Europe's Great Palace Museum

The **Hermitage**, one of the world's largest museums, comprises six buildings – the Winter Palace, the Hermitage Theater, and four others constructed specifically for the museum. With its 3 million exhibits, the Hermitage is not to be taken lightly. Even with restoration and staffing problems, which have forced the closure of huge areas, it would take half a day just to walk round without looking at anything.

Founded in 1764 by Catherine the Great, this museum has none of the democratic beginnings of Peter's Kunstkammer. Only the Empress and her court could admire its treasures. Today, things are very different, with crowds, particularly tour groups, being at times unbearable. Fortunately for the art lover, excursions tend to favor the most palatial rooms, and it is easy to slip away to ones of greater interest for the canvasses that hang there. Even the galleries with Rembrandts and da Vincis are relatively less crowded, and visitors to the Impressionists on the third floor will find the multitudes there more discerning. The ancient Roman and Greek sections on the ground floor, impressive in their size and blending well with the classical interior, are almost ignored by the public. They provide, however, a gentle and subtle "back-door" introduction to the museum. In contrast to its dour sister in vastness, the Louvre, the Hermitage's architecture and interiors are so splendid that they claim an attention equal to that bestowed on the exhibits.

Hermitage staircase detail

Another architectural gem is the newly restored **Hermitage Theater**, the city's first stage and a favorite of Catherine the Great's cultural elite. With its columns, balustrades and statues in wall niches, it was both the brainchild and the ultimate dream of Italian architect Giacomo Quarenghi. The theater's perfect acoustics can be appreciated during performances by some of the city's premiere artistic groups.

a second appeared, the **Alexander Column**, designed by August Monferrand, hewn from a cliff and hauled by 2,500 men to its current site. The angel bearing a cross which surmounts it, symbolizing Peace, bears a portrait likeness to Alexander. The arch, the column, and the main entrance of the palace are in straight alignment, and the column serves to unite the ensemble.

From Palace Square walk west across to the gardens in front of the **Admiralty**, whose centerpiece is the yellow and white building with gilded spire crowned by a frigate that is the symbol of the city. The Admiralty was established as a fortified shipyard; this building was constructed in 1823 as the headquarters of the navy, by a

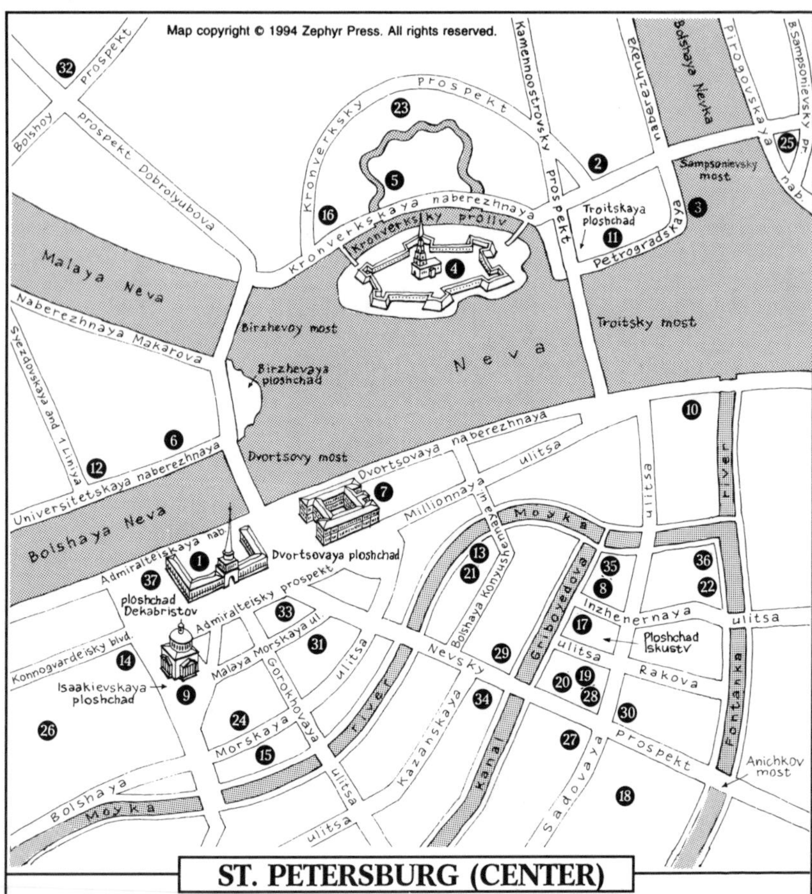

ST. PETERSBURG (CENTER)

Admiralteiskaya naberezhnaya
Адмиралтейская набережная

Admiralteisky prospekt
Адмиралтейский проспект

Anichkov Most
Аничков мост

Birzhevaya ploshchad
Биржевая площадь

Birzhevoy Most
Биржевой мост

Bolshaya Konyushennaya ulitsa
Большая Конюшенная улица

Bolshaya Morskaya ulitsa
Большая Морская улица

Bolshaya Neva River
Большая Нева

Bolshaya Nevka River
Большая Невка

Bolshoy prospekt
Большой проспект

Bolshoy Sampsonievsky prospekt
Большой Сампсониевский проспект

Ploshchad Dekabristov
Площадь Декабристов

Prospekt Dobrolyubova
Проспект Добролюбова

Dvortsovaya naberezhnaya
Дворцовая набережная

Dvortsovaya ploshchad
Дворцовая площадь
Dvortsovoy Most
Дворцовый мост
River Fontanka
Река Фонтанка
Gorokhovaya ulitsa
Гороховая улица
Kanal Griboyedova
Канал Грибоедова
Inzhenernaya ulitsa
Инженерная улица
Isaakievskaya ploshchad
Исаакиевская площадь
Ploshchad Iskusstv
Площадь Исскуств
Kamennoostrovsky prospekt
Каменоостровский проспект
Ulitsa Kazanskaya
Улица Казанская
Konnogardeisky bulvar
Конногвардейский бульвар
Kronverkskaya naberezhnaya
Кронверкская набережная
Kronverksky Proliv
Кронверкский пролив
Kronverksky prospekt
Кронверкский проспект
Naberezhnaya Makarova
Набережная Макарова
Malaya Morskaya ulitsa
Малая Морская улица
Malaya Neva River
Река Малая Нева
Millionnaya ulitsa
Миллионная улица
Moika River
Река Мойка
River Neva
Река Нева
Nevsky prospekt
Невский проспект
Petrogradskaya naberezhnaya
Петроградская набережная
Pirogovskaya naberezhnaya
Пироговская набережная
Ulitsa Rakova
Улица Ракова
Sadovaya ulitsa
Садовая улица
Sampsonievsky Most
Сампсониевский мост
Syezdovskaya Liniya
Съездовская линия
Troitskaya ploshchad
Троицкая площадь
Troitsky Most
Троицкий мост
Universitetskaya naberezhnaya
Университетская набережная

MAP KEY

1. **Admiralty**
   Адмиралтейство
2. **Ksheshinskaya Mansion**
   Усадьба Ксешинской
3. **Cruiser Aurora**
   Крейсер «Аврора»
4. **Peter and Paul Fortress**
   Петропавловская крепость
5. **Kronverk**
   Кронверк
6. **Kunstkammer**
   Кунсткамера
7. **Hermitage**
   Эрмитаж
8. **Russian Museum**
   Русский музей
9. **St. Isaac's Cathedral**
   Исаакиевский собор
10. **Peter the Great's Summer Palace**
    Летний Дворец
11. **Peter the Great's Cottage**
    Домик Петра Первого
12. **Menshikov Palace**
    Дворец Меньшикова
13. **Pushkin Apartment Museum**
    Дом-Музей Пушкина

Russian architect, A.D. Zakharov. The entrance is the ultimate symbol of Russian sea power, its main body and spire decorated with statues and bas-reliefs depicting, among other themes, Neptune surrendering his trident to Peter the Great. Turn 180°, putting the Admiralty at your back, and you will find yourself standing at a focal point of the city plan. From here you can look down three major streets – Nevsky prospekt to the left, Gorokhovaya ulitsa in the center, and Vosnesensky prospekt to the right. These three spokes are crossed by concentric streets, rivers, and canals. The natural landscape was thus incorporated and adapted to the pattern of the city.

While walking across the garden, notice the bust of a man with a camel

14. **Manezh**
    Манеж
15. **Artists' Union**
    Союз художников
16. **Zoo**
    Зоопарк
17. **Maly Opera and Ballet Theater**
    Малый Театр Оперы и Балета
18. **Pushkin Drama Theater**
    Драматический театр имени Пушкина
19. **Philharmonia Large Hall**
    Большой Зал Филармонии
20. **Philharmonia Small Hall**
    Малый зал филармонии
21. **Cappella**
    Капелла
22. **Circus**
    Цирк
23. **Russian American Theater**
24. **Astoria Hotel**
    Гостиница «Астория»
25. **St. Petersburg Hotel**
    Гостиница «Санкт Петербург»
26. **Central Post Office**
    Центральная почта
27. **Gostiny Dvor**
    Гостиный двор
28. **Passazh department store**
    Пассаж
29. **Dom Knigi Bookshop**
    Дом книги
30. **Tsentralny Food Store**
    Центральный гастроном
31. **Donon 24-Hour Shop**
32. **Holiday 24-Hour Shop**
33. **Aeroflot office**
    Кассы Аэрофлота
34. **Kazan Cathedral**
    Казанский собор
35. **Church of the Savior on Spilled Blood**
    Церковь Спаса-на-Крови
36. **Mikhailovsky Castle (Engineer's Castle)**
    Михайловский замок
37. **Peter the Great statue**
    Памятник Петру Первому

Decembrists' Square: Peter the Great statue, with Senate and Synod Building. Visits by wedding couples are a local tradition.

at its base. This is N.M. Przhevalsky (1839–88), an explorer of Asiatic Russia and Mongolia. Anything more than a casual glance should reveal a marked resemblance of this figure to "Papa Joe" Stalin.

When you cross the garden, with the Admiralty to your right, you'll find yourself on the **Decembrists' Square** *(Ploshchad Dekabristov)*, which is open to the Neva. In the center stands Falconet's **Statue of Peter the Great** (1768–80). The sculptor was invited to Petersburg by Empress Catherine for this special task, upon the recommendation of the philosopher Diderot. A masterpiece of sheer dynamism, it can only be fully appreciated by walking right round – each angle presents a different view, a different meaning, the Tsar calm or threatening, the horse striving forward into the unknown or stopping on the brink of the abyss. The snake under the horse's hooves symbolizes the Tsar's enemies. The statue and its ambiguous stances were immortalized by Pushkin in his long poem, *The Bronze Horseman*. The great aspirations of the Tsar, his striving for good, run up against the elements, in the form of a flood, and against the man in the street, whose representative is the civil servant Yevgeny, for whom the statue of Peter is a heartless bringer of death.

Among Pushkin's friends were several young officers who came to this square with their troops on December 24, 1825. In their attempt to change the course of Russian history and create a constitutional monarchy, they moved to prevent the **Senate** (situated in the building directly across the square) from swearing loyalty to the new Tsar, Nicholas I, who sent 3,000 troops to meet them. The Senate had already secretly taken their oath, and the building was empty when the insurrectionists arrived. The revolt was crushed, and the leaders hanged or exiled.

The side of the square opposite the

river is completed by **St. Isaac's Cathedral**, surmounted by an immense cupola whose dome often serves to orient the visitor lost in the confusing nearby back streets. Its observation deck provides the best view of the city: looking over the flat, skyscraperless cityscape, interspersed with expanses of water, it's not difficult to imagine the marshlands over which the city rose. Impressive statistics for the Cathedral are easy to come by: 43 types of stone and marble were used; 100kg of pure gold cover the dome; and the sanctuary can accommodate some 14,000 people. Equally astonishing is the sacrifice that went into creating it, not only from ordinary laborers, who included an army of serfs, but from its creators. St. Isaac's proved to be the death of August Monferrand, the architect who took 30 years to build it (1818–48). He died an unhappy man a month after its completion; Alexander II had refused to let him be buried there. Karl Bryullov, the artist who painted the main frescoes, caught a chill from which he never recovered while working inside the dome. Today St. Isaac's is a museum, and is used for services on major church holidays. Among other fineries, note the mosaic iconostasis with malachite columns and Orthodoxy's only stained glass window, depicting Christ shimmering mysteriously under gas light.

Klodt's Nicholas I statue and St. Isaac's Cathedral

St. Isaac's both links and separates Decembrists' Square and another one named for the cathedral. In the center is a **Statue of Nicholas I**, the same Tsar who quelled the Decembrists. Pyotr Klodt's Nicholas, although a bit pompous, is a graceful ornament, as well as a technical rarity: its entire

Petersburg Floods

If you leave Decembrists' Square, walking to the left of St. Isaac's Cathedral in the direction of its eponymous square, you will see a yellow and white classical building with a portico, and lions guarding the entrance. Pushkin's hero, Yevgeny, saved himself by climbing onto one of those lions during the terrible flood of 1824, an all too historical event. Floods are a constant threat hanging over the city. The worst two occurred in 1824, and exactly 100 years later. Plaques indicating the high-water marks of various floods can be found throughout the city. You can see one of them on a stele on the right hand side of the Sinyy bridge as you face the Mariinsky Palace.

weight rests upon just two points.

Opposite St. Isaac's stands the **Mariinsky Palace**. Originally built by Nicholas Schtakenschneider in 1844 for Nikolay's daughter Maria, it took on a political significance after her death, housing the Tsarist Council, and now the city council. You may not notice at first a peculiar feature of this square. Its greater part comprises the **Sinyy Bridge**, the city's widest, which spans the Moika River.

The second, optional, part of this walk provides a contrast to the grandeur of Catherine's and Nicholas' cities. With St. Isaac's behind you, cross the Sinyy Bridge, and turn to the right along the Moika River. You immediately enter into calmer surroundings. Here lived some of the participants in the dramatic events that occurred nearby. No. 72 Moika Embankment is the former house of the Decembrist leader Ryleyev. Here the plotters held their last meeting, on the 13th of December, and a day later Ryleyev was arrested.

No. 86 is Monferrand's house, where the great architect lived as he supervised the building of his masterpiece. It was built with materials left over from the construction of St. Isaac's.

The most interesting house in this part of town is the **Yusupov Palace** at No. 94, an early Classical building owned in pre-Revolutionary years by the eccentric and conspicuously wealthy Prince Felix Yusupov, rumored to have a fortune the size of the Tsar's. Here on 17 December 1916 Yusupov and friends killed the Tsar's favorite, the mystic monk Grigory Rasputin, in what proved to be a last-ditch attempt to save the monarchy. Their task was not an easy one, as Rasputin was an immensely strong man. After poisoning and shooting their adversary to little effect, they finally succeeded by tying him in a sack and heaving him into the river. Today guided tours take visitors round the luxurious white-columned hall and the private theater upstairs. The palace also houses an exhibition on Rasputin, and chamber music concerts are frequently performed there.

Continue along the Moika until it crosses the Kryukov Canal. The triangular island beyond the junction on your right is **New Holland**, with a timber warehouse, canal system and shipyard dating from the 1760's. Tourists are not allowed inside – the premises are in use as a factory making military uniforms. But the massive entrance arch, flanked by four huge Tuscan columns, is worth the walk in itself. Not frequented by the crowds, New Holland provides an opportunity for contemplation.

Retracing your steps to the Moika bridge, turn right toward the gleaming church in the distance. This is Ulitsa Glinki, named after Mikhail Glinka (1804–57), the composer of *Life for the Tsar*, and it will bring you shortly to **Teatralnaya ploshchad**, where a monument to him stands. This square for most of the city's history has been the center of its musical life, and indeed the country's. At the end of the 18th century the Bolshoi Theater was built there, and was for some time the largest in Europe. In the 1880's, it was replaced by the **Conservatoire**, Russia's first musical institute. Among the first graduates was Pyotr Tchaikovsky.

On the other side of Glinki, the **Mariinsky Theater**, circular in shape, was built in 1860 in honor of another Maria, the wife of Alexander II. Now better known as the Kirov Ballet Theater (although recently returned to its original name), the Mariinsky's reputation spread throughout the world by the turn of the century, with the fame of the great dancers Anna Pavlova, Tamara Karsavina, and Mikhail Fokine who performed there.

Left: ***Tamara Karsavina and Mikhail Fokine dancing Stravinsky's*** **Firebird. Right:** ***St. Nicholas Cathedral***

Another name associated with the theater is opera singer Fyodor Chaliapin; an exhibition is devoted to his life and work.

The final goal of this walk lies just beyond the end of the street, the baroque **Cathedral of St. Nicholas**, which dates from the middle of the 18th century. Its five domes and central body are lavishly decorated with statuettes and columns. Nicholas is the patron of sailors, who came there to worship. Note the anchors atop each entrance gate, and another unusual feature – the cathedral is surrounded on all sides by water. It is actually two churches on separate levels. St. Nicholas was one of the few Petersburg churches not closed during the Soviet era.

Turn left along Ulitsa Sadovaya to the metro at Sennaya Ploshchad.

WALK 3: NEVSKY PROSPEKT AND THE MURDERED TSARS

This walk begins on the city's main thoroughfare, the crowded, noisy and tourist-ridden **Nevsky prospekt**. (Take the metro to Nevsky Prospekt/ Gostiny Dvor station.) Anyone visiting the city for the first time could be forgiven for walking up and down it incessantly – the chances of getting lost if you stray are great. But this is not the way to see St. Petersburg, and true lovers of the city try for the most part to avoid Nevsky. Nonetheless, parts of it are historically interesting, and should be visited.

Nevsky prospekt, or the Great Perspective Road as it was first called, was laid out in the early 18th century to provide a direct route between the Admiralty and Ligovsky prospekt, the road to Novgorod. It soon became the city's main street, with churches, palaces and markets springing up all the way from the Neva to the Fontanka River, then the edge of town.

You emerge from the metro opposite **Our Lady of Kazan Cathedral**, completed in 1811 by architect Andrey Voronikhin. The church proper is deceptively small, all but the dome effectively hidden behind a semicircular Corinthian colonnade. In fact, the cathedral doesn't face onto the avenue; instead its façade looks east toward the Admiralty. This peculiar orientation was the product of clashing requirements: Tsar Paul I wanted *Kazansky sobor* modeled after St. Peter's in Rome, while the church authorities required that the altar face east; practice also dictated that the main entrance be located opposite the altar. Furthermore, Voronikhin wished to set up a dramatic relationship between the cathedral and Nevsky prospekt, in keeping with the pattern established in the siting of other major city landmarks. His solution was to add the colonnade, and to open it on the north side to Nevsky as you see it.

Our Lady of Kazan Cathedral, view from Nevsky prospekt and bridge over Griboyedov canal

Opposite is a small square with ornamental railings, also designed by Voronikhin. The cathedral itself, converted in Soviet years into a museum of atheism, now houses an exhibition on Orthodox Christianity, which enhances the splendor of its marble floor, red granite columns and Borovikovsky paintings. After the war with Napoleon, the cathedral became a repository for trophies from the victory, as well as the resting place of Field Marshall Mikhail Kutuzov, who expelled French troops from Russia. On the square in front of its colonnade you can see his statue, as well as a statue of one of his less successful predecessors in command, Barklay DeTolley. This square is again a popular place for demonstrations, just as it was in tsarist days. At the end of this walk, you will find yourself back at this very spot, and your landmark will be the globe that crowns Dom Knigi, the art nouveau building opposite the cathedral.

Walk down Nevsky, with the Admiralty spire at your back. On the left are two early classical churches, built for communities from far-flung regions of the empire. The first is **St. Catherine's Catholic Church**, where the last Polish king, Stanislaw, lies buried. Cowed by Catherine the Great in 1795, he lived out his life in St. Petersburg. The second is Felten's **Armenian Church**.

You are now entering the commercial heart of St. Petersburg. On the right is the huge early Classical

Gostiny Dvor, once a guest house for visiting merchants but now a vast shopping complex. The *dvor* is perhaps most interesting today for the crowds outside it, including nationalist booksellers, giving way to seedy mafia types near the metro, and in turn to buskers in and around the underpass.

Next on the right after Gostiny Dvor is the **Saltykov-Shchedrin Public Library**, the country's second largest after Moscow's Lenin Library. Works include the *Ostromir Lectionary*, two 1,000 volume Chinese encyclopedias, manuscripts by Immanuel Kant and the smallest book in the world – a collection of Krylov's Fables the size of a postage stamp. Proceed past the library, and you will see that its façade opens onto a garden, which is called Ostrovsky Square. This part of the building, designed by Carlo Rossi, is topped by a statue of Minerva. You can see another Russian Minerva, Catherine II, in the middle of the square, which is better known to Petersburgers as "Catherine's Garden." She stands on a pedestal, high above her principal courtiers, some of whom were also her lovers. The garden is bordered opposite Nevsky by the gracious façade of the **Pushkin Drama Theater**, built as a royal theater. It is surmounted by another classical god, Apollo on his chariot, the patron of muses.

Just past Ostrovsky Square, as you continue along Nevsky, is a garden adjacent to the Anichkov Palace, built for Empress Elizabeth's favorite, Count Razumovsky. In order to see its marvelous façade, you'll have to enter the grounds by the gate on Nevsky. In the 18th century, Petersburg's rivers were more important arteries than its streets. So the façade of this palace, as well as those of many others, looks toward water. Although Razumovsky lived there for a few years, and it later became a minor royal residence, it is named after Lieutenant-Colonel

Fontanka River and Anichkov Bridge, with the Beloselsky-Belozersky Palace* (right), *from the Anichkov Palace. Artist: V.I. Serdyukov

Anna Akhmatova: Muse of Petersburg

In a rear wing of Fontanny Dom, which forms part of a quiet courtyard park, is the **Anna Akhmatova Museum**. Here the great poet lived during most of the years from 1920–52, and endured most of the tragic events of her long life. Her first husband, poet Nikolay Gumilyov, was accused of conspiring against the regime and was shot in 1921; her son Lev and third husband Nikolay Punin were arrested and incarcerated in the 1930's; and her soul-mate, the poet Osip Mandelstam, died at the end of the same decade in a labor camp. This was also the time of her greatest persecution by the authorities. Here she composed *Requiem*, her supreme elegy to the victims of Stalin's reign of terror, but dared not write it down – she committed the 200-line poem to memory, as did a few of her trusted friends, until the arrival of a more open era long after the Second World War.

"Into what dirt they've trampled me!" she said toward the end of her life. "I've had everything – poverty, prison lines, fear, poems remembered only by heart, and burnt poems. And humiliation and grief." Nevertheless, her experiences did not cow her. She recognized at an early age that she was marked for both great fame and suffering.

This museum could easily have become a slavish history of the poet, or simply a collection of her personal effects, but it is neither. It expresses the full power of her works and the stark simplicity of her material life, while bringing her contemporaries, such as Mandelstam and Pasternak, to life as well.

(Note that entrance to the Museum may not be possible from the Fontanka embankment. Another entrance is off Liteiny prospekt, one block down Nevsky after crossing the Anichkov Bridge. Look for a plaque next to a courtyard entrance, then follow the signs.)

Anna Akhmatova, 1921
India ink on paper
by Yuri Annenkov

We met for the last time
On the embankment, where we
had always met.
The Neva was high
And they were afraid the city would flood.

He spoke of the summer, and he also said
That for a woman to be a poet
was – absurd.
I can still see the tsar's tall palace
And the Peter and Paul fortress! –

Because the air was not ours at all,
But like a gift from God – so miraculous.
And at that moment was given to me
The latest of all my mad songs.

– Translated by Judith Hemschemeyer

Anichkov, the military engineer whose team was stationed on the site while they were building the city's first river bridge, across the Fontanka, a few meters ahead. A later bridge on the same spot, the city's most famous and most central, is also named after Anichkov. It was built by Alexander Bryullov, brother of the victim of St. Isaac's, and its four statues of a man and horse by Pyotr Klodt were added later. The theme of this composition, one central to the origins of the city, is Man taming Nature.

Turn left along the far side of the **Fontanka**, a small tributary of the Neva, flowing out from the delta and back into it again at the mouth. It is named for the fountains which once graced the nearby Summer Garden, and which were fed by the river waters. The Fontanka became a very stately river, crossed by ornamental bridges and with numerous palaces constructed on its banks. One of these is **Fontanny Dom** (Fountain House), built in the mid-18th century for the wealthy Sheremetyev family.

To the right of the bridge ahead, tucked away on Mokhovaya Ulitsa, is the unusual **Church of St. Simeon and Anna**, built by Zemtsov in 1734. With its octagonal drum and cupola, both made of wood, and its tall belfry, it combines Petrine and ancient Russian styles.

Cross the bridge toward the building of the Circus and cut through until you reach an avenue flanked by outbuildings of the **Mikhailovsky Castle**. This is the **Klenovaya Alleya** (Maple Avenue). The lower part is now occupied by a large souvenir market, where, if you enter, you will have to spend some time in order to locate worthwhile items among the generally poor quality *matryoshka* dolls and paintings on offer. Turn right toward the castle. Rastrelli's statue of Peter the Great possesses none of the fluid effect of Falconet's statue, but celebrates the triumphant warrior. In the bas-reliefs below, he pursues his Swedish enemies. The inscription on its pedestal reads, "From grandfather to grandson," Paul's contribution to the memory of his grandfather. The monument was created earlier, not long after Peter's death, and Paul had it removed from storage and placed before his castle.

Mikhailovsky Castle, view from the Summer Garden

Paul hated his mother, Catherine, and sought to do everything in a contrary fashion. This monument became Paul's argument against Falconet's Bronze Horseman, commissioned by Catherine, just as the castle in front of you was opposed to her Winter Palace. Because his father, Peter III, had been murdered, Paul erected for himself a real fortress. The cold battle regalia on either side of the entrance, the masonic symbols and the claustrophobic octagonal courtyard leave the visitor feeling chilled and oppressed. The Mikhailovsky Castle was completed in 1800 by the architects Vassily Bazhenov and Vincenzo Brenna in the waning days of Paul's reign as he tried to shut himself away from court conspiracy. It was bordered on two sides, as it is today, by the Moika and Fontanka Rivers; Paul had two canals (since filled in) dug to complete his protective encirclement. But all his measures failed: after just 40 days in residence he was strangled by his closest courtiers, and his ghost is said to wander regularly hereabouts. The palace later became an engineering college (hence the new name, "Engineers' Castle"), and Dostoyevsky, among others, studied there. The influence it had on his work is not difficult to imagine.

Follow Sadovaya ulitsa back toward Nevsky and take the first right turn onto Inzhenernaya ulitsa. Passing the **Ethnography Museum** on the right you reach **Ploshchad Iskusstv** (Art Square), brainchild of the great Italian Carlo Rossi. He built its centerpiece, the **Mikhailovsky Palace** (now the Russian Museum), for Grand Duke Mikhail, brother of Tsar Nicholas I. The other buildings came later, their architects conforming perfectly to Rossi's grand classical plan.

It is now time to gaze in a counterclockwise direction, beginning with the building to the left of the Russian Museum, Alexander Bryullov's rather modest **Maly Theater**, which is a good place to come for opera and ballet. Through the archway to the left and into a courtyard is the site of a unique café, the **Brodyachaya Sobaka** (Stray Dog). This was the center of bohemian and artistic life in St. Petersburg in the years leading up to the First World War. Artists and writers gathered to watch and participate in a special kind of improvised cabaret. Anna Akhmatova (1889–1966) was one of the stars of this world. It was at the Stray Dog that she met Natan Altman, who painted one of the most famous portraits of the poet; it now hangs across the square in the Russian Museum. Nothing remains now of the café; only a few images of dogs painted on a wall in the next archway hint at its existence.

Next comes the opening of Mikhailovsky Street, connecting to Nevsky prospekt; to the right you can see the façade of the Grand Hotel Europe. On the opposite corner is the former Noblemen's Assembly, which was frequently used for concerts because of its excellent acoustics. It is now the **Shostakovich Philharmonia**. In 1942, during the darkest days of the siege of Leningrad, Dmitry Shostakovich's Seventh ("Leningradian") Symphony was performed there and broadcast live throughout the country, a dramatic testament to the city's courage and resolve.

Rather than complete the circle, turn now to its center. The statue of **Pushkin** in the garden is the most recent addition to Art Square's composition, dating from the 1950's. Its siting is perfect, as you are surrounded there by the Petersburg of Pushkin's time.

Cross the garden, from statue to museum, to return to Inzhenernaya ulitsa, which leads to the Griboyedov Canal. Turn right to face the large Church of the Resurrection, better known as **Our Savior on the Spilled Blood**. The name arises from the spot on which it was built, site of the assassination of Tsar Alexander II (1 March 1881). In another irony of Russian history, an intelligent, reform-minded ruler who emancipated the serfs was blown apart by a terrorist bomb, while his successor, the reactionary Alexander III, died peacefully in his bed. The church, begun in 1883, seems to demonstrate a classic gambit by authorities both Tsarist and communist – effectively to kill the

A Banquet of Russian Art

The Mikhailovsky Palace shelters the oldest and largest public collection of Russian art, the **Russian Museum**. Of the 300,000 works kept here, the fraction on display provides unforgettable insights into the national consciousness.

Begin with the icons on the first floor, where the first Byzantine-style works give way to the more original and expressive paintings of Russian masters like Rublyov and Daniil. The museum allows a good opportunity to compare the various icon-painting schools, including those of Pskov and Novgorod. In gallery 5 the first secular painting begins with the prim portraiture of the 18th century. Note particularly the severe metal sculpture of the arrogant Tsarina Anna Ioannovna with a Moorish boy by Carlo Rastrelli and the almost comical portrayals of Peter III and his son Paul, by Antropov and Shubin respectively. The first floor ends with the seascapes of Aivazovsky and Bryullov's famous *Last Day of Pompeii*, in company with other canvasses of epic subject and prodigious proportions.

The ground floor and Benois wing sections are impossible to describe in full. The museum's collection of late 19th century and early 20th century works is incomparable – Vassily Polenov's dark, spiritual paintings, whole rooms full of the lively realism of Ilya Repin, the Russian heroism of Vasnetsov, Vrubel and Nesterov, and Valentin Serov's thoughtful, brightly dressed young ladies. The Russian Museum, like the Hermitage, must not be missed on any account.

Art Square, with Pushkin statue and the Russian Museum

Although once very conservative in its exhibitions, the Museum has in recent years organized several shows of 20th century and avant-garde art. They now accept into their collection previously rejected independent art.

memory of such deviant or inconvenient personalities as the poet Vladimir Mayakovsky and the Leningrad party leader Sergey Kirov, whom Stalin is suspected of murdering in 1934, by means of paying fulsome tribute in the naming of public buildings and other places after their deaths. This is indeed a lavish tribute to the assassinated Tsar – an extraordinary feast of patterned and colored domes echoing St. Basil's in Moscow, and reviving forms of 17th century Moscow and Yaroslavl architecture.

The final leg of this walk, back down the right side of the canal to

Nevsky, brings us to St. Petersburg at the turn of the century, the city of bankers and industrialists. Two buildings stand out, both designed by architect Pavel Syuzor. At #13 is the **Mutual Credit Society**, a masterpiece of eclecticism lavishly decorated with statuettes. Further down, opposite the Kazan Cathedral, is the art nouveau **Dom Knigi** (House of Books). Formerly owned by the Singer Sewing Machine Co., this is one of the landmarks of Nevsky, with its glass tower and globe.

WALK 4: SUMMER PALACE TO SMOLNY

(Directions: Go to metro Nevsky Prospekt/Gostiny Dvor, which exits at the intersection of Nevsky prospekt and Sadovaya ulitsa.) With the Admiralty Spire visible on your left at the end of Nevsky, and Gostiny Dvor department store at your back, cross Nevsky and walk along Sadovaya until you reach the Neva embankment. Along the way, you will pass the Engineers' Castle, seen earlier in this walk. Sadovaya ulitsa leads to the **Field of Mars**. A former parade ground, it was converted into a monument to the fallen of the February Revolution of 1917. Past military glory is commemorated by the monument to 18th century General A.V. Suvorov, who is depicted as Mars, the Roman god of war.

Walk past the statue and out onto the Neva Embankment, turning to the right. You will cross a small stone bridge which spans the Swans' Canal. From the embankment, enter the **Summer Garden**, begun in 1704 as Peter's attempt to imitate, or even surpass, the splendor of Versailles. In this he may not have succeeded, but the overall effect is one of great serenity and restraint. The quiet and orderly avenues are lined with sculptures of Roman gods and goddesses, together with allegorical statues, even one of maverick Swedish Queen Christina, who achieved a kind of notoriety by snubbing both the Catholic and Lutheran hierarchies. Here as elsewhere in and around the city, the statuary was buried during World War II to protect it from bombing. The Dutch-styled **Summer Palace**, mentioned earlier in Walk #1, is open as a museum. The decor, preserved from Petrine times, is tasteful, with green and red brocade walls, a bedroom in velvet and a Dutch tiled kitchen. A weather device made by the Dresden firm of Dinglinger hangs in room 5, showing time, wind direction and force. Its indoor water pipes were the city's first.

Summer Garden

Walk down through the Summer

Garden and exit at the end, turning left and crossing the Panteleimon Bridge to enter Ulitsa Pestelya. The little baroque **St. Panteleimon's Church** just ahead was built in honor of Russia's first naval victories over Sweden. It is all that remains of the **Partikulyarny Wharf**, an area where townspeople came to build their own ships in the early 18th century. Later it was replaced by salt and wine warehouses, earning itself the name **Solyanoy Gorodok**, "Salt Quarter."

In the nearby Solyanoy pereulok is the **Mukhin School of Art and Design**. Built with the funds of Baron Stieglitz in 1881, it now fills two buildings including the glass-roofed former exhibition center behind. The students and staff don't seem to mind visitors – you can walk through the magnificent halls, admire the Byzantine-style ceilings and watch new talent at work in the galleries of the huge exhibition hall.

Returning to Ulitsa Pestelya, the seemingly modest archway straight ahead formerly had a sinister significance. In Tsarist days this was the back entrance of the notorious **Third Department** (Fontanka, 14), described by Alexander Herzen as the "Central Office of Spies." Famous visitors included Fyodor Dostoyevsky, detained here in 1848 for participation in an illegal club, and Lenin, who was refused a foreign passport in 1891. The archway was the "staff" entrance – they crept in incognito.

Transfiguration Cathedral

Turn left down Pestelya, and you will see that it runs between two churches, both built in honor of Russian military victories. The **Cathedral of the Transfiguration**, now ahead of you, loudly proclaims the defeat of Russia's traditional 18th century enemy, Turkey, by means of upturned cannon barrels incorporated into the wrought iron fence that surrounds it. En route, you pass the **Dom Muruzi**, a large apartment block that amazed Petersburgers of the end of the 19th century with its lush, oriental ornamentation. Later, the luxurious residences were divided into cramped communal flats. In one of them, Nobel Prize winning poet Joseph Brodsky spent his childhood and early adult years, an experience memorably described in his essay, "A Room and a Half." Spirited attempts by fans of the poet to proclaim this fact are regularly scrubbed off the wall.

Leave the cathedral square to the left and turn right onto Ulitsa Saltykova-Shchedrina. Cross Prospekt Chernyshevskovo and continue until you reach the **Tauride Garden**, on your left. This small landscape garden, designed by Ivan Starov in 1783, was once regarded as one of the finest in Europe. Now a children's park, and still quite lovely, it is nevertheless threatened by over-use and lack of funding. Enter the park at the gate and proceeed diagonally toward a large duck pond; you'll see a building with a tall glass roof on the other side. This is the **Tauride Palace**, one of the city's

Tauride Palace from the Gardens

finest examples of strict Classicism, the style prevalent during the reign of Catherine the Great. The palace was a gift from the empress to her favorite, Grigory Potemkin. It, too, was a celebration of the victory against the Turks; Potemkin had been made Prince of Tauride in honor of his conquest of the Crimea (*Tauris* or *Tavriya*) in 1788. The palace has an interesting history. Tsar Paul converted it to stables to show his contempt for his mother's lover, and during much of the 19th century it was in disuse. In 1906 it was taken over by the State Duma, and ever since then jealous politicians have hidden its luxurious interiors from public view. In 1917 the Tauride became the epitome of dual power in Russia, as both the Provisional Government and the Petrograd Workers' and Peasants' Soviet worked under the same roof. Until recently a Higher Party School, it now houses the Interparliamentary Assembly of the Commonwealth of Independent States (IACIS), a body with no obvious powers or purpose.

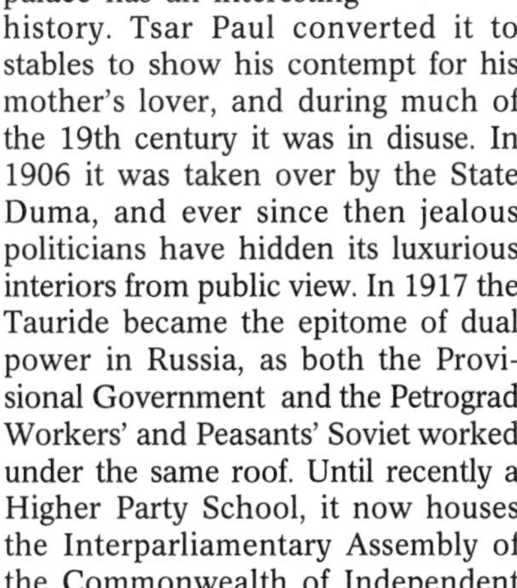

Now, turn to the right down Ulitsa Voinova, and behold the gleaming **Smolny Convent**, Rastrelli's fairy-tale baroque masterpiece. But first on the left you will come upon a much earlier building, the Petrine **Kikin's Chambers** (Ulitsa Stavropolskaya, 9), probably the only building in St. Petersburg to have benefited from World War II. A.V. Kikin, the impetuous boyar who owned it, was a court advisor and in charge of the *Smolny Dvor* (tar yard, used in ship construction and repair) which was later replaced by the con-

Smolny Convent

vent. An opponent of Peter's reforms, Kikin joined forces in 1718 with the Tsar's son Alexey to overthrow him, and was subsequently put to death. After temporarily housing the Kunstkammer, it gradually lost its original appearance in the course of successive modifications. Nazi bombing revealed some of the 18th century facade, and restorers were able to reconstruct it.

The Convent was commissioned by Empress Elizabeth, and Rastrelli, who is considered its principal architect, began work in 1748. The complex is dazzling in its unity. The basic plan is rectangular, with chapels situated at the corners of the wall surrounding the central **cathedral**. The ensemble's airy colors and patterns spread from the cathedral to the smaller buildings, and all the way round the courtyard at the back. (As you circle the cathedral, look up and your gaze will meet the astonished eyes of cherubs peeping from the tops of upper windows.)

The interior of the cathedral is now white, its paintings gone, but the effect upon entry is nonetheless dramatic. Unfortunately, the floor is partly taken up by a rather out-of-place Gzhel porcelain exhibition. The best time to come here is the evening, when its faultless acoustics can be heard during frequent choral concerts.

Smolny Convent was never used for its intended purpose, and was soon converted into the first school for the daughters of noble families. Later, a further building was added. **Smolny Institute** (1806–08) stands to the right, down a long driveway. Giacomo Quarenghi built it in high classical style, with a typical long façade and eight-columned portico. Its greatest historical moment arrived in 1917, when the Workers' Soviet (assembly) transferred its headquarters there from the Tauride. Two months later,

Smolny Institute

the **October Revolution** was planned and carried out from within these walls by Leon Trotsky and other Bolsheviks, who outmaneuvered their erstwhile allies in the Soviet, the Mensheviks and the Social Revolutionaries. Smolny was the seat of Soviet power until March 1918, when the government was transferred to Moscow. Now the building is the St. Petersburg mayor's office, and though the Communist Party is no more, a famous statue of a gesturing Lenin stands on a high pedestal before the building's portico, and the 1920's colonnades at the entrance to the drive still proclaim, "Workers of the World, Unite!"

From here you can cross the square and walk to Ploshchad Vosstaniya/ Mayakovskaya metro via Suvorovsky prospekt, some 15 blocks (2 km) distant. As an alternative to this lengthy walk, go one block on Suvorovsky instead, to its intersection with Tulskaya ulitsa and board the #7 trolleybus, travelling in the same direction you have been walking, that of Nevsky prospekt and the metro.

Once you have reached metro Ploshchad Vosstaniya you can, if you wish, add a final excursion. Cross Nevsky and board the #1, 14, 16, or 22 trolleybus, riding along Old Nevsky prospekt as far as Ploshchad Alexandra Nevskovo. Rising behind this square is another marriage of Baroque and Classicism, the **Alexandro-Nevskaya Lavra**, a monastery of Russia's highest category. Commissioned in 1710 to mark the canonization of Novgorod's hero, Prince Alexander Nevsky, famous for his victories over the Swedes and the German knights, it brought together the varied talents of Petrine builder Domenico Trezzini (who designed the monastery's **Annunciation Cathedral**), the Tauride's Ivan Starov (the **Trinity Cathedral**) and baroque specialist Mikhail Rastorguyev (the **Metropolitan's residence**).

But the *lavra* is most famous for its necropoles, which flank the main entrance path. To the left the **Lazarevskoye Cemetery**, founded in 1716, is principally a burial place of the capital's nobility, but also includes the graves of architects such as Voronikhin, Rossi and Quarenghi, and of the great scientist and humanist Mikhail Lomonosov. Opposite, in the **Tikhvinskoye Cemetery**, or **Artists' Necropolis**, repose Russia's greatest 19th century composers, including Tchaikovsky, Glinka, and Rimsky-Korsakov, as well as novelist Fyodor Dostoyevsky. (The #1 trolleybus will take you back along the entire length of Old Nevsky and Nevsky prospekts.)

Memorial to prima ballerina Vera Kommizharshevskya

WALK 5: PETROGRAD SIDE

This walk through turn-of-the-century Petersburg begins at the cruiser ***Aurora***, anchored in the Bolshaya Nevka. (Directions: Take the metro to Gorkovskaya station; walk south a few hundred meters to the Bolshaya Neva River, then left [east] along the Petrovskaya Embankment, passing Peter's log cabin [Walk #1], until you reach the juncture of the Bolshaya Neva and the Bolshaya Nevka.)

The *Aurora* achieved fame during the Revolution, firing a symbolic shot at the Winter Palace to signal its storming by the Bolsheviks. It also saw real action, most notably in 1904, shortly after its launching, during the disastrous defeat of the Russian fleet by the Japanese at Tsushima Strait,

Cruiser Aurora

and continued in service throughout the Civil War and World War II. The ship is now a free exhibition, recently deideologized and presenting a history of the cruiser from its launching to the raising of the St. Andrew's flag on its mast in 1992.

On the shore adjoining the *Aurora* stands the **Nakhimov Naval Institute**, built in a perfect imitation of Petrine Baroque style in 1909–11. Follow the Bolshaya Nevka as far as the first bridge. Turn left onto Kuybysheva ulitsa to the **Kshesinskaya Mansion**, an asymmetrical house with a granite foundation and walls of light-colored tile, one of the most distinct examples of Art Nouveau in Petersburg. It was built by Alexander Gogen in 1904 for Tsar Nicholas II's mistress, the ballerina Matilda Kshesinskaya, who danced at the Mariinsky Theater. Pay attention to the intricate ironworking of the gates and fence.

Next door is an early 20th century

On Exhibit: History in the Making

Abandoned by its owner in 1917, the Kshesinskaya Mansion then became an early headquarters of the Bolsheviks, and subsequently the Leningrad Museum of the Revolution. Now, in post-Communist St. Petersburg, its exhibitions, tracing many ideological crosscurrents, provide fascinating insights into the past as well as into today's situation.

The ground floor is occupied by a Museum of Political Parties, which traces their development from the days of the Tsarist Duma to the Revolution, then resumes with Perestroika and continues with today's variegated political spectrum, from the anarchists to extreme rightists like the Pamyat society.

The upper floors, almost bereft of visitors, remain frozen in time, drenched in Red regalia and heroism. One room is "Lenin's Study," containing a replica of the desk where he worked. The curious can ask to be shown another room, generally closed to visitors. This too is deeply Red, but in one corner a surprise is in store – a display about the abortive coup of August 1991!

But the greatest draw for the student of post-Communist psychology may be the newly opened, privately operated wax museum, dubbed the Museum of Political Terror. During guided tours through a display of 29 wax figures, visitors will ask themselves, Why is the Russian experience so tragic? The first room displays some of building of a very different kind. The city's main **Mosque** is easily identified by of its two tall minarets. It was built in 1912 by a Russian, Stepan Krichinsky, and modelled after Tamerlane's mausoleum in Samarkand.

Walking past the Gorkovskaya metro and up Kamennoostrovsky (formerly Kirovsky) prospekt, with the Neva at your back, you are soon in quite a different city. Indeed, you could be forgiven for doubting that you are still in St. Petersburg. With its absence of grand palaces, canals and ornamental gardens, and its abundance of stately town houses in Neo-Classical and Art Nouveau style, interspersed with courtyards and little squares, this district may even suggest that other great art nouveau city, Gaudí's Barcelona – albeit a restrained, northern version. From its conception in the 1890's, Kamennoostrovsky was the home of the creative intelligentsia.

This street pleases the eye virtually from beginning to end. First on the right is the **Lidval House**, with interesting animal bas-reliefs. A few hundred meters on, **Ploshchad Mira** (not to be confused with the now renamed Sennaya Ploshchad on the other side of the Neva) is a pretty art nouveau ensemble, an octagon surrounded by graceful towers, spires and cupolas.

Compare this with the neo-gothic grandeur of A.Ye. Belogrud's **Ploshchad Lva Tolstovo**, to your right at the intersection with Bolshoy prospekt. Here the first part of the walk ends. You can re-board the metro here at Petrogradskaya station.

Otherwise, the second half of the tour continues straight on toward the northern end of the island. As you proceed, you should be aware that you are in the Neva delta, crossing a series of large islands. After a few more blocks, you will cross a bridge over the Karpovka river onto Aptekarsky Island, the "Island of Medicinal Gardens," founded in the early days of the city. These were transformed gradually

Europe's greatest thinkers pondering the problem – figures as varied as Marx, Dostoyevsky and Sakharov, the latter looking particularly strained in thought, his head bent painfully over the table. The emphasis then shifts to political casualties – the Decembrists, the Tsarist reformer Stolypin, and Nicholas II before their deaths, and ends with recent leaders, from Lenin to Yeltsin. Groups of schoolchildren may be forgiven for becoming confused here; the lively philosophizing of the guides is a lot more difficult for young minds to follow than traditional Marxist spoon-feeding. This is a good place to visit in the company of an opinionated Russian acquaintance!

"Literacy Paves the Way to Communism" (poster)

Ploshchad Lva Tolstovo

into a botanical garden, a calm and serene spot. If you like, you can reach it by turning right along Karpovka naberezhnaya. Returning to Kamennoostrovsky prospekt, you can continue to walk (although less interesting, the early 20th century theme continues), or board any trolleybus across the Malaya Nevka river to **Kamenny ostrov** (Stone Island).

Originally the estate of Peter the Great's Chancellor, Gavriil Golovkin, Kamenny ostrov became in the early 19th century a site for hunting lodges and mansions, a small-scale alternative to the vast estates being built at that time south of the city. After 1917 it was renamed Worker's Island, and trumpeted as a great new health and recreation resort for the working man. The reality, however, was rather different. Much of the island was sealed off with high fences and barbed wire as the country's new bosses moved in to take their plots of land and build their dachas. It remains today a weekend haunt for the city's religious and political elite.

On the eastern tip of the island, the **Stone Island Palace** was built in 1776–84 by Quarenghi and Felten for the future Tsar Paul. The hand of Paul can be sensed almost immediately, at the entrance to the palace from the road. Here stands Felten's eccentric little neogothic **Church of John the Baptist**, complete with Masonic symbols. Inside the gates are another characteristic feature, the remains of a horse cemetery. Just two gravestones are left, dedicated to Paul's favorite steeds. The palace (now a sanatorium) seems neglected and forlorn, despite the presence of holiday-makers and proximity to civilization in general.

Turn back to the larger, western part of the island, crossing Kamennoostrovsky prospekt, and follow the embankment of the Malaya Nevka river. At No. 11 is the **Dolgorukov** (or **Oldenburgsky**) **Dacha,** one of several fine examples of classical wooden architecture on the island, a cube with columned porticos on each side and a wide, flat dome on top. It even boasts a pair of sphinxes on the waterfront. The dacha was reconstructed after a fire to the original designs from the ground up. It is worth going inland to explore the island and its numerous interesting buildings. At No. 25 (the address is on the embankment but the house inland) is the dacha of Vladimir Bekhterev, the psychoneurologist who diagnosed Stalin as insane. Walk down the Naberezhnaya Reki Krestovki beside the island's central waterway. At the beginning stand the remains of an oak planted by Peter the Great in 1714. Here, the early 19th century mansions of the royal court give way to houses in Art Nouveau style, such as the

Kamenny Ostrov dacha

fairytale wooden castle now occupied by the **Danish Consulate**, built by R.F. Meltzer in 1901–04 (Polevaya Alleya, 8).

Visit also the north embankment. The fine neo-classical palace at #6, with its hint of Art Nouveau, was **Senator Polovtsov's Dacha,** built on the site of a house where Alexander Pushkin spent his last summer. One of the city's last prerevolutionary constructions, it soon found itself with new owners, the Union of Metalworkers.

We've saved the best for last. The **Stone Island Theater**, an attractive early 19th century classical building with triangular pediment and eight-column portico on the far side of the island, does not at first sight appear out of the ordinary. What is peculiar is that it is made entirely of wood, and was built in just 40 days. Though flammable (it was seriously damaged by fire in the middle of the last century), wood has its advantages. During summer performances, the actors removed the back wall and used the park behind as their set.

Cross the bridge ahead onto **Yelagin Island**, noting the façade of the **Yelagin Palace** on your right. This island was once a summer residence of the tsars; in 1917, it really was given to the people. Now the Kirov Culture and Recreation Park, it tends to get noisy and crowded in summer. In 1818–22 Carlo Rossi built the palace complex here. Today, much of the palace is open to the public as temporary exhibitions.

Cross by the island's northern bridge to the mainland and Primorsky prospekt, and turn right toward metro Chornaya Ryechka (2 km). At No. 91 is a **Buddhist Temple**, built at the beginning of this century by a Russian, Gavriil Baranovsky, in collaboration with Lhasa scholar Agwan-Khamba. This recreation of Tibetan medieval forms makes a distinctive finish to this walk. (If you prefer, walk one block inland from the temple to Savushkina ulitsa, and board a #2, 3, 31, or 37 tram to the metro, traveling through a district of three- and four-story apartment buildings constructed after World War II by German P.O.W.s.)

The western tip of Yelagin Island

The Blockade Cemetery and Museum

This century's most deeply etched memory for Petersburgers remains World War II, and the terrible siege (called the Blockade by Russians) to which Leningrad was subjected by German Army Group North in 1941–43. A bombing raid reduced the main food warehouses to rubble. The daily ration during the worst winter of 1941–42 was 125 grams (4 oz.) of "bread," a dense, wet, barely nourishing product composed mainly of grain substitutes such as cellulose. About 650,000 people died from starvation, bombardment, and winter frost. Often, there was no one to bury the dead, as whole families perished. A Leningrad historian wrote, "Each day in the besieged city was the equal of many months of ordinary life. It was terrible to see how from hour to hour there vanished the strength of those near and dear." And a Komsomol (Young Communist) official recalled, "Human beings simply slipped away. They no longer could stand."

Barrage balloons over the Admiralty

There was no wood for coffins; everything that could burn was burned for heat. The frightful level of casualties required a new burial place, and the health authorities were forced, with great regret, to prepare mass graves. One such place was on the northern outskirts of the city, near the village of Piskaryovka. Pits were blasted and filled, sometimes with hundreds of bodies. Four hundred seventy thousand people are buried there.

In 1960 a memorial museum and park were established, with well-ordered flower gardens and lawns. It exhibits documents and photos of the dead, as well as enlarged photographs of the diary of a young girl, Tanya. Almost every page marks the death of a relative. The last entry reads, "Everyone is dead. Only Tanya remains." In critical condition, she was evacuated from the city and died shortly thereafter. Other exhibits describe the city's defenses and the Road of Life, the crucial winter ice route across Lake Ladoga which saved the city from complete starvation.

Behind the buildings is an **Eternal Flame,** lit by a torch brought from the Field Of Mars, and at the other end, the **Motherland statue,** six meters of bronze, laying her wreath of oak and laurel on the graves of the victims.

The **Piskaryovskoye Cemetery** is at Prospekt Nepokoronnykh, 74. Take the metro to Ploshchad Muzhestva ("Courage") station. Board a #123 bus on Prospekt Nepokoronnykh ("the Unconquered"), and ask someone to point out the stop for *Piskarovskoye memorialnoye kladbishche.*

Courage

We know what lies in the balance at
this moment,
And what is happening right now.
The hour for courage strikes upon our clocks,
And courage will not desert us.
We're not frightened of a hail of lead,
We're not bitter without a roof overhead –
And we will preserve you, Russian speech,
Mighty Russian word!
We will transmit you to our grandchildren
Free and pure and rescued from captivity
Forever!

– Anna Akhmatova, 1942. Translated by Judith Hemshemeyer

24 January 1942

Forty degrees below zero!

The blackout curtain has frozen to the window: in the room there is semi-darkness. The walls, smeared with oil paint, are covered with moisture. Thin streams of water trickle down to the floor.

Going to get bread, I wrapped myself up in Lena's flannel blanket, leaving only a crack for my eyes.

When I came out onto the street, the sky was so bright that I squinted my eyes shut. The trees growing near our doorway, covered with snow and hoarfrost, glittered unbearably.

Under the tree lay two corpses wrapped haphazardly in a sheet. The naked feet of one of them stuck out, with the big toes protruding.

The water pipes don't work. I have to go to the Neva for water. The bakery stopped working for lack of water. Thousands of Leningraders who were still in condition to move came out of their dens. Forming a living conveyor from the Neva to the bakery, they handed buckets of water to one another with hands numb from the cold.

The bread got baked!

Excerpted from Elena Kochina, *Blockade Diary*, trans. by Samuel C. Ramer (Ann Arbor: Ardis Publishers, 1990)

ALTERNATIVE PETER: UNDERGROUND HEROES OF THE BREZHNEV ERA

While much has been written about the traditional sights of St. Petersburg, history continues to be made, though often it is not yet recognized as such. The Brezhnev stagnation period and early *perestroika* also have their heroes, the artists and musicians of the underground who worked their days as caretakers and street-sweepers and spent their nights creating art for the young and rebellious.

Little now remains of the world of private apartment concerts and exhibitions; there is simply no longer a need for them. But the people who created it are still around, as well as a few places where they gather.

One place which perhaps embodies this spirit more than any other is the complex at Ulitsa Pushkinskaya 10, home of the **Free Culture Foundation**. To get there, take the metro to Ploshchad Vosstaniya/Mayakovskaya station. Upon exiting, turn right on Nevsky prospekt and then right again on Pushkinskaya ulitsa, near a monument to the poet which stands in the center of a small, attractive garden. The initial impression is uninspiring. "Gallery 10-10," the foundation's official outlet, is up a long flight of stairs and is often closed; a tiny secondhand record shop is nestled beside an archway. Only after passing through here do things start to get interesting, as you find a churned-up courtyard dotted with the odd mural. You have entered the **Exhibition of Contemporary Fresco**. Any one of the stairways ahead will take you into a world created by one or more artists. Painted or graffiti-covered stairwells and doorways announce that you are on "neutral territory," a land of flamingoes and radiant suns.

The courtyard has a second archway, and in the left side of it is a door, entrance to the **Shrine of John Lennon**, an otherwise ordinary communal apartment filled with rock memorabilia and home of one of the most colorful figures of the Leningrad underground. Kolya Vasin is the city's, in fact the country's, #1 Beatles fan. Once an organizer of underground concerts in the city, Vasin's current aim is to build a temple to Lennon on the Gulf of Finland. His collection includes a T-shirt worn by Lennon, a signed record sent by him in 1971 and a Campbell's soup can from Andy Warhol, among many other artifacts. But most significant is the way this museum expresses the spirit of an era. For Vasin's generation, the youth of the 1960's and '70's in Russia, rock music, and the Beatles in particular, was an escape from Soviet reality, one of the first windows on a West that is now fully open to them, for good or ill.

Home-grown rock music was always a factor too, often crudely aping Western styles and stances. It wasn't until the late '70's that a genuinely Russian style of rock emerged, and Leningrad was its nucleus. At last Russians had their own rock hero, someone whose words they could identify with on a more everyday and personal basis. This was Boris ("Bob") Grebenshchikov, poetic vocalist of the group Aquarium, who lived in a top floor apartment on Ulitsa Sofiyi Perovskoy, 5 (now **Malaya Konyushennaya Ulitsa, 5**), just off the Griboyedov Canal. Although he has moved away, the spirit remains, and graffiti proclaims "Bob, you're a saint!" or "Beatles, have faith in Bob, he knows the truth." When you reach the top landing you find the "Door to Nirvana," and below these words is painted a Russian Orthodox cross decorated with the Aquarian symbol, a testament to Grebenshchikov's religious beliefs.

Grebenshchikov also used to sketch occasionally, and his band was closely associated with a motley group of artists, the *Mitki*, united by their hippie-like tolerance and feelings of brotherhood toward all people. Their primitivist art reflects both Rousseaus, borrowing from the philosopher's tenets and the painter's style. Now they are respectable – they even have some canvasses in the Russian Museum – but their lives are studio- rather than gallery-oriented. Their self-styled headquarters are the **Tikhomirov brothers' apartment** (tel. 245-0175) on Aptekarsky Pereulok, 6/42. Centrally located, it is used as a studio by two prominent *Mitki*, the educated and sophisticated Viktor, and his more down-to-earth, primitivist brother Andrey. They welcome visitors, both to their studio and to the roof above, which rivals St. Isaac's for its panoramas of the city, including the best view imaginable of the Church of Our Saviour on Spilled Blood. Perhaps they will consider an offer, if you should find a painting that strikes your fancy.

Ulitsa Pushkinskaya, 10/42

OLD & NEW STREET NAMES

Former ("Soviet") Name	New Name
Anny Ulyanovoy ulitsa	Polozova ulitsa
Bratstva ulitsa	Maly Sampsonievsky prospekt
Brodskovo ulitsa	Mikhailovskaya ulitsa
Voinova ulitsa	Shpalernaya ulitsa
Voytika ulitsa	Vitebskaya ulitsa
Gaza prospekt	Staro-Petergofsky prospekt
Dzerzhinskovo ulitsa	Gorokhovaya ulitsa
Zhelyabova ulitsa	Bolshaya Konyushennaya ulitsa
Kalyaeva ulitsa	Zakharevskaya ulitsa
Karla Marksa prospekt	Bolshoy Sampsonievsky prospekt
Kirovsky prospekt	Kamennoostrovsky prospekt
Kommunarov ploshchad	Nikolskaya ploshchad
Krasnoy Konnitsy ulitsa	Kavalergardskaya ulitsa

OLD & NEW STREET NAMES (Continued)

Krushteyna kanal	Admiralteysky kanal
Mayorova prospekt	Voznesensky prospekt
Maksima Gorkovo prospekt	Kronverksky prospekt
Marii Ulyanovoy ulitsa	Grafsky pereulok
Mira ploshchad	Sennaya ploshchad
Smirnova prospekt	Lanskoy shossé
Ogorodnikova prospekt	Rizhsky prospekt
Olega Koshevovo ulitsa	Vvedenskaya ulitsa
Petra Lavrova ulitsa	Furshtatskaya ulitsa
Podbelskovo pereulok	Pochtamtsky pereulok
Profsoyuzov bulvar	Konnogvardeysky bulvar
Rakova ulitsa	Italyanskaya ulitsa
Skorokhodova ulitsa	Bolshaya Monetnaya ulitsa
Sofi Perovskoy ulitsa	Malaya Konyushennaya ulitsa
Tolmachyova ulitsa	Karavannaya ulitsa
Fotievoy ulitsa	Eletskaya ulitsa
Fofanovoy ulitsa	Enotaevskaya ulitsa
Khalturina ulitsa	Millionnaya ulitsa
Shchorsa prospekt	Malyy prospekt P.S.
Kirovsky most	Troitsky most
Komsomolsky most	Kharlamov most
Pestelya most	Panteleimonovsky most
Pionersky most	Silin most
Svobody most	Sampsonievsky most
Skver na Ostrovskovo ploshchad	Ekaterininsky skver
Detsky park	Yusupovsky sad
Sad im. F.E. Dzerzhinskovo	Lopukinsky sad
Park Chelyuskintsev	Udelnyy park
Ploshchad Vostanniya	Znamenskaya ploshchad
Griboyedova kanal	Ekaterininsky kanal
Dekabristov ploshchad	Senatskaya ploshchad
Ostrovskovo ploshchad	Aleksandriyskaya ploshchad
Pestelya ulitsa	Panteleimonskaya ulitsa
Revolyutsii ploshchad	Troitskaya ploshchad
Stachek ploshchad	Narvskaya ploshchad
Truda ulitsa	Blagoveshchenskaya ulitsa
Truda ploshchad	Blagoveshchenskaya ploshchad

Source: *The Traveller's Yellow Pages for Saint Petersburg* (1993)

Note. You will find that people often continue to use the old names. It is possible, too, that some of the new names may never be adopted in popular usage; for example, Griboyedova kanal or Dekabristov ploshchad.

St. Petersburg Metro

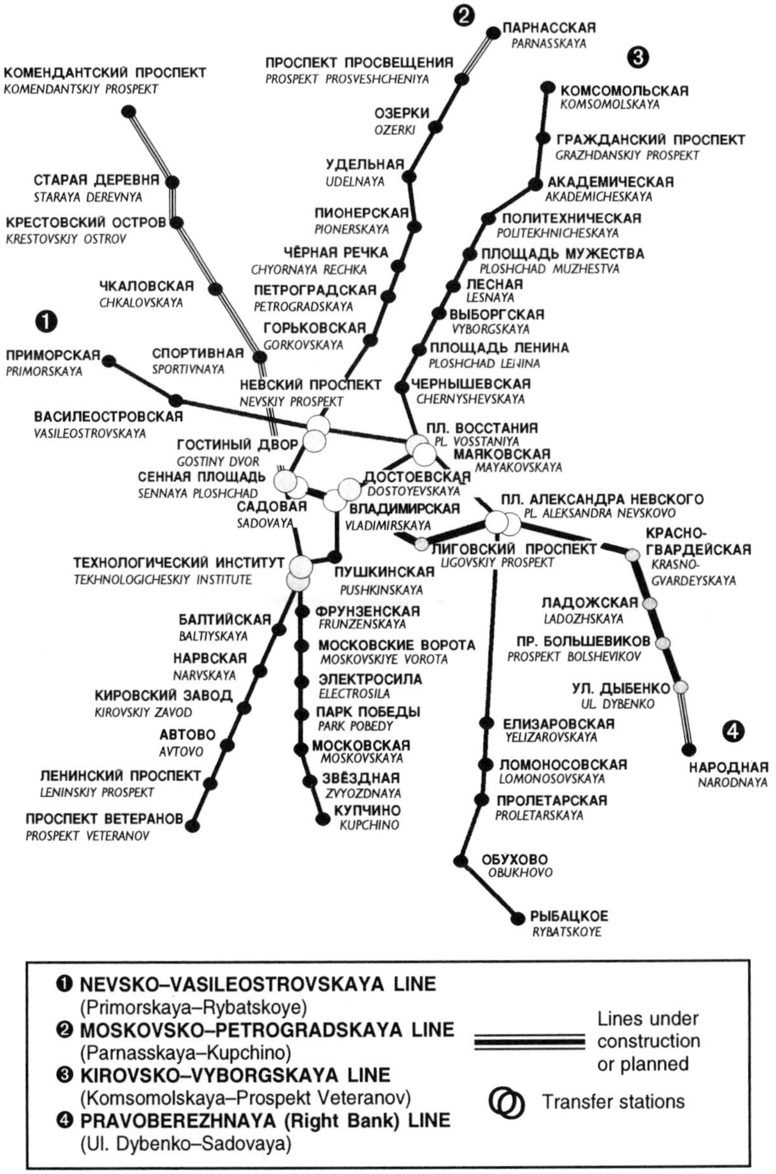

❷
ПАРНАССКАЯ
PARNASSKAYA

❸

ПРОСПЕКТ ПРОСВЕЩЕНИЯ
PROSPEKT PROSVESHCHENIYA

КОМЕНДАНТСКИЙ ПРОСПЕКТ
KOMENDANTSKIY PROSPEKT

КОМСОМОЛЬСКАЯ
KOMSOMOLSKAYA

ОЗЕРКИ
OZERKI

ГРАЖДАНСКИЙ ПРОСПЕКТ
GRAZHDANSKIY PROSPEKT

УДЕЛЬНАЯ
UDELNAYA

СТАРАЯ ДЕРЕВНЯ
STARAYA DEREVNYA

АКАДЕМИЧЕСКАЯ
AKADEMICHESKAYA

ПИОНЕРСКАЯ
PIONERSKAYA

КРЕСТОВСКИЙ ОСТРОВ
KRESTOVSKIY OSTROV

ПОЛИТЕХНИЧЕСКАЯ
POLITEKHNICHESKAYA

ЧЁРНАЯ РЕЧКА
CHYORNAYA RECHKA

ПЛОЩАДЬ МУЖЕСТВА
PLOSHCHAD MUZHESTVA

ЧКАЛОВСКАЯ
CHKALOVSKAYA

ПЕТРОГРАДСКАЯ
PETROGRADSKAYA

ЛЕСНАЯ
LESNAYA

ВЫБОРГСКАЯ
VYBORGSKAYA

❶

ГОРЬКОВСКАЯ
GORKOVSKAYA

ПЛОЩАДЬ ЛЕНИНА
PLOSHCHAD LENINA

ПРИМОРСКАЯ
PRIMORSKAYA

СПОРТИВНАЯ
SPORTIVNAYA

НЕВСКИЙ ПРОСПЕКТ
NEVSKIY PROSPEKT

ЧЕРНЫШЕВСКАЯ
CHERNYSHEVSKAYA

ВАСИЛЕОСТРОВСКАЯ
VASILEOSTROVSKAYA

ПЛ. ВОССТАНИЯ
PL. VOSSTANIYA

ГОСТИНЫЙ ДВОР
GOSTINY DVOR

МАЯКОВСКАЯ
MAYAKOVSKAYA

СЕННАЯ ПЛОЩАДЬ
SENNAYA PLOSHCHAD

ДОСТОЕВСКАЯ
DOSTOYEVSKAYA

САДОВАЯ
SADOVAYA

ВЛАДИМИРСКАЯ
VLADIMIRSKAYA

ПЛ. АЛЕКСАНДРА НЕВСКОГО
PL. ALEKSANDRA NEVSKOVO

КРАСНО-ГВАРДЕЙСКАЯ
KRASNO-GVARDEYSKAYA

ЛИГОВСКИЙ ПРОСПЕКТ
LIGOVSKIY PROSPEKT

ТЕХНОЛОГИЧЕСКИЙ ИНСТИТУТ
TEKHNOLOGICHESKIY INSTITUTE

ПУШКИНСКАЯ
PUSHKINSKAYA

ЛАДОЖСКАЯ
LADOZHSKAYA

БАЛТИЙСКАЯ
BALTIYSKAYA

ФРУНЗЕНСКАЯ
FRUNZENSKAYA

ПР. БОЛЬШЕВИКОВ
PROSPEKT BOLSHEVIKOV

НАРВСКАЯ
NARVSKAYA

МОСКОВСКИЕ ВОРОТА
MOSKOVSKIYE VOROTA

ЭЛЕКТРОСИЛА
ELECTROSILA

УЛ. ДЫБЕНКО
UL. DYBENKO

КИРОВСКИЙ ЗАВОД
KIROVSKIY ZAVOD

ПАРК ПОБЕДЫ
PARK POBEDY

ЕЛИЗАРОВСКАЯ
YELIZAROVSKAYA

❹

АВТОВО
AVTOVO

МОСКОВСКАЯ
MOSKOVSKAYA

ЛОМОНОСОВСКАЯ
LOMONOSOVSKAYA

НАРОДНАЯ
NARODNAYA

ЛЕНИНСКИЙ ПРОСПЕКТ
LENINSKIY PROSPEKT

ЗВЁЗДНАЯ
ZVYOZDNAYA

ПРОЛЕТАРСКАЯ
PROLETARSKAYA

ПРОСПЕКТ ВЕТЕРАНОВ
PROSPEKT VETERANOV

КУПЧИНО
KUPCHINO

ОБУХОВО
OBUKHOVO

РЫБАЦКОЕ
RYBATSKOYE

❶ **NEVSKO–VASILEOSTROVSKAYA LINE**
(Primorskaya–Rybatskoye)

❷ **MOSKOVSKO–PETROGRADSKAYA LINE**
(Parnasskaya–Kupchino)

❸ **KIROVSKO–VYBORGSKAYA LINE**
(Komsomolskaya–Prospekt Veteranov)

❹ **PRAVOBEREZHNAYA (Right Bank) LINE**
(Ul. Dybenko–Sadovaya)

Lines under construction or planned

Transfer stations

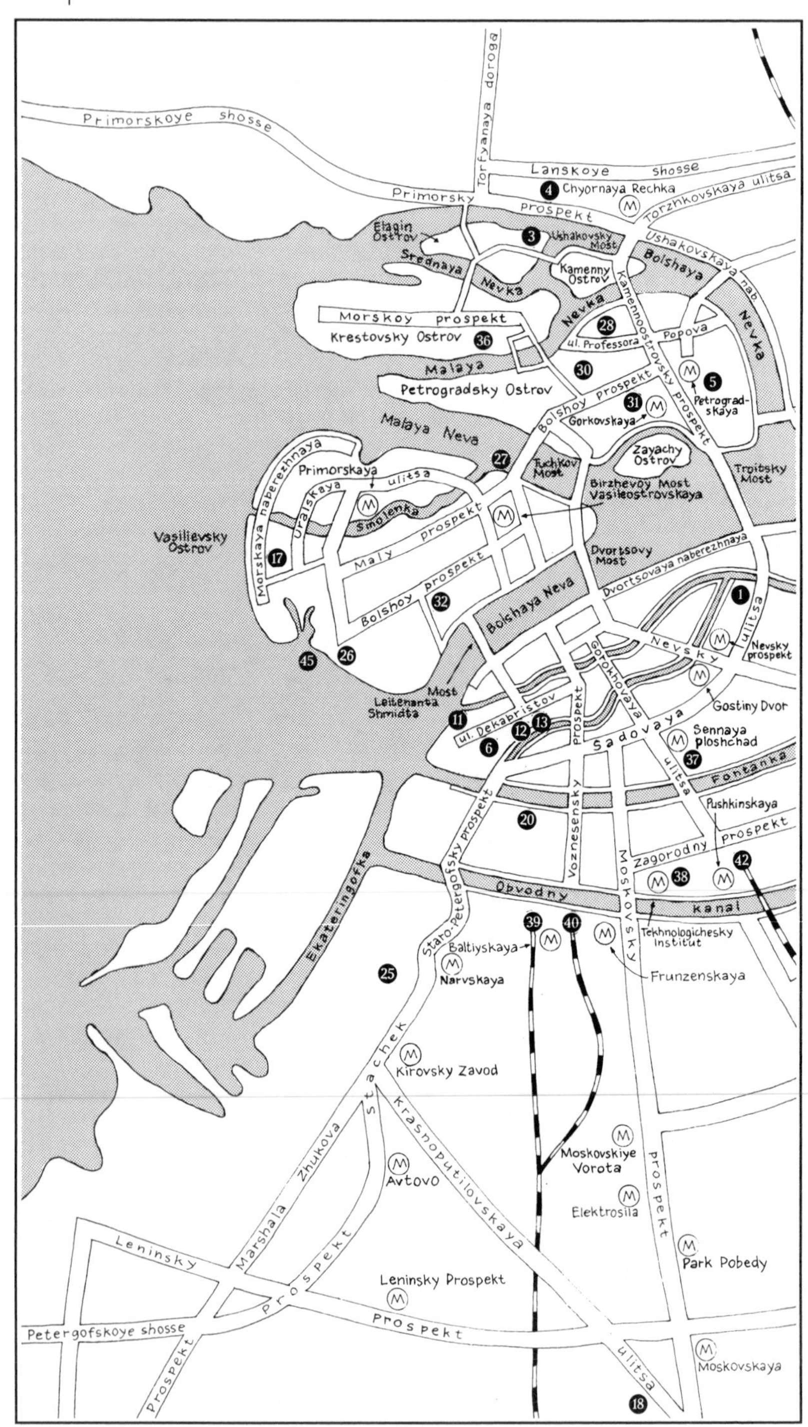
Primorskoye shosse
Torfyanaya doroga
Lanskoye shosse
Chyornaya Rechka
Primorsky prospekt
Torzhkovskaya ulitsa
Elagin Ostrov
Ushakovsky Most
Ushakovskaya nab
Srednaya Nevka
Kamenny Ostrov
Bolshaya Nevka
Kamennoostrovsky prospekt
Morskoy prospekt
Krestovsky Ostrov
ul. Professora Popova
Malaya
Petrogradsky Ostrov
Petrogradskaya
Bolshoy prospekt
Gorkovskaya
Malaya Neva
Zayachy Ostrov
Tuchkov Most
Troitsky Most
Primorskaya
Birzhevoy Most
Vasileostrovskaya
Morskaya naberezhnaya
Uralskaya
ulitsa
Smolenka
Maly prospekt
Vasilievsky Ostrov
Bolshoy prospekt
Dvortsovy Most
Dvortsovaya naberezhnaya
Bolshaya Neva
Nevsky
ulitsa
Nevsky prospekt
Gorokhovaya
Gostiny Dvor
Most Leitenanta Shmidta
ul. Dekabristov
prospekt
Sadovaya
Sennaya ploshchad
Fontanka
ulitsa
Pushkinskaya
Staro-Petergofsky prospekt
Voznesensky
Zagorodny prospekt
Moskovsky
Obvodny kanal
Ekateringofka
Baltiyskaya
Tekhnologichesky Institut
Frunzenskaya
Narvskaya
Kirovsky Zavod
Stachek
Krasnoputilovskaya
Marshala Zhukova
Avtovo
Moskovskiye Vorota
Elektrosila
prospekt
Park Pobedy
Leninsky
prospekt
Leninsky Prospekt
prospekt
Petergofskoye shosse
prospekt
ulitsa
Moskovskaya
1
3
4
5
6
11
12
13
17
18
20
25
26
27
28
30
31
32
36
37
38
39
40
42
45

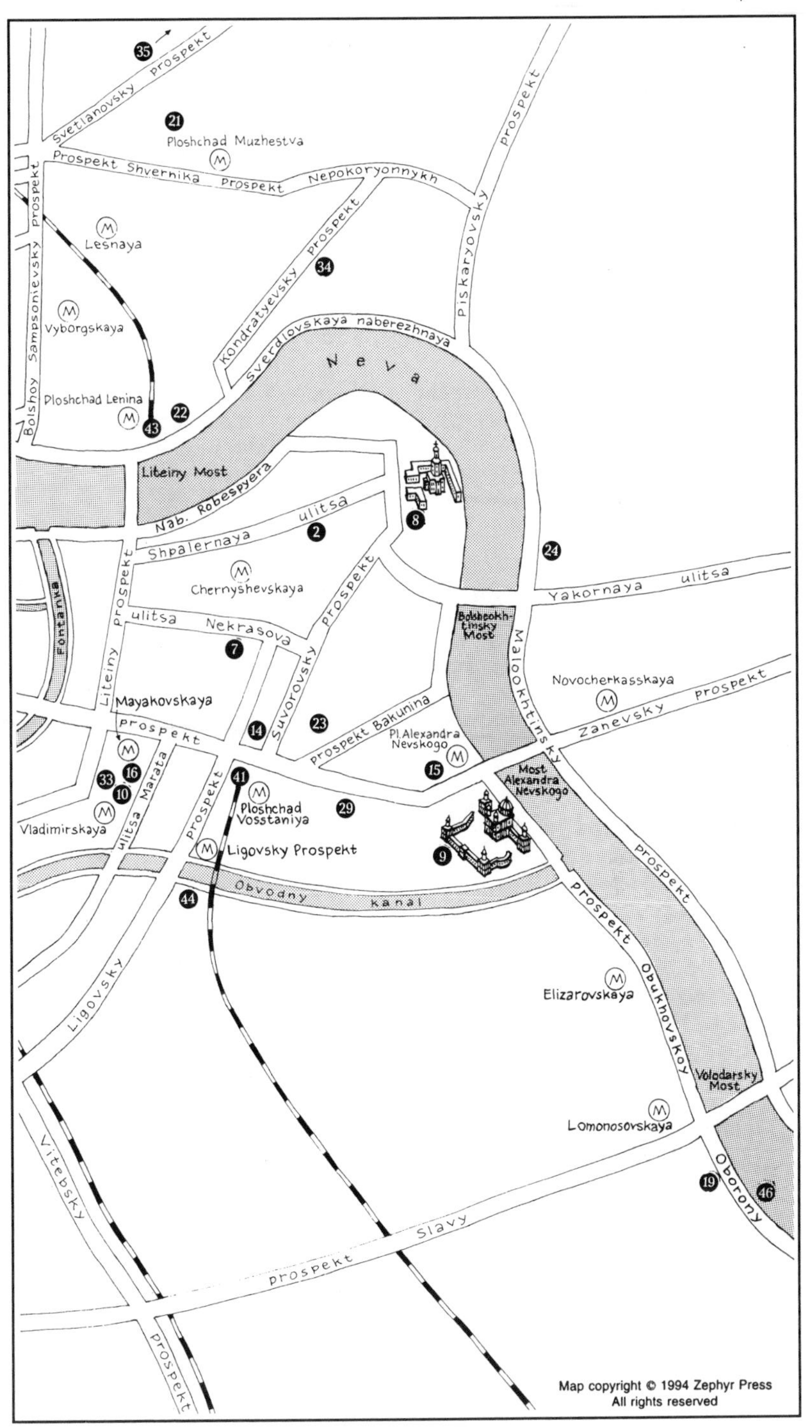

Svetlanovsky prospekt
Ploshchad Muzhestva
Prospekt Shvernika
prospekt Nepokoryonnykh
Bolshoy Sampsonievsky prospekt
Lesnaya
Kondratyevsky prospekt
Piskaryovsky prospekt
Vyborgskaya
Sverdlovskaya naberezhnaya
Neva
Ploshchad Lenina
Liteiny Most
Nab. Robespyera
Shpalernaya ulitsa
Chernyshevskaya
Fontanka
Liteiny prospekt
ulitsa Nekrasova
Suvorovsky prospekt
Yakornaya ulitsa
Bolsheokhtinsky Most
Malookhtinsky
Novocherkasskaya
Zanevsky prospekt
Mayakovskaya
prospekt
prospekt Bakunina
Pl. Alexandra Nevskogo
Most Alexandra Nevskogo
ulitsa Marata
Ploshchad Vosstaniya
Vladimirskaya
Ligovsky Prospekt
Obvodny kanal
prospekt
Obukhovskoy prospekt
Elizarovskaya
Ligovsky
Volodarsky Most
Lomonosovskaya
Oborony
Vitebsky prospekt
prospekt Slavy
35
21
34
22
43
8
2
24
7
14
23
15
41
33
16
10
29
9
44
19
46

ST. PETERSBURG

Most Aleksandra Nevskovo
Мост Александра Невского
Ploshchad Aleksandra Nevskovo
Площадь Александра Невского
Prospekt Bakunina
Проспект Бакунина
Bolsheokhtinsky Most
Большеохтинский мост
Birzhevoy Most
Биржевой мост
Bolshoy Sampsonievsky prospekt
Большой Сампсониевский проспект
Ulitsa Dekabristov
Улица Декабристов
Ekateringofka
Екатерингофка
Kamenny Ostrov
Каменный остров
Kondratyevsky prospekt
Кондратьевский проспект
Krasnoputilovskaya ulitsa
Краснопутиловская улица
Krestovsky Ostrov
Крестовский остров
Lanskoye shossé
Ланское шоссе
Most Leitenanta Shmidta
Мост лейтенанта Шмидта
Leninsky prospekt
Ленинский проспект
Ligovsky prospekt
Лиговский проспект
Liteiny Most
Литейный мост
Liteiny prospekt
Литейный проспект
Malaya Nevka River
Река Малая Невка
Inzhenernaya ulitsa
Инженерная улица
Malookhtinsky prospekt
Малоохтинский проспект
Maly prospekt
Малый проспект
Ulitsa Marata
Улица Марата
Morskaya naberezhnaya
Морская набережная
Moskovsky prospekt
Московский проспект
Ulitsa Nekrasova
Улица Некрасова
Prospekt Nepokoryonnykh
Проспект Непокорённых
Prospekt Obukhovskoy Oborony
Проспект Обуховской обороны
Obvodny Kanal
Обводный канал
Petergofskoye shossé
Петергофское шоссе
Petrogradsky Ostrov
Петроградский остров
Piskaryovsky prospekt
Пискарёвский проспект
Primorskoye shossé
Приморское шоссе
Primorsky prospekt
Приморский проспект
Ulitsa Professora Popova
Улица профессора Попова
Shpalernaya ulitsa
Шпалерная улица
Naberezhnaya Robespyera
Набережная Робеспьера
Prospekt Shvernika
Проспект Шверника
Prospekt Slavy
Проспект Славы
Smolenka
Смоленка
Srednaya Nevka River
Река Средняя Невка
Prospekt Stachek
Проспект Стачек
Staropetergofsky prospekt
Старопетергофский проспект
Suvorovsky prospekt
Суворовский проспект
Sverdlovskaya naberezhnaya
Свердловская набережная
Svetlanovsky prospekt
Светлановский проспект

САНКТ-ПЕТЕРБУРГ

Torfyanovaya doroga
Торфяновая дорога
Torzhkovskaya ulitsa
Торжковская улица
Uralskaya ulitsa
Уральская улица
Ushakovskaya naberezhnaya
Ушаковская набережная
Ushakovsky Most
Ушаковский мост
Vasilyevsky Ostrov
Васильевский остров
Vitebsky prospekt
Витебский проспект
Volodarsky Most
Володарский мост
Voznesensky prospekt
Вознесенский проспект
Yakornaya ulitsa
Якорная улица
Yelagin Ostrov
Елагин остров
Zagorodny prospekt
Загородный проспект
Zanevsky prospekt
Заневский проспект
Zayachy Ostrov
Заячий остров
Prospekt Zhukova
Проспект Жукова

MAP KEY

1. **Church of the Savior on Spilled Blood**
Церковь Спаса на Крови
2. **Taurida Palace**
Таврический дворец
3. **Yelagin Palace**
Елагинский дворец
4. **Buddhist Temple**
Буддистский храм
5. **Mosque**
Мечеть
6. **Synagogue**
Синагога
7. **Roman Catholic Church**
Костел
8. **Smolny Convent**
Смольный монастырь
9. **Alexander Nevsky Lavra**
Александро-Невская Лавра
10. **Dostoyevsky Museum**
Музей Достоевского
11. **Blok Museum**
Музей Блока
12. **Mariinsky Theater**
Мариинский театр
13. **Conservatory**
Консерватория
14. **Hotel Oktyabrskaya**
Гостиница «Октябрьская»
15. **Hotel Moskva**
Гостиница «Москва»
16. **Nevsky Palace Hotel**
17. **Pribaltiiskaya Hotel**
Гостиница «Прибалтийская»
18. **Pulkovskaya Hotel**
Гостиница «Пулковская»
19. **Rechnaya Hotel**
Гостиница «Речная»
20. **Sovyetskaya Hotel**
Гостиница «Советская»
21. **Sputnik Hotel**
Гостиница «Спутник»
22. **“Holiday” Youth Hostel**
23. **Youth Hostel**
24. **Okhta Hotel**
Гостиница «Охта»
25. **Tsenturion Hotel**
Гостиница «Центурион»
26. **Olympia Hotel**
Гостиница «Олимпия»

27. Hotelship Peterhof
28. Hostel in "Youth Palace"
Гостиница в Дворце Молодёжи
29. Express Market
30. Super Babylon Market
31. Sytny Market
Сытный рынок
32. Vasilyeostrovsky Market
Васильеостровский рынок
33. Kuznechny Market
Кузнечный рынок
34. Kondratyevsky Market
Кондратьевский рынок
35. Institute of Traumatology
Институт травматологии
36. City Hospital No. 31
Городская больница №31
37. American Medical Center
38. Polyclinic No. 2
Поликлиника №2
39. Baltiisky Vokzal
Балтийский вокзал
40. Varshavsky Vokzal
Варшавский вокзал
41. Moskovsky Vokzal
Московский вокзал

The Hermitage Museum and the Admiralty
Artist: V.I. Serdyukov

PRACTICAL MATTERS

Transport

Metro. St. Petersburg's metro system is not as extensive as Moscow's, though it now covers most areas of the city. Two lines (the red and the blue) run between the city's northern and southern suburbs; the green line connects Vassilyevsky Island with the southeast; and the new orange line joins the right bank of the River Neva with the center at Sadovaya. Payment is by metal jeton (a token; now also used in public phone boxes), while monthly passes good on all forms of public transport are sold near the beginning of each month. Though it still opens at 5:30 a.m., the metro now closes earlier, at around 12:30 a.m. instead of 1 a.m., so be careful not to get stranded. (See metro map, p. 219.)

Overland Transport. The city has frequent bus, tram, and trolleybus services, the latter two usually more convenient for major routes – for instance, on long streets like Nevsky prospekt or areas like Vassilyevsky Island poorly served by the metro.

Suburban and Inter-city Transport. St. Petersburg's train, bus, and boat stations (*vokzaly*) and airports are as follows:

Moskovsky Vokzal (metro Ploshchad Vosstaniya): trains to Moscow and beyond, and northern Russia (tel. 168-0111; 168-4374)

Finlandsky Vokzal (metro Ploshchad Lenina): trains to Vyborg, Helsinki, and western Karelia (tel. 168-0111; 168-7685)

Varshavsky Vokzal (metro Baltiyskaya): trains to the Baltics, Poland, western Ukraine, and Pskov (tel. 168-0111; 168-2611)

Vitebsky Vokzal (metro Pushkinskaya): trains to Bielarus, central Ukraine, and Moldova, and local trains to southern suburbs including Pushkin and Pavlovsk (tel. 168-5390)

Baltiysky Vokzal (metro Baltiyskaya): local trains along the Baltic coast (tel. 168-0111)

Avtovokzal No. 1 (metro Baltiyskaya, outside Varshavsky Vokzal): buses to destinations you are unlikely to need, though there are rumored to be some services to Vyborg and Lake Ladoga (tel. 292-1683)

Avtovokzal No. 2 (metro Ligovsky Prospekt, nab. Obvodnovo Kanala, 36): buses to Vologda, Petrozavodsk, Pskov, Novgorod and the Baltics (tel. 166-5777)

Morskoy Vokzal (metro Primorskaya, then #10a trolleybus, pl. Morskoy Slavy): passenger terminal for sea-going vessels (tel. 355-1902; 355-1310)

Rechnoy Vokzal (metro Proletarskaya, pr. Obukhovskoy Oborony, 195): riverboat terminal for Lakes Ladoga and Onega, and the islands of Valaam and Kizhi (tel. 262-1318)

Pulkovo 1 Airport (bus #39 from metro Moskovskaya or express bus from Ulitsa Gertsena, 13): domestic flights (tel. 293-9911; 293-9021; 293-9031)

Pulkovo 2 Airport (infrequent bus #13 from Hotel Pulkovskaya, otherwise 30 minutes by taxi): international flights (tel. 104-3444; 291-8913)

Rzhevka Airport (suburban train to Rzhevka from the Finlandsky Vokzal): flights to some destinations in Russia's north (tel. 227-8562)

Ticket Offices. Rail (for foreigners): Nab. kanal Griboyedova, 24. The Intourist *kassa* is #104 – turn right after the entrance and follow the Intourist signs upstairs. ***Air*** (domestic flight tickets for foreigners): Nevsky pr., 7/9 (tel. 293-9031)

Car Hire. While many firms provide car hire with drivers, generally cheaper than driverless cars but with greater restrictions, here are some that do rent driverless cars, which can allow greater freedom for longer trips, if you speak Russian and are suitably prepared:

InNis, Hotel Astoria and Motel Olgino (tel. 210-5858; 238-3709): Japanese cars, unlimited travel within CIS

Interavto (Hertz), ul. Ispolkomskaya, 9/11 (tel. 277-4032): Volvos, Mercedes, and Volkswagens for travel within St. Petersburg and Leningrad Region. Reservations can also be made at the Grand Europe and Moskva Hotels.

TransWell Troikka Ltd., Lermontovsky pr., 37 (tel. 113-7253): unlimited travel.

Car Repair. Garages specializing in the servicing of Western cars include: InNis AutoService, Motel Olgino (tel. 238-3709); Inavtoservis (Volvo), Vitebsky pr., 17/2 (tel. 298-3910); Sovinteravtoservis, Preportoviy proyezd, 5 (tel. 290-1510); TDV-Auto (Ford), ul. Kommuny, 16 (tel. 521-4612).

Accommodation

While the range of hotel accommodation in St. Petersburg is far from perfect, it is fast becoming reasonable, with at least some choice in every category.

To help with advance bookings in all categories, we recommend the **"Shakti" Center for Advanced Studies of History and Culture** (Kovenskiy per. 29/3, tel. & fax: 279-5198, metro Ploshchad Vosstaniya; or book from the U.S. through **Russian Travel Service,** phone & fax: [603] 585-6534). They offer extensive bed-and-breakfast listings, as well as widespread contacts in the hotel and apartment rental business. They can also provide rooms in cheap, unpublicized hostels for as little as $7 a night. (For more information, see their advertisement.)

The Reso-owned **Grand Hotel Europe** (ul. Mikhailovskaya, 1/7) and Marco Polo's **Nevsky Palace** (Nevsky pr., 57) are top of the line, though for style the "Europe" wins hands down, with its magnificent decor and the city's best restaurants. Intourist's stately **Astoria** is not far behind, both in comfort and price, charging $180 for a single while the other two are over the $200 mark.

For about $100 there is plenty of choice, with the highest standards offered by two floating hotels. Reso's **Olympia**, (pl. Morskoy Slavy; metro Primorskaya, $150 a single) has the excellent Piccolo restaurant and the open-air White Nights Bar on the roof. For $120, the Swiss-owned **Hotelship Peterhof** is much better located, at nab. Makarova near the spit of Vassilyevsky Island (tel. 213-6321). Most of the others in this category are Intourist or ex-Intourist, including the new but tacky **Okhta**, the monstrous **Pulkovskaya**, the group-filled **Pribaltiiskaya**, the mediocre **Moskva**, and the over-priced and poorly located **Sovyetskaya**. The best value is probably the **St. Petersburg** (Vyborgskaya nab. 5/2, tel. 542-9123; metro Ploshchad Lenina), at $65 for good service and facilities. There are also two smaller, cozier medium-rangers, the Finnish **Hotel Helen** (Lermontovsky pr. 45/1, tel. 251-6101; metro Tekhnologichesky Institut and the **Hotel Mercury** (Tavricheskaya ul. 39, tel. 278-1977; metro Chernyshevskaya).

The situation for the budget traveler has been changed radically by the appearance of two **youth hostels**. The first (3rd Sovyetskaya 28, tel. 277-0569; metro Ploshchad Vosstaniya) is run by an American and is now firmly

In St. Petersburg May We Recommend

"Shakti"

Center for Advanced Studies of History & Culture

The Center is now in its second year of facilitating the visits of scholars, journalists, and other professionals, as well as those of tourists and students. By special arrangement, the publishers of *An Explorer's Guide to Russia* are pleased to offer bed & breakfast, guide/interpreter, and other contacts through the Center for Advanced Studies of History & Culture, bookable from the U.S. at a cost substantially below other such services.

The Center can provide virtually any assistance you might need in St. Petersburg, from the basic (which might comprise visa support, meeting you at the airport or train station, bringing you to your bed & breakfast host, and picking you up at the end of your stay) to individualized literary, architectural, or other tours, support for business research and negotiations, Russian language instruction, or organization of scientific and cultural seminars and meetings with Russian colleagues.

For **bed & breakfast**, daily rates range between $20 and $35, depending upon whether your host speaks English and the location of the apartment (the center or suburbs). Rooms or apartments without host are also available. **Guide/interpreters** are available for individual sight visits, or for engagements of several days or more; the rate is between $25 and $50, depending upon level of experience and other factors. Guides with less formal training are suitable for most tourists. A **car and driver** may be engaged for traveling within the city or outside. The Center can also book an interpreter (with or without a car) to accompany you on explorations of such regions as Karelia, Novgorod. and Pskov. For further information, please contact the Center or their U.S. agent, at:

Russian Travel Service
Attn: Helen Kates
P.O. Box 311
Fitzwilliam, NH 03447
tel. & fax:
(603) 585-6534

"Shakti" Center
Ekaterina Cherkasova, Director
Kovenskiy pereulok, 29/3
191014 St. Petersburg, Russia
tel. & fax:
(7)(812) 279-5198

◆ SAMPLE LISTINGS ◆

These are some of the Petersburg bed & breakfast hosts and guide/interpeters who are available for booking through the Center.

BED & BREAKFAST

Metro PETROGRADSKAYA, in the old suburbs of Petrogradsky district. **Tatyana**, an English teacher, lives with her spry grandmother and 21-year-old son, who speaks German. They have a 4-room apartment, and can offer one or two rooms to accommodate guests.

BED & BREAKFAST (Continued)

Metro VLADIMIRSKAYA, in the center. **Ludmila** is an artist, and her husband a massage therapist. They live in a 3-room apartment with their 9-year-old son. Ludmila speaks English, and they have a pet doberman. They offer 2 rooms for guests.

Julia's apartment is four bus stops from metro PROSPEKT PROSVESHCHENIYA, in new suburbs of the Primorsky district. She is a doctor, and does not speak English. She is 28, likes playing tennis, and has a dog. She can rent one room, or two adjoining rooms.

Near Metro NOVOCHERKASSKAYA, in the old suburbs of Krasnoguardeisky ("Red Guard") district, which used to be the name of the metro stop as well. **Anatoly** and **Lidiya** are a 27-year-old couple, who speak English. Their 3-room apartment is near a large department store on the shore of the Neva. They like having guests, and offer to drive them around the city. The three rooms can be rented with or without the presence of hosts.

Olga and **Nikolay** and their daughter (18) live near Metro VLADIMIRSKAYA, in the center. Their daughter speaks English. They live in an excellent, unusual apartment just a few steps off of Nevsky prospekt, and can host one guest. Interests: music, travel.

Near Metro PRIMORSKAYA, in the center of the old suburbs district of Vasilyevsky Island. **Irina** lives with her husband and *babushka* (grandmother) in a 2-room apartment. The whole apartment, or a single room can be rented. Irina speaks English; they like to go down-hill skiing.

Near Metro PIONEERSKAYA, in the new suburbs of the Primorsky district. **Anna** lives with her husband, **Sergey**, and 15-year-old daughter Natasha, who is studying English. They love to travel in the country, and their apartment is near a wooded area. They have a 3-room apartment, and offer one room for rent, for either one or two persons.

Metro MAYAKOVSKAYA, in the center, Kuybishevsky district. **Klara** and her 28-year-old son **Yuri**, who speaks English, live in a 3-bedroom apartment. They offer two rooms for rent. Interests include science, art, sports. They also invite guests to visit their second home in Novorossiysk, on the Black Sea.

Metro PROSPEKT PROSVESHCHENIYA, in new suburbs of the Vyborg district. **Tatyana** and **Vladimir** and their three children live in a 4-room apartment. They have a 22-year-old daughter and twin boys of 14. Two family members speak English. They especially welcome college students as guests, one or two at a time.

Inna and **Marina** live near metro PETROGRADSKAYA, not far from the center and close to the beautiful central park of the city on Kamenny and Yelagin Islands. Marina speaks English. They can accommodate one guest, or a couple in a double bed.

Metro PRIMORSKAYA, near the Gulf of Finland. **Herman** and **Margarita** offer one room for rent in their household of four people, located in the district of Vasilyevsky Island. Their interests include history, psychology, and sociology. They can also send monographs of their research in these fields, and are especially interested in meeting other scholars. They can accommodate one or two guests with a double bed.

Metro PROSPEKT VETERANOV, south of the city in new suburbs. **Nikolay** and **Maria** live with their 21-year-old son, Leonid, and a *babushka*, Tamara, who is a wonderful cook. Their son speaks English. They can accommodate two people in one bed.

GUIDE / INTERPRETERS

Irina is 27 years old, and a graduate of Moscow State University. She has studied the architecture of St. Petersburg and worked for Intourist. She is also competent interpreting at business meetings or translating documents. She can work full-time, either in St. Petersburg or traveling outside the city.

Thirty-nine-year old **Yelena** studied English at St. Petersburg University, and also took many courses in art, literature, and architecture. She has a guide's certificate from the "Intourist Travel Company," and is skilled in business English. She can work part-time as a guide, either in St. Peterburg or outside the city.

Yelena, 32, has studied at St. Petersburg University, Department of English Language and Literature. She has a guide's certificate from Intourist, and is capable of translating business talks. She is available part-time as a guide, for Petersburg or outside.

Natalya is 39, a graduate of St. Petersburg University, Department of English Language and Literature. She likes art, music, and architecture, and can work part-time as a guide.

Tatyana is a student at St. Petersburg University, speaks fluent English, has working knowledge of German, and is available as a part-time guide in St. Petersburg and outside. She plays guitar and sings, and also likes chess.

Anna is a student in the Foreign Languages Department of the Russian State Pedagogical University. English is her main language of study, but she can also translate German, and is available part-time as a guide.

on its feet, providing pre-arrival visa support for travelers and soon to have IYHA affiliation. Reservations can be made through Russian Youth Hostels, 409 N. Pacific Coast Highway, Bldg. 106, Suite 390, Redondo Beach, CA 90277 (U.S. tel. [310] 379-4316). Unfortunately, for Russians the $15 a night charge is usually prohibitive. This factor, combined with a midnight curfew, somewhat dampens the friendly international spirit normal to the youth hosteling movement. The second, newer hostel, **Holiday** (ul. Mikhailova 1, tel. 572-7364), promises to avoid this problem, with slightly cheaper beds ($12) and a youthful Russian staff who hope to create a festive atmosphere. Its location is original, too, with views of the river, the Peter and Paul Fortress, and the dour Kresty (Crosses) Prison from its Stalin-era building.

If the hostels are full, there are other options. You could do a lot worse than the central **Oktyabrskaya** (Ligovsky pr. 10, tel. 277-6330; metro Ploshchad Vosstaniya, $25 a night). Similar in price are the **Druzhba** (ul. Chapygina 4, tel. 234-1844; metro Petrogradskaya), owned by the International Kingswood Trust, and a floor of the **Rechnaya Hotel** (Obukhovskoy Oborony pr. 195, tel. 262-8400; metro Proletarskaya) owned by a Liechtenstein firm (doubles only). The **Sputnik** seems to promise a great deal, except for its location (Morisa-Toreza pr. 34, tel. 552-5632; metro Ploshchad Muzhestva). It offers single rooms with baths and satellite TV for just $20. At least two other small places offer lower, hostel-type prices: the **Dvorets Molodyozhi** (Prof. Popova ul. 47, tel. 234-3278; metro Petrogradskaya; doubles only) and the tiny but very decent **Ritm Tsenturion** (ul. Turbinnaya 11, tel. 186-7689; metro Narvskaya).

Apartment rental can be a dodgy business, with the large summer influx of often unknowing foreigners providing easy prey for varying degrees of deceit. However, it is the cheapest option if you go about it the right way. For instance, when arriving from Moscow on the train, it makes sense to avoid the numerous sharks at the station and head for the Oktyabrskaya Hotel nearby. In the reception area is an apartment bureau offering accommodation for $8–$10 a night. Freelancers operating in the vicinity generally charge about the same. You can get even cheaper – a firm called **Yuzhny Dvor** (tel. 315-0438) charges as little as $3 a day for stays of 3 or more days.

Drinking Water. Visitors to St. Petersburg should take care not to drink tap water, unless it has been boiled first. It contains a bacterial organism called *giardia* that makes many visitors sick. Although Petersburgers generally have developed an immunity to *giardia*, many boil their water anyway. This should not be a problem when eating at restaurants, as long as you confine your water drinking to bottled mineral water.

Eating Out

St. Petersburg has its share of expensive restaurants, usually well publicized and not in great need of extra praise. Apart from the sumptuous Hotel Europe–type restaurant, "expensive" in this case means $20–$50 a head without drinks. Here are a few worth mention: **Sankt-Peterburg**, nab. kan. Griboyedova 5, tel. 314-3586; metro Nevsky Prospekt. Mirrors make this restaurant look much bigger than it really is. Food is Russian, excellent and imaginatively arranged.

Bella Leone, Vladimirsky pr. 9, tel. 113-1670; metro Vladimirskaya. An odd mix of Mexican and Russian cuisine, but it works well – the food is excellent.

Literaturnoye Café, Nevsky 18, tel. 312-8536; metro Nevsky Prospekt. Not what it should be, in terms of food and service. Still, it is a tourist attraction (Pushkin spent his last evening there before his fatal duel) and its early 19th century atmosphere and soothing music should not be missed.

Ambassador, nab. Fontanki 77; metro Nevsky Prospekt. Not quite ambassadorial, but its extravagant interior is a good attempt. Food and service are good and not over-priced, but menu prices are a well-kept secret.

Unlike Moscow, St. Petersburg has been inundated of late with cheap eating places. Of course, standards vary, but most serve edible food. If you're in any of the central areas, with the possible exception of Vassilyevsky Island, it should rarely take you more than 15 minutes to find a place for lunch or an early evening meal. Here are the best of a good bunch:

Zhemchuzhina, 2 Shkipersky Protok; metro Vassilyeostrovskaya. Good, inexpensive Azeri food, though portions are small.

Demianova Ukha, Gorkovo pr. 53, tel. 232-8090; metro Gorkovskaya. Crowded, cheap, and tasty fish restaurant, but not for the feeble-hearted: Even the tomato salad drips with oil.

Baghdad, ul. Furstadtskaya 35; metro Chernyshevskaya. Excellent, cheap Uzbek food and lightning-fast service.

Nevsky, Nevsky 71, tel. 311-8093; metro Ploshchad Vosstaniya. An old-style Soviet restaurant that's trying hard. The evening $20 cover charge is prohibitive, so come at lunchtime for the soft piano music and soothing fountain.

Tbilisi, Sytninskaya ul. 10, tel 232-9391; metro Gorkovskaya. Friendly, fast service and imaginative Georgian fare. Herby, spicy, healthy, and one of the very cheapest restaurants near the center.

Café Cat, Stremyannaya 22, tel. 311-3377; metro Mayakovskaya. Quiet, inexpensive, small, clean, and tasteful, with decent Russian cuisine. Evening entertainment for a small cover charge.

Café Saigon, ul. Plekhanova; metro Sennaya Ploshchad. The Vietnamese decor is faultless, the food, too, except for one thing – it's Russian! The mushroom soup is delicious.

Café Europa, ul. Rimskovo-Korsakova 11; metro Sennaya Ploshchad. Not to be confused with the hotel, but that's not to say the food isn't excellent. Book in advance.

Schwabsky Domik, Novocherkassky pr. 28, tel. 528-2211; metro Novocherkasskaya. As well as the well-publicized hard-currency section, there is actually a very good ruble restaurant and buffet next door. Authentic German cuisine for very reasonable prices.

Tete-a-Tete, Bolshoy pr. 67, tel. 232-7548; metro Petrogradskaya. A restaurant for couples. Most tables are for two with low, intimate lighting, and dinner dress is required in the evening.

Priboy, nab. reki Moiki 19; metro Nevsky Prospekt. Modern black mirrored interior. Delicious food but small portions.

Sankt-Peterburg Restaurant Café, nab. kan. Griboyedova 3. Good choice of snacks, very crowded; interesting, art-student atmosphere.

Charodeika, Nevsky 88; metro Mayakovskaya. Go downstairs for coffee and snacks. Prices are not the lowest, but the location is good.

Na Zagorodnom, Zagorodny 20; metro Vladimirskaya. Pleasant interior, crowded, good choice of snacks including wide range of seafood and sausages.

Café bar, Suvorovskaya 42; metro Chernyshevskaya. Bustling, close little café with gritty Turkish coffee and earthy Russian food.

Rassana, ul. Furmanova 19; metro Chernyshevskaya. Tiny, hot, and crowded, but the snacks, atmosphere and stylish-but-penniless clientele are appealing.

Fast food. Although there is no shortage of cafés serving tasteless microwaved food, St. Petersburg has only two genuine fast food joints to date. They are **Polyar**, Moskovsky pr. 222, metro Moskovskaya, only convenient if you're staying at the Pulkovskaya Hotel, and about the last place you would expect – the **Hermitage Museum Café**.

Tea and Cakes. Three other cafés, which don't serve food, should also be mentioned: **Zerkalnoye**, Zagorodny pr. 8; metro Vladimirskaya. The perfect place for morning coffee or afternoon tea.

Kalamis, Kamennoostrovsky pr. 19; metro Petrogradskaya. Tiny, pretty, and cozy café, owned by the cosmetics salon next door.

Petrograd, Bolshoy pr. 2l; metro Petrogradskaya. A U.S. joint venture, and corresponding cakes and cookies.

Nightlife

Though there is a burgeoning nightlife in St. Petersburg now, it has largely followed the Moscow pattern of casinos, erotic cabarets, and prostitute-frequented discos, many of them distinctly unsafe for foreigners. Only a handful of places are genuinely interesting, but for the sake of completeness, here is a list of those you can visit without feeling too intimidated to enjoy yourself.

Foul play, unexpected romance, or just a cold and lonely night...

Any of these can happen to Petersburgers (or visitors) who get stranded on one of the city's islands when the bridges open nightly for the passage of big ships. This occurs at varying times between 1:25 and 5:45 a.m. Check in advance before traveling late at night, and remember that taxi drivers don't like being stranded either! Some bridges close again briefly around 3 or 4 a.m.

Discos

Melody, Sverdlovskaya nab. 62, tel. 227-1596; metro Novocherkasskaya. A Swedish-run complex with restaurant, bar, and casino. Full of foreigners chatting up prostitutes, but probably the most decent mainstream disco, its prices made bearable by a happy hour.

Europa Plus Dansing, Kamennoostrovsky pr. 68; metro Chornaya Ryechka. Uninspiring disco and floor show organized by local radio station in an uninviting sports hall. Occasionally organizes pop concerts.

Joy, corner of nab. kan. Griboyedova and Lomonosova; metro Nevsky Prospekt. Mainstream disco with a hint of soul and a black DJ. Lively and popular.

Estrada, ul. Bolshaya Konyushennaya; metro Nevsky Prospekt. An irregular Friday night gay disco in the appalling innards of the Estrada Theater. With an element of straight, and an element of high camp, the crowd here is lively and generally stylish.

Café caprice, ul. Krzhizhanovskaya 3/1; metro Prospekt Bolshevikov. A serious gay disco with prison-like security at the back of beyond, Wednesdays and Saturdays only. If you're looking for a fun evening, think twice before making the trek.

Tunnel, ul. Zverinskaya; metro Gorkovskaya. Cheap, popular, and the trendiest club in town at the time of writing. Its setting is perfect – in a bomb shelter, permanently cool and without fire risk. Just in case, there are huge water tanks behind the bar.

Rock and Jazz Venues

Tam Tam Club, corner of Maly pr. and 16-aya liniya; metro Vassilyeostrovskaya. A platform for up-and-coming indie bands. Dirt cheap admission and beer, interesting decor. Music tends toward the hardcore, but check listings for other styles.

Indie Club, metro Proletarskaya. More typically for Russian rock venues, this one is set in a Culture House. Though it loses to Tam Tam on atmosphere, the range of music is wider and there's a disco in the foyer.

Jazz Philharmonic Hall, Zagorodny pr. 27, tel. 164-8565; metro Vladimirskaya. As the name suggests, this is a very formal place, and there is little opportunity to wander around or talk during performances. Still, there are late night jam sessions Friday and

Saturday. Type of jazz generally depends on the day of the week.

Bars

Chaika, nab. kan. Griboyedova 14; metro Nevsky Prospekt. The best of several German beer bars and a favorite meeting place for foreigners. The food is nothing special, so come here to drink.

Beer Garden, Nevsky 86; metro Mayakovskaya. One of the city's few outdoor watering holes. Food is good but pricey.

John Bull Pub, Nevsky 70; metro Mayakovskaya. Waitress service makes it rather un-publike, but with its cheerful atmosphere and reasonable decor, it's a cut above Moscow's various attempts to ape Englishness.

Grand Café Antwerpen, Kamennoostrovsky pr., opposite metro Gorkovskaya. This good but expensive restaurant with authentic Belgian-style interior makes an ideal setting for a quiet daytime drink.

Warsteiner Forum, Nevsky 120; metro Ploshchad Vosstaniya. Friendly but rather nondescript German beer bar, convenient for the Moskovsky Vokzal.

Cabarets

We will let one suffice for all. **Kan Kan**, Izmailovsky pr. 7, whose $50 cover charge limits the clientele largely to guests at the top-class hotels, features palatial decor and professional acts that recently combined comedy, singer Natalya Sorokina, a gypsy band, and dance routines that got racier as the night wore on. Also serving drinks and dinner.

Shopping

Department Stores

St. Petersburg's major department stores are all within a few yards of each other around Nevsky prospekt and Sadovaya ulitsa. The biggest, **Gostiny Dvor**, is seedy, bland, and nightmarishly labyrinthine, though you can find just about anything there if you look hard enough. Avoid changing money with black-marketeers. Upstairs is **Littlewood's**, a hard-currency store with a full range of Western goods. The **Passazh** is just opposite on Nevsky – shopping is easier there, with a single row of well-signposted shops, a smaller version of Moscow's GUM. On the opposite side of Gostiny Dvor on Sadovaya is the smaller **Apraksin Dvor**.

Tsentralny Gastronom, formerly Gastronom No. 1, Nevsky prospekt

Most hotels have some kind of hard-currency store selling clothes, souvenirs, alcohol, and other selected items, although usually the choice is not good. The best are probably the **Neva Star** in the Hotel Moskva and the **Baltic Star** in the Pribaltiiskaya.

Food

You won't find Moscow's plethora of Western-type foodstores here, but the abundance of good Russian shops makes up for it.

St. Petersburg's **Stockmann Kalinka**, Finlandsky pr. 1, metro Ploshchad Lenina, takes credit cards, and nearby, in the Hotel St. Petersburg, there is another smaller, equally expensive grocery store called **Intour Duty Free**. For fresh fruit, try the Finnish **Express Market**, with two shops, one at Nevsky 113 (corner of Kharkovskaya ul.), metro Ploshchad Vosstaniya, and the other at Moskovsky pr. 73, metro Frunzenskaya.

Wealthy Russians tend to favor **Super Babylon**, Maly pr. 54, metro Petrogradskaya, which is nothing short of a Western supermarket. Several other shops in the Babylon chain stock food, notably at Nevsky 69, metro Ploshchad Vosstaniya. Two other ruble shops worth mentioning are **Donon**, Gertsena 17, metro Nevsky Prospekt, and **Holiday**, Bolshoy pr. 2, metro Gorkovskaya, both open **24 hours** a day. If you like shopping in style, brave the crowds at the magnificent **Tsentralny Gastronom**, Nevsky 56, metro Gostiny Dvor.

The city's main central covered markets are as follows:

Kondratyevsky, Polyustrovsky pr. 45, metro Ploshchad Lenina; **Kuznechny**, Kuznechny pr. 3, metro Vladimirskaya; **Nekrasovsky**, ul. Nekrasova 52, metro Ploshchad Vosstaniya; **Sennoy**, Moskovsky pr. 4/6, metro Sennaya Ploshchad; **Sytny**, Sytninskaya pl. 3/5, metro Gorkovskaya; **Vasilyeostrovsky**, Bolshoy pr. 16, metro Vasilyeostrovskaya.

Souvenirs, Works of Art

Ordinary souvenirs are never hard to find, whether on Nevsky prospekt or at any of the major tourist spots. Here, then, is a guide to places offering more sophisticated gifts:

Griffon, Gertsena 33; metro Nevsky Prospekt. A small art salon with quality handicrafts.

The Russian Arts, ul. Saltykova-Shchedrina 53; metro Chernyshevskaya. Art shop with especially interesting glasswork.

Most of St. Petersburg's new private galleries tend to put profit before art. Here are a few which nevertheless deserve attention:

Borey, Liteiny pr. 58; metro Mayakovskaya. A small, noncommercial gallery with rapidly-changing exhibitions much loved by the artists for its informal atmosphere.

Navicula Artis, pl. Truda 4; metro Sennaya Ploshchad. The high prices here (up to $15,000) are a sign of quality in this case – this is the city's finest experimental gallery, set in the magnificent Nikolayevsky Palace. Come to have a look at least.

Pushkin, **Gogol**, (currently no permanent address). Exhibitions of the older generation of St. Petersburg underground, mounted at various locations. Look for write-ups in the press or ask around.

Artists' Union of Russia, Gertsena 38; metro Nevsky Prospekt. Located in another palace, this one from the time of Catherine the Great, the Artists' Union holds up to five exhibitions at a time. Chances are you'll find something to interest you.

Books

The huge book market which spreads daily along Nevsky prospekt should cater for most of your art book and guidebook needs. However, **Mir** bookshop at Nevsky 13 (metro Nevsky Prospekt) has a wider selection, plus even some trashy fiction in English and books in other languages. The **Writers' Book Corner** at Nevsky 66 and another shop at Nevsky 20 should also be investigated, likewise **Dom Knigi** at Nevsky 28 if you can stand the crush. The best antiquarian bookshop is the **Bukinist** at Liteiny 59.

Illustration by M.V. Dobuzhinsky for Dostoyevsky's Byeliye Nochi (White Nights)

Theater, Concerts, Circus

Mariinsky Theater, Teatralnaya ploshchad 1, tel. 114-5924; metro Sennaya Ploshchad. Known in Soviet times by its more familiar name, the Kirov, this is probably good enough reason on its own to come to St. Petersburg... and ticket prices are much lower than at Moscow's Bolshoy.

Maly Theater of Opera and Ballet, Ploshchad Iskusstv 1, tel. 219-1988; metro Gostiny Dvor. Second only to the Mariinsky, and a good substitute if you're here in July when the other's season has finished.

Large Hall of Philharmonia, Brodskovo ul. 2, tel. 311-7333; metro Gostiny Dvor. The best of the city's concert venues.

Glinki Philharmonic Hall, Nevsky 30, tel. 312-4585; metro Gostiny Dvor. A small, intimate venue with a good concert program.

Academic Capella, nab. reki Moiki 20, tel. 233-0243; metro Nevsky Prospekt. Excellent choir concerts.

Smolny Cathedral, pl. Rastrelli 3/1, tel. 542-0942. Even better choir concert space.

Circus, nab. Fontanki 3, tel. 210-4390; metro Gostiny Dvor. On a par with Moscow circuses.

Russian American Theater, Baltic Home International Theater Center, Lenin Park 4, tel. 232-8576; metro Gorkovskaya. Drama in English, using American and Russian actors.

Bolshoy Drama Theater, nab. reki Fontanki 65, tel. 310-9242; metro Gostiny Dvor. For those with a knowledge of Russian, the best dramatic theater in town.

Theater on Liteiny, Liteiny 51, tel. 273-5335; metro Mayakovskaya. Experimental theater at its best.

Leisure

One is readily attracted to the parks of St. Petersburg, but while many of them are beautiful, they are usually quite crowded. The large, out-of-town palace parks can be just as congested, but only on the well-trodden routes. The **Alexandrovsky Park** at Tsarskoye Selo (see Leningrad Region) seems particularly mysterious, abandoned and lightly visited. If you're looking for fresh air and virgin forest, though, take a local train anywhere north from the Finlandsky Vokzal and you won't be disappointed.

For beaches, most local people tend to go out to Gulf of Finland resorts like **Sestroretsk** and **Solnechnoye**, but this is becoming increasingly hazardous. There is supposed to be a pollution-free beach just west of the Peter and Paul Fortress but this would seem to defy logic.

Places of Worship

Russian Orthodox:

Cathedral of the Holy Trinity at Alexander Nevsky Lavra (monastery), Reki Monastyrki nab. 1, metro Ploshchad Aleksandra Nevskovo; tel. 274-0409. Services at 9 a.m. and 6 p.m. daily; 7 & 10 a.m. and 6 p.m. on Sundays.

Church of St. John the Baptist, Kamennoostrovsky pr., just across Bolshaya Nevka River bridge, south of metro Chornaya Ryechka; tel. 234-1324. Services at 5 p.m. Saturdays and 9 p.m. Sundays. This church especially welcomes those who want to speak about Orthodoxy with Russian people who know English.

Other Faiths:

Baptist Church, Bolshaya Ozyornaya 29a, tel. 553-4578; metro Ozerki

Buddhist Temple, Primorsky pr. 91, tel. 239-0341; metro Chornaya Ryechka, then #2, 3, 31, or 37 tram

International Church, Nevsky 39, tel. 315-8446 or 352-2015; metro Gostiny Dvor

Lutheran Church, ul. Proletkulta 4, tel. 470-9963; in the town of Tsarskoye Selo (see Leningrad Region)

Mosque, pr. Gorkovo 7, tel. 233-9819; metro Gorkovskaya

Roman Catholic Church, Kovensky per. 7, tel. 272-5002; metro Ploshchad Vosstaniya

Synagogue, Lermontovsky pr. 2, tel. 206-0078; metro Sennaya Ploshchad

Medical Care

Like Moscow, St. Petersburg now has an **American Medical Center** (AMC), at 77 nab. reki Fontanki, tel. 119-6101; metro Gostiny Dvor. It has a small emergency room and Western GPs who will see non-members during working hours Monday–Friday. It provides immunization, and can arrange evacuation home. The alternative is **Polyclinic No. 2**, Moskovsky pr. 22, tel. 292-6272, for emergencies 110-1102; metro Tekhnologichesky Institut. This is the former outpatient clinic for diplomats and foreign VIPs, with fully stocked Western pharmacy and dental clinic and 24-hour emergency service.

For inpatient care, the AMC has several recommendations:

City Hospital No. 31, pr. Dinamo 3, Krestovsky Ostrov, metro Petrogradskaya (tel. 235-1202), a former VIP hospital.

Institute of Traumatology, ul. Akademika Baikova 8, metro Politekhnicheskaya (tel. 556-0831).

Children's Hospital No. 1, Avangardnaya ul. 14, metro Prospekt Veteranov, then #30 trolleybus (tel. 135-1207). For gynecological care, there are as yet no firm recommendations, though a fuller list of these and other hospitals with good reputations can be found in *Where in St. Peters-*

burg or *The Traveller's Yellow Pages.*

The AMC and Polyclinic No. 2 have the best selection of Western drugs at their pharmacies. For emergencies, try the 24-hour pharmacy at Nevsky 83, tel. 277-7966, but check beforehand for availability of the product you need.

Publications in English

Newspapers and Magazines

Compared with Moscow, standards here are low, so it's just as well that the *Moscow Times* and *Moscow Tribune* are available here, too.

St. Petersburg News: a quarterly glossy magazine with features, listings, and a pull-out section in Russian. Available for dollars in most hotels.

St. Petersburg Press: a decent, free weekly newspaper à la *Moscow Times*, with local and CIS news.

Neva News: Twice monthly, badly written and edited. Definitely not worth the $1 charged for it in hotels, but can be obtained for rubles at street kiosks.

St. Petersburg for You: a monthly review for tourists and businessmen. Unedited and therefore incomprehensible. For rubles.

Guides and Directories

St. Petersburg Yellow Pages: a dry and exhaustive bilingual directory, not really much use for travelers.

Traveller's Yellow Pages: everything that the above isn't. It selects only the best in each category and provides essential advice for the first-time visitor, as well as vital information such as nightly opening times for the city's bridges (see box). Published by Info Services International, 1 St. Marks Place, Cold Spring Harbor, NY 11724; tel. (516) 549-0064.

Where in St. Petersburg: a guide for independent travelers, providing similar kinds of information to the above, plus a business telephone directory and a very useful sectional street map, good for finding your bearings without broadly advertising that you're a foreigner. Published by Russian Information Services, 89 Main Street, #2, Montpelier, VT 05602; tel. (800) 639-4301.

Tours

The following offer excursions for the discerning tourist:

Union of Architects, Gertsena 52, tel. 312-0400; metro Nevsky Prospekt. Tours of the city and out-of-town palaces by professional architects.

Architectural Tours of St. Petersburg, tel. 298-4359. As above; also organizes canal tours.

"Shakti" Center for Advanced Studies in History & Culture, Kovenskiy pereulok 29/3, tel. 279-5198; metro Ploshchad Vosstaniya. Tours of museums, churches, archives, literary places, and other sites. (See advertisement.)

Two **Dostoyevsky experts** offer tours of the city: call Sergei Belov at 227-3572 or Alexander Raskin at 510-4450.

Another interesting way to see the city is by canal, and there are now several private operators offering trips, ranging between $10 and $25 an hour.

RUSSIAN GLOSSARY

Academy of Arts
Художественная академия

Apraksin Dvor
Апраксин двор

Aptekarsky pereulok
Аптекарский переулок

Artists' Union of Russia
Союз художников России

Baghdad Café
Кафе «Багдад»
Bukinist
Букинист
St. Catherine's Catholic Church
Екатериниский костел
Café Charodeika
Кафе «Чародейка»
Children's Hospital No. 1
Детская больница №1
Demianova Ukha restaurant
Ресторан «Демьянова уха»
Estrada Disco
Дискотека «Эстрада»
Café Europa
Кафе «Европа»
Exhibition of Contemporary Fresco
Выставка современной фрески
Fontanny Dom
Фонтанный дом
Institute of Traumatology
Институт травматологии
Shrine of John Lennon
Храм Джона Леннона
Café Kalamis
Кафе «Каламис»
Kikin's Chambers
Кикины палаты
Klenovaya alleya
Кленовая аллея
Lazarevskoye Cemetery
Лазаревское кладбище
Theater Na Liteinom
Театр «На Литейном»
Mukhin School
Мухинское училище
Nakhimov Institute
Нахимовский институт
Café Na Zagorodnom
Кафе «На Загородном»
Nekrasovsky Market
Некрасовский рынок
New Holland
Новая Голландия
St. Panteleimon's Church
Пантелеймоновская церковь
Café Priboy
Кафе «Прибой»
Pulkovo Airport
Аэропорт Пулково
Rassana Café
Кафе «Рассана»
Rzhevka Airport
Аэропорт Ржевка
Café Saigon
Кафе «Сайгон»
Sennoy Market
Сенной рынок
Church of SS. Simeon and Anna
Церковь Симеона и Анны
Sinyy Bridge
Синий мост
Stock Exchange
Биржа
Strelka
Стрелка
Summer Garden
Летний сад
Tbilisi Café
Кафе «Тбилиси»
Tikhvinskoye Cemetery
Тихвинское кладбище
Tunnel Disco
Дискотека «Туннель»
Writers' Book Corner
Лавка писателя
Yusupov Palace
Юсуповский дворец
Café Zerkalnoye
Кафе «Зеркальное»
Café Zhemchuzhina
Кафе «Жемчужина»

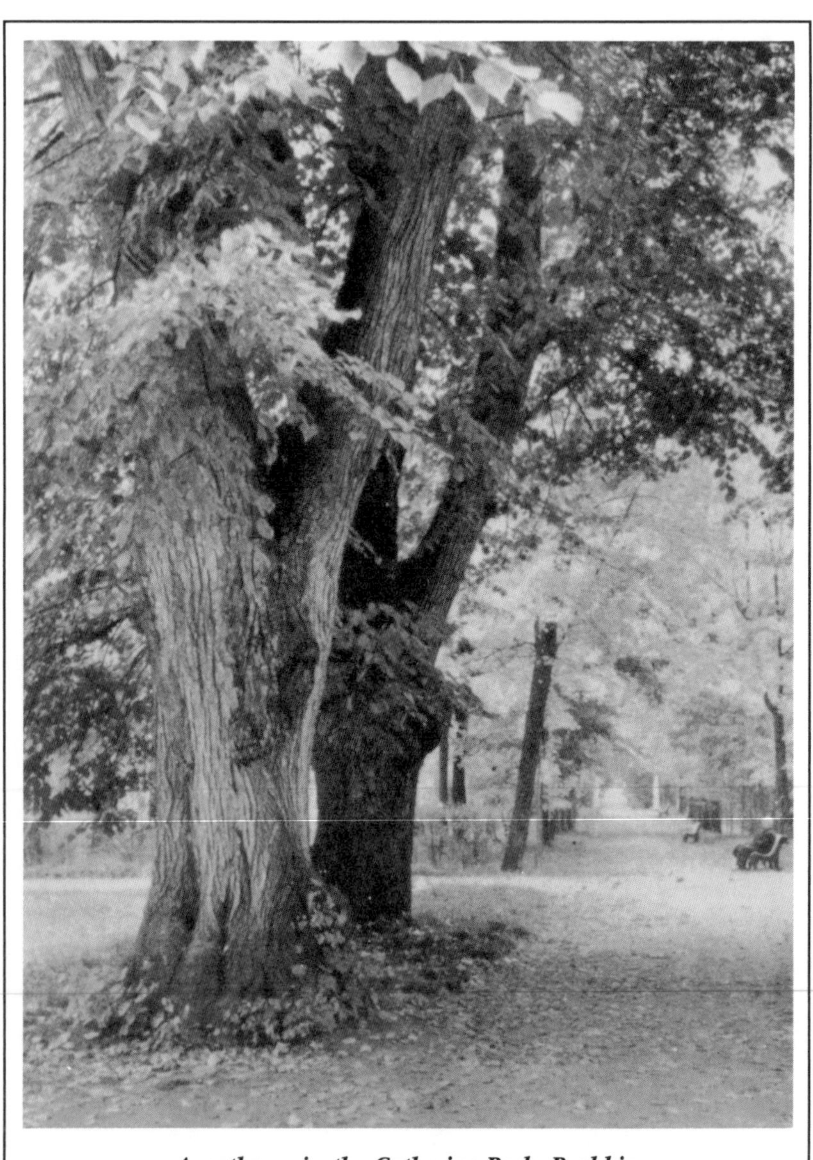

A pathway in the Catherine Park, Pushkin

LENINGRAD REGION

LENINGRADSKAYA OBLAST

St. Petersburg and its formerly eponymous *oblast* now bear different names as a result of referenda which took place in 1991. While the citizens of Leningrad voted to restore their city to its pre-World War I name, those of the surrounding region did not follow suit.

This sprawling region spreads from the Gulf of Finland to Lake Onega, from Novgorod to Karelia. While the suburbs of St. Petersburg are renowned for their summer palaces and parks, go further afield and you will find a much older heritage – the towns and fortresses which defended first Novgorod's, then Moscow's, northern borders during the 11th century and after. The region, like other parts of northwest Russia, is also blessed with forests, beautiful lakes and traditional wooden architecture.

THE PALACES AND PARKS: PETRODVORETS

In the years following the founding of St. Petersburg, the city was not the only focus of intensive building. On an island in the Gulf of Finland, the citadel of Kronstadt was raised, and the Tsar's courtiers laid out seaside plots for themselves along the nearby coast. Peter had a wooden palace built for him in his favorite spot, which was to become known as **Peterhof**. Here he received guests, monitored the progress across the water at Kronstadt, and planned a system of parks at Peterhof to join the lower plain near the sea with higher ground inland. In 1712, Russian victory in the sea battle of Gungut made Peterhof secure from attack by the Swedes. Two years later, work began in earnest on the site, and Peter's dream to create a new Versailles began to take shape. The Upper Chambers, now the Grand Palace, came into being, as well as gardens with fountains and cascades, and the favorite haunt of the Tsar, the snug, seaside Monplaisir Palace.

During the next two centuries, St. Petersburg's most famous architects and sculptors reworked and perfected Peterhof. In 1745, the Empress Elizabeth commissioned Rastrelli to redesign the Grand Palace, adding side wings and two domed blocks, one a church, the other topped by the coat-of-arms. At the same time, the palace was infused, inside and out, with the extravagant baroque decoration that is its hallmark.

Grand Palace, Petrodvorets

The current century's upheavals were deeply felt at Peterhof. The Revolution opened to the general public what was once a sanctuary of the privileged, while the Second World War all but destroyed it. Today's palace is the splendid result of decades of restoration.

Petrodvorets is the most grandiose of St. Petersburg's palace ensembles and also the most open, visible at a great distance both from land and sea. There is always something to admire, and it is well worth visiting even if you don't see the interiors. The only disappointment is the fountains of the Grand Cascade, which seem constantly under repair.

The **Grand Palace** can be exhausting for its sheer size and countless halls, all but a few of them devoid of human warmth or even an accumulation of royal splendors. It is obviously a reconstruction, its vast spaces never inhabited but only admired. Note the gilded wood carvings of the main staircase, the legions of innocent maidens portrayed in the picture gallery, the carved wood panels of Peter's study, and the exotic mixed parquet of the Chinese rooms.

If you arrive by sea, your first sight will be the **Grand Cascade**, a feast of spurting torrents, spraying mist and gold statues. It was built to celebrate Russia's beginnings as a naval power. The statues and fountains throughout the park are united by a marine theme, while at the cascade's focal point, a Russian Samson pries open the jaws of a Swedish lion, which send a jet of water 20 meters high.

On the west side of the Lower Park can be found the quieter beauty of the **Marly Palace**, a temporary residence for guests or family of the Tsar, built in 1723 by Johann Braunstein. Its modest form is in perfect harmony with its surroundings. Walking back to the east along the shore of the Gulf brings you to the **Hermitage**, another Braunstein masterpiece, which was offered to members of the Tsar's entourage for merriment or solitude.

Continuing east and crossing a canal brings you to **Monplaisir**, a palace in whose construction Peter the Great personally participated. It has many details associated with Peter, including wood paneling, Chinese rooms and a Dutch kitchen. Next door is a block once occupied by Catherine the Great, as she waited to assume power while her hapless husband, Peter III, was overthrown.

Inland of Monplaisir, the aquatics of Petrodvorets assume a more playful tone. Two trick fountains, designed to drench unsuspecting passers-by, give way to Chessboard Hill, perhaps the most extraordinary of the park's cascades. Three brightly colored dragons guard the entrance to a small grotto, spurting water over a sloping chessboard. The cascade is oddly flanked by traditional classical statues by Italian masters from the early 18th century.

Continuing east, you will arrive at the gates of the Alexandria Park, a much wilder and less trodden place that was once the domain of Peter's right-hand man, Prince Menshikov. In due course, it was given to Nicholas I's wife Alexandra.

The Hermitage* (left) *and the Umbrella* (right), *a trick fountain in the Lower Park

Alexandria Park could scarcely make more of a contrast with its neighbor. It is essentially a landscape garden, or rather a seascape one; the sea plays a major role in its composition. Full of small romantic buildings and follies, its overriding style is gothic, notably the towering Germanic capella, devoted to Alexander Nevsky, and Alexandra's own residence, the Cottage Palace, its early nineteenth century interior the finest of all in Petrodvorets.

ORANIENBAUM

A short journey to the west from Petrodvorets brings you to another former Menshikov property, the palace and park of Oranienbaum, still sometimes known by its Soviet-era name, Lomonosov. Prince Menshikov once again sought to outdo everyone in the splendor of this palace. After his fall, the estate eventually came into the hands of Grand Prince Peter and his German wife Catherine, later the Great, who commissioned the architect Rinaldi to build more palaces for them.

Oranienbaum survived World War II intact, the only one of St. Petersburg's palaces to do so. Today it is a quiet park and museum complex, each of its buildings displaying splendidly festive interiors. Be sure to study the map at the gate before entering – signposts in the park are rare and often misleading, and thick plantings of trees make orientation difficult.

Menshikov's palace, its main façade obscured by trees, is currently under restoration, so walk round to the left of it to **Peter III's Palace**. This odd little cuboid was once the center of Peterstadt, a mini-fortress used by the infantile prince for parading his "toy" soldiers. Now it is simply set in a quiet garden. Its interiors, often in Chinese style, are cloyingly rich.

This theme is continued in Catherine's palace, also known as the **Chinese Palace**, on the western end of the park. This building's fate was also to be merely a toy, a showpiece, as it was never lived in by the future empress. With its restrained exterior and extravagant interior, it is the most complete and outstanding example of rococco in Russia – a sea of damask wallpaper, paintings on plaster and canvas, fake marble and parquet containing 20 species of wood. The culmination of all this is the Great Chinese Study, a free interpretation by European masters of Chinese art, with a ceiling fresco representing the union of Asia and Europe, a theme in keeping with the expanding Russian Empire.

Finally, visit the Coasting-Hill Pavilion. This was built in 1762–64 for an early Russian prototype of the roller-coaster. First known as the "Russian Hill," its popularity spread all over the world. In addition to further rococco interiors, the Pavilion includes a model of the roller-coaster; the original fell into disuse and was dismantled long ago.

PUSHKIN

Formerly known as Tsarskoye Selo (Tsar's Village), this settlement's original name was a corruption of the Finnish *saari*, meaning island, but later came to mean just what it suggests. Tsarskoye Selo became the tsars' main country residence, complete with a dependent town to serve it.

Tsarskoye Selo's beginnings were modest. The acquisitive Prince Menshikov came by this farmstead south of St. Petersburg in 1707. But not for long – three years later Peter bequeathed it to his future wife, Yekaterina Alexeyevna. From her, **Catherine's Palace** took its name.

However, serious work on constructing the palace, gardens and outbuildings commenced only under Empress Elizabeth. Rastrelli created a baroque palace of unprecedented glamour and glitter. Unfortunately, materials used in building were of poor quality, and Elizabeth's successor Catherine the Great set about a major reconstruction almost immediately after her accession. The interior was redecorated in classical style, and much of the baroque extravagance of the exterior toned down. This was the heyday of Tsarskoye Selo, and it became, as well as Catherine's favorite residence, a playground for aristocratic youth. Work was begun on a second palace for Alexander, the Tsarina's grandson.

Catherine's son, Tsar Paul, virtually abandoned Tsarskoye Selo in favor of nearby Pavlovsk, and the palace complex was threatened for a time with oblivion. However, Alexander I, true to his grandmother's ideals, returned there, and development continued through much of the 19th century. This time it was the town's turn – it became the first in Russia to have a railway line (1837) and electricity (1880). Up until the Revolution, it was a model town, with the best sewage system, cleanest roads and best schools in the country. Poets Alexander Pushkin and Anna Akhmatova both studied in Tsarskoye Selo, Pushkin in the Lyceum attached to the Catherine Palace.

After the Revolution, the town was given a new role, as a center for childrens' sanatoria, and correspondingly a new name, Detskoye Selo (Childrens' Village), retained today only at the railway station. Pushkin, as it was renamed in 1937, 100 years after the poet's death, was virtually destroyed during the war and is still undergoing restoration today. The Catherine Palace is again intact, and its glittering, golden halls and 20,000 works of art surpass Petrodvorets completely. The jewel of its crown is the Great Hall. Once a venue for banquets and masquerade balls, its walls form a vast gallery of windows, mirrors and gilded carving.

The 300m southeast façade, turquoise and studded with the large forms of gold atlantes seeming to support white columns, displays Rastrelli's glamorous artistry. The contrasting northwest side was redone in a more subdued classical style by Catherine the Great's chief architect, the Scot Charles Cameron.

The palace is surrounded on two sides by the large **Catherine Park**. Adjacent to Rastrelli's façade is a nearly rectangular formal garden. Its centerpiece, three-quarters of the way between the palace and the Lower Ponds, is the **Hermitage**, a building in the plan of a cross used for meals and balls. An elaborate system of pulleys and ropes enabled courtiers to dispense with servants and set up tables or dance floors as they pleased and with a minimum of effort.

Away to the right is the Great Pond, Catherine's favorite place for strolling, located in the larger, landscaped portion of the park. A superb place from which to view it is the **Cameron Gallery** (1780–85), adjacent to the south

Catherine Palace, and the "Girl with a Jug," along the Great Pond

corner of the palace, which stands between the formal and landscape parks. The many surprises in and around the pond include a rostral column which rises from the water in honor of the sea victory against the Turks at Cesme, Turkish Baths in the form of a diminutive mosque and minaret, and a pyramid nearby which marks the grave of three of Catherine's pet dogs, Sir Tom Anderson, Zemir and Duchess. As you walk along the shore, you will also encounter a simple statue of a girl with a broken pitcher; this was a favorite of Pushkin and Akhmatova, each of whom wrote poems about her.

Spreading to the north are other buildings and follies, this time in Chinese style. Their focus is a Chinese Village, also designed by Cameron; I found a company of twelve-year-olds parading there in prerevolutionary uniforms. Does it now house a school for monarchist children?

Several other parks and palaces complete the Pushkin complex. To the northwest, the **Alexander Park** is overgrown and mostly in ruins, but a magnet for the intrepid explorer. The palace's exterior is severely classical, and the interior is off limits; it is Defense Ministry property. Worth seeing are the towering gothic ruin of the Arsenal, at the intersection of paths in the center of the park, as well as a pavilion where the Tsar's elephants used to be kept.

On the park's edge are the most recent structures in the area, the Fyodorovsky Village, which dates from the years immediately prior to the Revolution. Built in ancient Russian style to resemble a kremlin, they were intended to house the tsar's bodyguards. The gates sport white-stone carvings echoing the Vladimir-Suzdal style of centuries past. Nearby is St. Fyodor's Cathedral, also in pseudo-Russian style. The foundation stone was laid by Nicholas II, a bust of whom stands in the yard behind. A native of Tsarskoye Selo, he was a frequent visitor to the village, which is where he was arrested by the Bolsheviks. Erected just last summer, this is the first monument on Russian territory to the last tsar.

Finally, Babolovsky Park, which lies beyond the Orlov Gate at the southern extreme of the Catherine Park, is the largest of the three, and was used mainly for horse-riding. Its remote palace was built in Anglo-gothic style in 1784 for Catherine's favorite, Grigory Potemkin.

PAVLOVSK

The Pavlovsk ensemble just south of Pushkin was a much later construction than its neighbor. It was begun by Catherine the Great for her son, the future Tsar Paul. But Charles Cameron's work, like most of the things his mother initiated, failed to please the prince, who during the 1790's engaged Vincenzo Brenna (1745–1820), Cameron's understudy, to redo it. During the half century consumed in building the palace, one of the finest landscape parks in Europe was fashioned around it.

Postwar restoration was completed in 1970, much earlier than at the other outlying royal residences. Unfortunately, the palace is too small to withstand large numbers of people, and admission at certain times is by group excursion only.

This classical palace has a rather compact core surmounted by a low dome. A pair of wings on the courtyard side, added by Brenna, form nearly a complete circle around a courtyard. It is a delight to approach the palace from this side, along Treble

Lime Alley. (The courtyard is where you will enter, find the *kassa*, and put *tapochki*, protective slippers, over your shoes.)

After ascending from the ground floor to the first, you will see two contrasting modes of decoration in the rooms of the central portion of the palace, announced by Paul's Hall of War and tsarina Maria Fyodorovna's Hall of Peace. Paul's taste at Pavlovsk often recalls his oppressive Mikhailovsky Castle in St. Petersburg, with its battle regalia and masonic symbols. Happily, Maria's contributions to the appearance of many interiors provide a saving balance. Her suite of rooms (Hall of Peace, library, boudoir, and bedroom) include splendid patterned parquet floors and exquisite wall paintings.

Among the most pleasing furnishings of the palace – which were all removed for safekeeping ahead of the German advance in 1941 – are a collection of intricately detailed silver and gilt clocks. Most rooms include a large black and white photograph showing their ruination at the time of the German withdrawal. What has been accomplished since is an astounding act of re-creation, carried out by skilled craftspersons and ordi-

Above: ***Pavlovsk Palace from Centaur Bridge.*** **Below:** ***Slavyanka River***

nary citizens alike. Their story is movingly told by Suzanne Massie in her book, *Pavlovsk: The Life of a Russian Palace*.

But the greatest pleasure of Pavlovsk is its splendid landscape park, essentially the work of Charles Cameron. He shaped the Slavyanka river valley into **Pavlovsk Park**'s defining central landscape, later elaborated with picturesque pavilions and rustic bridges. The park is especially stunning in autumn, the mix of trees chosen for maximum colorful effect. Allow time to explore the park's many special places, including the Centaur's Bridge, hidden unobtrusively in the shadow of the palace; the Old Woods, where bronze statues of the Twelve Muses stand in an étoile formed by converging paths; and the Pil Tower, a cylindrical folly further afield in a portion later designed by Brenna.

GATCHINA

This stern palace with Italianate features which lies to the south of Pavlovsk is quite distinct in aspect from all of the other suburban palaces. It was originally designed by the Italian architect Antonio Rinaldi for Count Orlov, Catherine the Great's favorite, when Orlov was at the height of his influence. Tsar Paul later commissioned Vincenzo Brenna to replace its intimacy with pomp and ceremony.

Gatchina's recent history is notable only for its harshness – the palace was even more badly damaged than its neighbors in World War II. As a result, a great deal of restoration work remains to be done. Nevertheless, there is little evidence of this. The main entrance is magnificent and often eerily calm, with few human figures in sight other than the statue of Tsar Paul.

The palace museum contains collections of art and artifacts from all

Priory Castle, Gatchina

over the world which were preserved from the Nazis, but only a limited number of rooms are open. Many of the principal rooms, including the White Hall and the throne of Tsar Paul's widow, Maria, have recently been restored.

The park, also the work of Brenna, is now almost completely wild. Its leafy romanticism is marred only by the poorly cared for paddleboats on the White Lake. A string of islands, connected by a peculiar variety of bridges, stretches across the lake. But don't hope to cross to the other end – one bridge has been removed, for no perceptible reason other than to frustrate the leisurely stroller.

For the best view of the palace, walk around the lake to the Island of Love, where the twin towers can be seen looming over dense greenery. The ceiling of the island's Venus Pavilion is decorated with an 18th century painting of the plump, self-satisfied goddess. On this day, she was being kept company by a talkative, elderly attendant.

There are three other parks – the strictly geometric Silvia Park, and the Menagerie and Priory hunting grounds. The latter contains the extraordinary **Priory Castle**, built by architect Nikolay Lvov at the end of the 18th century for the emigré French Prince Conday, Prior of the Maltese Knights of St. John, who never chose to reside there. A Germanic fairy-tale castle, it may also be Russia's only adobe (earthen) building.

The town of Gatchina has many attractive 18th century wooden houses and a charming Lutheran church at the southern end. Lovers of Art Nouveau should visit the Rozhdestvensky House on Ulitsa Khokhlova, now a wedding palace, and the odd triangular house of the caricaturist Shcherbov at #4 Ulitsa Chekhova.

THE FORTRESSES: ORESHEK

This island in a corner of Lake Ladoga is known for its peanut shape (the name comes from the Russian word *orekh*, meaning "nut"), an impregnable position guarding the entrance to the river Neva, and for the political prisons established there.

Originally built as part of Novgorod's northern fortification system in 1323, it became an entry point into Russia for merchant shipping. In the 17th century it fell to the Swedes, but Peter the Great regained it in the Northern War, and had it converted into a prison. An early inmate was his unloved wife, Yevdokia; Catherine and others kept up this tradition.

After the Revolution, the Bolsheviks abandoned the prison. Still, Oreshek played a major part in World War II, when its garrison held the Germans at bay throughout the siege of Leningrad, thus preventing the complete encirclement of the city.

Today, Oreshek, a short day trip from St. Petersburg and well away from the crowds, is a grim and mysterious place. The wreckage inside the walls is almost unchanged since the war. The ruined Assumption Cathedral is a far cry from its former twin, the SS. Peter and Paul Cathedral in St. Petersburg. Within is a memorial to the garrison.

At the far end are the former prison blocks. Within the citadel of the fortress is the Secret House (1798), where members of nearly every generation of revolutionaries have languished. Oreshek was also a place of execution. Alexander Ulyanov, Lenin's brother, was shot there; a plaque on the courtyard wall commemorates him.

Ladoga's Secret Sanctuary

The 50 islands of the Valaam Archipelago, granite outcrops with sheer cliffs cut by glaciers, are a distinctive feature of northern Lake Ladoga. Their remoteness suited them for monastic life, and by the 14th century a community of monks had settled here.

Plundered several times by the Swedes, Valaam only became truly established as a monastery in the 18th century, under the protection of the normally anti-clerical Peter the Great. A new abbott, Father Nazary, built *skeets*, small monastic dwelling-places which functioned outside the traditional monastery framework.

They were populated by monks who chose to live an even more austere way of life than that of the main monastic community. Some took vows of silence and limited their diets to the strictest form of veganism. Others took vows not to wash; after years of this their clothes would graft to their bodies and had to be scraped off. One hermit, Damaskin, slept in a coffin; he would later preside as abbot over Valaam's most prosperous era.

Father Damaskin brought Valaam international fame, sending missionaries as far afield as Alaska. At home, everything was rebuilt, using bricks baked from local clay; the islands again became self-sufficient, housing a wide variety of workshops and agricultural activities.

After 1917, Valaam's luck continued: as part of newly-independent Finland, it escaped the Bolshevik scourging of Russian Orthodoxy. When the Soviet Union invaded in 1940, the monks of Valaam made use of their new citizenship and fled, founding New Valaam further west. This descendant of the parent monastery still exists today.

In 1989, the original Valaam was reconsecrated; six monks returned to the monastery that year. Today, they are twelve in number. Although a triumph for the Russian Orthodox Church, this development is proving to be a mixed blessing for others. New Valaam, entirely Finnish but still in possession of the old monastery's treasures, puts forward its claims to the islands, but the Russians shun any contact and deny the Finns' legitimacy. For them, no real Christian could live by the Gregorian calendar.

Meanwhile, the island's 600 villagers resent what they see as insensitive treatment by church authorities. The mainland housing they were promised has not materialized, and many villagers are reluctant to leave their remote island home for flats in a modern city. The villagers tend to view the monks as lazy strangers, far removed from the natives' devout and self-sacrificing traditions. Mutual respect so far seems to elude both parties. The donation of 23 million rubles authorized by Boris Yeltsin two years ago seems to have evaporated, stalling the monastery's protracted restoration process.

Whatever Valaam's internal conflicts, it is a perfect place for an extended day or weekend outing from St. Petersburg. Boat trips and wanders through the hills, plus the never-ending surprises of the islands – skeets, chapels, and crosses in unexpected places – will please romantics and the pious alike.

The settlement's focal point is the

Cathedral of the Transfiguration, within the monastery, a lofty church that's been decked in scaffolding for 15 years, some indication of the task its restoration poses. Inside, the picture is a sad one of crumbling 19th century tempera paintings and forlornly empty iconostasis frames. Here and there are the monastery's service blocks, the work of St. Petersburg architect Alexey Gornostayev. Life continues in its shadow, although the handful of shops and single café hardly buzz with activity. The town will probably dissolve if the monastery takes full control; liquor and tobacco could be banned from the islands as in former times.

A wild forest road takes you to Skitsky Island, and the now functioning All Saint's Skeet, the one most restricted to visitors, where the psalter is read 24 hours a day, each monk taking a two-hour shift. Always the largest of the dependent communities, Skitsky also has Gornostayev's most notable commission in the islands, a skeet designed in the manner of a white fairytale castle rising through the trees.

On the southern end of Valaam Island, sites were named by an enraptured abbot after places in the Holy Land, following his return from a pilgrimage to Jerusalem.

Valaam Monastery

The New Jerusalem's Resurrection Church hosts concerts of Valaam's unique chanting, while the Gethsemane Skeet is a handsome wooden church in eclectic style.

Some of the skeets are in far-off corners of the islands, so you would do well to allow more than a day to explore them. However long you're here, you'll enjoy this haven, where even blustery weather does not mar the idyllic calm.

IVANGOROD

If you're traveling to Estonia along the shores of the Gulf of Finland, a stop on the border will give you an opportunity to visit two great fortresses on opposite banks of the Narova river. **Ivangorod** and **Narva** have always been rivals; now they are once again on opposing sides, as Russia and Estonia squabble over citizenship, frontiers, and other post-Soviet matters.

Narva's fortress came first, built by the knights of the Livonian Order in the 13th century in traditional European style. It was known as "Long German" for its slender walls which surrounded a high central watchtower, or keep.

Ivangorod followed in 1492, decreed by Ivan III shortly after the unification of Rus' under Moscow's leadership. He made the most of a brief lull in the raids by the Livonians. In the space of a single summer, a great fortress went up before the very eyes of the Narvans, and suddenly Long German seemed a mere toy by comparison.

Blown up during the last war, Ivangorod is under restoration but its complex of towers and battlements, a paradise for war-game enthusiasts, is accessible and allows magnificent views of the river valley, Long German and Estonia. Inside it's weed-ridden and empty, except for two small churches and an 1891 mortar cannon in a corner, looking very much in need of an overhaul.

VYBORG

This town near the Finnish border is almost completely non-Russian in appearance. Vyborg's old town is, in terms of plan and architecture, entirely European.

Russia's claim on Vyborg (*vee*-borg) has always been shaky. Sweden founded it in 1293 on former Novgorodian land. When it finally joined Russia after the Northern War (1700–17), it was already decidedly Finnish in ethnicity, and in 1917 it became a part of the new state of Finland. After the Red Army regained the territory between the Gulf and Lake Ladoga in 1944, Stalin's policy was to populate it with Russians.

Today it is a strange mixture. There sometimes seem to be an inordinate number of drunks on the streets, but some locals are prospering, selling goods to Finns attracted by Vyborg's new status as a Free Enterprise Zone. Emerging from the railway station, you are confronted by a host of hard currency shops and notices in Finnish. And there is more; Vyborg must have the only bus station in Russia boasting a hard currency bar, complete with prostitutes. A few yards away is the Finnish-built Hotel Druzhba, where you can stay in relative comfort, but for a price – over $100 a night for a single.

Busloads of foreign tourists elicit great interest. As they park in the town's central square, Russians surround them brandishing their wares, mostly locally produced wicker baskets.

Sociology and commerce aside, Vyborg is filled with ancient monuments, notably the fortress. Built on an island in the gulf, it was once known as the most impenetrable fortress in Scandinavia. Now only its foundations remain; it was replaced in the 19th century by a tower shaped like an old Russian warrior's helmet. Surrounding buildings are packed with souvenir shops and galleries of Finno-Ugric folk art, while the castle museum, still primarily devoted to socialist achievement, awaits deideologization.

The old town's straight, narrow streets contain a hodge-podge of Germanic and Scandinavian architecture from several eras. Note particularly the slender 15th century clock tower and the 16th century Merchant's Guild House, now the Vyborg Dog-Lovers Club.

The lower town is interesting too, and for more than the basket sellers. The market square has a rather austere Finnish covered market, and nearby a round tower, actually oval, was once part of the Swedes' defense system. Now it houses a decent restaurant.

Across the gulf is the estate of Monrepo (from the French *mon repos*, "my rest"). Its classical mansion, pavilions and landscape garden blend perfectly, giving it the name "Fairytale of the North".

DIRECTIONS

Petrodvorets: a short ride by suburban train from Baltiisky Station to Novy Petergof, then by local bus to the palace entrance. In summer a "Raketa" hydrofoil service operates from the pier outside the Hermitage. By car, leave St. Petersburg by Prospekt Stachek, and take a right in the suburbs along the coastal A121, about 35 km altogether.
Oranienbaum: by train to just beyond Petrodvorets; get off at Oranienbaum 1 station. The palaces are slightly inland. Summer Raketas are less convenient, leaving from the Morskaya pier near Tuchkov Most on Vassilyevsky Island.
Pushkin: a short suburban train journey from the Vitebsky Station to Detskoye Selo, then by local bus #371. By car, leave by Moskovsky prospekt and turn left just before Pulkovo airport, 25 km overall.
Pavlovsk: as for Pushkin, then one stop further by train. The park entrance is just opposite the station, and a long but very pleasant walk to the palace. Buses also connect station and palace.
Gatchina: an hour's journey from the Baltiisky Station on Gatchina-bound trains only. By car, leave on Moskovsky prospekt and continue south past Pulkovo on the M20 Kiev road, 40 km.
Oreshek: just over an hour by Dubrovka-bound suburban trains from Finlandsky Station to Petrokrepost, then by riverboat to the island. By car, leave by the M18 Petrozavodsk road, and after 45 km cross the Neva bridge and turn left for the town of Petrokrepost.
Valaam: Though in Karelia, the islands are best reached from St. Petersburg. An irregular boat service from the River Station takes you there and back in 36 hours, and includes guided tours of the monastery and some of the skeets. Obtain timetables and tickets from the Central Tourist Bureau on Ulitsa Bolshaya Konyushennaya. The only means of individual travel to Valaam is by overnight train to Sortavala (from St. Petersburg or Petrozavodsk), then by infrequent boat (journey time 2 hours).
Ivangorod: 3 hours by bus from Petersburg's No. 2 Bus Station. By car, leave on the M11 Tallinn road and follow for 115 km to the Estonian border.
Vyborg: 2½ hours by suburban train from Finlandsky Station or 120 km along the M10 (north) Helsinki road.

RUSSIAN GLOSSARY

Alexandria Park
Александринский парк
Alexandrov Park
Александровский парк
All Saints Skeet
Всесвятский Скит
Assumption Cathedral
Успенский Собор
Babolovsky Park
Баболовский парк
Chinese Palace
Китайский Дворец
Chinese Village
Китайская деревня
Coasting-Hill Pavilion
Катальная горка
Detskoye Selo
Детское Село
Dubrovka
Дубровка
Fyodorovsky Village
Фёдоровский городок
St. Fyodor's Cathedral
Фёдоровский Собор

Gatchina
Гатчина
Gethsemane Skeet
Гефсеманский Скит
Grand Palace
Большой Дворец
Ivangorod
Ивангород
Lake Ladoga
Ладожское озеро
Lower Park
Нижний парк
Marly Palace
Дворец Марли
Monplaisir
Монплезир
Monrepos
Монрепо
Novy Petergof
Новый Петергоф
Oranienbaum
Ораниенбаум
Oreshek
Орешек
Pavlovsk
Павловск
Peter III's Palace
Дворец Петра Третьего
Petrodvorets
Петродворец
Petrokrepost
Петрокрепость
Priory Castle
Приоратский Дворец
Pushkin
Пушкин
Resurrection Church
Воскресенская церковь
Skitsky island
Скитский остров
Slavyanka River
Река Славянка
Sortavala
Сортавала
Transfiguration Cathedral
Преображенский Собор
Valaam Archipelago
Архипелаг Валаам
Vyborg
Выборг
White Lake
Белое Озеро

Samson Fountain, Petrodvorets

TVER REGION

TVERSKAYA OBLAST

In a convenient location between Moscow and St. Petersburg, Tver region is justly famed for its rivers, lakes, reservoirs and other waterways, to which everything else seems to take second place. The Volga River has its source near the town of Selizharovka, and its upper reaches have fashioned beautiful landscapes, as in the little town of Staritsa. Not far from Selizharovka is a series of lakes, the largest of which is Seliger, a popular holiday area. On the Moscow–St. Petersburg route, the little town of Vyshny Volochok is the site of Russia's first man-made waterway system, designed by Peter the Great in 1789.

TVER

This ancient Volga city was founded by Novgorodians in the 12th century, but was annexed soon after by Vladimir-Suzdal prince Vsevolod Big Nest. Tver reached its zenith only after the collapse of the Tatar Yoke, when it became Moscow's chief rival, thwarting for a time the latter's attempts to establish an all-Russian state.

Fifteenth century Tver was powerful and wealthy, its namesake city beautiful and famed for masons, jewelers and icon painters. It was brought to heel by Muscovite Prince Ivan III in 1485, and now possesses no visible remains of its former glory.

A great fire of 1763 destroyed much of the city. By the end of the century, it had a grand, new center in classical style and was an important stop on the Moscow–St. Petersburg road.

In 1931, Tver was renamed Kalinin, after the titular head of the Soviet state during Stalin's dictatorship, who was born there. It changed back in 1990, though the restored name does not seem to have caught on firmly yet in people's minds.

Tver today is a rather sterile mixture of classical and modern, punctuated here and there by the octagonal drum of a baroque church. Still, it is a lively and progressive enough city, and an acceptable base from which to see the surrounding area.

If you have time to spare in Tver, the best place to spend it is at the **Royal Palace**, built for Catherine the Great as a respite on the Moscow–St. Petersburg road; additions were made by Carlo Rossi at the turn of the 19th century. Today, it looks faded and worn, but inside are a very decent history museum and art gallery, the latter

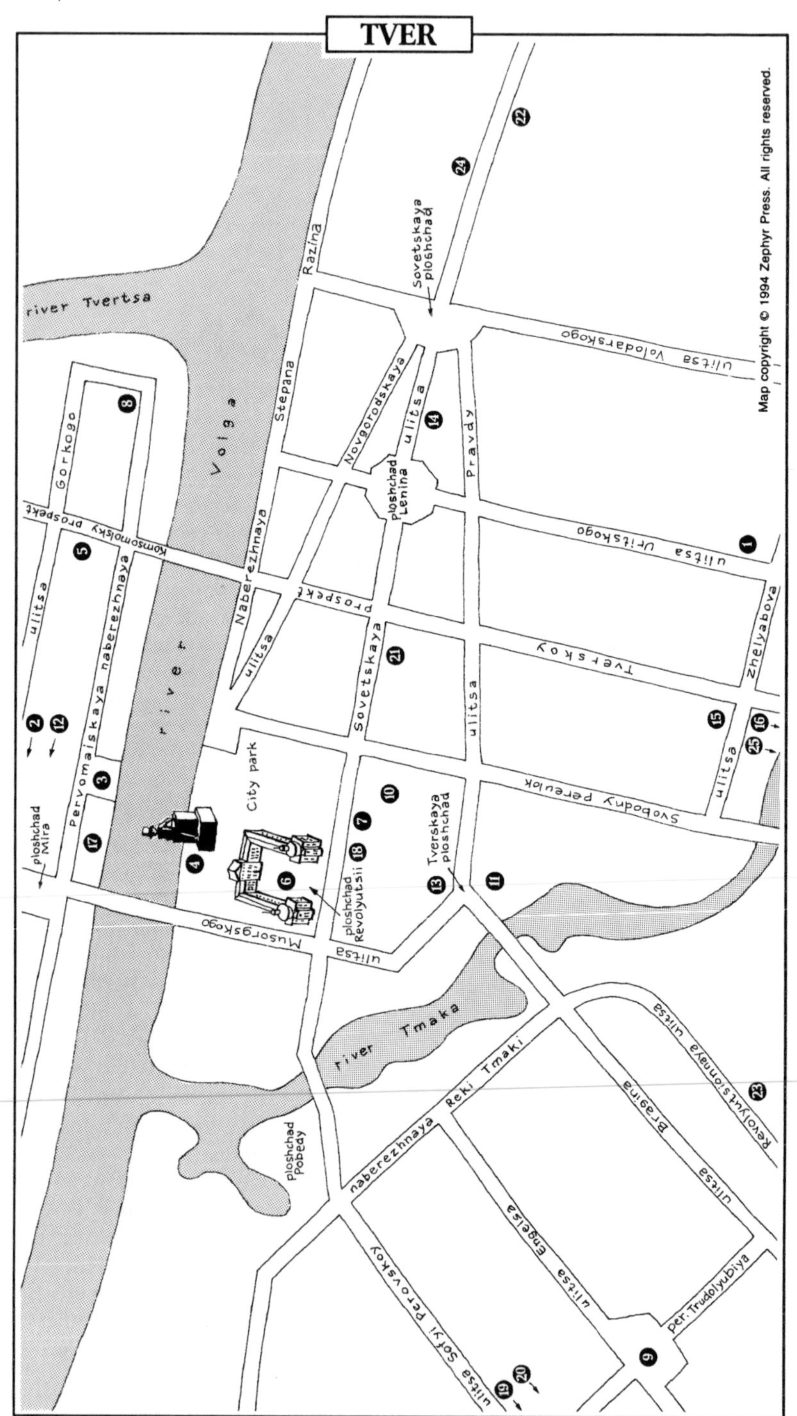
TVER
river Tvertsa
river Volga
Razina
Stepana
Novgorodskaya
ulitsa
Sovetskaya ploshchad
ulitsa Volodarskogo
Pravdy
ploshchad Lenina
ulitsa Uritskogo
Naberezhnaya
Komsomolsky prospekt
Gorkogo
ulitsa
Pervomaiskaya naberezhnaya
prospekt
ulitsa
Sovetskaya
Tverskoy
Zhelyabova
ulitsa
ulitsa
City park
ploshchad Mira
ploshchad Revolyutsii
Tverskaya ploshchad
Svobodny pereulok
ulitsa Musorgskogo
river Tmaka
naberezhnaya Reki Tmaki
ploshchad Pobedy
ulitsa Bragina
Revolyutsionnaya ulitsa
ulitsa Engelsa
ulitsa Sofyi Perovskoy
per. Trudolyubiya
1
2
3
4
5
6
7
8
9
10
11
12
13
14
15
16
17
18
19
20
21
22
23
24
25
Map copyright © 1994 Zephyr Press. All rights reserved.

ТВЕРЬ

Ulitsa Bragina
Улица Брагина
Ulitsa Engelsa
Улица Энгельса
Ulitsa Gorkovo
Улица Горького
Komsomolsky prospekt
Комсомольский проспект
Ploshchad Lenina
Площадь Ленина
Ploshchad Mira
Площадь Мира
Ulitsa Musorgskovo
Улица Мусоргского
Ulitsa Novgorodskaya
Улица Новгородская
Pervomaiskaya naberezhnaya
Первомайская набережная
Ploshchad Pobedy
Площадь Победы
Ulitsa Pravdy
Улица Правды
Revolyutsionnaya ulitsa
Революционная улица
Ploshchad Revolyutsiyi
Площадь Революции
Ulitsa Sofiyi Perovskoy
Улица Софии Перовской
Sovyetskaya ploshchad
Советская площадь
Sovyetskaya ulitsa
Советская улица
Naberezhnaya Stepana Razina
Набережная Степана Разина
Svobodny pereulok
Свободный переулок
River Tmaka
Река Тьмака
Naberezhnaya reki Tmaki
Набережная реки Тьмаки
Trudolyubiya pereulok
Переулок Трудолюбия
Tverskaya ploshchad
Тверская площадь
Tverskoy prospekt
Тверской проспект
River Tvertsa
Река Тверца
Ulitsa Uritskovo
Улица Урицкого
River Volga
Река Волга
Ulitsa Volodarskovo
Улица Володарского
Ulitsa Zhelyabova
Улица Желябова

MAP KEY

1. **Excursion Bureau**
   Экскурсионное бюро
2. **Intourist**
   Интурист
3. **Afanasy Nikitin Monument**
   Памятник Афанасию Никитину
4. **Pushkin Monument**
   Памятник Пушкину
5. **Arefiev House**
   Дом Арефьевых
6. **Royal Palace**
   Путевой Дворец
7. **Nobles' Assembly**
   Дворянское Собрание
8. **Assumption Cathedral of the Otroch Monastery**
   Успенский собор Отроч монастыря
9. **White Trinity Church**
   Церковь Белой Троицы
10. **Philharmonia**
   Филармония
11. **Circus**
   Цирк
12. **Tver Motel**
   Мотель «Тверь»
13. **Tsentralnaya Hotel**
   Гостиница «Центральная»
14. **Seliger Hotel**
   Гостиница «Селигер»
15. **Volga Hotel**
   Гостиница «Волга»
16. **Turist Hotel**
   Гостиница «Турист»
17. **Yakor Restaurant**
   Ресторан «Якорь»

18. **Nadezhda Café**
    Кафе «Надежда»
19. **Okolitsa Café**
    Кафе «Околица»
20. **Russky Dom Restaurant**
    Ресторан «Русский дом»
21. **Souvenir Shop**
    Сувениры
22. **Bookshop**
    Книжный магазин
23. **Market**
    Рынок
24. **Post Office**
    Почта
25. **Bus and Train Stations**
    Вокзалы

Royal Palace and Kalinin Monument, Tver

containing, in addition to icons and later Russian paintings, a collection of 16th and 17th century western European art.

Behind the palace is a riverside park, its embankment graced by a recent statue of Pushkin in a contemplative pose and wearing a top hat, silhouetted against the river. The poet was a frequent visitor to Tver, where he had many friends.

On the opposite bank, another famous local figure, Afanasy Nikitin, is remembered with an unusual monument resembling the prow of a ship. Nikitin was one of many merchant explorers from Tver who travelled far and wide during the 15th century in search of new business. In 1466 he reached India, and his observations were collected in a book called *Journey Beyond Three Seas*, one of the "best-sellers" of the day.

Other places to visit are: the merchant Arefiev's house, across the Volga, now a museum of 17th century life in the city; Tver's oldest church, the lovely little 16th century White Trinity, to the west of the center across the Tmaka river; and Ulitsa Uritskovo, a modest provincial version of Moscow's Arbat.

STARITSA

Tradition links the name of this attractive little Upper Volga town to the "Time of Troubles," when Polish armies ravaged the settlement and left only a single living soul, an old woman, *staritsa* in Russian. Early coats-of-arms depict a rather emaciated hag (if the term can be forgiven), though in later, more prosperous days she was replaced by a plumper version.

The legend errs, however; the town was already known by this name in the 13th century. The Tver princes built a fortress there, on a peninsula with a commanding view over two river valleys.

With the demise of Tver, Staritsa became part of the centralized Russian state, but remained an independent-minded princedom right up to the reign of Ivan the Terrible. Fearing Staritsa's Prince Vladimir as a possible champion of his boyar enemies, the Tsar invited him to Moscow and forced him to drink from a poisoned chalice. With Vladimir out of the way, Ivan was now able to deal with Novgorod, his remaining Russian rival.

Staritsa's main landmark today is the **Assumption Monastery**, down in the Volga valley, nestled in a bend of the river. It makes a spectacular sight from almost every angle, but especially from the high Volga bridge and the Kremlin battlements opposite.

In its center is the grand, five-domed Assumption Cathedral, a contemporary of St. Basil's in Moscow. Empty and neglected today, it reportedly has dungeons and a secret passage leading to the Volga. There may once have been a political prison here – chains and human bones have been found. In 1819 a small classical building was added to the rear of the church, the burial vault of the Tutolmin family, local philanthropists. Although it bears a close resemblance to Napoleon's tomb, it was built ten years earlier.

The nearby tent-roofed Church of the Presentation of the Virgin, now the local **museum**, arose slightly later. Ivan the Terrible built it to mark his newly-established authority over the town.

Other buildings in this densely packed monastery include a bell-tower which used to house a library, the mausoleum of Generalissimo Glebov-Terestreshnev, a man of Catherine the Great's time, and a forlorn-looking gate church on the Volga side, abandoned due to constant flooding. They are all now empty and, sadly, subject to continual vandalization.

The other side of the river also has notable features, including the earthen ramparts of the former Kremlin, still keeping an exhilarating vigil over the two rivers. The Pyatnitskaya Church, just below the hill, is a strange, palace-like structure – note its side chapels, miniature versions of the classical Cathedral of SS. Boris and Gleb on the hill above.

Staritsa's oldest and most renowned trade was blacksmithing, and seven smithies remain, all part of an unusual complex built into the hillside.

TORZHOK

This extraordinary town on the little Tvertsa river could not have been better named. *Torzhok* means "market" and that's just what it is. People have always traded here, and even today a walk through its streets leaves an impression that the entire local population is bustling and haggling, as they have done throughout their lives and history.

Torzhok appeared early on the map of Russia. In the 10th century there was already a trading settlement there, an important link between the north-west – Pskov and Novgorod – and central Russia: Tver, Suzdal and Ryazan.

A great wooden fortress once stood

Backwaters of Distinction

Central Russia would be much the poorer without beautiful **Lake Seliger** and the chain of Upper Volga lakes – Sterzh, Vselug, Peno and Volgo. People come not only for the area's excellent swimming, fishing, hunting and canoeing, but to convalesce as well. The mild, humid climate, an abundance of oxygen from the pine forests and constantly changing water supply provide a very healthful environment.

The lakes are rich in wildlife, too. Animals and plants abound, particularly on Khachin, Seliger's central and largest island. The lake contains 21 species of fish.

The main holiday center of the lakes is **Ostashkov**, on the southern shore of Seliger. Yet it remains remarkably unspoiled by tourism. It seems to combine the quiet charms of Scandinavian lakeland and rural New England, though its cupola-punctuated landscape remains unmistakably Russian.

The townspeople, indeed, are deeply religious. Avidly observing church holidays, they retain ancient pious customs, such as congratulating the bereaved after a funeral on the memory of their dead.

Ostashkov's streets of wooden houses are exquisitely pretty. The oldest street in the town is Myasnitskovo, with a handful of 17th century buildings, most in bad repair. On Lenina, one house, the most derelict, bears a notice threatening prosecution of anyone attempting to demolish it.

Lake Seliger

The lakeside promenade is the most idyllic of all, especially at the approach of sunset. Groups of small children play mischievously,

Continued next page

there which put up a stiff resistance against the Tatars in 1238. It held out for 14 days against Batiy, and thereby probably preserved Novgorod from the enemy. When it fell, the women and children were burned alive in the wooden cathedral where they had sought refuge.

After another 19 burnings and resurrections (we are told), Torzhok emerged by the 18th century as a prosperous trading hub, enhanced by its position on the Moscow–St. Petersburg road. While Moscow was built on seven hills, Torzhok arose on twenty-seven, graced by two cathedrals, eleven monasteries and thirty-six parish churches. Architects such as Carlo Rossi, Matvey Kazakov and Nikolay Lvov worked there, and created a townscape of highly original form and color.

while the water's edge is strewn with their discarded clothing.

Tours by lake steamer are available at weekends from Ostashkov, and there are regular boat services on other days. Trips to Khachin Island are recommended, and to the tiny nearby Stolbnoy Island, site of the Nilova Pustyn monastery. A labor camp existed on the grounds of the latter in the '20s and '30s. In 1939–40, it took in Polish gendarmes and reserve policemen captured during the Soviet invasion. Unlike the officers at Katyn, their fate has not yet been discovered.

The ideal way to stay on Lake Seliger is to camp, though you should be prepared to cope with the frequent short rainfalls. Try the long, sinuous **Selizharovsky Plyos Lake**, with its wooded shorelines, to the southeast of Ostashkov. The grim hotel in Ostashkov should be your last resort – there are plenty of tour bases (*turbazi*) here, the greatest concentration being at Zarechye, across the lake.

And so it has remained, at least in part. Despite Bolshevik looting of its main churches and Nazi bombs which levelled the town center, Torzhok still harbors today a priceless part of Russia's cultural heritage.

The **Kremlin**, near the main road bridge on the west bank of the Tvertsa, is now occupied by Rossi's contribution to the architectural landscape, the five-domed, classical Transfiguration Cathedral. This magnificent landmark once contained Russia's most treasured icon, the Virgin of Smolensk, now hidden away in a private collection.

Looking away from the center along the riverbank, you will see Torzhok's greatest masterpiece, Lvov's **Monastery of SS. Boris and Gleb**, a UNESCO-listed landmark. The first monastery on this site was founded in the 10th century by Yefrem, son of Kievan Prince Vladimir, who sought solace in religion after viewing the headless bodies of his brothers Boris and Gleb, murdered by yet another brother, Svyatopolk.

Lvov's churches were added in 1796 (the Cathedral of SS. Boris and Gleb) and 1811 (the Church over the Gate). The first is low, massive and simple, and was once adorned by 37 icons painted by Vladimir Borovikovsky, whose work may be appreciated inside St. Petersburg's Kazan Cathedral. All were lost after the Revolution. The second church, by contrast, is tall and slender, perfectly proportioned with porticos and rotundas, and topped by a belvedere and spire. It once contained bells which could be heard from Tver, 60 km away.

Corner tower of Borisoglebsky Monastery and Tvertsa River

The monastery's festive, candle-shaped corner tower, overlooking the river, was the stage for a bizarre meteorological ritual. Every morning a monk would appear on the balcony; the manner of his dress was supposed to reveal the day's weather.

Walk further along the embankment to the five-tier, wooden **Old Ascension Church**, which crowns the highest hill. Over 350 years old, it was erected in a day by a single man with an axe. There is an extraordinary view

Old Ascension Church

of Lvov's two churches: the top of the gate church seems to rise straight out of the cathedral. The Resurrection Convent is also visible across the river. The nuns occupied themselves by day with the craft of sewing with gold thread, but their alleged nighttime pursuits made the integrity of their holy vows suspect: secret passages lead from the convent under the river to the monastery!

Return to the central marketplace, home of the famous twice-yearly Torzhok fair, known for its lavish stalls of flax, yuft and morocco. But it was also a "market" of a different kind: it was the custom for boys to come there to chose their favorite girl.

Cross the footbridge and climb the hill on the other side by the "limping steps," so called because it's impossible to climb them without shortening your stride. At the top you will find the town "boulevard," scene of the next stage of the courting ritual. The girls would stroll there, giving the boys a chance to propose. A girl might refuse, but it seems the boy had the upper hand: if he asked to accompany her on four occasions, she was obliged to wed him.

Behind the boulevard is Kazakov's Royal Palace, another stopping-place for Catherine the Great during her travels, and at the end of the square behind, Pozharsky's Hotel, loved by Pushkin because of the tasty cutlets served by the hostess. A plaque on the wall is engraved with a couplet by the poet praising them.

Pushkin had a good reason for visiting Torzhok. As well as seeing his friend Pyotr Olenin (whose house is now a museum devoted to the poet), he came to admire the "pedigree women" of Torzhok. Absurd as it may seem, the most beautiful girls in the town were put on show on the ground floor of the hotel. But this was no slave market – each girl was accompanied by an "object" (*predmyet*), as their boyfriends were called.

THE UPPER VOLGA PUSHKIN RING

Around Torzhok and Staritsa are many places connected with Alexander Pushkin, and a special tourist route has been fashioned of them. You'd have to be a serious Pushkin devotee to want to see every one, but two or three at least are worth making the effort. Both the beautiful park at Malinniki and the estate at Bernovo belonged to the Wulf family, Pushkin's friends and neighbors at Mikhailovskoye (see Pskov Region). Perhaps even more spectacular is the large mansion and park with waterfalls at Gruziny, occupied by the Poltoratskys, relatives of the poet's sweetheart, Anna Kern.

PRACTICAL MATTERS

Tver's best hotel is the **Volga**, on Ulitsa Zhelyabova, quiet, clean and inexpensive. Alternatively try the **Seliger** at Sovyetskaya, 52 or the **Tsentralnaya** at Pravdy, 33/8. The **Turist** is convenient to the stations, but pricier.

Eating out is relatively easy, too. The businessmen's association **Russky Klub** has recently opened a restaurant on Prospekt Lenina, 18/1 (tel. 45397, 46443), evenings only, requiring dress in "classical style." The non-classical should try instead the **Café Nadezhda** at Sovyetskaya, 12, popular, friendly and serving delicious food. Just make sure you can cope with their innovative *modus operandi* – you are expected to write the order down yourself. Another alternative is the **Yakor** restaurant at Nab. Nikitina, 27 (tel. 15386), refurbished, reasonably elegant and quiet. If you're staying at the Volga Hotel, try not to be tempted by their restaurant's delicacies (frogs' legs etc.); it isn't worth it.

For further information, Tver has a very useful 1993 directory (in Russian, available at most bookshops), with everything from trolleybus routes to addresses of functioning churches.

DIRECTIONS

Tver: just over 2 hours by local train from Moscow's Leningradsky Vokzal. By car follow the M10 Leningradskoye shossé for about 200 km.

Ostashkov: 11 hours by daily train from the Leningradsky Vokzal. By car take the M10 to Torzhok (270 km), then another 150 km on the A111.

Staritsa: 1½ hours by bus from Tver, or 80 km down the A112.

Torzhok: 1½ hours by bus or local train from Tver, by car 65 km NW, just off the M10.

Gruziny, **Bernovo** and **Malinniki** are all on the P88 Torzhok–Staritsa road, Gruziny 12 km from Torzhok, Bernovo and Malinniki 60 and 50 km from Staritsa respectively.

RUSSIAN GLOSSARY

Assumption Monastery
Успенский монастырь

Bernovo
Берново

Monastery of SS. Boris and Gleb
Борисоглебский монастырь

Gruziny
Грузины

Khachin Island
Остров Хачин

Malinniki
Малинники

Nilova Pustyn
Нилова Пустынь

Old Ascension Church
Старовознесенская церковь

Lake Peno
Озеро Пено

Lake Seliger
Озеро Селигер

Selizharovka
Селижаровка
Selizharovsky Plyos
Селижаровский Плёс
Staritsa
Старица
Sterzh
Стерж
Stolbnoy Island
Остров Столбной
Torzhok
Торжок
Transfiguration Cathedral
Преображенский собор
Upper Volga Pushkin Ring
Верхневолжское Пушкинское кольцо
Lake Volgo
Озеро Волго
Lake Vselug
Озеро Вселуг
Vyshny Volochok
Вышний Волчёк
Zarechye
Заречье

Pushkin and Volga River

YAROSLAVL REGION

YAROSLAVSKAYA OBLAST

Despite comprising an area smaller than Estonia, which by Russian standards is small, Yaroslav Region is quite remarkable in encompassing four cities which at various times in Russian history could be called great. The powerful merchant city of Yaroslavl, once Russia's second largest, is just an hour's drive from Rostov, which in earlier days was the capital of an enormous princedom. At one point in the 12th century, the princedom of Pereslavl-Zalessky succeeded in subordinating Rostov. In the 15th century another city, Uglich, reached its zenith, controlling lands well beyond the bounds of today's region. What is more, in all four, monuments have been preserved through the ages which few other Russian cities can match.

YAROSLAVL

There is a joke among Soviet-era historians about Yaroslavl. As they were busy systematically destroying the heritage of Russian Orthodoxy, the Bolsheviks had an alphabetical list of towns marked out for "reconstruction." While Kostroma and Nizhny Novgorod, for example, went as expected, the planners never quite got down to the "Ya's" ("Ya" is the transliteration of "Я," the last letter in the Russian alphabet) before perestroika came along. Graced as it is by the cupolas and bell-towers of over a hundred churches, this is one of the few large provincial Russian cities that can genuinely be called beautiful.

Legend has it that Yaroslavl was founded by Yaroslav the Wise, son of the Kievan Prince Vladimir. Happening on a pagan tribe who worshipped bears, he killed all the local members of the species, and the tribe succumbed to him as their leader. The symbol of the bear remains a part of the town's coat-of-arms to this day.

A minor princedom since the 13th century, Yaroslavl grew and prospered, reaching its peak in the 16th/17th centuries. Its merchants became extraordinarily rich and powerful, and commissioned church after church from skilled local and Kostroma-based masons and artists, who worked at a rate that surpassed even Moscow's builders.

The development of St. Petersburg took a lot of the wind out of Yaroslavl's sails, but it remains

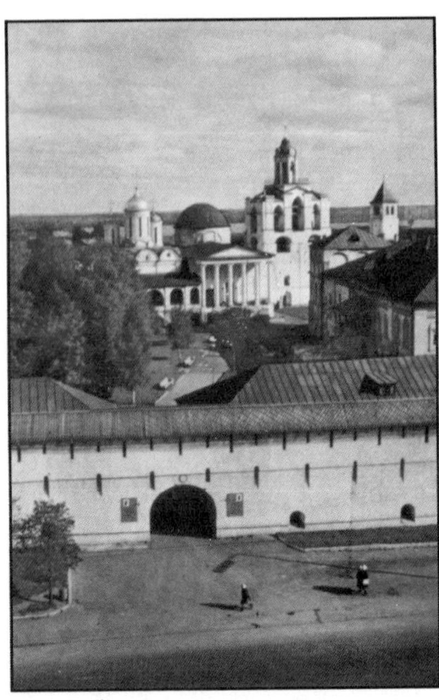

Monastery of Our Savior, with the Transfiguration Cathedral (left center) and its bell-tower (right)

nonetheless a major provincial industrial center, and projects something of a cosmopolitan atmosphere.

The Center

The best place to begin your exploration of the town is the **Monastery of Our Savior**, whose thick white walls dominate the center. This was once a mighty fortress and a seat of learning – here the great epic poem, *The Lay of Igor's Host*, was rediscovered in 1790 after centuries of oblivion.

Today, the monastery serves as the central Yaroslavl **history museum**. Much of it, including the 1516 Transfiguration Cathedral, is currently closed for repairs. The cathedral is the city's oldest building, and contains some of the finest 16th century frescoes in existence. Also of interest is an exhibition of manuscripts from the library, and a collection of amusing 17th century baked tiles.

Climb up the bell-tower to get your bearings and a better view of the patchy but architecturally rich landscape.

Leaving the monastery, follow the embankment of Yaroslavl's smaller river, the Kotorosl, to the left in the direction of the Volga. You will pass the site of the city's Kremlin, commonly known as Log City, where the local prince's palace once stood. The only remaining building is the simple and modest Log Church of St. Nicholas, its slender bell-tower and five drums revealing a masterful sense of proportion. The market Church of the Savior-in-the-Town, meanwhile, on the nearer mound, is a more bulky and squat affair, but beautifully sited. Even the athletic track placed between them does not seem to detract from their appearance.

Continue beside the placid Kotorosl to its convergence with the stately and dramatic Volga. This part of town offers a profusion of architectural styles, and museums. The Volga Fortress Tower, a relic of the former 17th century town wall, looms over the river side. Opposite stands the classical Church of SS. Elijah and Tikhon, and the solid and ornate Metropolitan's Chambers. Now an **icon museum**, the chambers were built by Iona, the

Volga Tower

wealthy 17th century Rostov metropolitan.

Another **art museum** is in the nearby Provincial Office Building. Nearly every notable Russian artist is represented, including a fine collection of works by turn-of-the-century artist Konstantin Korovin (1861–1939), the first Russian artist to be directly influenced by the French Impressionists. According to art historian Camilla Gray, Korovin was also the key figure in the late 19th century revolution in theatrical design, whose effects were to be felt far beyond Russia.

With the approach of the River Station and the noise of the bridge beyond, the embankment starts to lose some of its intimate charm. Turn left down Narodny pereulok and enter a courtyard to the right to see the little **Church of St. Nicholas-Nadeyina**. This is Yaroslavl's oldest parish church, built in 1622 by a merchant named Nadey Sveshnikov with ideas above his station. He added a side chapel for his own personal use, a practice in those days only considered acceptable for princes. The interior, open mornings as a museum, has a beautiful baroque iconostasis, and frescoes depicting, in meticulous detail, the life of Nicholas the Miracle-Worker, Russia's best-loved saint.

Just off to the right is Yaroslavl's second merchant church, the Church of the Nativity of Christ, and one of its finest, if only for the gate church and bell-tower that introduce it. Its various layers are unique – first gateway, then gallery, then church, then bell-tower. For the first time, glazed tiles were used as decoration, a feature repeated and perfected on many later churches in the city.

Continuing down Narodny pereulok and coming out on Sovyetskaya ploshchad brings you to the magnificent **Church of St. Elijah the Prophet**, built by the Skripin family, who were favored by both Tsar and Patriarch. Despite the very basic quincunx church at the center, its side chapels and bell-tower give it an odd, dissonant harmony. The southwest chapel is particularly impressive, built in the tent-roof style just before it was banned by Patriarch Nikon. No less impressive is the interior, with its bright and breezy frescoes by Kostroma's Guri Nikitin.

St. Elijah's took on a special role during the town planning of the late 18th century. Catherine the Great's architects used it to full effect, making it the focal point of the city, with five major roads leading off the square.

Take one of these branches to Ploshchad Podbelskovo, the vast city square flanked by the Monastery of Our Savior. Here is one more church, typical of Yaroslavl's later style: pillarless but with layers of purely decorative *kokoshniki* to disguise the fact. The Epiphany Church is open as a

Detail of fresco by Guri Nikitin. Church of Elijah the Prophet

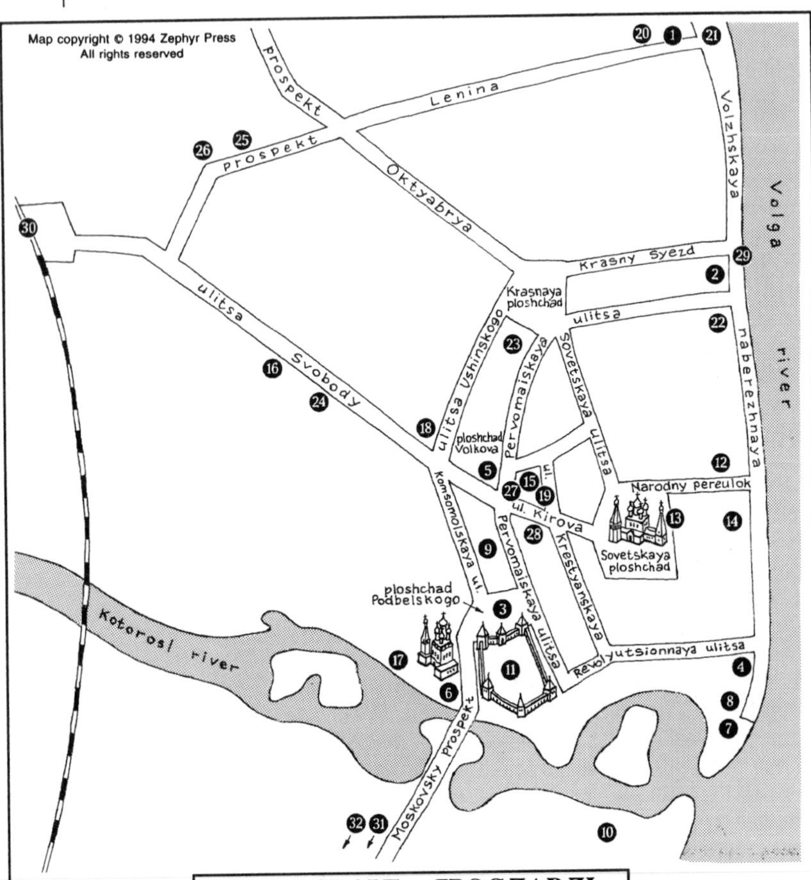

YAROSLAVL • ЯРОСЛАВЛЬ

Ulitsa Kirova
Улица Кирова
Komsomolskaya ulitsa
Комсомольская улица
Krasnaya ploshchad
Красная площадь
Krasny Syezd
Красный съезд
Ulitsa Krestyanskaya
Улица Крестьянская
Prospekt Lenina
Проспект Ленина
Moskovsky prospekt
Московский проспект
Narodny pereulok
Народный переулок
Prospekt Oktyabrya
Проспект Октября
Ulitsa Pervomaiskaya
Улица Первомайская
Ploshchad Podbelskovo
Площадь Подбельского
Revolyutsionnaya ulitsa
Революционная улица
Sovyetskaya ploshchad
Советская площадь
Ulitsa Sovyetskaya
Улица Советская
Ulitsa Svobody
Улица Свободы
Ulitsa Ushinskovo
Улица Ушинского
Ploshchad Volkova
Площадь Волкова
Volzhskaya naberezhnaya
Волжская набережная

MAP KEY

1. **Tourism Office**
   Туристическое бюро
2. **Nekrasov Monument**
   Памятник Некрасову
3. **Yaroslav the Wise Monument**
   Памятник Ярославу Мудрому
4. **Volga Tower**
   Волжская башня
5. **Vlasius Tower**
   Власиевская башня
6. **Annunciation Church**
   Благовещенская церковь
7. **Metropolitan's Chambers**
   Митрополичьи палаты
8. **SS. Elijah and Tikhon Church**
   Ильинско-Тихонская церковь
9. **Gostiny Dvor**
   Гостиный двор
10. **Korovniki Churches**
    Коровники
11. **Monastery of the Savior**
    Спасский монастырь
12. **St. Nicholas Church**
    Никольская церковь
13. **Church of St. Elijah the Prophet**
    Церковь Ильи Пророка
14. **Art Museum**
    Художественный музей
15. **Philharmonia**
    Филармония
16. **Circus**
    Цирк
17. **Hotel Yubileinaya**
    Гостиница «Юбилейная»
18. **Yaroslavl Hotel**
    Гостиница «Ярославль»
19. **Volga Hotel**
    Гостиница «Волга»
20. **Turist Hotel**
    Гостиница «Турист»
21. **Severny Region Express Bar**
    Экспресс-бар «Северный регион»
22. **Café Lira**
    Кафе «Лира»
23. **Golden Bear Café**
    Кафе «Золотая медведь»
24. **Hungaria Restaurant**
25. **Chaika Restaurant**
    Ресторан «Чайка»
26. **Souvenirs**
    Сувениры
27. **Bookshop**
    Книжный магазин
28. **Souvenirs**
    Сувениры
29. **River Station**
    Речной вокзал
30. **Main Vokzal**
    Вокзал Ярославль Главный
31. **Moskovsky Vokzal**
    Московский вокзал
32. **Bus Station**
    Автовокзал

museum, providing a chance to see Yaroslavl's later church artists, noted for their realistic backgrounds, and for saints that look like real people.

The latest addition to the square is a statue of Yaroslav the Wise, opened with great ceremony by President Yeltsin and Ukrainian President Leonid Kravchuk in October 1993. The ancestral prince holds a piece of the Kremlin in his hand and looks toward Moscow.

The Outer Settlements

If you looked across the river Kotorosl from the end of the embankment, you would have noticed an ensemble of two churches in the distance. They are in Korovniki, once a settlement devoted to the rearing of cattle. Though not the easiest place to get to, it is considered the most picturesque spot in the city.

The **Church of St. John Chryso-**

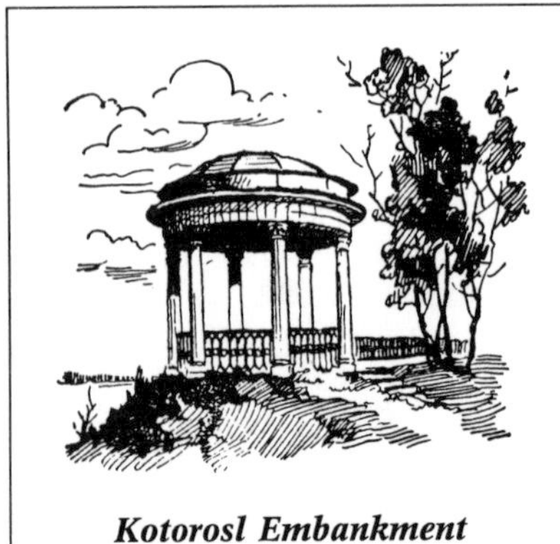

Kotorosl Embankment

stom, on the right if observed from the Volga, is a masterpiece. Built in 1654, shortly after St. Elijah's, it was the first Yaroslavl church to have a single centralized mass. Its tent-roofed side chapels and low gallery give it a pyramid-like appearance.

The nearby Church of the Virgin of Vladimir was built 15 years later as a heated winter church. The belfry was added in 1680. Slender and positioned skilfully between the two churches, it became known as the "Candle of Yaroslavl."

Also across the Kotorosl (but on the other side of town) is the settlement of Tolchkovo, once inhabited by the city's wealthy leather dressers and traders, whose wares were highly valued throughout Russia. They intended to build a church to be remembered by, and they succeeded. Richer residents gave money, poorer ones gave their labor, and the result was the **Church of St. John the Baptist**, regarded as the peak of Yaroslavl's architectural excellence. Its greatest innovation is the side chapels. Instead of tent-roofs, banned by 1671 when construction commenced, these unusually tall annexes are each topped by a cluster of five domes, thus giving the church fifteen domes in all. Note also the vase-shaped main cupola, a later addition.

The Tolg Convent

Half an hour's boat trip up the Volga from the River Station is the Tolg Convent, set peacefully in a tiny village. Now functioning again, it presents a beautiful view from the river, and if you're lucky enough to arrive when the bells are ringing, its spirit can be overwhelming.

Founded in 1314, this relatively poor convent acquired its magnificent stone buildings only in the 17th century. Among them is the imposing Cathedral of the Presentation of the Virgin, now undergoing painstaking restoration. The convent is famous for its main icon, the 17th century Virgin of Tolg, now in the Yaroslavl Art Museum.

ROSTOV THE GREAT

First mentioned in chronicles of 862 but in fact even older, Rostov is the oldest city in the region. It was made famous by Prince Yuri Dolgoruky, who ruled there in the 12th century. Dolgoruky gave it the name "Great," although he later moved his capital to Suzdal in fear of the local nobles.

The princedom gradually broke into smaller pieces. Surprisingly, the Tatar invasion had an almost beneficial effect, as Rostov became a center of resistance to the yoke. However, Moscow proved a stronger focus for attempts at unification, and finally put Rostov in its shadow.

The city retained its position in the church as a rich diocese, and by the 17th century had amassed considerable wealth from its hinterland of farms and villages. Its Metropolitan, Iona, having bungled an opportunity to become Patriarch, threw all his remaining strength into building an enormous and luxurious Kremlin on the banks of Lake Nero.

Rostov Kremlin and Cathedral Square

Rostov's prestige lasted only another 100 years. When Catherine the Great confiscated all church land, the see moved to Yaroslavl and the Kremlin gradually fell into disuse. Only at the end of the 19th century was it restored and made a museum, which it has remained ever since.

Nothing remains today of Rostov's secular glory, and only three churches date from pre-Iona days. Everything centers round the Kremlin, which seems almost a town in itself. Within its walls are a cellar café, a souvenir shop, and the **International Youth Tourism Center**, currently providing the only accommodation in town.

Even those who feel indifferent to most Russian architecture cannot fail to be astounded by the drama of this enormous conglomeration of towers and cupolas. Try to get a view from the road south where it rises, dreamlike, across the lake.

Paradoxically, the main buildings are outside the Kremlin proper. Iona deliberately built it away from the 16th century **Assumption Cathedral**, leaving the latter as a link with the town. But the Cathedral is also a link in another sense. Its simple form, with flat pilasters topped by keel-shaped *zakomary*, continues the tradition of Rostov's early churches.

The nearby belfry is a masterpiece too, with 13 bells whose sounds are unmatched in all of Russia. They are capable of performing a series of complex and unique chimes, led by the largest, Sysoy, over 30 tons in weight and audible 20 km away.

Move next into the Kremlin, with its five churches and numerous chambers. The walls, mighty and imposing, actually have no value whatsoever as fortifications. Rather, they are a monument to the wealthy indulgence of Iona.

Of the churches, the most interesting is Iona's private one, the Church of the Transfiguration-above-the-Cellars. Its uniqueness lies in the position of the solium, with its gilded columns, brass Holy Doors and lavish frescoes, elevated practically to head height of the worshippers below.

The main part of the museum is in the Metropolitan's House, the three-storey building in the center of the courtyard. Apart from the icon and 18th–20th century art collections, it contains a display of a local craft known as *finift,* enamel ware painted and fired in such a way that the gloss created seems to be everlasting.

Apart from a rather appealing town

The Land of Ugly Murders

The name Uglich may suggest dark images of Soviet city life, but nothing could be further from the reality of this pretty Volga town. The beauty does, however, have a sinister side, including several cases of violent premeditated homicide.

Uglich dates from the 10th century, although as it was a key point on the Volga trade route, people had settled there much earlier. Arab coins from as early as the 6th century have been found. It became part of the Rostov princedom by the early 13th century, and flourished between sackings by the Tatars, yet was never fully independent.

In the 16th century, Ivan the Terrible used Uglich as a base for launching attacks on the Tatars. After Ivan's death, his son Dmitry moved there with his mother, and seven years later was brutally murdered by Boris Godunov. As a result, local townspeople revolted, which lead to their own massacre. This was how one of Russia's most bloody periods, the Time of Troubles, began. Indignation did not die with the massacre. The city's coat-of-arms portrays a haloed Dmitry with a fierce-looking dagger in his right hand.

Most people see Uglich for the first time from along the river. The magnificent Kremlin's walls have fallen, but this only emphasizes the beauty of the **Church of St. Demetrius on Spilled Blood**, built on the site of the Tsarevich's death. In a style found throughout Uglich, the bright red building with its blue, starred cupolas combines a church, a trapezium (Russian: *trapeznaya*), and a bell-tower.

Princes' Chambers, Uglich

In contrast to Yaroslavl and Rostov, Uglich's historical monuments suffer acutely from neglect and lack of money. The fine Kremlin **museum** cannot afford to pay attendants for all its rooms, sometimes preventing individual visitors from seeing the bright, dissonant colors of the wall-paintings in the Cathedral of the Transfiguration of the Savior, or the craft exhibition in the 15th century **Princes' Chambers**.

Just down Ulitsa Karla Marksa sits the **Resurrection Monastery**, a highly unusual complex now falling into ruin. Built on sand, it sank several centimeters in the 1930's and '40's when a hydro-electric power station was constructed nearby. (During the same construction, another monastery was blown up and submerged in a spate of Stalinist fervor.) Inside, ceramic tiles depicting fairytale animals and monsters, as well as other wall paintings, are hidden from public view. Local authorities guard their treasures jealously;

though this protects them from vandals, it also thwarts the explorer.

Opposite is the Church of the Nativity of St. John the Baptist, similar in style and origins to Dmitry's church. Here, a 17th century psychopath murdered the son of wealthy local merchant Nikifor Chepolosov, and the church was built in the boy's honor.

For a picturesque walk, follow the Volga embankment back past the Kremlin, away from the power station, and cross the Kamensky Stream. Passing the Chaika watch factory, one of the most famous in Russia and the town's largest employer (there is a museum here and weekend tours can be organized) you will see a little ruined church in the next village high on a cliff above the Volga. It perfectly complements the beauty of the view along the northern Volga valley.

Inland, Uglich has yet more charms. At Ogneva Gora, a hill at the rear of the town, stands the St. Alexius Monastery, its unusual Assumption (also called "Wondrous") Cathedral boasting a triple tent roof. Once a pagan sanctuary, it retains even now a mysterious, highly-charged atmosphere. Nighttime wanderings are not recommended.

Out toward the rail and bus stations is the Church of St. Demetrius Na Polye (in the Field). Built when the Tsarevich Dmitry's remains were dispatched to Moscow, it is now again a working church. Alongside lies the town cemetery.

center with passable shops (the local cheese is delicious), Rostov's other attractions are its two **monasteries**. At the Yaroslavl end of town on Ulitsa Zhelyabova is the older Monastery of St. Avraamy of Rostov. Founded in the 12th century, its Epiphany Cathedral is the oldest building in Rostov, dating from after the fall of Kazan in 1552. The Russian victory was attributed to a crozier which the Tsar took with him, used according to tradition by St. John the Apostle to smash a pagan idol, and later presented to the metropolitan.

The second, the Monastery of our Savior and St. Jacob, is at the approaches to the town from Moscow. A rather disorganized ensemble, its most interesting building is the chaotic but ingenious Church of St. Demetrius, built by the serfs of the rich Moscow noble Count Sheremetyev at the end of the 18th century.

PERESLAVL-ZALESSKY

Founded as a major fortress by Yuri Dolgoruky in 1152, just five years after Moscow, this settlement on Lake Pleshcheyevo became something of a buffer for various invading armies. Perhaps it is no coincidence that Russia's earliest military hero, Alexander Nevsky, was born there.

Pereslavl was often visited by the Tsars in the 16th century, who poured much wealth into the construction of monasteries and churches. Even the anti-clerical Peter the Great took an interest. In his youth he built a flotilla there, whose launching delighted the entire Moscow nobility and clergy.

Today, Pereslavl shows few signs of the prosperity that is its due, with such a rich past and a guaranteed place on the Intourist map. In fact, it has a feel of almost disastrous neglect, and the small, semi-rural community here doesn't seem to know how to cope with its numerous monuments.

There's no problem with accommodation, however. The relatively new Fregat hotel, restaurant, and bar complex should satisfy most of your needs.

The center of town is the Krasnaya ploshchad (Red Square), just across the river Trubezh from the hotel. The beautifully simple white stone Transfiguration Cathedral in its center is one of the oldest in the land of Vladimir-Suzdal, built at the same time as Kideksha's Church of SS. Boris and Gleb (see Vladimir Region). Alhough its three-apse body has survived well, it lacks the decoration associated with pre-Mongolian churches of the area. Unfortunately it is firmly padlocked (though no frescoes have survived) and visitors will have to be content to admire it from the outside.

Pereslavl is very spread out, an inconvenience for those on foot, though it has only one major road and everything is easy to find. First go south, to the massive **Goritsky Monastery** on a hill to the right. Most of the buildings of this rich and powerful monastic establishment date from the time of Empress Elizabeth, who desired a splendid residence for her confessor, Archbishop Arseny. Unfortunately Catherine the Great had other ideas and abolished the diocese. The new ensemble was never used for its intended purpose. Today, it is Pereslavl's museum, with an excellent collection of religious wood carvings. The Assumption Cathedral is a rare example of provincial Russian baroque; its magnificent interior is currently under restoration.

Turn left at the bottom of Museiny pereulok onto Podgornaya ulitsa, and walk for 15 minutes until you reach the lakeside. Here you will find the Botik Museum, where the only surviving boat of Peter's flotilla is kept. While a fire reduced all the other craft to cinders, the *Fortuna*, partly built by Peter himself, remains intact. This is also the best place to view Lake Pleshcheyevo, rather than tramping through the mud-churned streets of the town. It is famous for its herring, once used to supply the tsar's table during coronation feasts.

Goritsky Monastery and Koshkin Monument

Of the town's four other monasteries, only the southernmost, the Convent of St. Theodore, founded in the 14th century on the site of a battle between the Moscow and Tver princedoms, seems to have a future. It is to house a children's computer center.

Slightly closer to the center (opposite the Goritsky Monastery) is the Monastery of St. Daniel. The 16th century Trinity Cathedral is the second oldest in the town, with a form resembling that of the Transfiguration Cathedral. It was built in thanks for the birth of Ivan the Terrible, whose conception was deemed due to the prayers of the local abbot. The interior, with frescoes by Guri Nikitin, is almost always closed, and the rest of the monastery buildings have an abandoned appearance.

The two monasteries of SS. Boris

and Gleb and of St. Nikita have suffered even grimmer fates. The former, in the center of town, has been taken over by gangs of teenage boys, who proudly show visitors the ancient artifacts they have dug up. The latter, at the northern end, associated with a 13th century miracle-worker, is literally falling to ruin. The roof of one of its churches has caved in, and the other is accessible only by ladder.

Such is the fate of a small Golden Ring town, a victim of centralized Intourist bureaucracy. While tourists passed through here in their hundreds, Pereslavl received none of the material benefits.

PRACTICAL MATTERS

For no obvious reason, hotels in Yaroslavl are a lot cheaper than in many cities, without being any less comfortable than, say, neighboring Kostroma. The modern **Yubileinaya** (Kotoroslnaya naberezhnaya, 26) is decent and clean, and very affordable, about $12/night for a single in the fall of 1993. If you want cheaper still, the **Turist** (Prospekt Lenina, 2) is lower grade, but still provides conveniences. It's probably best to avoid the older **Yaroslavl** (Ploshchad Volkova) and **Volga** (Ulitsa Kirova, 10), both without conveniences and not much lower in price.

Eating out here is best accomplished by avoiding the state restaurants, though the private establishments rarely excel, either. An exception is the **Golden Bear Café** (#3 Pervomaiskaya, tel. [0852] 32-85-32) with smart interior, waitresses and clientele, and delicious salads. Don't be fooled by the unattractive exterior – its purpose is exactly that, to fool people. For atmosphere, another place to try is the **Hungaria** (Ulitsa Svobody, 43). Intimate and often crowded, the "Hungarian" food nevertheless leaves a lot to be desired. Along the same lines, locals are much enthralled by a Chinese restaurant, the **Chaika** (Lenina, 26). Though the soups and flavors are definitely Chinese and very tasty, other ingredients are obviously Russian (like sweet and sour chicken bones, and gristle wrapped in batter), and there is no rice.

For a quick snack, you won't do better than the convenient, efficient and faintly arty **Severny Region Bar Express**, situated in the basement of the Center for Scientific and Technical Information, on the Volzhskaya Naberezhnaya next to the Turist Hotel. Poor students, however, head for the **Café Lira**, also on the Naberezhnaya but near the River Station. Another passable café, the **Yartek**, is centrally located, on Ulitsa Deputatskaya, 7.

One state restaurant, the **Volga**, works late into the night. It provides good entertainment, not because of any variety program, but rather by displaying the more comical elements of provincial Russian society in action. It's located in the river station.

DIRECTIONS

Yaroslavl: Almost every long distance train from Moscow's Yaroslavsky Vokzal stops here, journey time 5 hours. By car take the M8 Yaroslavskoye shossé (280 km). It is also a major stop on Moscow-Nizhny Novgorod Volga cruises.

Rostov: by train an hour short of Yaroslavl, or 1½ hours by local train or bus from Yaroslavl. By car the same, 60 km SW on the M8.

Uglich: 6 hours by daily train from Moscow's Savyolovsky Vokzal. By car take M8 as far as Rostov, then left on the R153, about 250 km. On the way you will pass a picturesque monastery in the settlement of Borisoglebsky. Uglich is also a stop on the above-mentioned Volga cruises.

Pereslavl-Zalessky: by bus three hours from Moscow (metro Sholkovskaya). By car about half way between Moscow and Yaroslavl.

RUSSIAN GLOSSARY

St. Alexius Monastery
Алексеевский монастырь
St. Avraamy Monastery
Аврамиевский монастырь
Borisoglebsky
Борисоглебский
Monastery of St. Daniel
Даниловский монастырь
Church of St. Dmitry on Spilled Blood
Церковь Дмитрия-на-крови
Hotel Fregat
Гостиница «Фрегат»
Goritsky Monastery
Горицкий монастырь
International Youth Tourism Center
Международный центр молодёжного туризма
Ulitsa Karla Marksa
Улица Карла Маркса
Krasnaya ploshchad
Красная Площадь
Museiny pereulok
Музейный переулок
Monastery of St. Nikita
Никитинский монастырь
Ogneva Gora
Огнева Гора
Pereslavl-Zalessky
Переславль-Залесский
Lake Pleshcheyevo
Плещеево озеро
Podgornaya ulitsa
Подгорная улица
Resurrection Monastery
Воскресенский монастырь
Rostov Veliky (Rostov the Great)
Ростов Великий
Monastery of Our Savior & St. Jacob
Спасо-Яковлевский монастырь
Convent of St. Theodore
Фёдоровский монастырь
Tolchkovo
Толчково
Tolg Convent
Толжский монастырь
River Trubezh
Река Трубеж
Uglich
Углич
Yaroslavskoye shossé
Ярославское шоссе
Café Yartek
Кафе «Яртек»
Ulitsa Zhelyabova
Улица Желябова

Title page illustration: ***Yaroslavl Coat of Arms***

KOSTROMA REGION

KOSTROMSKAYA OBLAST

If there's one thing that Kostroma Region can treasure, it's forest, which covers over 70 percent of its territory. These are not the friendly birch woods of central Russia, but wild northern terrain, where bears and wolves prowl. It is inhabited, though sparsely; Slavs have lived there since the 9th century. This guide, however, will restrict itself to the southwest corner of the region, which is part of the Volga Valley.

KOSTROMA

This northern city on the Volga was founded in 1152 by Yuri Dolgoruky during his colonization of the river valley. Surrounded on three sides by thick forests, it gained a reputation as an impenetrable fortress. Nevertheless, it was destroyed by the Tatar sacking of 1238, although it remained a useful hiding place for Muscovite princes during the period of the yoke.

The appearance of the Godunov family in Kostroma has its origin in legend. In 1330 their ancestor, a Tatar noble called Chet, who had been sent by the Khan to keep an eye on Muscovite prince Ivan Kalita, fell ill just outside the city. Two saints appeared to him in a dream and promised him recovery if he became a Christian. He converted, recovered, and decided to found a monastery here, called St. Ipaty's, dedicated to one of the subjects of his vision. His family, meanwhile, became a mighty boyar clan.

It was a potent mixture. St. Ipaty's became one of Russia's most influential monasteries, and the Godunovs, anxious to be considered cultured, poured copious amounts of money into stone building, icon- and fresco-painting there.

Kostroma reached its zenith under Mikhail Romanov. As Russia's third largest city after Moscow and Yaroslavl, it was an important commercial center. Its stonemasons and painters travelled far and wide, working in Yaroslavl, Rostov, Suzdal, and in Moscow's Kremlin.

In 1773, tragedy struck again. A great fire destroyed all but two monasteries and a handful of churches, the town's only stone buildings. And yet the timing could not have been better, as this was Catherine the Great's era of city planning. Soon Kostroma had a new center, a grandiose classical ensemble stretching from the Volga up to the main square.

Stalin, as if to "compensate" for

Panorama of Kostroma, Moscow Province. 19th century drawing by L.R. von Klenze. Collection of the New York Public Library

Kostroma's not being bombed to rubble in World War II, more or less did the job himself – beforehand. In the 1920's and '30's, the city's church-filled skyline was gradually transformed into the semi-industrial wasteland it is today. That said, there's still much of interest left.

The city's main attraction remains the **Monastery of St. Ipaty,** located compactly on the banks of the Kostroma River and opposite the main part of the city. The original Godunov Trinity Cathedral was blown up in the mid-17th century by careless monks who brought candles into the powder cellar. But the disaster may have been beneficial, as the new church was painted by the renowned Kostroma artist, Guri Nikitin. His fluid figures and portrayals of historical and biblical events are best seen here. In addition to the paintings in the main body of the church, which are still intact today, there is one in the foyer – the Last Judgement – an entertaining portrayal of eternal damnation. Under the church is the Godunov family's burial vault, in which four coffins still remain.

A second section of the monastery, out through a gate to the right, encloses the pretty, wooden **Transfiguration Church from Spas-Vezhi**, rescued from the flood plain of the River Volga when the Gorky Reservoir was built. The building to the right houses a natural history museum. One half is devoted to the flora and fauna of the region, including a host of stuffed beasts – bears, wolves, boars and wildcats – all meticulously cared for. Downstairs, you can admire a fine collection of the most beautiful butterflies and the most hideous scorpions and spiders, assembled by Ivan Rubinsky, a turn-of-the-century fanatic.

Behind the monastery is a **wooden architecture museum**, notable for its little octagonal chapel in the village square, bathhouses on stilts across the river, a well-tended cabbage patch, and the beautifully carved Serov

Birthplace of the Romanov Dynasty

Kostroma occupies an odd position in the life of the family that ruled Russia for 304 years. No noble or Tsar was born here, nor did any member of the family live here by his own volition. Yet every Romanov monarch except Peter the Great visited and patronized the city. In England, it would no doubt have had the same status as "Royal" Tunbridge Wells or Bognor "Regis."

At the beginning of the 17th century, Russia was in disarray. Polish intervention complicated the infighting between noble families, and two "false Dmitrys" (impostors claiming to be Ivan the Terrible's son) divided loyalties further. At the time, Kostroma was patronized by Boris Godunov, the ruling Tsar, whose family was the traditional enemy of the boyar Romanovs.

In 1600, Godunov exiled Fyodor Nikitich Romanov, who was then head of the family, to Kostroma's St. Ipaty Monastery. Thus his son Mikhail became acquainted with the area. In 1613, he happened to be there at the time he was elected Tsar by the Land Assembly and offered the throne by its delegates.

In honor of the event, Mikhail revived the monastery, reinforcing the prestige it had received from the Godunovs. Notably, he transformed the rather non-descript building where Mikhail had taken the throne into the festive Romanov's Chambers, and every successive Tsar made it his duty to enter it.

The town itself was to reap the benefits of its position much later, benefits still visible today. In the 18th century, Catherine the Great endowed it with provincial Russia's finest trade and administrative centers, including a special hotel for members of the Tsar's family.

In commemoration of the dynasty's triumphant yet inauspicious 300th anniversary, a museum (now the local art gallery) was built in 1913 to house a special exhibition on the Romanovs. In the city park, a monument was commissioned, including statues of Peter the Great, Nikolay II, Mikhail Romanov and others. World War I and the Revolution intervened, and in the 1920's all excess decoration was removed, while Vladimir I. Lenin, leader of the world proletariat, in glorious reinforced concrete, usurped the pedestal.

Romanovs' Chambers, St. Ipaty Monastery

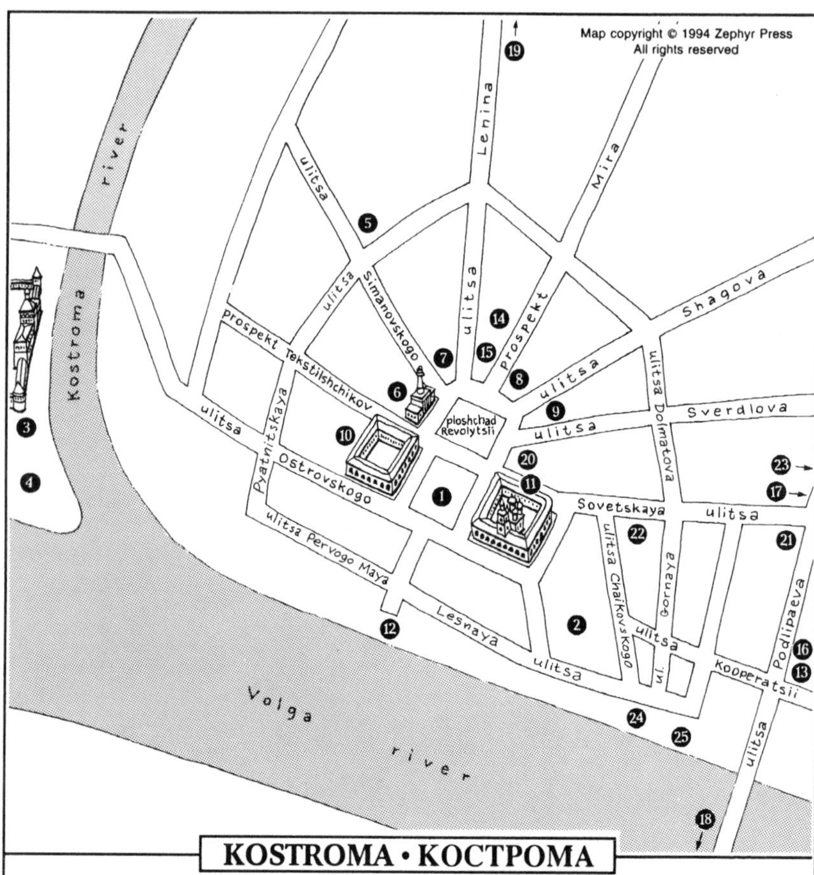

KOSTROMA • КОСТРОМА

Ulitsa Chaikovskovo
Улица Чайковского
Ulitsa Dolmatova
Улица Долматова
Ulitsa Gornaya
Улица Горная
Kostroma River
Река Кострома
Ulitsa Kooperatsiyi
Улица Кооперации
Ulitsa Lenina
Улица Ленина
Lesnaya ulitsa
Лесная улица
Prospekt Mira
Проспект Мира
Ulitsa Ostrovskovo
Улица Островского
Ulitsa Pervovo Maya
Улица Первого Мая
Ulitsa Podlipaeva
Улица Подлипаева
Pyatnitskaya ulitsa
Пятницкая улица
Ploshchad Revolyutsiyi
Площадь Революции
Ulitsa Shagova
Улица Шагова
Ulitsa Simanovskovo
Улица Симановского
Sovyetskaya ulitsa
Советская улица

Ulitsa Sverdlova
Улица Свердлова
Prospekt Tekstilshchikov
Проспект Текстильщиков
Ulitsa Tereshkovoy
Улица Терешковой
Volga River
Река Волга

MAP KEY

1. **Susanin Monument**
   Памятник Сусанину
2. **Lenin Statue**
   Памятник Ленину
3. **St. Ipaty Monastery**
   Ипатьевский монастырь
4. **Wooden Architecture Museum**
   Музей деревянного зодчества
5. **Epiphany Monastery**
   Богоявленский монастырь
6. **Fire Tower**
   Пожарная каланча
7. **Registry**
   Здание гауптвахты
8. **Courthouse**
   Суд
9. **Town Hall**
   Городской Совет
10. **Trading Arcade**
    Торговые ряды
11. **Intercession Church**
    Покровская церковь
12. **Moskovskaya Zastava**
    Московская застава
13. **Resurrection Church**
    Воскресенская церковь
14. **Art Museum**
    Художественный музей
15. **Tsar's Hotel**
    Царская гостиница
16. **Hotel Volga**
    Гостиница «Волга»
17. **Hotel Kostroma**
    Гостиница «Кострома»
18. **Motel**
    Мотель
19. **Berendeyevka Restaurant**
    Ресторан «Берендеевка»
20. **Skazka Café**
    Кафе «Сказка»
21. **Philharmonia**
    Филармония
22. **Post Office**
    Почта
23. **Bus and Train Station**
    Вокзалы
24. **River Station**
    Речной вокзал
25. **Cruise Terminal**
    Речной вокзал (круизы)

house, complete with mirror, samovar and even a gramophone for a well-to-do peasant. Another house, belonging to the Tsipelev family, has an exhibition of pottery, an important regional craft.

Returning to the town, visit the late 18th-century center. Paradoxically, a city famous for its architects has a center built entirely by outsiders. **Susanin Square**, with its fire tower (listed by UNESCO), house of offices, and hotel for royal guests, was built mostly by St. Petersburgers, true to the classical canons of the day.

Incidentally, the name of the square comes from Ivan Susanin, a hero in the 1613 war against Poland. An elderly peasant in a nearby village, he offered to take a gullible Polish detachment to Mikhail Romanov, but instead led them into the nearest swamp, where they all drowned, Susanin included.

Nearby are the labyrinthine **trade rows,** bursting with souvenir shops.

Kostroma Trading Arcade

They are the largest in the country, and contain 96 merchant stalls in the two main squares alone. Each row has its own product – tobacco, butter, cakes and pastries, fish, flour, beer... the list is almost endless.

The final part of the complex is the descent to the Volga, and the **Moskovskaya Zastava**, the formal entrance to the city from the capital, with recently replaced Tsarist eagles on its gates.

The entire area is planned to become a kind of open-air museum, and all new building in the area has been forbidden.

Also be sure to visit the newly reopened Epiphany Monastery, with its miracle-working icon of the Fyodorovsky Virgin, used by Alexander Nevsky in battle, which later became the Romanov family icon.

Finally, have a look at the Resurrection Church "In the Thicket," just behind the Volga Hotel. It's typical of Kostroma's merchant churches built, in this case, by a paint trader. This trader bought from England such marvelous paint that each barrel cost a barrel of gold. The story is told that on one occasion his English partner returned him a barrel of gold with his paint by mistake, and that he used this money to build the church. Unlike the city's monastery churches, this one is almost obscenely festive in its exterior decorations. Inside are Kostroma's earliest surviving, pre-Nikitin, frescoes.

NEREKHTA

Situated between Kostroma, Yaroslavl and Ivanovo, this major railway junction and pottery center has always inspired the envy of Kostromians. Yet Nerekhta is only a small town, with extraordinarily strong and well-kept traditions, and defended effectively against the rigors of the outside world.

One such tradition is its unique dialect, a scrambling of words and stresses that leaves most Russians wincing in disbelief. Here is one entertaining example: if a Nerekhtian wants to tell you to get out of the way, instead of the normal Russian word *otoidi*, he'll probably say *otdaisya*, which to anyone else means, "give me your body."

Although its cluster of churches was all but destroyed by the Bolsheviks, Nerekhta has been undergoing major restoration work for years. Now it's almost completed, and just last fall a treasure was uncovered – beautiful paintings on the *zakomary* of the St. Nicholas Church, unseen since the 1920's.

Now civil architecture is the target, with a new, progressive mayor attracting investment to rebuild the 19th century trade rows, and even planning to pull down the local Lenin statue.

Local businessmen, however, remain stereotypically selfish. The little **Convent of St. Parkhomy** just outside of town is penniless and virtually without hope of getting financing for restoration. Just last May, nine nuns, mostly young girls, moved into buildings that can only be described as derelict. Now stoppage of work on a crucial part of the main roof of the cathedral is threatening their future, and still no help comes.

KRASNOYE-ON-VOLGA

This village south of Kostroma was he site of a bloody battle here between Russians and Tatars. The casualties were so high that the Volga turned red with blood (red in Russian is *krasny*).

Yet the real reason for Krasnoye's fame is much happier. For over a thousand years it has been a center for the making of jewelry. Begun by Finno-Ugric tribes in the 9th century, the craft was adopted by Slavs when they arrived, and the village's fame spread throughout Russia along the Volga. Today, a school specializing in the craft attracts pupils from all over the CIS.

The local museum exhibits treasures from the 9th century to the present, including frames for Old Believers' icons and graduation work by the most recent students.

The village's Epiphany Church, built in 1632, is a particularly attractive example of tent-roof construction, banned by Patriarch Nikon later in the century for being un-Russian.

PRACTICAL MATTERS

You will need to stay in Kostroma, although accommodation in the city leaves much to be desired. For some reason Intourist never got around to building the hotel that was planned, and despite Intourist-scale prices, the municipal Hotel Volga is not of the same standard. The brand new Intourist Motel is quieter and cleaner, but too far out of town to be any use to those lacking a car. Budget travellers will have to make do with the older, seedier, and crowded **Kostroma**, on the way to the railway station.

As for restaurants, there is nothing really outstanding, though the above hotels all provide passable food. Try also the **Berendeyevka** restaurant, set in a park north of the city which once served as a set for the film *The Snow Maiden*, and the **Skazka Café** on Ulitsa Sovyetskaya, near the center (till 7 pm only).

DIRECTIONS

Kostroma: by train 7 hours from the Yaroslavsky Vokzal; by car take the M8, turning onto the A113 just before Yaroslavl, 350 km.

Nerekhta: an hour by bus from Kostroma, on a minor road off the A113.

Krasnoye-on-Volga: an hour by bus from Kostroma. By car, leave the city on the Zavolzhsk road, down the Volga without crossing the bridge.

RUSSIAN GLOSSARY

Krasnoye-na-Volge
Красное-на-Волге

Nerekhta
Нерехта

Convent of St. Parkhomy
Пархомиевский монастырь

Zavolzhsk
Заволжск

IVANOVO REGION

IVANOVSKAYA OBLAST

This small region northeast of Moscow owes its existence mainly to the industrial city which has been growing at its heart since the end of the last century. It has two other features worth special mention. As Ivanovo comprised part of the ancient lands of Vladimir and Suzdal, village icon-painting centers developed there, being replaced after the 1917 revolution by a lacquer miniature industry. Its countryside, bordered to the north and east by the Volga, became a favorite haunt of late 19th century artist Isaac Levitan and other painters of the Itinerant (Wanderers) movement.

IVANOVO

This textile center has often been described as the "Russian Manchester." But at textiles the similarity ends. Combining potholed streets of gray wooden houses with Soviet industrialism, Ivanovo offers little to tempt the traveller. The city was once well known for its gender imbalance. With women flooding in from the country to work at the looms, men were in short supply. Nowadays population figures in the "city of women" differ little from the norm, but some women are still shockingly aggressive in their sexual pursuits. If you're young and male, consider yourself forewarned!

Ivanovo is also sometimes called "the Cradle of the Revolutionary Movement." Strong trade unions developed at the end of the last century, and in 1905 the first workers' Soviet was formed there.

PLYOS

With its steep hills and valleys and pleasant Volga waterfront, Plyos is among the most graceful of Russian towns.

Though a settlement existed there prior to the Tatar invasion of 1238, Plyos's real history began in 1440, when Vassily the Dark, son of Muscovite Prince Dmitry Donskoy, built a fortress on the river as a defense against further attacks from the east. Between sackings by Tatars and Poles, Plyos was the gathering point for a 15th century Muscovite campaign to throw off the yoke completely.

The town's role changed over the

The Miniaturists of Vladimir/Suzdal

Icons and lacquer boxes may not seem to have a great deal in common, but for the villages of Palekh, Kholuy and Mstyora, the two crafts are interlinked.

All three villages were once icon-painting centers of the Vladimir/Suzdal school, inhabited by artists who fled the Tatar invasion in the 13th century. Their traditions ran deep, embodying significance both as religious and folk art.

Kholuy style lacquer box

Over the centuries, communications between far-flung regions of Russia improved, and the styles of the many different icon schools tended to merge. This trend was felt in the three villages, whose craftsmen adopted some features of the Moscow and Novgorod schools. But most valued was their ability to work in miniature, a skill they developed from the days of the yoke, when believers first sought small, personal icons.

Following the Revolution, the icon workshops of the three villages were closed, and their highly-trained craftsmen had to seek other, less skilled work. Something else was badly needed to provide an alternative application for their skills, and a solution was found in the lacquer miniature craft of Fedoskino, outside Moscow. In 1924, the raw materials, papier mâché boxes, were brought to Palekh and Mstyora, and ten years later to Kholuy. All three began to develop and produce their own characteristic interpretations of fairy-tales, literary and historical themes, developing a craft which has become highly prized on the world market, and even one of the symbols of Russia today.

The reawakening of Christianity in Russia has been felt in Palekh, Kholuy and Mstyora. Lacquer boxes with religious themes, as well as icons, are in increasing demand. And there is an interesting twist. Some Palekh artists have taken to painting icons on papier mâché, a material which is proving more suitable than the traditional wooden surface. They have only the Bolsheviks to thank for this discovery!

Of the three centers, **Palekh** is today the best known and most visited, being a stop on the Golden Ring with a top class restaurant and a wealth of interesting sites and museums. This was not always the case – unlike in Kholuy and Mstyora, Palekh had no navigable river. Only the publicity and help given its craftsmen by writer and literary *apparatchik* Maxim Gorky, a close friend of local artist Pavel Korin, put Palekh on the map.

The slender, five-domed **Church of the Elevation of the Cross**, the village's central landmark, is functioning now, its fine 19th century wall paintings the best monument there is to Palekh's older craft. Restored in oil paint from an earlier original, they are in fine condition today, or at least the part that is visible – in the adjoining winter church changes in temperature have made them peel badly.

One of the greatest Palekh artists of this century, Ivan Golikov, had a fate typical of those born at the end of the last. Trained in Palekh's iconographic traditions, he was faced in 1917 with the choice of unemployment or less fulfilling work. After seven years making a living outside his native village on costumes and stage sets, he became one of the pioneers of the lacquer miniature craft. He is remembered in his former cottage, a tiny museum on the corner of the village's two main streets.

Just opposite is the main museum, organized by Gorky himself. It displays the exquisite festival icons that were Palekh's specialty, and the work of its lacquerists in presentation cabinets. Note the bright features of the figures portrayed on the boxes, and the abundance of gold used in illustration.

Buying souvenirs is no problem in Palekh, and there is little risk of ending up with any of the numerous fakes that have flooded Moscow's markets. There is a tiny souvenir kiosk outside the museum, and an exhibition/sale in the school, at the Ivanovo end of the village. The **Traditions of Palekh** firm, an association of teachers at the school who sell their work at much reduced prices, is also based there.

Palekh craftworkers: pressing papier mâché (left) and lacquering boxes (right)

Palekh's lacquer miniatures are

far from cheap, though, with the smaller items beginning at $10, and pieces at the **Tovarishchestvo Palekha** at #33 Ulitsa Lenina can only be for the serious collector. But as a showcase for about 40 members of the Russian Artists' Union, this is the best Palekh has to offer.

Palekh has a very primitive but friendly village hotel just opposite the main road junction.

Just an hour's bus ride away, **Kholuy** has different traditions. Situated on the banks of the Teza river, it flourished in the last century, sending its icons to France, Ethiopia, and even to Goethe's private collection. Its specialty was the so-called *raskhozhiye* or "marketable" icons for ordinary people.

When Kholuy finally turned to lacquer miniatures in the early 1930's, the features of its iconography were transferred to the new craft. Kholuy's boxes are more like realist paintings, and, unlike on Palekh ware, the black background is totally excluded from the picture itself. Kholuy's masters have a tendency toward romantic themes, such as the poetry of Lermontov and Yesenin, or the landscapes of Suzdal.

Today's Kholuy is well off the beaten track, but this permits it to be picturesque in a way that Palekh, pierced by the thundering Ivanovo–Nizhny Novgorod highway, can only dream of being. The central Trinity Church is sadly abandoned, but with the pretty wooden houses around it and a little river bridge, it is fetchingly attractive. The village **museum** has an excellent presentation of Kholuy crafts, and takes the trouble to demonstrate, unlike others, how the crafts of the three towns differ from each other.

The third village, **Mstyora**, is equally scenic but even more remote. Closer in style to Palekh, its miniatures tend to emphasize patterns and color details, while human figures become secondary and tend to fade into the background. They favor blues, greens and violets to depict nature, and this has earned them the nickname, "Russian Dutchmen."

Trinity Church and Tesa River, Kholuy

centuries. In the 17th century, it was a church diocese stretching north to Kostroma and Galich, then in the late 18th became a major trading center on the Volga. Toward the end of the 19th, it lost this role to the nearby town of Kineshma, which had acquired a railroad. It became a place of rest, a favorite retreat of the artists Ilya Repin and Isaac Levitan, and of singer Fyodor Chaliapin. Today it continues to attract holiday-makers as a stop on Moscow-Nizhny Novgorod river cruises.

However you arrive in Plyos, it seems sensible to begin by surveying it from above at the site of the fortress, now known as Cathedral Hill. Sheltered within the rampart rim is the **Assumption Cathedral**, a small church built in classical style by conservative local churchmen who wished to rebuke the extravagance of the then fashionable Naryshkin Baroque. Nearby is a bust of Vassily the Dark, a brooding, bearded figure set on an elongated pedestal.

The view from the east side of the rampart is magnificent, and includes the part of the town beyond the Shokhonka River where Levitan lived, dominated by the bell-tower of St. Barbara's Church and a tiny, winding cobbled street, one of many in Plyos that leads down to the riverside.

The west side is more wooded, but passing through a beautiful birch avenue you can get glimpses of the main trade square below. The next hill is occupied by the local *dom otdykha* and by little pavilions which jut in dilapidated splendor above the expanses of the Volga.

Take any cobbled street down to Ulitsa Lenina, running parallel to the river, a very attractive street with some fine wooden houses. To the right Lenina comes out into the trade square beside the **Resurrection Church**, a five-domed cube typical of this area but with a classical afterthought – a columned portico at the entrance. This church was built in celebration of the victory of 1812 and is a major Volga River landmark.

Follow the embankment east (right)

Plyos lane

into a quieter part of town. Just across the little bridge over the Shokhonka is the **house museum of Isaac Levitan**. Although Levitan (1860–1900) spent just a couple of years in Plyos, the man considered by many to be Russia's greatest landscape painter drew great inspiration from its valleys, churches and river views. In fact, it is often said that Levitan and Plyos discovered each other. A gallery here combines his works with those of other *peredvizhniki*, including several by his Moscow teacher, Vassily Polyenov. The studio and kitchen upstairs, where he lodged, seem alive with his memory.

Ascend rickety wooden steps to Levitan's Hill, the artist's favorite place, which he visited every evening. The little wooden Resurrection Church from nearby Bilyukovo now stands there, but the best view is from the steps themselves.

PRACTICAL MATTERS

If you really need to stay in **Ivanovo** (and if you're visiting the craft villages, this may be the case) there are three passable hotels, the best being the **Tsentralnaya** on Ulitsa Engelsa. The others are the **Sovyetskaya** on Prospekt Lenina and the **Turist** on the corner of Ulitsas Baturina and Kalinina, centrally located by the river.

 DIRECTIONS

Ivanovo: by train from Moscow's Yaroslavsky Vokzal, journey time 6–7 hours, or by bus from metro Sholkovskaya. By car take the M7 to Vladimir and leave by the A113 through Suzdal. It's approximately 100 km from Vladimir.
Palekh: there is one daily direct bus from Moscow, otherwise change at Ivanovo. Bear in mind that if you're travelling directly to Palekh, it is best to go by bus all the way, as Ivanovo's train and bus stations are far apart. By car leave Ivanovo on the Nizhny Novgorod road; it's about 60 km.
Kholuy: by bus from Ivanovo to Yuzha (2 hours), then by local bus. By car when in Palekh follow signs to Yuzha, then on the outskirts of the latter take a right turn to Kholuy.
Mstyora: by local train from Vladimir. Some long distance trains from Moscow to Nizhny Novgorod also stop there. From the station, take a local bus to the village. By car turn off the M7 about 80 km beyond Vladimir.
Plyos: 1½ hours by bus from Ivanovo. By car take the A113 (50 km from either Ivanovo or Kostroma) to Privolzhsk and go east another 15 km. Plyos is also a stop on Moscow–Nizhny Novgorod Volga cruises.

RUSSIAN GLOSSARY

Assumption Cathedral
Успенский Собор
St. Barbara's Church
Варваринская Церковь
Ulitsa Baturina
Улица Батурина
Church of the Elevation of the Cross
Крестовоздвиженская Церковьр
Ulitsa Engelsa
Улица Энгельса
Golikov House-Museum
Дом-музей Голикова
Ulitsa Kalinina
Улица Калинина
Kholuy
Холуй

Prospekt Lenina
Проспект Ленина
Levitan House-Museum
Дом-музей Левитана
Mstyora
Мстёра
Palekh
Палех
Plyos
Плёс
Privolzhsk
Приволжск
Resurrection Church
Воскресенская церковь
Shokhonka River
Река Шохонка
Hotel Sovyetskaya
Гостиница «Советская»
Tovarishchestvo Palekha
Товарищество Палеха
Traditons of Palekh
Традиции Палеха
Hotel Tsentralnaya
Гостиница «Центральная»
Hotel Turist
Гостиница «Турист»
Yuzha
Южа

Plyos: Shokhonka River pavilion

NIZHNY NOVGOROD REGION

NIZHEGORODSKAYA OBLAST

Today's Nizhny Novgorod Region was once at the eastern edge of Russia, and even now it remains something of a boundary between east and west, marking the transition from the Russian heartlands of Vladimir and Ryazan to the Finno-Ugric republics of Mordovia and Chuvashia. The Volga creates a north-south boundary, between the fertile farmland of the area around Arzamas and the bleak forests of the north.

This is truly an area of contrasts. It contains some of the oldest cities in Russia (Nizhny Novgorod was founded in the 13th century, Gorodets even earlier, in 1150), and yet in this century much of it has been uglified to excess by heavy industry. While being home to some of the most familiar Russian village crafts, including the *matryoshka* doll, it boasts a car factory which stretches 5 km across the city of Nizhny Novgorod, plus almost every other heavy industry from ships to paper. For the Orthodox Church it is also important – in the 18th century St. Serafim of Sarova lived and worked in the south. Yet Sarova itself (now just across the *oblast*'s southern border in Mordovia), where Seraphim spent his formative years, is now the highly secret closed town of Arzamas 16, known for its production of neutron bombs. (One map which shows holy places connected with the saint discreetly blots out Sarova with an index.)

The people of Nizhny are said to be thick set, surly, and categorical in their judgements. While they keep strongly to traditions (an example is the persistence of Old Believer sects in some areas), they somehow combine this with a readiness to take on board new ideas. Their cuisine is quintessentially Russian – this is the home of such dishes as pancakes with caviar (*bliny s ikroy*) and meat hotpots. The most flamboyant dish, however, is the *kurnik*, a chicken or fish pie of ample proportions made for weddings and other feasts. It is cut up like a cake in a ritual that resembles the breaking of bread.

NIZHNY NOVGOROD

Russia's third largest city, in Soviet times renamed Gorky but now returned to its former name, is perhaps best known in the West as the place of exile of human rights activist Andrey

Sakharov. Its rich history and character have been obscured for decades by its closed status.

Founded in 1221, it grew to become Russia's most important commercial center. As an old saying goes, St. Petersburg was the head of Russia, Moscow the heart and Nizhny Novgorod the pocket. During the past century, however, it has become a huge industrial city, with 80 percent of its production geared towards defense. During the past few years it has seen the rise of an entrepreneurial class, and is developing a strange dual personality, consisting of the old Gorky and the even older but revived Nizhny.

Though not bristling with churches like, say, Yaroslavl, another great Volga merchant city, it has a unique charm that non-Russians are only just beginning to discover. Nizhny has not fully learned how to cater to tourists yet, but it has certain advantages over even the best provided of Russian cities. While hotel accommodation is still a problem, fast-track privatization has meant a mushrooming of restaurants, cafés and shops which, while expensive for locals, fall far short of the prohibitive hard currency prices of Moscow.

Nizhny is situated at the confluence of the Oka and Volga rivers, occupying both banks of the former. The old city is built around the great Kremlin on the right bank. On the left is the commercial heart, comprising the Yarmarka (fair) and industrial zones centered on the Volga car factory and Sormovo shipyards.

History

According to legend, Nizhny dates from much earlier than its official founding. Supposedly what is now the Kremlin was in the 6th century occupied by a Mordovian prince with 18 wives and countless children. On a visit to his local shaman, he was informed that Mordva would be prosperous if his children did not quarrel. This of course they did, and Russians began to take over the area.

Nizhny was founded as a military outpost in the 13th century during the eastward Russian colonization; it retained this status for the next 500 years. It suffered destruction during the Mongol-Tartar invasion. With the fall of Byzantium, however, the Volga became the main trade artery between Europe and the east, and Nizhny's commercial significance grew.

Another important stage in the city's development came at the beginning of the 19th century when the Fair arrived, brought upriver from the Makaryev Monastery, where its original buildings had been destroyed by fire. By this time, the merchant class was already well established, and was giving the city a new face.

The late 19th century brought industrialization, including the development of shipyards in the Sormovo suburb. Emancipated serfs flocked from the surrounding villages, and a robust proletariat came into being. In 1905 the shipworkers put up barricades in the streets. In 1917, only the small city garrison put up a brief resistance against the Bolsheviks.

In Soviet times, industrialization continued, with the building of the huge Volga car factory, and Nizhny's commercial traditions, if not forgotten, became dormant. In 1932 the city took the name of its famous son, Maxim Gorky.

Increased concentration of defense industry factories made Gorky a "closed city," and in 1980 it achieved notoriety as the virtual prison of nuclear physicist Andrey Sakharov, silenced for his condemnation of the Afghan War.

The Kremlin

Nizhny's huge 16th century fortress, whose walls and 11 towers straddle a steep hillside above the Volga, is the administrative center of both the city and the region. Its military garrison and abundance of black cars lend it a seriousness second only to that of Moscow's Kremlin.

Nothing remains of the original buildings inside. The only church is the Cathedral of the Archangel Michael, tent-roofed and dating from the 17th century. During the summer months (the church has no heating), there is an exhibition devoted to the victorious 1612 volunteer army sent by local merchant Kosma Minin and Suzdal Prince Dmitry Pozharsky to liberate Moscow from the Lithuanians and Poles. Minin's sarcophagus is inside the church.

Other buildings of interest are the House of Soviets, Nizhny's best example of late 20s constructivism and now the garrison headquarters, and the former Governor's house. The latter, built in 1840, is now occupied by a branch of the Art Museum, home to a high quality but somewhat unadventurous collection of almost every Russian artist of note from Borovikovsky to Falk.

Nizhny Kremlin

The main monuments in the Kremlin are all military. An obelisk dating from 1828 devoted to Minin towers over the Volga, while hardware from World War II below the walls on the town side is a favorite playground for toddlers. Not far from the obelisk, the city's eternal flame is guarded by solemn schoolchildren.

Around the City Center: Three Walks

Walk #1: Pokrovka

A good place to begin a tour of Nizhny Novgorod is on the main square, named after Minin and Pozharsky, outside the Kremlin. The statue to local hero Kosma Minin in the square has been the butt of many a joke. The original was built in 1712 for the centenary of his victory, but was taken to Moscow. The city didn't get a new statue until 1942, when it was erected to boost morale during the darkest days of the Leningrad siege. But the statue's outraised arm was too heavy, and began to fall, ironical since the man had an arm crippled by polio. The hapless statue was removed and replaced, absurdly, by a cardboard cut-out. The current three-dimensional statue is only three years old.

Ploshchad Minina is also the beginning of Ulitsa Bolshaya Pokrovka, formerly Sverdlova, Nizhny's main street and a lively pedestrian precinct, stretching for about a mile south to Ploshchad Gorkovo. The first crossroads is with Ulitsa Piskunova, which runs round to the Volga embankment. Facing you as you walk up Pokrovka

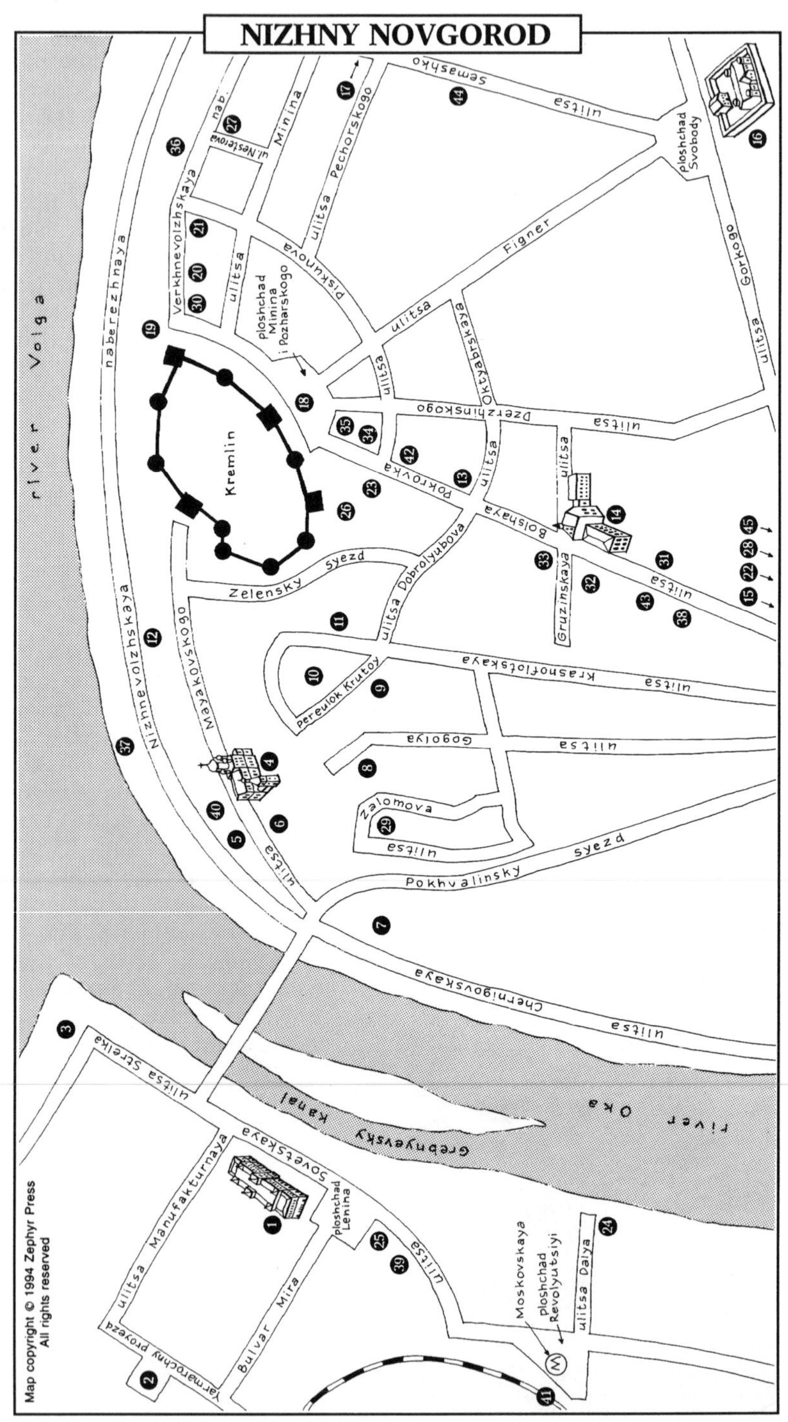
NIZHNY NOVGOROD
river Volga
river Oka
Kremlin
naberezhnaya
Nizhnevolzhskaya
Verkhnevolzhskaya
ulitsa
ul.Nesterova
nab.
Minina
ulitsa Pechorskogo
Semashko
ulitsa
ploshchad Svobody
Figner
ulitsa
ulitsa Gorkogo
Piskunova
ploshchad Minina i Pozharskogo
ulitsa
Oktyabrskaya
ulitsa
Dzerzhinskogo
ulitsa
Pokrovka
Bolshaya
ulitsa
ulitsa
Gruzinskaya
Zelensky syezd
Mayakovskogo
ulitsa
ulitsa Dobrolyubova
pereulok Krutoy
Krasnoflotskaya
ulitsa
Gogolya
ulitsa
Zalomova
ulitsa
Pokhvalinsky syezd
Chernigovskaya
ulitsa
Grebnyevsky kanal
ulitsa Strelka
Sovetskaya
ulitsa Manufakturnaya
Yarmarochny proyezd
Bulvar Mira
ploshchad Lenina
ulitsa
Moskovskaya
ploshchad Revolyutsiyi
ulitsa Dalya

НИЖНИЙ НОВГОРОД

Ulitsa Bolshaya Pokrovka
Улица Большая Покровка
Ulitsa Chernigovskaya
Улица Черниговская
Ulitsa Dalya
Улица Даля
Ulitsa Dobrolyubova
Улица Добролюбова
Ulitsa Dzerzhinskovo
Улица Дзержинского
Ulitsa Figner
Улица Фигнер
ULitsa Gogolya
Улица Гоголя
Ulitsa Gorkovo
Улица Горького
Grebnyevsky kanal
Гребневский канал
Gruzinskaya ulitsa
Грузинская улица
Ulitsa Krasnoflotskaya
Улица Краснофлотская
Kremlin
Кремль
Pereulok Krutoy
Переулок Крутой
Ploshchad Lenina
Площадь Ленина
Ulitsa Manufakturnaya
Улица Мануфактурная
Ulitsa Mayakovskovo
Улица Маяковского
Ulitsa Minina
Улица Минина
Ploshchad Minina i Pozharskovo
Площадь Минина и Пожарского
Bulvar Mira
Бульвар Мира
Metro Moskovskaya
Станция метро «Московская»
Ulitsa Nesterova
Улица Нестерова
Nizhnevolzhskaya naberezhnaya
Нижневолжская набережная
River Oka
Река Ока
Ulitsa Oktyabrskaya
Улица Октябрьская
Ulitsa Pechorskovo
Улица Печорского
Ulitsa Piskunova
Улица Пискунова
Pokhvalinsky Syezd
Похвалинский съезд
Ploshchad Revolyutsii
Площадь Революции
Ulitsa Semashko
Улица Семашко
Ulitsa Sovyetskaya
Улица Советская
Ulitsa Strelka
Улица Стрелка
Ploshchad Svobody
Площадь Свободы
Verkhnevolzhskaya naberezhnaya
Верхневолжская набережная
River Volga
Река Волга
Yarmarochny proyezd
Ярмарочный проезд
Ulitsa Zalomova
Улица Заломова
Zelensky Syezd
Зеленский съезд

MAP KEY

1. **Fair**
   Ярмарка
2. **Old Fair Church**
   Староярмарочная церковь
3. **Alexander Nevsky Church**
   Церковь Александра Невского
4. **Stroganov Church**
   Строгановская церковь
5. **Stroganov Mansion**
   Строгановская усадьба
6. **Excursion Bureau**
   Экскурсионное бюро
7. **Annunciation Monastery**
   Благовещенский монастырь
8. **Pushnikov Chambers**
   Пушниковы палаты
9. **Olisov's Chambers**
   Олисовы палаты
10. **Assumption Church**
    Успенская церковь
11. **Chapygin House**
    Дом Чапыгина
12. **Rukavishnikov House**
    Дом Рукавишникова

13. **Nobles' Assembly**
Дворянское Собрание
14. **State Bank**
Банк
15. **Shcholokovsky Khutor**
Щёлоковский хутор
16. **Ostrog (old prison)**
Острог
17. **Pechora Monastery**
Печорский монастырь
18. **Minin Monument**
Памятник Минину
19. **Chkalov Monument**
Памятник Чкалову
20. **Art Museum**
Художественный музей
21. **History and Architecture Museum**
Историко-архитектурный музей
22. **Sakharov Flat-museum**
Музей-квартира Сахарова
23. **Gorky Drama Theater**
Драматический театр имени Горького
24. **Circus**
Цирк
25. **Tsentralnaya Hotel**
Гостиница «Центральная»
26. **Moskva Hotel**
Гостиница «Москва»
27. **Oktyabrskaya Hotel**
Гостиница «Октябрьская»
28. **Oka Hotel**
Гостиница «Ока»
29. **Nizhegorodskaya Hotel**
Гостиница «Нижегородская»
30. **Rossiya Hotel**
Гостиница «Россия»
31. **Kolisei Restaurant**
Ресторан «Колисей»
32. **Vitalich Restaurant**
Ресторан «Виталич»
33. **Lykova Damba Café**
Кафе «Лыкова дамба»
34. **U Shakhovskovo Restaurant**
Ресторан «У Шаховского»
35. **Harbin Chinese Restaurant**
Ресторан «Харбин»
36. **Gardinia Café**
Кафе «Гардиния»
37. **River Station (Raketa boats)**
Речной вокзал
38. **Khudozhestvenniye Promysly Shop**
Магазин «Художественные промыслы»
39. **Bookshop**
Книжный магазин
40. **Market**
Рынок
41. **Moscow Station (Moskovsky Vokzal)**
Московский вокзал
42. **Dmitriyevsky Cheese Shop**
Дмитриевский магазин
43. **Puppet Theater**
Кукольный театр
44. **Gorky Flat-museum**
Музей-квартира Горького
45. **Alexey Peshkov's House**
Дом Алексея Пашкова

is the famous **Dmitriyevsky** cheese shop. The abundance of tempting edibles there reflects the general situation in a city virtually free of a hard currency superculture. Just opposite is Teatralnaya ploshchad and the Gorky Drama Theater, which is best appreciated from the outside, and not recommended for lovers of the stage.

Further on up the left hand side is the former house of the Nobles' Assembly, an early 18th century classical structure with six massive columns, but Pokrovka's real treat is yet to come. Again on the left, past crossroads with Ulitsa Grusinskaya, is the **State Bank**. This huge block of Art Nouveau, with its tower-shaped protuberances either side of the entrance and tent roof in traditional Russian style, had an unfortunate beginning. It was built in 1913 to commemorate 300 years of the Romanov dynasty, just four years before its overthrow. If you can talk your way inside, the ceilings, decorated by the Pashkov brothers, icon-painters from Moscow, are breathtaking.

The upper reaches of Pokrovka are graced by the modern Puppet Theater on the right, reminiscent of the Obraztsova Theater in Moscow. Performances are well worth seeing. The arts and crafts shop, **Khudozhestvenniye Promysli**, slightly further on the right, has departments for each of the region's main craft centers.

State Bank

Walk #2: Down the Volga

At the end of Ploshchad Minina take a right toward the Rossiya Hotel along Verkhnyevolzhskaya Naberezhnaya, with its superb views of the Volga. The **Art Museum** on your right has no permanent displays, but the standard of its temporary exhibitions is very high. Slightly further is the **History Museum**, incorporating exhaustive displays about the geology and natural history of the region. However, most interesting of all is the building. It was completed in 1877 as the family home of the extravagant merchant Sergey Rukavishnikov. The façades, whose balconies and overhangs are supported by nymph statues and herms, were sculpted by Smolensk craftsman Mikhail Mikeshin.

The embankment continues for a kilometer or more, then ends abruptly with several huge ski jumps. Just beyond them you can see a cupola topped by a crescent, the **city mosque**.

Down below on the right is the former **Pechora Monastery**. From where you stand, it is quite a complicated place to reach; it's better to walk inland and along the nearest main road, Ulitsa Rodionova, as far as the bus station, then take a left before the Pechory Cinema. Be aware before making the descent, though, that the grounds of the monastery are often muddy. Though currently occupied by the harmless-sounding City Restoration Board, there are "Beware of the Dog" signs everywhere (but no dogs).

Pechora began as a cave monastery (from the Russian *peschery*, meaning caves), founded in the 14th century by a monk from the first monastery of this type in Kiev. The first stone monastery, a mile downstream from the present site, became a major center of learning in the 14th century. However, it was swept away by a landslide in 1597, though it is said that on church holidays the ghostly sound of bells can be heard from the sea.

The rebuilt version is certainly worth admiring for its architectural skill, even if only from afar. The centerpiece Ascension Cathedral, with its five cupolas, is perfectly complemented by two tent-roofed churches on either side, whether viewed from the river or from land. One of them, the Church of St. Euphemius, is the only surviving tent-roofed church-over-the-gate in Russia.

Walk #3: Up to the confluence

Returning to Ploshchad Minina, you can descend the ornamental steps by the Kremlin's St. George's Tower

Traditional Crafts

Because the poor soil of the northern part of the region made farming difficult, much of the peasant population today makes their living from traditional crafts, such as wood-carving or painting, or metalwork. It is there that most items you now find in souvenir shops – *matryoshka* dolls, wooden spoons, paintings, chopping boards – originate.

There are several major centers worth visiting, and in some factories tours can be arranged. **Gorodets**, a town situated upstream of Nizhny on the Volga, near the entrance to the Gorky Reservoir, should be a priority. Though virtually nothing remains of the original settlement, and all but one of its more recent churches have been demolished, its wooden architecture is very appealing. The intricately carved platbands (decorative window framing) you may have noticed occasionally on houses in other places are on every single house here, and the craftmanship is superior.

Platband carving, or *nalichniki* (see photo on p. 300) has remained a cottage industry to this day, and there are also two factories which provide a rich variety of goods. **Gorodets Painting**, (*Gorodetskaya Rospis'*) carries on the tradition of painted chopping boards. Originally made of oak and decorated with carvings, in the last century these boards began to be painted. The wood was simply varnished, then the light background painted over with cheerful scenes such as tea-drinking or merrymaking. As well as mass-producing souvenirs, the factory, founded in Soviet times, has a number of talented craftsmen, and a showroom with a collection of its choicest work.

Across town, the **Tatyana** joint stock society produces patterned scarves and shawls, traditionally with gold thread but nowadays using cheaper metal. In Soviet times, it invented "Gorky guipure," heavy stitched lace nets superimposed with a threaded pattern. In the 1970s an ancient lace-weaving craft from the nearby town of Balakhna was resumed in a branch of the Gorodets factory.

All of these crafts and more can be seen in the excellent local museum, though unfortunately at the time of writing the town didn't have a single souvenir shop, and prospective buyers will have to go to Nizhny or elsewhere.

The town of **Semyonov** may not be as old as Gorodets, but its crafts are probably better known. The surrounding area, remote from the Volga valley, was settled by Old Believers in the 17th century as they sought refuge from their persecutors. Though little now remains of their religion, their creative traditions have lasted as almost no others'.

Khokhloma Painting (*Khokhlomskaya Rospis'*) has organized all the crafts from surrounding villages into a single center. (None are native to Semyonov itself.) Here the principles applied are very different from those at Gorodets, requiring a much more intricate preparation procedure. Cups and dishes were the main products. After turning, the wood was treated, painted, varnished, then baked. The end product was black, cinnabar and gold in color, the last created as the effect of baking aluminum powder. Today the most famous product of the factory is its wooden spoons.

Just to the north is the **Semyonov Painting** (*Semyonovskaya Rospis'*) factory. From the gigantic pictures on the gates it is immediately obvious that this is the home of the famous *matryoshka* doll. Like many things Russian, the *matryoshka* principle originated from abroad, in this case from Japan. Its beginnings in Russia are uncertain, though the first are believed to have been made in the Sergiyev Posad area outside Moscow. However, in 1922, a Semyonov turner called Arsenty Mayorov brought back a plain wooden doll from the market and made the industry his own. Though other local centers like Maidan also produced *matryoshkas*, the best always came from Semyonov, where the traditions were strongest and most suited to the new product. Now visitors to the factory will find a friendly and relaxed atmosphere where all stages of production can be observed.

Semyonov matryoshka factory

The local museum, just off the main square to the right of the fire station, is also worth a visit. Its display of local crafts is exhaustive, and the life of Old Believers in the area well portrayed. A craft shop opposite was only recently opened, a fact betrayed during my visit by the zeal of the assistant.

Another important craft of the region is the casting of copper alloys in the Oka valley town of **Pavlovo**. The Pavlovo locksmiths became famous in the 18th century for their depictions of animals and fabulous beings in miniature, often using the grotesque motifs of 9th and 10th century Russian art. Now a souvenir industry has developed there, and tourists travelling by boat often visit the riverside museum and shop.

to begin the second riverside walk. The huge statue at the top is of Valery Chkalov, the first man to fly over the North Pole. Jutting out into the river at the bottom is another monument, a boat from the little Volga Flotilla, which was instrumental in defeating the White armies in the 1918–19 civil war, and the Germans at Stalingrad in 1942–43.

Turn left and walk for less than a kilometer, turning left again after the art nouveau Rukavishnikov Bank. This brings you to Ulitsa Mayakovskovo, once the domain of Nizhny's richest merchant family, the

House with platband carving (now a newspaper office)

Stroganovs. But first you might want to climb up the hill in front of you, Ilyinskaya Gora. The little **Assumption Church**, visible at the top, is considered a pearl of 17th century Russian architecture, built by a merchant called Olisov. Its cupolas are decorated with glazed tile friezes, while the church itself was constructed in a style known as "a crossed barrel with four faces," normally reserved for wooden structures. It is the only stone church of its kind left in Russia. Just behind the church are Olisov's Chambers, one of a number of 17th century secular buildings in the city dating from the early days of the Fair. Peter the Great spent his 50th birthday there. Nearby at 27 Ulitsa Pochainskaya is the house of the merchant Chatygin, also known as Peter the Great's House, where he stayed on the way to his southern campaign in 1695.

But Peter the Great was not on good terms with all Nizhny merchants. Salt and potash baron Grigory Stroganov, whose wealth exceeded even the Tsar's, aroused Peter's ire when he built the **Church of the Nativity** (on Ulitsa Mayakovskovo, reached by returning to the route of the walk). This fine example of Moscow Naryshkin Baroque (see Glossary) was carved by some of the country's best craftsmen, who were then blinded by Stroganov in fine Russian tradition so that they could not surpass their own excellence. But the source of Peter's anger lay in the interior, where a glittering iconostasis painted by a Byzantine master included an Archangel Michael bearing an uncanny resemblance to Stroganov! While praying in the church, the Tsar looked up to find himself staring into the face of his host. Disgusted by what he suspected was Stroganov's vanity, he stormed out. Stroganov promptly closed the church until Peter's death.

Ulitsa Mayakovskovo leads out onto a square, to the right of which is the Oka bridge, the city's main link with the left bank.

Beyond the bridge, walk along Ulitsa Chernigovskaya to the **Annunciation Monastery**. Founded in the 13th century by Prince Yuri Vsevolodovich, it served to guard the approaches to the Kremlin and the ferry across the Oka. Unfortunately, none of the original buildings have survived, only their 18th century replacements, which have now been returned to the church. Like the Pechora, it is muddy and hard to reach, and is probably best seen from the Yarmarka opposite.

The Left Bank

Whether you're looking from across the Oka or driving down the left side you cannot help but notice the huge building of the **Yarmarka**. Built in neo-Russian style in 1890, it will remind those familiar with Moscow of the GUM Department Store, which was built later. During Soviet times it became a children's shop, but is now being used once again for its original purpose. The fair takes place monthly, for three or four days, while the rest of the time the building is empty save for a handful of commercial shops and stalls.

Several blocks behind the Yarmarka and unfortunately obscured by modern housing is the pretty white **Church of the Transfiguration of the Savior**, otherwise known as the Staroyarmarochnaya, or Old Fair Church. This is the only remaining building of a huge complex built at the beginning of the last century. Its architect was Monferrand, who also designed St. Isaac's Cathedral in St. Petersburg. But this church is small, white and neat, hence its nickname, "the Toy St. Isaac's."

Apart from the areas around the Fair and the Moscow Station just to the south, the left bank is almost exclusively working class and industrial. To the west is **Sormovo**, one of the cradles of the revolutionary movement. The action of Gorky's novel, *Mother*, took place in the shipyards there. The revolutionaries of 1905 are still lovingly remembered by countless monuments, and a statue of Lenin is engraved with his prophetic words, "1905 is a dress rehearsal."

To the south is a district capturing the spirit of an altogether different era, the utopian socialism of the 1930s. It was during this period of mass industrialization that the Volga car plant and others were built, inspiring names like "Socialist Town" and "Engine of the Revolution," the latter now the name of a stop on the metro. Workers were housed in flats with connecting corridors, supposedly to give them a sense of community. This was not achieved, and the corridors were removed. In any case, this type of housing was only completed for a small portion of the workers; most lived in wooden barracks, the last of which were not replaced until the 1960s.

Other Places of Interest

Although the city itself no longer bears his name, Nizhny has far from forgotten **Maxim Gorky**. Two rather ordinary museums are dedicated to him: the house of Alyosha Peshkov, his grandfather, on Ulitsa Korolenko; and the one on Ulitsa Semashko where he spent his later years.

The **flat-museum of Andrey Sakharov** is a modest affair, situated on the southern edge of the city in the house where he and his wife lived in exile. Although most of the original furniture was removed after his departure, this was more than compensated for during my visit by the vivid stories and descriptions of the guide. A room of the museum is dedicated to prisoners of conscience of Nizhny Novgorod, a condition set by Sakharov's wife, Yelena Bonner, for opening the museum. The address is 214 Ulitsa Voennykh Kommissarov, reached by any bus bound for the Shcherbinka 2 housing estate. The museum even has a bus stop named after it (Musei Akademika Sakharova).

To the east is a large area of recreational parkland known as **Shcholokovsky Khutor**. In its center is the regional wooden architecture museum, displaying buildings brought from nearby villages and reassembled on site. One unusual exhibit is the little Old Believers' Church, dating from the 17th century. The museum has plans to exhibit Mordovian, Mari and Tatar farmsteads as well as the traditional Russian. It is situated at the end of Okhotnichya ulitsa, the last stop on the #28 bus route.

MAKARYEVO

The original site of the Fair was not in Nizhny Novgorod itself but rather about 100 km downstream on the edge of the Volga's Yellow Lake (*Zholtoye Ozero*). But here the Fair, which was destroyed by fire in 1816, was both preceded and outlasted by a huge and powerful monastery, the **Makaryevsko Yellow-Water**. Founded originally in 1435, it was sacked by the Tatars and rebuilt only 200 years later. But even then the newly created two-wall fortification, impenetrable as it may have seemed, fell in a single day to Ataman Osipov, one of the lieutenants of peasant revolt leader Stenka Razin, in 1670. Nowadays the monastery is a picturesque stop-off on Volga cruises or a pleasant day-trip on the river.

Just a few miles up from Makaryevo, the **Kerzhenets** river flows into the Volga. Its lower reaches are an area of outstanding natural beauty, and a favorite destination for trips in the traditional *baidarka* boats.

PRACTICAL MATTERS

Where to stay

Accommodation in Nizhny is in very short supply. The most expensive hotel is the **Oktyabrskaya** on Verkhnyevolzhskaya naberezhnaya, the former Communist Party hotel, which charges $50 a night, though even for this price you may not get a room. The several medium range hotels are for rubles, but cannot cope with demand and have to be booked well in advance.

They are the **Nizhegorodskaya** (Ulitsa Zalomova, 2); **Rossiya** (2a Verkhnyevolzhskaya Naberezhnaya); **Oka** (Prospekt Gagarina, 27); and the **Tsentralnaya** (Ploshchad Lenina). The **Moskva** on Teatralnaya ploshchad was being renovated at the time of writing.

There are cheaper places which generally have rooms available, but conditions are basic. The most central is the **Dom Krestyanina** at 6 Ulitsa Dzerzhinskovo. Otherwise some locals rent out flats short-term for around $10 a night. A local newspaper, *Birzha* (Stock Exchange), has ads for apartment rentals.

Getting Around

Public transport in Nizhny is more frequent and less horribly packed than in many Russian cities. As well as the usual books of tickets, you can get daily or five-day passes for buses (not for trams or trolleybuses), which can be cheaper still than the ticket books.

The metro is of no interest architecturally, and has only one line, running from Moskovskaya (the train station) south through the industrial suburbs on the Oka left bank. Completed in 1985, it was meant to be extended to the city center. This project, however, fell foul of local opposition. Townspeople who were concerned that vibrations would destroy the city's old buildings staged a sit-in on Ploshchad Gorkovo, and forced the authorities to back down.

Eating Out and Nightlife

The quickest and easiest place to eat in Nizhny is without a doubt the **Gardinia** on Verkhnyevolzhskaya naberezhnaya. Opened in 1992 by a Palestinian American couple, its concrete-and-glass Soviet-style exterior is matched by tacky Americana inside. It doesn't appear to have fixed opening hours, and though the choice of food is not always good, at this writing it's probably the only Western-style fast food joint in the country outside of Moscow and St. Petersburg.

Cafés in the city center are otherwise both numerous and seedy. **Lykova Damba**, on the corner of Ulitsa Bolshaya Pokrovka and Ulitsa Dobrolyubova has salads to supplement the usual sausage sandwich and pastry fare. Pizza and hot-dog stands are probably best avoided.

As for restaurants, the picture is much rosier, and seems likely to improve further. There is now a healthy choice of places offering substantial meals, tasteful decor and polite, friendly service, all for reasonable ruble prices. The best all-rounder is definitely **U Shakovskovo** in the Dom Aktyora on Ulitsa Piskunova, which offers passable music as an added bonus. Smart dress may be required. Try also **Vitalich** and **Kolisei** on Bolshaya Pokrovka, the top floor of the River Station on Nizhnyevolzhskaya naberezhnaya, and a new place called **Assambleya** in the Social and Cultural Center on Oktyabrskaya ploshchad. If you're tired of Russian food, there is a Chinese restaurant called **Harbin** on the corner of Bolshaya Pokrovka and Ploshchad Minina.

For nightlife, Nizhny is still a long way behind Moscow. There is only one hard currency bar, in the Oktyabrskaya Hotel. For late night drinkers, however, there are also casinos, on Bolshaya Pokrovka at the Kremlin end and on Ulitsa Vorobyova.

DIRECTIONS

Nizhny Novgorod: by overnight train from the Kursky or Yaroslavsky Stations, two trains from each. Recently a luxury commercial train with supplement has started running from the Kazansky station. By car just keep going straight east out of Moscow on M7 Gorkovskoye shossé. The distance is approximately 400 km.

Gorodets: by Raketa speedboat up the Volga, or by bus from the bus station next to the Moskovsky Station in Nizhny. By car north on the R150 to Zavolzhye, then right across the locks at the entrance to the Gorky Reservoir, 50 km.

Semyonov: by suburban train on the Vetluzhsky line from the Moskovsky Station. By car northeast on the R159, 65 km.

Pavlovo: by Raketa speedboat up the Oka, or by suburban train from the Moskovsky Station. By car south on the R125, 65 km.

Makaryevo: by Raketa speedboat down the Volga, otherwise access by dirt road only and indirect.

RUSSIAN GLOSSARY

Dom Aktyora
Дом Актёра
Dom Krestyanina
Дом Крестьянина
Ulitsa Gagarina
Улица Гагарина
Gorodets
Городец
Dvoriki
Дворики
Kolisei
Колизей
Ulitsa Korolenko
Улица Короленко
Makaryevo
Макарьево
Moscow Hotel
Гостиница «Москва»
Nizhegorodskaya Oblast
Нижегородская область
Nizhny Novgorod
Нижний Новгород
Okhotnichya ulitsa
Охотничья улица
Pavlovo
Павлово
Pechory Cinema
Кинотеатр «Печоры»
Ulitsa Pochainskaya
Улица Почаинская
Rukavishnikov Bank
Рукавишников банк
Semyonov
Семёнов
Shcherbinka 2
Щербинка 2
Teatralnaya ploshchad
Театральная площадь
Tsentralnaya Hotel
Гостиница «Центральная»
Ulitsa Voennykh Kommissarov
Улица Военных Комиссаров
Ulitsa Vorobyova
Улица Воробьёва
Zavolzhye
Заволжье

Bolshaya Pokrovka Street, Nizhny Novgorod.
Title page photo: ***City mosque***

VLADIMIR REGION

VLADIMIRSKAYA OBLAST

The Vladimir Region is an area of farmland and forest immediately east of Moscow, a diminished version of the former Vladimir-Suzdal Princedom, which from the mid-12th century until the rise of Moscow in the 14th was considered the most influential in Russia. Before it was taken over by the Tatars in 1238, Vladimir was Russia's cultural center; its limestone masonry and carvings have never been surpassed. This rich heritage, and later treasures, have in part survived to the present. Because of Vladimir's position on the Golden Ring of Russia and the abundance of attractions – by no means confined to the regional center and Suzdal – tourism is better organized than in most regions. There are plenty of museums, often with colorful brochures and special effects, and the visitor should have little trouble finding interesting places to visit.

VLADIMIR

Despite its history, today's Vladimir (Vla-DEE-meer) is not the most attractive of Russian cities. First of all it is an industrial center, producing electric motors, tractors, watches and shoes; these factories tend to encroach on the historic part. The main street is reasonably pleasant, and a walk along the top of the ledge past the cathedrals would be beautiful, were it not for the railway line spoiling the view of the Klyazma River.

Along with its ancient churches, Vladimir has a number of other interesting architectural monuments and many well-kept museums. The greatest concentration is around the Golden Gate. Approaching from the center of town, the city's 12th century earthen ramparts, now known as **Kozlov Val**, are on the left. An old water tower, resembling a disembodied tower from a city wall, houses an exhibition of 19th century life in Vladimir, and the top floor is a viewing platform. Across the square to the left is the huge Old Believers' **Trinity Church** with its exhibition of local crafts – embroidery and lacquer boxes from Mstyora and glass from Gus Khrustalny included. Further left, the large modern building is the acclaimed **Lunacharsky Drama Theater**.

Descending from the Golden Gate by Ulitsa Pervomaiskaya will bring

Kozlov Val Museum

you to the striking green baroque **Church of St. Nikita**. Turn right here and proceed to the small church ahead to the left. This is the 16th century **Assumption Cathedral of the Princess' Convent**, the earliest of Vladimir's post-Mongolian churches. It replaced 12th century buildings where the sisters Maria and Anna, both wives of Vsevolod Big Nest, were buried. The present church has no carvings, but several tiers of *kokoshniki* tapering to a single dome, giving it a different kind of charm. Formerly a museum, it has now been returned to the Church.

Walking back along Ulitsa Tretyevo Internatsionala toward the cathedrals, you pass the **Arcade** (*Gostiny Dvor*) on your left, an example of late 18th century Russian Classicism and now a row of shops, then on your right a bookshop at #44, before crossing a bridge into Ploshchad Svobody. Continuing past the cathedrals, you come to the **History Museum** at #64. This contains the original coffin of Alexander Nevsky, once buried nearby in the **Monastery of the Nativity**. You may need a guided tour here (available at the museum), because written information is sparse.

SUZDAL

About 32 km north of Vladimir on the Kamenka River is the ancient city of Suzdal (*sooz*dahl), which from the 12th to the 18th centuries played a major role in the life of Russia. Since then, it has barely been altered, keeping a special, old-world charm.

Suzdal first achieved fame in 1152, when Yuri Dolgoruky moved his seat of government there, and built his fortress at nearby Kideksha. It grew to become a rich trading city, greater than contemporary London, and continued to flourish, despite the move of the capital to Vladimir by Dolgoruky's son Andrey Bogolyubsky.

Even after the Tatar-Mongol invasion, Suzdal remained a political center, and as late as the 15th century it rebelled against Moscow's rule, for which Muscovite Prince Vasily the Dark cruelly punished the city.

Suzdal's religious significance continued, and its accumulation of architectural and artistic wealth was hindered only by repeated invasions by Poles, Lithuanians and Crimean Tatars.

Suzdal today covers an area of about 7 square kilometers, in which there are over a hundred architectural monuments. It can be negotiated easily on foot, but requires several days to be seen in full. If you get tired, in summer there are always horse-drawn carriages for hire in the center.

Just out of town is the Main Tourist Complex, with good, motel-like facilities, and several of the **monasteries** also have accommodation. Food, as in

Vladimir, is of a reasonable standard and restaurants are fairly numerous. You can accompany your meal with Suzdal's specialty, *myedovukha* or mead, fermented honey whose taste is similar to English scrumpy cider.

Tours should begin in the Kremlin, and with the Cathedral of the Nativity (see box). The ensemble also includes the **Archbishop's Chambers** and the **Cross Chamber**, a huge vaulted hall without a single pillar, the first of its kind in Russia. The museum here contains a history exhibition, and among other things china made by Russia's first manufacturer, the Suzdalian Dmitry Vinogradov in the 18th century. There is an exhibition in the refectory church of icons, from the early days of the Vladimir school to the blossoming of the art in Suzdal in the 15th and 16th centuries and beyond. Note The Intercession, with its expression of lyrical imagery and an individual spiritual world for each of the characters portrayed.

It would be impossible to describe all of Suzdal's churches here, especially the large number among them built in the early 18th century. However, as we pass through the center of the city from the Kremlin some are especially worthy of mention. Most churches in or around the market place are in pairs, with large, lavishly decorated summer churches and smaller, more modest places of worship which could be more easily heated during the winter. An example of this is the **Church of the Resurrection**, with the **Church of our Lady of Kazan.** The first of these is in the shape of a flattened cube and almost without decoration. Yet it has miniature *kokoshniki* in a band below the roof. Continuing north along Ulitsa Lenina towards Red Square (Krasnaya Ploshchad), you will pass the **Churches of St. Lazarus and St. Antipius** on the left hand side. The distinguishing feature of the former, the summer church, is again the *kokoshniki*. Built in 1667, this was one of the first churches where the formerly functional *zakomari* (arched gables that follow the contours of the vaulting of 11th and 12th century Russian churches), became purely ornamental as a result of changes in construction techniques. The winter church nearby is notable for its bell tower, colored tastefully in maroon, cream and white and topped by an unusual concave tent roof.

The huge yellow bell tower ahead of you and opposite Krasnaya Ploshchad indicates the **Monastery of the Deposition of the Robe**. The Cathedral of the same name, built in the first half of the 16th century, is unusual for its shallow helmet domes on elongated two-tier drums, which make them resemble minarets. The most notable building in the ensemble, however, is the **Holy Gate** with one large and one small arch, each surmounted by an elegant octagonal tent roof with tiny cupolas.

Take the road to the left after the Monastery (now, or formerly, Ulitsa Engelsa), and head for the churches of the **Monastery of Alexander Nevsky**. Very modest in comparison with the huge Nevsky Lavra, on whose site it was built, this handsome ensemble is a good location from which to view the Convent of the Intercession, across the Kamenka River.

Returning to Lenina, and continuing north, you come to the **Monastery of the Savior and St. Euthimius**, Suzdal's largest and most powerful monastery, with a 1200m wall and 12 towers. It was founded in 1352, but most construction dates from the 16th or 17th centuries. The **Cathedral of the Transfiguration** is the centerpiece, a huge five-domed cube with numerous side-chapels, influenced by the Assumption Cathedral in Moscow's Kremlin. Inside is a mu-

The White Stone Architecture of Vladimir

With the disintegration of Kievan Rus' in the middle of the 12th century, a golden age of Russian architecture began in various regional centers. Princedoms like Vladimir and Suzdal began to seek new forms of expression and to move away from the gigantism of Kiev and Byzantium.

Vladimir became the foremost of these various schools, mainly because of the skill shown in positioning its churches in natural surroundings and the high standard of its stone carving.

After suffering destruction under the Tatars and later undergoing alterations, six such churches and two other buildings have survived, at least in part, to the present day.

The oldest of the six is also the simplest. The **Church of SS. Boris and Gleb at Kideksha**, outside Suzdal, is all that remains of a fortress built by Yuri Dolgoruky in 1152. The outside has almost no ornamentation apart from a band of blind arcading, later developed in the more decorative Vladimir churches.

The inside of the church is part of the Vladimir-Suzdal museum, displaying two 12th century frescoes, believed to depict Dolgoruky's Greek wife and his two sons Boris and Gleb. Boris and his wife Maria are buried there.

Time and 17th century restorers have not been kind to the church. Its original huge helmet dome and roof were replaced and new windows cut, making it appear today rather forlorn. However, in combination with the 17th century St. Stephen's Church and bell-tower, and the low wall surrounding them, it does have a gentle and unassuming charm, and is worth the 2 km trek from Suzdal.

Vladimir's huge **Assumption Cathedral** is the next of the surviving pre-Mongolian churches,

Church of the Nativity and St. Nicholas wooden church, Suzdal

built in 1160 by Prince Andrey Bogolyubsky and meant to be the successor to St. Sophia's in Kiev. (Andrey had moved his capital to Vladimir two years earlier, having despaired of uniting Rus' from a divided Kiev.) As the Assumption is the name given to the time when the twelve apostles gathered from the corners of the earth round the Virgin's death bed, it was hoped that the building of the cathedral would unite the Russian princedoms.

In 1185 the cathedral was damaged by fire, then virtually rebuilt by the craftsmen of the then leader Prince Vsevolod Big Nest. New walls went up around the old, and four domes were added to the original one. Apart from a bell-tower and connecting chapel added in the 19th century, this is the form in which the cathedral has reached us today. Even now, it towers over the city, and from a distance even seems to be floating, separated from the ground by the foliage that surrounds it.

Inside, the cathedral is no less stunning, with a 25m iconostasis, boasting several icons painted by Andrey Rublyov. (Now they are in the collection of Moscow's Tretyakov Gallery.) Rublyov's frescoes still remain in some spots, and there are possibly more to be uncovered. A common theme is The Last Judgement, in which the hatred and despairs of the day, portrayed by the sinners, were contrasted with the ultimate goal of love and harmony, as expressed in one fresco, The Procession of the Righteous into Heaven.

Vladimir's greatest Princes, Bogolyubsky and Big Nest, are buried in the vaults, and their sarcophagi can be seen in one of the niches hewn out of the original wall and leading to the newer one.

The reasons for the building of the **Church of the Intercession on the Nerl** at **Bogolyubovo** are not entirely clear, considering its distance from any civilization and lack of any apparent practical use. But whether it was put there in memory of Prince Andrey's son who died fighting the Volga Bulgar tribe or to impress visitors arriving in the princedom by boat, the main thing is that it is there, and can simply be admired for its surpassing charm and beauty.

Church of the Intercession on the River Nerl

Situated on a flood plain at the confluence of the Nerl and

Continued on page 312

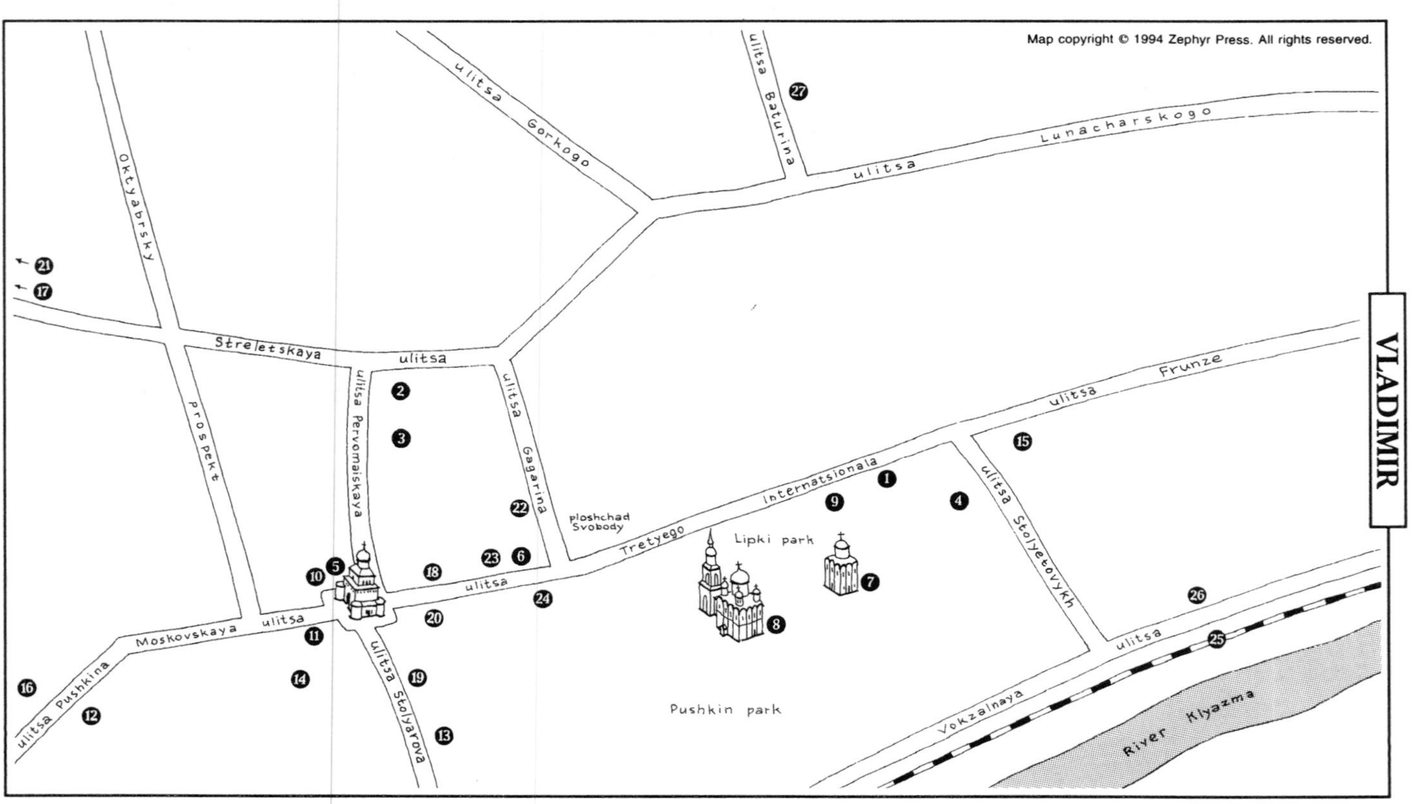
VLADIMIR
Map copyright © 1994 Zephyr Press. All rights reserved.
ulitsa Gorkogo
ulitsa Baturina
ulitsa Lunacharskogo
Oktyabrsky prospekt
Streletskaya ulitsa
ulitsa Pervomaiskaya
ulitsa Gagarina
ulitsa Frunze
ulitsa Internatsionala Tretyego
ploshchad Svobody
Lipki park
ulitsa Stolyetovykh
Moskovskaya ulitsa
ulitsa Pushkina
ulitsa Stolyarova
Pushkin park
Vokzalnaya ulitsa
River Klyazma

ВЛАДИМИР

Ulitsa Baturina
Улица Батурина
Ulitsa Frunze
Улица Фрунзе
Ulitsa Gagarina
Улица Гагарина
Ulitsa Gorkovo
Улица Горького
River Klyazma
Река Клязьма
Lipki Park
Парк Липки
Ulitsa Lunacharskovo
Улица Луначарского
Moskovskaya ulitsa
Московская улица
Oktyabrsky prospekt
Октябрьский проспект
Ulitsa Pervomaiskaya
Улица Первомайская
Ulitsa Pushkina
Улица Пушкина
Pushkin Park
Парк Пушкина
Ploshchad Svobody
Площадь Свободы
Ulitsa Stolyarova
Улица Столярова
Ulitsa Stolyetovykh
Улица Столетовых
Streletskaya ulitsa
Стрелецкая улица
Ulitsa Tretyevo Internatsionala
Улица Третьего Интернационала
Vokzalnaya ulitsa
Вокзальная улица

MAP KEY

1. **Monument to Alexander Nevsky**
Памятник Александру Невскому
2. **Assumption Cathedral of the Knyaginin Convent**
Успенский собор Княгининова монастыря
3. **Church of St. Nikita**
Церковь Святого Никиты
4. **Walls of the Monastery of the Nativity**
Стены Рождественского монастыря
5. **Golden Gates**
Золотые Ворота
6. **Trade Rows**
Торговые ряды
7. **Cathedral of St. Demetrius**
Собор Святого Дмитрия
8. **Assumption Cathedral**
Успенский собор
9. **Historical Museum**
Исторический музей
10. **Military Museum**
Военный музей
11. **Glass Museum**
Музей стекла
12. **Clocks and Time Museum**
Музей часов и времени
13. **Old Vladimir Museum, Viewing Gallery**
Музей старого Владимира. Смотровая галерея
14. **Drama Theater**
Драматический театр
15. **Hotel Vladimir**
Гостиница «Владимир»
16. **Hotel Zarya**
Гостиница «Заря»
17. **Hotel Zolotoye Koltso**
Гостиница «Золотое Кольцо»
18. **U Zolotykh Vorot Restaurant**
Ресторан «У Золотых Ворот»
19. **Traktir Restaurant**
Ресторан «Трактир»
20. **Slavyanka Restaurant**
Ресторан «Славянка»
21. **Bookshop**
Книжный магазин
22. **Souvenir Shop**
Сувениры
23. **Arts and Crafts**
Художественные промыслы
24. **Bookshop**
Книжный магазин
25. **Train station**
Железнодорожный вокзал
26. **Bus station**
Автобусная станция
27. **Market**
Рынок

White Stone Architecture of Vladimir, *continued from page 309*

Klyazma rivers, this is a perfect place for contemplating and feeling harmony with nature, and admiring the splendid isolation of this single-domed, simple white church.

Approaching closer, you can see the church's modest carvings of King David entrancing birds and lions with his psaltery playing, a symbol of the ultimate triumph of peace and goodness.

In the later part of Vladimir's ascendancy, intricately detailed and lavish white stone carving came to be the hallmark of its cathedrals. The earliest such example is the **Cathedral of St. Demetrius**, also in Vladimir, built by Vsevolod Big Nest in 1197. This church, like the Church of the Intercession, is fascinating for its simple charm, but is distinguished by the ornamentation of its upper tier.

The most striking thing about these carvings is that they are shamelessly pagan, prompting church chroniclers to ignore the cathedral completely. The abundance of mythological creatures is reminiscent of early Russian woodcarving, while the presence of the enthroned Vsevolod among them shows his aspirations to power and divinity. A parallel is drawn with Alexander the Great, depicted in another section, embodying hopes that Russia would become as great as expansionist Macedonia.

The **Cathedral of the Nativity** at **Suzdal** would surely have looked even more magnificent with its carved exterior, had anything other than the lower tier survived. Built in 1225, the single dome and upper tier collapsed in 1445, and only the lower part as far as a band of blind arcading remained. This section, however, is richly decorated with female heads, lions, birds and mythological animals, most strikingly on the arches of the portals.

Exterior carving, St. Demetrius Cathedral

Inside, little has survived of the original frescoes, but two "Golden Gates," at the south and west portals, date back to the 13th century. Made by etching patterns into black lacquer covered copper plate, then filling the grooves with a gold/mercury mixture, they depict biblical scenes on sections divided by copper bars.

After various alterations, fires, and attack by the Poles and Lithuanians, the cathedral's present appearance is very different. The five blue star-studded onion domes added in 1750 have not diminished its majesty.

The last of the Vladimir churches, **St. George's Cathedral** at **Yuryev-Polsky**, was intended to surpass all others in its exterior carvings. This it did, and just in time. It was finished in 1234, four years before the Mongol/Tatar yoke descended on the princedom.

This small cathedral suffered as much as its predecessors from the rigors of time. In fact it nearly didn't survive at all, collapsing in the 1460's but then being reconstructed stone by stone by Moscow builder Vassily Yermolin. Unfortunately, after reassembly it lost its tall, graceful appearance, becoming the somewhat heavy, squat structure it is today.

Nevertheless, much of the carving has survived, though it was beyond Yermolin's abilities to fully fit them back together properly. While the themes are already familiar from the churches so far discussed, St. George's is distinguished by the way two types are combined. The figures of men and animals were carved on individual stones, then added to the walls, while in other places much lighter, abstract patterns were etched directly into the walls.

Inside the church, part of the Yuryev-Polsky Museum, there is an exhibition of pieces of the original stone found after the rebuilding.

Two other buildings remain from 12th century Vladimir, one military, one civil. Vladimir's **Golden Gate** was built between 1158 and 1164; as part of Andrey Bogolyubsky's complex defense system, though all that now remains is the frame for the oaken copper-covered doors, whose copper was stripped off by the Tatars.

The structure is now topped by the tiny 19th century Church of the Deposition of the Robe and buttressed by round towers on each side. Inside is the local Military History Museum, with a dramatic and graphic model of the Tatar siege.

St. Demetrius Cathedral, Vladimir

The first seat of the Vladimir princes at **Bogolyubovo** was entirely destroyed over the centuries by Tatar Hordes, and virtually nothing is left of Andrey's palace and churches. However, one part of the complex has survived – the **Staircase Tower** and passageway connecting it to the original **Cathedral of the Nativity**. It is immediately distinguishable from the building beside it by the color of the stone and the familiar blind arcading and semi-columns.

In the adjoining building, a museum displays some of the foundations of the cathedral.

seum, devoted to the frescoes and murals of the Kostroma artist Gury Nikitin. Though painted over in the last century, the original work is now being gradually uncovered - be attentive to make out the more faded colors.

The stout 16-17th century belfry is reminiscent of the Rostov Kremlin belfry. The extraordinary sound created by these bells will be heard on the hour if there happens to be a tour group on hand to listen.

The rest of the monastery is taken up with museums: of ancient books, decorative and applied art, and folk art from every conceivable corner of the Russian Federation. Perhaps the most fascinating is a prison that was built on the grounds for religious and political offenders, and was used as an isolation block in Soviet times. Its two most famous inmates were the Decembrist Shakhovsky and Von Paulus, the German commander at Stalingrad. Von Paulus, released in 1946 in exchange for a Soviet pilot, never made it home – he died of food-poisoning on the way.

Prince Dmitry Pozharsky, who liberated Moscow from the Poles and Lithuanians in 1612, is buried in the monastery grounds.

Opposite on Ulitsa Lenina is a rare 17th century secular building, the house of a tavern and bakery owner. The tiny museum inside is an exhibition of 18th century peasant life.

The Convent of the Intercession, which you will have seen several times sitting tantalizingly across the river, unfortunately requires considerable walking to reach from here. You will need to retrace your steps to Krasnaya ploshchad, turn left onto Ulitsa Krupskoi, cross the river, then fork right again along the bank. From this direction, you will be able fully to appreciate its siting. Compared with the towering walls of the St. Euphimius Monastery, the Convent, in its much lower meadow, exudes a more feminine beauty and surpasses its masculine rival in charm.

Although founded in 1364, the Convent's current buildings date from the 16th century. It, too, has a history involving much grief, having been used as a place of banishment for noblewomen. This trend was initiated by Muscovite Grand Prince Vasily III, who sent his barren wife Solomonia there. According to a legend, though, she gave birth to a son after taking the vows. He went on to become the robber Kudeyar, a kind of Russian Robin Hood.

The central church here, the **Cathedral of the Intercession**, is clearly reminiscent of the pre-Mongolian Vladimir school, though built several centuries later. The combination of *zakomari*, lower built-on galleries and the two tiny "toy" side domes give it a lavish but airy feel. A mausoleum containing the convent's unhappy inmates is in the vault.

The **Refectory Church of the Conception of St. Anne**, probably built by a Polish architect, has a broad band of red diamond shapes running immediately under the cornices. It now houses a restaurant.

Nowadays, the Convent's purposes are divided somewhat awkwardly among the church (it is a nunnery once again), hotel accommodation in wooden chalets, and a tiny museum.

The final stop on this tour of Suzdal, reached from the Convent directly by tarmac road, is the **Museum of Wooden Architecture and Peasant Life**, also accessible from the Kremlin end of town via Ulitsa Lenina. The most prominent structure here is the **Church of the Transfiguration**, built in 1756 and brought to the site from the village of Kozlyatovo. It catches the eye from a distance with its four octagonal tiers of decreasing volume and three shingled cupolas. Various houses of prosperous peasants on the site have been restored fully, and visitors are greeted as they enter by peasant women in traditional costume. However, these buildings can only be viewed inside during the summer months.

MUROM

This medium-sized town on the river Oka was once a great fortress, and for centuries an outpost of Rus'. It is the oldest town in the Vladimir region, first mentioned in the chronicles in 862, when it was settled by Finno-Ugric tribesmen. The Slavs arrived in the 10th century, and Murom became part of Kievan Rus'. Over the centuries, it developed as a trading center.

Though nothing now remains of the original city (the Kremlin was pulled down by the Empress Elizabeth in the 18th century), Murom was given much of its current appearance in the 17th century by its rising merchant class. Today it is an attractive and well-preserved town, and a good stop-off point on both river cruises and road trips east. It is easy to negotiate, being square in plan, and, in an unusual aid to visitors, town maps are displayed on the streets. The main hotel, the **Rus'**, is just opposite the bus station on Ulitsa Moskovskaya.

Murom's oldest monument is the 16th century **Church of SS. Cosmas and Damian**, on a small hill overlooking the Oka. This tiny church, whose tent roof collapsed in the last century, has a connection with St. Basil's Cathedral in Moscow: both were built in honor of Ivan the Terrible's defeat of the Tatars. It was from this spot that Ivan observed his troops crossing the Oka on their way to Kazan.

In the center of town, the main landmarks are the adjoining **Trinity Convent** and **Annunciation Monastery**, now both revived. The Trinity is distinctive for its central church with green and brown decorative tiles beneath the cornices. The griffons and double-headed eagles depicted seem to serve as a reminder of the glorious pre-Mongolian days. The Annunciation Monastery, while externally plainer, has a main cathedral which is resplendent inside, with a magnificently carved and painted west portal and an 18th century baroque wooden gold-painted iconastasis.

St. Cosmas and Damian

Murom is amply blessed with picturesque churches, their beauty enhanced by the backdrop of the Oka river. One such is the baroque **Church of St. Nicholas on the Embankment**, built for the local fishing community, who supplied the Tsar's family with fish. Slightly further out of town to the north are the remains of the **Convent of the Resurrection**, a very pleasing ensemble now converted into a children's sports club. Built in the 17th century, again with merchants' funds, the Presentation and Resurrection Churches should please those who find the decoration of the town's central monasteries to be overwrought.

The historic center of the city is the **Zvorykin Mansion**, where the scientist Vladimir Zvorykin (1889-1982) spent his early years before emigrating to the U.S. and becoming "the father of television." It now houses the local history and art museum, which is remarkably worthwhile for a town of this size. It contains 15th century icons of the Murom school, as well as a collection of western European and Russian paintings. The latter came from the **Uvarov Mansion** just out of town, the home of a noted Russian archaeologist who also emigrated after the Revolution. This crumbling house is currently on the grounds of a military base, but still hopes for a new lease of life from the local authorities.

Finally, don't miss the railway station, a neo-Russian style building designed by Shchusev, architect of the Kazansky Station in Moscow.

YURYEV POLSKY

The Vladimirskiye Opolya, a large area of open, rolling plains, encompasses the three cities of Vladimir, Suzdal and Yuryev Polsky. This terrain is especially evident in the last of these; with its wide, flat streets and palisaded shopping arcade, this little town seems more akin to the windswept American prairies than the Russian heartland.

St. George's Cathedral aside (see box), the local museum, housed in the nearby **Monastery of the Archangel Michael**, has a few surprises. The eponymous cathedral houses a rare collection of wooden sculptures. Most are from nearby wooden churches, but one, a figure of St. George on horseback, is from the cathedral, and is thought to have been sculpted by

St. George's Cathedral, with exterior carving

Yermolin himself.

Another hall has displays about the Napoleonic Wars. One of the senior generals in the Russian army, Prince Bagration, came to his cousin's estate at Sima, 24 km north of here, after being wounded in the leg at Borodino. Having refused amputation, he died of gangrene. A museum is currently being organized on the former estate, and here, too, there are some interesting exhibits, including Bagration's carriage and a French vase depicting Napoleon's retreat from Moscow, brought back from Paris by a wealthy Vladimir merchant.

ALEXANDROV

This sleepy old Russian town on Vladimir's north-west border was once of vital importance for the Russian Empire. The fortress of **Alexandrovskaya Sloboda** took Ivan the Terrible's fancy in 1565, and he moved the entire court there from Moscow, building a huge wooden palace and receiving foreign ambassadors in it. The fortress also became the base of the *oprichnina*, a special terror zone created by the Tsar to control his boyar enemies with oppressive laws and a brutal secret police.

The Tsar had an extensive network of underground passages dug below the fortress, leading some archaeologists to believe that Ivan's legendary library may be hidden there. Though the mainstream of opinion disagrees – the Moscow Kremlin is the most likely site – local experts think there is buried treasure of some kind. Digging is under way, and results are expected soon.

But not all Alexandrov's 16th century treasures lie underground. The **Trinity Cathedral** contains booty from Ivan's conquests, including copper doors in the same style as in the Cathedral of the Nativity in Suzdal, stolen from Novgorod and Tver.

After being sacked by Poles and Swedes, Alexandrov re-emerged in the 17th century as the **Convent of the Intercession**, a place for unruly nuns similar to its namesake in Suzdal. However, it seems this community may not have been so cultured – a document in the museum tells of a nun banished here for picking fights and "using foul and undesireable language." One famous exile, though, was Peter the Great's sister Marfa Alexeyevna, who supported the Streltsy rebellion against him.

Today there is once again a convent here, coexisting with a well-kept museum. You can see Marfa's chambers, cellars from Ivan's time, and a collection of printed cotton from the local Baranovo factory.

Vasnetsov wall painting, Gus Khrustalny Glass Museum

GOROKHOVETS

A tour of the lands of Vladimir would not be complete without this little town on the banks of the Klyazma. Nowhere else in Russia has an entire town center been so well preserved as it appeared in the 17th century. In addition to its churches, Gorokhovets has no less than seven secular stone buildings from the same period, rare elsewhere even if they stand alone.

Gorokhovets shares a similar history with many of its neighbors, beginning as a fortress, falling prey to Tatar attacks and then prospering as a merchant town. Its position on the main Moscow–Nizhny Novgorod route made it particularly wealthy in the 17th century, and its leading merchants tried to outdo one another in the lavish decorations of the churches they sponsored.

The center can be easily negotiated on foot in a matter of hours. To get a good view of Gorokhovets, walk up **Puzhalova Gora**, meaning Scary Hill, where legend says that during a 16th century Tatar raid a ghostly giant, sword in hand, loomed before them in the rays of the setting sun, causing them to flee in terror.

Just across a cherry-orcharded ravine is St. Nicholas' Hill, site of the former fortress, which became the **St. Nicholas Monastery** when settlers moved down to the valley. Built by the merchant Semyon Yershov in 1681, the **Trinity Cathedral** is a forlorn sight today, though still magnificent from a distance. But while the St. Nicholas Monastery is lofty and austere, the **Convent of the Purification of the Virgin** in the town is more intimate and pleasing from close quarters. Its auxiliary buildings, backing onto the town square, conjure an odd effect, as if the town itself was part of the convent and not the other way around. The **Cathedral of the Annunciation**, towering over the central square, and the **Monastery of the Apparition of the Virgin**, standing isolated across the Klyazma, both built by Yershov, complete the tangible picture of Gorokhovets' spiritual heritage.

For the best in secular architecture, the honors go once again to Semyon Yershov. His mansion on the edge of Puzhalova Gora, now the historical museum, looks built to last, its stout white walls immediately visible on two sides from the entrance gate. The restored interior includes the Red Chamber, where guests were received and feasts held. Other such buildings include the **Shiryayev House**, more decorative and Western-influenced, and the **Belov** and **Rumyantsev Houses**, single-chamber dwellings owned by ordinary townspeople.

Though Gorokhovets lost most of its significance in the 19th century, some wooden buildings remain from the beginning of the 20th in neo-Russian style. Particularly striking are the **Shorin House** at 43 Ulitsa Moskovskaya and the **Military Commander's House** at 50 Ulitsa Lenina.

GUS KHRUSTALNY

Established as a major glass center of world renown, Gus still manages to look well despite the overpowering presence of three factories in its center.

Originally started in Mozhaisk outside Moscow in 1723, the glassworks was moved here in 1756, after a Senate decree banned it from operating near the capital. Since then it has built up a reputation comparable with Murano in Italy or Baccarat in France.

The best place to see Gus glass is in

the town's grandiose museum, located in the former St. George's Cathedral. This fascinating church, set among trees in an attractive central square, seems more Catholic than Orthodox. It was completed in 1903 to designs of Leonty Benois. Viktor Vasnetsov was commissioned to create mosaics both outside and inside, and his *Last Judgement*, painted on the west wall, is considered the best of his monumental works. (Vasnetsov, painter and stage designer, and his brother Apollinarius were both members of the Abramtsevo artists' colony outside of Moscow.)

The museum itself traces the glassworks' history, and includes a huge, multi-faceted sculpture, called *A Hymn to Glass*, at the former altar. Works of recent artists are displayed on a central table.

There are no souvenir shops as such in the town, but almost every other shop seems to sell them, and even the museum attendants may furtively slip you an item of a tea-set for perusal.

(For Mstyora, see Ivanovo Region.)

PRACTICAL MATTERS

Facilities in Vladimir are passable, especially since the new **Zolotoye Koltso** (Golden Ring) **Hotel** was built in a western suburb on the corner of Ulitsas Balakireva and Chaikovskovo. It boasts the best restaurant in town. The **Hotel Vladimir** at 74 Ulitsa Tretyevo Internatsionala is central but very basic, while the **Zarya** at 36 Ulitsa Pushkina is seedy and roach-ridden.

Restaurant standards are reasonable —this is the heartland of traditional Russian dishes like mushrooms (try *griby po-Vladimirski*) and hotpots of every imaginable variety. **Traktir** (2 Ulitsa Stolyarova), **U Zolotykh Vorot** (17 Ulitsa Tretyevo Internatsionala) and the new private **Slavyanka** on the latter street are all worth a visit. For fast food, there is a decent pizzeria on the same street, though lines can be long.

(For comments on accommodation in Suzdal and Murom, please refer to the main text.)

DIRECTIONS

Vladimir: by long distance or local train from the Kursky station, or bus from the main Moscow Bus Terminal at metro Sholkovskaya. By car along M7, Gorkovskoye shossé; 170 km.

Bogolyubovo is reached by local bus from Vladimir's Ulitsa Gagarina and is situated just east of the town on M7.

Suzdal: one daily bus from Moscow, otherwise best reached by the frequent service from Vladimir (journey time ½ hour). By car from Vladimir take the A113 Ivanovo road (left off the M7 if coming from Moscow). **Kideksha** is 5 km east of the town past the bus station.

Murom: by train from the Kazansky Station or by 2½ hour bus journey from Vladimir. By car there is no obvious direct route, so best take the M7 until about 13 km before Gorokhovets, then turn right onto the R76 and continue for about 73 km.

Yuryev Polsky: by bus from the main Moscow Bus Terminal (3 hours) or from Vladimir (1½ hours). By car take A103 Sholkovskoye shossé through Kirzhach and Kolchugino, or from Vladimir take the scenic R74.

Alexandrov: by local train from the Yaroslavsky Station (2½ hours). By car take the M8 as far as Dvoriki (161

km), turn right and continue for 24 km. Can also be combined with a trip to Sergiyev Posad. (See Moscow Region.)
Gorokhovets: best reached by bus from Nizhny Novgorod. Local trains from Nizhny stop in the middle of nowhere, and you'll need to go on further by local bus. By car 486 km from Moscow on M7, 195 from Vladimir and 130 from Nizhny.
Gus Khrustalny: by 3 hour bus from Moscow or 1½ hour bus or train (on the Tumskaya line) from Vladimir. By car from Vladimir 73 km on the R73.

RUSSIAN GLOSSARY

Alexandrov
Александров
Ulitsa Balakireva
Улица Балакирева
Bogolyubovo
Боголюбово
Ulitsa Chaikovskovo
Улица Чайковского
Dvoriki
Дворики
Gorokhovets
Гороховец
Gorkovskoye shossé
Горьковское шоссе
Gostiny Dvor
Гостиный Двор
Gus Khrustalny
Гусь-Хрустальный
Ivanovo
Иваново
Kideksha
Кидекша
Kirzhach
Киржач
Kolchugino
Кольчугино
Krasnaya ploshchad
Красная площадь
Ulitsa Krupskoi
Улица Крупской
Ulitsa Lenina
Улица Ленина
Ulitsa Moskovskaya
Улица Московская
Murom
Муром
Sergiyev Posad
Сергиев Посад
Sholkovskaya metro
Станция метро Щёлковская
Sholkovskoye shossé
Щёлковское шоссе
Slavyanka
Славянка
Ulitsa Stolyarova
Улица Столярова
Suzdal
Суздаль
Traktir
Трактир
Tumskaya (Tuma) train
Поезд на Туму
Vladimir
Владимир
Yuryev Polsky
Юрьев-Польский
U Zolotykh Vorot
У Золотых Ворот

RYAZAN REGION

RYAZANSKAYA OBLAST

Immediately southeast of Moscow, the Ryazan Region was part of a powerful independent princedom which became a worthy rival to Muscovy in the 14th century under Prince Oleg.

When it finally emerged from centuries of destruction by Tatars, the region became in many ways the epitome of rural Russia. While traditional crafts, *izby* (Russian wooden village huts) and peasant life are far from exclusive to Ryazan, they have become closely linked to the region through poet Sergey Yesenin, whose verses extol the virtues of the Russian *muzhik* (yokel). For an area so far removed from city culture, Ryazan is surprisingly blessed with architectural monuments. Until recently, many points of interest were completely cut off from the outside world. Construction of the Great Ryazan Ring tourist route has facilitated access, but you still won't find many tourists there. This region is for those who enjoy voyages of discovery.

A detailed trip around the Ring merits a book in itself; but a visit to its furthest and most interesting point, the town of Kasimov, will whet the appetite of those who wish to explore further.

RYAZAN

The present regional center became the capital of the Ryazan princedom only in the 14th century, during its Golden Age. Formerly known as *Pereyaslavl Ryazansky*, it replaced the old capital to the south, which was razed by Batiy in 1237.

Throughout the centuries, Ryazan kept up at least a nominal independence from Moscow, which saved it from the worst excesses of the Hordes. Even when that danger had passed, Moscow continued its "hands off" approach. This held true particularly in architecture, where Ryazan's classical and baroque buildings retain a distinct flavor.

Despite a quite pleasing outward appearance, modern-day Ryazan can feel a little intimidating for the visitor. Until recently, it had one of Russia's most reactionary local governments. On at least one occasion, police beat demonstrating democrats mercilessly in the streets. The ubiquitous presence of young men with skinhead haircuts denotes a mixture of army cadets (the city has four military academies) and mafia thugs.

What is now known as Ryazan's

Assumption Cathedral

Kremlin is not, strictly speaking, a Kremlin at all. Nothing remained of the city's original wooden fortress when the present structures were built. The space is now occupied by the former Metropolitan's residence, which houses the city's museum, and by the **Assumption Cathedral**.

The Cathedral serves as Ryazan's massive monumental centerpiece. Built in an incredible seven years (1693–99) by the serf architect Yakov Bukhvostov, it was one of the first examples of Naryshkin Baroque, a style characterized by an abundance of vertical highlights, carved portals, and platbands. Naryshkin Baroque is named after the westernizing family of Peter the Great's mother, Natalya Naryshkina, who favored it. The style originated in Ryazan, although Moscow masters perfected it.

Along with the bell-tower added in the 19th century, the Assumption Cathedral stands out for a considerable distance, remaining visible as far as 25 km upriver. The positioning of the two creates an arresting sight within the town. Approaching from the main street, the bell-tower's golden spike, flanked by two of the cathedral's blue starred cupolas, rises dead ahead through the trees in perfect symmetry.

Other buildings surround the cathedral in a pleasing disorder. Just behind, and totally dwarfed by it, stands the early 16th century **Church of the Archangel Michael**, the oldest building in Ryazan and the only structure to survive from the days of the independent princedom. It is now part of the city museum, as is **Prince Oleg's Palace**, actually the metropolitan's chambers. Also baroque, it boasts especially handsome red and white platband ornamentation.

KIRITSY

Just south of Ryazan lies one of the finest architectural monuments of the region, the former estate of the von Derviz family at **Kiritsy**. The mastermind of this 1889 pseudo-gothic mansion was Fyodor Shekhtel, normally associated with Art Nouveau, and famous for such buildings as the Yaroslavsky Station and Ryabushinsky House in Moscow. This was one of his earlier works, and despite the absence of the flowing forms of his

later style, its Romanticism is almost overpowering.

Kiritsy lies today at the back of the local sanatorium, abandoned and derelict. With its pavilions, statuettes and weed-ridden terraces, it has all the makings of a haunted castle. A hulking bridge spans the ravine to the left, where rooks caw madly overhead as if waiting for some terrified mortal to plunge to his death. Beyond it, Chestnut Alley takes you down to the fairytale main gates, now scarred by vandalism and graffiti.

YESENIN COUNTRY

Ryazan's most famous literary figure was **Sergey Yesenin** (1895–1925), "perhaps the most Russian poet of all time," write the editors of *Silver and Steel: An Anthology of 20th Century Russian Poetry* (Doubleday, 1993). "The poetry of no one else was so formed from the rustling of birch trees, from the soft patter of rain-drops on thatch-roofed peasant huts, from the neighing of horses in mist-filled morning meadows, from the clanking of bells on cows' necks, from the swaying of chamomile and cornflower, from the singing in the outskirts of villages. Yesenin's verses were not so much written by pen as breathed out of Russian nature." A complex character, Yesenin committed suicide in disillusionment in 1925, but he is remembered fondly in the Ryazan Region. In the city of Ryazan, on the Kremlin embankment, a monument of Yesinin's head, arms and chest rises up as his poetry arose, from the Russian earth. And in Spas-Klepiki, a tiny museum remembers his school days there.

Yesenin Monument, Ryazan

For a revealing glimpse of Yesenin's childhood and youth, visit his birthplace at Konstantinovo. This tiny village is best approached along the river Oka, where you will see the Church of Our Lady of Kazan, lonely and forlorn, peeping over the hilltop. This work of austere 18th century Classicism is slowly being brought back to life by its small congregation.

The museum of Yesenin's home is a tiny plain wooden cottage hidden in the trees. Nearby stands a simple wooden barn, where he wrote several poems, including "Return to my Country." At the other end of the village, an exhibition of literary work traces his life from early childhood through to his death. (Despite his love for his native landscape, Yesenin is buried far away, in Moscow's Vagankovskoye Cemetery.)

Just down river from Konstantinovo stands the Monastery of St. John the Divine at Poshchupovo, marked by a huge bell-tower visible from a considerable distance. Now a working monastery, its unassuming history is compensated by legends. Appearing in a vision to the great Tatar Khan Batiy, the monastery's patron saint is said to have stopped Batiy in his tracks, which induced him to give up his siege. More plausible is the proposition that Peter the Great had a prison there. On a hill-

A Meeting of Two Worlds

Well within overnight train distance of Moscow, Kasimov is an unusual sight for those approaching along the River Oka. Situated on its banks, this city of two hills represents two different civilizations. On one, the Orthodox cupolas of Cathedral Square (*Sobornaya ploshchad*) reach to the sky, while on the other a gleaming white tower dominates the horizon. This is a 15th century minaret, the town's oldest surviving structure, and beside it stands a mosque.

Kasimov, however, was always predominantly a Russian town. Founded in 1152 by Yuri Dolgoruky as Meshchersky Gorodets, it was an eastern outpost of the Suzdal-Nizhny Novgorod princedom. In the 15th century, when it became the home of Kasim, a Tatar prince who fled Kazan after a feud, Kasimov took its present name. In exchange for allegiance to Moscow and defense of Russia's eastern borders, Kasim was given his own kingdom, which stretched 225 km to the south. Although it lasted until 1681, its rulers left a subtle mark.

The Tatar hill now lives apart from the bustle of the town center. The 18th century **mosque** is now the local museum, and invites visitors to ascend the ancient, whitewashed minaret. From here, there is a picturesque view of the Oka and the Russian town. Nearby is the 16th century **Tekiye** (tomb) **of Shah Ali Khan**, named for the prince who helped Ivan the Terrible destroy the Kazan khanate. The plain, square, stone cuboid, typically Islamic in form, defiantly asserts its foreignness with an Arabic inscription above the door.

Shah Ali Khan mausoleum and River Oka from minaret

The only other Tatar structure, the 17th century **Tekiye of Afghan Muhammed Sultan** is a considerable walk from the town proper. This building is fundamentally Russian in style, hailing the approaching integration and virtual disappearance of Islamic culture in Kasimov.

In contrast to the well-kept museum and sparkling white minaret, nearby Sobornaya ploshchad epitomizes contemporary Russian economic decay. The stately classical and empire mansions and churches of the former merchant center are dangerously derelict. In places, low-roofed, columned **Trade Rows**, built in the 1830's by china manufacturer I.S. Gagin and once the pride of the town, are little more than ruins.

The tastefully columned **Nastavin House**, in the near right corner of the square if you approach from the main street, exemplifies the tremendous effort made by this particular merchant family to improve Kasimov. Nikolay Nastavin also designed a tree-lined boulevard, named after him, and brought piped water to its inhabitants.

side beyond the monastery, just above a holy spring, is a network of caves. These caves, dwelling-places of the first monks, are believed to have been the place of incarceration for some of the leaders of the Streltsy Rebellion.

PRACTICAL MATTERS

If you need to stay in Ryazan, the best hotel is the **Lovetch**, beside the Ryazan 2 rail station. Its restaurant is also quite decent, and if you can't get a place you can always pay a small admission fee for the casino upstairs, where they'll bring you food from the kitchen. The **Pervomaiskaya** on Pervomaisky prospekt and the **Moskva** on Ulitsa Lenina are more central, but seedier and best avoided.

DIRECTIONS

Kasimov: difficult to reach by public transport – there are buses from both Moscow and Ryazan, but even the latter takes 3½ hours. The R123 from Ryazan takes a semi-circular route (the top half of the Ryazan Ring) 150 km long. If coming from Moscow, you have the alternative of turning off the M6 at Lyubertsy for Yegoryevsk and following a smaller road through that town, which joins the Ring at Spas-Klepiki.

Ryazan: by almost any non-Kazan/Siberia bound train from the Kazansky Station, journey time 4 hours. By car 195 km down the M6.

Kiritsy: by the Shatsk bus from Ryazan. By car 65 km beyond Ryazan on the M6. Just beyond the stream crossing, turn left toward the sanatorium.

Konstantinovo: by local bus from Ryazan. By car, turn left at Rybnoye, 6 km short of Ryazan, and continue for another 23 km.

Ryazan, **Kasimov** and **Konstantinovo** are all stops on the route of state-run *Rechflot* boats, tickets for which may be purchased at either of Moscow's river stations, or at the central Rechflot bureau (see Moscow Services). These trips do not include meals or excursions, but you can leave the boat where you please.

RUSSIAN GLOSSARY

Kasimov
Касимов
Kazansky vokzal (station)
Казанский вокзал
Kiritsy
Кирицы
Konstantinovo
Константиново
Ulitsa Lenina
Улица Ленина
Lovetch Hotel
Гостиница «Ловечь»
Lyubertsy
Люберцы
Moskva Hotel
Гостиница «Москва»
Pervomaiskaya Hotel
Гостиница «Первомайская»
Pervomaisky prospekt
Первомайский проспект
Poshchupovo
Пощупово
Ryazan
Рязань
Ryazanskaya oblast
Рязанская область
Shatsk
Шацк
Spas-Klepiki
Спас-Клепики
Yegoryersk
Егоревск

TULA REGION

TULSKAYA OBLAST

For an area of Russia so green and pleasant, washed by the Oka and Don rivers, it seems odd that Tula's greatest distinguishing feature should be its heavy industry. But this is the case. In the area around Novomoskovsk lie the vast majority of the mines in the Moscow coal field, while in the city of Tula, Russia's oldest weapons industry continues to uphold traditions of quality craftsmanship.

TULA

This major industrial city on the river Upa only emerged as a town in the 14th century, when it was a craft center in the Ryazan princedom. After Moscow's victory against Mamai's Tatars at Kulikovo Field in 1380, its Prince, Dmitry Donskoy, took control of Tula. Over the next 200 years it was gradually fortified against the still-dangerous enemy. Tula's *zaseka* fortifications became the most important ones along Russia's southern frontier. When the town finally recovered from the ravages of the Tatars in the 17th century, its arsenal ensured continuing prosperity. Today Tula is one of the largest cities in the Moscow area.

Tula is not a physically attractive city by any stretch of the imagination. Its bare and plain Kremlin is obscured from the river side, while an accumulation of rubbish, rubble and modern building further detract from its appearance.

Museums are its greatest attraction. The **Regional Art Museum** on Ulitsa Engelsa is one of provincial Russia's best. It boasts Western European collections accumulated by local merchants which provide an excellent survey of Italian, Dutch and Flemish art of the 16th–18th centuries. Another room displays pottery, with examples of Wedgwood, Meissen and Sevres ware. The museum's decent collection of Russian art includes Valentin Serov's portrait of industrialist and art patron Savva Mamontov.

Apart from the Weapons Museum, the Samovar Museum, just outside the Kremlin entrance, exhibits another product associated with Tula. Production of samovars began there in the late 18th century as a peculiar offshoot of the weapons industry, and also achieved nationwide fame. Of the many samovar museums around the country – one in Kaluga even claims to *be* the Tula museum! – this is definitely the best. Among the more

The Gunsmiths of Tula

In the early days of the Russian state, Tula was on the southern border of the nation; marauding Tatars from Kazan and the Crimea frequently sacked and looted. In the 16th century a *zaseka*, a fortification made from felled trees stacked lengthwise with sharpened branches facing the enemy, was constructed in Tula and in other places in the borderlands. (The English term for this construction is an *abatis*.)

This defensive system needed to be manned, and its defenders needed arms. At the time, the only available weapons came from Moscow's Kremlin Armory, far from their place of application. Because the Crimean Tatars regularly attacked, the *zaseka* constantly needed fresh supplies.

A solution was at hand. An area rich in iron ore, Tula was able to attract local craftsmen to repair old and make new weapons. The city's gunsmiths gradually developed their own community, and in 1595 received special status and a *sloboda*, or freemen's village, behind the town's Kremlin.

A century later, the escalation of military activity during the reign of Peter the Great proved to be a strain for the small, free and privileged band of gunsmiths. Stringent production quotas and the threat of reprisals for bad workmanship increased outputs by a factor of 30 in the space of a half century, from 242 arquebuses (see Glossary) a year to 7,000 by the end of the 17th century.

But Peter needed even more weapons in the course of his campaign against Sweden for an outlet to the Baltic Sea. After he tried unsuccessfully to organize further the labor of the gunsmiths, he decreed in 1712 the building of a factory.

Tula soon became established as Russia's arms capital. Tula's gunsmiths had such skill that they acquired reputations of almost mythical expertise. A case in point is Nikolay Leskov's short story, "Lefty," which tells of a Tula craftsman who met a task set by the tsar: to create shoes that would fit an English-made steel flea. Napoleon made the city one of his prime targets in 1812, but after the capture of Moscow, his exhausted army could make no further conquests.

The **Tula Weapons Museum**, in the Kremlin's former **Epiphany Cathedral**, traces the work of Tula masters, from muskets to Kalashnikovs. The ground floor shows weapons used in the campaigns of pre-revolutionary Russian armies – 16th century muskets that took eight minutes to load and fire, 18th century Russian rifles, pepperboxes (pistols) made after English and Belgian designs employed in the Crimean War, versions of Burton rifles which the Americans regarded as superior to their own, and the first magazine weapons, notably the home-made Mosin rifle.

There are also some curiosities, like the "Velodog," a tiny pistol intended for the English market. Its designers thought that with the abundance of dogs and cyclists in England, the latter would undoubtedly need protection from the interesting exhibits are a fine art nouveau *teremok* samovar, a water-boiling model of the Lenin Mausoleum and a 70th birthday present for Stalin.

To the right of the Samovar Museum are the **Odoyevskiye Gates** of the **Kremlin**. Though hardly imposing today, this 16th century fortress was considered a formidable defensive structure in its day. Its walls seem low, but were surrounded by natural obstacles and bristled with arquebuses. Even if the enemy penetrated the wall, it still had to deal with the corner towers, each a fortress in its own right.

former! Instead, the pistol became a favorite among women. There are trophies as well, such as Napoleon's Mendome Column, which he ordered while punch drunk from his victories to commemorate his "conquest" of Russia; he later had to leave it behind. Also, take a look at the collection of late 18th century Eastern swords, daggers, and pistols which the great Russian general Suvorov captured in his Eastern campaigns.

The center of the hall has a recently opened exhibition of tsars' weapons, made to order or presented on the occasion of imperial visits to the factory. These include a hunting carbine given to Catherine the Great in 1775, and an 1887 example encrusted with ivory and presented to Tsarina Maria Fyodorovna. There is also a unique collection of dueling pistols from Western countries, because domestic production, like the act of dueling itself, was illegal.

The first floor display brings you into the 20th century, but in an unexpected way. The church-like interior seems to clash violently with the awesome array of modern military hardware. The crude socialist realist paintings on the ceiling that exalt Tula weapons production and Soviet military might add an extra dimension of tackiness.

The exhibits fascinate nonetheless. They begin with the inefficient but innovative Maxim Gun, an early, turn-of-the-century machine-gun which Tula produced. There are numerous Kalashnikovs, and trophies captured from the Nazis in World War II. Take a look as well at the guns in the center of the hall – numerous sporting pistols, some of them Olympic medal-winning, made individually to suit each marksman; hunting pistols for cosmonauts, intended to protect them if they landed from space in some wild, remote part of the world; and miniatures, including 1½ inch long revolvers and 1.5mm bore cannons, all capable of firing.

Tula Weapons Museum

As yet, no private workshops or forges exist in the city, and the factory remains enveloped in tight security. This museum remains the best, if not the only, way of seeing the work of Tula gunsmiths.

Nothing remains of the original city inside the walls, and only two churches stand in this vast area. The monumental **Assumption Cathedral** dates from 1764, and is notable for its sheer size and intricate baroque carvings. Now reconsecrated, its soulful interior displays late 18th century frescoes. The Soplyakov brothers painted them in the Yaroslavl style, distinct for its realistic portrayal of landscapes and cityscapes. The iconostasis, currently on display in the art museum, will be breathtaking when returned to the sanctuary, as planned.

YASNAYA POLYANA

Just 15 km south of Tula lies the country estate of the writer Lev Tolstoy, author of *War and Peace* and *Anna Karenina*. The estate is now a museum complex with acres of serene parkland. Tolstoy's wife, Sofiya Andreyevna, once described Yasnaya Polyana as "his cradle and his grave," and his memory lives in the place. The museum's exhibits were evacuated before the Nazi occupation, and those you see today are all authentic.

Tolstoy's great-grandfather Count Volkonsky bought the estate, and through him and his heirs it became a place of beauty, solitude, and learning. The young writer was brought up on its traditions, and, since he took his inspiration there, he seldom left for long. In his later years Tolstoy spent more and more time there as he worked on his great novels. Like Konstantin Levin, one of the heroes of *Anna Karenina*, he took to farming and living a simple life, and he also became progressively more ascetic and isolated from the modern world.

Lev Tolstoy

The main museum here amply illustrates the many stages of Tolstoy's life, albeit in a slightly jumbled manner. Most impressive is the dining room, with its portraits of the author and his family, and its corners for "young people" and "serious conversations." This scene reflects the prime of his life, when he relished social occasions and the company of the young. Just next door, the study he used in his youth and extreme old age contains the sofa on which he was born, while the bedroom suggests the simplicity of his later period, complete with a traditional Russian flaxen shirt, hanging on a peg.

The **Literature Museum** nearby is Tolstoy's former school for peasant children, which the local gendarmes once closed down for being too radical. The former **Volkonsky Mansion**, the original main house, is the administrative center of the museum and not open to visitors. A short walk through the woods will bring you to **Tolstoy's grave**, in a place known as **Stary Zakaz**. Tolstoy chose this site as a result of one of his son Nikolay's whims. The boy told a story about a green stick there which contained the secret of happiness, and the whole house, charmed by him, believed it. Several kilometers south of the estate is the **Kochakovsky Necropolis**, a pretty churchyard by a lake which contains the graves of most of Tolstoy's relatives.

BOGORODITSK

While Yasnaya Polyana has been popular with both Russian and foreign tourists for years, this no less interesting estate away to the east has received too little attention. Count Bobrinsky had Bogoroditsk built at the end of the 18th century. This colorful personality was the illegitimate son of Catherine the Great by her favorite Grigory Orlov. Renowned for his love of fire-fighting, he was held in much affection by the local peasantry.

But an even more fascinating character planned the estate. Andrey Bolotov was an obscure 18th century genius whose activities covered almost every sphere of art and science. After he brought the potato to Russia and published exhaustive dissertations on agriculture in a journal which he wrote and edited on his own, he built at Bogoroditsk Russia's first English landscape garden, with marble statues, romantic ruins and waterfalls. On its grounds, he directed performances of Russia's first children's theater.

Little now remains of this masterpiece, but you can admire one of Bolotov's innovations. From the classical mansion which overlooks a lake and houses the museum, you can see how he designed the town. The Oval Room has five windows, upon which each of the town's streets, across the lake, converge. Today, in an effort to make a little extra money, the museum uses the room as a private marriage registration office. On "registration day," museum visitors may find it difficult to brave the happy crowds of well-wishers.

While the ground floor has an exhibition devoted to Bolotov, the upstairs rooms give an idea of how the Bobrinskys lived and include fine 18th century furniture made by local serfs. These are the only authentic exhibits – the estate suffered badly during the war and has only recently been restored.

An exhibition of precious and semiprecious stones from the town's factory awaits up another flight of stairs. Souvenirs are very inexpensive in the museum's shop.

The gatehouse nearby dates from the time when a part of the *zaseka* defensive system occupied the site. It now blends in harmoniously with the rest of the ensemble.

POLYENOVO

As his museum estate in the Oka valley demonstrates emphatically, the life of Vassily Polyenov, the late 19th century landscape artist and member of the *peredvizhniki* group, has a cultural significance which goes far beyond the bounds of painting.

After he lived in France and served as a volunteer in the Russo-Turkish war of 1877–78, the already established artist came home to settle down at the age of 34. He wanted to start a museum that functioned as an educational center for Russian and foreign culture. To this end, he purchased a sandy hillock on the riverbank and immediately began to build a house and garden. The museum opened in 1892, while in the nearby studio Polyenov continued to immortalize

Byokhovo Church, Polyenovo

Oka scenes in his landscapes.

The Polyenov family remained after the Revolution and Vassily lived there until his death in 1926. Although the house was nationalized, his heirs continued to run the museum. Today his grandson's wife directs it.

You notice upon arriving that Polyenovo departs from Russian traditions. The main house and Abbey Studio are built in Art Nouveau style with a Scandinavian flavor. The buildings have a sturdy and spacious, but also a homely feel. The gardens follow Polyenov's whim, and use the surrounding topography and flora to maximum effect.

The museum appeals. Fresh flowers and a music box ready to play a melody of that era accent the mood of each room. The museum exhibits portraits, landscapes, folk art, ceramics, and even collections of ancient Greek and Egyptian archaeological finds. Upstairs a diorama depicts a "Voyage Round the World." Polyenov painted and narrated the scenes himself, and used to entertain the local village children with them.

About 2½ km down river is the village of Byokhovo, with its Trinity Church that rests scenically on ancient earthen fortifications. It might not surprise you that Polyenov also built this church in 1906, as a tribute to the landscaping skills of the Novgorodian architects of the 12th century. The church incorporates some of their stylistic features, notably in its façade and cupola. Polyenov's grave is in the cemetery nearby, on the site of an ancient burial mound.

KULIKOVO FIELD

In 1380 one of Russia's greatest military triumphs took place on this huge open space beside the Don river. The victory loosened the Mongol-Tatar yoke and established Moscow as the leading Russian princedom.

The Tatar Khan of the day, Mamai, had sought to renew his grip on Russia (established in the middle of the previous century on the basis of submission to the Khan and payment of heavy annual tribute) and to check the rising power of Muscovy under its Prince, Dmitry Donskoy. To ensure victory, he enlisted the help of Moscow's other enemies, Lithuania and the jealous Ryazan princedom, before setting out to reconquer the nation which had so feared his predecessors.

When he heard of the danger, Dmitry gathered a great army, and marched far out of Moscow, crossing the Don so as to face Mamai alone and isolate him from his allies. The military expertise and higher morale of the Russians brought them complete victory.

An unusual church now graces the Field. The architect Alexey Shchusev, who designed the Lenin Mausoleum and the Kazansky Station in Moscow, completed it. Although begun in the early part of this century, work on the church dragged on into World War I.

The church deserves a look if you happen to be passing. As well as the traditional five central cupolas, it has two towers at the entrance. A cupola tops one, while the other has a tent-roof in the form of a helmet, to represent the Russian fighting spirit.

Nearby you will find a monument of cast iron in the form of an obelisk topped by a cupola and a cross. The architect Alexander Bryullov, brother of painter Karl (some of whose work can be seen in St. Isaac's Cathedral, Petersburg), built it in 1848.

PRACTICAL MATTERS

The only special advantage of accommodation in Tula is its centralized booking system for hotels. The best hotel, and the place to book, is the **Moskva**, outside the Moskovsky Station. You can also get a room in the lower-grade **Tula**, on Prospekt Lenina outside the bus station, or the **Yunost** on Ulitsa Sverdlova. For food, you're unlikely to do better than the friendly **Pizzeria** on the 8th floor of the Moskva.

DIRECTIONS

Tula: by almost any southbound train from the Kursky Station, or by car 195 km along M2.
Yasnaya Polyana: by #114 Shchekino bus from the stop outside the bus station on Tula's Ulitsa Benina to the Shkolnaya stop, then turn right from the main road and walk down past the school to the museum car park. For the cemetery, go two stops further to Vremenny. By car continue along the M2 from Tula to the village of Yasnaya Polyana and turn right.
Bogoroditsk: by bus 1½ hours from Tula. By car 225 km from Moscow by M4 or 30 from Tula, taking the Kimovsk road and turning right at Uzlovaya.
Polyenovo: by train from the Kursky Station to Serpukhov, then by local bus, or by daily river boat in summer. It is also accessible from Velegozh station on foot. By car take the M2 to Malakhovo (105 km), turn right onto the R144, then after 13 km go right again and continue for another 5 km.
Kulikovo Field: almost unreachable by public transport, it can be seen by taking a detour from the M4, turning left after Bogoroditsk onto the R142, continuing for 48 km, turning left again at Kresty and driving for another 13 km.

RUSSIAN GLOSSARY

Bogoroditsk
Богородицк
Byokhovo
Бёхово
Kresty
Кресты
Kulikovo Field
Куликово поле
Marakhovo
Марахово
Moskva Hotel
Гостиница «Москва»
Novomoskovsk
Новомосковск
Polyenovo
Поленово
Serpukhov
Серпухов
Shchekino
Щёкино
Shkolnaya
Школьная
Stary Zakaz
Старый Заказ
Tula Hotel
Гостиница «Тула»
Tulskaya oblast
Тульская област
Uzlovaya
Узловая
Velegozhsky station
Велогожский вокзал
Yasnaya Polyana
Ясная Поляна
Yunost Hotel
Гостиница «Юность»

KALUGA REGION

KALUZHSKAYA OBLAST

Situated immediately to the southwest of Moscow, Kaluga shares many of the features of its neighbors – the fighting spirit of Smolensk and Bryansk, and a natural beauty comparable to that of Tula and Oryol.

The first quality manifests itself in the heroism of the little town of Kozelsk. In 1238 it was threatened by the Tatar hordes. While the great cities of Moscow, Smolensk, Vladimir, Ryazan and Chernigov were falling to the enemy, little Kozelsk held out for seven days. Batiy Khan labeled it "the evil city" (*zloy gorod*), and ordered not a soul to be spared. In the massacre that ensued, 4,000 Tatars were killed, and a handful of townspeople survived to rebuild Kozelsk.

In literature, the Kaluga Region provided inspiration to Gogol, Tolstoy, Dostoyevsky, Pushkin and Chekhov, who all spent a substantial part of their lives there. And little Tarusa was the childhood summer home of Marina Tsvetayeva, one of the great quartet of 20th century Russian poets that also included Boris Pasternak, Anna Akhmatova, and Osip Mandelstam.

KALUGA

Like so many of Russia's towns, this regional center on the Oka river has retained some of its past glory despite present-day deterioration and poverty. But perhaps most unusual is the completeness of Kaluga's preservation, making it the country's best museum, after St. Petersburg, of early 19th century classical architecture.

Kaluga realized its importance much later than many of its neighbors. It became a princedom only in 1505 and thirteen years later fell completely under Moscow's influence. During the "Time of Troubles" of the early 17th century, however, it revealed a rebellious spirit, supporting first Ivan Bolotnikov's peasant revolt and then the second False Dmitry. The latter was murdered there by his former Tatar allies as he prepared to attack Moscow.

In the 17th and 18th centuries, Kaluga suffered sacking by the Poles and Crimean Tatars, several fires, and two epidemics, leaving it desolate and poverty-stricken. Its luck changed with the arrival of Catherine the Great in 1775, and a year later it became a *guberniya* center. In 1786 a new town

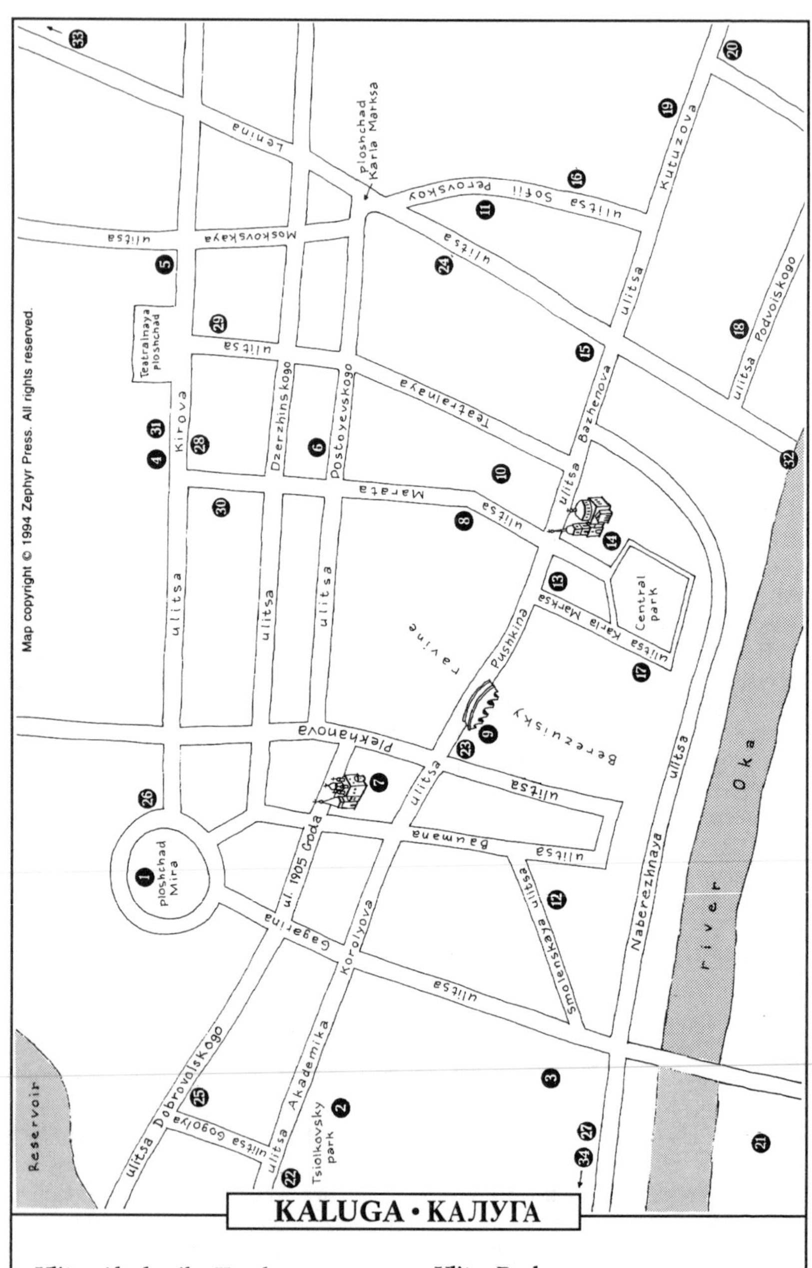

KALUGA • КАЛУГА

Ulitsa Akademika Korolyova
Улица Академика Королева
Ulitsa Baumana
Улица Баумана
Ulitsa Bazhenova
Улица Баженова
Bereziusky Ravine
Березуйский овраг

Central Park
Центральный Парк
Ul. Dobrovolskovo
Улица Добровольского
Ulitsa Dostoyevskovo
Улица Достоевского
Ulitsa Dzerzhinskovo
Улица Дзержинского
Ulitsa Gagarina
Улица Гагарина
Ulitsa Gogolya
Улица Гоголя
Ulitsa Karla Marksa
Улица Карла Маркса
Ulitsa Kirova
Улица Кирова
Ulitsa Kutuzova
Улица Кутузова
Ulitsa Lenina
Улица Ленина
Ulitsa Marata
Улица Марата
Ploshchad Mira
Площадь Мира
Moskovskaya ulitsa
Московская Улица
Naberezhnaya ulitsa
Набережная Улица
Ulitsa 1905 Goda
Улица 1905 Года
River Oka
Река Ока
Ulitsa Plekhanova
Улица Плеханова
Ulitsa Podvoiskovo
Улица Подвойского
Ulitsa Pushkina
Улица Пушкина
Reservoir
Водохранилище
Smolenskaya ulitsa
Смоленская Улица
Teatralnaya ulitsa
Театральная Улица
Tsiolkovsky Park
Парк Имени Циолковского

MAP KEY

1. **Tsiolkovsky Monument**
   Памятник Циолковского
2. **Tsiolkovsky Grave**
   Могила Циолковскому
3. **Tsiolkovsky House Museum**
   Дом-Музей Циолковского
4. **Church of the Peace-Bringing Wives**
   Церковь Жен-Мироносиц
5. **Church of St. John the Baptist**
   Церковь Иоана Предтечи
6. **Assumption Church**
   Успенская Церковь
7. **St. George's Church**
   Георгиевская Церковь
8. **Church of the Intercession**
   Покровская Церковь
9. **Stone Bridge**
   Каменный Мост
10. **Post Office**
    Почта
11. **Pestrikov Almshouses**
    Пестриковская Богадельня
12. **Church of Our Savior**
    Спаская Церковь
13. **House of Offices**
    Здания Присутсвенных Мест
14. **Trinity Cathedral**
    Троицкий Собор
15. **Trading Rows**
    Торговые Ряды
16. **Church of St. George-behind the-Trade Rows**
    Церковь Георгия-за-Лавками
17. **Noblemen's Assembly**
    Дворянское Собрание
18. **Church of Our Lady of Kazan**
    Казанская Церковь
19. **Epiphany Church**
    Богоявленская Церковь
20. **Archbishop's Estate**
    Архиерейская Усадьба
21. **Church of the Nativity**
    Церковь Рождества
22. **Space Museum**
    Музей Космонавтики
23. **History Museum**
    Исторический Музей

24. **Art Museum**
Художественный Музей
25. **Hotel Zul**
Гостиница «Зул»
26. **Hotel Kaluga**
Гостиница «Калуга»
27. **Hotel Sputnik**
Гостиница «Спутник»
28. **Kolos Restaurant**
Ресторан «Колос»
29. **Café Rus'**
Кафе «Русь»
30. **Market**
Рынок
31. **Bus Station**
Автовокзал
32. **River Station**
Речной Вокзал
33. **Kaluga 1 Train Station**
Вокзал Калуга 1
34. **Kaluga 2 Train Station**
Вокзал Калуга 2

Russia's Spiritual Powerhouse

Few places have as important a role in Russia's religious life as the monastery of **Optina Pustyn.** In the dying years of the Romanov dynasty, it gained a reputation unmatched in the Orthodox Christian world for bringing spiritual renewal to its visitors.

It was founded by Opta, a repentant robber, in the 15th century near Kozelsk. For over 400 years, it was relatively insignificant – and poor. At the end of his reign, Peter the Great closed the monastery as part of his campaign against monastic power. It subsequently housed some of the host of wounded produced in the course of the Tsar's military exploits.

Optina's fortunes changed in 1821 with the arrival of Moisey and Antoniy Putilov, two disciples of St. Seraphim of Sarova. Seraphim, a religious thinker and contemporary of Pushkin's who is said to have spent fifteen years living unarmed in the forest among bears, believed that "silence is the sacrament of the world to come, words are the weapons of this world." His disciples built the **Skit of St. John the Baptist** in a nearby wood, and gathered round them the wisest religious thinkers of the day, the *startsy*. With Moisey as prior, the monastery also flourished; a trapezium, cells, hostels, a library, several churches, and a farmstead were built.

People came to Optina from all over the Christian world. Everyone from English Lords to the local peasantry knelt before the *startsy*. "The spiritual intensity generated by the new monastic communities which Seraphim set up began to attract a new kind of pilgrim – secularized intellectuals – for visits if not pilgrimages. Optina Pustyn… became a center of counseling and of spiritual retreats for many of

Russia's most famous 19th-century thinkers: beginning with the Slavophile Ivan Kireyevsky, who spent much of his later life there, and extending on through Dostoyevsky, Tolstoy, and [the philosopher] Vladimir Solovyev," writes James H. Billington in *The Icon and the Axe: An Interpretive History of Russian Culture.* Dostoyevsky regularly stayed in a little house in the Skeet, which is now a museum to him. He based the monastery of Alexey Karamazov in *The Brothers Karamazov* on his impressions of Optina. Father Amvrosy, one of the most noted of the *startsy*, became the model for the enigmatic Father Zossima. Lev Tolstoy, nearing the end of his life and already completely alienated from Orthodoxy, came here nonetheless for spiritual peace. Nikolay Gogol, however, failed to find solace – his tormented life was already nearing its even more unhappy end.

After the revolution, Optina Pustyn met a familiar fate. It was closed completely in 1923 and its monks exiled, sent to camps, or shot. Subsequently, it became a museum, a *dom otdykha* (holiday resort), a military base, and an agricultural college. During the early stages of World War II, it was a POW camp for Polish officers. Within a space of six months, its inmates were either recruited by the NKVD or doomed to execution at Katyn.

In 1987, Optina Pustyn was returned to the Church, and since then restoration work has produced constant progress. Two churches, the **Presentation of the Virgin** and **St. Mary of Egypt**, have been rebuilt virtually from scratch. The former now houses the remains of Father Amvrosy, exhumed from the necropolis beneath the monastery in 1988. While grappling with economic problems, Optina is gradually getting back on its feet, both physically and spiritually.

Tourists, pilgrims, and those seeking to be cured at the two holy springs are welcomed with food and hostel accommodation. The monastery has even recently acquired martyrs. In April 1993 three monks were savagely murdered by a satanist Afghan war veteran; their graves stand near its enclosing wall.

Dostoyevsky house in skeet

The Skit, where restoration work has almost been completed, is the most interesting site. The ensemble is satisfyingly homely and tidy, with vegetable patches and a ring of neat wooden houses around the central **Church of St. John the Baptist** – a rare example of early 19th century wooden architecture based on a classical stone prototype. There are two museums behind the church, the smaller one dedicated to Dostoyevsky and, to its left, the house where Gogol stayed, his interest aroused by the other writers who visited Optina.

plan was drawn up by Vassily Bazhenov's pupil, Yasnygin, and the city thus laid out has remained to this day.

A walk around Kaluga should begin with its imposing central landmark, the **Trinity Cathedral** (in the central park on Ulitsa Bazhenova), a centerpiece of Yasnygin's plan. Its main attraction is the massive cupola, almost 20 yards in diameter, making it even wider than Voronikhin's Cathedral of our Lady of Kazan in St. Petersburg. Local architects opposed the plan, saying the cupola's size would make it insupportable, but they were proved wrong.

Returning to the road, you will have already noticed two archways, to the right and left. This, more than anything, has given Kaluga the nickname of "little St. Petersburg." They are part of the town's administrative offices (*prisutstvyenniye mesta*), the series of linear buildings flanking Bazhenova and Ulitsa Karla Marksa. Sections were used as a seminary in the last century.

Turning left and passing under one of these arches, you will see the **Nobles' Assembly**, dating from the mid-19th century, on the left. Ahead is the **Stone Bridge** (*Kamenny most*), perhaps Kaluga's greatest architectural treasure. Built by P. Nikitin shortly before the Yasnygin plan, it resembles a Roman viaduct, with two levels of arches in the center. There is nothing quite like it anywhere else in Russia. It crosses the **Berezuisky Ravine**, a picturesque, almost unspoilt gully running from the Oka to the center of town.

Just beyond the bridge on the left is the house of the merchant Zolotaryov. In the beginning of the 19th century, this was an ordinary provincial town mansion. Today, however, its rarity has made it infinitely more precious, and like the local **History Museum** its richly decorated interior is accessible to the visitor. While the exhibits inside are relatively ordinary, and often totally unconnected with the decor, the marble columns, bas-reliefs and romantic landscapes on the walls and ceilings serve as a reminder of Moscow's great 18th century palaces, burned out during the Russian retreat from Napoleon in 1812.

Vostok *rocket, Kaluga Space Museum*

Outside of the center, though, the town has an all-too-familiar Brezhnev era feel: Victory Square has its massive Socialist statue, uniformed schoolchildren with red flags patrol the tomb of the unknown soldier, and giant letters on the nearby building proclaim, "Hail to the Soviet nation, the victorious nation!"

Kaluga was also the hometown of Konstantin Tsiolkovsky, an eccentric professor who designed zeppelins in his attic, and, when finally recognized as a genius after the Revolution, became known as the father of cosmonautics. The huge **Space Museum** at Ulitsa Akademika Korolyova is full of rockets and capsules, both models and others that actually completed missions. On the green outside is a life-size model of *Vostok*, the ship Yuri Gagarin used on his first space flight. For about $1 a head you can get a guided tour in English. Tsiolkovsky is buried in the nearby park, and his home is preserved as a museum at 79 Ulitsa Tsiolkovskovo.

TARUSA

Few Russian villages can match the beauty of this charming place on the river Oka in the north of the region, an inspiration for many Russian and Soviet writers and artists.

Tarusa's most famous daughter is the passionate emigrée poet Marina Tsvetayeva. She spent her childhood summers there, and her muse was subtly nurtured in its very Russian landscape. The village still lives and breathes her today. The **Tsvetayeva Museum** is perhaps not the best choice of sites – the **Dom Pesochnovo**, where she grew up, was leveled after the war to make way for a *dom otdykha*'s dance floor. The current exhibition is in her grandfather's house at 30 Ulitsa Rozy Lyuksemburg. After the revolution, Tsvetayeva moved first to Czechoslovakia and then to France, and returned here only briefly in 1939. She always expressed the wish to return and die there. Now a stone marks the place at the riverside where she wanted to be buried.

On the hill above this stone, in a tiny enclosure, lies the grave of the artist **Victor Borisov-Musatov**, covered by the forlorn sculpture of a young boy lying supine. Art critic/historian Camilla Gray writes that Borisov-Musatov (1870–1905) was, after Vrubel, "the most significant and influential painter in Russia at this time," and the only one to combine certain stylistic elements of the classical-oriented Petersburg artists, with the color experiments of contemporary Moscow painters.

Note also the little **Church of the Re-**

You, rushing past on your streets
To some dubious magic you've tasted,
If only you knew how much heat,
How much lifeblood I've already wasted,

How much heroic passion I threw
At a random shadow or rustling...
How each time my heart flamed anew
And spent its powder for nothing.

O trains flying into the night,
Making off with the sleep of the station...
But I know nevertheless that you might
Never answer – if you heard it – the question:

Why are my words so strong and so sharp
To my cigaret's perpetual smolder.
How much gloom and imperiling dark
In the light-haired head on my shoulders.

– Marina Tsvetayeva, 1913

translated by Nina Kossman in *The Inmost Hour of the Soul* (Clifton, N.J.: Humana Press, 1989), reprinted by permission

surrection with a bell-tower that lends to the village an almost Swiss feel.

Returning to the center of town, the **Art Gallery** has a modest collection of works by Tarusa's famous inhabitants. Of special note are the canvases of **Vassily Polyenov** (1844–1927), one of the first painters to focus on the Russian countryside and a great friend of Tolstoy and Turgenev. His estate, now a museum, lies in a beautiful setting across the river not far from the village, in the neighboring Tula Region (see p. 330).

PRACTICAL MATTERS

In many respects, today's Kaluga is a challenging destination, possibly because of poor management by the local authorities or simply due to grinding poverty. Hotel prices, though still low by Western standards, are unusually high for Russia, and for no apparent reason–facilities are worse, if anything, than in most cities. The **Hotel Kaluga** at 1 Ulitsa Kirova, doesn't live up to its reputation as the best; try instead the **Zul** on Ulitsa Gogolya or the **Priokskaya** on Ulitsa Suvorova. Restaurants are also poor. The best option may be to visit in passing and bring your own food.

DIRECTIONS

Kaluga: by almost any train from Moscow's Kievsky Station. Kaluga 2 station is far from the town, but an alternative is to take a slow suburban train to Kaluga 1. By car take the M3 Kiev road for about 160 km and turn left.

Optina Pustyn: 2 hours by bus from Kaluga to Kozelsk, followed by a lengthy walk, or by M3 55 km SW beyond Kaluga, then left for another 25 via Sukhinichi to the town of Kozelsk. The road to the monastery is straight back through the town from the bus station, which is on the Sukhinichi road.

Tarusa: by suburban train from the Kursky station to Serpukhov, then a 1½ hour bus ride. By car as to Serpukhov (see Moscow Region), then right on the Obninsk road (8 km), then left, 18 km.

RUSSIAN GLOSSARY

Dom Pesochnovo
Дом Песочного
guberniya
губерния
Kaluga
Калуга
Kaluzhskaya Oblast
Калужская Область
Obninsk
Обнинск
Optina Pustyn
Оптина Пустынь
Ulitsa Rozy Lyuksemburg
Улица Розы Люксембург
Serpukhov
Серпухов
Sukhinichi
Сухиничи
Ulitsa Suvorova
Улица Суворова
Tarusa
Таруса
Ulitsa Tsiolkovskovo
Улица Циолковского

BRYANSK REGION

BRYANSKAYA OBLAST

In the southwest corner of Russia, bordering on Ukraine and Bielarus, lies the Bryansk Region. Its greatest wealth lies in its forests – over a million hectares (12,000 sq. km), covering over a third of its surface. The timber there comprises a total volume of 145 million cubic meters. Wild boar, brown bears and elk roam this forest, and in a nature reserve to the south at Trubchevsk, the rare black stork is protected. Writers, including Alexey Tolstoy and Fyodor Tyutchev, have found inspiration in Bryansk. A century later, the same forests shielded a powerful partisan army from the Nazis.

The Bryansk Region has shouldered more than its share of suffering. Its forests still haven't recovered from clearing by the Germans during their campaign against the partisans. A more recent catastrophe, Chernobyl, brought untold hardship to the inhabitants of Klintsy and Novozybkov in the southwest. Radiation levels there are still high, and the area should be avoided.

BRYANSK

Few places in the world, even in long-suffering Russia, compare to the town of Bryansk in the way its rich history has been so brutally obliterated. Once an ancient settlement on the Desna river, Bryansk was transformed during the present century into a huge regional industrial center.

The city was founded in 985 by Prince Vladimir, who united the Vyatichi and Rodimichi tribes across the river. Bryansk's position, surrounded by forest, protected it from the Tatar raids other cities were so vulnerable to in the 13th century. In fact its original name, Debryansk, comes from the Russian *debry*, meaning thick forest. It flourished during this period; Prince Roman moved his capital there after the sacking of Chernigov. But in the 14th century the Tatars finally moved in, closely followed by Lithuanian princes, who stayed for 150 years.

When finally rejoined with Russia, Bryansk became a frontier town; by the mid-16th century, its southern neighbor, Ukraine, was part of the Kingdom of Poland. Trade developed at the local fair, outside the Sven monastery on the town's outskirts. In Peter the Great's time, Bryansk became a

The Forest Fighters of Bryansk

In 1941, when Germany occupied vast tracts of the western Soviet Union, many people took to the forest and formed partisan units. Nowhere was this more common than around Bryansk, where 60,000 men, women and children hid in dug-outs in dense forest and ravines, sleeping on pine branches and making superhuman efforts to remain alive and yet unnoticed in the extreme cold.

Their activities posed such a threat to the Germans that the latter were forced to cut down vast areas of forest around the city of Bryansk in order to retain control. Near the town of Dyatkovo, where the movement was strong and the Germans weak, partisans were able to set up a "republic" behind enemy lines in 1942. It was four months before the occupiers finally resolved to remove this threat to the west, although the more remote areas of the region were never really under their control.

Bryansk's fighters took a heavy toll on the enemy, killing 150,000, putting hundreds of artillery pieces out of action and, in the later stages, blowing up railway lines. Nowadays, they are still remembered with respect, and children play "partisans" instead of "soldiers."

The best place to get an impression of all this is **Partizanskaya Polyana** (Partisan Field), a unique memorial complex just outside Bryansk on the Oryol road. Here, an indoor museum with diorama and preserved outdoor dugouts shows how the partisans lived. In the nearby clearing are several monuments. On a wall, names of the 8,000 partisans who died are listed. Below it is an "eternal" flame, lit only on special occasions because of the fire hazard. The centerpiece of the complex, a huge concrete triangle, is graced with the image of Lenin, who, despite having died twenty years prior to the war, still managed to have something prophetic to say about it. Just beyond Partizanskaya Polyana is the **Beliye Berega** (White Shores) tour base (*turbaza*), highly recommended for its natural surroundings.

shipbuilding center, and Catherine the Great decreed the building of an arsenal there.

However, in pre-revolutionary times Bryansk was a district, rather than a *guberniya,* or province, and developed as such. Only after the Revolution did it become a sprawling industrial city. During the war, it was virtually wiped off the map by the Germans; only seven percent of its pre-war buildings remain.

Present-day Bryansk is divided into four districts, effectively four separate towns, by three rivers, the Desna, the Bolva and the Snezhet. The oldest district, and the only one of real interest, is the Sovyetsky in the southwest.

The old city center is on Pokrov hill, just above Ulitsa Kalinina. A monument to the "city of military glory" dominates the skyline. Nearby is Bryansk's oldest church, the 1626 **Intercession Cathedral**, now functioning again.

Bryansk's forests are given a lavish tribute in the **Alexey Tolstoy Museum Park** on Bulvar Gagarina. An indoor exhibition provides a rather lengthy slide-tape presentation, three-dimensional forest scenes for each of the four seasons (accompanied by readings from literature), and stuffed animals, complete with the appropriate bellowing sounds on tape. If this experience of "canned" nature proves excessive, the park outside, with its collection of imaginative wooden sculptures of historical and fairy tale characters, provides an alternative. The sculpture park came about in the 1950's as a creative way to salvage the trunks of the park's elms when they were struck down by Dutch Elm Disease. Now oak sculptures have replaced them, but the spirit of the originals has been preserved. Unfortunately the varnish suppliers are at Lvov in Ukraine, and economic links have been broken. Consequently, many sculptures are beginning to crack, and the local artists who made them are too busy weathering economic difficulties to craft replacements. Most impressive is a wooden fountain given to the park in 1985, Bryansk's millenium. It consists of a watermill and wheel, with two demons pouring water onto it from buckets, while the miller and his son look on. Even when the water is turned off, it presents a vivid scene.

Alexey Tolstoy Wooden Sculpture Park

Two other places in Bryansk, both on the edge of the Sovyetsky District, are more interesting for their history than for what is there today. **Chashin Kurgan**, just off Bezhitskaya ulitsa and the #3 trolleybus route, is the site of the original fortress town. It was there in 1976 that archaeologists established the true founding date of the city, which had existed for more than 100 years before moving to the

Pokrov Hill. Earthworks remain, providing a view of the rivers and factories beyond.

The **Sven Monastery** to the south on Ulitsa Frunze, at the end of the #1 and #4 trolleybus routes, was actually founded in 1288, though the current buildings date from the 17th century – the golden age of the Sven Fair, when Bryansk was a gateway to Europe, and trade in furs and jewelry in particular was flourishing. Of the monastery's churches, the massive **Assumption Cathedral**, built by Ivan the Terrible, is today little more than a pile of rubble. Only the gate churches survive, interesting for their mixture of Moscow and Ukrainian baroque. There is a very fine view from outside the monastery. Overlooking the river stands an oak tree, under which it is said that Peter the Great liked to sit. He stayed at the monastery on his way to head off a Swedish attack on Ukraine.

THE LITERARY BRYANSHCHINA

Bryansk's forests have provided inspiration for many writers, one of whom has now been immortalized in his former home.

Just to the northwest of Bryansk is **Ovstug**, the birthplace of Fyodor Tyutchev (1803–73), generally regarded as the greatest nature poet Russia has produced. The Tyutchev estate, though completely destroyed in World War II, has been rebuilt from scratch and now contains a sizable museum. Unfortunately bereft of Tyutchev personal possessions (the museum doesn't have the resources to protect them from pilferers), it is almost entirely made up of letters, documents and photographs. Its setting is idyllic – the little house stands above a sloping garden, a statue of Tyutchev in contemplation, and a gnarled old oak, the poet's contemporary.

There is, at the first beginning of fall
a brief, but extraordinary time –
The whole day turns as it were to crystal,
and the evenings are sublime…

Where a lively sickle felled the grain,
Nothing but emptiness everywhere –
glimmering in an idle furrow
only a spiderweb's thin hair…

– Fyodor Tyutchev (1857)
(translated by J. Kates)

DYATKOVO CRYSTAL

Just north of Bryansk is the town of Dyatkovo, famous for its cut-glass. Though the original factory didn't survive the war, its reputation has. Founded by industrialist and local celebrity Ivan Maltsev in 1790, the Dyatkovo factory has recently received a number of major international honors, including the Gold Mercury Award in 1980 and the 1993 International Diamond Star for Quality, unusual recognition for a Soviet enterprise and unheard of in the glass industry.

The factory is 200 meters north of the center of town. You can take a tour round the various workshops, including the cutting and hand-blowing sections. The museum opposite has a huge if unimaginatively arranged collection of the factory's finer output. The shop beside the factory entrance is not really for souvenirs, but for the factory's ordinary production, and any hint of commercialism is belied by the empty boxes and wood chips on the floor.

PRACTICAL MATTERS

All the hotels and facilities of Bryansk are also located in the Sovyetsky District. The top hotel is the **Bryansk**, at 98 Prospekt Lenina. Food in the city is unremarkable, though proximity to Ukraine means that the coffee is drinkable.

DIRECTIONS

Bryansk: by almost any train from Moscow's Kievsky Station. By car take the M3 Moscow–Kiev road for 325 km, then take the A141 right toward Roslavl into the town.

Dyatkovo: (from Bryansk) by bus on the regular Star and Ivot services from the central bus station on Ulitsa Peresveta. By car take Bezhitskaya ulitsa towards Roslavl, then just outside the city turn right onto Liteinaya ulitsa, driving straight through Bezhitsky District and on for 65 km.

Ovstug: by bus from the central bus station; by car leave by the Roslavl road, drive for 48 km and take a right into the village.

RUSSIAN GLOSSARY

Beliye Berega
Белые Берега
Bezhitskaya ulitsa
Бежицкая улица
Bryansk
Брянск
Bryanskaya oblast
Брянская область
Bulvar Gagarina
Бульвар Гагарина
Chashin Kurgan
Чашин Курган
Dyatkovo
Дятьково
Ulitsa Frunze
Улица Фрунзе
Ivot bus service
Автобусный маршрут "Ивот"
Ulitsa Kalinina
Улица Калинина
Prospekt Lenina
Проспект Ленина
Liteinaya ulitsa
Литейная улица
Ovstug
Овстюг
Partizanskaya Polyana
Партизанская Поляна
Ulitsa Peresveta
Улица Пересвета
Roslavl
Рославль
Sven Monastery
Свенский монастырь

SMOLENSK REGION

SMOLENSKAYA OBLAST

Smolenskaya Oblast, which lies between Moscow and Russia's western border, established itself very early as an integral part of Rus'. By the 7th century it was trading with Greeks via the Dnieper and Bulgars via the Volga. Smolensk city became one of the nation's leading cultural centers by the 1200's. The position of the "Smolenshchina" (smahl*yen*shina"), as it is sometimes called, on Russia's western edge has had two effects on Smolensk's development. It has absorbed cultural elements from other nations, Poland and Byelarus in particular, and earned a long history of heroism on the battlefield against Russia's numerous western enemies.

SMOLENSK

The city of Smolensk, situated grandly on the upper reaches of the Dnieper River, has always been commercially important. In the 9th century it was a way station for river traders bound for Kiev. The name originates from the Russian word *smol,* meaning tar – this is where they tarred their boats. The original citadel was built on present-day Cathedral Hill. Two hundred years on, the Smolensk princedom was formed, and its extravagant princes began a massive stone building program, of which a handful of churches survive.

Smolensk's independence was lost to the Lithuanians in 1404 and was never regained. By the city's liberation in 1514, Moscow was already establishing its authority. It has remained a powerful and important provincial center ever since.

The city today is not so easy to negotiate: there are steep hills everywhere, public transport is appalling and even the joy of walking around the town walls is denied to all but rappellers – every few hundred meters there are pieces missing, knocked out after the last war by desperate locals with no bricks to rebuild their bombed-out homes.

A tour of the city should best begin from Cathedral Hill, the old center. The bright green of the Assumption Cathedral (see box) is accompanied by an entire architectural ensemble, built later and colored similarly. Most interesting is the Archbishop's Residence, a long two-story building on the western slope, built by renowned architect Pyotr Obukhov in 1774.

Undoubtedly the city's biggest attraction, though, is its walls, still magnificent today despite the considerable damage done to them over the centuries. They took just six years to build, with as many as 300,000 people working on the project from dawn until dark. During the period of construction, Boris Godunov forbade private stone building anywhere else in Russia, punishable by death. The final length of the walls was 6 kilometers, and they were reinforced by 38 defensive towers. The best preserved section today is east of the town, and though access is difficult, the **Veselukha Tower** provides fine views of the Dnieper and surrounding hills. The most attractive section, though, is on the riverside, where the **Hodigitria Gate Church** and bell-towers at either end provide a welcome break from the grey stonework.

None of Smolensk's three 12th century churches is close to the center, but one, the **SS. Peter and Paul**

The Campaigns through Smolensk

Though one of the few parts of Russia virtually untouched by the Tatars, Smolensk has had more than its share of invasions, occupations, sieges and sackings. At first these took the form of random forays by Poles and Lithuanians in the 13th century, culminating in its inclusion in the Great Lithuanian Principality in 1404. But when Moscow became Russia's capital, Smolensk's strategic significance became greater than ever.

In the space of the next five centuries, Smolensk was to come under fire on three further occasions. Each time neither the sturdiness of its defenses nor the heroic resilience of the defenders was enough to save the city from occupation. Yet each time Smolensk encumbered its attackers sufficiently to prevent Moscow itself from collapsing, and to allow Russia time to recover and drive out its invaders.

The Polish-Lithuanian invasion of 1609 provided an immediate opportunity to test Russia's largest stone fortress, built here by Boris Godunov to cope with just this threat. Sure enough, it required two years to take the city, and only then by treachery from within. By this time, however, Kosma Minin and Dmitry Pozharsky had already gathered their volunteer army and Russia was saved. Not Smolensk, though – the city remained in enemy hands for another forty years.

Two hundred years later, Russia was again in danger, this time from Napoleon. The suddenness of the attack on Smolensk was quickly neutralized by the city walls and their brave defenders, and the French advance was halted. Only Russian Marshal Kutuzov's policy of retreat and consolidation allowed the French to enter the city. But the siege had weakened Napoleon and united the Russian armies of de Tolly and Bagration.

The process was repeated in World War II. Hitler's troops reached Smolensk, almost 500 km into Soviet territory, on 10 July 1941, just a month after the beginning of Operation Barbarossa. But

Continued on page 351

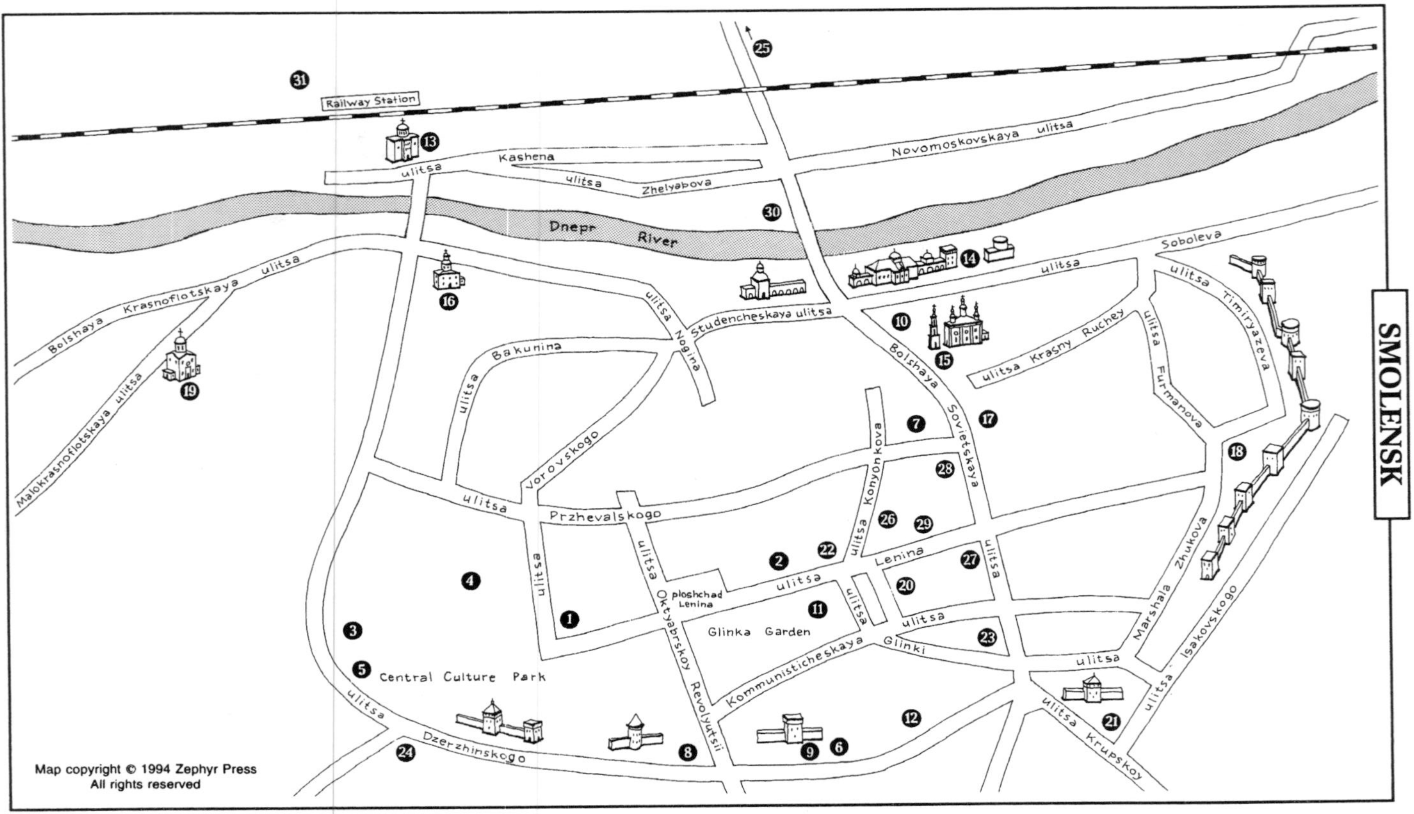
SMOLENSK
31
Railway Station
25
13
ulitsa Kashena
ulitsa Zhelyabova
Novomoskovskaya ulitsa
30
Dnepr River
Soboleva
ulitsa
14
16
Bolshaya Krasnoflotskaya ulitsa
Malokrasnoflotskaya ulitsa
19
Studencheskaya ulitsa
Nogina
ulitsa Bakunina
Vorovskogo
10
15
Bolshaya Sovietskaya
ulitsa Krasny Ruchey
ulitsa Furmanova
ulitsa Timiryazeva
17
18
7
ulitsa Konyonkova
28
26
29
ulitsa Przhevalskogo
ulitsa
2
22
Lenina
27
ulitsa
4
ulitsa
ploshchad Lenina
ulitsa Oktyabrskoy Revolyutsii
11
20
1
Glinka Garden
ulitsa Glinki
23
Kommunisticheskaya
Marshala Zhukova
ulitsa Isakovskogo
ulitsa
3
5
Central Culture Park
12
21
ulitsa Krupskoy
ulitsa Dzerzhinskogo
24
8
9
6

СМОЛЕНСК

Ulitsa Bakunina
Улица Бакунина
Bolshaya Krasnoflotskaya ulitsa
Большая Краснофлотская у́лица
Bolshaya Sovietskaya ulitsa
Большая Советская улица
Central Culture Park
Центральный Парк Культуры
Dnepr River
Река Днепр
Ulitsa Dzerzhinskovo
Улица Дзержинского
Ulitsa Furmanova
Улица Фурманова
Glinka Garden
Сад Глинки
Ulitsa Glinki
Улица Глинки
Ulitsa Isakovskovo
Улица Исаковского
Ulitsa Kashena
Улица Кашена
Kommunisticheskaya ulitsa
Коммунистическая улица
Ulitsa Konyonkova
Улица Коненкова
Ulitsa Krasny Ruchey
Улица Красный Ручей
Ulitsa Krupskoy
Улица Крупской
Ulitsa Marshala Zhukova
Улица Маршала Жукова
Ploshchad Lenina
Площадь Ленина
Ulitsa Lenina
Улица Ленина
Malokrasnoflotskaya ulitsa
Малокраснофлотская улица
Ulitsa Nogina
Улица Ногина
Novomoskovskaya ulitsa
Новомосковская улица
Ulitsa Oktyabrskoy Revolyutsii
Улица Октябрьской Революции
Ulitsa Przhevalskovo
Улица Пржевальского
Ulitsa Soboleva
Улица Соболева
Studencheskaya ulitsa
Студенческая улица
Ulitsa Timiryazeva
Улица Тимирязева
Ulitsa Vorovskovo
Улица Воровского
Ulitsa Zhelyabova
Улица Желябова

MAP KEY

1. **Tour and Excursion Bureau**
   Экскурсионнное бюро
2. **Intourist Bureau**
   Интурист
3. **Korolevsky Bastion**
   Королевский Бастион
4. **Monument to the Heroic Defenders of Smolensk**
   Памятник Героическим Защитникам Смоленска
5. **Monument to the St. Sophia Regiment**
   Памятник Софийскому Полку
6. **Monument to the Heroes of 1812**
   Памятник Героям 1812
7. **Memorial to the Victims of Fascism, October 1941**
   Мемориал жертв фашизма, Октябрь 1941
8. **World War II Smolensk Liberation Monument**
   Памятник Освобождения Смоленска в войне 1941-1945гг.
9. **The Immortality Mound Memorial and Eternal Flame**
   Мемориал "Курган бесмертия"
10. **Kutuzov Monument**
    Памятник Кутузову
11. **Glinka Monument**
    Памятник Глинке
12. **Kutuzov Bust**
    Бюст Кутузова

13. **SS. Peter and Paul Church**
Церковь Петра и Павла
14. **Dnieper Gate**
Днепровские Ворота
15. **Assumption Cathedral**
Успенский собор
16. **Church of St. John the Divine**
Церковь Иоанна Богослова
17. **Trinity Monastery**
Троицкий монастырь
18. **Main fragment of town wall**
Фрагмент крепостной стены
19. **Church of Archangel Michael**
Церковь Архангела Михаила
20. **Konenkov Sculpture Museum**
Музей скульптора Коненкова
21. **Art gallery**
Музей изобразительных искусств
22. **Hotel Tsentralnaya**
Гостиница Центральная
23. **Hotel Smolensk**
Гостиница «Смоленск»
24. **Hotel Rossiya**
Гостиница «Россия»
25. **Restaurant Vityaz**
Ресторан «Витязь»
26. **Cafe Zarya**
Кафе «Заря»
27. **Bar Russky Chai**
Бар «Русский Чай»
28. **Bookshop**
Книжный магазин
29. **Souvenir Shop**
Сувениры
30. **Market**
Рынок
31. **Railway Station**
Вокзал

Church (1146) is conveniently but unfortunately placed. Beside the railway and bus stations, its austerity and simplicity of design (Byzantine cruciform) hardly suits its chaotic modern surroundings. Inside, restorers and priests struggle to coexist.

The **Church of St. John the Divine**, just to the south on Bolshaya Krasnoflotskaya, was built just 20 years later in a similar style. Today, little remains of the original church and the likeness to its predecessor has been all but lost.

In the late 12th century, Smolensk architects began to digress from Byzantine and Kievan canons, producing churches which were noticeably taller, narrower and more elegant, with an especially narrow drum. The only one of these to survive is the **Church of the Archangel Michael**, on the western edge of town on Ulitsa Malokrasnoflotskaya. Except for minor late additions, it has remained intact, and from the opposite shore of the river provides a moment of relief in an area that is hardly picturesque.

Two art museums in the town are worth a visit. The **Art Gallery** at #7 Ulitsa Krupskoi houses a range of Russian canvases typical of provincial museums, featuring such painters as Aivazovsky and Levitan, as well as some European works, including Juan de Arellano and H. Cassel. The building itself is a fine example of art nouveau, designed by Sergei Malyutin and Viktor Vasnetsov.

At #7 Ulitsa Mayakovskovo is a sculpture museum featuring the works of native son Sergey Konyonkov. Portraying events and personalities of the last century, he drew his inspiration from ancient Greece. Indeed, he used the finest marble from the quarries at Mount Pentelikon. The most famous work here is a *Self Portrait*, the solemn, bearded head of the sculptor rooted firmly in a stone block.

The Road to Katyn

Taking the road to the west out of Smolensk will bring you to a number of interesting monuments and sites. In the midst of the forested area of sana-

continued on page 354

The Campaigns through Smolensk, *Continued from page 347*

the defenders held out there for another two, virtually ruining the Nazis' chances of taking Moscow by winter.

These struggles have all left their mark on Smolensk, as well as on other towns in the region, and not purely in a negative sense. Altogether, the number and variety of war memorials here is great. Smolensk Region is an ideal place for gaining insight into how Russians remember past glories and griefs.

For those interested in Smolensk's history, the west-east road, the hope and despair of every invading army, tells its own story.

Starting from **Rudnya**, on the western border of Russia with Bielarus, you will find two World War II memorials. At a road junction to the east of the town is a *katyusha,* the first ever reactive mortar battery, mounted on a concrete pedestal. Hurriedly commissioned just a day after being tested, this weapon stopped the furious German attack for a week in July 1941. To the south is "The Grieving Mother," the face of a woman carved into stone, looking down at

Continued on page 352

"They were not mourners, but communicants."

"As we wandered up the slope, plunged in its ash and concrete ghosts, it threw out shadows which I was to encounter again and again at Russian memorials – not only of grief, but of something darker and less reducible. It seemed to me that those who came here – guided groups of somber men, women clutching carnations – were not mourners, but communicants, and that this was a necessary pilgrimage into their atrocious past, a ceremonial opening of wounds. ... They came here, I sensed, less in sorrow for the collective unimaginable dead, than in a pantheistic tribute to the motherland – the scarred and holy womb which must never be desecrated again."

– Colin Thubron, from *Where Nights Are Longest: Travels by Car through Western Russia* (New York: Atlantic Monthly Press, 1987)

The Campaigns through Smolensk, *continued from page 351*

the grave below with great sorrow. This is the site of a mass-killing by the Nazis; 3,000 died here in October 1941 in reprisals against the partisans.

Reaching Smolensk itself, you will find it difficult to miss the largest war memorial of them all: the massive, 60 meter high green **Assumption Cathedral**, which dominates the city skyline from the site of the original citadel of Prince Vladimir Monomakh. It was commissioned by Tsar Alexey Mikhailovich to commemorate the heroic defense against the Poles, but construction dragged on to the end of the 18th century. The spacious interior is accented by an iconostasis that stretches from floor to ceiling. Executed between 1730 and 1740 by the Ukrainian Sila Trusitsky, it is a masterpiece of 18th century wood carving.

Smolensk's 1812 monuments are numerous and varied. Perhaps the most interesting is that erected by Nadolsky and Shutsman in 1913, dedicated to the "Heroes of the Patriotic War of 1812" and depicting a Gallic soldier grappling with eagles as he tries to climb into their nest. The two fierce birds, one in combat and the other shielding the nest, represent the armies of de Tolly and Bagration, united to defend Russia. Those who distinguished themselves in the August 4–5 battle are remembered by a black obelisk surmounted by a cupola and cross, erected by D. Adamini in 1841. And the St. Sophia Regiment has another obelisk, this one crowned by an eagle with outspread wings and built by one of the regiment's own footsoldiers a hundred years later. Field Marshal Kutuzov has two monuments in the city, one a bust at the entrance to the **Heroes' Memory Garden** (1912), the other a full statue, only 40 years old. All are in the city park except the last, which is at the foot of Cathedral Hill.

This same Garden provides the focus for remembrance of World War II (also known to Russians as "the Great Patriotic War") in Smolensk. At the foot of the town wall are marble plaques inscribed with the names of the fallen. On Pokrovskaya Gora is the **Bayonet Monument**, put up by townspeople to remember the defenders. And in a central square beside the Pioneer Palace, local hero Volodya Kurilenko, who died aged 18 after blowing up five enemy columns in 1941, is remembered with a statue. A survey of Smolensk's memorials would be incomplete without mention of the city's liberators. On the corner of Ulitsas Oktyabrskoy Revolyutsiyi and Dzerzhinskovo is an artillery crew carved in granite. Finally, Smolensk's biggest monument, dedicated to the Soviet war effort as a whole, is situated in the **Readovsky Park** out of town. This is the **Immortality Mound**.

Leave Smolensk by the southerly Old Smolensk Road, the route taken by Napoleon. At the village of **Tsaryevo-Zaimishche** stands a column of birch trees dating from Catherine the Great's time. It was there that on 17 August 1812, Kutuzov took command of the Russian army. A memorial plaque stands on the hill above. Just a few kilometers further is **Solovyovo**, scene of battles in both 1812 and

Yefremov Monument

1941. In the latter year, a Dnieper river crossing was held for a fortnight, saving two Soviet armies from encirclement and destruction. Another *katyusha* marks the spot; 893 men are buried there.

The next town on the route, **Dorogobuzh**, achieved fame during Napoleon's journey back to France. A bloody battle took place there on 26 October 1812, as a result of which the Russian troops gained a commanding position on the town's ancient earthworks. A century later, a 12 meter column was erected on the bank of the Dnieper to mark the victory.

About 21 km west of **Vyazma** is another World War II monument, this time to the *Baumantsy*, a division formed in the Baumansky District of Moscow. Exhausted and almost out of ammunition after battling the enemy for a week, these men somehow found the strength to break out of their encirclement and save their banner from capture.

The town of Vyazma was the scene of fierce fighting during the 1812 war. In battles lasting two days and 10 hours respectively, the Russians and French contested the town before and after Moscow. During the French retreat, Napoleon lost 7,000 men there and had to dump his booty in a lake in nearby Semlevo. It has never been recovered. Now all that remains are the familiar double-headed eagles, one outside the History Museum on the main square, the scene of the battle, the other on the grounds of the Arkadievsky Convent up the hill.

Pride of place in the town now goes to the **Yefremov Monument**, a dramatic sculpture depicting wounded men fighting for the liberation of Vyazma. This process took almost a year, as hundreds of thousands died in the so-called "Vyazma Pot," leaving the ground studded with shrapnel and bone splinters. Lieutenant-General Mikhail Yefremov was a shock-troop commander who was killed there and is now buried in the town's military cemetery.

toria beyond the city stands a little concrete bunker a few hundred yards from the road on the left. It is said that Hitler came here in 1941 to gloat over newly-won territory.

Slightly further, in the village of **Gnyozdovo**, are the remains of some unique 12th century burial mounds. There are 4,000 of them, making this the largest such site in Russia. Nothing to compare has been discovered in Kiev or Novgorod, Russia's largest cities at the time. It is still a mystery to archaeologists why they are so far from Smolensk itself.

Now marked by a roadside sign, **Katyn Forest** is open to visitors, though once this was the grounds of the regional party committee's sanatorium, surrounded by barbed wire. Here lie the bodies of the cream of the Polish officer corps, massacred there in 1940 with German ammunition by Stalin's secret police. A crude but lasting cover-up ensued, effected by the terrorizing of eyewitnesses; only in 1990 did the Soviet government finally admit to the crime.

The officers' graves are tastefully arrayed in a clearing set back from the road. The Nazis, too, helped to make Katyn infamous: a small memorial commemorating a massacre of their own lies en route to the main site.

Flyonovo

South of Smolensk off the Roslavl road, this village was once the home of the artist and patron Princess Maria Tenisheva, wife of a wealthy industrialist. Following the example of Savva Mamontov at Abramtsevo, she turned her estate into an artists' community, with studios and a school. Like Abramtsevo, the museum there is a feast for lovers of Art Nouveau.

One of the former workshops is the **Teremok**, a colorful, richly-carved fairy-tale house designed by the artist Sergei Malyutin and now a museum of folk art. On top of the nearby hill, the pretty **Church of the Holy Spirit** is another art nouveau classic, with layered *kokoshniki* and a mosaic of Christ by Nikolai Roerich, another artist who took inspiration from Russian folk traditions.

VYAZMA

Wartime heroics (see also box) were not the only hallmark of this pretty and peaceful town, and it is worth an hour or two's stroll.

Founded in the 13th century, Vyazma went through the usual cycle of prosperity and destruction before slipping into provincial insignificance after the 1812 war. Its heyday was the 17th century, when Mikhail Romanov fortified it. There is even a legend that under Alexei Mikhailovich it briefly became Russia's capital – stranded between the plague-ridden cities of Moscow and Smolensk, the Tsar was forced to stop there.

Vyazma's most striking landmark is the 1676 **Trinity Cathedral**, its slender central cupola rising majestically from a jumble of *kokoshniki* and a low, broad base. The 19th century belfry beside it is well proportioned, dominating without dwarfing the church. Just across the ravine is the **Spassky Tower**, the only remaining structure of the city fortress. Its squat, sturdy appearance suggests that its survival was not accidental.

But among Vyazma's liberally scattered 17th and 18th century churches, one is truly outstanding. From the center, look for the triple spires in the distance across the Vyazma river. This is the **Hodigitria Church of the Mon-**

astery of St. John the Baptist (now functioning again), built in 1638. Examined from close-up, this church has all the trappings of festive pre-Petrine Russian architecture – demi-columns, pediments, and three layers of *kokoshniki*. Its most unusual feature, though, is the tent roofs – three together in a row. Only one other such stone church still exists, the Divnaya Church in St. Andrew's Monastery, Uglich.

PRACTICAL MATTERS

Though Smolensk is probably best seen as a stop-off point on the Moscow-Brest road, reasonable but unexceptional accommodation and restaurants are available. The best city hotel is the Rossiya on Ulitsa Dzerzhinskovo, 23/2, though the Tsentralnaya on Ploshchad Lenina, 2/1 has a hard currency shop and some Intourist facilities. For those with a car, the Intourist Motel Phoenix is 16 km west of the city on the Minsk road.

DIRECTIONS

Smolensk: by almost any long distance train from the Byelorussky Station, journey time 7½ hours. By car take the M1 Minskoye shossé, 389 km.

Flyonovo: from Smolensk, there are buses to Flyonovo and Talashkino, the latter requiring a further half-hour walk at the end. By car take the A141 Roslavl road for about 15 km, then turn left through the village of Talashkino and continue for another 1½ km.

Katyn: from Smolensk by Smetanino-bound buses. By car, leave Smolensk by the A141 Vitebsk road.

Vyazma: By both train and car, follow the same directions as Smolensk, with journey times halved.

The Old Smolensk Road runs between Vyazma and Smolensk, parallel and to the south of Minskoye shossé.

RUSSIAN GLOSSARY

Dorogobuzh
Дорогобуж

Flyonovo
Флёново

Gnyozdovo
Гнёздово

Katyn
Катынь

Minskoye shossé
Минское шоссе

Roslavl
Рославль

Rudnya
Рудня

Smetanino
Сметанино

Smolensk
Смоленск

Smolenskaya oblast
Смоленская область

Solovyovo
Соловьёво

Talashkino
Талашкино

Tsaryevo-Zaimishche
Царёво-Займище

Vitebsk
Витебск

Vyazma
Вязьма

Trinity Cathedral, Vyazma

PSKOV REGION

PSKOVSKAYA OBLAST

Sandwiched between Novgorod and the Baltic States, between St. Petersburg and Bielarus, the area that is today the Pskov Region has for most of its history been on Russia's border. While its beautiful lakes, mixed forests and vicious mosquitos are all typical of northern European Russia, its history is unique.

Pskov was Russia's main buffer against her northwestern enemies. When Lithuanians, Swedes, Teutonic Knights of the Livonian Order, and Poles came against Russia, they almost always fell foul of Pskov's fortresses: Pechora, Izborsk and Pskov itself. Although overshadowed by the more powerful Novgorodian princedom in the east, and known periodically as its "suburb" or "younger brother," Pskov remained independent for some time, and developed distinctive schools of art and architecture. Perhaps more than any other style in Russia, Pskov's church architecture has retained its identity over the centuries. In this century, some churches destroyed during World War II have been faithfully restored. The squat, single-dome structures of rough-hewn white limestone, with their characteristic vertical-wall belfries, distant cousins of the belfries of Spanish "mission style" churches in the New World, still grace the city and countryside of Pskov.

PSKOV

Situated at the confluence of the Velikaya (meaning "great") and Pskova rivers, Pskov is one of the most appealing of Russia's old cities. Few kremlins can match the majesty of Pskov's Krom, while nearly all of the city's many churches are handsome.

The exact founding date of Pskov is not known, though it existed as early as 862. In its first few centuries, Novgorod ruled it, but it became independent in 1137 when Prince Vsevolod Mstislavich, grandson of Vladimir Monomakh, was thrown out of Novgorod and sought refuge here.

While the Tatars overran the rest of Russia, Pskov had the Livonian Knights to worry about. Indeed, the local boyars betrayed the city to them in 1240, and it took the intervention of Alexander Nevsky to liberate it two years later at the battle of Lake Chud. With the discrediting of the local

The Museum Reserves

Although the natural beauty of the Pskov Region may be exceeded elsewhere, the architects and builders who worked here in early centuries demonstrated a genius for siting. The resulting harmony between the works of man and of nature is difficult to surpass, and in two places nears perfection. Both have been restored or preserved in all their subtlety.

The Izborsk and Maly Valleys

The ancient settlement of Izborsk, one of the ten oldest cities in Rus', the seat of Prince Truvor and site of a powerful frontier fortress, is a much-loved stop on tour itineraries. The views of Gorodishchenskoye Lake from the town are dramatic, and the fortress has the look of a northern English castle. But the more adventurous of spirit should explore further – you won't regret the difficulties of reaching the valleys' hidden sanctuaries.

Start from the fortress (built in 1330) and head for the **Kukovka Tower** past the 14th century **St. Nicholas Cathedral**. This tower was the fortress dungeon, and last refuge from the enemy. As you pass through to the outside, you find yourself on a ledge above a lake, with a lovely view. A path winds down to the **Slavenets Springs**, a series of little waterfalls which gush down into the valley. As you go, look around you, down at the lake, back at the fortress, and forward to the **Truvorovo Settlement**. Almost nothing here is out of step with its natural setting.

As you continue past the springs, head up toward the copse on the hill above to the left. This is the cemetery, close to Izborsk yet calm and little-frequented. As you reach the exit, you will see a large stone cross on the right. This is **Truvor's Cross**, which commemorates the founder of the town who ruled here for two years in the 9th century. But the cross is not authentic – Truvor was a pagan and could not have had one. As you emerge from the cemetery you see at once the settlement (*gorodishche*) and the little **St. Nicholas Church** at its edge. This is the original site of the town, where sheep-ridden earthen ramparts look over the lake and beyond.

Izborsk Fortress

Now the going starts to get difficult. Descend to the lakeside to the

Church of St. Sergius of Radonezh, Izborsk

sound of frogs in the reeds and follow the track at the bottom, which crosses a stream and comes out into a field with allotments owned by the nearby village. Rather than continuing toward the village (on the other side of the river), bear left immediately and climb up the side of the hill. For this part of the journey you really need rubber boots – streams break the track at regular intervals. Unfortunately there is no regular path along the valley at this point and you have to keep climbing. The field at the top seems endless, but keep looking down toward the valley and eventually you will see the **Maly Monastery**, whose little square belfry peeps up through the trees. The path is now clear again, and you descend through the woods. You don't see the monastery again until you get there. It's invisible from all directions save that of the lake itself. Go down to the bottom of the little cemetery where a spring of holy waters trickles, then go up to the belfry, typically Pskovian with its square form. Finally, go down to the lake to feel really cleansed by the beauty of Maly.

Mikhailovskoye

The **Pushkin Museum Reserve** poses a challenge for its many visitors. Its vast area and great distance from any major population center make any kind of day-trip either very rushed or incomplete. Yet that should not deter anyone from enjoying its natural beauty and literary charm.

Pushkin's family first came to Mikhailovskoye in 1742. Empress Elizabeth made a gift of the estate to Abram Hannibal, the poet's Ethiopian great-grandfather, who was known as "the Arab of Peter the Great." Pushkin visited frequently, but his longest stay was during his exile. Destroyed during the last war, this and other nearby estates have been painstakingly restored. The result is a beautiful and well-kept museum, reverent enough to avoid the label of theme park.

Mikhailovskoye is the centerpiece, but is unexceptional on its own. Pushkin was often unhappy there, as he preferred St. Petersburg society to the solitude he experienced in this house. When the rest of his family was present, there was often friction, partly because his father feared for his own position when his son was in trouble with the authorities. Yet Pushkin had a savior in his poetry, and various

Continued on page 360

The Museum Reserves, *continued from page 359*

drafts of his work are now on display. The house looks out onto Lake Kuchanye, and beyond it lies the **Petrovskoye Estate**. The museum there is dedicated to Pyotr Hannibal, Pushkin's great uncle and evening drinking partner. Petrovskoye is 4 km away, reached by walking around the lake to the right.

Mikhailovskoye's surroundings show a remarkable taste, both in their original form and in the way they have been restored. Its traditional French park is crossed by linden and fir avenues and dotted with surprising landmarks, such as the Pushkin family chapel and the very appealing statue of the poet, whose slender form reposes thoughtfully in an orchard.

Turning right off the fir alley before the chapel, you will find yourself on the gentle wooded path where Pushkin strolled on the way to see his neighbors. If you pass another lake, Malenets, and cross through more woods and pasturelands, you will eventually reach **Trigorskoye**, the home of the Osipov-Vulfs, a cultured and sociable family who attracted Pushkin with their extensive library and delicious peasant food. If Mikhailovskoye meant solitude for Pushkin, at Trigorskoye he found its opposite. He whiled away the hours there chatting with his host or partying with the numerous young people in the house. The park, in English landscape style, is highly romantic. It contains a giant sundial, a bench where the poet and his verse hero Yevgeny Onegin loved to sit, and the "green room" – a clearing surrounded by linden trees where young people danced in summer.

About 5 km to the south is **Pushkinskiye Gory**, the administrative center of the reserve. Here you can stay in the reasonably priced **Hotel Druzhba** and see the poet's homeland at your leisure. Pushkin is buried nearby; at a bend in the road, women sell flowers to the many well-wishers who come to pay tribute. His grave is on a hilltop in the **Svyatogorsky Monastery**, a kind of corrective center for monks who are sent here to repent for drinking and blaspheming.

aristocracy that resulted, power shifted, as in Novgorod, to the *veche,* a popular assembly with the Prince as titular head of state.

Wars against the Livonians continued for the remaining 250 years of Pskov's independence. During this period the city moved gradually out of Novgorod's sphere of influence and into Moscow's, and finally united with the latter in 1510 under Grand Prince Vassily III. Relations between the two cities were never completely harmonious, and Pskov frequently revolted. The *veche* even returned to power briefly in 1608–11 when the townspeople supported the second False Dmitry.

Pskov's military significance remained, and on three further occasions she saved Russia. In 1581 the city held off an army of 100,000 under Polish king Stephen Batory. In 1615 it was evacuated and destroyed before Russia was able to defeat Swedish king Gustavus Adolphus. Finally, Peter the Great used Pskov as a base for his campaign against the Swedes.

A Message to Siberia

Deep in the mines of Siberia
Preserve your self-respecting patience;
Not for nothing your hard labor
And your thought's high aspirations.

Hope, who is misery's faithful sister,
Down in the grimmest dungeon will
Arouse your spirits and your zeal.
The time will come that you have
wished for:

Love and friendship will pass through
Into your dismal prison cells
Just as, in those bestial holes,
My voice, unfettered, comes to you.

Your heavy chains will fall apart,
The dungeon walls cave in – and freedom
At the gate receive you gladly,
And brothers render you your sword.

– Alexander Pushkin, 1827
(translated by J. Kates)

In this war, the Russians captured the port of Narva and gained access to the sea. From this time on, Pskov lost its strategic importance.

Unlike most western Russian towns, Pskov does not immediately betray the destruction it suffered in World War II. Although only 18 buildings stood in the city when the Nazis left, today the city walls, numerous churches and even some fine examples of 17th century secular stone architecture have been rebuilt or restored. Pskov's abundance of historic buildings put it on a par with cities such as Yaroslavl, which were never occupied.

Though relatively small and compact, it would be difficult to see Pskov in a day. Only the most perfunctory coach tour could take in everything and negotiate river crossings quickly enough.

The Krom

Pskov's mighty Kremlin stands on a promontory between the Velikaya and Pskova rivers, and is especially impressive from the banks of the second, smaller river. It is entered from the land, which is the weakest side, and was once protected by a deep moat. Today the wall has sunk into the ground and the entrance is through a hole cut above the ancient gate. A magnificent view of the huge Trinity Cathedral opens up inside. This is the original center of the city and the site of a miracle. St. Olga, who passed

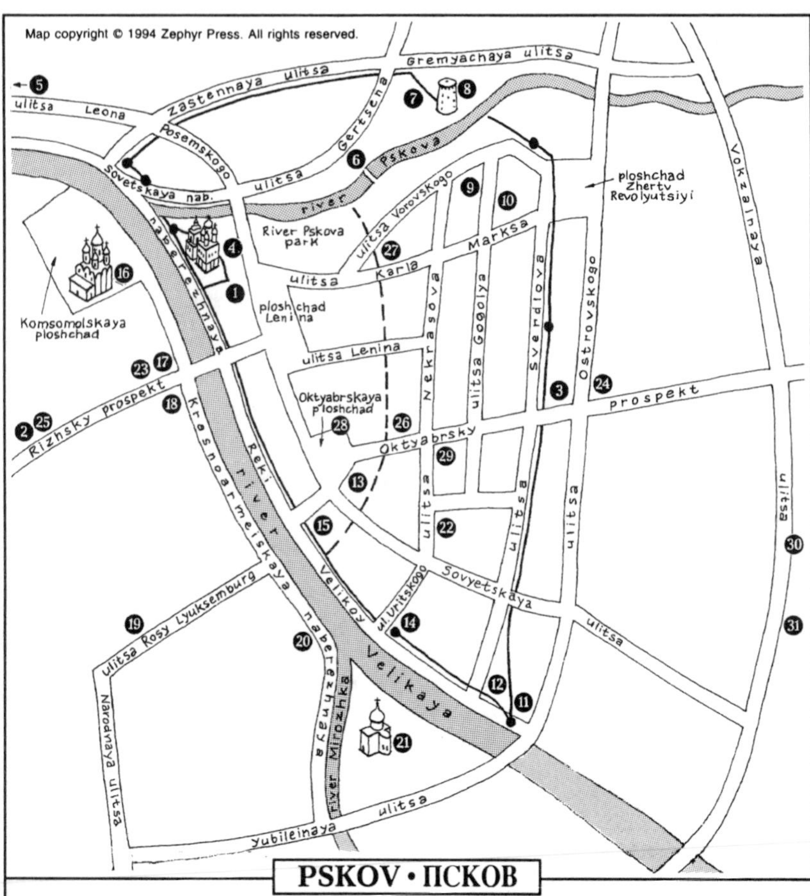

Ulitsa Gertsena
Улица Герцена
Ulitsa Gogolya
Улица Гоголя
Gremyachaya ulitsa
Гремячая улица
Ulitsa Karla Marksa
Улица Карла Маркса
Komsomolskaya ploshchad
Комсомольская площадь
Krasnoarmeiskaya naberezhnaya
Красноармейская набережная
Ploshchad Lenina
Площадь Ленина
Ulitsa Lenina
Улица Ленина
Ulitsa Leona Posemskovo
Улица Леона Посемского
River Mirozhka
Река Мирожка
Narodnaya ulitsa
Народная улица
Ulitsa Nekrasova
Улица Некрасова
Oktyabrskaya ploshchad
Октябрьская площадь
Oktyabrsky prospekt
Октябрьский проспект
Ulitsa Ostrovskovo
Улица Островского
River Pskova
Река Пскова
River Pskova Park
Парк реки Псковы
Rizhsky prospekt
Рижский проспект

Ulitsa Rozy Lyuksemburg
Улица Розы Люксембург
Sovyetskaya naberezhnaya
Советская набережная
Sovyetskaya ulitsa
Советская улица
Ulitsa Sverdlova
Улица Свердлова
Ulitsa Uritskovo
Улица Урицкого
River Velikaya
Река Великая
Naberezhnaya reki Velikoy
Набережная реки Великой
Vokzalnaya ulitsa
Вокзальная улица
Ulitsa Vorovskovo
Улица Воровского
Yubileinaya ulitsa
Юбилейная улица
Zastennaya ulitsa
Застенная улица
Ploshchad Zhertv Revolyutsii
Площадь Жертв Революции

MAP KEY

1. **Travel Bureau**
Бюро путешествий
2. **Intourist**
Интурист
3. **Pushkin Monument**
Памятник Пушкину
4. **Kremlin**
Кремль
5. **Snetogorsky Monastery**
Снетогорский монастырь
6. **Epiphany Church**
Богоявленская церковь
7. **SS. Cosmas and Damian Church**
Козмодемьянская церковь
8. **Gremyachaya Tower**
Гремячая башня
9. **Malt House**
Солодёжня
10. **Pachenko House**
Дом Паченко
11. **Intercession Tower**
Покровская башня
12. **Twin Churches of the Intercession and the Nativity of the Virgin**
Храм Покрова и Рождества
13. **St. Basil's on the Hill**
Церковь Василия на Горке
14. **St. George from Vzvoz**
Церковь Георгия со Взвоза
15. **Hodigitria Church**
Церковь Одигитрия
16. **Cathedral of St. John**
Иоанновская церковь
17. **Assumption Church by Ferry**
Церковь Успения с Пароменья
18. **St. Anastasia Chapel**
Часовая святой Анастасии
19. **St. Nicholas at the Stone Wall**
Церковь Николы Каменоградского
20. **St. Clement's Church**
Климентовская церковь
21. **Mirozhsky Monastery**
Мирожский монастырь
22. **City Museum**
Городской музей
23. **Turist Hotel**
Гостиница «Турист»
24. **Oktyabrskaya Hotel**
Гостиница «Октябрьская»
25. **Rizhskaya Hotel**
Гостиница «Рижская»
26. **Bookshop**
Книжный магазин
27. **Market**
Рынок
28. **Post Office**
Почта
29. **Telephone Exchange**
Телефон
30. **Train Station**
Железнодорожный вокзал
31. **Bus Station**
Автовокзал

through in the 10th century, saw a sign from heaven and ordained the building of a cathedral. The first stone church was built in the 12th century. The current giant is 17th century, built in Moscow style, when the capital was finally imposing its will on Pskov.

The wall on the south side of the

Pskov Krom

cathedral was the meeting place of the *veche*. Here the city's entire male population met and voted on local issues. A podium stood above the square, where present and former mayors, the military commander, and the Prince sat. The bell tower is the former Snetnaya Tower, and is older than the cathedral itself. It stands in unusual fashion outside the city walls. A walk to the far left corner brings you to the Kutekrom Tower, Pushkin's favorite place for contemplation during his visits.

The archaeological excavations you will have passed on your way into the Kremlin are known as **Dovmont's Town**. It is named after Prince Dovmont Timofey, a popular 13th century Pskov ruler who had a palace within the second ring of city fortifications. Twenty churches once stood there, and their lower parts are only now being rediscovered and reconstructed.

After you exit through the second wall you come to Lenin Square, once the trade center of the city and scene of a revolt by townspeople in 1476 against an unpopular Moscow appointee, Prince Yaroslav Striga-Obolensky. The revolt occurred when one of the Prince's men stole cabbages from a local trader, whose colleagues subsequently rallied to his defense.

Zavelichye (Beyond the Velikaya)

As you cross the Velikaya River from the Krom, the first eye-catching landmark is the 16th century **Church of the Assumption at the Ferry**, distinguishable by its five-row belfry in traditional Pskov style. On the opposite side of the road is the tiny **Chapel of St. Anastasia**. Built to a project by architect Alexey Shchusev in 1911, its interior is covered with frescoes painted by Nikolay Roerich (1874–1947), a painter and set-designer whose background included studies of archaeology and Russian folk art. They can be viewed on request to the Mirozhsky Monastery museum.

A right turn along Krasnoarmeiskaya Naberezhnaya will bring you to the **Cathedral of St. John.** It is one of two surviving 12th century churches in Pskov and the only remaining city church built by the Pskov princes, many of whose wives are buried there. Its original form has either been maintained or restored, although the plastering and whitewashing betray later alterations.

If you return to the bridge and continue along the embankment, you will see ahead **St. Clement's Church** at the water's edge and beyond it the Mirozhsky Monastery. But first take a right down Ulitsa Rozy Lyuksemburg to the little church of **St. Nicholas at the Stone Wall**, the best example of a small, pillarless church in Pskov.

The **Mirozhsky Monastery of the Savior** has a special place in Pskov's history. It emerged at a time when Christianity was being spread through Russia and became Pskov's main center of learning. It had a vast library and scriptorium, and developed a prestigious icon-painting school. It now sits peacefully by the river, shying away from the busy road on one side and the noisy town beach on the other. Its centerpiece is the **Transfiguration Cathedral,** built in the 12th century, Pskov's first church with painted interiors. The Greek frescoes inside are miraculously well preserved and are now under UNESCO protection. The paints used here came from all corners of the earth. Note particularly The Ascension, the imposing figure of Christ in the dome, surrounded by rings of angels and then apostles, and the Virgin Orant in the central apse.

Cathedral of St. John

The 16th–17th century St. Stephen's Church and other surrounding buildings are currently being prepared to house a fresco museum.

The Outer City

Recross the Velikaya River from the Mirozhsky Monastery to return to the outer fortified area of the city. These walls enclose a section of the Pskova river, which meant that in times of siege the city had a constant supply of water and as a result was practically invincible. This is known as the **Okolny Town**. On your left as you cross is the **Intercession Tower,** and just inside the corner of the wall is a unique double church. In fact, the two parts, the **Intercession** and the **Nativity,** are separated by a common wall. The original Intercession Church was built in memory of the defenders of Pskov against Stephen Batory in the 16th century, and a monument to them stands in front of it.

Pass along the embankment and turn inland after passing the late 15th century **St. George's Church**. On Ulitsa Nekrasova are the **Pogankin Chambers**, a huge white stone merchant house from the beginning of the 17th century. It occupies an entire block, a testament to the owner's great wealth, the source of which remains a mystery even today. The house contains Pskov's **History and Art Museum**. The icon collection is of particular interest. Though the best examples of the Pskov school are now in Moscow or St. Petersburg, the city has a number of interesting exhibits from the Mirozhsky and Pechora Monasteries and elsewhere. The earliest are 14th century, when the icon of St. Juliana established the Pskov tradition of narrow, expressive faces. In the 15th century, Pskov masters developed their own special color scheme, which used a dazzling cinnabar brought from India in combination with softer local colors like rain-washed grassy green. Later icons show the growing Moscow influence on Pskov art, with the long slender Dionysian-like figures of St. Nicholas, or the full length Deesis Range, both from the early 16th century. One unique exhibit is the Virgin Orans of Mirozh (the Great Panagia), a 16th century copy of a 13th century icon made by an enraptured Ivan the Terrible. The fate of the original is unknown. Other exhibits of the museum are Prince Dovmont's sword, used to gird princes at their coronations, and a collection of 17th–18th century bibles from Moscow.

Around the central Oktyabrskaya Ploshchad are a number of interesting churches. Note the city park, with the **Church of St. Vassily-on-the-Hill**, whose design gives the impression that the sheer force of gravity is pulling it into the slope from all sides. Across Sovyetskaya in a square behind is the unusual 17th century **Hodigitria Church**. Follow Ulitsa Gogolya after crossing Oktyabrsky Prospekt and you'll come to two more 17th century secular buildings, the **Malt House** and the **Pachenko House,** and beyond them one of the most picturesque spots in Pskov. After you descend into the Pskova riverside park, you will see opposite the **Gremyachaya** (Thundering) **Hill**, with the **Tower** of the same name and the **SS. Cosmas and Damian Church**. This is the site of the outer wall's northern river crossing, and is desperately romantic. The ruined tower and its reflection in the river allow for quiet meditation, a far cry from the feelings of awe inspired by the Krom.

Zapskovye (Beyond the Pskova)

As you walk down toward the Kremlin, turn right across a footbridge to reach the most peaceful part of the town. There was never any trading here, and merchants generally refrained from building. The large church on your left is the **Epiphany Cathedral,** the site for *veche* meetings on this side of the river.

Near the Kremlin, take the #1 bus out to the **Snetogorsky Monastery,** perched on a high ledge above the Velikaya on the outskirts of town. The ensemble's oldest building, the **Church of the Nativity of the Virgin**, is an early post-Mongolian structure. Its exterior dimensions match the interior ones of its prototype, the Transfiguration Cathedral at the Mirozhsky Monastery. Extensive 14th century frescoes have survived, unfortunately without the upper layer of paint. Some of these paintings deviate from Byzantine canons and demonstrate a more Russian style. Another interesting structure is the belfry. Built by the Italian architect Frazilov in 1526, it resembles a wasp's nest. Occupying armies have also left their mark on Snetogorsky – Stephen Batory's Poles left scratched drawings in the cathedral choir, while the German Army Group North put in drains in 1941.

PECHORY MONASTERY

To the west of Pskov, on the Estonian border, is the small town of Pechory, where in 1473 a cave church was founded by hermits. In the 16th century it became a monastery and by 1568 a powerful frontier fortress. Through a strange twist of fate it escaped the wrath of the Bolsheviks – Lenin signed it away to the newly-formed state of Estonia in 1920, and it

Assumption Cathedral, Pechory Monastery

has remained in use throughout the century. Although Stalin returned Pechory to Russia after the war, Estonia now claims it once again and border tensions are growing. This issue is guaranteed to make any Russian's blood boil.

Today's monastery is as sturdy, imposing and colorful as ever. It is best seen from a viewing platform down to the left of the main gate. The walls follow the natural contours of the land, spreading over both sides of a ravine with the River Kamenets running through beneath.

As you enter the monastery compound you will see the classical columns of the St. Michael's Cathedral ahead. But to reach the main, lower part take a left through the small **Church of St. Nicholas the Gateman**, painted by Nikolay Roerich in the last century, then wind down to the right on what is known as the "Blood-stained Road." Legend claims that Ivan the Terrible personally decapitated Kornily, the Father Superior, as he came out to greet the Tsar with bread and salt; Ivan believed Kornily was supporting the boyars. In fact Kornily was killed later in Pskov.

The main square of the monastery cannot fail to impress. Straight ahead is the magnificent **Assumption Cathedral** with decorated panels on the walls, and tiered domes with painted drums. This part was built in 1759, but below it is the original cave church, now a burial vault – seven galleries contain no less than 10,000 bodies, including ancestors of Alexander Pushkin and 1812 General Mikhail Kutuzov. Now the caves are accessible, but only for one hour in the morning, and occasionally at additional times for tour groups. On the feast of the Assumption, the 27th of August, the forecourt and steps of the cathedral are used for a festive open-air service.

No less stunning is the belfry to the left. A weight in the form of a large barrel full of stones operates the clock. Ropes link the mechanism to the bells.

The building in the center of the arc formed by the Cathedral and belfry is the vestry, distinguished by its red walls, white platbands, blue cupolas and slit-windowed roofs. It contains manuscripts and incunabula, including early local records.

Snetogorsky Monastery fresco

PRACTICAL MATTERS

Hotel accommodation in Pskov has been made bearable by the appearance of the **Rizhskaya** on Rizhsky prospekt. Its restaurant can be excellent on a good day, fortunate because nowhere else in town provides this quality. Other hotels are the **Tourist** on Krasnoarmeiskaya Naberezhnaya, or if you're really desperate, the old and crumbling **Oktyabrskaya** at 36 Oktyabrsky prospekt.

DIRECTIONS

Pskov: two trains run overnight from Moscow's Leningradsky Station. By car take the M9 Riga road as far as Pustoshka, then right on the M20 St. Petersburg-Kiev highway.
Izborsk and **Pechory:** by bus from Pskov, total journey time 1 hour. By car take the A212 out of Pskov, turning right for Pechory at Izborsk.
Pushkinskiye Gory: by bus, 3 hours from Pskov. By car go south on the M20 to Novgorodka (85 km) and turn left (22 km).

Gremyachaya Tower, Pskov

RUSSIAN GLOSSARY

Gorodishchenskoye Lake
Городищенское озеро
Izborsk
Изборск
Krom
Кром
Mikhailovskoye Estate
Усадьба Михайловское
Novgorodka
Новгородка
Pechory
Печоры
Pskovskaya oblast
Псковская область
Pushkinskiye Gory
Пушкинские Горы
Pustoshka
Пустошка
Svyatogorsky Monastery
Святогорский монастырь
Trigorskoye Estate
Усадьба Тригорское

NOVGOROD REGION

NOVGORODSKAYA OBLAST

Few of old Russia's provinces have as much of interest to the visitor as Novgorod, or as much potential for prosperity in that nebulous future beyond today's economic woes. In the north, a regional center which is also one of Russia's oldest and grandest cities brings visitors from all over the world to admire its cultural heritage and famous early churches, scattered along the banks of the Volkhov river and Ilmen Lake. In the southeast, the Valdai Uplands, with their invigorating forest air and clear lakes, provide relief from the predominant flatness of European Russia.

When you consider the Novgorod Region's position, half way between St. Petersburg and Moscow, it is difficult to imagine that it could still have room for deserted or forgotten places. But it has, and in abundance.

NOVGOROD THE GREAT

In Russian, the word Novgorod means new town and that, extraordinary as it may seem, is just what it is. True, a city existed here since the ninth century, but to say it survived World War II would be something of an exaggeration. Only eight people lived through the war here, and not many more buildings. Therefore, surveying the city today with its beautifully proportioned and positioned churches, people can admire the work not just of the original builders, but also the spectacular achievements of recent restorers.

The city's origins are cloaked in legend. Slovena and Rus, two Slavic brothers, built a town here called Slovensk. The lake whose shores they inhabited was called Ilmen, after Slovena's daughter, and the river Volkhov, after his son. Novgorod arose later, when the old settlement had fallen into ruin. Slovensk was probably at the site of the Rurik fortress (*Gorodishche*), downstream from today's city.

Novgorod was founded in the 9th century, and quickly became a key point on the Scandinavia–Byzantium trade route which conveyed furs, fish, honey and leather between the northern and southern extremes of Europe. Within Rus, it never fully respected Kiev's authority, and in 1014 its Prince, Yaroslav, refused to pay tribute to his Kievan masters. Two centuries later, Novgorod was an independent state.

Novgorod quickly established itself as Russia's most progressive and enlightened city. The *Ostromir Lec-*

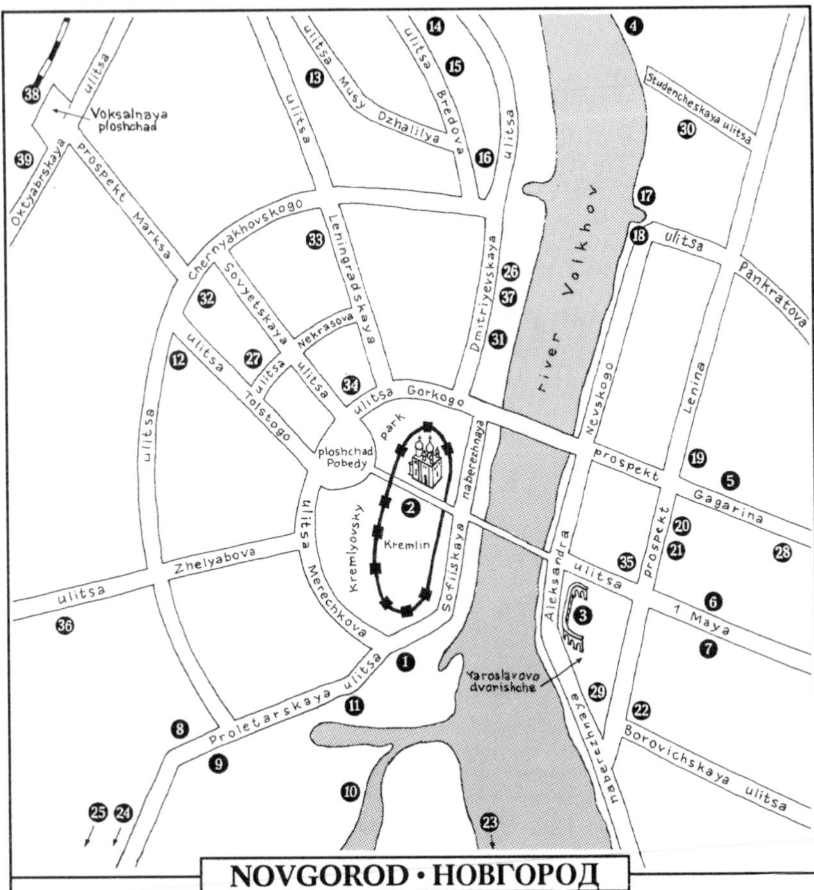

NOVGOROD • НОВГОРОД

Naberezhnaya Alexandra Nevskovo
Наб. Александра Невского
Borovichskaya ulitsa
Боровичская у́лица
Ulitsa Bredova
Улица Бредова
Dmitriyevskaya ulitsa
Дмитриевская у́лица
Prospekt Gagarina
Проспект Гагарина
Ulitsa Gorkovo
Улица Горкого
Kremlyovsky Park
Кремлёвский парк
Prospekt Lenina
Проспект Ленина
Ulitsa Leningradskaya
Улица Ленинградская
Prospekt Marksa
Проспект Маркса
Ulitsa Meretskova
Улица Мерецкова
Ulitsa Musy Dzhalilya
Улица Мусы Джалиля
Ulitsa Nekrasova
Улица Некрасова
Oktyabrskaya ulitsa
Октябрьская улица
Ulitsa 1 Maya
Улица 1 Мая
Ulitsa Pankratova
Улица Панкратова
Ploshchad Pobedy
Площадь Победы
Proletarskaya ulitsa
Пролетарская улица

Sovyetskaya ulitsa
Советская улица
Studencheskaya ulitsa
Студенческая улица
Ulitsa Tolstovo
Улица Толстого
Voksalnaya ploshchad
Вокзальная площадь
Yaroslavovo dvorishche
Ярославово дворище
Ulitsa Zhelyabova
Улица Желябова

MAP KEY

1. **Victory Monument**
Памятник Победы
2. **St. Sophia's Cathedral**
Софийский собор
3. **Arcade of the Yaroslavl Court**
Ярославово Дворище
4. **Cathedral of the Nativity of Our Lady, St. Anthony's Monastery**
Церковь Рождества Богородицы, монастырь святого Антония
5. **Church of St. Theodore Stratilates**
Церковь Фёдора Стратилата
6. **Church of the Transfiguration of the Saviour**
Преображенский собор
7. **Church of Our Lady of the Sign**
Знаменская Церковь
8. **Church of SS. Peter and Paul**
Церковь святых Петра и Павла
9. **White Tower**
Белая Башня
10. **Church of St. John**
Церковь святого Иоанна
11. **Trinity Church**
Церковь Троицы
12. **Church of the Twelve Apostles**
Церковь Двенадцати Апостолов
13. **Trinity Cathedral**
Троицкий собор
14. **Zverin Monastery**
Зверин монастырь
15. **Church of St. Nicholas the White**
Церковь Николы Белого
16. **Church of SS. Peter and Paul, Kozhevniki**
Церковь святых Петра и Павла в Кожевниках
17. **Church of St. John the Divine**
Церковь святого Иоанна Чудотворца
18. **Church of SS. Boris and Gleb**
Церковь святых Бориса и Глеба
19. **Church of St. Nikita**
Церковь святого Никиты
20. **Church of St. Demetrius of Thessalonika**
Церковь Дмитрия Солунского
21. **Church of St. Clement**
Церковь святого Клемента
22. **Church of St. Michael**
Церковь святого Михаила
23. **Church of St. Nicholas**
Церковь святого Николая
24. **Vitoslavlitsy Museum**
Музей "Витославлицы"
25. **St. George's Monastery**
Монастырь святого Георгия
26. **Hotel Intourist**
Гостиница «Интурист»
27. **Hotel Volkhov**
Гостиница «Волхов»
28. **Hotel Sadko**
Гостиница «Садко»
29. **Hotel Rossiya**
Гостиница «Россия»
30. **Beresta Palace Hotel**
Отель «Береста Палас»
31. **Feniks Restaurant and Casino**
Ресторан и казино «Феникс»
32. **Rossiya Cinema**
Кинотеатр «Россия»

33, 34. **Bookshops**
Книжный магазин

35. **Souvenirs**
Сувениры
36. **Market**
Рынок
37. **Intourist office**
Интурист

38, 39. **Railway Station, Bus Station**
Вокзал, Автобусная станция

tionary, written there in 1057 for the city governor, is the oldest Russian book. Meanwhile, ordinary towns-people were becoming remarkably literate, communicating by means of scratch marks on pieces of birch bark. Simplicity and rationality were the hallmarks of Novgorodian art and architecture.

Escaping direct Mongol-Tatar attack, but not the payment of tribute, Novgorod kept alive a measure of Russian independence throughout the years of the yoke. Right up to the 15th century it remained a powerful state, with a remarkably democratic political system. Important issues were settled by convening the *veche*, a gathering in which every adult male freeman had a vote.

In 1478, Moscow's Ivan III finally got jealous of Novgorod's independence and unceremoniously swallowed it up. His Terrible successor broke the power of the local boyars (landowners and merchants) and massacred 40,000 people.

Whether in the land itself, or in the blood of its inhabitants, an independent spirit still endures here. Astrologists are predicting a rosy future for Novgorod, and there's definitely something in the air.

Magdeburg Gate, St. Sophia's Cathedral. Photo: William C. Brumfield

Today's city is anything but a backwater. It is working hard to exploit its many assets, and is achieving at least a facade of prosperity. Novgorod's great appeal to visitors is exploited to the full, by the city authorities as much as by souvenir peddlers. For example, museum admission for foreigners can be as much as 100 times what it is for Russians.

But while group tourism is booming here, Novgorod also has a great deal to offer the independent traveler. No organized excursion can possibly encompass the entire feast of church architecture, or even of frescoes, which it offers. But at the same time, some form of transport is definitely needed – monuments are scattered and some are nearly inaccessible. The once highly efficient and convenient river steamers are now nowhere to be seen.

Seeing Novgorod: The Kremlin

Almost always the best place to start a city tour wherever you are in Russia, in the case of Novgorod the Kremlin is definitely the focus of attention. Lacking the administrative significance of, say, Moscow's, it is overrun by tour groups, tacky souvenir sellers and all the usual accessories, but that does not detract from its enormous historical and cultural significance.

While most of the ensemble is 15th century, its greatest treasure is the functioning **Cathedral of St. Sophia**, built by Prince Vladimir in the 11th century as a symbol of the city's independence. Nevertheless, it's based on its namesake in Kiev, and external dimensions match the older St. Sophia's internal ones. Inside, the cathedral is equally magnificent, with five aisles and a lofty u-shaped choir. Most of the current murals are 19th

Russian Lakeland

The acres of taiga forest, where bears and wolves roam, and the deep blue lakes of the **Valdai Uplands** are today, as they always have been, a favorite holiday place for ordinary, and not so ordinary, Russians. The region has become even more appealing now that the Crimean and Baltic coasts are in different countries, and the Caucasus resorts are in the shadow of the strife-torn regions of Abkhazia, Ossetia and Ingushetia.

Centered around a town of the same name, a bustling little district center on the Moscow-St. Petersburg road, the Valdai Uplands are the beginning of a range of hills extending southwards through the Smolensk and Tver regions, all the way to Kharkov in Ukraine. Lakes Valdai and Uzhin (no connection with the Russian word for "supper") are dotted with sanatoria and health resorts.

But there is one *dom otdykha* (holiday resort) that's a cut above the rest. "Valdai," snuggled in a remote but stunning corner of Lake Uzhin, was once the site of a dacha built for Stalin, though no one seems to know for sure whether he ever used it. Now top government officials relax there in idyllic surroundings.

Arriving from land, nothing initially betrays the exclusive nature of the place. The crumbling neoclassical facade of the administrative block could mark any lowly Trade Union sanatorium in the country. Only the imposing iron gates of the compound suggest something else.

Once you've talked your way through the main gates, or slipped in undetected through the back door of the administrative block, a short walk through beautifully tended pine groves brings you to the resort itself, a six-year-old complex bizarrely reminiscent of bland postwar British red-brick universities. In fact, it is a 320-place luxury hotel which has hosted prime minister Yegor Gaidar and possibly Boris Yeltsin, as well as foreign diplomats and businessmen.

The facilities are almost inconceivable for provincial Russia, including a coffee bar with luxurious sofas, a cafeteria with a respectable choice of food including vegetables grown organically on site, lakeside

Continued on page 374

century, but there are occasional fragments of 12th century work, such as the famous Constantine and Elena. The presence of the first Christian Roman Emperor here is not accidental – Novgorod's Cathedral was built at a time when Christianity was first establishing itself in Russia. A few of the icons in the iconastasis, such as the Church Feasts, painted by Greek and Serbian artists, date back to the 14th century. Note also its great **Magdeburg Gates,** made in Germany in the 11th century and decorated with biblical scenes in bronze relief. They were carried away as booty from the Varangian fortress of Sigtuna in 1117 by Novgorodian warriors.

The cathedral belfry is perhaps the most eyecatching structure in the Kremlin. Its six rectangular pillars separating the bell chambers, erected after the original structure in the 16th century, give it a powerful, burly appearance.

The Kremlin has two **museums**. The main part is in the three-story former Administrative Chambers on the opposite side from St. Sophia. Passable archaeology (including some of the birch-bark letters discovered in the 1950's) and 18th–19th century painting sections are complemented by an excellent icon collection, which is surpassed only by those of the Russian Museum and Tretyakov gallery. Look particularly for the 11th century SS. Peter and Paul icon, painted for St. Sophia's Cathedral. Its color harmony is astonishing for its age, though

Continued from page 373

cottages and three-room suites, skiing, windsurfing, and a full sports complex. Prices are "negotiable," i.e. steeper for foreigners, but relatively affordable at the time of my visit.

Returning to the town of Valdai, note the cupolas in the distance across Lake Valdai from the waterfront. They belong to the **Iversky Monastery**, founded in the 17th century by the church reformist Patriarch Nikon. A huge building project

Pontoon bridge to Iversky Monastery

was undertaken here, and a fortress built, enclosing the enormous five-dome **Assumption Cathedral**. The monastery became a major landowner, and the life of Valdai, then just a village, became centered around it. I was told more than once about underground passages beneath the lake linking monastery and village.

Nowadays, unfortunately, access is not so easy. Until recently, two steamers made the short journey across the lake. Both, however, have been sold off, and one now stands high, dry and derelict on the shore. The land route is much longer, and the last three miles, which includes the crossing of a rickety pontoon bridge, will have to be done on foot; the monastery is actually on an island. But the walk can be a pleasant one.

Just before reaching the monastery, a marvelous view of it opens up over the water on the right hand side. Further on to the left is a clearing in the trees with a campfire and several seats carved out of logs. This is a memorial to Todd Erik Francis, a young American who died during a visit in 1990.

The town itself has one interesting landmark. Perched above the main road is **Catherine's Church**, a tiny round building in classical style built by the architect Lvov for the eponymous empress in 1793. Although she raised money for the project partly through local taxes, Catherine refused the townspeople entry, reserving it for her own private worship.

The church now houses a museum incorporating an exhibition of bells from the famous 19th century factory run by the Usachov brothers. There is a legend that the Novgorod *veche* bell, symbol of the city's independence, was lost in Valdai on the way to Moscow. Falling from a cart, it smashed into dozens of tiny bells. Thus, it is told, Valdai's bell-making tradition began.

the Russianness of the saints' faces betrays their later addition (in the 14th century) to the Byzantine bodies. The processional icon of Our Lady of the Sign, from the 12th century, is no less significant. It was believed to have delivered the city from its Suzdalian invaders.

The **Palace of Facets**, behind the Cathedral, houses Novgorod's modest version of Moscow's Kremlin Armory, accessible only by guided tour (once a day, early afternoon for individual visitors). Treasures of this exhibition of Russian decorative and applied art from the 11th to the early 20th centuries include the Great Zion, an elaborate gilded chalice with apostles on its doors and a deesis (saints portrayed in relief) on the cupola, and a unique panagiarion (repository for ceremonial medallions) made in 1435.

Millenium Monument

No visitor to the Kremlin can fail to notice the **Millenium of Russia Memorial**, sculpted in bronze by Mikhail Mikeshin in 1862. It is crowned by Russia herself, a woman kneeling before the cross. Below the sphere on which she stands are Russia's greatest leaders – Rurik, Vladimir, Dmitry Donskoy, Mikhail Romanov, Ivan III and Peter the Great in dramatic poses. The base of the monument is ringed with writers, artists, generals, and statesmen engaged in thought and discussion.

Yaroslav's Court

Crossing the Volkhov River by a footbridge from the Kremlin, you will see to your right on the opposite side a row of columns. These are the remains of the city's market stalls, and the beginning of Yaroslav's Court, the seat of power of Novgorod's princes, and later the meeting place of the *veche*. The only surviving building of the court is the **St. Nicholas Cathedral**, built in 1113. Unfortunately, the building is heavily obscured by scaffolding while its 12th century frescoes undergo long-term restoration.

The cluster of nearby churches, all completely rebuilt since the war, have something of the air of a theme park about them. Most are empty, none have been used for worship since their reconstruction and one even contains a souvenir shop. Most interesting is the brick **Church of St. Parasceve Piatnitsa** (originally dating from 1207), which has three side chapels, an absurdly small cupola and walls that taper peculiarly to the ground. Crossing through the park and continuing down Ulitsa Pervovo Maya (Ilyina ulitsa), you come to the **Church of the Transfiguration**, one of Novgorod's most colorful and treasured monuments. Note the four-gabled roof and the delicate harmony of its rich exterior carvings and tiny windows. The church was built in 1374, and just four years later, the fresco-painter Theophanes the Greek was commissioned to work here. Today it is the only survivor of the 40 churches he painted. Though what remains of his work is fragmentary, it is nevertheless enough to give an idea of his sketchy, impressionistic style.

Transfiguration Church

Just across the road, the **Church of our Lady of the Sign,** a massive five-domed Moscow-style cathedral, contains a striking array of 18th century frescoes by Kostroma masters, now beautifully and thoroughly restored.

Turn north from here towards Prospekt Gagarina and you will come to the **Church of St. Theodore Stratilates on the Stream.** Though built a decade earlier and more restrained in appearance, its influence on the design of the Transfiguration Church is immediately apparent.

Churches by the River

Continue north through the market side as far as the earth rampart and turn left down toward the river. Two churches at the bottom, on either side of the stream, are worth taking a look at. The **Church of St. John the Divine** is a miniature version of the two just mentioned and was once envied for its attractive location. Nowadays, it's surrounded by a very shabby marina, really little more than a rubbish dump. On the left, opposite, the **Church of SS. Boris and Gleb at Plotniki** has fared rather better. A tasteful and picturesque cathedral-type church built in the 16th century, it stands at the end of a pleasant promenade.

Take a right past St. John's and follow the riverbank, picking your way through the brave locals bathing amidst the twisted metal debris, then past the Beresta Palace Hotel. Further upstream is the **St. Antony's Monastery**. The **Cathedral of the Nativity of Our Lady** was built in 1119, but you wouldn't think so to look at it – 17th and 19th century alterations have transformed it within and without. Twelfth century frescoes remain in the altar area, but were mostly obscured by scaffolding when I visited. In their haste to open a museum here, the restorers, it seems, failed to realize that almost nothing was visible.

The Nerev End

On the opposite side of the river from St. Antony's, behind the Intourist Hotel on Ulitsa Bredova, is perhaps the most beautiful of Novgorod's fresco museums. Passing another post-Mongolian masterpiece, the **Church of SS. Peter and Paul in Kozhevniki** (the leather-tanners' district), continue to the **Zverin Monastery,** built on the site of the *zverinets*, or prince's hunting grounds. Inside, the **Church of St. Simeon the God-Receiver** was built in 1467 in memory of victims of the plague. Entering the church, you find yourself in the middle of a silent spiritual assembly where every piece of wall space is used, and every saint in Christendom portrayed.

Myachino and Vitoslavlitsy

Downriver on the Kremlin side, toward the Volkhov delta and Lake Ilmen, lies the smaller Myachino Lake, and on its shore **Vitoslavlitsy**,

Peter, Novgorod's earliest known builder. As with other Novgorod churches of this era, its roofline originally followed the contours of the vaulting, evidenced on the exterior by the arches of each bay. Though reconsecrated, the monastery is as yet without monks.

In contrast with this monumental splendor is the **Church of the Nativity of our Lady at Peryn**, a modest chapel hidden in a glade downstream. This is Novgorod's last pre-Mongolian church, built in a former pagan sanctuary dedicated to the God Perun. It is just one of Novgorod's many isolated churches that blend in with nature, a little known side of the city's character.

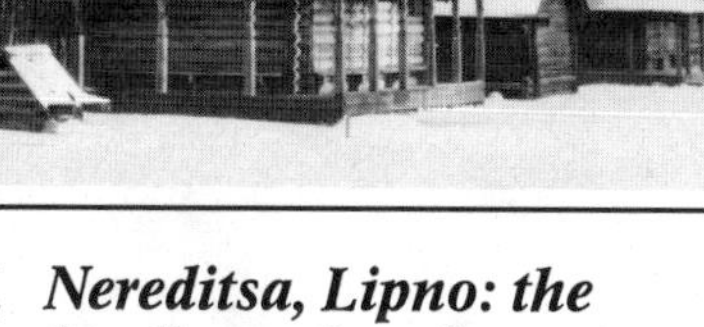

Vitoslavlitsy Museum of Wooden Architecture.* Above: *Chapel from village of Kashira.* Right: *17th century* izba *from village of Pyshevo.

Novgorod's museum of wooden architecture. Comprising churches, mills, cottages and an indoor folk art museum, it testifies to the high standard of building and craftsmanship of Novgorodians from the 16th century onwards. Note particularly the hip-roofed **Assumption Church from Kuritsko**, the museum's first exhibit, standing in splendid isolation by the lake, or the **Church of St. Nicholas from Tukholya**, with its unusual elongated base, seemingly stretched upwards.

Straight down the road to the river, a huge layered bell-tower built in the 1830's by Carlo Rossi marks out the **Yuryev Monastery**, Novgorod's oldest. St. George's Cathedral is a triumph of 12th century architecture by Master

Nereditsa, Lipno: the far-flung churches

Unless you make a special effort, you're unlikely to see these places except from a great distance. At one time there was a steamer service to the **Rurik Fortress**, near the first of these, but now the only options for reaching it are taxi or private motorboat. In Nereditsa, you can see the remains of the **Annunciation Church**, the original building of which dates from 1103, Novgorod's second stone structure after St. Sophia. It was once the home of the famous *Mstislav Lectionary*, now kept in the State Historical

Museum in Moscow. The current church, badly damaged in World War II, is 14th century. Inland on **Nereditsa Hill** is the **Transfiguration Church**, powerful, austere and noble. The church was totally destroyed, then rebuilt after the war. In a remarkable restorative feat, its fresco is being recreated from tiny fragments.

Finally, for the most romantic and wildest of all Novgorod's churches. **St. Nicholas on Lipna Isle** is so completely on its own that it seems unchanged since the 13th century. Access is by boat only, and there may be problems going ashore: the monument is jealously guarded by a *babushka*, so be tactful but persuasive.

STARAYA RUSSA

Best known as the summer home of writer Fyodor Dostoyevsky, this town on the southern side of Lake Ilmen was once an important spa and, even earlier, a salt-producing center. Its oldest building is the **Transfiguration Cathedral** (1198), now a museum containing 12th century frescoes. In the adjoining halls, an exhibition tells the story of the local theater, made up of famous St. Petersburg actors who came to perform for celebrities taking cures at the baths.

The **Resort** itself is a down-at-heels shadow of its former self. As you stroll around the broken fountain and rusty benches, it's difficult to imagine that theater director Konstantin Stanislavsky and writer Maxim Gorky once took the waters here. Even the salt springs seem tasteless and lifeless.

Dostoyevsky House Museum

The riverside **Dostoyevsky House Museum**, however, has lost none of its charm. The little green house will not take up much of your day – the museum has just four upstairs rooms but the austere furnishings, softened by the luscious browns and greens of the fabrics, make for minutes, if not hours of contemplation. If you're interested in information, though, you'll need a guided tour, as there is nothing written in the whole museum. This is where Dostoyevsky wrote much of *The Brothers Karamazov*. In fact, the fictitious town of Skotoprigonyevsk, where the murder of old man Karamazov took place, is modelled on Staraya Russa. A map in the museum marks places mentioned in the novel. Just up the road is the little **St. George's** church, where Dostoyevsky attended services.

PRACTICAL MATTERS

There is quite a decent range of accommodation in Novgorod. At the top is the year-old **Beresta Palace Hotel** (address: Rayon 3, "Third District"), one of the Austrian Marco Polo chain and the only foreign-owned hotel outside of Moscow and St. Petersburg. For $136 (for a single room) you'll be pleased to know the luxury accommodation is supplemented by a cosmetic institute, dental clinic, swimming pool, sauna, massage parlor, solarium, night club, pub and a conference hall seating 160. For lesser mortals, its coffee bar allows a welcome break from sightseeing in the north part of the market quarter.

If you're prepared to pay dollars, but not that many, the **Hotel Intourist** on the opposite side of the river (Dmitriyevskaya ulitsa, 16) charges $40 a night and has decent facilities. Ruble alternatives are the **Sadko** (Prospekt Gagarina, 16) or the **Rossiya** (Naberezhnaya Alexandra Nevskogo, 19/1), both typical modern Soviet monstrosities, also the older and more stately **Volkhov** (Ulitsa Nekrasova, 24). Next door to the Volkhov, the horribly named **Azot**, despite being the hotel of the Mineral Fertilizer Ministry, is actually a decent fall-back option.

Obvious choices for meals are again the Beresta Palace and Intourist, also the **Detinets** inside the city kremlin, which serves decent hotpots, and mead superior to Suzdal's. The last two are generally clogged with tour groups in summer, so book or arrive early.

A number of night bars also serve food at unsocial hours, in addition to having an occasionally lively atmosphere. Try the casino bar in the **Rossiya** cinema or **Singapur** (no obvious relation to its Asian namesake) at the north end of Ulitsa Chernyakhovskogo. The latter has a rather repetitive disco which nonetheless delights the local youth. Another casino, the **Feniks** on the sixth floor of the Drama Theater (next door to the Intourist), has a restaurant and bar but is expensive, empty, and atmospherically dead.

SS. Boris and Gleb at Plotniki

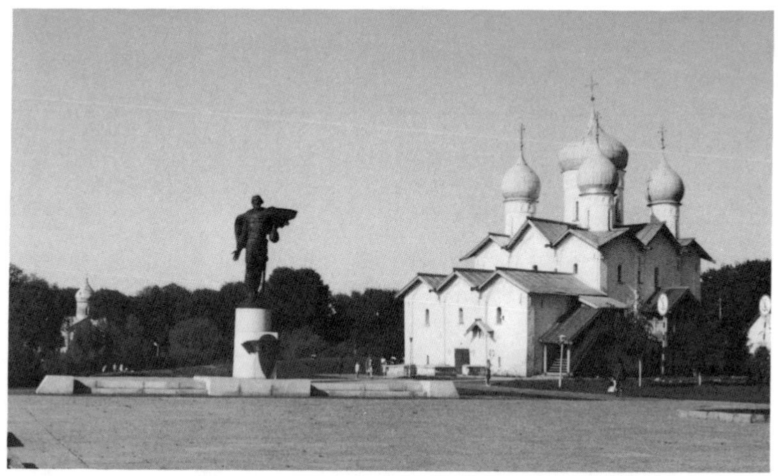

DIRECTIONS

Novgorod: by daily train from Moscow (9 hours) and St. Petersburg (4 hours). The latter also now has a fast luxury Sunday service taking a little over 2 hours. By car Novgorod is just off the Moscow–St. Petersburg road. **Vitoslavlitsy**, the **Yuryev Monastery** and **Peryn** are reached from the city by #7 bus.

Valdai: served by Moscow-Pskov trains. From Novgorod the bus journey is about 2½ hours. For the **Dom otdykha**, take the Roshchino bus from the center. By car, Valdai is on the Moscow-St. Petersburg road, slightly closer to the latter. For the **Iversky Monastery**, turn right toward Borovichi just before the town (if coming from Moscow), then left after 450 meters. For the **Dom otdykha**, turn right after the town and continue going right round the lakes.

Staraya Russa: served by Moscow-Pskov trains. From Novgorod the bus journey is two hours. By car from Moscow, take a left at Yazhelbitsy, just after Valdai and continue for about 95 km through Demiansk. From Novgorod, leave by the A116 Pskov road and turn left at Shimsk.

RUSSIAN GLOSSARY

Azot
Азот
Borovichi
Боровичи
Demiansk
Демьянск
Detinets
Детинец
Dom otdykha
Дом отдыха
Iversky Monastery
Иверский монастырь
Novgorod
Новгород
Novgorodskaya oblast
Новгородская область
Peryn
Перун
Rayon 3
Район 3
Roshchino
Рощино
Shimsk
Шимск
Singapur
Сингапур
Staraya Russa
Старая Русса
Valdai
Валдай
Yazhelbitsy
Яжелбицы

VOLOGDA REGION

VOLOGODSKAYA OBLAST

A vast northern region stretching from Lake Onega halfway to the Urals, Vologda marks a transition from the tamer, more populated country of central Russia to the wild taiga forest of the north. Peasant life here is simple, yet its products surprisingly sophisticated – lace patterned dresses, woven birch bark and a uniquely flavorful butter. Vologda is also a place of spiritual pursuits; numerous monasteries command its rivers and lakes.

VOLOGDA

It's easy enough to explain the recent rush of tourists to this northern city. Few places can claim so much living history and have remained little known to foreigners for so long.

Relatively undisturbed by the political and military upheavals of the center, Vologda has led its quiet provincial life for hundreds of years. History began here in the 12th century, when Novgorod colonized the area during campaigns against the Finns. But the latter's influence was never as great as elsewhere: first Rostov and later Moscow had a stronger presence. Vologda proved a powerful ally of Muscovy against Novgorod prior to Russia's unification.

This reputation as Moscow's favorite was enhanced in the 16th century. Arriving for one of his exhaustive bouts of boyar-bashing, Ivan the Terrible took an immediate fancy to the city and came to live there for several years. Legends concerning his desire to move the capital to Vologda seem far-fetched, but his influence is undoubted.

In 1568 he began building the city's most distinctive structure, **St. Sophia's Cathedral**. Inspired by the Moscow Kremlin's Assumption Cathedral, there is nothing unique about its architecture, but even during construction it made a lasting impression on locals and visitors alike. This huge church took just two summers to build: no doubt Ivan had local craftsmen working literally to save their lives.

But things did not end well for St. Sophia's. Legend has it that when the Tsar entered the building for the first time, a brick fell on his head, and he stormed back to Moscow in a rage. For whatever reason, he left Vologda in a hurry and never returned. The finishing touches were added only after his death, years later.

St. Sophia's was a scene of tragedy

during the Lithuanian invasion of 1612. Vologda's only stone building, the cathedral became a refuge as the enemy burned the city to the ground. Unfortunately the domes were wooden, and those inside were suffocated.

Somehow Vologda survived this calamity, and has remained peripheral to conflict ever since. Steeped in tradition, it is a microcosm of provincial life, neither a bustling cosmopolitan center nor a backward town.

The former Kremlin, now mostly occupied by the walled **Archbishop's Palace**, is the obvious place to begin exploring Vologda. St. Sophia's Cathedral now stands outside the walls. Try to get a view from the bell-tower, and to persuade the reluctant museum attendants to let you see the frescoes inside, painted by the Yaroslavl master Dmitry Plekhanov in the 16th century.

If you venture into the Palace grounds, head for the local crafts exhibition rather than the dull main museum. There you will be able to see the sophisticated cottage industries native to the region. *Beresta*, or birch bark, famous in Novgorod as the forerunner of writing paper, is woven into shoes, boxes and many other items.

But the pride of Vologda is its lace scarves, dresses and even summer coats, and every self-respecting local woman learns how to work with lace. Brides would prepare lace marriage garments, sometimes working steadily for up to two years. Patterns are numerous, and each has its own name, such as "frost," "birch tree," or "cake."

Leaving the Palace, take a walk to the left along the riverside. Except for the receding rumble of traffic on the bridges, Vologda seems a sleepy backwater here. Bearing right with the river brings you to the oldest and quietest part of town. A granite monument marks its founding.

Turn back down Ulitsa Burmaginykh and continue inland after crossing Ulitsa Mayakovskovo to see one of the city's most striking and picturesque churches. The Church of St. Varlaam of Khutyn, one of two churches that form the remains of the Monastery of St. Elijah, was built in 1780 in classical style by a merchant with St. Petersburg connections and tastes. Its very attractive rotunda with ionic columns and dome appears pressed from the sides into an oval.

Following the river in the opposite direction from St. Sophia's and the Kremlin, passing three bridges and a slow bend of the river on the way, will bring you to another curiosity, a little square building known now as the "Cottage of Peter the Great." In fact, the Tsar only stopped off here for the night on journeys north, its owner being his Dutch friend Ivan Gutman, one of many foreign merchants to settle here in the 18th century. It is

Entrance to Monastery of Our Savior at Priluki

The Wooden Houses of Vologda

In a country where wooden buildings are about as common as the forests that supply them with timber, their ubiquity in Vologda is hardly a surprise. But if elsewhere you find the occasional interesting building worth remark, rest assured that in Vologda you won't know where to look first.

Vologda's wooden houses are veritable mansions and stately homes, splendid architectural combinations that seem almost unreal. While the city's stone architecture is derivative and provincial, its wood builders were masterful.

When Peter the Great began designing "model plans" for stone dwellings, Vologda architects responded with wooden versions. Today, the earliest one to survive dates from the end of the 18th century. The **Zasetsky House** (Ul. Leningradskaya, 25) is a rather modest town residence for a rich nobleman, with mezzanine and balcony supported by four simple columns.

Zasetsky's house is only an appetizer, however, for what Vologda has in store. A few decades later, Greek and Roman styles would inundate the town, as with the **Volkov House** (Leningradskaya, 28), fronted by a massive six-column Tuscan portico that is made entirely of wood. Unlike in Moscow, outer decorations

Continued on page 387

#37 Ulitsa Gertsena, a wooden architectural monument in Russian classical style (1829)

now a rather uninspiring museum with exhibits mostly borrowed from St. Petersburg.

A short bus ride to the northern edge of town brings you to the **Monastery of our Savior at Priluki**, a contemporary of St. Sophia's. It was founded in the 14th century by a certain Dmitry, a pupil of St. Sergius of Radonezh, who later became a powerful landowner and guardian of Muscovy's northern borders. When disaster struck Moscow in 1812, all the treasures of the Kremlin and Sergiyev Posad were brought here for safekeeping.

Now functioning again, it is in the throes of new construction, and, like many other monasteries, its courtyard oozes with mud. The poet Konstantin Batyushkov, a contemporary of Pushkin, is buried there.

Unfortunately the attention being given to the monastery by the Orthodox Church is not shared by the local village church just outside, which is pretty but derelict and waterlogged beneath a collapsed roof.

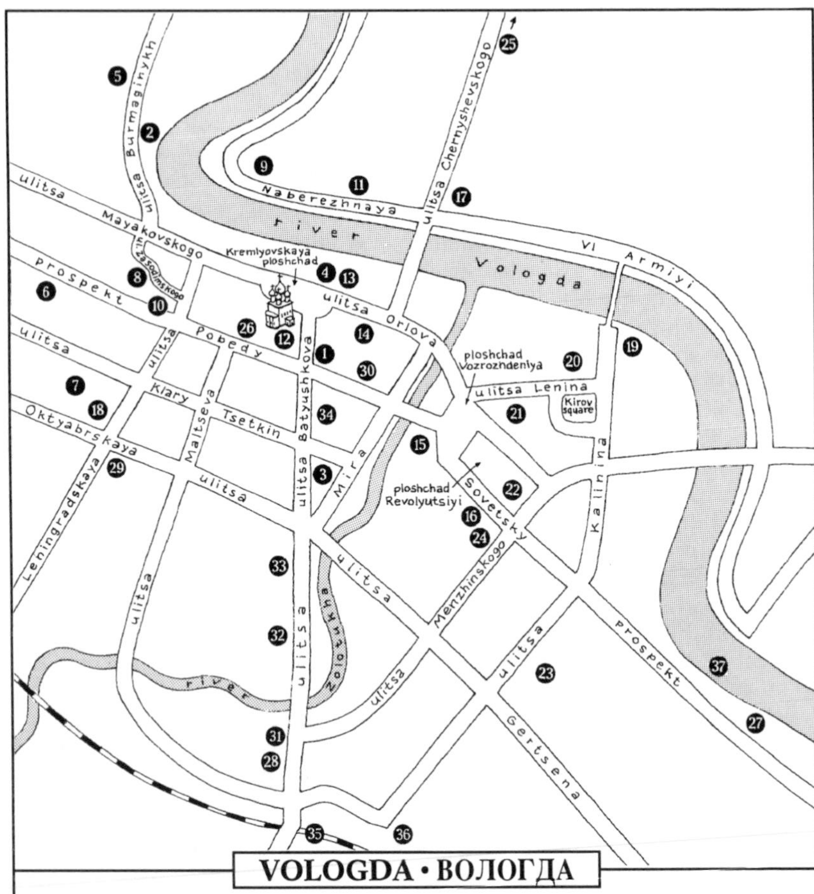

VOLOGDA • ВОЛОГДА

Ulitsa Batyushkova
Улица Батюшкова
Ulitsa Burmaginykh
Улица Бурмагиных
Ulitsa Chernyshevskovo
Улица Чернышевского
Ulitsa Gertsena
Улица Герцена
Ulitsa Kalinina
Улица Калинина
Ploshchad Kirova
Площадь Кирова
Ulitsa Klary Tsetkin
Улица Клары Цеткин
Kremlyovskaya ploshchad
Кремлёвская площадь
Ulitsa Lenina
Улица Ленина
Leningradskaya ulitsa
Ленинградская улица
Ulitsa Maltseva
Улица Мальцева
Ulitsa Mayakovskovo
Улица Маяковского
Ulitsa Menzhinskovo
Улица Менжинского
Ulitsa Mira
Улица Мира
Oktyabrskaya ulitsa
Октябрьская улица
Ulitsa Orlova
Улица Орлова

Prospekt Pobedy
Проспект Победы
Ploshchad Revolyutsiyi
Площадь Революции
Naberezhnaya Shestoy Armiyi
Набережная Шестой армии
Sovyetsky prospekt
Советский проспект
River Vologda
Река Вологда
Ploshchad Vozrozhdeniya
Площадь Возрождения
Ulitsa Zasodimskovo
Улица Засодимского
River Zolotukha
Река Золотуха

MAP KEY

1. **Excursion Bureau**
Экскурсионное бюро
2. **Monument to Founding of Vologda**
Монумент 800-летия Вологды
3. **Ilyushin Monument**
Памятник Ильюшину
4. **Batyushkov Monument**
Памятник Батюшкову
5. **Assumption Monastery**
Успенский монастырь
6. **SS. Constantine and Elena Church**
Церковь Константина и Елены
7. **Churches of St. Vladimir**
Владимирские церкви
8. **Church of St. Varlaam of Khutyn**
Церковь Варлаама Хутынского
9. **Church of the Purification of the Virgin**
Церковь Сретенья
10. **Zasetsky House**
Дом Засецкого
11. **Church of St. John Chrysostom**
Церковь Иоанна Златоуста
12. **Archbishop's Palace**
Архиерейское подворье
13. **Alexander Nevsky Church**
Церковь Александра Невского
14. **Intercession Church "na torgu"**
Покровская церковь «на Торгу»
15. **Former Hermitage Hotel**
Бывшая гостиница «Эрмитаж»
16. **Former City Duma**
Бывшая Городская Дума
17. **Church of St. Demetrius of Priluki**
Церковь Дмитрия Прилуцкого
18. **Volkhov House**
Дом Волкова
19. **Wooden House**
20. **Former Governor's House**
Бывший Губернаторский дом
21. **Nobles' Assembly**
Дворянское Собрание
22. **Church of St. John the Baptist**
Церковь Иоанна Предтечи
23. **Intercession Church "na Kozlyonye"**
Покровская церковь «на Козлене»
24. **Former Ulyanov House Museum**
Бывший Дом-музей Ульяновых
25. **Monastery of Our Savior in Priluki**
Спасо-Прилуцкий монастырь
26. **History Museum**
27. **Peter the Great Museum**
Домик Петра Первого
28. **Vologda Hotel**
Гостиница Вологда
29. **Oktyabrskaya Hotel**
Гостиница «Октябрьская»
30. **Sever Restaurant**
Ресторан «Север»
31. **Pizzeria**
Пиццерия

32. **Vologda Souvenirs**
Вологодские сувениры
33. **Bookshop**
Книжный магазин
34. **Market**
Рынок
35. **Train Station**
Железнодорожный вокзал
36. **Bus Station**
Автобусный вокзал
37. **River Station**
Речной вокзал

KIRILLOV

North of Vologda on Lake Siverskoye, this small town is dominated by the **Monastery of St. Cyril of Beloozersk**, once one of Russia's largest. It was founded by a monk of the same name in 1397, acting under instruction from the Virgin Mary, who had appeared to him in a vision. From its modest beginnings – the hermit's hovel of Kirill and a small church, now preserved in a corner of the main monastery – it acquired a reputation for power and invincibility; only Lithuanian sacking prompted its masters to construct today's thick stone walls.

Of the buildings still extant, most date from the 17th century, the monastery's zenith. Disgraced princes and boyars were exiled there, along with Patriarch Nikon, who spent the last five years of his life within its walls. All provided it with lavish gifts, and Nikon seems to have turned to carpentry, having made an armchair here. Most are contained in the museum (in the Church of the Presentation of the Virgin), along with a fine collection of icons from the surrounding area.

Just outside Kirillov is a monastery of a different kind in the village of **Ferapontovo**. Founded in 1399 by a Muscovite monk, this tiny sanctuary was graced by the Cathedral of the Nativity of the Virgin almost 100 years later, the first stone building in the Russian north. Sated with life in the capital, the famous fresco-painter Dionysius came here to paint the church, and stayed until his death.

Almost all the interior surfaces are his work, and are the best-preserved examples anywhere. While his color schemes and content are starkly simple, his gestures are highly expressive. Note the copies of four pictures of the Virgin Mary in the museum, her expressions and postures changing gradually from disbelief to acceptance of the Immaculate Conception.

The cathedral is not closed to visitors, as seems to be the case; the museum attendants simply assume that no one can afford the admission fee – so be persistent!

N.B. On the way to Kirillov you'll pass the village of **Molochnoye**, an important dairy center. This is where Vologda butter, the area's most famous food product, is made. Churned to a secret recipe which somehow involves the addition of nuts, this is a product you'll have difficulty finding in the shops, so a pilgrimage here might be in order.

USTYUG THE GREAT

At the eastern edge of the region, as far from Vologda as Moscow is, this picturesque little town may be the most remote place mentioned in this guidebook. But that's no reason to leave it off the itinerary.

Founded in the beginning of the 13th century, Ustyug was to become the northern gateway to Siberia. With the opening up of trade routes in the 16th century, it was a key transit point, earning itself the title *Veliky*, the Great, which it shares with only Novgorod and Rostov.

As well as trading in Siberian fur and Rostov *finift*, Ustyug had its own smiths, potters, icon-painters, and other craftspeople who became known throughout the country. The city prospered even through the Petrine era, when the opening of the Baltic precipitated a permanent decline in other northern towns. Only when bypassed by the railway did it begin to recede.

However, prosperity endured long enough for Ustyug to build a host of glittering churches and monasteries, most of which remain, dominating the town's gently rolling hills and the peaceful River Sukhona.

The best way to arrive in Ustyug is by boat. From whichever direction you come the tiny cupolas, five to a

Cathedral Courtyard bell-tower. Ustyug the Great.

continued from page 383

are wooden as well; Vologda's trademark.

By the 1840's, Vologda's aristocracy was on the wane and its merchants on the rise. The **Sokovnikov House** (Sovyetsky prospekt, 20) seems like a noble's residence; two pairs of columns frame its main first floor window; with a balcony below and portico above. Yet it is closer to the people; details like carved railings and chimney are in a local folk, not classical style.

By mid-century, architects in Vologda had reached their creative peak, replacing the imitation of stone-building with their own unique style. They built mainly two-storey houses, whose balconies, instead of jutting out in front, are recessed in a side corner over the main doorway; both balcony and entrance are set back from the main façade. The town's skilled woodcarvers went to work here, creating intricate archways, columns and railings; see the houses at Klary Tsetkin, 20 or Naberezhnaya Kedrova,18. While on the former street, in a favorite locale for building in the latter part of the century, note the square at the crossroads with Ulitsa Maltseva, its historic houses diagonal to the roads.

Unfortunately it is not easy to explore the interiors of Vologda's houses. Only one is open, the former place of exile for Lenin's mother and sister, at Sovyetsky prospekt, 26A. Now deideologized, it provides a glimpse into life in a late 19th century rented flat.

church atop slender drums, and supported by compact, cuboid bodies serve as a landmark. Common in late 17th century Russia, these cupolas dominate the town's every corner.

Ustyug's focus is **Cathedral Courtyard**, a bristling ensemble right on the riverbank, gleaming under a recent gloss of paint. In contrast, just inland is the Monastery of the Archangel Michael, quietly magnificent, built with the same kind of intricate mastery employed in Rostov's Kremlin.

Parish churches are absurdly numerous. Almost every local merchant must have had one of his own. The most stunning of these is the **Ascension Church**, near the River Station. It has a very festive decor, reminiscent of Moscow churches like the Trinity in Nikitniki. As the oldest surviving stone building in the town, it was supposed to set the style for future constructions. But local craftsmen kept their churches plain and the Ascension church was left in splendid isolation.

Ascension Church, Ustyug

Ustyug's museum is in the attractive Usov mansion by the river, sporting exhibits of metal engraving (on silver covered by a black alloy), and of Shemogodsk carvings – boxes, whose lid is a thin layer of carved *beresta* superimposed on a colored background.

Ustyug's carving traditions are also reflected in its iconostases. A ten minute boat-ride out of town takes you to the Monastery of the Trinity at Gleden, which has a five-row iconostasis so magnificent it outshines the very icons within it. Note particularly the carved figures of the apostles on the Tsar's Gates.

PRACTICAL MATTERS

The hotels of Vologda are average. Both the cheap **Oktyabrskaya** (Ulitsa Oktyabrskaya, 25) and the even cheaper **Hotel Vologda** (Ulitsa Mira, 92) are bearable. No restaurants here really excel, though the Oktyabrskaya is the best, and the noisy **Sever** in the center runs a not-so-close second. The Vologda restaurant, in the hotel, seems to have an older clientele. If you're sick of restaurant food, slip round the back of the Vologda to the little pizzeria in the neighboring block.

DIRECTIONS

Vologda: 8 hours by train from Moscow's Yaroslavsky Voksal, or by car 500 km straight up the M8.

Kirillov: 2 hours by bus from Vologda (**Ferapontovo** is another, local bus ride away). By car leave

Vologda to the north west on the Vytegra road; both monasteries are signposted off it, about 120 km away. The Vologda tourist office also organizes river trips.

Ustyug the Great: from the Yaroslavsky Voksal by Kotlas- or Vorkuta-bound train to Kotlas (journey time about 20 hours), then by boat or local train (another 1½ hours). River boats run from Vologda during springtime high water. By car (good luck to you on this one!) take the M8 to Chekshino north of Vologda and turn left to Totma. After Totma, things start to get difficult, since there are two roads: one direct but inferior that follows the Sukhona river valley; the other taking a detour south via Nikolsk. Both have non-asphalted sections — in the case of the first, half the length of the road. From Vologda the distance is about 300 km overall.

RUSSIAN GLOSSARY

Monastery of Archangel Michael
Михайло-Архангельский монастырь

Ascension Church
Вознесенская церковь

Cathedral Courtyard
Соборная площадь

Chekshino
Чекшино

Monastery of St. Cyril of Beloozersk
Кирилло-Белозерский монастырь

Ferapontovo
Ферапонтово

Kirillov
Кириллов

Kotlas
Котлас

Molochnoye
Молочное

Cathedral of the Nativity of the Virgin
Собор Рождества Богородицы

Nikolsk
Никольск

Church of the Presentation of the Virgin
Введенская церковь

Lake Siverskoye
Озеро Сиверское

River Sukhona
Река Сухона

Totma
Тотьма

Monastery of the Trinity at Gleden
Троицко-Гледенский монастырь

Ustyug the Great
Великий Устюг

Vytegra
Вытегра

ARCHITECTURAL ELEMENTS: WOODEN CHURCHES
Church of the Presentation, 1684. Osinovo (Arkhangelsk Region)

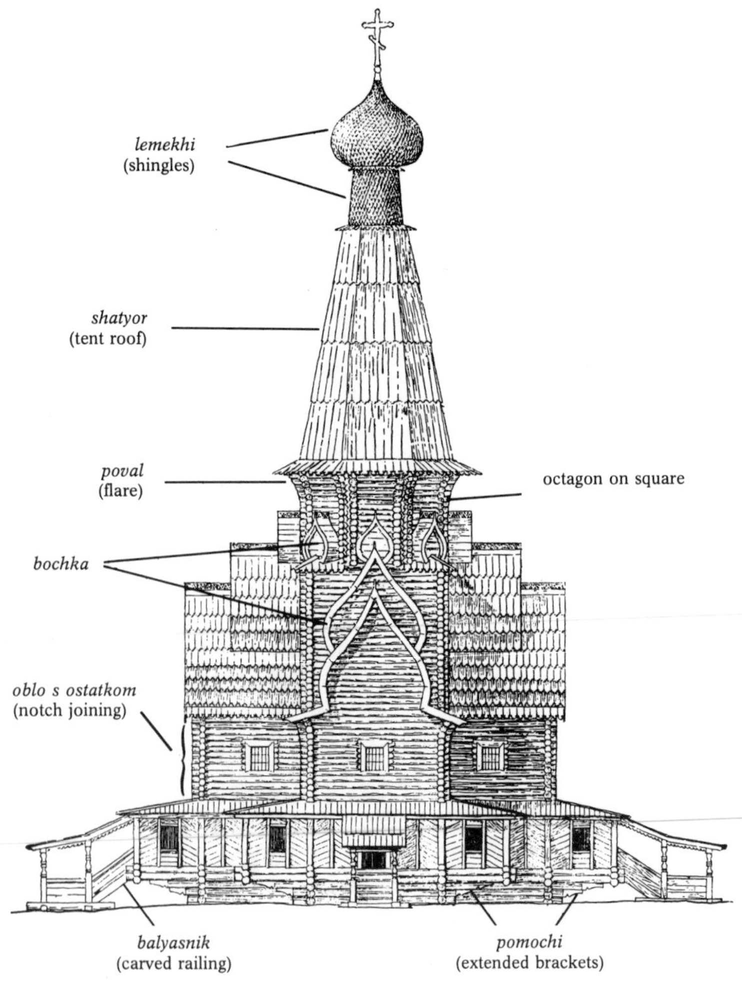

Adapted from *A History of Russian Architecture*
by William C. Brumfield (Cambridge University Press, 1993),
by permission of the author

ARKHANGELSK REGION

ARKHANGELSKAYA OBLAST

This immense area occupying the northwest corner of Russia's main land mass has a surface area considerably larger than France. About half of it is taken up by the island of Novaya Zemlya, notorious for its nuclear testing site, and by an Autonomous Area of the Finno-Ugric Nenets nation. The rest is mainly forested, broken by dramatic river valleys. In the center of the region, the almost inaccessible Pinega Nature Reserve boasts unrivalled formations of gypsum karst and over 60 caves, some with cathedral-like interiors and names borrowed from St. Petersburg churches to fit. In the more settled areas, like the Northern Dvina and Onega valleys, village life goes on as it has for centuries, among the charming wooden dwellings and churches of the *Pomory*.

They have always cherished their freedom from feudalism, from bullying by the center and from outside occupation. But while they roam freely through their lakes and forests, hunting, fishing and mushrooming, they also have a tendency to withdraw into themselves and drown their sorrows in drink. This self-involvement seems even to be reflected in their speech, which is not fully comprehensible to other Russians.

Most popular pastimes involve the gathering of food. Men go out with their *kuzovy*, special metal backpacks, to collect the area's flavorful giant mushrooms, or they fish for salmon. Food is simple but healthy – guests are met with barrels of salmon or roe, *shang'i*, the local bread made with *tvorog* (cottage cheese) or other cheeses, and pies filled with fish, mushrooms or cranberries.

ARKHANGELSK

If you're visiting Solovki, you'll probably have some time to kill in this rather uninspiring modern port. Founded by Ivan the Terrible in 1584 after a British vessel was shipwrecked there, it is notable chiefly as the cradle of the Russian merchant fleet, which Peter the Great launched in 1694. Later, it vied for a while with St. Petersburg for designation as Russia's new capital.

The best way to get a feel for this once stately city is to take a walk along the waterfront west of the sea/river station to the Pur Navolok Cape, site of the city's foundation. Landmarks are

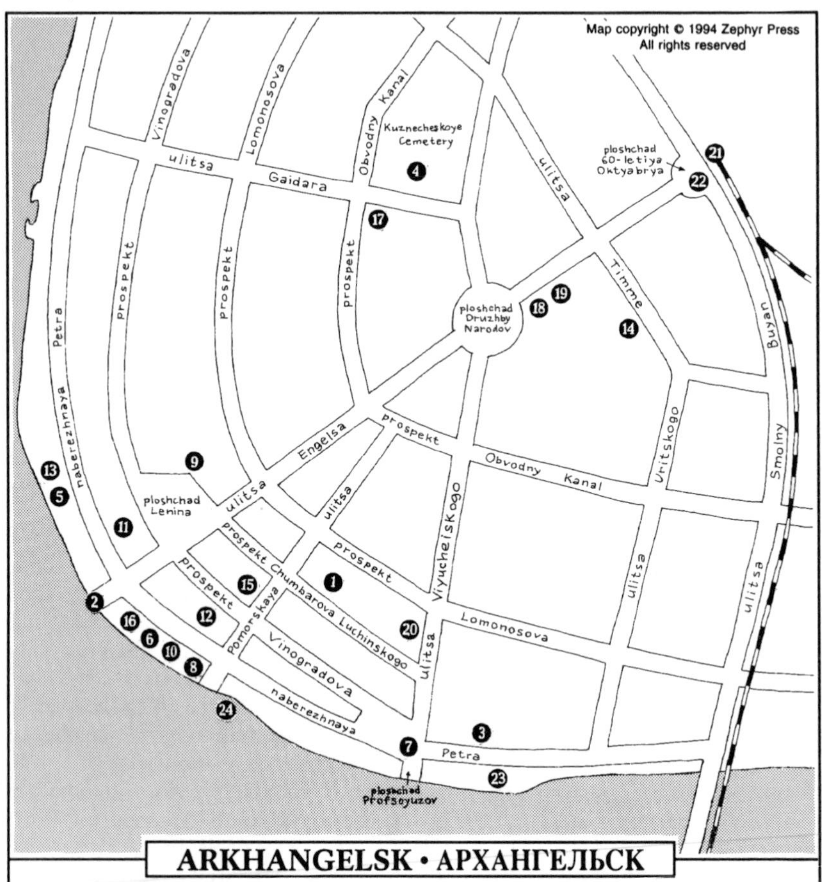

ARKHANGELSK • АРХАНГЕЛЬСК

Prospekt Chumbarovo Luchinskovo
Проспект Чумбарова Лучинского
Ploshchad Druzhby Narodov
Площадь Дружбы Народов
Ulitsa Engelsa
Улица Энгельса
Ulitsa Gaidara
Улица Гайдара
Kuznecheskoye Cemetery
Кузнеческое Кладбище
Ploshchad Lenina
Площадь Ленина
Prospekt Lomonosova
Проспект Ломоносова
Prospekt Obvodny Kanal
Проспект Обводный канал
Naberezhnaya Petra
Набережная Петра
Pomorskaya ulitsa
Поморская улица
Ploshchad Profsoyuzov
Площадь Профсоюзов
Ploshchad Shestidesyatiletiya Oktyabrya
Площадь 60-летия Октября
Ulitsa Smolny Buyan
Улица Смольный Буян
Ulitsa Timme
Улица Тимме

Ulitsa Uritskovo
Улица Урицкого
Prospekt Vinogradova
Проспект Виноградова
Ulitsa Viyucheiskovo
Улица Выучейского

MAP KEY

1. **Regional Council for Tourism**
Областной Совет по Туризму
2. **Peter the Great statue**
Памятник Петру Первому
3. **Mikhail Lomonosov statue**
Памятник Ломоносову
4. **Monument to "Victims of Intervention" (in cemetery)**
Памятник Жертвам Интервенции
5. **Monument to Founding of Arkhangelsk**
Монумент 400-летия основания Архангельска
6. **Monument to "Victims of Intervention" (on waterfront)**
Памятник Жертвам Интервенции
7. **Monument to "Defenders of the North"**
Памятник Защитникам Севера
8. **Museum of Northern Seafaring**
Музей Северного Мореплавания
9. **Art Museum**
Художественный Музей
10. **Schooner "Zapad"**
Шхуна «Запад»
11. **Trade Rows**
Торговые ряды
12. **Solovyetsky Monastery Mission**
Соловецкое подворье
13. **Pur Navolok Hotel**
Гостиница «Пур Наволок»
14. **Hotel Belomorskaya**
Гостиница «Беломорская»
15. **Hotel Dvina**
Гостиница «Двина»
16. **Alyosha restaurant**
Ресторан «Алёша»
17. **Petrovsky restaurant**
Ресторан «Петровский»
18. **Souvenirs**
Сувениры
19. **Art Salon**
Художественный салон
20. **Market**
Рынок
21. **Train Station**
Железнодорожный вокзал
22. **Bus Station**
Автовокзал
23. **Sea-River Station**
Морской-речной вокзал
24. **River Station (for local services)**
Речной вокзал

the crumbling 17th century Gostiny Dvor and a statue of Peter the Great which marks the site of his wooden cottage, now moved to Kolomenskoye Museum Preserve, Moscow.

Venturing inland is likely to leave you lost in the concrete jungle which has all but overpowered the old wooden city; on only one street, Ulitsa Chumbarova-Luchinskovo, is Arkhangelsk's past being preserved and restored.

For an idea of how Arkhangelsk used to look, go to the excellent model of Old Arkhangelsk, built by a local pensioner and housed in the Sailors' House of Culture at Prospekt Lomonosova, 269 – the difference is both dramatic and saddening. Also not to be missed is the well-organized

The Groaning Islands

The mixed emotions roused by the Solovyetsky Islands may be unsettling, but their landscapes are unforgettable. This archipelago in the White Sea offers a stark combination of painful history and natural beauty in a splendidly isolated setting.

The islands even have their own micro climates. Closer in temperature to central Russia than to Arkhangelsk, their weather can change in summer within minutes from gray and chilly to unbearably humid. While several smaller islands are covered by tundra, most are thickly wooded and infested with 30 breeds of mosquitoes, the dominant topic of conversation among visitors who arrive during the biting season.

Founded in the 15th century by hermit monks, the Solovyetsky Monastery became rich and powerful in the 16th when abbot Philip Kolychev built smithies, craft workshops, canals, a brick factory and – most important – the massive stone Kremlin.

This fortress would later become an invincible defender of Russia's northern borders, but its most immediate effect was to cause a headache for reformist Patriarch Nikon, when its monks refused to accept reforms and held out against the Tsar's troops for eight years. They only surrendered after betrayal from within.

The decline of Solovki, as it is nicknamed, was to be reversed dramatically during the Crimean War. When two British frigates tried to induce surrender, their warning shot was answered by the monks (who knew nothing of naval military code) with a lethal salvo which severely crippled one vessel. This

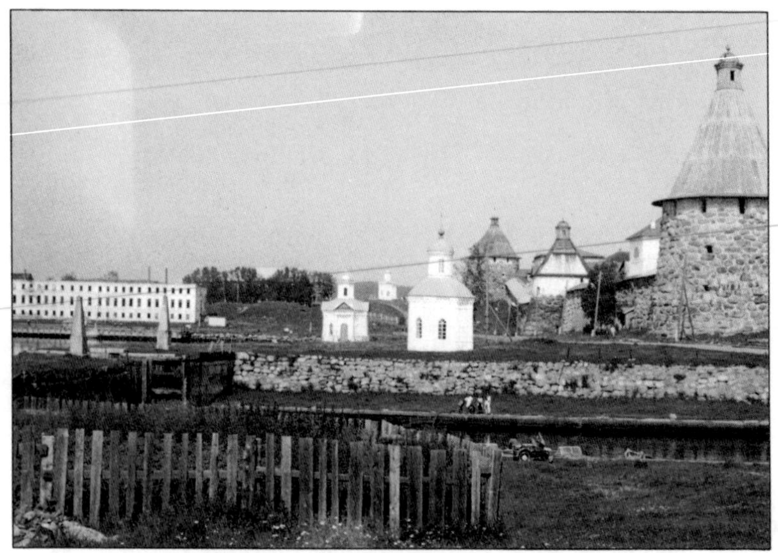

Solovki monastery, chapels, and drydock

plucky defense gained the approbation of Tsar Alexander II, who renewed government support of the monastery.

But the rally did not last long. By 1920, when the Bolsheviks arrived, Solovki had already died a natural death; the monks saw what was coming and departed.

Three years later Lenin established a labor camp there. Though the camp was harsh from the beginning, the 1920's authorities allowed inmates to practice their old vocations. Priests prayed and held services, scientists studied meteorology and natural history, and actors created a theater company that even toured the mainland.

The 1930's buried any liberal tendencies. As *kulak* peasants and old guard Bolsheviks joined their erstwhile victims in the prisoners' ranks, Solovki's status changed in 1936 from camp to prison, acquiring the initials STON – aptly, the Russian word for "groan." Solovki's name became one of those Russian words everyone knew but no one dared to utter.

The prisoners were dispersed in 1939 to other camps, and a naval cadet school replaced them. For the past 25 years Solovki has been a museum reserve, with some property recently returned to the church for monastic purposes. But traces of tragedy remain – every visitor feels the sorrow of these islands.

Arriving by sea you'll moor near the **Kremlin**, the natural starting point for any tour. It hasn't lost any of the brawn that put the wind up the British 140 years ago; its thick stone walls have never needed repair. Inside, though, it lends a contrasting impression; mainly 16th century buildings combine to offer interesting nooks, crannies, and picturesque courtyards. Though greatly altered over the centuries, the central **Transfiguration Cathedral** reflects the era that produced St. Basil's Cathedral and the Kolomenskoye churches in Moscow. Ivan the Terrible invested 1,000 rubles in its building; in those days you could come by a sturdy milk cow for 2 kopecks.

Transfiguration Cathedral

During the prison camp years, the cathedral became the reception area for new arrivals. Many died in its cramped and chilly recesses. Their fellow prisoners would hide their deaths for days, hoping thereby to receive extra rations.

Nearby is the **Trapezium Chamber**, the second largest building of its kind in Russia after Moscow Kremlin's Palace of the Facets. This solid white structure, however, was built by Russians, not Italians.

Not far from the Church-over-the-Gate, the island's only functioning place of worship, is a small **museum**, mainly devoted to the camp. It presents a bitter roll call of the more notable inmates.

The settlement outside its walls is also of interest, partly on account of its 2,000 inhabitants, not natives so much as vestiges of Solovki's layered history. Local youths seem particularly aggressive – some think nothing of cursing drunkenly in the monastery grounds within earshot of surprised tour groups.

A short walk to the south brings you to a series of **neolithic stone labyrinths,** estimated to be 25,000 years old. Their original purpose is not clear; theories variously posit them to be fish traps, sun dials, temples or flying saucer landing pads. Walking through them is supposed to cleanse the soul, so if you get lost you must be a hopeless sinner.

Distances on these islands are great, so other excursions will require a half day at least, or some form of transport. One attractive option is to travel by boat, which allows you to penetrate some of the 500 lakes which the monks connected with tiny canals. This will, however, require some skill in punting – the canals are only just wide enough to accommodate the boats, which are available for rent from a small wharf reached by turning right off the main road just outside the town.

This road also leads to **Khutor Gorka** botanical garden. Started in 1822, its appeal is more as a quiet sanctuary than as a display of bright color. Its cedar and apple trees and larch avenues are guarded by a classic haunted house on the hilltop. (If you hear creaking boards you know the "gray monk" is abroad.)

Khutor Gorka botanical garden

Further out of town is **Sekirnaya** ("Whipping") **Hill**, so called after a bizarre legend about a fisherman who tried to settle on the island, but whose wife was flogged by angels, thus demonstrating the monks' exclusive right to live there. The chapel-cum-lighthouse later served as an infamous prisoners' quarters during the 1920's. No one sent there expected to survive. The view, of the surrounding forest and of Savvatyevo, the island's first settlement, is magnificent.

Of the other islands in the archipelago, the most interesting is Anzer, with its pretty Trinity and Golgotha skeets. Unfortunately it is a closed nature reserve and virtually inaccessible to tourists. You will need special permission to go there.

Art Museum on Ploshchad Lenina, with a rich collection of 16th century wood carvings from local village churches.

MALIYE KARELY

Windmill from Bolshaya Shalga, Maliye Karely Wooden Architecture Museum

This large wooden architecture museum 24 km east of Arkhangelsk may disappoint those who have seen Kizhi. Its exhibits are numerous, but few are really outstanding. A tour round a few local villages, where such monuments are preserved in their natural environment, should prove equally, if not more, rewarding. Still, the countryside in which the museum is located is very pretty, if you have time to admire it before the mosquitoes devour you. And one building alone, the Resurrection Church from the village of Kushereka, with its onion-shaped roof characteristic of the area, might make a visit worthwhile.

KARGOPOL

This tiny, remote town on Lake Lachye in the south of the region is almost as old as Moscow. Colonized by Belozersk and Novgorod princes since the 12th century, it gained both prosperity and notoriety in the 16th as a crossroads of north-south and east-west trade routes. Local merchants were given exclusive rights to bring salt from the White Sea, but they angered their southern countrymen by mixing it with limestone.

In Ivan the Terrible's time, white stone building began here, and Kargopol's masons created a simplified version of Moscow's five-dome church style. Their legacy remains, and even today the town is an isolated northern outpost of stone construction.

Approaching Kargopol from across the Onega river, several clusters of cupolas can be seen. In the center is **Cathedral Square**, and the town's first stone church, the Cathedral of the Nativity of Christ. With its elaborate apses, side chapels and porch, and its widely-spaced five domes, it is a testament to Ivan's glorious age of battlefield triumphs and commercial prosperity. The nearby John the Baptist Church was built in 1751, when the town was already in economic decline. Only then did Kargopol architects perfect the cubic form of their churches, as here. Note also its Ukrainian-style, pear-shaped baroque cupolas.

The third Church of the Presentation of the Virgin houses a compact **museum** of local life. Among other things, it tells of Alexander Baranov, a Kargopolian who administered Russia's American colonies from 1804–08. In 1799, he founded New Arkhangelsk, now the Alaskan town of Sitka.

Kargopol's second ensemble, down the street in the direction of Lake Lachye, is **Annunciation Square**. The cathedral of the same name is another masterpiece, unusual for two things – the carved patterns on its exterior, and its very existence; its funding was so meager that it's a miracle it was built at all.

Another late 17th century church, of the **Resurrection**, completes the architectural landscape of Kargopol. Just downriver of Cathedral Square, it makes a powerful impression, standing alone on one of Kargopol's spacious, grassy squares. While the others have straight roofs, the Resurrection Church is topped by *zakomary*, giving it a more ancient, venerable appearance.

While in Kargopol, be sure to visit the clay doll workshop on Arkhangelskaya ulitsa. Craftsmen always welcome visitors, and souvenirs go for very reasonable prices.

Clay doll workshop, Kargopol

The surrounding countryside is also worth a tour; pretty wooden churches and bell towers grace almost every village. Saunino is the closest, within walking distance of the town, and Lyadiny the most attractive, suggesting comparison with Kizhi.

Kargopol is too remote to work as a day trip from anywhere, and the **hotel** at Lenina, 83 is pretty primitive. Help can be sought from the local tourist office at #60a Ulitsa Tretyevo Internatsionala, tel. (81822) 22-170, or 21-282. In addition to providing excursions for individuals to nearby village churches, and for groups on the lake, they can arrange private accommodation at ridiculously low rates.

PRACTICAL MATTERS

What **Arkhangelsk** lacks in sights, it makes up for in services. The **Pur Navolok Hotel**, formerly used by members of the Central Committee of the Communist Party, allows a very pleasant stay if you can swing $80 a night. For half that you can get a room in the dark and uninspiring **Meridian**, and for less still in the two seedy ruble hotels, the **Dvina** and **Belomorskaya**.

The lively and excellent **Petrovsky** restaurant has jazz on alternate nights and crowds every day, so be sure to book. A quieter alternative is the **Alyosha** restaurant and bar, beside the *Zapad* museum/schooner. The **Topaz** café, in the Sports Palace opposite the sea/river station, is handy for snacks. Arkhangelsk even has a decent night club – the **Iskra** ("Spark") discotheque – in the Sailors' House of Culture.

An English language monthly newspaper called *Arkhangelsk Business News* is available in hotels, and provides some information about events of interest to visitors.

DIRECTIONS

Arkhangelsk: by train from Moscow's Yaroslavsky Vokzal, journey time approximately 20 hours, by plane 2 hours from Sheremetyevo-1. By car, take the M8 all the way to the end, distance 1,100 km.

Solovyetsky Islands: by weekly boat from Arkhangelsk, departing Friday and returning Monday. A package including full board and excursions can be booked through Arkhangelskturist (speak Russian), tel. (8182) 43-9797. Alternatives are irregular boats from Kem (for directions, see Republic of Karelia chapter) and Belomorsk in Karelia, both just two hours away (contact the local tourist offices for details), chartered flights, and yachts from Arkhangelsk (the latter bookable through the local yacht club on [8182] 43-7711). Individual travel (on the daily flight from Arkhangelsk) is by invitation only – this is a frontier zone.

Maliye Karely: by regular local bus from the sea/river and bus stations in Arkhangelsk.

Kargopol: by train to Nyandoma, 7 hours short of Arkhangelsk, then another 2 hours by bus. By car, turn left off the M8 after Velsk and continue for about 250 km.

RUSSIAN GLOSSARY

Annunciation Square
Благовещенская площадь
Anzer Island
Остров Анзер
Belomorsk
Беломорск
Cathedral Square
Соборная пдощадь
Church of St. John the Baptist
Церковь Иоанна Предтечи
Kargopol
Каргополь
Kem
Кемь
Khutor Gorka Botanical Garden
Хутор Горка
Lake Lachye
Озеро Лачье
Lyadiny
Лядины
Maliye Karely Museum
Малые Карелы
Cathedral of the Nativity of Christ
Собор Рождества Христова
Nyandoma
Няндома
Pinega Nature Reserve
Пинежский заповедник
Church of the Presentation of the Virgin
Введенская церковь
Resurrection Church
Воскресенская церковь
Sailors' House of Culture
Дом Культуры Моряков
Saunino
Саунино
Sekirnaya Gora
Секирная Гора
Solovyetsky Islands
Соловецкие Острова
Stone Labyrinths
Каменные Лабиринты
Transfiguration Cathedral
Преображенский Собор
Ulitsa Tretyevo Internatsionala
Улица Третьего Интернационала

Title page photo: ***Monument to Victims of British/American Intervention, 1918–20. Arkhangelsk waterfront***

REPUBLIC OF KARELIA

RESPUBLIKA KARELIYI

This flat and remote region resembles its neighbor, Finland, in all but living standards and primarily Russian ethnicity. Its endless forests and lakes make for an ideal holiday in the wilderness, though much of its territory is swampy, impassable and mosquito-ridden during the relatively hot summer. Fifteen percent of the population are Karelians, members of a Finno-Ugric nation closely related to the Finns. The size of this group led to Karelia's designation as an Autonomous Republic (and even a Union Republic for a while) during the Soviet years. As a result, Finnish generally receives equal status to Russian. Even in mainly Russian Petrozavodsk, signs are bilingual.

PETROZAVODSK

Despite its location in beautiful lakeland and closeness to rich deposits of copper and iron ore, Karelia's capital has a grim and colorless history. Peter the Great founded it in 1703 as a cannon factory with a sideline soon added in decorative iron railings. Most of the canal bridges in St. Petersburg have parts which originated there. But despite its reputation for metalcraft, Petrozavodsk was always a backward provincial town. Until this century it only had one stone street. It became a common place of exile for political dissenters, who coined for it the nickname, "Siberia-near-the-capital." As if this wasn't enough, the city suffered a devastating Nazi occupation of exactly 1000 days.

Indeed, there is practically nothing to see in Petrozavodsk. However, the city makes up for this with a friendly and seemingly literate atmosphere: it must be the only Russian city where bookstalls outnumber liquor kiosks. In any case, Petrozavodsk is the main base from which to visit Kizhi, and in that role it is tolerable enough. (See Practical Matters.)

KIVACH

This lakeland nature reserve to the north of Petrozavodsk includes Europe's second largest waterfall, exceeded only by Switzerland's Reichenbach Falls. This watery cascade inspired 18th century Russian poet Gavrila Derzhavin, who was governor

continued on page 404

Russia's Greatest Wooden Sanctuary

It would be a crime to visit Petrozavodsk or Lake Onega without going to Kizhi Island, the country's largest and finest wooden architecture museum. The **Monastery of our Savior** (*Spassky Pogost*) is probably the most picturesque ensemble in the country, and is further enriched by the surrounding buildings and landscape.

The monastery's churches and belfry astound with the harmony of their setting as you approach the island. The structures impress from every angle and at any time of day. From behind, the sun intricately silhouettes the clustered cupolas of the **Cathedral of the Transfiguration**.

Unknown craftsmen built the cathedral in 1714, during the reign of Peter the Great. Twenty-two domes rise festively to a large central dome, making the whole resemble a great fir tree. Its strikingly simple plan consists of an octagonal central frame with four stepped sections, each one topped by a cupola. As if to make the "tree" bristle, the third row down has an additional cupola on each of the four "bare" sides of the octagon. A roof beneath each cupola keeps rain off the walls. The Transfiguration Cathedral became the prototype for church-building in the Onega area, of which many splendid examples remain.

The Cathedral has not always enjoyed its current international recognition. As an unheated and rarely maintained summer church, it has

Monastery of Our Savior, Kizhi. **Left:** ***Church of the Intercession of the Virgin.*** **Right:** ***Cathedral of the Transfiguration***

often suffered neglect. UNESCO lists it as a monument in urgent need of restoration, but work is unlikely to begin for some time since no one knows quite how to go about the job. So far it is in no danger of collapse, but 12 percent of its beams are rotten, which causes concern. The public is not at present allowed inside, where an unsightly metal carcass that supposedly reduces fire risk has hampered reconstruction.

The **Church of the Intercession of the Virgin** opposite is much sturdier. As a winter church, it was looked after more carefully; it now houses a museum. Its much simpler construction contrasts favorably with the Transfiguration Cathedral, while its impressive nine-domed roof complements the other's 22.

After you enter the trapezium, you will find an exhibition devoted to a peasant revolt of 1769–71, which broke out after Catherine the Great introduced an unpopular "soul tax." Cannon fire which killed five men bludgeoned the peasants into submission. The ringleaders suffered horsewhipping, branding, and permanent exile to the mines of Siberia.

The rest of the church is devoted to icons of the Onega area, which include some from the Transfiguration Cathedral and culminate with the church's own magnificent iconostasis. These local treasures are smaller and more intimate than their southern counterparts, with round and often appealing faces of saints and savior alike.

The church's modest, free-standing **belfry** (1874) replaces previous towers that had fallen into ruin in the 19th century. It attracts little interest in itself but nicely completes the ensemble. From some directions it seems to stand immediately between the two churches and acts as a pivot around which they revolve.

St. George, from the iconostasis of the Transfiguration Cathedral

You should not forget the walls and entrance gate of the monastery. The original structures date from the early 16th century, but the current walls are modelled on those at the nearby monastery of St. Elijah.

The rest of the museum lies beyond the monastery at the southern end of the island. Two buildings stand out among the many barns and traditional north Russian bathhouses, with direct access between the steam rooms and the water of the lake below. They are the middle peasants' houses from **Oshevnevo** and **Seredka**, which are typical of Onega area dwellings of the late 19th century, combining home and barn under one roof. Both are open to visitors and impress with their

Oshevnevo peasant farmstead, with decorative board of granary in foreground. Kizhi Island.

interior spaciousness and functionality and their exterior decorated beams and platbands. The second house has an interesting collection of sleighs and boats.

The little **Chapel of the Archangel Michael from Lelikozero** sparks interest in the multitude of wooden churches on this and surrounding islands. Its octagonal tent-roofed belfry and single tiny cupola on a triangular roof are hallmarks of Onega wooden architecture.

The next exhibit, a **windmill from Volkostrov**, provides a good view of the monastery. If you stand a few feet in front of the windmill you see the two churches as if they were one. Only the light on the cupolas betrays their different shades.

The tiny **Church of the Resurrection of Lazarus** recalls an era in wooden architecture now almost forgotten. Built in 1390, it formed part of the Muromsky Monastery. Pre-Christian beliefs were particularly persistent in Karelia, and these monasteries were only able to establish Orthodoxy there in the 14th century.

When you leave this area of the museum, you should plan to walk at a leisurely pace through the remaining part of the island. Take a calorie-rich picnic to sustain you during the remaining 5 km.

The village of **Yamka**, on the eastern side, consists of buildings from other islands on the lake. But this is no theme park, since the people who live here are just ordinary peasants who are struggling to survive. Don't be surprised to see people dipping their laundry into the murky waters of Onega.

On the other side of the island, the village of **Vassilyevo** has the best of Kizhi's secular buildings. These include the rich peasant Sergin's 19th century mansion from Munozero with its carved platbands and gables. Nearby is the island's earliest native church, the little 17th century **Assumption Church**, which has a "cage" construction, so called because of its large octagonal bell-tower with an open-air drum which could be used as a watch-tower. This kind of bell-tower is common to small northern wooden churches.

Kizhi's two remaining landmarks should not be hard to find. You will have already seen the **Chapel of the Assumption of the Virgin**, which sits on the island's central hill, on the way to Vassilyevo. At the north end, past the rather plain Pudozh Sector village, is the **Chapel of the Three Prelates**, whose huge, tent-roofed bell-tower entices visitors with its apparent proximity.

If you still have energy and time, the villages and chapels of the surrounding islands and mainland give further insight into the life of Onega. Visit the villages of **Korba** and **Voroby** on Bolshoy Klimenetsky Island, or **Podyelniki**, on the mainland to the north.

Village of Vassilyevo, Chapel of the Assumption

continued from page 400

of Petrozavodsk at the time, to write "The Waterfall," his best-known poem. Unfortunately, its flow was sharply reduced by construction, in 1936, of a dam upriver at Girvas. Until a year ago visitors could only enter this tiny part of the reserve, but foresters now can accompany them into other areas.

The main town on the road to Kivach is the district center of **Kondopoga.** If you have time, visit this old village and its beautiful **Assumption Church**. This tall and slender landmark, which towers gracefully over Onega's Chupa inlet and the flat lands behind, was once a landmark for lost ships. It was erected in 1774 during the last great era of wooden church construction. No later church has surpassed in beauty its unusual tower-like form. It also offers a rare opportunity to see a functioning wooden church from the inside. The pillars of the trapezium have the appearance of musclebound giants whose arms hold up the roof, making the building seem more like a pagan temple than an Orthodox church.

If you have a car, you can also visit Martsialniye Vody, a spa village just to the east. Peter the Great's patronage popularized this place. After their discovery in 1714, its iron-rich waters earned the name "Martial Waters," after the Roman god of war and iron. Forgotten after Peter's death, the spa was revived only in 1964. Today you can see a small wooden church, built under Peter's supervision, a museum, and a pavilion that stands over the original spring.

KEM

This nondescript town in northern Karelia is the closest point on the mainland to the Solovyetsky Islands (see Arkhangelsk Region), so you might conceivably find yourself there. If you do, be sure to visit the **Assumption Cathedral**, Kem's only landmark. Two twin side chapels flank this massive tent-roofed church, which is a worthy contemporary of Kizhi's Transfiguration Cathedral. Its construction was inspired in part by the euphoria following Russia's victory over Sweden in the Northern War.

(For Valaam Island, see Leningrad Region.)

PRACTICAL MATTERS

Accommodation is definitely **Petrozavodsk**'s strong point, thanks to entrepreneur Pyotr Leshberg, who opened Russia's first private hotel there in March 1993. Small, clean and pleasant, the **Hotelli Pietari** (Shuiskoye shossé, 16; tel. [81400] 4-53-97) cost less than $20 in mid-1993 for a single, and offers a bar, sitting room for guests, swimming pool and sauna. This compares very favorably with the city's two main state-run hotels, which offer considerably fewer amenities for similar prices. The **Severnaya** at #21 Lenina is the older and more central of the two, while the tourist-oriented **Karelia** on Naberezhnaya Gyullinga is the most expensive in town. Of the several private hotels which sprang up in Pietari's wake, the only well-located one is **Karel Skan** at #28 Ulitsa Murmanskaya. Situated in a gray, five-story block, it provides youth hostel-type accommodation in double and triple rooms for under $5 a night.

Eating out can be a pleasure in Petrozavodsk. **Russkaya Starina**, tucked awkwardly in a dark corner of the former House of Political Enlightenment at 12 Ulitsa Kirova, qualifies as the town's best restaurant. It features fast, friendly service and good Russian cuisine, with cabaret and striptease late into the night. If you're looking for somewhere down-to-earth, and at the same time tasteful, try the **Neubrandenburg** at 23 Lenina, named after one of Petrozavodsk's many twin cities. The hotel restaurants are reasonable but loud, while the cavernous **Petrovsky** at 1 Andropova tends to fill with drunken, singing Finns.

Cafés also satisfy. The **Taide Gallery** at 13 Lenina is a good place for coffee and a cheese sandwich while you contemplate the paintings on offer around you. Petrozavodsk can also claim the best ice cream parlor in Russia, with **Ben & Jerry's** in the House of Pioneers at 8 Krasnaya ulitsa. But be forewarned, as Ben & Jerry's sells inexpensively enough for lines to stretch out into the street. It's also worth remembering that **Russian ice cream** (*morozhenoye*) generally is excellent. Ice cream in Petrozavodsk comes in a number of flavors, of which orange is the best, though curiously it actually tastes of peach. You should readily find it sold on street corners or from special kiosks, as in other Russian cities.

DIRECTIONS

Petrozavodsk: by car from Moscow NW on the M10 to Chudovo, then right on the A115 to Novaya Ladoga and right again on the M18 (1076 km overall), or on the M18 direct from St. Petersburg, 412 km. There are several daily trains from St. Petersburg's Moskovsky Vokzal and Moscow's

Leningradsky (journey time from Moscow, 16 hours). Flights from Sheremetyevo-1 airport take 2 hours.
Kizhi: by hydrofoil from Petrozavodsk. There are special excursion services, but the best bet is to take the local service bound for Velikaya Guba. The early morning boat guarantees seeing the island before the crowds arrive. For **Korba** and **Voroby**, alight at Sennaya Guba; for **Podyelniki**, go on to Velikaya Guba.
Kivach: continue north on the M18 for about 50 km, then turn left into the reserve. Buses go as far as Kondopoga, though if you're lucky you'll find a local bus to take you further.
Kem: another 400 km up the M18, or a further 8 hours on the Murmansk railroad.

RUSSIAN GLOSSARY

Hotelli Pietari
Гостиница «Петр»
Church of the Intercession of the Virgin
Покровская Церковь
Karel Skan Hotel
Гостиница «Карел Скан»
Karelia Hotel
Гостиница «Карелия»
Republic of Karelia
Республика Карелии
Kem
Кемь
Kivach
Кивач
Kizhi Island
Остров Кижи
Kondopoga
Кондопога
Korba
Корба
Ulitsa Lenina
Улица Ленина
Martsialniye Vodi
Марциальные Воды
Monastery of Our Savior
Спасский погост
Oshevnevo farmstead
Усадьба из Деревни Ошевнево
Petrovsky restaurant
Ресторан «Петровский»
Petrozavodsk
Петрозаводск
Podyelniki
Подъельники
Russkaya Starina restaurant
Ресторан «Русская Старина»
Sennaya Guba
Сенная Губа
Seredka
Середка
Severnaya Hotel
Гостиница «Северная»
Taide Gallery
Галерея Тайде
Transfiguration Cathedral
Преображенский собор
Valaam Island
Остров Валаам
Vassilyevo
Васильево
Velikaya Guba
Великая Губа
Voroby
Воробьи
Yamka
Ямка

MURMANSK REGION

MURMANSKAYA OBLAST

The most common name for this part of northwest Russia is the Kola Peninsula (*Kolsky Poluostrov*). Forests rather than tundra cover this atypical arctic territory which has a very mild climate, and possesses deposits of almost every mineral known to man.

But Kola's natural riches have been under heavy attack for some time. As if accidents at its own notorious power station weren't enough, its proximity to the nuclear testing area at Novaya Zemlya has surely affected it. Chemical pollution has had much more glaringly obvious effects. Sulfur dioxide fumes emitted by the *Severnikel* combine at Monchegorsk in central Kola have killed off 15 square kilometers of forest in the Lapland nature reserve. In the north, a mysterious invisible cloud with an odor of stale socks shrouds the Murmansk road 50 km south of the city.

These blemishes might seem to deter tourism, but Kola exerts a strange allure as an outpost of civilization 300 km above the Arctic Circle. Here you can see the deepest man-made hole in the world, the most northerly botanic gardens, bird reserve, electrified railway, sanatorium, scientific research institute, electric power station and even trolleybus depot in the world!

MURMANSK

The Arctic Circle's largest city is a strange phenomenon. Its modern sprawl over several hills shelters hundreds of thousands of people, who endure constant darkness for two months of the year and a never-setting sun for another two. It has bats that hunt in broad daylight, lilacs that blossom in August and a harbor that never freezes.

The port of Murmansk appeared only this century, in the dying months of the Tsarist regime. During World War I, the enemy blockaded the Baltic and Black seas, Russia's main western seaboards. The Kola Peninsula, with the Gulf Stream that washes its northern shore, emerged as a perfect alternative. Construction began on Romanovo-on-the-Murman, as Murmansk was originally to be called.

Then came the Revolution and Civil War. In 1918, British and American troops arrived and occupied the peninsula for two years. They also brought supplies to the White armies in the region. The Bolsheviks assumed control in 1920.

In the Soviet era Murmansk grew

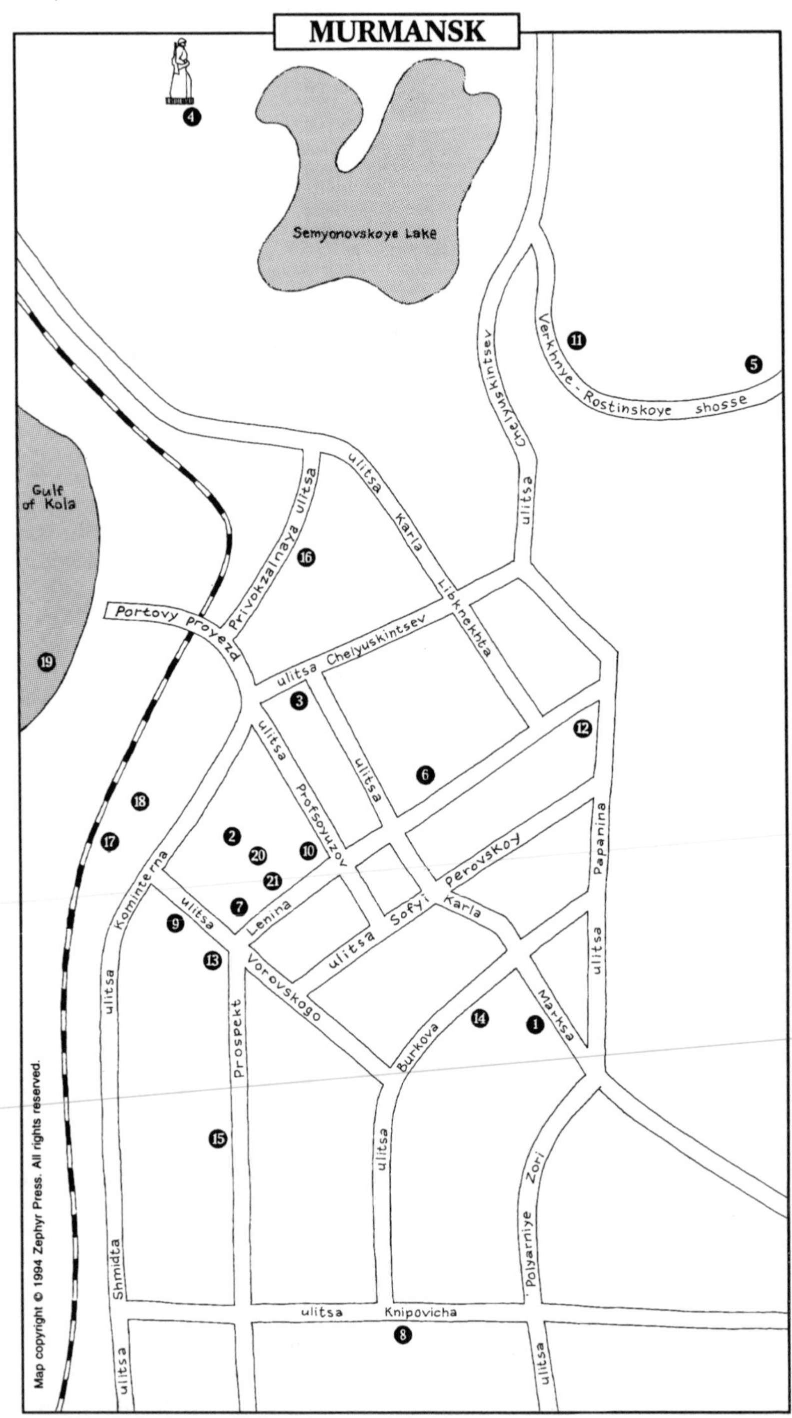
MURMANSK
Semyonovskoye Lake
Gulf of Kola
Verkhnye - Rostinskoye shosse
ulitsa Chelyuskintsev
ulitsa Karla Libknekhta
Privokzalnaya ulitsa
Portovy proyezd
ulitsa Chelyuskintsev
ulitsa
ulitsa Profsoyuzov
ulitsa
Perovskoy
Papanina
ulitsa Kominterna
ulitsa Lenina
ulitsa Sofyi
Karla
ulitsa
Vorovskogo
Prospekt
Burkova
Marksa
ulitsa
Polyarniye Zori
ulitsa Shmidta
ulitsa Knipovicha
ulitsa
ulitsa
1
2
3
4
5
6
7
8
9
10
11
12
13
14
15
16
17
18
19
20
21

МУРМАНСК

Ulitsa Burkova
Улица Буркова
Ulitsa Chelyuskintsev
Улица Челюскинцев
Ulitsa Karla Libknekhta
Улица Карла Либкнехта
Ulitsa Karla Marksa
УлицаКарла Маркса
Ulitsa Knipovicha
Улица Книповича
Gulf of Kola
Кольский залив
Ulitsa Kominterna
Улица Коминтерна
Prospekt Lenina
Проспект Ленина
Ulitsa Papanina
Улица Папанина
Ulitsa Polyarnye Zori
Улица Полярные Зори
Portovy proyezd
Портовый проезд
Privokzalnaya ulitsa
Привокзальная улица
Ulitsa Profsoyuzov
Улица Профсоюзов
Semyonovskoye Lake
Семеновское озеро
Ulitsa Shmidta
Улица Шмидта
Ulitsa Sofyi Perovskoy
Улица Софьи Перовской
Verkhnye-Rostinskoye shossé
УВерхне-Ростинское шоссе
Ulitsa Vorovskovo
Улица Воровского

MAP KEY

1. **Excursion Bureau**
Экскурсионное бюро
2. **Monument to the Victims of Intervention**
Памятник Жертвам Интервенции
3. **Monument to the anti-Hitler Alliance**
Памятник анти-Гитлеровской Коалиции
4. **"Alyosha" Monument**
Памятник «Алёша»
5. **War Cemetery**
Воинское кладбище
6. **City Museum**
Городской музей
7. **Arktika Hotel**
Гостиница «Арктика»
8. **Polyarniye Zori Hotel**
Гостиница «Полярные Зори»
9. **Meridian Hotel**
Гостиница «Меридиан»
10. **Yunost Café**
Кафе «Юность»
11. **Panorama Restaurant**
Ресторан «Панорама»
12. **Medved Restaurant**
Ресторан «Медведь»
13. **Art Salon**
Художественный салон
14. **Bookshop**
Книжный магазин
15. **Souvenirs**
Сувениры
16. **Market**
Рынок
17. **Train Station**
Железнодорожный вокзал
18. **Bus Station**
Автовокзал
19. **Sea Station**
Морской вокзал

20, 21. Post Offices
Почта

rapidly only to be levelled to rubble in World War II. Today, tangled dock-lands, railway sidings, and high-rise buildings nearly obscure its older center.

Murmansk's status as an international port and its closeness to the Norwegian and Finnish borders ensure a plentiful supply of foreigners and make it relatively expensive. Sailors and fisherman of every description abound, as do prostitutes.

As should now be clear, people do not come to Murmansk for sightseeing – it is better experienced through its everyday life. Nevertheless, you should visit the local **museum** at Lenina, 90 for insights into the specific nature of the region. There you will find minerals of every imaginable description, flora and fauna of the forest and tundra, and halls on Russian and Saami life. Two models of the Resurrection Church in Kola, a masterpiece of wooden architecture which matched the beauty and genius of the Kizhi churches, highlight the collection. In 1854, this Kola jewel fell victim to those great civilizers the British, who, in a nasty sideshow of the Crimean War, bombarded it with cannon fire. The church and fortress around it burned to the ground.

"Alyosha" statue

From the museum, take the #3 trolleybus away from the center to **Lake Semyonovskoye**. This hilltop body of water seems about to spill onto the road climbing toward it. Take a left turn off the road before you reach the lake in order to reach "**Alyosha**," the giant statue of a soldier looking over Murmansk harbor. This is the city's main war memorial, dedicated to the defenders of the Soviet polar region, and is also the best place to view the harbor and city.

Next, take the hillside road past the Panorama restaurant to the World War II cemetery. Slightly beyond the Soviet graves is a section dedicated to fallen US and British Commonwealth troops. If you're looking for graves from the 1918–20 occupation, you won't find them there despite the insistence of many locals and even some guidebooks. This cemetery is in another part of town, away to the southeast, abandoned and forgotten during the Soviet years. There is now talk of restoration.

Unless you've really got time to kill, the 16 km trip to Kola is hardly worth the effort. Originally the capital of the peninsula, it never quite recovered from the 1854 fire, and Murmansk now threatens to swallow it up altogether. Only the massive squat cupola of a 19th century church distinguishes the place.

KIROVSK

Khibiny is one of Russia's most unusual ski resorts. Constant darkness prevails during much of the season, and yet by May, when it is still possible to ski, the sun shines all night. Its long winter has earned it the name "little Antarctic." The slopes of the Aikuaivenchorr ("sleeping beauty" in Saami) and **Kukisvumchorr** ("mountain over a long valley") host the "Khibiny Spring" international competition every year. The Hotel Khibiny

The Dying Villages of Kola

Russians were not the first settlers on Kola. Finno-Ugric tribes like the Saami, whom we know as Laps, arrived first. Only a small number of these people remain in Russia, 2,000 of them in the remote town of Lovozero. Their culture survives, with factories that produce traditional costumes and handicrafts and a local concert hall that holds exhibitions and shows, even though Lovozero is by and large a gray Soviet town. Most external distinguishing features have disappeared.

In the case of remote Russian communities, the story is very different. All-wooden villages preserve traditional ways of life in settings that seem to have frozen centuries ago.

Russians, or *Pomory* as they are known here, arrived on Kola from Novgorod in the 13th century and occupied mainly the southern White Sea or Tersky coast of the peninsula. The salmon found here in abundance proved a profitable commodity for Novgorod merchants, and the town of Varzuga in particular, flourished.

Life has gone on here for hundreds of years almost unaffected by war, progress and revolution, but now the potent mixture of economic decay and greater freedom of movement is proving lethal. Since most younger people have left, only handfuls of pensioners struggle on in their dilapidated wooden hovels, as food supplies and communications become less and less affordable for them.

One such place is Kovda, 100 km south of the southern district center of Kandalaksha. As you arrive there in summer from the main road, you will find Kovda's bridge – its only land link with civilization – submerged and impassable. Yet the little village and its pretty 17th century wooden church and belfry provide a tangible incentive not to admit defeat. People in a nearby settlement will row you across the water, if you make inquiries.

If you arrive by boat, the most immediate landmark is the large, ancient roofed cross on the ridge above. A common feature of *Pomory* villages, such a cross is a focal point of their civilization, a symbol of their courage and source of strength during hard times.

Just down the hill is the 17th century **Church of St. Nicholas**, caged in scaffolding but unlikely to be restored in the near future. This fine architectural monument certainly shows its age, just like its elderly *babushka* caretaker, for whom the entrance ladder and huge lock on the door are gargantuan obstacles. She doesn't complain about that, however. She reserves her indignation for those

St. Nicholas Church, Kovda

who have left the church to decay. If properly looked after, and not used merely as dissertation fodder by visiting specialists, St. Nicholas would now be as sturdy as it was 300 years ago. If someone cared, its severe interior would be softened by icons for worship. Instead, floorboards buckle in all directions while the depleted locals hope for a miracle.

In a pine copse behind the hill above the village is Kovda's third ancient monument, a traditional north Russian cemetery. Long ago, the settlers here did not actually bury their dead, but sealed them in wooden boxes above the ground. Later on, the boxes assumed a purely symbolic significance, marking and covering the graves underneath. Today, these frail wooden structures stand neglected and open to the elements. Only one or two remain. Like the village itself, they might not exist for much longer.

provides accommodation.

Several miles out of Kirovsk is the **Vudyavr Valley**, site of **Botanical Gardens** where scientists experiment with the adaptation to polar conditions of plants from as far away as the subtropics. The results are extraordinary: violets and bluebells blossom in the open fields during the short arctic summer.

KANDALAKSHA

Once a simple *Pomory* fishing village, this dreary industrial town is at the center of a remarkable bird reserve that covers islands in the nearby gulf and on the north coast of Kola, in the Barents Sea. Over 240 species of birds have been recorded there, though most migrate south for the winter. Of the twenty species permanently resident, the most notable is the eider, once hunted nearly to extinction for the down it uses to make its nests. In the last century Russia "produced" 10,000 metric tonnes of eider down a year. After the Revolution the government moved to protect the bird. Naturalists still collect down on the reserve, but only after nesting has finished.

One of the White Sea islands, **Medvezhy Ostrov**, is the site of Russia's oldest silver mine, opened in 1669. Both this mine and a source of lead ore discovered later functioned for just a few years before they were flooded.

The local excursion bureau (tel. 50396) arranges tours to the islands, but only in July and August, after the nesting season. The headquarters of the reserve plus a small museum are in the old village, which is a short bus ride from the center of town. For a view of the islands, head for the village of **Rnyazhnaya Guba**, just across the river, and accessible by a bridge further along. Here there is a Civil War monument on the headland and a derelict ski jump. On a clear day, the view from the top of the hill above is impressive.

PRACTICAL MATTERS

Most hotels are for hard currency. The central Intourist **Hotel Arktika** costs $80 a night minimum for a single room, while the **Polyarnoye Zory** and inconvenient **69th Parallel** work out somewhat cheaper. If you're looking for a reasonable ruble hotel, look no further than across the square from the Arktika to the fishermen's **Meridian**.

Eating out in Murmansk ought to be a pleasure for the fish lover, but unfortunately the choice is hardly better than in many inland cities. Still, there are a few good eateries here. If you're well-dressed, and feeling rich and exclusive, try the private **Medved** restaurant at the northern end of Ulitsa Lenina. Its mirrored ceiling and grandiose seating contrast sharply with the drab gray building that houses it. The ruble-equivalent cover charge of $4 is worth it for the smooth saxophonist, excellent mulled wine and chocolate animals in the ice cream. The more traditional **Panorama** on Lake Semyonovskoye is smoke-free and also comfortable, though its seating is reminiscent of passenger ferry lounges. The Arktika and Polyarnoye Zory hotel restaurants are also passable. The former has the advantage of a room without evening band and some screened tables for absolute privacy. For a quick snack try the **Café Yunost**, but beware of fishbones in the pizza.

DIRECTIONS

Murmansk: 39 hours by train from Moscow's Leningradsky Vokzal, slightly less from St. Petersburg's Moskovsky. By plane 2½ hours from Sheremetyevo-1 airport. By car from Moscow on the M10 to Chudovo, outside St. Petersburg, then right on the A115 to Novaya Ladoga and right again on the M18 through Petrozavodsk. From St. Petersburg direct on the M18.

Kirovsk: 4 hours closer than Murmansk. Change trains at Apatiti or turn off the M18 north of Kandalaksha.

Kandalaksha: another hour closer.

Kovda: On a minor road off the M18 just north of the Karelian border. Buses are infrequent and run only in winter from Kandalaksha.

RUSSIAN GLOSSARY

Aikuaivenchorr
Айкуайвенчорр
Apatiti
Апатиты
Botanical Garden
Ботанический сад
Chudovo
Чудово
Kandalaksha
Кандалакша
Hotel Khibiny
Гостиница «Хибины»
Khibiny
Хибины
Khibiny ski resort
Лыжный курорт Хибины
Kirovsk
Кировск
Knyazhnaya Guba
Княжная Губа
Kola
Кола
Kola Peninsula
Кольский Полуостров
Kovda
Ковда
Kukisvumchorr
Кукисвумчорр
Lovozero
Ловозеро
Medvezhy ostrov
Медвежий Остров
St. Nicholas Church
Никольская Церковь
Novaya Ladoga
Новая Ладога
Petrozavodsk
Петрозаводск
Semyonovskoye Lake
Семёновское Озеро
69th Parallel Hotel
Гостиница «69-я Параллель»
Varzuga
Варзуга
Vudyavr Valley
Долина Вудъявр

Village of Kovda

Glossary

arcade. A series of arches supported by columns, piers, or pillars.

apparatchik. A Communist party official, generally a mid- to low-level one. Maxim Gorky's status (see Ivanovo chapter) was actually higher than this.

arquebus. The earliest generic name in English usage for early firearms, dating from the 16th century. From Old French.

belvedere. A raised turret or lantern on the top of a house or other structure, situated so as to command a view.

beresta. Birch bark, famous in Novgorod as the forerunner of writing paper. It is woven today into shoes, boxes and other items by craftspersons, particularly in Vologda Region.

blind arcading. Purely decorative rows of arches carved into or applied to the outsides of walls, a particularly common feature of Vladimir-Suzdal architecture which was later adopted by the Moscow school.

boyars. The higher nobility, generally subordinate to the princes, a class whose origins lay in intermarriage between Varangians and other Scandinavian peoples and the native Slavic aristocracy. The boyar class was abolished by Peter the Great.

cupola. An onion dome of any size on a cylindrical base, or *drum,* crowning a church, bell tower, mosque or other structure.

crozier. A staff capped by a crook or cross, borne by or before a bishop, metropolitan, or other high eccliastical official, on ceremonial occasions.

drum. The cylindrical base of a *cupola.*

dom otdykha. A rustic holiday resort.

finift. Enamel ware painted and fired in a such a way that an extremely durable gloss is created.

herm, also *herma.* A statue consisting of the head of the Greek god Hermes mounted on a square stone post.

kokoshniki. Semicircular, gabled decorative panels that ring the bases of spires or of drums, in single or multiple courses, and of uniform or varying sizes. Derived from the peaked *kokoshnik* headgear of medieval Russian women.

kulak. In Bolshevik terminology, a comparatively prosperous peasant farmer. The definition was never exact, but it might include those who employed others, who owned a horse or other livestock, etc. During the period of Stalinist collectivization of agriculture, those peasants deemed to be "kulaks" were often driven off their land and exiled or even killed, while the poorer peasants were organized into collective farms.

lavra. Russian word for "monastery"

Naryshkin Baroque. An architectural style incorporating an abundance of vertical highlights, carved portals and *platbands*. It is named after Peter the Great's mother, Natalya Naryshkina, who favored it.

platband. A decorative window surround of wood, tile, or carved stone.

peredvizhniki. Members of the Society for Traveling Art Exhibitions, founded in 1870, who included most of the best painters of the time. The *peredvizhniki* had three guiding principles: realism, populism, and national consciousness. They believed that it was not enough merely to sympathize

Glossary

with the common people in their painting; "they must reveal the strength, the moral worth and the natural intelligence of the people they painted." (Dmitry V. Sarabianov, in *Russian Art: From Neoclassicism to the Avant Garde, 1800–1917*. New York: Harry N. Abrams, 1990)

quincunx. An arrangement of five objects, with one placed at each corner of a rectangle and the fifth at the center.

risalits. In architecture, sections of the exterior walls of a building that project from the main line of the façade. They are usually symmetrical to the building's central axis. From the Italian *risalita*, meaning projection.

see. In the church, the seat from which a bishop, archbishhop, or (in the case of Russian Orthodoxy, a metropolitan or other head of a diocese) exercises jurisdiction.

solium. The raised floor at the front of a church sanctuary.

tent roof. A steeply pitched church roof, generally constructed in the form of hexagonal or octagonal panels, diminishing in width from base to top. Similar to the steeples of Western churches.

trapeza or *trapeznaya*. The western addition to a church, built to supplement the sanctuary, the worship space beneath the *cupola(s)*. This extension may also, in small village churches, have been used for other purposes, such as public meetings.

zakomari. Arched gables that follow the contours of the vaulting of 11th and 12th century Russian churches.

Russian Booklist

Art & Architecture

Brumfield, William C. *A History of Russian Architecture*. Cambridge University Press, 1993. Well-written and beautifully illustrated survey, probably the definitive work on the subject in English. This is an expanded version of the exquisitely designed 1983 book by the same author, *Gold in Azure: One Thousand Years of Russian Architecture* (Boston: David R. Godine, Publisher; o.p.).

Gray, Camilla. *The Russian Experiment in Art, 1863–1922*. New York: Thames & Hudson, 1986. The best introduction to the art of this period.

History

Billington, James H. *The Icon and the Axe: An Interpretive History of Russian Culture*. New York: Vintage, 1970. "A rich and readable introduction to the whole sweep of Russian cultural and intellectual history from Kievan times to the post-Khrushchev era." –*Library Journal*

Literature & Memoir

Akhmatova, Anna. *The Complete Poems of Anna Akhmatova*. Trans. Judith Hemschemeyer. Boston: Zephyr Press and Edinburgh: Canongate Press, 1992. "A magnificent achievement whose like as an event in poetic scholarship is not likely to be equalled in our day" – Harrison Salisbury

An Age Ago: A Selection of Nineteenth-Century Russian Poetry. Selected and translated by Alan Myers. New York: Farrar, Straus & Giroux, 1988.